Human Nature in American Thought

HUMAN NATURE
IN
AMERICAN THOUGHT

A History

Merle Curti

THE UNIVERSITY OF WISCONSIN PRESS

Published 1980

The University of Wisconsin Press
114 North Murray Street
Madison, Wisconsin 53715

The University of Wisconsin Press, Ltd.
1 Gower Street
London WC1E 6HA, England

First printing

Printed in the United States of America

For LC CIP information see the colophon

ISBN 0-299-07970-8

In Memory of
Frances Becker Curti

Contents

In the contradictory and confused situation of the travellers' reports at the very beginnings of literature in America, one finds a central, underlying question: what is human nature?

ALDO SCAGLIONE, 1976

Deformities and misgrowths, especially of the human species, are rarer in America (where everything is truer to nature) than elsewhere.

JOHANN DAVID SCHÖPF, 1783–84

It is, perhaps, no inconsiderable Proof of the Truth of Religion, that amidst the insuperable Errors which bewildered the Philosphers in their contemplations of Human Nature, it is Revelation alone which hath dispelled the Darkness, and at once discovered the indelible Characters of our Grandeur, and the deplorable Fountain of our Corruption.

WILLIAM LIVINGSTON,
The Independent Reflector, 1753

Of course men, if not wolves, have made great progress since those days. But man, being reasonable, should humor his helpmate's fancies and understand the workings of her mind.

WILLIAM BYRD II, 1728

Can it be natural to men thus to degenerate into a state of brutal stupefaction? So many millions of rational beings, endowed with moral capacities, having the full exercise of the corporal functions, to submit to be treated like brutes, what a shocking consideration.

HERMON HUSBAND, 1761

The ill treatment which this unhappy part of Mankind receives here, would almost justify them in any desperate attempt for Gaining that *Civility* & *Plenty* which tho denied them, is here, commonly bestowed on Horses!

PHILIP FITHIAN, 1774

Preface

IN THE history of American thought the idea of human nature, though largely overlooked by scholars, has been a major theme. If in a three-hundred-year span the persistent concern of intellectual leaders with the nature of man was sometimes the result of curiosity, it was more often associated with concrete interests, values, and involvement: ideas about human nature in America have functioned as exposition, explanation, and vindication in the private and public spheres of historical experience. Throughout our history some idea about the nature of mankind has informed religious discussion, literature, education, and political, social, and economic theory and practice. Assumptions and reflections about human nature have in turn left their mark on all these. Many years ago it seemed to me that the time had come to examine this aspect of our intellectual history. This book is the result, then, of a long-standing interest.

Another justification for such an inquiry stems from the fact that the discussion of human nature has been especially widespread and lively in times of great change or preparation for it, whether in public experience or in emerging movements of thought. Striking examples include the extensive use of the term in the late eighteenth and the late nineteenth and early twentieth centuries—decades of remarkable change in old patterns of living and in outlook as well as of new scientific discoveries. The revival of interest in human nature in our own day gives this study added contemporary significance.

Monographs exist on the idea of human nature in ancient and contemporary China, classical Greece, Renaissance and post-Renaissance Europe, and the Soviet Union. A few scholars have studied the image of man in one or another aspect of its American career: John Dewey, Arthur O. Lovejoy, Reinhold Niebuhr, Perry Miller, and Cecilia Kenyon come to mind. Moreover, historians of religion, philosophy, education, the family, sex roles, literature, and the natural and social sciences could hardly avoid giving it some attention. Only two scholars, I believe, have tried their hand at anything like an overall survey: Don M. Wolfe, in his affirmatively suggestive essays published as *The Image of Man in America* (1957, 1970), and Floyd W. Matson in his sketchy but useful little book *The Idea of Human Nature* (1976). I have learned a good deal from all these pioneers. Even so, no one knows better than I the hazards of an attempt at a more systematic, full-scale study.

Complex problems face anyone who tries to write such an account. By and large the meanings of the term *human nature* have been so taken for granted that the historian rarely finds formal definitions. At different times and in any given time the term suggested various meanings. Nowadays *human* implies to some, as it did to almost everyone in the past, whatever sets mankind apart from God and whatever distinguishes it from the rest of the animal world. Characteristics assumed to be unique to humans have included the capacity for reason, judgment, and planning, for restraint and self-discipline, and for creating culture, including such symbolic systems as language, myths, religion, and metaphorical thinking, all presumably related to God's plan or to the evolution of special physiological equipment. Intellectuals usually assumed, also, that similarities between groups of humanity outweighed differences, however striking, in physical appearance, custom, and behavior. Yet we shall see that in situations of marked tension between the dominant whites and Indians and blacks, some denied that these dark-skinned creatures were or even could become true human beings. Darwinian and post-Darwinian theory assigned to many animals characteristics commonly associated with human beings, such as anxiety, fear, and anger, and at least in the case of the higher primates, still-more-complex behavior. Indeed, some evidence today suggests that certain insects and mammals communicate with each other regarding the location of food and signs of danger.

The matter of the constancy or flexibility of man's innate endowment has long presented problems. From the time of the ancient Chinese and Greeks the idea has persisted that human nature, being ineluctable, cannot be changed. Yet for an equally long time others have endowed man with a capacity for creative adaptation to changing environments and even for making new ones. Long before present-day behavior modification, some noted and cherished a plasticity sufficient to insure the possibility of changes in conduct—indeed, even in the human constitution itself. Such changes have been related to conscious and unconscious modifications of the culture, largely through scientific discoveries and their application to child-rearing, education, and other aspects of life.

This, of course, is another way of saying that ideas about human nature, like other ideas, have often been functionally related to changing interests and needs.

The word *nature*, like *human*, also suggested a rich variety of meanings. In conjunction with *human* it implied that something in man's makeup explains behavior or at least conditions it. That which is defined as *natural* (innate or predispositional) has often, but not always, been considered as universal.

Such connotations and others related to them have found expression over the entire span of American experience. It would therefore be quite unhistorical to impose on our whole discussion any particular meaning for the term.

Whatever the understanding of the phrase *human nature*, its history, as we have noted, stretches back to ancient civilizations if not to primitive man. Several heritages have influenced its American exploration. These include the classical legacy and, above all, the dominant and subordinate movements of thought in the Old World both at the time of colonization and in the centuries that followed. Throughout, the constant factor was the Hebraic-Christian view of man, though this was by no means monolithic and changeless.

In view of unique historical experiences in America, one might expect the discussion here to have distinguishing characteristics. We shall see the extent to which this has been true. Looking back on this experience, the transmitted heritage of the Old World and its modification in the New, it becomes possible to identify successive meanings given to the phrase. So the first task of the historian might be regarded as the identification of its principal meanings in the American discussion.

Although many have held human nature to be an autonomous entity, others have regarded it as a generalized abstraction. To them it was derived in some cases from a given doctrine or creed or philosophical system, in others from observations of specific conduct in particular situations. In any case, human nature as an abstract concept has not always been distinguished from other abstractions. Thus a special need arises for keeping in mind the limitations of categorizing the meanings given to the term over time. Yet it is still permissible to identify these at least in broad outline. They can, I believe, be described in terms of supernatural dualism, total depravity including the domination of the "deceptive heart," mechanistic materialism, basic goodness, environmental malleability, the autonomous individual, the social and cultural conceptions of man's makeup and performance, biological determinism, and more recently, the biosocial or biocultural view.

Though one can identify specific ideas about human nature one often has to extract them from the contexts, in the absence of formal defini-tions. Furthermore, views about human nature did not always appear as conscious, conceptually refined or coherent ideas. One often finds mere attitudes that imply ideas, prejudices, or convictions. To repeat, times of social crisis engendered open, explicit inquiry and cultural debate.

Such identifications of what human nature has meant emerge from a study of the voluminous and widely varied materials at hand. For the pre-Darwinian period these include the writings of religious leaders, philosophers, medical authorities, pioneer ethnologists, and men and women of letters. In the last century, however, when science has pre-scribed the dominant methods for studying human nature, the records include reports of experimental work in biology, psychology, the social sciences, field studies in anthropology, and interdisciplinary investiga-tions embracing two or more traditional subjects. The examples I have chosen in both the earlier and later periods seem on the basis of much reading over a long time, to be fairly representative.

Were one to limit the history of the American examination of human nature to systematic discussions, it would not be hard to break down ideas about the image of man into their components. Despite difficulties, I have, however, also given some attention to the bearing on the main theme of informal remarks of members of the intellectual community and extrapolations from them.

As we shall see, ideas about man's nature raised and stimulated efforts to answer questions about influences on behavior—astrological, super-natural, biological, environmental, and social-cultural. More specifi-cally, influences on the actions of men and women took form in the Christian plan of sin and grace, the operation of the faculties in the body-mind relationships, and environmental conditions, whether geograph-ical, economic, or social. Writers varied in regarding motives as con-scious or unconscious, though the emphasis on the latter came relatively late—as rational, irrational, and nonrational; as selfish and benevolent, separately or in conjunction. Major views associated motives and con-duct with such issues as rationality and madness, free will or deter-minism, uniformity and diversity in the great groupings of mankind, the malleability or fixity of original endowment, equality or inequality of native talents, and the role of *nature* and *nurture* in character formation and achievement. Also significant was the way in which participants in the discussion viewed the effects of human nature on social arrange-ments and historical change. Some believed that human nature sanc-tioned existing institutions, even made them imperatively necessary. Others held that these and prevailing customs violated the true nature of man. Still others felt that an understanding, or better, precise knowledge of human nature might enable men and women to achieve identity and self-fulfillment. Skeptics, however, questioned whether knowledge could have any real value for such objectives, for prediction and control, or for solving elusive mysteries.

Most views involved at least some of these assumptions and convictions. Such was the case even before the images of man found expression in unfamiliar and complex vocabularies. New conceptions, though, often raised new problems and invited further exploration.

When new concepts appeared, older ideas lingered and did not always vanish. To be sure, even when they persisted, whether in something like their original form or in a modified form, they seldom played as important a role as they once had. I have tried to sort out those that appeared to be most widely held at any given time.

An obvious task involves finding the reasons for changes in the vogue or credentials of different ideas about human nature. Clearly one reason for change relates to actual intellectual conflict and debate on issues that often seemed to have only an indirect relation to the human constitution and predispositions. The list is a long one. Examples include the meaning of sin, the causes of crime and aggression, sumptuary legislation, the right or wrong of slavery, the propriety of integration or segregation of minorities and the loss or maintenance of group identity, sexuality and the character and roles of male and female, and the objectives of formal education, together with pedagogic methods thought to promote these objectives. On some issues the conflicting views of man's nature met head on. We see this in the debates between pacifists and those who believed in the inevitability of war. We see it in disputes over free enterprise, social control, and socialism. On the psychological level, another kind of conflict questioned whether instincts or cognition explained behavior. Challenging the view that instincts dominated, some denied their very existence. Again, the growing importance of universities with research programs and the rise of specialized scholarly organizations also influenced the flavor and outcome of disputes bearing directly or indirectly on shifting ideas about human nature.

A major factor in explaining changes in the acceptability and vogue of certain ideas involves distinctively American conditions and historical events. These included the American Revolution, tensions between church and state, conflicts with Indians, slavery and its aftermath, the drift of people to the West and to cities, immigration and ethnicity, population growth, and the exploitation of natural resources. Of importance on quite a different level were a variety of inventions ranging from labor-saving devices to sophisticated apparatus in biological and psychological laboratories with refined statistical techniques for quantifying data. The relation of all this to the prediction and control of behavior in a world which witnessed genocide, mass hunger, atomic war, and terrorism frightened not only humanists but divided the scientific community itself.

In taking account of the persistence of old ideas and the emergence of new ones, and of the impact of distinctive American problems and conditions, I have been faced by the problem of organizing a great amount of information from both monographs and what were primarily sources for this investigation. I have combined a chronological, topical, and biographical organization of the ideas of intellectuals. I have shown the relation of their views on human nature to the rest of their thought. The influence of predecessors on their ideas about man, as well as that of their own social status, has been taken into account. I have especially emphasized the social and other uses made of these ideas, though no effort has been made to assess the influence of such appeals to one or another view of human nature in situations of conflict. If some such appeals to human nature were a matter of habit, in other cases they seemed to have indicated a serious belief in the relevancy of the appeal.

My debts are numerous. The footnotes and bibliographical note indicate the scholars on whose work I have drawn. My first wife, Margaret Wooster Curti, who had a lively interest in the history of American psychology, urged the need for broadening the scope of existing studies written from a technical point of view for a specialized audience. We discussed many of the problems of a larger undertaking. Several students in my seminars at the University of Wisconsin–Madison contributed in masters' essays and doctoral dissertations to my knowledge of American attitudes toward genius, controversies over eugenics, and ideas of particular leaders about man's nature: the list includes Gretchen Kreuter, Mark Haller, and Charles Townsend. I am also indebted to research assistants who helped me in one or another phase of the investigation. The list includes Richard S. Kirkendall, Thomas Meehan, Peter Karsten, Paul O'Keefe, George Rawick, and William Tillman. My friends Charles A. Barker, David F. Hawke, Hamilton Cravens, Theodore Brameld, and David Fellman read in whole or in part the manuscript in one or another draft, and made useful suggestions. To David Fellman I owe, in addition, a great deal for encouragement and support. I am also deeply grateful to David F. Allmendinger, Jr., and to John Higham. Both made searching conceptual criticisms of the first draft and suggested fruitful ways of getting around many obstacles. They and other friends encouraged me to go on with the study when I had all but decided to drop it. My daughter Martha Curti saved me from many errors by a close reading of the manuscript; she also made many useful suggestions. Many others, including Robert L. Schneider, Fulmer Mood, Louis C. Hunter, William A. Williams, LaWanda Cox, and the late Harry Hayden Clark eased the path in one way or another. My editor for the University of Wisconsin Press, Mary Maraniss, did a great deal to improve the manuscript, and I will always be deeply grateful to her.

I want also to express my appreciation for suggestions from colleagues and staff at the Center for Advanced Studies in the Behavioral Sciences at Stanford during the year I was a Fellow. I also thank the Research Committee of the University of Wisconsin for generous support. I shall not forget the help of the staffs of the Wisconsin State Historical Society, the Memorial Library of the University of Wisconsin, and other libraries. Of these I am especially grateful to the Henry E. Huntington Library. The time I spent at San Marino as a Visiting Scholar in 1969 proved to be both enjoyable and fruitful. I recall especially the helpful comments of Ray A. Billington and the late Allan Nevins.

Norma W. Lynch retyped all the footnotes in record time. I owe a special debt to Roberta Schambow for retyping the mauscript itself several times with accuracy, efficiency, and unfailing good spirit.

The history of the idea of human nature in America needs to be further probed, supplemented, and interpreted from angles of vision different from my own. Recent and forthcoming research in the behavioral sciences needs to be integrated in the general picture. I should like to think that my work may be useful to future scholars and that in the meantime it may interest those working in American Studies and intellectual history. I hope, also, that it may attract many of the informed public who have followed current writing about human nature and behavior in relation to personal problems and to the larger issues of our time.

HUMAN NATURE IN AMERICAN THOUGHT

1

Traditional Ideas in New Situations

IDEAS ABOUT human nature resemble rivers with vague banks, and in exploring the history of such ideas the place to begin is with the tributaries. When the first university-educated men and those of some learning came to the Atlantic seaboard, they brought with them the thinking familiar to them and to their peers at home. In the long span of American interest in human nature, ideas transmitted from England overshadowed all others. Yet those which Spanish and other explorers, missionaries, and commentators expressed about the relation between the newly discovered Indian and traditional ideas of the human constitution and destiny can hardly be ruled out altogether. As we shall see, their discussion influenced early English views about the relation of the Indian to human nature.

Identifying those early ideas that the settlers brought with them brings other questions to mind. Did new situations in America help to shape first the selection and then the emphasis given the ideas? In what way, if any, did distinctive experiences in America raise new questions about man's nature? How did the changing cultural and social environment invite new uses for accepted ideas about it? In the century and a half of colonial experience, did the casual references to human nature and more sustained discussion of it show any notable changes? If so, how can these be explained? Such questions suggest a structural framework for the exploration of American ideas of human nature.

In the social, economic, and intellectual ferment and thorny conflicts of Elizabethan England, the interplay of medieval and Renaissance ideas

3

understandably brought out varying views about human nature. In such times, as we shall see more than once, controversies about the nature of man tend to be sharply explicit. Social change in the seventeenth century and the vogue of new ideas widened the perception of differences between assumptions about human nature and actual character and conduct. These several heritages, traditional and upsurging, shaped the outlook of the better educated among both the second and third generations of colonists and new arrivals on the Atlantic seaboard. Of whatever vintage or commitment, parsons, magistrates, merchants, and planters of some formal education did not at once give up or even greatly modify Old World ideas about man's nature.

The first Europeans of some book learning who settled the Atlantic seaboard and the Spanish borderlands viewed human nature in terms of a traditional cosmic scheme. This had taken shape in the Graeco-Roman world, and the medieval church and the Christian humanists of the Renaissance and Reformation sanctioned it with appropriate amendments and revampings. Whatever the defining criteria of man's nature and destiny, Catholics, Anglicans, and dissenters in the main accepted this cosmic and eclectic pattern of thought.

The picture envisioned a universe marked in the first place by plenitude—whatever could possibly have been created had been created. It was also an orderly, hierarchical universe of living beings and inanimate objects all alike governed by God's law. The Creator embodied divine nature, ineffably different from the natures of all other constituents of the universe. Closest to God stood the angels. Perfect in their gift of understanding and adoration, blessed with a free will always obedient to him, the angels served as God's messengers to and protectors of human beings. Opposed to God and his angels stood Satan and all his wicked satellites, the fallen angels who, having broken God's law, waged a never-ending struggle to control mankind with tempting promises of supernatural powers. Human nature, though sharply contrasting with divine nature, nevertheless bore some kinship to it in embodying an immortal soul. Human nature also, of course, partook of the material cosmos. Here everything of a physical character consisted in varying combinations of the four basic elements—air, water, earth, and fire. In the hierarchical Great Chain of Being, animals, plants, and nonliving objects took their designated places below man. However distinct, each bore some relation to the others.[1] Even man himself resembled the beast in ambiguous and disputed ways.[2]

1. E. M. W. Tillyard, *The Elizabethan World Picture* (London, 1960), pp. 24–66; also Arthur O. Lovejoy, *The Great Chain of Being* (Cambridge, Mass., 1936), esp. chaps. 3–6.

2. For dissident views about the creation of man and the relationships between man and animals see Don Cameron Allen, *Doubt's Boundless Sea: Skepticism and Faith in the Renaissance* (Baltimore, 1964), pp. 24–25, 60, 67–68, 137, 188, 205–6.

Divisions of human beings by sex and by fixed social class did not negate the concept of mankind. The Book of Genesis supported this view. So did the belief that every human being, a duality of perishable physical body and immortal soul, represented a unique microcosm of the universe itself.

Within this frame, supplemented, as we shall see, by the influence of the planets, sun, and moon on human destiny, colonial thinking differed in the emphasis given to one or another aspect of the image of man. Even so, most early Americans of some light and learning accepted the tradition of Aristotle, Galen, and their medieval commentators in conceiving of human nature as a function of a complex organism both physiological and psychological in character and mode of operation. English writings, some encyclopedic, some specialized, provided the outline or filled in the details.[3]

According to this heritage, the human organism consisted of closely interacting, mutually influential physical components and corresponding mental or spiritual functions or faculties. Like all other created matter, the bodily organs were made up of the basic, universal elements (earth, water, air, fire). The liver, the heart, and the brain outranked all other organs. Each created humours or subtle fluids. In varying combinations these humours—blood, choler, phlegm, and black bile or "melancholy" (each with its own qualities)—explained the temperament or personality of every individual. In imbalance, the humours also accounted for every conceivable ailment, including mental disarray. Remedies for these could be found in some antidote in the mineral, vegetable, or animal world that, by God's grace, bore an identifiable "signature" or "correspondence." At least until William Harvey's discovery of the circulation of blood, colonists subscribed to the doctrine of humours. Thus Anne Bradstreet, in one of her didactic poems, assessed the role of the humours in the makeup of various types of personalities.[4] Finally, each of the chief organs, liver, heart, and brain, in cooperation with the humours, created various kinds of essences or "spirits" that, in somewhat the fashion of the later nervous system, served as agents of communication with the psychological aspects of human nature.

On this interwoven and interacting psychological level, the soul (to some, related but discrete souls) corresponded to the distinctively corporeal parts of human nature, the humours, the "spirits," and the liver,

3. Thus, for example, Harvard students had access to Johannes Magirus's *Physiologiae Peripateticae*, first published in 1596, which presented Aristotle's and Galen's views about the relation of the four elements to the human body. See Theodore Hornberger, *Scientific Thought in the American Colleges, 1638–1800* (Austin, Texas, 1945), p. 39.

4. *The Works of Anne Bradstreet*, ed. Jeannie Hensley (Cambridge, Mass., 1967), pp. 33–50.

heart, and brain. The soul's vegetative functions or faculties included nutrition, growth, and reproduction. The sensitive soul embraced the five outward senses and the "internal senses" of memory, imagination, and sometimes common sense. These faculties accounted for the appetites or passions, especially the emotions of love and hate, desire and aversion, hope and despair, courage and fear. The rational soul, man's unique possession among worldly creatures, involved the faculties of reason, or understanding, and will. Authorities differed on the relative force of reason and will, though most held that the latter could make free choices. God had meant the rational soul to govern the vegetative and sensitive souls; but in fallen man, the opposite proved only too often the case. Thus tumult, chaos, and disorder in the psychological functions of human nature replaced the intended equilibrium. Ceaseless war raged between reason and the corrupted will and unruly passions.[5]

Any one of several writers might be chosen to illustrate this overall scheme. A summary in Sir Walter Raleigh's *History of the World*, begun in the Tower of London before his release in 1616 for another American voyage, is especially appropriate because of its popularity in the colonies.

> And whereas God created three sorts of living natures, to wit, angelicall, rationall, and brutal; giving to angels an intellectuall, and to beasts a sensual nature, he vouchsafed unto man both the intellect of angels, and sensative of beasts, and the proper rational belonging unto man; and therefore—man is the bond and chaine which tieth together both natures; and because, in the little frame of man's body there is a representation of the Universal, and (by allusion) a kind of participation of all parts thereof, therefore was man called Microcosmos, or the little world.[6]

Though Raleigh's own unfortunate experiences might have given him reason for doubt, he still accepted the idea that man in some ways partook of divinity, the microcosm, man, being

> internal endued with a divine understanding, by which he might contemplate and serve his Creator, after whose image he was formed,

5. For this oversimplified summary I am indebted to Lilly B. Campbell, *Shakespeare's Tragic Heroes, Slaves of Passion* (Cambridge, 1960; rept. ed., New York, 1969), chaps. 5 and 6; Theodore Spencer, *Shakespeare and the Nature of Man* (New York, 1942); Patrick Critwell, "Physiology and Psychology in Shakespeare's Day," *Journal of the History of Ideas* 12 (1951): 75–81; and, especially, Herschel Baker, *The Image of Man: A Study of the Idea of Human Dignity in Classical Antiquity, the Middle Ages, and the Renaissance* (Cambridge, 1947), chap. 17.

6. Sir Walter Raleigh, *Works*, 8 vols. (Oxford, 1829; 2d ed., New York, 1964), 2:58.

and endued with the powers and facilities of reasons and other abilities, that thereby also he might govern and rule the world, and all other God's creatures therein.

Assuming that the will is free to choose between real alternatives, as fit a faculty of the rational soul, Raleigh with some optimism held that in spite of its appetitive quality, the will makes us

> desire that good which the understanding comprehendeth to be such indeed or in appearance, and flieth the contrary; this is our will, which we use to stir us up to seek God and heaven, and heavenly things, by which we rest also in these things, and are delighted and satisfied in them, being gotten. This is a part of the reasonable soul; this is one point by which we are men, and do excel all other creatures living upon the earth.[7]

Though modified and challenged, as we shall see, by competing Renaissance and post-Renaissance movements of thought, this scheme governed the outlook of well-informed early colonists and later arrivals.[8]

Like their contemporaries across the sea, the first generation of colonial men of education accepted the ancient and complex doctrines of astrology. Natural astrology concerned itself with the influence of the planets and signs of the zodiac on such material things as eclipses, the weather, and the well-being or ills of the human body. Judicial astrology dealt with the ways in which the movements of the planets influenced the human mind, including emotions and the will. In the late seventeenth century and the early eighteenth century, students at Harvard, like those at William and Mary and Yale, were expected to be familiar with astrology. By the 1720s, however, its accuracy, if not its validity, came under question. Still, the makers of almanacs, who professed some scholarship, included throughout the eighteenth century astrological advice in matters affecting the movements of ships, the planting and harvesting of crops, and diseases of the human body. Thus in the words of E. M. W. Tillyard, "the orthodox belief in the stars' influence, sanctioned but articulated and controlled by the authority of religion, was not always kept pure from the terrors of primitive superstition."[9]

In seventeenth-century America, as in the Old World, the learned, like the unschooled, believed that human nature involved behavior resulting

7. Raleigh, "Treatise of the Soul," *Works*, 8:586–87.
8. Edward Eggleston, in *The Transit of Civilization from England to America in the Seventeenth Century* (Boston, 1959), gives examples.
9. Tillyard, *The Elizabethan World Picture*, p. 53. The best treatment of colonial astrology is that in Herbert Leventhal's *In the Shadow of the Enlightenment: Occultism and Renaissance Science in Eighteenth-Century America* (New York, 1976).

from Special Providences. These divine interventions in human affairs presumably took place within natural law as opposed to miracles. Inscrutable though the interventions were, men might, through reason, at least approximate God's intentions, whether these signified disapproval for sin or timely warnings against a given course of action. Thus the appearance of comets, of huge flocks of pigeons, and of swarms of flies before Bacon's rebellion in 1676 was later remembered as a divine warning of imminent tumult. Again, angels might give warnings to people through apparitions, specters, or nocturnal dreams. The most cherished of these unusual mediations, however, took the form of wonderful "Deliverances" from calamities—from lightning, fire, storms, shipwrecks, dread diseases, and Indian captivities. Abundant examples of all these found faithful reporters, sometimes with corroborating affadavits from eye-witnesses. Captain John Smith, the Jesuit missionaries, John Winthrop, Jasper Danckaerts, Increase and Cotton Mather, Samuel Sewall, John Syles, and Mary Rowlandson illustrate the genre.[10]

In the war between God and Satan, the Devil and his cohorts also intervened in human behavior. Demoniacal possession of the wretches who fell prey to such machinations might find expression in seizures, hysteria or outright madness, and far worse, witchcraft.

Were the only aspect of the colonial acceptance of the Judeo-Christian belief in witchcraft the conviction that evil intentions and behavior resulted from human weakness and depravity and from the power of an incorporeal Satan, the persistence of this still widely held attribute of human nature would need little comment. Several circumstances, however, gave special meaning to witchcraft in the seventeenth-century discussions. One was the seeming likelihood that an unsettled and wild country offered unusual opportunities to the Devil in his never-ending war against God and the effort of his Chosen People to build a truly Christian order. The commonly accepted reality of witchcraft became spectacularly implemented when anxieties, tensions, and bitter strife in a community encouraged some to charge others with its overt practice, a situation which led to tragic consequences in Salem. No less significant was the division among ministers, physicians, and magistrates over the interpretation of theological, medical, and legal guideposts for testing the authenticity of evidence in the accusations, denials, motives, and use and misuse of psychological and physical torture to extract confessions

10. Richard M. Dorson has collected, with comment, representative selections from the sources in *America Begins: Early American Writings* (New York, 1950). See also the illuminating notes and fine selections from the sources in John Demos, ed., *Remarkable Providences, 1600–1700* (New York, 1972).

of accusers and accused.[11] The most thorny issue concerned the validity of spectral evidence or the actual appearance of the image of the witch to threaten and abuse the victim. Some of those involved in making judgments questioned or rejected spectral apparitions. They regarded them as fantasies and illusions resulting from undue pride, lust for public attention, or unconscious or downright deceit. Cotton Mather, like his father Increase Mather, rejected spectral evidence in the trials. Yet in his *Memorable Providences* Cotton Mather, the most erudite parson of his day, wrote that "though it be folly to impute every dubious incident, or unwonted Effect of Providence, to Witchcraft: yet there are some things which cannot be excepted against, but must be ascribed thither."

Evidences of black magic from the Invisible World, like Special Providences and Deliverances, proved that whatever the limitations of human freedom and responsibility, men and women could still thank and praise God for his marvellous blessings and take steps to set their community straight with the just and angry God whom it had offended.

Though most participants in the Salem hangings did not, like Cotton Mather's friend Judge Samuel Sewall, express public repentance, belief in witchcraft waned with the growing vogue of rationalism, skepticism, and scientific method. Among the new generation Josiah Cotton, Thomas Hutchinson, and Benjamin Franklin, for example, used the tools of historical analysis and satire to weaken lingering credulity among the unlettered.

As belief in Special Providences, Special Deliverances, and witchcraft, along with other articles of Christian faith and tradition, suggests that the formally educated and lesser folk shared many of the same attitudes toward man's nature, so did various usages mainly secular in character. An example is the proverb. Rooted in classical, biblical, and other literary sources as well as in folk wisdom, proverbs served the learned and the unlearned in different ways. They can be thought of as means for making acceptable or endurable much that was painful, and of easing the malaise that stemmed from the mysterious and the uncertain. The significance of the fact that some proverbs contradicted others is that the very contradictions served useful purposes. Of these, none was more important than the temporary and partial satisfaction provided by a

11. The scholarly literature on colonial witchcraft is voluminous. In addition to the printed sources I am especially indebted to John Demos, "Underlying Theses in the Witchcraft of Seventeenth-Century New England," *American Historical Review* 75 (1976): 1311–26; Chadwick Hansen, *Witchcraft at Salem* (New York, 1969); and Paul Boyer and Stephen Nissenbaum, *Salem Possessed: The Social Origins of Witchcraft* (Cambridge, Mass., 1974). Boyer and Nissenbaum have also edited *The Salem Witchcraft Papers*, 2 vols. (New York, 1977). Leventhall's discussion, *In the Shadow of the Enlightenment*, chap. 3, was helpful on the relation between the attitudes of intellectuals and the common people.

given proverb or saying when self-interest conflicted with what a presumed consensus held to be the group welfare, and when this conflict yielded to no rational or complete resolution. So it was said that there are two sides to every story. The ambivalence of many proverbs also suggested that what seemed reasonable and true in one situation did not seem so at other times and under other circumstances. In addition to all this, William Penn's comment about proverbs probably had a special bearing on their use by those with some formal education. "The wisdom of nations," he wrote, "lies in their proverbs, which are brief and pithy; collect and learn them; they are notable measures and directions for human life; you have much in little; they save time and speaking; and upon occasion may be the fullest and safest answers. . . ."[12]

The proverbs of the first settlers, like those of the ancients long before them and of their near predecessors the Elizabethans, reflected the belief, on the one hand, that man's conduct was largely determined, and on the other, that he was free and responsible for his actions. The importance of caution, foresight, of frugality in shaping an outcome and one's own responsibility for that outcome were reflected in *Look before you leap; Good watch prevents misfortune; An ounce of prevention is worth a pound of cure; Things hardly attained are long retained; First deserve and then desire; He that maketh his bed ill lies there;* and *Where the will is ready the feet are light.* Unworthy passions and emotions, however powerful, need not be all-determining: *Where reason rules, appetite obeys; A man without reason is a beast in season; Envy never enricheth; He that doth what he will often doth not what he ought.* Ambition might be checked too: *Grasp no more than the hand will hold* and *A bird in hand . . . is worth ten flys large.* The belief that man was responsible for his acts and that he could learn from witnessing punishments metely dealt to those who broke the laws of God and man found expression in *He that chasteneth one amendeth many.*

On the other hand, forces beyond man's control also played a role in the human condition. These forces included heredity, habit, and an environment that a man had no part in choosing or shaping: *Blood will tell; You will never make a satin purse of a sow's ear; Custom is a master that makes a slave of reason; As the twig is bent, so the tree inclines; He is proper that hath proper conditions; Noble plants suit not a stubborn soil; Gnaw the bone that falls to thy lot;* and *There's no flying from fate.* It was not clear whether inborn temperament or effort was implied in *A man of gladness seldom falls into madness.* In any case, there was a tendency to blame one's lot not on his own shortcomings but on something else: *Everyone puts his fault on the times.*

12. Frederick B. Tolles and E. Gordon Alderfer, eds., *The Witness of William Penn* (New York, 1957), p. 199.

With all the attributes men shared in common, each was different by nature. *None is a fool always, everyone some time; All tread not in one shoe; There could be no great if there were no little.* Thus appearances are often deceptive: *A tree is known not by its leaves but by its fruits; Good words without deeds are rushes and weeds;* and *Everyone's faults are not written on his forehead.*[13]

All this—cosmology, theology, psychology, and the common wisdom of the proverbs—summed up much in the older heritage, including the dominant image of man that settlers in the New World brought with them. But it was not everything. The complex and often contradictory Renaissance views of human nature made up part of the intellectual baggage of literate explorers, developers, and colonizers of the Atlantic seaboard.

Some leaders of the Renaissance, discussing human nature in secular terms, projected a more or less pessimistic image of man. Machiavelli's commentaries on the power struggles for military dominance and commercial expansion in the ancient world and in the Italy of his time offered a complex view of man that stressed the dominant role of inborn and unchangeable passions and emotions. These included the will to survive and dominate and the dislike of being dominated. But a paradoxical readiness to succumb and to imitate led the many to fall prey to clever, manipulative, and ambitious leaders in never-ending conflicts. In spite of the strength of the emotions in relation to reason in the human makeup, Machiavelli held that it was still possible for both leaders and people to have some control over their immediate present and future in the ceaseless conflicts between *fortuna* or chance and contingency, on the one hand, and on the other, dynamic *virtú* or the soldier-like qualities of boldness, will power, self-discipline, and ability to work with others against corruption and for survival. To be sure, in *The Prince,* the most widely known of his writings, Machiavelli explained success and failure in power struggles through examples of the manipulability of the people by a shrewd, clever, and deceitful ruler. But in his *Discourses on Livy* and in other writings, he suggested such political devices as separation of powers and checks, balances, and relative economic equality as means by which patriots might, in the face of corruption and usurpation of power, safeguard their liberty.[14]

13. Most of these proverbs appeared in John Ray, *A Collection of English Proverbs* (Cambridge, 1670; London, 1837). Also useful are Ronald Rideout and Clifford Whitting, *English Proverbs Explained* (London, 1917); Edwin M. Fogel, "Proverbs of the Pennsylvania Germans," in *The Pennsylvania German Society* 36 (1929): 1–221; David Kin, ed., *Dictionary of American Proverbs* (New York, 1955); and Bartlett J. Whiting, *Early American Proverbs and Proverbial Phrases* (Cambridge, Mass., 1977).

14. Niccolò Machiavelli, *The Discourses of Machiavelli,* ed. Dr. W. Stark, vol. 1 (London, 1950), pp. 166, 274–75, 315.

Machiavelli, often misread and misunderstood, influenced the satirical pessimism of French and English writers about human nature. He interested Franklin, Jefferson, John Adams, and other founders of the American republic.[15]

In the meantime, scholarly colonists often had some acquaintance with other secular Renaissance and post-Renaissance thinkers who also took a dim view of human nature. Montaigne, with skepticism and irony, questioned the traditional Christian view of the orderly and beneficent laws of nature and human rationality and uniqueness. Thomas Hobbes argued that man was by nature a selfish, brutish animal engaged in constant warfare with all other men unless restrained by an all-powerful sovereign. His principal ideas found expression in the years of troubled conflict that stimulated much migration to the New World.

The theme of universal self-interest also informed the views of Virginia's early leaders. This was evident in the often-quoted explanation for the failure of the initial policy of communal planting and harvesting. "When our people were fed out of the common store, and laboured joyntly together . . . ," wrote Ralph Hamor, "glad was that man who could slip from his labor; nay, the most honest of them in a generall businesse, would not take so much faithful and true paines, in a weeke, as now he will do in a day, neither cared for the increase, presuming that howsoever their harvest prospered, the generall store must maintayne them."[16]

On the other hand, the Renaissance and post-Renaissance also offered a brighter view of human nature than that set forth by Hobbes and Machiavelli. Christian humanists emphasized the dignity of man and his capacity for both spiritual and intellectual development. This was to be reflected in colonial writing. Later, the Cambridge Platonists too, seeking to clarify the religious confusion of the early seventeenth century, opposed the deprecation of human reason and human nature. These were identified with an abstract conceptualized spirituality—the only true reality—that suffused and in truth constituted the whole universe.[17]

At the opposite end of the spectrum, the new science also reenforced the brighter view of man's constitution. It is of course true that Copernicus and Galileo verified laws of nature that, in contradicting Ptolemaic astronomy, denied the central spot previously given the earth

15. J. C. A. Pocock, *The Machiavellian Moment: Florentine Political Thought and the American Republican Tradition* (Princeton, 1975), esp. chaps. 6 and 15. See also Anthony J. Pansini's introductory essay in his new translation of Machiavelli's writings, *Machiavelli and the United States of America* (Greenvale, N.Y., 1969).

16. Ralph Hamor, in Samuel Purchas, *Hakluytus Posthumus, or Purchas His Pilgrimes*, 20 vols. (Glasgow, 1905–7), 19:95.

17. Basil Willey, *The Seventeenth-Century Background* (London, 1934), pp. 133 ff.

and its human inhabitants in the whole scheme of the universe. The new science had implications beyond this for the understanding of human nature, however. In empirical and inductive inquiries, experimenters and philosophers found a promising key for unlocking the secrets of a nature that had subordinated human powers to it. Chemists and physicians, in probing the mysteries of the body, challenged much received doctrine in physiology and psychology. Building on their work, Francis Bacon eloquently preached man's ability and duty to maximize knowledge through exploiting nature for the bettering of the human lot. Bacon hoped that in time science would enable man to control his passions and to minimize the role of the "idols" or "conceits" that kept him from applying scientific truth for the improvement of man's estate.[18] Needless to say, the growing commercial class and the promoters of colonization hailed this view of expanding human powers over nature and fate in a world of new initiatives and untold opportunities for gain and fame at home and overseas.

Man's capacity for inductive reasoning based on observation was seldom displayed in positive statements or even very often implied in the early reports of hitherto unknown geological and biological marvels of the New World. Settlers and explorers more often revealed traditional attitudes about the makeup and functions of human nature. Belief in God's endowment of his children with the gift of reason implied the duty to use it for the glorification of the Creator by finding new marvels in nature and by putting them to good use. Some reports of botanical and geological wonders reflected the Renaissance stress on man's intellectual curiosity as an earmark of human dignity. In many reports, readiness to attribute the unusual to some sort of supernatural magic appeared in the mixture of fact, fancy, and hearsay. Now and then a discovery led to conflicting explanations bearing directly on man's nature. Thus some believed that the indigenous rattlesnake had a supernatural power of making human beings as well as birds and animals powerless to feel or move. The snake presumably exercised this power through the fixed gaze of the Evil Eye. On the other hand, the more skeptical looked for rational explanations: perhaps the snake's eyes emitted powerful effluvia.

The presence of Indians and blacks provided a far more telling focus on interest in human nature than the wonders of plants, trees, fish, birds,

18. Francis Bacon, *The Works of Francis Bacon*, 15 vols. (New York, 1863–72), 8:383–529; 9:13–357; Karl R. Wallace, *Francis Bacon on the Nature of Man* (Urbana, Ill., 1967); and George H. Nadel, "History as Psychology in Francis Bacon's Theory of History," *History and Theory* 5 (1966): 275–87. See also Theodore D. Boseman, *Protestants in the Age of Science: The Baconian Ideal and Antebellum American Religious Thought* (Chapel Hill, 1977), for references to Bacon in colonial writing.

and beasts. In relation to concepts of man, what views did Europeans have about these peoples when colonization began? How did the first colonial experiences with Indians and Negroes fit the current ideas about human nature? The images of these newly perceived peoples had much in common. Yet there were differences.

With the discovery of the New World, conflicting reports about its strange inhabitants challenged existing views about the nature of man, views which now seemed to leave many questions blurred and unsettled. The problem Indians posed for views of man were complicated by ambiguities and contradictions in the reports of discoverers, explorers, and missionaries and by the ways that commentators at home read the reports. Further, in serving various needs of Europeans, these differing views compounded the difficulties.[19]

The essence of the Christian view of man was, to be sure, clearly enough understood: the human being was a creature capable of receiving divine grace. A few Spanish and other explorers and commentators, citing the Indians' entrenched heathenism and resistance to Christianization, denied them the right to be considered human beings. The Church ruled otherwise. Still, the decision left many matters up in the air.

The classical heritage paradoxically both helped and confused efforts to solve the problem of the Indians' humanity. That heritage defined man as a being capable of living in society, of being civilized, and of reasoning. Reports of Indians with complex social organization and architectural monuments indicated that at least many met these criteria. Also relevant was the classical myth which envisioned a long lost golden age in which an innocent people lived happily in an idyllic land. Early reports of Indian hospitality, childlike curiosity, primeval purity, and

19. My discussion of the Indians is indebted to many authorities, especially to Margaret Hodgen, *Early Anthropology in the Sixteenth and Seventeenth Centuries* (Philadelphia, 1964); J. H. Elliott, *The Old World and the New, 1492–1950* (Cambridge, 1970); Fred Chiapelli, ed., *First Images of America: The Impact of the New World on the Old*, 2 vols. (Berkeley and Los Angeles, 1976); Lewis Hanke, *Mankind Is One* (DeKalb, Ill., 1974); Henri Baudet, *Paradise on Earth* (New Haven, 1965); Edward Dudley and Maximillian E. Novak, eds., *The Wild Man Within: An Image in Western Thought from the Renaissance to Romanticism* (Pittsburgh, 1973); Gilbert Chinard, *L'Amérique et le rêve exotique dans la litterature française au XVIIe au XVIIIe siècle* (Paris, 1913); Roy Harvey Pearce, *The Savages of America: A Study of the Indian and the Idea of Civilization* (Baltimore, 1953); and James Levenier and Hennig Cohen, eds., *The Indians and Their Captives* (Westport, Conn., 1977). Robert F. Berkhofer, Jr.'s commanding analysis in *The White Man's Indian: Images of the American Indian from Columbus to the Present Day* (New York, 1978) came to my attention after my discussion had been written. For the approach of a distinguished historical geographer consult Carl O. Sauer, *Sixteenth-Century North America: The Land and the People as Seen by Europeans* (Berkeley, 1971).

simple, intimate dependence on nature suggested that America and its people verified the appealing myth. Montaigne and other humanistic critics of the corruption, hypocrisy, and pretensions of the European nobility used this myth, more or less satirically, to criticize all that they scorned in the Old World. The Noble Savage was embarked on his career.

Still another ancient myth, embroidered in the Middle Ages, played a part in what explorers and commentators perceived the Indian to be. This was the fantasy of the beast-man, half human, half animal, reared beyond the reach of civilization. When the Indian was described as a naked savage, sexually potent and promiscuous, crafty and cruel, it was easy to associate him with the beast-man. In Christian idiom this suggested the disturbing and frightening idea that the Indian symbolized the evil in every human heart. The Indian, then, must be either the acme of degeneration or the Devil incarnate. The assimilation of the Indian to the myth warranted his exploitation and enslavement. It also justified his virtual annihilation in case of obstinate, bloody resistance to European occupation of the lands over which he freely roamed.

Even after the Church decided that the newly discovered inhabitants of America must be regarded as members of the family of man, it was hard to fit such strange and forbidding human beings into the familiar picture in the Book of Genesis. In his *History of the World* Sir Walter Raleigh, though reporting the existence of semihuman beings, nevertheless faced the problem of race in relation to human nature by projecting a monogenetic view. This held that, as children of God, the newly found red people possessed the capacity for leading rational as well as moral lives. Other writers tried to explain how the wandering and "lost" offspring of Adam and Noah had got to where they were and why they so bafflingly differed from the rest of the human family.[20] Explanations varied almost as much as the diverse judgments of explorers, geographers, and commentators on the character of the Indians.

Favorable and unfavorable views there were. A good many explorers, like Amadas and Barlowe, whom Raleigh sent to the New World, described the natives in such phrases as "very handsome and Godly," and contended that their behavior compared well with that of Europeans. Such comment might, of course, have been meant to quiet fears of prospective investors and colonists. On the basis of such reports Peter Martyr, echoing the classical myth, depicted Indians as seeming to live in a "golden Worlde of which the olde Wryters speak so muche."[21]

20. Don Cameron Allen, *The Legend of Noah: Renaissance Rationalism in Art, Science and Letters* (Urbana, Ill., 1948), chap. 6, esp. pp. 119 ff.
21. Hodgen, *Early Anthropology*, p. 371.

More characteristic was the view of the Indian as the faulted European, degenerate and degraded, but still having the capacity for leading a rational and moral life. William Strachey in his *Historie of Travell into Virginia Britania* (1612), after tracing Indian descent from the wandering Ham, expressed the hope that patient effort might civilize and Christianize the wayward savages.[22] Some decades later Roger Williams, after noting similarities between Indian and Hebrew words, concluded: "The wandering Generations of Adam's . . . posteritie having lost the true and living God their Maker have created out of the Nothing of their own Inventions many false and fained Gods and Creators."[23] But, like Strachey, Williams had no doubt that as children of the true God, Indians deserved to be so regarded and so treated.

Not everyone who held the monogenetic view of the unity of mankind with its varied races accepted the orthodox Christian explanation. Thus some secular-minded Renaissance writers on the origins of Indians, though holding to the monogenetic view, questioned biblical exegesis. They fell back on the classical conception of natural decay or rhythmical change. Or, sympathetic with the empiricism of the new science, they hypothesized (as Jean Bodin did) that environment might be the key to the riddle of human variance. Or, again, Montaigne, with his skeptical, satirical, and relativist outlook, held that what seemed barbaric in savage behavior stemmed only from its very strangeness: in many ways, the customs and conduct of these peoples, even their cannibalism, were no worse than the ways of so-called civilized Europeans.[24]

At the other extreme, some writers, in dehumanizing the Indians, laid the ground for a later rejection of the monogenetic view of race in favor of a polygenetic one. The Indian, if admittedly a human being, resembled animals in lacking rational and moral capacity. One such spokesman perceived the Indians as "bad people, having little of Humanitie but shape, ignorant of Civilitie, of Arts, of Religion; more brutish than the beasts they hunt, more wild and unmanly than their unmanned wild Countrey, which they range rather than inhabite."[25] In

22. William Strachey, Gent., *The Historie of Travell into Virginia Britania*, ed. Louis B. Wright and Virginia Freund (1612; London, 1953), pp. 65, 69, 74 ff., 93–94.

23. Roger Williams, *A Key into the Languages of America*, with an introduction by Howard W. Chapin, 5th ed., 2 vols. in one (New York, 1973), pp. 24–25, 147. See also Williams's letter to Gov. John Winthrop in *The Complete Writings of Roger Williams*, 7 vols. (New York, 1903), 6:114.

24. Michel Montaigne, *The Essays of Michael Seigneur de Montaigne*, 3 vols. (London, 1684), 1:375 ff.

25. "Virginias Verger: Or a Discourse shewing the benefits which may grow to this Kingdome from American English plantations," in Purchas, *Hakluytus Posthumus*, 19: 231.

asking whether the English were justified in planting colonies on lands inhabited by Indians, Robert Gray contended that their near inhumanity disqualified them from the right to hold land. "Although the Lord hath given the earth to the children of men the greater part of it [is] possessed and wrongly usurped by wild beasts, and unreasonable creatures, or by brutish savages, which by reason of their godless ignorance, and blasphemous Idolotrie, are worse than those beasts which are of most wilde and savage nature."[26] Before the end of the seventeenth century, Dr. William Petty of the Royal Society rejected the concept of man as a unified whole in the hierarchy of being—an idea implied much earlier by Isaac de la Peyère—and regarded races as separately created kinds of men innately differing in capacities associated with human beings. Each had a fixed place in the Great Chain of Being.[27]

These colliding preconceptions played a part in the bewildered and contradictory reactions of the newcomers themselves to their first encounters with the aborigines. How they related Indians to their inherited images of man varied according to particular native cultures. The settlers' views of their ambiguous neighbors further reflected their own religious and social group characteristics.[28] Personal factors also, of course, affected reactions.[29] In short, preconceptions brought from England, place, time, and situation all figured in views set forth about the Indian and human nature.

Early Virginia provided examples of the ways in which the two broad preconceptions of the Indian interacted with the social status and personalities of those reporting interracial experiences.[30]

In the eyes of Captain John Smith, who seems to have stood for the prevailing position, the Indians were "inconstant in everrie thing, but what feare constraineth them to keepe. Craftie, timerous, quicke of apprehension, and very ingenuous." But Smith noted individual differences too. "Some are of disposition fearful, some bold, most caulteous." But all, just the same, were savage. He saw them "soone

---

26. Robert Gray, A Good Speed to Virginia (London, 1609), quoted by Gary B. Nash in "The Image of the Indians in the Southern Colonial Mind," William and Mary Quarterly, 3d ser. 29 (1972): 210.

27. Hodgen, Early Anthropology, pp. 419 ff., 450.

28. For a discussion of New England Puritan views see chap. 2.

29. For example, note the differences between John and William Bartram, father and son, and both Quakers. John Bartram wrote, "But unless we bang the Indians stoutly, and make them fear us, they will never love us, nor keep the peace long with us." His son, two decades later, pictured the Indian as the Noble Savage. Carl Bridenbaugh, Myths and Realities: Societies of the Colonial South (Baton Rouge, 1952), p. 119.

30. See the illuminating introductory essays in Wilcomb E. Washburn's collection of documents, The Indian and the White Man (Garden City, N.Y., 1964).

moved to anger, and so malitious, that they seldome forget an injury. They seldome steale one from another, least their conjurers should reveale it, and so they be pursued and punished." In other words, while Smith found in the Indians motives of fear, covetousness, and anger, as he found them among whites, and while he acknowledged special abilities, he took on the whole a dim view of their nature. He summed up the matter laconically: "And in this lamentable ignorance doe these poore soules sacrifice themselves to the Divill, not knowing their Creator."[31]

But Captain John Smith did not express the views of everyone in early Jamestown. Hear the admonition of the Reverend Alexander Whitaker: "Let the miserable condition of these naked slaves of the Divill move you to a compassion toward them. They acknowledge that there is a great good God, but know him not; . . . wherefore they serve the Divill for feare, after a most base manner."[32] But Parson Whitaker believed the Indians to be capable of better things and urged home support for their conversion to Christianity.

The familiar story of John Rolfe and Pocahontas was pertinent because it lent, at least for a time, support to the brighter view of Indian nature. Parenthetically, it was also relevant because the explanation Rolfe made in 1614 to Sir Thomas Dale was a rare example of self-analysis of motives on the part of an early Virginia settler.[33]

The tragic events of 1622 blasted the hope that the Rolfe-Pocahontas alliance might, with other factors, sustain the uneasy peace and lead to a lasting accommodation of the two racial variants of mankind. Indian leaders had now come to face the fact that the colony would not fail and

31. John Smith, *The Generall Historie of Virginia, New-England and the Summer Isles*, in Edward Arber, ed., *Travels and Works of Captain John Smith*, 2 vols. (Edinburgh, 1910), 1:361, 374. For Smith's character and an evaluation of the *Generall Historie* see Philip L. Barbour, *The Three Worlds of Captain John Smith* (Boston, 1964).

32. The Rev. Alexander Whitaker, part of a tractorate written at Henrico in Virginia, in Purchas, *Hakluytus Posthumus*, 30:110.

33. Rolfe assumed, in true Christian fashion, that human nature is at bottom frail and given to corruption. "I forget not to set before mine eyes the frailty of mankinde, his prones to evill, his indulgence in wicked thoughts, with many other imperfections wherein man is daily ensnared, and oftentimes overthrowne." He is aware that his love for Pocahontas may have been the work of the Devil. At the same time Rolfe testifies to the power of Christian teaching and faith in remarking that had he merely given vent to his passion he would have done so with a "seared conscience." In not doing so, he obviously believed or at least stated that his action stands in contrast with "the vulgar sort" who attributed to him mere sexual motives. His contrast of his own capacity for restraint of the basic passions and "filthiness" of the "vulgar sort" suggests that in his view the differences demarking a gentleman from the common herd may be "in the blood." Lyon Gardiner Tyler, ed., *Narratives of Early Virginia* (New York, 1907), pp. 243 ff.

that white encroachment, having no bounds, threatened their whole way of life. Hence the surprise massacre of at least 347 whites and the near annihilation of the colony. English revenge, no less brutal and merciless, found its justification: "Because our hands which before were tied with gentleness and faire usage, are now set at liberty by the treacherous violence of the Savages, not untying the Knot, but cutting it; So that we, who hitherto had possession of no more ground than their waste, and our purchase at a valuable consideration of their own contentment, gained; may now by a right of Warre, and law of Nations, invade the Country, and destroy them who sought to destroy us."[34]

Successive massacres, mounting strife on the frontier, and horror stories of unspeakable cruelty toward white captives nourished the dim view of the Indian. Several writers looked on him as a hopelessly brutal beast, even as subhuman. A traveler among southeastern tribes held that such unnatural men must have been separately created.[35] A witty western Pennsylvania lawyer wrote, "They have the shapes of men and may be of the human species, but certainly in their present state they approach nearer the character of Devils."[36] With such opinions fairly common, colonial Americans, with notable exceptions, gave up the early hope of converting and civilizing creatures now viewed as not having the capacity either to lead civilized lives or to receive God's grace. Human nature had long been identified with these capacities. It implied equality in God's eyes and in natural law. Since the implementation of such a view of human nature seemed impossible and to conflict with white interests as well, it was easy to shift to the position that the Indian as "bound inextricably in a primitive past, a primitive society, and a primitive environment" was thus designed "to be destroyed by God, Nature, and Progress to make way for Civilized Man."[37]

Yet there were varying exceptions to this image of the Indian in relation to ideas about human nature. One view, deriving in part, as Wilcomb E. Washburn has shown, from the accounts and comments of early explorers, travelers, and European writers, continued to perceive

34. Edward Waterhouse, "A Declaration of the State of the Colonie and Affaires in Virginia [1622]," *Records of the Virginia Company*, 4 vols. (Washington, D.C., 1906–35), 3:556–57.

35. Bernard Romans, *Concise Natural History of East and West Florida* (New York, 1775), p. 39, cited in Pearce, *The Savages of America*, pp. 47–48.

36. Hugh Henry Brackenridge, "The Animals, Vulgarly Called Indians," in Washburn, ed., *The Indian and the White Man*, p. 116.

37. Pearce, *The Savages of America*, p. 4. For reason for the failure of the assumption that the Indian would in time adapt to a European pattern of life see Wesley Frank Craven, *White, Red and Black: The Seventeenth-Century Virginian* (Charlottesville, Va., 1971), pp. 52–53.

the Indian as a child of nature unspoiled by the anxieties, competitiveness, and complexities of civilization.[38] This image, while present in America, found much less favor there than in the intellectual circles of Europe.

Nevertheless, firsthand experience now and then lent support to something like this view. The Maryland Jesuits found in the Pascataways a gentle, peaceful, hospitable tribe, and shaped their views of Indian nature accordingly. "The naturall wit of these men is good," wrote Father Andrew White in 1634; "conceiving a thing quick to. They excell in smell and taste, and have far sharper sight than we have." Father White observed no levity in sexual matters. "There is small passion amongst them," he added. And he was convinced that "if these were once Christian, they would doubtlesse be a vertuous and renowned nation."[39] Experience taught, according to another "Relation of Early Maryland," that "by kind and faire usage, the Natives are not onely become peaceable, but also friendly." It appeared that Indian life mirrored the way all men had lived "whilest the world was under the law of Nature"—freedom for all, "yet subject to command for the publicke defence."[40] The Jesuits blamed their failure to convert large numbers of these likely candidates on Lord Baltimore's refusal to recognize their jurisdiction in the large grants of land they had got directly from Indians.

The Quakers held a similarly bright, though distinctive, view about the relation of Indians to human nature. Impressed much less by the differences between the two races than by similarities, the Friends convinced themselves that the natives, as children of God, had the universal human capacity to receive the Light of the Holy Spirit and to live the life of love. Without the Catholic ritual and pageantry generally dear to Indian taste, the Quakers could convey this message only by example. It was, for some time, fairly effective as a means of keeping peace: the Quakers made little or no effort to induce the Indians to accept the white man's civilization. In the context of conflicting commercial interests and imperial strife, the Quakers could not always square their behavior with their convictions. Thus they could not persuade the frontier Indians to keep a one-sided peace that threatened their way of life. The Quaker experiment failed. It failed, however, without undermining the conviction of a commonly shared human nature that

38. Wilcomb E. Washburn, "The Moral and Legal Justification for Dispossessing the Indians," in James W. Smith, ed., *Seventeenth-Century America* (Chapel Hill, 1959), pp. 22–25.

39. Clayton C. Hall, ed., *Narratives of Early Maryland 1633–1684* (New York, 1910), p. 44.

40. Hall, ed., *Narratives of Early Maryland*, p. 84.

endowed Indians as well as whites with the capacity to respond to love in kind.[41]

The eighteenth century, with new situations and fresh currents of thought, witnessed other efforts to understand Indian nature without changing it or making praise or blame the dominant note. On the one hand, the retreat of "savage" danger from older, settled areas figured in the new appraisals. In looking back on the long period of strife and bloodshed, now happily past, Robert Beverley, a Virginia gentleman and historian, regretted that intermarriage between whites and Indians had been so exceptional, for such alliances, he thought, might have prevented much warfare between the two races.[42] If only rare individuals shared Beverley's opinion,[43] it received fresh attention toward the end of the century when Enlightenment views meshed with empirical observations.

The experiences of missionaries living among Indians also contributed to some shift in mid- and late-century views about the Indian in relation to human nature. Learning their languages and observing their customs, these bold and hardy men sometimes provided in their reports documentation for the traditional image of the Indian, but more to the point, also expressed a rudimentary empirical realism. John Gottlieb Heckewelder, a Moravian able to use tribal tongues in working with Indians, assessed their capacity for friendship. He held that their passion for revenge owed little to an inborn malicious disposition. It stemmed rather "from violence of natural feelings, unchecked by social institutions, and unsubdued by the force of revealed religion." Heckewelder also attributed much Indian behavior to their conviction that good never comes from evil, nor evil from good.[44]

Such traders and forest diplomats as Conrad Weiser, William Johnson, and George Croghan also lived in close touch with Indians. They learned their speech. They tried to comprehend their ways. Often, finding their women sexually attractive, these traders made casual or formal arrangements which led to an interbreeding that somewhat softened sharp differentiations in views of human nature. Of the traders James Adair was, in his realistic understanding of the Indians, of special note. After living for thirty-three years with the southeastern tribes, he described in detail their customs and beliefs. Now and then he stereotyped natives in

41. William W. Comfort, *William Penn, 1644–1718: A Tercentenary Estimate* (Philadelphia, 1944), p. 44.

42. Robert Beverly, *The History of the Present State of Virginia*, ed. Louis W. Wright (Chapel Hill, 1947), p. 38.

43. For the best-known example see Louis B. Wright, ed., *The Prose Works of William Byrd of Westover* (Cambridge, Mass., 1966), pp. 221–23.

44. John Heckewelder, *An Account of the History, Manners and Customs of the Indian Nations Who Once Inhabited Pennsylvania and the Neighboring States* (Philadelphia, 1819), p. 272. The manuscript was written much earlier than the publication date.

such traditional clichés as the red man's indigence and procrastination and the like. Adair was, though, remarkably free from moral judgments on the inherent inferiority or superiority of Indian nature. He believed that "with proper cultivation, they would shine in the higher spheres of life" and, in some aspects of everyday affairs, provide models for Europeans. Adair came close to suggesting something like a modern theory of culture.[45]

Having no more firsthand knowledge of Africans than of Indians, the original colonists brought with them ready-made attitudes that had taken shape in Elizabethan England.[46] The little that was known about the Dark Continent south of the Sahara came in part from contacts with Portuguese and Spanish traders and in part from such sixteenth-century travelers and writers as Antonio Malefante, Leo Africanus, and Peter Heyln. With some exceptions, such reports pictured the Negroes as wretched, naked, and animal-like in habits and appearance. The Elizabethan linking of blackness with ugliness, baseness, and evil accounted in part for such a grim judgment. Presumed facial likeness of Africans and apes also lent itself to the speculation of affinity or even kinship. Writing in 1626 of the Hottentots, Sir Thomas Herbert reported that "their words are sounded rather like that of Apes, then Men. . . . And comparing their imitations, speech, and visages, I doubt many of them have no better Predecessors then Monkeys."[47] Then too, the heathenism of the blacks appeared to go beyond that of any other savages. They seemed to lack any religion at all. Moreover, they were thought to indulge in unchecked lust and sexual depravity. Viewed in the frame of the Great Chain of Being idea, Negroes ranked far below Indians. In the distinctive qualities credited to man, the blacks seemed to be "utterly destitute of reason" and "like unto beasts."

The image of the African as almost subhuman was further sharpened by the fact that the Old World and emigrants to Anglo-America knew the blacks only as slaves. This central fact had its own implications in discussions of the relation of the Negro to human nature. David Brion Davis has shown that the paradoxical problem of slavery in classical

45. James Adair, *The History of the American Indians*, with a new introduction by Robert F. Berkhofer, Jr. (New York, 1968), pp. vi–vii.

46. John W. Blake, ed., *European Beginnings in West Africa, 1454–1578* (London, 1937); and *Europeans in West Africa, 1450–1560*, 2 vols. (London, 1942), Hakluyt Society Publications vols. 86 and 87, 1:150–52, 159–61, 163; 2:343–45, 367–68; Winthrop D. Jordan, *White over Black: American Attitudes toward the Negro, 1550–1812* (Chapel Hill, 1968), chap. 1; and Felix N. Okoye, *The Image of Africa* (Buffalo, N.Y., 1971), pp. 15–21.

47. Hodgen, *Early Anthropology*, pp. 412, 417.

antiquity remained insoluble on the eve of colonization. The paradox stemmed from the incompatibility of regarding the slave as both an object and a human being. Classical thought in general reduced the humanity of the slave by depriving him of such necessary attributes as the possession of an autonomous will. According to Aristotle, complete subordination made the slave a mere extension of his master's will and interest. Nor did Christianity change the basic situation very much. The Bible sanctioned slavery. To be sure, the Church admonished masters to treat slaves with compassion. Still, in Davis's words, slavery implied "the ultimate in dependence, disability, powerlessness, sinfulness, and the negation of autonomous self-consciousness."[48] Matters were not helped much when the leading political theorists of the sixteenth and seventeenth centuries justified slavery on grounds of utility and social order.

The paradox in the assumption that the Negro slave was both a thing and an inferior human being was further complicated by the fact that freedom had come to be thought of in England as an indestructible part of at least the British exemplification of human nature. The apparent easy susceptibility of Africans to enslavement raised questions about their capacity for the human earmark of freedom. Moreover, the profitable role of British buccaneers in the Spanish slave trade further defined the dim view of the Negroes' relation to human nature.

It is not clear just when and how the first Africans brought to Jamestown in 1619 began to be treated differently from white indentured servants. In view of the ideas colonists carried with them about Africans, some categorization of their inferiority must have operated from the start. In any case, laws in effect by 1660 permanently bound to slavery imported and native-born blacks as well as their offspring.

As slavery developed in other colonies in varying degrees and in patterns influenced by the economy, social structure, and ratio of whites to blacks, the institution was accepted almost without challenge. This was true even though white labor sufficed to cultivate staple crops.

The more numerous the slaves in relation to the white population the more tensions and anxieties stemmed from their presence. Interbreeding took place despite the law, and menaced the assumed superiority and purity of white blood. Strains and apprehensions also sprang from actual or threatened slave insurrections, which jeopardized not only rights in slave property but white control itself. Brutal retribution followed a bloody and dreadful uprising in New York in 1741. The court told two condemned Negroes that, in contrast to the loyalty of the ox, the ass, and

48. David Brion Davis, *The Problem of Slavery in the Age of Revolution 1770–1823* (Ithaca, 1975), p. 40. My discussion of slavery is deeply indebted to this splendid analysis.

the dog to their masters, they, like most of their complexion, had shown "such an untowardness, as it should seem, in the very nature and temper of ye, that ye grow cruel by too much indulgence, so much are ye degenerated and debased below the dignity of the human species, that even the brute animals may upbraid you."[49]

Such diatribes did not change the fact that Christian doctrine affirmed the unity of mankind. Thus opinion in both the Old World and the New felt compelled to allow human status to Negroes, which pushed into the background the occasional linking of blacks with ape-like beasts but did little to lessen the fears and tensions associated with slavery. In fact, these fears and tensions focused attention more and more on the relation of the Negro to human nature.

One aspect of this discussion inevitably related to the black skin color. Though its causes remained a mystery, Europeans and in due course colonial Americans advanced various explanations. At first, in the seventeenth and early eighteenth centuries, the most widely accepted theory held that Africans, as the descendants of Ham, were black and thus inferior by virtue of God's curse. This explanation continued to affect the categorization of Negroes as inherently and ineradicably the basest of the base. This was true even after the rising vogue of environmentalism in the eighteenth century tried to explain dark skin as a result of the burning equatorial sun. Since whites living in the tropics remained white and since blacks in temperate climates remained black, as did offspring unless modified by miscegenation, the environmental explanation was not altogether satisfactory.

Two other movements of thought still further confused the picture. On the one hand, the popularity in the eighteenth century of the Great Chain of Being idea seemed to warrant grading man in terms of more or fewer human attributes. On the other hand, in the 1730s the renowned Swedish naturalist Linnaeus, having classified mankind of whatever color and body type as an integral part of animal creation, refused to make color or its absence a badge of either inferiority or superiority. If Linnaeus's view of man as part of animal creation held, who could entirely escape the fear that the bestial in human nature might gain the upper hand? In a new land, lacking the institutional restraints of the Old World, slaveowners in particular and whites in general determined to make sure, by social discipline, that the genuinely human aspect of man, identified with their own color, their own Christianity, their own

49. A *Journal of the Proceedings in the Detection of the Conspiracy Formed by Some White People, in Conjunction with Negro and Other Slaves, for Burning the City of New York, and Murdering the Inhabitants* (New York, 1744), p. 339. See also Daniel Horsmanden, *The New York Conspiracy* (New York, 1810).

civilization, be dissociated so far as possible from the presumed dominant brutality of the blacks. Thus, as Winthrop Jordan has noted, early Americans, with notable exceptions such as Dr. John Mitchell of Virginia, went further than most European scientists in continuing to identify blackness with inferiority, physical, mental, and moral.[50]

Doubts about the basic sameness of whites and blacks partly explained the reluctance of most slaveowners in the southern colonies to act on the obligation to convert slaves, a clear implication of the Christian doctrine of the unity of mankind and an explicit biblical command. Would not Christian teaching, holding as it did that all souls are equal in God's sight, encourage converted blacks to edge toward equality in everyday worldly matters? Anglican and sectarian leaders alike, in emphasizing the obligation to Christianize slaves, brushed aside these objections: blacks after all were not only human beings with rational souls, they were also property, and their status as such could in no way be changed by conversion. Actually, the argument went, Christianity would instill the biblical command to accept one's worldly lot, to obey the master, thus making the slaves more docile servants. In so often failing to heed such admonitions by trying harder to Christianize their blacks, slaveowners became vulnerable to the charge of looking upon Negroes as beasts rather than as human beings. Few owners actually seem to have so regarded blacks. The fact, though, that they sometimes treated their slaves as beasts gave some point to the charge.

Human nature was thus with some reluctance and qualification conferred on Negroes, both in colonies where the economy seemed to make them indispensable as slaves and in those where white labor was ample for cultivating staple crops. Inherited views as well as experience strengthened convictions about universal and immutable black inferiority. As we shall see, quite different views also grew out of American conditions and new international movements of thought.

Thus American experience, in heightening and in time modifying traditional ideas about Indians and Africans, channeled thought about the relation of race to human nature in distinctive directions.

Considerable evidence, however, indicates that the classical and especially the Christian tradition provided anchors against any marked or easy change in attitudes toward human nature. One example was the "noble dirge" written by a devoted follower of Nathaniel Bacon shortly after his enemies crushed the rebellion he led in Virginia. The writer

50. This is based on Jordan, *White over Black*, pp. 177, 210, 239, 255.

explained Bacon's condemnation in terms of a feeling of community guilt directed against a sacrificial victim:

> *Mars* and *Minerva*, both in him concurd
> For arts, for arms, whose pen and sword alike
> As *Cato* did, may admiration strike
> Into his foes; while they confes witall
> It was their guilt sti'd him as Criminal.[51]

In nearby Maryland, the Jesuits bore witness to their belief that God affected what men did in transcending the power of corporeal nature. Divine mercy gave courage to resist evil. In his compassion, the Lord did not suffer his servants to be tested beyond the point they could endure, "but with temptation had always made a way to escape, that we may be able to bear it." Again, effort, reenforced by divine pleasure, led to satisfying conversions among early settlers. These conversions affected "great reformation of morals," at least in the case of a sinner and heretic who came to shed "abroad the very sweet favor of a good example upon all who are acquainted with him." Moreover, in a society "not usually supplied with the best class of men," God's blessing kept vice from springing up among new converts. On the other hand, God did not always bestow repentance, conversion, and reform. A letter of 1654, for example, mentioned the execution of a little old woman accused of sorcery and disabling the ship on which she was bound for Maryland. The record, moreover, admitted that even the Catholic rulers, sharing the human thirst for property and authority, stymied the Jesuits' legitimate claims to lands. To trust in the goodness of God and in the piety of Catholics was thus the best the fathers could do under the circumstances.[52]

By the end of the seventeenth and beginning of the eighteenth century several felt that colonial life was changing human conduct, which under any term of reference was a function of human nature. Some ascribed this in part or even largely to the hand of God. Francis Daniel Pastorius, the learned founder of Germantown in Pennsylvania, for example, who had sought the New World in the hope of living the Christian way more readily than Europe made possible, noted the necessity of both hard work and divine aid in achieving sobriety and good character. Pastorius expressed his faith that God's vengeance would in His own time drive off the "chaff" to which human nature was subject, his picturesque way of describing "coiners of false money and other persons."[53]

51. *Proceedings of the Massachusetts Historical Society* 9 (1866–67): 324.

52. Hall, ed., *Narratives of Early Maryland*, pp. 123, 141.

53. Albert Cook Myers, ed., *Narratives of Early Pennsylvania, West New-Jersey and Delaware 1630–1707* (New York, 1912), p. 400.

Even without any reference to the Deity, many held that conduct and character in the New World reflected the unique conditions of life that brought out the good and the bad. George Alsop, a London artisan, Anglican, and Royalist who came to Maryland as an indentured servant, lent his witty pen to the celebration of much that he found. In baroque prose he satirized the foibles of the Puritan Commonwealth he had fled in disgust, as well as Maryland's "money-mad" and troublesome dissenters. Yet his *Character of the Province of Maryland* might have served as a promotion tract. What struck him most were the differences in the lot of his class in his new and his old home. "Those whose Lives and Conversations have had no other gloss nor glory stampt on them in their own Country, but the stigmatization of baseness, were here (by the common civilities and deportments of the Inhabitants of this Province) brought to detest and loathe their former actions."[54] At about the same time John Hammond, who knew both Maryland and Virginia at first hand, made the point that "many who in *England* have been lewd and idle, there in emulation or imitation (for example moves more than precept) of the industry of those they finde there, not only grow ashamed of their former courses, but abhor to hear of them, and in small time wipe off those stains they have formerly been tainted with."[55]

The absence of beggars and other social derelicts in the colonies was contrasted with the prevalence of those unfortunates in England. Hammond declared that he found, in the four months after he returned to England, "more deceits and villanies (and such as modesty forbids me to utter) then I either ever saw or heard mention made of it in *Virginia*, in my one and twenty years abroad in those parts."[56] Writing about Pennsylvania at the end of the seventeenth century, Gabriel Thomas asserted that it was "a Shame and Disgrace to the State that there are so many [beggars] in *England*." He attributed the lack of them in America not only to economic opportunities, but, explicitly, to the fact that in America man did not have "the least Occasion or Temptation to take up that Scandalous Lazy Life, Jealousie among Men is here very rare." Thomas even thought that New World conditions had a wholesome eugenic effect on the American-born. After noting that it was unusual to find an "old Maide" in Pennsylvania and that barrenness was extremely rare, he declared that "the *Christian Children* born here are generally

---

54. George Alsop, "A Character of the Province of Maryland," in Hall, ed., *Narratives of Early Maryland*, p. 351. For a discussion of Alsop and his writing see J. A. Leo Lemay, ed., *Men of Letters in Colonial Maryland* (Knoxville, Tenn., 1972), pp. 48–69.

55. John Hammond, *"Leah and Rachel"*; or, *the Two Fruitful Sisters Virginia and Maryland* (London, 1656). Reprinted in Peter Force, ed., *Tracts and Other Papers Relating Principally to the Origin, Settlement and Progress of the Colonies in North America*, 3 vols. (Washington, D.C., 1836–44), 3 (tract no. 14):16–17.

56. Hammond, *"Leah and Rachel,"* p. 17.

well-favored, and *Beautiful* to behold. I never knew any come into the World with the least Blemish on any part of its Body, being in the general, observ'd to be *better Natur'd, Milder*, and more *tender Hearted* than those born in *England*."[57] Nor were these exceptional verdicts. William Smith, an eighteenth-century historian of New York, a jurist, and ultimately a Loyalist, believed that inhabitants, despite the unfortunate effects of the British policy of sending criminals to the colony, were "in general healthy and robust, taller but shorter lived than Europeans and, both with respect to their minds and bodies, arrive sooner to an age of maturity." Moreover, being "more uprightly in their natural tempers than the people of England, . . . instances of suicide are here very uncommon."[58] Such views persisted. The well-trained and careful observer Johann David Schöpf, chief surgeon to the Hessian troops in the Revolution, noted that "deformities and misgrowths, especially of the human species, are rarer in America (where everything is truer to nature) than elsewhere."[59]

The realistic comment that even America had its wicked people sometimes tempered such optimism. "Some natyres will never be reformed" was John Hammond's way of putting it. For such, in his view, but one thing could be done—trust to "severe and wholesome laws and remedies made, provided, and duly put into execution." Here was an expression of the general reliance on the idea that penalizing laws inhibited evil conduct, provided a deterring example to others, and, conceivably, induced those who had strayed to return to the path of righteousness or at least of decency.

The best-known literary achievement of the Chesapeake country, *The Sot-Weed Factor; or a Voyage to Maryland* (1708), recognized the complexity of human nature in any environment. Its author, Ebenezer Cook, was an old Maryland settler and established lawyer in Prince Georges County. Writing as a young greenhand come to trade in tobacco, Cook was presumably satirizing the crudity and dubious character of Marylanders:

> Many Canniballs transported o'er the Sea
> Prey on these Slaves, as they have done on me.

57. Gabriel Thomas, *An Historical and Geographical Account of the Province and Country of Pennsylvania, and of West New-Jersey in America* (London, 1698), pp. 44, 41–42.

58. William Smith, Jr., *The History of the Province of New-York*, ed. Michael Kammen, 2 vols. (Cambridge, Mass., 1972), 1:223, 227.

59. Johann David Schoepf, *Travels in the Confederation: New Jersey, Pennsylvania, Maryland and Virginia* (Philadelphia, 1911), p. 95.

> May they turn Savage, or as *Indians* wild,
> From Trade, Converse, and Happiness exild,
> Where no Man's Faithful, nor a Woman Chast.

Actually, the humorous and often ribald mock-poem was a put-on designed to ridicule British misconceptions of the New World. Yet since it was received as a satire on unscrupulous, shrewd colonists, it implied that whether by selective immigration or by the impact of the environment, behavior had been transformed from reasonable decency into shocking deceptions and dishonesty.[60]

That Ebenezer Cook was not an isolated Chesapeake literary figure was clear from the notable writing published mainly in Annapolis and Williamsburg newspapers in the mid-eighteenth century. Teachers, lawyers, planters, and clergymen contributed sermons, satirical verse in the manner of Butler's *Hudibras*, and essays, some on political, some on trivial themes. Well read in the Latin classics, especially Cicero and Horace and in the contemporary literature of England, these Chesapeake writers reflected several views of human nature, largely derivative but nevertheless reflecting American experience.

The Anglican clergy took into account the limitations of human nature as well as its brighter side. Commissary James Blair recognized human depravity but defended free will and an innate capacity for prudence, restraint, and moderation. He opposed "leveling," but as an ardent champion of the Society for the Propagation of the Gospel in Foreign Parts, favored instruction of Indians and Negroes in the catechism and Apostles' Creed. In dedicating his published sermons (1722) to the Bishop of London, Blair noted that colonial clergy, unlike the English, did not find it necessary to stress doctrinal points or to resist deism, atheism, or Socinianism and other heresies, since these were mainly nonexistent. "Yet we find Work enough . . . to encounter the usual Corruptions of Mankind, Ignorance, Inconsideration, Practical Unbelief, Impenitence, Impiety, Worldlymindedness, and other Common Immoralities." In this he was emphasizing the pastoral, practical, and moral aspects of religion as necessary for regulating human nature.[61]

60. See Lawrence C. Wroth's extensive commentary on Cooke's writings, "The Maryland Muse by Ebenezer Cooke: A Facsimile, with an Introduction," *Proceedings of the American Antiquarian Society* 44 (1934): 267–335; Robert D. Arner, "Ebenezer Cooke's *The Sotweed Factor:* The Structure of Satire," *Southern Literary Journal* 4 (1971): 33–47; Lemay's *Men of Letters in Colonial Maryland*, pp. 77–110; and especially, Edward H. Cohen, *Ebenezer Cooke: The Sot-Weed Canon* (Athens, Ga., 1975).

61. Parker Rouse, Jr., *James Blair of Virginia* (Chapel Hill, 1971), p. 23; this is the standard biography of Blair. See also Gerald J. Goodwin, "The Anglican Middle Way in Early Eighteenth Century America" (Ph.D. diss., University of Wisconsin, 1965), p. 144.

The sermons of the Reverend Thomas Cradock of Maryland, an erudite scholar, reflected the Latitudinarian emphasis on benevolence and joyfulness as a worthy aspect of human nature. Although Cradock courageously denounced the worldly parsons in his midst,[62] he found Christian sanction for the human capacity for happiness. "Can a gloomy outward Soul," he asked, "answer the ends of [Christ's] Coming: can a morose Pharisaic Temper be suitable to so blessed a Design as our Lord's?" Since man was formed for society, how could society function without "a cheerful and benevolent Disposition? How can a Man be desirous to produce the happiness and Benefit of his Neighbour, when he has not a Soul susceptible of Generous Sentiments? When he's wholly absorbed with himself, and looks with an evil eye on every Thing that is sociable? Can the Soul promote Harmony that hath no Harmony in itself? No, the morose, surly, uncheerful man can never answer the End of his Creation; he can never be a good Man or a good Christian; the good Neighbour, or the good Friend! He may say what he will, but if he wants a *Merry Heart*, he wants a very great characteristic of the Human Mind."[63] For Cradock religion, instead of being grim and fearful, was comparable rather to "wine red in the glass" with "laughter and joy."

If Cradock might be thought to take too cheery a view in squaring human nature with religion, no such judgment could be made of Richard Lewis. After a brief sojourn at Oxford, this young Welshman migrated to Maryland in 1718 to teach in Prince William Free School in Annapolis. His poetry, published locally and in England before his death sixteen years later, reflected his knowledge of the Latin classics and mythology. In heroic couplets reminiscent of Vergil's epic, he celebrated the founding of Maryland and the leadership of Lord Baltimore. Lewis's work also showed his debt to Addison, Pope, Thompson, and Young. His view of man reflected a sympathetic sensitivity to Newtonianism and to the perception psychology of Locke. He was the earliest American poet of nature, regarding the lush cornucopia of the pastoral Chesapeake area and the strange beauties of the American wilderness as superior to anything in the Old World. Yet in his melancholy view, the Edenic Wilderness and its Noble Savage were destined to be destroyed by civilization. In "Rhapsody" as in other poems, he wrote of a human nature dominated by such frailties as self-love, conceit, and a proud heart. Reason often failed to control the passions. Lurking beneath a calm surface, the precarious mental makeup easily tipped toward

62. Lemay, *Men of Letters in Colonial Maryland*, pp. 191, 193, 197, 208, 229, 325, 326; and Richard Beale Davis, *Literature and Society in Early Virginia* (Baton Rouge, 1973), pp. 185 ff.

63. Thomas Cradock, *Two Sermons, with Preface* (Annapolis, Md., 1707), pp. 2–3.

madness. Note the correspondence between the description of a beach and the mental condition of an individual:

> When I reflect on this, methinks I find,
> Drawn on these Waves, the Picture of my Mind;
> Tho' now, my Bosom all serene and calm,
> Seems fill'd with soft Content, and pleasing Balm;
> Yet soon, perhaps, with rude resistless Sway;
> Shall rising Passion drive this Calm away;
> The Mind disturb'd, and mad with raging Woe,
> Shall to the Sight a loathsom Bottom show;
> And those Ideas which my Fancy store,
> May be dispers'd like Sands upon the Shore.

The poet fell back on a possible stoicism:

> Whatever Views employ my musing mind
> My weakness, and thy wondrous Pow'r I find.
> Such Pow'rs my fickle Mind endue,
> That I my future Course may safe pursue.

Lewis's widely known and technically competent poem "A Journey from Patapsco to Annapolis" pictured man allegorically in the several stages of his journey through life. Human inconsequentiality in the face of the vast, beautiful, and ordered universe led the poet to question not only the efficacy of man's reason, but immortality, and even a wise and benevolent Creator. Yet, to quote the leading authority on his work, Lewis, after raising doubts, achieved a final religious affirmation "made in the face of, and partly by including and transcending the major modern currents of thought."[64]

Although not inclined toward deism as Lewis was, Thomas Reid shared some of his ideas about the limitations of human nature. A Scot, a Presbyterian, a widely read scholar, a tutor, and probably an indentured servant on a Virginia plantation, Reid sent his essays and verse to the *Virginia Gazette*. In one piece he held that man minds "not how his fellow fares if he himself don't perish," and in another that God in making man had stamped on him a conscience which was identified with the Holy Spirit. Reid's most telling piece, at least in terms of a discussion of human nature, was an essay, "The Religion of the Bible and the Religion of K[ing] W[illiams] County Compared" (1768–69).[65] This

64. Lemay, *Men of Letters in Colonial Maryland*, p. 148.
65. Richard Beale Davis, ed., *The Colonial Virginia Satirist: Mid-Eighteenth-Century Commentaries on Politics, Religion, and Society*, Transactions of the American Philosophical Society, n.s., vol. 57, pt. 1 (Philadelphia, 1967), pp. 44 ff.; and *Literature and Society*, chap. 9.

bold satire contrasted the ideal of the Renaissance gentleman, which the local gentry professed, with the actuality of class snobbishness, arrogance, pride, social gluttony, money-lust, vanity, and sexual alliances with slaves who were all too often treated without human consideration. In Reid's view the gentry hypocritically spoke of themselves as "gentlemen born." In truth, though, every man was born equal, helpless, naked, and poor. How many so-called gentlemen came far from meriting the title! He would have made short shrift of the attitude conveyed in James Fitzhugh's remark that it was "better never to be born at all than to be ill-bred."[66] "Every man," Reid wrote in a similar vein, "praises his own and condemns the ruling Passion of his neighbours." If such well-meant task-taking brought recrimination, never mind, he went on: "For take mankind in gross, two thirds of them will come under the denomination of fools or knaves, and what opinion they form of us is not worth our while to know."[67] Yet he could also say,

> True love to mankind in your writings show,
> Nor vent thy spite and malice 'gainst thy foe;
> Defend your cause with all the skill you can,
> And, though you hate his errours, love the man.[68]

An anecdote about a brutal four-man fist fight, related by Philip Fithian, another tutor to Virginia families, suggested that Reid was not alone in his evaluation of human nature in a new society dominated by a self-styled gentry. "Every diabolical Strategem for Mastery is allowed & practised, of Bruising, Kicking, Scratching, Pinching, Biting, Butting, Tripping, Throtling, Goughing, Cursing, Dismembring, Howling etc. This spectacle," Fithian continued, "(so loathesome & horrible) generally is attended with a crowd of People! In my opinion (others may think for themselves) animals which seek after & relish such odious and filthy amusements are not of the human species, they are destitute of the remotest pretension to humanity; I know not how they came by their form, by the help of which they are permitted to associate with Men,

66. Richard Beale Davis, ed., *William Fitzhugh and His Chesapeake World* (Chapel Hill, 1963), p. 48. For a discussion of child-rearing see Edmund S. Morgan, *Virginians at Home: Family Life in the Eighteenth Century* (Colonial Williamsburg, 1952). It is worth noting that Philip Fithian, a tutor in Virginia, commended Robert Carter for the superior manner of dealing with children, who were "more kind and complaisant to the servants who constantly attend them than we are to our superiors in age and condition." Hunter D. Farish, ed., *Journal and Letters of Philip Vickers Fithian 1773–1774* (Colonial Williamsburg, 1957), p. 26.
67. Davis, ed., *The Colonial Virginia Satirist*, pp. 62–63.
68. Davis, *Literature and Society*, pp. 63, 180.

unless it has been . . . by an intermixture of the meaner kind of Devils with prostitute Monkeys!"[69]

Several decades before this diatribe, a Virginia-born aristocrat, William Byrd II of Westover, commented on human relations in enough detail to reconstruct an outstanding if not entirely representative planter's image of man. The human mind, Byrd thought, was endowed by the Creator with enough reason to distinguish between right and wrong and thus to promote happiness and well-being. But like Mandeville, Swift, and Pope, he held human passions to be more powerful than reason. In a self-analysis written in early manhood, he admitted that "he liv'd more by the lively movement of his Passions, than by the cold and unromantich dictates of reason."[70] He did not conceal in his diary his own vanity, ambition, and lust, which he laid at the door of human weakness and regarded with a bemused tolerance. Without shame, but with regret and hope of God's forgiveness, he noted in a matter-of-fact way his frequent violations of the ideal of reasonable restraint admonished alike by the ancient classics and the Augustan literature of England, which he knew at first-hand. Thus: "I took leave and went home in the chair and said my prayers, and kissed the maid till I polluted myself, for which God forgive me."[71] He kept his flirtations with the ladies of his own class within the bounds of propriety, an evidence of the role of status in his view of conduct and human nature. If Byrd recorded his sexual indulgence in an offhand way, he was not without anxieties. This was clear from his concern with the portents of dreams; he wrote of one in which a coffin was brought into the hall when he couldn't find his wife. Notwithstanding his own derelictions, William Byrd II assumed that the common clay was even less able than the gentry to control passions and to realize the virtues of moderation, efficiency, frugality, and compassion. His association of such virtues as achievement, success, and the utilitarian use of science with his own class narrowed somewhat his tolerant and relaxed view of the human kind. It was not entirely clear from his sharp criticisms of the sloth and primitivism of the woodsmen and traders of the backcountry whether he felt their shortcomings resulted from inborn limitations or from their way of life. In *The History of the Dividing Line* he accounted on one occasion for the lazy behavior of a "younker" by his "constitution." But

69. Farish, *Philip Vickers Fithian*, p. 183.

70. Maude H. Woodfin, ed., *Another Secret Diary of William Byrd of Westover for the Years 1739–1741* (Richmond, Va., 1942), p. 277. The standard biography is Pierre Marambaud, *William Byrd of Westover 1674–1744* (Charlottesville, Va., 1971).

71. Louis B. Wright and Marion Tinling, eds., *The London Diary and Other Writings of William Byrd of Westover* (New York, 1958), entry of Jan. 30, 1718, p. 72.

on another occasion: "To speak the truth, 'tis through aversion to labor that makes people file off to North Carolina, where plenty and a warm sun confirm them in their disposition to laziness for their whole lives." Here he parted company with earlier writers who had viewed optimistically the effect of nature's bounty on character and conduct.

Byrd's assessment of the influence of the natural environment was more evident in his generally sympathetic account of the Indians than in his attitudes toward Africans. Of the former he wrote that "all nations of men have the same natural dignity, and we all know that bright talents may be lodged under a very dark skin. The principal difference between one people and another proceeds only from the different opportunities for improvement."[72] In holding that the only way the settlers could have Christianized the red men would have been through intermarriage, and in describing some of the native customs in terms of natural religion, Byrd expressed a rational and humane view of the unity of mankind. His attitude toward the blacks was not entirely inconsistent with this idea, at least in theory: he congratulated the Earl of Egmont on the exclusion of slavery from Georgia, an institution harmful, he remarked, to blacks and whites alike. The slave trade itself he spoke of as "unchristian," as "making merchandise of our fellow creatures."[73] His treatment of his own "people," some of whom he bought and sold, was moderately kind and definitely paternalistic.

To sum up, Byrd's concept of human nature, evident in his witty and often satirical comments on man's foibles and in his ascription of the turn of events, favorable and adverse, to God's providence, reflected relative detachment and realism. It was also related to his conviction that no sharp line should divide the precepts of religion and morality from everyday life, however wide the gap in reality and however acquiescent he was to that gap.

No one in the planting aristocracy of South Carolina seems to have left a record from which an image of man comparable in comprehensiveness to William Byrd's can be put together. The *South-Carolina Gazette* of Charleston did, to be sure, bear witness to the fact that planters, teachers, lawyers, and clergymen wrote verses and essays that were urbane, satirical, pastoral, elegaic, and nostalgic in tone. Derivative and imitative, this writing reflected the tastes and values current in the mother country. The point can be made in a representative example that reflected awareness of human weakness, the need of mutual tolerance, and the role of love in controlling the passions:

72. Louis B. Wright, ed., *The Prose Works of William Byrd of Westover* (Cambridge, Mass., 1966), p. 221.
73. Richard L. Morton, *Colonial Virginia*, 2 vols. (Chapel Hill, 1960), 2:524.

All men have Follies, which they blindly trace
Thro' the dark Turnings of a dubious Maze.
But happy those, who, by a prudent care,
Retreat betimes, from the fallacious Snare.
The eldest Sons of Wisdom were not free
From the same Failure you condemn in me.
If as the Wisest of the Wise have err'd,
I go astray and am condemn'd unheard,
My Faults you too severely reprehend,
More like a rigid Censor than a Friend.
Love is the Monarch Passion of the Mind.[74]

The derivative character of such a view of the emotions was plain enough. Nor can an American accent always be identified in examples of concrete behavior, whether the matter in question concerned trade, medicine and health, plantation management, slavery, or relations with the Indians.

On the religious level a case in point was the position of the Reverend Alexander Garden, rector of St. Philip's Church in Charleston for some thirty years and master of Greek and Latin in the "free" school. His efforts to check the influence of the eloquent itinerant evangelist George Whitfield included the publication of *Six Letters* (1740). Here he held that good works "do as necessarily spring from and accompany a true and *lively* Faith, whether *before or after* Justification, as Light and Heat do the Sun; or that, as *the Body without the soul is dead*, so Faith without Works, whether before or after justification, *is dead* also." In the Anglican way, Garden also questioned whether in view of the deep-rooted habits common to human nature, regeneration could be the work of the moment.[75] All this hardly reflected a distinctive impact of American conditions on attitudes toward man's nature.

Garden's exhortation indicated, as did Byrd's comments in his diaries, at least some awareness of the classical ideal of subordinating selfish interests and human weaknesses to civil virtue and public weal. Neither man, however, hinted at a view of human nature implicit in the "country ideology" which Professor Pocock has delineated in *The Machiavellian Moment*. Suggestions of this, though, appeared in the reactions of two Carolinians to the social, political, and economic situation in those colonies.

74. Henning Cohen, *The South Carolina Gazette 1732–1774* (Columbia, S.C., 1953), pp. 193–94.

75. Frederick Dalcho, M.D., *An Historical Account of the Protestant Episcopal Church in South Carolina* (Charleston, S.C., 1820; rept. ed., New York, 1972), pp. 137, 141 ff. Pithy, candid, zealous, Garden supported schools for Negroes and, in Dalcho's verdict, was "a good Shepherd of Christ's flock."

The conflict between the established order in the Carolina lowlands and the backcountry pioneers provided the context for these views of human nature. Underrepresented in the assembly and unfairly taxed, the backcountry people also suffered from the lack of courts, magistrates, and law-enforcing officers. The social disorganization resulting from weak family ties and the absence of schools and an instructed clergy opened the door to violence on the part of uprooted ruffians, who defied property rights and civilized morality. Thus the lack of established institutions invited violence and disorder when these brutal bullies took matters in their own hands by defying established institutions.[76]

Charles Woodmason, a onetime merchant, planter, and magistrate on the seaboard and finally an Anglican itinerant minister in the South Carolina backcountry, indignantly spelled out in his journal "the licentiousness of the People." This was evident in a concubinage in which wives were swapped as cattle and in other irregular behavior more blameworthy than that of Indians living in a state of nature. Although Woodmason lamented the way in which New Light Baptists bewildered people's minds, he laid the whole lamentable situation, not to "the Miseries of Human Nature," but to the social upheaval of the time and place. In his humanitarian role, he drew up protests for the property-respecting Regulators who sought redress of grievances inflicted both by the lawless ruffians and the extorting seaboard elite. Though against the violence that an unrestrained human nature invited, he now condoned it as a means to a righteous end—the protection of property, the virtue of women, and an orderly society necessary to straighten out the sad, prevailing chaos in the public and private behavior of the backcountry.[77]

In the pine barrens and foothills of North Carolina similar grievances found an eloquent spokesman in Hermon Husband. A former Maryland Presbyterian and for a time a Quaker, he acquired land and influence in the Sandy Creek country where he settled about 1755. Opposing violence, he insisted that enlightened, organized opinion could force the remote, grasping authorities to mete out justice. Husband wrote many of the Regulators' demands for redress of grievances and the abuses of power. He tried to explain how the common people could, throwing aside their reason and moral endowment, submit with brutish stupefaction to exploitation and to beastly domination, and ascribed this

76. Richard M. Brown, *The South Carolina Regulators* (Cambridge, Mass., 1963), pp. 135–42.

77. Richard J. Hooker, ed., *The Carolina Backcountry on the Eve of the Revolution: The Journal and Other Writings of Charles Woodmason, Anglican Itinerant* (Chapel Hill, 1953), pp. 15, 23, 109 ff., 165 ff.

to their failure to use the reason that Nature had given them. But he also blamed the leaders, lay and clerical. In the pursuit of self-interest, they reduced the people to ignorance and indolence, making them slaves by their own consent. Yet, he insisted, the oppressed could still struggle to free themselves from virtual slavery. Denounced as a libelous inciter of riots, Husband saw his plantation laid waste and a price set on his head. In effect outlawed, he fled to Pennsylvania, where he later took part in the Whisky Rebellion. He was condemned to death, but Washington, thanks to influential intercession, reprieved him. Thus this complex and turbulent egalitarian, in seeking to explain the behavior of the down-trodden, offered both a crude analysis of motives and a faith that reason and moral indignation, expressed in struggle, might overcome evil and extortion.[78]

The impact of frontier experience on ideas about human nature owed more to legend and myth than to the reports of such sojourners in the backcountry as Woodmason and Husband. In a monumental study, Richard Slotkin has traced the origin and growth of an American archetypal myth centering in the near-legendary hero Daniel Boone, the rugged, lonely, self-sufficient, simple, powerful, and serene hunter and pathfinder in the Kentucky wilderness.[79] The story told of the heroic adventures of Boone, symbol of countless other pioneers.[80] Its brief content and simple form merely suggested the later embroidered, allegorical myth. In mastering the wilderness, including the ferocious and terror-striking Indians, the hero used violence to counteract violence. The result was the redemption of the land, the transformation from a "howling wilderness" (however beautiful and serene in solitude) into a pastoral utopia. In expiating the guilt of violence, the redeemed hero also achieved a hitherto unrealized human power to control the darkest aspects of both nature and human nature by discovering and abiding by their laws. Such implications of the story may have seemed strained at the outset. The myth was nevertheless later used in these and other ways by gifted writers, who associated it with ways of looking at human nature in an American setting.

The middle colonies, as well as Virginia, the Carolinas, and Kentucky, provided material for discussions of human nature that also reflected in

78. Hermon Husband, *Remarks on Religion* (1761); *Informations Concerning the Province of North Carolina . . .* (1773); *An Impartial Relation of the Rise and Causes of the Recent Differences in Public Affairs* (1775); and *Sermons*; all in William K. Boyd, ed., *Some Eighteenth-Century Tracts Concerning North Carolina* (Raleigh, N.C., 1927).

79. Richard Slotkin, *Regeneration through Violence: The Mythology of the American Frontier, 1600–1860* (Middletown, Conn., 1973), pp. 268 ff.

80. John Filson, *The Discovery, Settlement and Present State of Kentucky* (Wilmington, Del., 1784).

some measure the impact of American experience on traditional views of man.

Take William Livingston, a leading figure in New York law, education, and politics.[81] Reared in the Dutch Reformed Church, he had become a Presbyterian with some sympathy for deism. As a disciple of Locke, he ardently championed religious and intellectual freedom and the shaping influence of early education. Orthodoxies of all kinds were anathema to him. He was thus alarmed when the Anglicans planned to make what was to become King's College a means for advancing the interests of the Church of England. A college under an authoritative religious body would, in his view, catastrophically give dogmatism and priestcraft the upper hand.

With two law partners, Livingston launched the *Independent Reflector* to spread their ideas and to combat the Anglican party. In turn, the Anglicans and other critics denounced Livingston as an atheist. In an essay entitled "Of Human Nature, the Immortality of the Soul, and whether it can Exist without Thinking," Livingston tried to meet the charge. He found truth in each of the leading views of man: that which stressed the abjectness and corruption of human frailty and that which emphasized man's nobility and gifts in the hierarchy of earthly creatures. Any proper view, he urged, must take both positions into account. It must rely on revelation—a statement indicating his conviction that natural religion and revelation supplemented and reenforced each other. In any case, man's "Grandeur and Wretchedness are alike conspicuous. He may without vanity reflect on himself, as capable of a Participation of the Divinity: and without Error rank himself with the meanest Reptile. He is in short, an infinite Insect, and a despicable Immortal."[82] Though the juxtaposition of these two views of man was not unfamiliar, this seems to have been the first time when, in any essay bearing the title human nature, the coexistence was made so unequivocally. Livingston left it to others to explicate motives and behavior in terms of the dichotomy he set forth.

An enduring classic far more profound in its discussion of human nature owed its existence to a remarkable Quaker who was at home in all the Middle Colonies. Long before the appearance of John Woolman's *Journal*, the seventeenth-century founders of the Society of Friends— George Fox, Robert Barclay, and the best-known convert, William

81. I am indebted to Harold W. Thatcher, *The Social Philosophy of William Livingston* (Chicago, 1938); and especially to Milton Klein, *The American Whig—Livingston of New York* (Ann Arbor, Mich.: University Microfilms, 1954), AC-1, no. 8699.

82. *The Independent Reflector*, no. 49 (Nov. 1, 1753). This journal was edited, with an introduction, by Milton M. Klein and others, and published at Cambridge, Mass., in 1963. The quotation is from page 412 of the Cambridge edition.

Penn—had spelled out a distinct image of man. Although adjustments to life in America posed special problems for the Friends, as for others, the Quaker image of man on both sides of the Atlantic was very much the same. Quakers everywhere believed that human nature itself did not make war, the swearing of oaths, and religious intolerance inevitable or even necessary. They likewise felt that pride did not need to dominate behavior, and thus belittled display in dress and demeanor. The frailty of human nature could be strengthened by useful work and above all by group discipline.

Yet Quakerism, related as it was to Puritanism and to the mystical anti-establishment sects of the Reformation, did not view human nature in roseate terms. In some ways the Friends held a more restrictive view of man than the Puritans.[83] It is of course well known that the Puritans believed that reason, though tainted by corruption, remained an important auxiliary in the search for knowledge of God's will. Quakerism drew a strict line between the spheres of the natural, to which reason belonged, and the supernatural, to which religion belonged. In Penn's words, men tend to "side with the passions against their reason" and to let selfishness overrule their "attachement to the good."[84] Nor did Penn, particularly in his later years as a Friend, view human nature with much optimism. In *An Essay Towards the Present and Future Peace of Europe* (1693) he wrote: "Not that men know not what is right, their excesses, and wherein they are to blame, by no means, nothing is plainer to them. But so depraved is human nature that, without compulsion some way or other, too many would not readily be brought to do what they know is right and fit, or avoid what they are satisfied they should not do."[85] His realism found expression in the maxims he set down in his later years. "Trust no man with the main chance, and avoid to be trusted . . ."[86]; or again, "Our resolutions seem to be vigorous as often as we reflect upon our past errors, but alas, they are apt to flat [slacken] again upon fresh temptations to the same things."[87]

But there was also another side to the Quaker view of human nature. In denying the doctrine of predestination and in making everyone responsible for his own salvation, Quakerism offered as its central belief the infusion of the "seed of God" or some part of divinity in every human being. This was manifested by the light of Christ and the Holy Spirit. Extending in each individual beyond conscience and intuition, the

83. J. William Frost, *The Quaker Family in Colonial America* (New York, 1973), p. 13.
84. Tolles and Aldefer, eds., *William Penn*, p. 107.
85. William Penn, "An Essay Towards the Present and Future Peace of Europe" (1693), in Tolles and Aldefer, eds., *William Penn*, p. 144.
86. "Fruits of a Father's Love" (1726), in Tolles and Aldefer, eds., *William Penn*, p. 198.
87. "Some Fruits of Solitude" (1693), in Tolles and Aldefer, eds., *William Penn*, p. 168.

"inner light" was the point of contact in the Friends' dichotomy between the natural and the supernatural. Whatever the worldly differences in wealth and status, men and women were thus all spiritually equal and to be treated as friends and brethren. Scripture, also inspired by the Holy Spirit, lay down guides for conduct. To cite just one example, the command to love one's enemies made war a sin. Nor would God require that which human nature made impossible.

Even the greatest piety did not insure perfect accomplishment in keeping to the path for which the inner light and Scriptures were reenforcing guides. Compromise between the ideal standard and the spotted actuality was regrettably the result of human weakness. In America the existence of slavery at the doorstep, the presence of Friends in the Pennsylvania Assembly, which was called on to support the imperial wars, and the opportunities for acquiring comfortable means or even wealth presented Quakers with special temptations and special tests. Compromises there were. Yet some felt that Quaker ideas were in considerable measure realized in Pennsylvania. To cite one example, Gottlieb Mittelberger, whose views of Penn were by no means uncritical and whose own experience in the colony led him to return to his fatherland, testified that "one rarely hears or sees a quarrel between the people in this country. The most distant strangers trust each other more than do acquaintances in Europe. Also, people are far more sincere and generous toward each other than in Germany. That is why our Americans live together far more quietly and peacefully than the Europeans. And all this is the result of the liberty they enjoy, which makes them all equal."[88]

The *Journal* of John Woolman, a simple tailor and careful student of the Scriptures, did more than replicate the Quaker view of human nature and the obstacles man's weakness imposed in striving to achieve the ideal. In his concrete analysis of motives he gave a new depth and dimension to the discussion of human nature. Woolman had no doubt that divine love penetrated the universe with an order and harmony which God intended men to share. Every human being was endowed not only with reason, however corrupt and unreliable it might be, but also with nonrational, mystical emotions, sometimes evident in dreams and visions but most often in everyday experiences. These provided the most important avenue for the voice of God. Since both reason and the mystical emotions, which included an inborn and inner principle inciting to goodness toward every living creature, were of God, there could be no real conflict between the two. "The true felicity of man in this life,

88. Oscar Handlin and John Clive, eds., *Journey to Pennsylvania by Gottlieb Mittelberger* (Cambridge, Mass., 1960), pp. 85–86.

and that which is to come, is in being inwardly united to the fountain of universal love and bliss."[89] One corollary indicated that child-rearing must emphasize the kinder endowments. Another implied that all humanity, being blessed by gifts and needs identical in kind, should be regarded by their fellows as brothers and treated with respect, justice, and love. Like Penn, Woolman recognized the actuality of human vanity, greed, and selfishness. These, in operating both consciously and unconsciously, led men to suppose that what seemed immediate interests were true interests. Greed and selfishness lay at the root of the exploitation of the weak by the strong and explained the injustice of the unequal distribution of wealth and its use for display, prestige, and power. Avarice and self-interest also explained man's proclivity to compete and to make war. Such impulses, hardened in deep-rooted customs, did not lend themselves easily to change. Nevertheless, this need not be, thanks to the even more powerful force of love exemplified in Christ's redemption and in the message and guidance of the Spirit available to all who patiently and silently waited for it.

Since in his view deeds were more powerful than words, Woolman set himself the task, in all humility, of helping his fellows recognize truth and mend their ways. In advance of most Quakers he opposed slavery as a denial of human equality and love. He spelled out the Quaker opposition to war by refusing to pay taxes for its support and in taking the consequences. Woolman's example of a life of voluntary simplicity and of sharing what he had with those in need reenforced his strictures against seeking wealth for display, power, and a happiness it could not yield. Examining his own motives and helping others to probe theirs, John Woolman demonstrated through self-discipline the power in human nature to overcome the evil within and without and to live a life of peace, happiness, and security in accord with the truth infused by the divine spirit.

The transfer of ideas and values from the Old World, in the first century and a half of the settlement of the New, understandably included attitudes toward human nature. In the middle and southern colonies references to these involved little explicit and systematic analysis of the term itself. It was largely identified with Christian supernatural dualism and assimilated Aristotelian-medieval ideas and with proverbs and adages in the classical and Renaissance traditions. The phrase also involved a recognition of the influence of biology (including heredity),

89. Phillips P. Moulton, ed., *The Journal and Major Essays of John Woolman* (New York, 1971), p. 249.

astrology, Special Providences, and the natural and social environment. As generally understood, human nature included a capacity for introspective probing of motives, both conscious and unconscious. Conflict between reason and the emotions and passions (including sex) was assumed to be an innate characteristic. The discussion of human nature likewise identified tension between selfishness and benevolence. On occasion, references to human nature touched on such matters as fixedness or malleability in the human condition and determination versus free will. The traditional uses of ideas about human nature included advisory maxims intended to help men and women resolve conflicts and meet sorrow. Moreover, the American environment accentuated older uses and even initiated new ones. These included some awareness of the stimulation provided by hitherto unheard and unseen wonders to the faculties of sensation and imagination, and the enlargement through the use of empirical science of man's ability to adapt himself to unusual circumstances and to transform inherent potentialities into new achievements. Even more important was the problem posed by the contrast between beggarly poverty in the Old World and self-sustenance of those who had known only impoverishment in England. The bounty and opportunities of the new land seemed, again, to expand human capacity. Also important was the need of justifying elites and social status in a relatively mobile society. Above all, attitudes toward human nature figured in questions raised by relations with Indians and Africans.

We shall look to the ways in which all these issues were more thoroughly probed in early New England Puritan thought and in the widespread mid-eighteenth-century revivals.

2

Puritan Views and Visions

Take heed of receiving truth into your head without the love of it in your heart, lest God give you up to strong delusions to believe lies, and / lest you find / that in the conclusion all your learning shall make you more fit to deceive yourself and others.

THOMAS SHEPARD, 1672

Man is made with his feet on the earth and with his posture erect and countenance toward heaven, signifying that he was made to have heaven in his eyes, and the earth under his foot.

JONATHAN EDWARDS

IT WAS, of course, not only in the middle and southern colonies that new situations and views about human nature, old and new, interacted. Until the Revolution, in fact, the most explicit analysis of the nature of man took place in New England and reflected the distinctiveness of the sixteenth- and seventeenth-century Puritan movement. As Larzer Ziff has argued,[1] this was a revolutionary culture, a rebellion of "have-nots" against the established order. In rebelling, Puritans identified themselves as an elite and justified their own participation in earthly enterprise and spiritual advance. In New England the Puritan image of man was also related to the conviction, present at the start and elaborated by the second generation, that "God sifted a whole Nation that he might send choice Grain over into this wilderness" to establish a Bible Commonwealth. Divine plan gave the chosen "saints" the most favorable opportunity in history to enact a great drama on a new stage, to establish a beacon light in a dark world.

In discussing views about human nature in seventeenth-century New England one must keep in mind the broad similarity between the Puritan and other versions of the Christian image of man, in their belief in a supernatural dualism, original innocence, the Fall, the faculty psychology of Thomas Aquinas, and the conflict between reason and the corrupted will on the one hand and the useful but also dangerous affections or emotions on the other. Like several Christian philosophies,

1. Larzer Ziff, *Puritanism in America: New Culture in a New World* (New York, 1973).

Puritanism incorporated aspects of classical thought and Renaissance humanism. Within the frame of divine sovereignty, its theology sought ways of alleviating the tensions between the corrupted will and the affections, of reconciling moral responsibility with errant reason and feelings, and of providing a convincing view of conversion and regeneration. Now this involved a revision of faculty psychology, a revision effected with some aid from French and British divines. Thomas Shepard, Thomas Hooker, and Samuel Willard, among other New England ministers, struggled with the problem of properly balancing the faculties in the model of normative hierarchy.[2]

All this was evident in Charles Morton's *Compendium Physicae*, a late-seventeenth-century synthesis written by Morton before leaving England, and used as a textbook by him and his successors at Harvard for a great many years. The *Compendium* harmonized the mental philosophy of Aristotle and Aquinas with the new learning of such scientists as Boyle and such philosophers as Descartes.[3] It would, however, be wrong to suggest that this or any other treatise or sermon constituted the New England Puritan view of human nature in its totality. That view was neither monolithic nor static: shifts in emphasis and modifications reflected generational differences and changes in ways of living.[4] The New England Puritan view owed its greatest debt to Calvinism. Indeed, the doctrines of the sovereignty of God and of the universal corruption of man were central to all that concerned the relations between man and his Creator and between man and his fellows.

Besides modifying the theology and polity of Calvinism, New England writers supplemented the *Institutes of the Christian Religion* with the humanistic and Platonic logic of Petrus Ramus, a Huguenot reformer. They came to conceive of man, despite his clouded reason and his stubborn and devious will, enamored of the self, as capable of at least

2. Of special note are Thomas Shepard's *Certain Select Cases Resolved* (London, 1648), pp. 123–34, 155–56; *The Parable of the Ten Virgins* (London, 1648; rept. ed., 1660); and *The Paradoxes of Puritan Piety: Being the Autobiography and Journal of Thomas Shepard*, edited with an introduction by Michael McGiffert (Amherst, Mass., 1972). For varying interpretations see Norman Petitt, *The Heart Prepared: Grace and Conversion in Puritan Spiritual Life* (New Haven, 1966); J. Rodney Fulcher, "Puritans and the Passions: The Faculty Psychology in American Puritanism," *Journal of the History of the Behavioral Sciences* 9 (1973): 123–39; and James G. Blight, "Solomon Stoddard's *Safety of Appearing* and the Dissolution of the Puritan Faculty Psychology," in the same journal, 10 (1974): 238–50.

3. Theodore Hornberger, ed., *Compendium Physicae*, Publications of the Colonial Society of Massachusetts, vol. 33, *Collections* (Boston, 1940).

4. Merle Curti, "Psychological Theories in American Thought," *Dictionary of the History of Ideas*, 4 vols. (New York, 1973), 4:16–19. See also Perry Miller, *The New England Mind: The Seventeenth Century* (New York, 1939), chap. 9.

glimpsing, though never fully comprehending, the mystery of God's great and noble design with its majestic order and beauty. The plan not only embraced the unlimited sovereignty of God and the helplessness and depravity of man, but also envisioned God's mercy in offering the covenant of grace, the salvation of the predestined elect, of those who, infused with God's grace, recovered sufficient integrity of the will to truly believe in Christ the Redeemer. Such men and women alone were justified by faith according to God's cosmic plan. God's fully given grace inclined the faculties toward spiritual growth. No one could be certain whether his faith was pure enough to justify his salvation. This tension and delicate balance between assurance and uncertainty, and the anxiety it fostered, explained in part the preoccupation with and fear of death.[5] Such anxiety was deepened by the conviction that no one could, by his own powers alone, achieve faith, grace, and election. Yet one was, by God's law, bound to use to that end his reason, his will, and his affections, the limited but indispensable gifts God had permitted fallen and sinful man to keep.

Such, in broad outline, was the conceptual frame within which the New England Puritans discussed human nature and sought to come to terms with the problems these assumptions and commitments posed. We shall see that, considered in relation to family, class, the economy, and the authority of church and state, the Puritan views of human nature found applications intended to serve as persuasive sanctions.

Much writing illustrated the first, basic idea in the Puritan discussion—man's innate and transcendent weakness and sinfulness, "the beast" within him. At the risk of injustice to the subtle arguments of many writers on religious themes, the sermons, diaries, letters, and histories of five New Englanders have been chosen to illustrate the Puritan image of man: William Bradford, governor of Plymouth Plantation and author of a *History* written between 1630 and 1651[6];

5. David E. Stannard, "Death and Dying in Puritan New England," *American Historical Review* 78 (1973): 1305–30.

6. My account of Bradford's image of man, briefly sketched in *Human Nature in American Historical Thought* (Columbia, Mo., 1968), is based on his *The History of Plymouth Plantation*, ed. Worthington C. Ford, 2 vols. (Boston, 1912). I also found helpful Bradford Smith's *Bradford of Plymouth* (Philadelphia, 1951); and David Levin's "William Bradford," in Everett Emerson, ed., *Major Writers of Early American Literature* (Madison, Wis., 1972). Two monographs merit special attention: George D. Langdon, Jr., *Pilgrim Colony: A History of New Plymouth 1620–1691* (New Haven, 1966); and John Demos, *A Little Commonwealth: Family Life in Plymouth Colony* (New York, 1970). Peter Gay, in *A Loss of Mastery: Puritan Historians in Colonial America* (Berkeley and Los Angeles, 1966), argues that Bradford's history suffers from its piety and the partisan and parochial character of Puritan culture. For a critique of Gay, see David Levin's review in *History and Theory* 7 (1968): 385–93.

John Winthrop, governor of Massachusetts Bay, whose Journal, composed in the same period, was ultimately published as *The History of New England*[7]; John Cotton, a leading first generation clergyman[8]; and two latter-day Puritans, Cotton Mather and Jonathan Edwards.[9]

Bradford's conception of human nature needs to be put in the context of the story he was telling of a contemporary but very special chapter in the age-old contest between God and Satan, a contest in which the Plymouth band was involved as pilgrims in a dangerous but glorious journey toward their true home—heaven. They survived only by the providential hand of God. But this did not release them from the necessity of trying to assess the complex motives of actors each of whom was unique. Nor were God's children spared from endless decisions in trying to follow the course He had willed. In everyday affairs that course had to be discovered in ambiguous worldly evidence.[10]

Bradford made much of the faltering weakness of man, particularly when accounting for the challenges to Plymouth leaders, whose action God presumably directed. Thus unwillingness to check behavior stemming from original sin explained the deviations of the traitors and troublemakers of the settlement. Above all, Bradford saw man's innate disposition to sin in the covetousness and wickedness of outsiders with whom he had to deal—creditors in England, magistrates and traders in neighboring settlements, Dutch rivals, and perfidious Indians.

Yet in explaining misdeeds and in justifying actions taken against culprits, Bradford fell back on innate sinfulness less often than did Winthrop. In his *History of New England* the Bay Colony leader found sin everywhere, both within and beyond himself. While man's spiritual gift pulled him one way, his flesh, the world, and the Devil tempted him elsewhere. Even though Winthrop conceived of himself as saved, he was convinced of his own unworthiness. He fully grasped the Puritan's obligation to debase himself if he were even to hope for grace. In a

7. I have used James Kendall Hosmer's edition of *Winthrop's Journal*, 2 vols. (New York, 1908); and *The Winthrop Papers*, 5 vols., Publications of the Massachusetts Historical Society, 1929–1947. Edmund S. Morgan's *The Puritan Dilemma: The Story of John Winthrop* (Boston, 1958) and Richard S. Dunn's *Puritans and Yankees: The Winthrop Dynasty of New England 1630–1717* (Princeton, 1962) provide a useful context.

8. Larzer Ziff has the most comprehensive treatment: *The Career of John Cotton: Puritanism and the American Expression* (Princeton, 1962).

9. The best treatment of Cotton Mather is that of Robert Middlekauff: *The Mathers: Three Generations of Puritan Intellectuals 1596–1729* (New York, 1971), pp. 191–367.

10. Peter Gay, *A Loss of Mastery: Puritan Historians in Colonial America*, pp. 34 ff. Cf. Alan B. Howard, "Art and History in Bradford's *Of Plymouth Plantation*," *William and Mary Quarterly* 28 (1971): 266.

probing mood he wrote of his "heart getting loose one Sav: daye throughe want to due watchfulness and firme resolution . . . it gats so deepe into the world as I could not get it free."[11] When Winthrop felt this way about himself, he understandably approved the banishment of Anne Hutchinson for claiming that some, in having achieved justification, were so infused by the Spirit that the law was irrelevant to their conduct. Winthrop also saw the inevitable thrust toward sin in man's social life, notably in his greedy economic dealings. He detected such sinfulness not only in farmers, laboring men, and servants, but also in the well placed who defied the laws designed to regulate the market in the interest of justice to producers and consumers.[12]

John Cotton, the leading ecclesiastical theoretician in early Massachusetts Bay, held that sin was too deeply ingrained for man to be capable of warranting salvation by anything he might himself do; to take satisfaction in good deeds was a sign of pride and self-centered will. "It is a like corruption," he warned, to "look for Justification from sinne in the sight of God by our own works."[13] Yet Cotton stressed the Christ and the Spirit in those who received grace. For a time this required him, uncomfortably, even elusively, to straddle the contradictory emphasis on the law, on the one hand, and the transcendence of law for those infused by the Spirit, on the other.

Corruption and sin were also evident in the unlawful indulgence of the sexual instinct, an instinct natural to man and necessary to propagation but likely, even in the marriage bed, to interfere with spiritual growth. If, as Robert Middlekauff has held, the frequency of premarital indulgence and fornication after wedlock indicated that the Puritans took sex in their stride,[14] there was no question about the heinous crime of "unnatural" behavior. Thus it was the beast in man that, in the narrative of Bradford, led to whole waves of sex crimes. These were discussed with unrivaled candor in the *History of Plymouth Plantation*. "Marvelous indeed," wrote Bradford, "it may be to see and consider

11. *Winthrop Papers*, 1:208.

12. For Winthrop's position on the charge that a wealthy merchant was guilty of economic oppression and excessive gains see *The Apologia of Robert Keayne*, ed. Bernard Bailyn (Boston, 1964), p. 49.

13. The Rev. J. Lewis Diman, ed., "Master John Cotton's Answer to Master Roger Williams," *Publications of the Narragansett Club*, 1st ser., 2 vols. (Providence, R.I., 1867): 2:110. See also Cotton's *The Keys of the Kingdom of Heaven* . . . (Boston, 1644; rept. ed., 1843), pp. 32 ff., 107.

14. Middlekauff, *The Mathers*, pp. 202–3. See also David H. Flaherty, *Privacy in Colonial New England* (Charlottesville, Va., 1972), which contends that the inherent desire of human beings for privacy in sexual as in many other relationships was not altogether successfully checked by supervisory watchfulness, the legal tradition of moral authority, and the prevalence of large families living in restricted quarters.

how some kind of wickedness did grow and breake forth here, in a land wher the same was so much witnessed against, and so narrowly looked into, and severely punisyed when it was knowne; as in no place more, or so much, that I have known or heard of." Bradford laid this in the largest part to "our corrupte natures, which are so hardly bridled, subdued, and mortified." In seeking to explain the wretched deviations at Plymouth, he thought it likely that the Devil "carried a greater spite against the churches of Christ and the gospell hear," for Satan might have more power over God's servants in lands long possessed by such heathens as the Indians. But another reason, and here Bradford's insight was profound, was "that it may be in this case as it is with waters when their streames are stopped or dammed up, when they gett passage they flow with more violence, and make more noys and disturbance, then when they are suffered to rune quietly in their owne channels. So wickedness being here more stopped by strict lawes, and the same more nerly looked unto, so as it cannot rune in a commone road of liberty as it would, and is inclined, it searches every where, and at last breaks out where it getts vente." This theory of repression merits respect. And so does yet another hypothesis of which Bradford was "verily persuaded," namely, that there "is not more evills in this kind, nor nothing here so many by proportion, as in other places, but they are here more discovered and seen, and made publick by due search, inquisition, and due punishment."[15]

Winthrop, too, assigned to man's original nature his wont of yielding to the lusts of the flesh. But he did not equal Bradford's keen psychological insight by taking into account special factors that heightened and publicized breaches of the moral law. At the same time, Winthrop was more explicit than Bradford in emphasizing the ways in which man could control or at least check the passionate urges. "I have founde," he wrote, "that a man may master and keepe under many corrupt lusts by the meere force of reason and morall considerations (as the heathen did) but they will returne again to their former strength: there is no way to mortifie them but by faithe in Christ, and his deathe"; or, as he wrote to his son John in 1623, "that through the continuall instigation of Sathan and our owne proneness to evill, we are always in danger of beinge turned out of our course, but God will preserve us to the ende if we trust in him and be guided by his will."[16]

But sinful though man must be by the very essence of his nature, he could use God's gift of reason in preparing for conversion by seeking God's truth and law. Once grace had been experienced, reason was an

15. Bradford, *History of Plymouth Plantation*, 2:309–10, 328–30.
16. *Winthrop Papers*, 1:237, 283

auxiliary in the probing self-examination that every saint must constantly subject himself to. However prone reason was to fall prey to the emotions and self-deception, it was still to be cherished, subject to faith and subordination to God's will and law.

Winthrop often expressed his belief in human capacities, including reasoning power. In urging his brethren to migrate to the New World, he assured them that by use of "the facultye of Reason" God had given them they could strengthen the fortifications always required to endure never-ending conflicts between the spiritual and worldly nature. Yet Winthrop knew the limitations and indeed the dangers of undue reliance on reason. Thus he warned his son against leaning too heavily on his rational powers: "Study well, my Son, the saying of the Apostle, Knowledge puffeth up. It is a good Gift of God, but when it lifts up the Mind above the Cross of Christ, it is the Pride of Life, and the High-way to Apostacy, wherein many Men of great Learning and Hopes have perished."[17]

John Cotton's "reply" to Roger Williams also took for granted both the rationality of man and the role of revelation in guiding reason. Biblical texts supplied the major premises and logic the means of unfolding inner truths. His obvious purpose was to convince the reader through reason. But, like Winthrop, Cotton was sure that reason alone was not enough: if argument was to prove effective, God must intervene to help Roger Williams in his flight from darkness.[18]

In explaining the actions taken to protect the patent and to check the encroachments of the Massachusetts Bay people, Bradford also appealed to reason. Moreover, he assumed the capacity of the rank and file to listen to reason. In addition to a capacity for reason, man had in his affectional or emotional endowment a gift for love. America, Winthrop urged, required, more than England, the growth of the capacity for loving and caring for each other. That men were capable of living in such a socially desirable way followed from the fact that "love cometh of God and every one that loveth is borne of God, soe that This love is the fruite of the new birth, and none can have it but the new Creature."[19] Bradford made the same point. He urged that "you which do as it were begin in a new world, and lay the foundation of social piety and humanity for others to follow," should suffer no such weeds in your garden as the tale-bearing and fickle shifting of old for new friends so common in England. The governor of Plymouth assumed that men could, through the

17. *Winthrop Papers*, 3:136; 4:367.
18. Diman, ed., "Master John Cotton's Answer," pp. 21, 63.
19. *Winthrop Papers*, 2:290.

covenant, bind themselves together in a blessed community dedicated to the Christian life. Bradford also took it for granted that he himself, as a loving father looking out for all others and in turn receiving from them affectionate appreciation, might play a special role.[20] Still, the Puritan view of love and affection included an awareness of its perils: it must be kept in tow by reason and it must, in conjugal and parental relations, never be allowed to rival the paramount obligation of love of God.[21]

Yet with all man's capacity for reason and for love he could not, weak vessel that he was, steer the course of his own affairs save in a narrow sphere. "The fleshe," wrote Winthrop, "is eagerly inclined to pride, and wantonnesse, by which it playes the tirant over the poore soule, making it a verey slave; the workes of our callings beinge diligently followed, are a special meanes to tame it."[22] But even diligent pursuit of one's calling was not always enough. A Boston woman, hanged for murdering her child, was "so possessed with Satain, that he persuaded her (by his delusions, which she listened to as revelations from God) to break the neck of her own child, that she might free it from future misery."[23] Again, Winthrop spoke of Anne Hutchinson as "an instrument of Satan so fitted and trained to his service for interrupting the passage [of the] Kingdom in this part of the world, and poysoning the Churches here planted, as no story records the like of a woman, since that mentioned in the *Revelation*."[24] The Governor of Massachusetts Bay also blamed the devious Devil for Roger Williams's challenge to authority when he denounced prevailing Church-State relations and failure to compensate the Indians fairly for their lands. It was, in short, customary to blame the Devil for misfortune unless it was seen as a punishment for the collective sins of the colony.

On the other hand, it was also common to see God's providences in every blessing and happy outcome. When brotherly love and care governed the Plymouth people's performance of their covenants, it "must needs be therefore the spetiall worke and hand of God." When

20. William Bradford, "Letter Book," *Collections of the Massachusetts Historical Society*, 1st ser. 3 (1794): 30–31. Cotton Mather called Bradford "a common father to them all." Smith, *Bradford of Plymouth*, p. 202.

21. For an informed discussion see Edmund S. Morgan, *The Puritan Family, Religion and Domestic Relations in Seventeenth-Century New England* (New York, 1966), chaps. 2 and 3.

22. *Winthrop Papers*, 1:193–94.

23. *Winthrop's Journal*, 1:283.

24. *Winthrop's Journal*, 1:251–52.

smallpox infested a nearby Indian tribe, Bradford knew that the marvelous goodness and providence of God spared the settlers, not one of whom fell prey to the scourge though several had nursed the wretched savages.[25] But none of Bradford's examples of providences in the contest between good and evil matched one of Cotton Mather's tales. Theophilus Eaton was, Mather surmised, spared the debauch of drinking to the health of the Danish king when that monarch was providentially seized by a "sort of fit."[26]

God's intervention played a special role in strengthening man's will to do the right thing. This belief explained why some Puritans had the courage to leave their old moorings for the New World venture. Thus John Winthrop wrote to those in the homeland who held back from crossing the seas: "Though miracles be ceased, yet we may expecte a more than ordinarye blessing from God upon all lawfull meanes, where the work is the Lordes, and he is sought in it according to his will: for it is usuall with him to increase the strengthe of the meanes, or to weaken them as he is pleased, or displeased with the Instrumentes and the Action: and yet bothe without miracle: else you must conclude that he hathe left the gov[ernment] of the world, and committed all power to the Creature, that the success of things should wholly depend upon second causes."[27]

The Puritan image of man included the recognition of differences between individuals, and Bradford explicitly took stock of such differences beyond distinguishing saints or the elect as a group from the unregenerate mass. In justifying the decision to give up the communal experiment, he made this clear in the often-quoted picturesque words of which he was a master: "Upon the poynte all being to have alike, and all to doe alike, they thought them selves in the like condition, and one as good as another; and so, if it did not cut off those relations that God hath set amongest men, yet it did at least diminish and take the mutuall respects that should be preserved amongst them. And would have beene worse if they had been men of another condition."[28] Winthrop, too, saw individual differences among men as earmarks of God's hand in the behavior and lives of his creatures. "God almightie in his most holy and wise providence hath soe disposed of the Condicion of mankinde, as in

---

25. Bradford, *History of Plymouth Plantation*, 2:194–95.
26. Cotton Mather, *Magnalia Christi Americana; or, the Ecclesiastical History of New-England*, 2 vols. (Hartford, Conn., 1853), 1:151.
27. *Winthrop Papers*, 2:137–38.
28. Bradford, *History of Plymouth Plantation*, 1:302–3.

all times some must be rich, some poore, some highe and eminent in power and dignitie; others meane and in subjection."[29]

The stewardship of the elite followed from the recognition of innate differences in men's talents. John Cotton, who ascribed the varied abilities of men to God's part in shaping human nature, wrote that "all magistrates are to be chosen . . . out of the rank of noblemen or gentlemen among them, *the best that God shall send into the country*, if they be qualified with gifts fit for government, either eminent above others, or not inferior to others." To be sure, since "there is a straine in a mans heart that will some time or other runne out to excess, unlesse the Lord restraine it, but it is not good to venture it: It is necessary therefore, that all power that is on earth be limited, church-power or other."[30]

Winthrop's remarks about the need for limiting the power of magistrates were sometimes less forthright. When the Puritans were about to set foot on American soil, he spoke of the obligations inherent in their status in society. He declared that "noe man is made more honourable than another or more wealthy, etc., out of any perticuler and singuler respect to himselfe but for the glory of his Creator and the Common good of the creature, Man; . . ."[31] Again and again he insisted that a few were chosen to govern the many, contending in well-known words that "Democratie is, among most Civill nations, accounted the meanest and worst of all forms of Government . . . and Historyes doe recorde, that it hath been allwayes of least continuance and fullest of trouble."[32] To Thomas Hooker, Winthrop pointed out that it would be dangerous to give the body of the people a large share in the governing of the Commonwealth for "the best part is always the least, and of that best part the wiser is always the lesser."[33]

Not every spokesman in early Massachusetts saw eye to eye with Winthrop. Even when there was agreement that the magistrate must protect the faith, morals, and integrity of the community, differences

29. Winthrop, "A Model of Christian Charity," *Winthrop Papers*, 2:282–83; cf. *Winthrop's Journal*, 2:319–20. John Hull, mint-master and treasurer of the Colony, agreed, lamenting, in 1644, "the want of subjection of inferiors to superiors, and too much the want of religious care to contain in subjection those under them is a visible evil among us." Diary of John Hull, *Transactions and Collections of the American Antiquarian Society* (Worcester, Mass., 1857), 3:211.

30. John Cotton, "An Abstract of the Laws of New England as they are now established" (printed in London in 1641), *Collections of the Massachusetts Historical Society*, 1st. ser. 5 (1798): 173–92; *An Exposition upon the Thirteenth Chapter of the Revelations* (London, 1656), pp. 71–73, quoted in Stephen Foster, *Their Solitary Way: The Puritan Social Ethic in the First Century of the Settlement in New England* (New Haven, 1971), p. 169.

31. *Winthrop Papers*, 2:282–83; cf. *Winthrop's Journal*, 2:319–20.

32. *Winthrop Papers*, 4:383.

33. *Winthrop Papers*, 4:54.

arose about the precise nature of his authority and the character of his actions. As T. H. Breen has noted, the Puritans expected little less than perfection from the magistrate.[34] Winthrop's belief in his own rectitude drew strength from his conviction that his rule had its authority from God. He did not hold, however, that magistrates were immune from the passions afflicting the mass of men. In reply to questions about the doctrine of a divinely appointed governing elite and protests against some of the things he did, Winthrop reminded the General Court that "When you see the infirmities in us, you should reflect upon your own, and that would make you bear the more with us, and not be severe censurers of the failing of your magistrates, when you have continual experience of the like infirmities in yourselves and others."[35] Man, by reason of his sinful tendencies, must be ruled with a strong arm. There was, in the authoritarianism he derived from his image of man, little room for the free play of ideas or for rugged individualism in economic matters. Without a restraining authority, the evil in man would grow, until human beings became actually worse than brute beasts. True liberty is "the proper end and object of authority and cannot subsist without it; and it is a liberty to do that only which is good, just, and honest. . . . Whatsoever crosseth this, is not authority, but a distemper thereof."[36] The governing elite interpreted the moral law in terms of what was good, just, and honest. To be sure, the magistrate might, in recognition of man's infirmities, treat those who had erred with moderation, if the erring was not too far out of bounds. But he was to decide his proper course. Thus Winthrop's conception of human nature, including his belief in innate individual differences, justified a ruling class.

William Bradford did not go quite so far in spelling out the implications of a similar view of individual differences, of an innately gifted elite and an innately frail and sinful people. He recognized the proneness of the rank and file to err, but he did not make this, as Winthrop did, the justification for a governing aristocracy. He felt rather that to have superior abilities merely laid on some men the burden of stewardship for the less gifted. The leaders provided not only guidance and discipline, but affection and security.[37]

Bradford and Winthrop agreed that men and women were born with unequal abilities. Neither nature nor reason, Bradford wrote in a letter

34. T. H. Breen, *The Character of the Good Ruler: A Study of Political Ideas in New England 1630–1730* (New Haven, 1970), pp. xii–xx. After 1689 the emphasis in this discussion tended to be on qualities associated with the protection of civil rights.

35. *Winthrop Papers*, 2:134; *Winthrop's Journal*, 2:238.

36. *Winthrop's Journal*, 2:238–39.

37. Bradford, *History of Plymouth Plantation*, 1:192–93.

in 1623, intended women to take part in government: he too had read the Epistles of St. Paul. As in the case of all unequal abilities he pointed to the will of God as the explanation. In 1645 Winthrop wrote that "Mr. Hopkins, the governor of Hartford upon Connecticut, came to Boston and brought his wife with him (a godly young woman, of special parts), who was fallen into a sad state of infirmity, the loss of her understanding and reason, which had been growing upon her divers years, by occasion of her giving herself wholly to reading and writing, and had written many books. Her husband, being very loving and tender of her, was loathe to grieve her: but he saw his error, when it was too late. For if she had attended her household affairs, and such things as belong to women, and not gone out of her *way and calling* to meddle in such things as are proper for men, whose minds are stronger etc. . . . she had kept her wits, and might have improved them usefully and honourably in the place God had set her."[38] As Winthrop observed elsewhere, a true wife recognized that her proper subjection to the husband she had chosen was a way of liberty, rather than of bondage. She "would not think her condition safe and free, but in subjection to her husband's authority."[39]

In spite of the many difficulties the Puritans had with the Indians, Winthrop did not, as far as his Journal shows, hold that they were a lower form of being. Like many others in the early years of settlement, he opposed the extermination of the Indians on the ground of an innate inferiority. "We received a letter at the general court from the magistrates of Connecticut and New Haven and of Aquiday," he wrote in October 1640, "wherein they declared their dislike of such as would have the Indians rooted out, as being of the cursed race of Ham, and their desire of our mutual accord in seeking to gain them by justice and kindness, and withal to watch over them to prevent any danger by them, etc. We returned answer of our consent with them in all things propounded. . . ."[40] Like other Puritans, Winthrop believed in the capacity of these "beastlike men" to accept Christianity. He recorded the example of "one Wequash Cook," who attained "to good knowledge of the things of God and salvation by Christ, so as he became a preacher to other Indians, and labored much to convert them, but without any effect, for within a short time he fell sick, not without suspicion of poison from them, and died very comfortably."[41]

38. Bradford's letter is printed in the *American Historical Review* 8 (1902–3): 299; *Winthrop's Journal*, 2:225. Sanford J. Fox in *Science and Justice: The Massachusetts Witchcraft Trials* (Baltimore, 1968), chap. 8, discusses Puritan attitudes toward mental illness.

39. *Winthrop's Journal*, 2:239.

40. *Winthrop's Journal*, 2:18–19.

41. *Winthrop's Journal*, 2:69.

Bradford, although generally inclined to a somewhat more charitable interpretation of human nature than Winthrop, took a dim view of the Indians. He did not know whether their limitations resulted from God having permitted Satan an absolute dominion over them or from other circumstances. Bradford lacked John Eliot's zeal for converting the Indians, nor did he go as far as Roger Williams in showing a special sense of brotherhood in his dealings with them. Shrewd diplomacy, fair treatment, and some kindness, he seemed to feel, might generally keep Indians within bounds. But when these failed, God's elect could "but exerceise force . . . to reduse the Narigansets and their confederates to a more just and sober temper."[42] At the time of the Pequot war, Bradford felt that the triumph over the enemy was clearly predestined by divine will. The English, in short, were justified in fighting the Indians when they resisted white advance: if most of the savages were wiped out, it would at least be possible to bring Christ's message to the survivors. As long, however, as the Indians resisted God's people, who could doubt their perfidiousness was the work of the Devil?

With all the emphasis on fixed characteristics, with all the stress on viewing behavior and history as the unfolding of God's design, it might seem that the Puritans could find no place for the idea that man's nature might change. In a major sense this was true. Yet it was not quite the whole truth. Two levels of experience, spiritual and secular, must be kept in mind, even though in Puritan eyes no such demarcation was ever truly possible.

Conversion, the reception of grace and the resulting regeneration, transformed sinners into the saints that God had meant them to be. Conversion affected every faculty and emotion. This was of some consequence, even though the battle between light and darkness could never be resolved in this life. In the technology of conversion, the accepted covenant theory might be interpreted in ways that reflected American conditions. Since God had selected the most promising "seed" for establishing Zion in the wilderness and for quickening ultimate regeneration, this very fact encouraged effort to exercise the responsibility the covenant laid on the faithful. To build an ideal society in the face of almost overwhelming obstacles seemed to throw on sinful man all the greater obligation for using his reason and moral sense and for subordinating his will to that of God.

There was also a hope, among many, that the clean slate of a new environment would curb the least worthy aspects of human nature. In

42. Bradford, *History of Plymouth Plantation*, 2:380.

citing reasons for leaving Holland, Bradford emphasized the importance of social surroundings, expressing his fear that Pilgrim offspring might be corrupted by the great "licentiousness of youth in that countrie and the manifold temptations of the place." America, "being devoyd of all civill inhabitants, wher ther are savages and brutish men, which range up and downe, little otherwise than wild beasts,"[43] offered an environment where the faithful could build a commonwealth that encouraged the best of which man was capable. Again, in speaking of Plymouth's leadership, Bradford held that the New World offered plain and untutored yeomen a chance to realize native talents that must have lain dormant in the old home.

Winthrop also argued that the transfer to America promised to bring out the better part of man's nature. In England, "the land groneth under her inhabitants soe that man the best of creatures is held more base than the earth they travel on. . . ."[44] As he put it, the hard work that life in the wilderness imposed might be the means by which God would bring us "to repent of our former Intemperance and soe cure us of that disease which sends many amongst us untimely to our graves and others to Hell."[45] Moreover, conditions in the New World required the expression of mutual love: Adam's fall had not robbed man of the capacity for this. In the interest of survival, people would also have "the care of the publique . . . oversway all private respects, by which not onely conscience, but meare Civill pollicy doth bind us."

Yet actualities worked against anything like a satisfactory realization of these expectations. In describing the degeneration of Weston's neighboring establishment, Bradford reminded his followers that Christian laws and piety were perhaps even more indispensable in a new land than in the Old World. He warned that the promising conditions in the New World did not mean that human beings would always put to the best use their talents of will and reason. Though creators, human beings were, wheresoever, still limited creatures.

As in England, most men continued to flaunt the Puritan law in buying as cheap and in selling as dear as they could. It was impossible to enforce the laws regulating wages, since workers could quickly and easily move to another place. In relating these facts, Winthrop confessed that the new environment often failed to draw out that love and public spirit he had thought it reasonable to expect. Since the laws of wages could not be enforced, it had seemed best to turn the whole matter over to the local communities and to trust to the example of the best-minded.

43. *History of Plymouth Plantation,* 1:55, 56.
44. *Winthrop Papers,* 2:111.
45. *Winthrop Papers,* 2:144.

In other words, Winthrop saw that the elbow room America offered, and the social mobility it invited, heightened reliance on voluntary persuasion and example and weakened the force of law in economic expressions of human nature.[46] Put differently, the dynamic character of the New England environment worked against the hoped-for change in motivation and human relationships.

Even if non-Puritans could have been kept from flooding into New England, compromises with the world would have been inevitable. As new towns were planted on the outskirts of the early settlements, as more and more men took to the sea for fishing and trading, the tightly knit communities could not be sustained or duplicated. Social controls exercised by the Church, the magistrates, and the community itself were relaxed as individualism and secularism took increasing hold. Without giving up the basic view that the center of gravity lay outside the individual, that is, in God, or the concept that Christian love alone made social living possible, the later Puritans adjusted to the shifting social structure. The death of the first leaders long before the end of the century dramatized the impact of change on the Puritan model of human nature.

Emerging movements of thought interacted with the social changes that challenged the old orthodoxy. We shall see that a new concern with the doctrine of natural law and natural rights had some bearing on the discussion of human nature.[47] So did German pietism and British humanitarianism. Cartesianism and Newtonianism also demanded a hearing. To some extent each was incorporated into the orthodoxy that had set much store on the rationality of man as a means for discovering the law. The challenge of Locke's sensational philosophy, which rejected the notion of innate ideas, was more troublesome.

All this influenced Cotton Mather's thinking. His interest in the new science led him to defy the idea of human helplessness by courageously championing inoculation against smallpox. Yet on the whole he asserted traditional ideas with fresh zeal. Like his predecessors and most of his clerical contemporaries, Cotton Mather clung to the doctrine of innate and total depravity, and he reaffirmed the dogma that saving grace could alone insure salvation. In stressing the emotional side of human nature in evangelical conversion, he followed his grandfather Richard Mather. At the same time he was responding to German pietism. He also related man's emotional gifts to the chiliastic doctrine of the millennium that increasingly fascinated him.

Yet this did not keep him, at least until late in life, from setting a good

46. *Winthrop's Journal*, 2:24.
47. See pp. 75, 77.

deal of store on the reasoning faculty, which in accordance with tradition he viewed as an innate endowment. He rejected as irrational the Lockean view which, in his words, pretended that "we have no *Ideas* in minds, but what are introduced from abroad by *Observation*."[48] Reason, he wrote in *The Christian Philosopher* (1721), was "a *Faculty* formed by God, in the *Mind* of *Man*, enabling him to discern *Maxims of Truth*, which God himself has established, and to make true *Inference* from them. . . . Whenever any *reasonable thing* is offered, I have God speaking to me."[49] To Mather, reason was not merely the capacity for handling logic and for reaching some perception of the nature of the universe, but by reenforcing love, it pointed to ways for meeting human needs in the new social order by "the doing of good to other Men." Thus he hoped to invigorate the old Puritan sense of community responsibility for moral uplift and for succoring those in want. Reason, engraven in human nature, was, though in far less degree than piety, a telling factor in morality and therefore in tempering the depravity inherited from Adam.

Within this frame, Cotton Mather spelled out his views on human nature in his chief monument, the *Magnalia Christi Americani* (1702). A defense of the Mathers, it was also a jeremiad. Mather nostalgically idealized the founders and lamented the growing secularization while urging a return to the piety of the first generation. His reaffirmation of the old Puritan creed included a belief in the reality of witchcraft, which after the Salem episode had become a touchy matter. His defense of his own role was both evasive and ambiguous.[50]

Mather's dim view of human nature, qualified for those who had received grace, was reflected in his treatment of New England dissidents. He viewed Quakers as "Hellish Fanatics" who contradicted every truth, which was "to abuse the creature," and whose main design was "to exalt man." Mather also condemned as an abominable heresy the Quaker belief that "there is in every man a certain excusing and condemning *principle*, which indeed is nothing but some *remainder* of the divine image, left by the compassion of God upon the conscience of man after his fall; and this principle the Quakers called a measure of 'the Man Christ'—the *light*, the *seed*, and the *word*."[51] Though he had informed the provincial government that "for every man to worship God ac-

48. Cotton Mather, *The Man of Reason* (Boston, 1708), p. 3.

49. Cotton Mather, *The Christian Philosopher* (London, 1721), p. 283.

50. Cotton Mather, *Magnalia Christi Americani; or, the Ecclesiastical History of New England*, 2 vols. (London, 1702; 1st American ed. from the London ed. of 1702, Hartford, 1820), 1:409 ff.; *On Witchcraft; Being the Wonders of the Invisible World* (Boston, 1692; rpt. ed., Mt. Vernon, N.Y., 1950). See also Middlekauff, *The Mathers*, pp. 158–61; and Miller, *The New England Mind*, pp. 191–206.

51. Mather, *Magnalia*, 2:523. See also p. 492.

cording to his conviction, is an Essential Right of Human Nature,"[52] he did not condemn the persecution of the Quakers nor spare words in denouncing the antinomianism of Anne Hutchinson.[53]

Although Mather did not exempt the elect from the law as revealed in Scripture and institutionalized in the Puritan civil covenant, he thought of them in exalted terms. "We are all of us compounded of these two things, *the man* and *the beast,*" he wrote, in recounting the life of John Eliot, "but so powerful was the *man* in this holy person that it kept the *beast* ever tyed with a short tedder, and suppressed the irregular *calcitration* of it."[54] Mather's view of the elect was expressed elsewhere in the advice given to a young clergyman: "Have not you upon your Soul, a divine Workmanship, far more excellent, than the most curious Clock-Work in the World? A work of grace, is a work of God."[55] Despite stress on his own utter unworthiness, Mather, like other Puritan clergymen, looked on himself as a chosen instrument for the Lord's work on earth.

Mather worked out his views on man in a state of grace within the terms of the modified faculty psychology of his time. One who had been saved was marked by an "anatomy" in which the Spirit of rational Mind assumed mastery over both the Soul (depraved by original sin) and the Body. Regenerate spirits could resist carnal temptations and desires. To be sure, they knew the allures of "natural man." They could, however, "properly" control these. The affections, it will be recalled, readied the sinner for conversion and for the endless struggle of the elect to grow in grace.

With such a view Mather attributed uniform characteristics to the ministers and magistrates of early New England who had experienced Divine Grace. His concept of the human nature of the elect was a stereotyped one. Of the judges of New England he wrote, "Though they were not *nobly born,* yet they were generally *well-born;* and by being *eminently exemplary for a virtuous and a sober life,* gave demonstration that they were *new-born.*"[56] If now and then Mather tried his hand at a rudimentary character analysis, he was on the whole, as R. E. Watters has observed, incapable of clearly depicting individual differences.[57]

52. Perry Miller, *From Colony to Province* (Cambridge, 1953), p. 165. Miller sagely remarked, "We should note this interesting use of 'human nature.'"

53. Mather, *Magnalia*, 2:512 ff.

54. *Magnalia*, 1:537.

55. *The Diary of Cotton Mather, 1631–1708*, 2 vols., Collections of the Massachusetts Historical Society, 7th ser. 7, 8(1911–12), 8:428.

56. Mather, *Magnalia*, 1:132.

57. R. E. Watters, "Biographical Techniques in Cotton Mather's *Magnalia*," *William and Mary Quarterly*, 3d ser. 2 (1945):154–63. On the other hand Kenneth B. Murdock,

Eager to idealize the elite, he viewed the great men of the past as God's instruments for carrying out His plans. Thus he had little real concern for human motivation, since in the last analysis these men were only carrying out the will of God in all they did. Still, the judges and magistrates responsible for setting up God's Zion in the wilderness did use the rational part of man's nature to enforce His law.

The social implications of all this were clear enough at the time. Chosen by God to govern and stamped with the highest excellence possible in human nature, the magistrates and ministers rightly ruled as they saw fit. It was a divine as well as a civil duty to follow their lead in humble obedience. This alone could stem the chaos inevitable when men were left free to indulge their corrupted will.

Despite his way of stereotyping the character of the elect, Mather never fully decided whether scholastic success resulted from innate ability or from unusual opportunity. Many of his heroes had shown ability as children, but they had also often profited from special advantages before matriculation at the College. John Cotton sprang from a family that was neither so rich "that the *Mater Antis* [native genius] could have no room to do her part, nor so poor that the *Res anguis doni* [straitened circumstances] should clog his progress."[58] John Sherman's "intellectual abilities, whether *natural* or *acquired*, were such as to render him a *first-rate* scholar."[59] Of Jonathan Mitchell he wrote that "the faculties of the mind, with which the God that forms the spirit of man," were notable; he had "a *clear head*, a copious *fancy*, a solid *judgment*, a tenacious *memory*, and a certain discretion."[60] It would be wrong to read into Mather the theory that intellectual capacity *per se* was inherited. While stressing the piety of the parents of the "Saints," he never implied that offspring necessarily inherited intellect.

Child-rearing seldom invited comment in the *Magnalia*. The goal was to implant an awareness in the young of their corrupt nature. Precept, example, and punishment could subject their will to that of God. Moral introspection was also in order. He fretted over the relaxation of parental authority, which should be consistent and absolute, not fashioned to the

---

while admitting that the biographies are eulogistic, didactic, and incomplete, holds that some, at least, reveal an effort to depict the personalities and temperaments of the subjects. Kenneth B. Murdock, *Literature and Theology in Colonial New England* (New York, 1963), pp. 129–30. Samuel Eliot Morison, who is critical of Cotton Mather, agrees to the extent of observing that he found the biography of John Eliot more helpful than those of subsequent writers. Samuel Eliot Morison, *Builders of the Massachusetts Bay Colony*, rev. ed. (Boston, 1964), p. 394.

58. Mather, *Magnalia*, 1:253.
59. *Magnalia*, 2:83.
60. *Magnalia*, 2:83.

peculiarities of a child. Of his own children: "They must resign all to me who will be sure to do what is best. My word must be their law." Alas, his precepts sadly failed to produce in his son Cressy the results he longed for. Yet Mather's experience with this wayward lad had little effect on his convictions.[61]

The biographies of the elect revealed the attitude toward sex which Mather and other Puritans held.[62] To them, the appetite of the flesh was an underlying part of "the natural man." The *Diary* and the *Magnalia* recorded cases of sodomy, adultery, and infanticide, for which Mather justified harsh penalties. The elect, having mastered the weakness of the flesh, expressed their sexual life only in their placid marriage to "pious genteel women." Sexual love did not enter into Mather's references to marriage among the Saints; the duty of a wife was to lessen the secular cares of her husband. In short, a Christian society must not base its sexual mores and laws on the observed conduct of men and women. Sexual morality derived rather from an abstract Christian theory.

Mather's view of human nature involved a racial as well as a sexual code. He included Indians and blacks as members of the human race, but regarded them as inherently inferior. The Indians, in fact, were the "spawn of the Devil," the "veriest *ruines of mankind* which are to be found anywhere upon the face of the earth." This was evident in their total betrayal of the sense of good and evil implanted by nature in their hearts, and in their scanty technology and deplorable way of life. Before the English came, Satan had held complete sway over the aborigines; thus if need be, the English were justified in fighting soldiers of the Devil no longer worthy of being regarded as reasonable men. White superiority warranted taking the Indians' lands. On the other hand Mather, a slaveowner, seems to have felt that the African was destined to be the ward of the whites, whose duty it was to guide these poor dark skins to Christianity.[63]

In Mather's eyes the superiority of God's chosen people obligated them not only to show concern for the unregenerate but also to look out for those in material need both within and without the fold. The duty of benevolence[64] toward the ailing, the poor, and the wayward was in part an American counterpart of a similar concern with humanitarianism in

61. Mather, *Diary*, 7:535. See also 7:239 and the fine account by Elizabeth Bancroft Schlesinger, "Cotton Mather and His Children," *William and Mary Quarterly*, 3d ser. 10 (1953):181–89.

62. For this subject see Morgan, *The Puritan Family*, chap. 3.

63. Mather, *Magnalia*, 1:558; *Diary*, 7:564–68, 8:562. For an excellent discussion see Roy H. Pearce, "The 'Ruines of Mankind': The Indian and the Puritan Mind," *Journal of the History of Ideas* 13 (1952):200–217.

64. Cotton Mather, *Bonifacius: An Essay upon the Good*, ed., with an introduction, by David Levin (Cambridge, Mass., 1966).

England. More important for Mather was his conviction that benevolence, in meeting a Christian duty, brought out some of the better aspects of human nature. The obligation "to do good" also reflected a growing awareness that social change had weakened the neighborliness of the tight little communities of bygone days. In truth, the old Puritan order that Mather piously upheld in the *Magnalia* as a model for his own degenerate times had crumbled. Yet he believed that in doing good, in stressing the right feelings, in sustaining faith, and in counting on the Second Coming, dedicated Christians might salvage some part of the Puritan virtue, even though worldly interests had the upper hand.

Cotton Mather did not live to see the evangelical revivals of the 1740s, whose sponsors, at least initially, ignored his own emphasis on doing good here and now; he would have rejoiced at their promise to restore Christian faith and piety. He would have seen the revivals as needed fortifications in the weakened defenses against secularism. The recognition of the crucial role of the emotional side of human nature would have appealed to him. His heart would have gone out to the man who described the phenomena of the Great Awakening and ably explained their meaning for regeneration.

Jonathan Edwards was the first American to win an international reputation in theology and to develop a comprehensive view of human nature. This he did in systematic treatises, sermons, and polemical essays, challenging both the critics of the Great Awakening and the Arminians for stressing free will and good works. Edwards defined terms carefully and proved his skill in logic. In defending the Calvinist tenets of the unlimited sovereignty of God and the total helplessness and depravity of man, he showed a profound knowledge of Scripture and familiarity with the work of the Cambridge Platonists, Newton, Locke, Hume, Mandeville, Hutcheson, and Shaftesbury. To be sure, his conception of human nature, synthesizing as it did theology, psychology, philosophy, and ethics, was only a part of his whole cosmic vision. Although his technical skill and originality won the respect of his contemporary critics, yet his system was challenged by competing movements of thought and by new social demands. Nevertheless Edwards's view of man was a landmark in the American discussion of human nature.[65]

65. Although most students of Edwards have considered his ideas about human nature, Clarence H. Faust and Thomas H. Johnson focused on them in the introductory essay in their anthology *Jonathan Edwards: Representative Selections*, rev. ed. (New York, 1962). Mention should be made of A. B. Crabtree's *Jonathan Edwards' View of Man* (Wellington, England, 1948, a University of Zürich dissertation). I owe much to the introductory essays

Edwards distinguished sharply between divine and human nature. It is true that he thought every atom in the universe an integral part of God's plan; but he met the contradiction between the organic unity of the whole and the basic distinction between divine and human nature by holding that although man could not make himself godly, God could exalt him into a "new creature" that partook of divinity.

Familiar though the distinction between divine nature and human nature was, Edwards spared no effort to drive it home. The guilt of sinful man was "like great mountains, heaped one upon another, till the pile is grown up to heaven." Men are wholly corrupt, "in every part, in all their faculties, and all the principles of their nature, their understandings, and wills; and in all their dispositions and affections, their heads, their hearts, are totally depraved; all the members of their bodies are only instruments of sin; and all their senses, seeing, hearing, tasting, etc. are only inlets and outlets of sin, channels of corruption."[66] Were it not for God's restraints, "there are in the souls of wicked men those hellish *principles* reigning, that would presently kindle and flame out into hell fire. . . . There is laid in the very nature of carnal men, a foundation for the torments of hell."[67] So dominant in man was the self-regarding affection or emotion that he was, without God's grace, unable to do a truly good act; what men desired above all else was, in terms of their immediate understanding, their own happiness and well-being.[68]

To this well-known Calvinist image of man Edwards added two ideas designed to confound its critics. How, they asked, if God was good, could He also, in view of the pervasiveness of sin, be omnipotent? How, if He was omnipotent, could He also be beneficent? Could a just God have infused His children, created in His image, with inevitable and never-ending sin merely because of the transgression in the Garden? Edwards replied by insisting that the human race was a unit and that every

---

in the Yale edition of *The Works of Jonathan Edwards:* Paul Ramsey, ed., *Freedom of the Will* (New Haven, 1957); John E. Smith, ed., *Religious Affections* (New Haven, 1959); Clyde A. Holbrook, ed., *Original Sin* (New Haven, 1970); C. C. Goen, ed., *The Great Awakening* (New Haven, 1972); and Stephen J. Stein, ed., *Apocalyptic Writings* (New Haven, 1977). My references to Edwards's writing are, wherever possible, to this edition of his works. Among many useful studies, the most helpful have been Perry Miller, *Jonathan Edwards* (New York, 1949), and *Errand into the Wilderness* (Cambridge, Mass., 1956); Alfred Owen Aldridge, *Jonathan Edwards* (New York, 1966); Edward H. Davidson, *Jonathan Edwards: The Narrative of a Puritan Mind* (Cambridge, Mass., 1968); and Conrad Cherry, *The Theology of Jonathan Edwards: A Reappraisal* (Garden City, N.Y., 1966).

66. Jonathan Edwards, "The Justice of God in the Damnation of Sinners," *The Works of President Edwards,* 4 vols. (New York, 1852), 4:230.

67. Edwards, "Sinners in the Hands of an Angry God," in *President Edwards,* 4:315.

68. Edwards, "The Future Punishment of the Wicked Unavoidable and Intolerable," in *President Edwards,* 4:260; "Dissertation on the Nature of True Virtue," in *President Edwards,* 2:261–304.

member therefore partook of its tragic flaw. To the related criticism that the sovereignty of God and the total impotence of man made the Creator the author of sin, he replied that because of man's original sin, God merely removed the universal grace and benevolence that at the beginning had insured freedom from sin.[69]

The human being, in Edwards's eyes, was a unity composed of a closely interdependent body and soul, a concept that anticipates much in modern psychology. Edwards, however, discussed the soul in terms of the psychology of the Middle Ages, which, as we have seen, endowed the mind with separate faculties or powers. These, according to Edwards, "in all nations, are alike."[70] Though the mind was a unified functioning entity, he defined the faculties of understanding and will as its chief components. The understanding was that "faculty of the soul by which it is capable of perception and speculation, or by which it discerns, and views, and judges of things." Its functions included sensation, imagination, memory, and judgment or reason. God dealt with man through these faculties, but as subjects rather than cause. Like Locke, Edwards held that all faculties depended on sensation, which evoked pictures of external objects or awakened recollections of earlier sense impressions. But sensations were not the exact replicas inherent in the object perceived—these existed only in God's mind and were communicated to the human mind by His will and His laws. "The world is, therefore, an ideal one," of which men's perceptions were only hazy images. "Man's days on the earth, are as a shadow. It was never designed by God that this world should be our home."[71] The sense organs conveyed ideas to the brain by "animal spirits," subtle vapors or fluids seated in the brain and filling the nerves as water filled pipes. The spirits played an important part in the functioning of the understanding and of the second main faculty, inclination or will.[72]

This faculty, in Edwards's words, was that "by which the soul does not merely perceive and view things, but is in some way inclined with

69. Holbrook, ed., *Original Sin*, pp. 389 ff.; Faust and Johnson, eds., *Jonathan Edwards*, pp. ix, xiv.

70. "Miscellaneous Observations on Important Theological Subjects," *The Works of President Edwards*, 10 vols. (New York, 1830), 7:254. Edwards explained the differences between the intellectual achievement of the Greeks and Scythians, who, he believed, had equal natural talents, in terms of commercial contacts with Egypt and Phoenicia.

71. Edwards, "The Christian Pilgrim," in Faust and Johnson, eds., *Jonathan Edwards*, p. 130.

72. Leon Howard, *The Mind of Jonathan Edwards: A Reconstructed Text* (Berkeley and Los Angeles, 1963), pp. 35–36, 94. For a discussion of the essential distinctions between men and beasts, see pp. 82–83; for Edwards's discussion of the mutual interactions of body and mind, pp. 108–9. For a later reference to the mechanism by which the sense organs convey ideas to the brain see Smith, ed., *Religious Affections*, pp. 96–98, 113–14.

respect to the things it views or considers." The will, in other words, was that faculty by which the mind chose, and what it chose was in accordance with its inclination. Inclination operated in terms of liking or disliking, the two major affections. Indeed, "these affections we see to be the springs that set men agoing, in all the affairs of life, and engage them in all their pursuits; these are the things that put men forward, and carry 'em along, in all their worldly business; and especially are men excited and animated by these, in all their affairs, wherein they are earnestly engaged, and which they pursue with vigor."[73] Of the two major affections, love was the more important, giving rise to desire, hope, joy, and gratitude, just as its opposite occasioned fear, anger, grief, and hatred. Some affections, to be sure, combined all these approving and disapproving impulses. Every volition stemmed from those preceding volitions or acts that seemed most agreeable or desirable, as perceived through the understanding, which in turn derived from the senses. Unlike Locke, who held that will and desire must not be confounded, Edwards argued that the affections of the soul were not properly to be distinguished from the will.[74]

Edwards's recognition of the devious relationship between desires and will was evident in an example of behavior that showed great insight. Thus a man who was kind and helpful to his neighbor's wife made a show of desiring her restoration to health, and acted to that end. There was reality in his sincere efforts to have her health renewed. Yet "perhaps the principle he acts from is no other than a vile and scandalous passion; having lived in adultery with her, he earnestly desires to have her health and vigor restored, that he may return to his criminal pleasures, with her."[75]

Edwards's *Treatise on the Freedom of the Will* was a reply, based on scriptural and philosophical arguments, to the Arminians, who appeared to claim freedom of choice. Since volition rested on causes external to it, man was passive in the generation of the impulses or emotions that defined the power of acting or the expression of the will. The strongest and most recent motives, as the understanding conceived them, were the determinants of the will. Man was free to will what he desired, but he was not free to choose his desires and thus the choices open to him. In other words, Edwards did not reject the freedom of the will: in defining freedom as the liberty of choosing what one at the time most wanted to choose, he denied that the will was self-determining.[76]

73. Smith, ed., *Religious Affections*, p. 101. Edwards differentiated the affections from the passions by identifying them with purely animal appetites or inclinations—reactions to stimuli without thought or reflection.

74. *Religious Affections*, pp. 97–98.

75. Ramsay, ed., *Freedom of the Will*, pp. 316–17.

76. Faust and Johnson, eds. *Jonathan Edwards*, pp. xliii–lxiv.

Edwards also sought to overthrow the argument of his opponents that if a man was without freedom of choice he could not be held morally responsible for his sins. He met this objection by distinguishing between natural and moral necessity: in the latter, motives were from within and thus the sinner was blameworthy. To put it differently, acts of sin were voluntary, in that the sinner wanted to sin even though his wanting was necessary. Men's actions, he held, were subject to ethical judgment "not so properly because they are *from* us, as because we are *in them, i.e.,* our wills are in them; not so much because they are from some property of ours, as because they are our *properties.*"[77]

In rejecting the separate and independent functioning of the faculties and in holding that an act involved the total soul or personality, Edwards's position has appealed to modern psychologists. Philosophers have divided in assessing his achievement. Some have held that he failed adequately to come to grips with the central problem of freedom and determinism, while others have found little in modern discussions to reflect on his contribution.

Theologians have admired Edwards's discussion of the "transcendental sense" or "sense of the heart," a sense which differed from all others in that it shaped the "soul into an image of the same glory that it beheld." In *A Treatise Concerning the Religious Affections,* Edwards set himself the task of determining the criteria by which genuine piety and "the sense of the heart" could be distinguished from illusionary and deceptive feelings and behavior. The problem was the more subtle in that the Saints who were thus blessed were not free from sin, which was inherent in human nature; it was not that the regenerate did not need any longer to try to be worthy of grace. The sense or experience of grace might still be merely the working of a disordered imagination directed by Satan. With rare psychological insight Edwards realized that even the most stringent tests, which he analyzed in detail, might fail to give assurance that the experience of the "supernatural sense" was not mere "enthusiastic delusion." Like his Puritan forefathers, he believed in the necessity of unrelenting self-examination of one's true state. Moreover, he recognized the importance that dreams might have in this quest, and examined his own dreams to that end.[78]

Thus for Edwards true religion was in good part a matter of the affections, particularly the holy affections. To be sure, God dealt with men as reasonable creatures. "Holy affections are not heat without light; but evermore arise from some information of the understanding, some spiritual instruction that the mind receives, some light or actual knowledge."[79] But reason could be an inhibiting factor in emotional

77. Ramsay, ed., *Freedom of the Will,* p. 428.

78. Edwards, "Extract from the Private Writings," in *President Edwards,* 1:9.

79. Smith, ed., *Religious Affections,* p. 266. See also Edwards, *President Edwards,* 4:3.

expression. His conviction that emotions, as the springs of action, were the most essential part of true religious experience led him to welcome the revivals that aroused so much opposition in many quarters. He gave the revivals intellectual support, and recorded those he knew at first hand with such skill of language and psychological insight that even now the reader, as John E. Smith has remarked, almost feels that he himself has taken part in the experience. Without the religious affections men stood no chance of experiencing the "supernatural sense" and the reception of God's grace, a gift that God alone dispensed with power, compassion, and wisdom.

This emphasis on the affections was not new, but Edwards probed the emotional nature systematically and imaginatively. His acceptance of the Lockean stress on the role of the senses in both understanding and will explained why he believed in instilling fear and even terror in sinners. His revival sermons testified to his mastery of images, metaphors, and rhetoric. Convinced that such opponents of the Great Awakening as Charles Chauncy unjustifiably emphasized reason as the center of religion, Edwards confronted him with vigor. *The Faithful Narrative of the Surprising Work of God* and *The Treatise on the Religious Affections* presented strong reasons for holding that the emotions were the vital source of experience and conduct and that the holy affections were the gate to the "supernatural sense."

In his posthumous essay *The Nature of True Virtue*, Edwards tried to square the doctrine of total depravity with the quest for virtue. He set up, in effect, a model of what man is and of what he ought to be. As he is, man was so dominated by the evil affection of self-love that much if not all of his apparently unselfish behavior was only a subtly concealed selfishness. Moreover, man was without any inborn inclination toward true virtue, which Edwards defined as the disinterested love of God, "that propensity and union of heart to Being in general, that is immediately exercised in a general good will."[80] True virtue was beautiful and lovely beyond comparison, because the object of its love was beautiful and lovely. Disinterested benevolence or the love of God in itself, without any ulterior ends, was the most holy of the affections. It was exemplified in the lives of the saints, and movingly illustrated in the biography of Edwards's young friend David Brainerd.[81] In the redeemed, true virtue blended disposition and will in perfect harmony. The gift of God's grace, it bridged the gap between man as he was and man as he ought to be. As such, it was the highest virtue in the universe.

80. *President Edwards*, 2:262.
81. Edwards, "Account of the Life of David Brainerd," in *President Edwards*, 1: 645–72.

The idea of the order of the universe was the key, at least on the intellectual level, to Edwards's social philosophy, insofar as it was made explicit. He believed that social order rested on the differences in talent that marked men. "There is," he wrote, "a beauty of order in society . . . as when the different members of society have all their appointed office, place and station, according to their several capacities and talents, and every one keeps his place, and continues in his proper business."[82]

To sum up, Edwards invigorated the Calvinist view of human nature by a skillful use of contemporary thought: no one succeeded so well in trying to reconcile traditional doctrine and faith with the new learning. It is true, as Perry Miller has argued, that Edwards looked forward in some part to the intuitionalism and mysticism of transcendentalism. It is also true that he provided a model for later evangelistic revivalism. Moreover, his image of man has something in common with twentieth-century neo-orthodoxy and with contemporary understanding of religious psychology. But in also looking backward, Edwards tried to restore Puritan piety and to buttress its traditional concept of man. If he failed, the failure was magnificent in logic, philosophical skill, and a poetical vision that transcended his time and his place.

The discussion of human nature in Puritan New England once again illustrates the transfer of attitudes and ideas from the Old World and their modification by new situations. In comparison with the offhand and often implied attitude toward human nature elsewhere in British America, the Puritan discussion was coherent and precise. It was also used more often to justify social policies. If, notwithstanding Samuel Sewall's notable tract against slavery, Puritan leaders showed slight interest in relating the Africans to the rest of mankind, they were as responsive as intellectuals elsewhere to the problem of Indian nature. Citing Scripture, leaders regarded women as inferior to men in the endowment of reason and thus designed to play their proper part in a patriarchal family. Individual differences between whites, the complexity of motivation, the issues of free will and determinism and of the immutability of human nature itself were all brought well above the surface of awareness. The shifting social structure and the influence of new movements of thought in Europe modified ideas about human nature without introducing any major change. Yet in reacting to these forces and in trying to salvage what had been thought of as an essential part of the older heritage, Jonathan Edwards made himself a major figure in the discussion of human nature. This was no mean achievement.

82. Edwards, *President Edwards*, 2:275.

3

The American Enlightenment

The plain Truth is an *enlightened Mind* and not raised Affection, ought always to be the guide of those who call themselves Men; and this, in the affairs of Religion, as well as other Things.

CHARLES CHAUNCY, 1784

By a natural right all men are born free; and Nature, having set all men upon a levell and made them equals, no servitude or subjection can be conceived without inequality.

JOHN WISE, 1710

It is the energy of the intellect that has taken cognizance of the rights of human nature: and it is alone this which can correct the errors and renovate the world.

ELIHU PALMER, 1797

We fought for the great, unalienable, hereditary rights of human nature.

WILLIAM WIRT, 1817

I am not so sanguine as to suppose, that it is possible for man to acquire such perfection from science, religion, liberty, and good government, as to cease to be mortal; but I am as full persuaded, that from the combined action of causes, which operate at once upon the reason, the moral faculty, the passions, the senses, the brain, the nerves, the blood and the heart, it is possible to produce such a change in his moral character, as shall raise him to a resemblance of angels—nay more, to the likeness of GOD himself.

BENJAMIN RUSH, 1786

THE TERM *human nature*, first commonly used in the eighteenth century, carried various meanings to both Americans and Europeans who considered themselves "enlightened."[1] But the core of the "enlightened" idea of human nature lay in the conviction that man's uniqueness was better understood by the use of natural faculties of the mind than by supernatural revelation and metaphysics.

The faculty most pertinent was reason. When implemented by empirical observation, critical analysis, and generalization, it showed that cause and effect, balance and harmony, and verifiable laws governed human nature no less than the rest of the Newtonian universe. In the words of young Benjamin Franklin, man's "regular Acting is requisite to the regular moving of the whole" of which he is a part. Thus the unchanging constitution and operation of human nature could be understood by the critical analysis of observed and experienced behavior.

1. Although general works on the Enlightenment give some attention to ideas about human nature, the discussion is more pointed in such specialized studies as Gertrude V. Braun Rich, *Interpretations of Human Nature: A Study of Certain Late Seventeenth and Early Eighteenth Century English Attitudes toward Man's Nature and Capacities* (New York, 1935); Arthur O. Lovejoy, *Reflections on Human Nature* (Baltimore, 1971); and J. A. Passmore, "The Malleability of Man in Eighteenth-Century Thought," in Earl R. Wasserman, ed., *Aspects of the Eighteenth Century* (Baltimore, 1965), pp. 21–47. Henry F. May has profitably distinguished between different sequences of ideas in *The Enlightenment in America* (New York, 1976); and Donald H. Meyer, in *The Democratic Enlightenment* (New York, 1976), has raised penetrating questions about the American reception of the Enlightenment.

As Locke put it, this enabled the mind to distinguish between objective reality and the perception of reality. In turn, the laws of human nature permitted man to shape the mind, since everyone, being born without innate ideas, was subject to the influence of experience and education. Americans of intellectual standing began in the first half of the eighteenth century to speak with respect of the mental as well as the political philosophy of "the Great Mr. Locke."

If belief in the reasonable faculty used empirically was the key to an enlightened understanding of human nature, it was not the whole picture. In both Britain and America some doubted, with David Hume, the ability of a fallible reason, however skillfully used, to distinguish between objective reality and what appeared to be reality. Moreover, many emphasized the blocking role of the powerful emotions and passions. These largely explained what men thought, said, and did. At their best, emotions were the source of behavior beneficial to competing individuals and society alike. At their worst, emotions and passions led to untold misery and evil. Some writers, notably Swift, Mandeville, and Rochefoucauld, believed that reason could never control selfishness, vanity, love of praise, anger, and lust, and in fact, that people deceptively justified as reasonable whatever their emotions impelled or encouraged them to do. Others felt that it was possible through self-training and persistent effort to balance emotions and reason. To still others, such as Shaftesbury, Adam Smith, Joseph Addison, and their American followers, the socially beneficent emotions of kindness and altruism, deeply imbedded in human nature, put such a disciplined subordination of evil within the common reach. Francis Hutcheson and the philosophers of the Scottish Enlightenment, a major influence on American thought from the Revolution to the mid-nineteenth century, emphasized a universal, innate moral sense. This gave added confidence in human ability to unmask evil and to choose the good.

Yet however much such ideas about human nature appealed to some well-schooled Americans, few cut themselves off altogether from older views.

With qualifications, this was especially true in religion. In accepting the idea that the human being was subject to the universal laws of physical nature, intellectuals committed to theism no longer assumed the constant interference of an angry but just God in men's daily affairs. Faith in a providential deity was more congenial. Others went beyond the Puritan acceptance of reason as a tool for confirming Scripture and reconciling it with science and in so doing often modified Christian doctrine. Sooner or later the results ranged from Unitarianism to moderate, or in some instances pronounced, deism. This implied new scope for conscious human action. On the other hand, many deeply devout scholars exempted religion from unlimited questioning. In the Great Awakening and later revivals, they reduced it to the test of direct, personal experience with the religious emotions.

Nor was it only in the religious sphere that those attracted by scientific empiricism clung to older ideas about human nature. In general, enlightened men cherished the wise insights of Greek and Roman moral philosophers, above all the stoics' belief in the capacity of all human beings for moral virtue. The Roman juridical expositors of the concept of a natural law and natural rights to life and liberty also continued to enjoy prestige. This venerable concept had provided justification for opposing unlimited secular authority in the Middle Ages and had later proved useful to the rising middle classes in defending their property, status, and individual freedom. Americans, convinced by reason, inference, and experience that the laws and rights of nature were embedded in human nature itself, eventually evoked them in their great political experiment of nation-building.

Meantime, colonists unhappy with what they regarded as imperial encroachments relied on yet another string to their bow, the doctrine of the rights of Englishmen to immunities and values won in hard struggles of the past. Above all, British rights stressed individual autonomy and freedom from the arbitrary authority of throne and altar. In the mid-eighteenth century, English and American Whigs cited James Harrington, Benjamin Hoadly, Algernon Sidney, and the contemporary authors of *Cato's Letters* in opposing extensions of royal prerogative and the elitism, corruption, and tyranny of Parliament.[2] The writings of these authors imbued human nature not only with innate weakness and evil but also with an inborn love of freedom and equality before the law. Such an image, together with the memory of earlier colonial struggles for rights and freedom, became part of the American rhetoric of enlightened protest.[3]

By 1776 remonstrating colonial leaders who sought justification in the available concepts of human nature carried to logical conclusions familiar ideas about man's makeup and behavior. The most patent example, of course, was the right of revolution as the last resort in the

2. The authoritative study is Caroline Robbins's *The Eighteenth-Century Commonwealthman* (Cambridge, Mass., 1959), esp. pp. 115 ff. See also, for the influence of these writers on colonial pamphleteers, Bernard Bailyn's *The Ideological Origins of the American Revolution* (Cambridge, Mass., 1967); and Peter Karsten, *Patriot Heroes in England and America* (Madison, Wis., 1978), chaps. 2 and 3.

3. Algernon Sidney, *Discourses on Government*, 3 vols. (New York, 1803), 2:463 and 3:154; and *Cato's Letters*, by John Trenchard and Thomas Gordon, 4 vols. (London, 1723), 1:243, 266; 2:43, 250–51, 253, 275; 3:40–41, 210–11.

defense of the natural rights of man to life, liberty, and property. Patriots remembered that Locke had justified the Revolution of 1689 under the rubric of natural rights. In view of the general familiarity with his thought, it is understandable that the authors of the Declaration of Independence borrowed his words as well as his ideas.

One of the first Americans to anticipate characteristic emphases of the early Enlightenment was the Reverend John Wise of Ipswich, Massachusetts.[4] He has long been well known in American religious history for his courageous efforts to keep the Mathers from substituting the less-democratic presbyterian polity for the traditional congregational system of church government. This struggle, together with his earlier opposition to James II's annulment of the province's charter, led Wise, in his several protests, to make use of a social philosophy of natural rights and a clearly outlined conception of human nature. In other words, he looked upon his image of man as an instrument in a conflict of ideas and interests.

Why John Wise used this particular instrument has never been altogether explained. It is hardly enough to point out his indebtedness to modern commentators on the Roman jurists, sources that were at hand for others. Nor did his democratic values seem to stem from some conflict with parental authority or from unique aspects of his upbringing. They may, however, have owed something to the fact that even though he was a graduate of Harvard and one of the ministerial elite, he was the son of an indentured servant and malt brewer.

Wise represented an early phase of the Enlightenment—the idea that the universe was infused with the principle of reason. With the supporting aid of Scripture man could identify and obey natural laws by "Right Reason." This ancient concept, present in Greek, Roman, medieval, and Renaissance thought, embraced more than the simple rational faculty. It combined reason with morality and virtue. Right Reason, implanted by the Creator in all human beings, linked them with God and set them apart from the world of beasts. Right Reason enabled them to know and obey the natural laws governing the universe, including interpersonal relations and connections with the state.[5] The concept of Right Reason provided the frame and pivot for Wise's view of human nature.

4. The most recent published biography, George Allan Cook's *John Wise: Early American Democrat* (New York, 1952), makes use of the manuscripts in the Boston University collection and in other repositories.

5. Robert Hoopes, *Right Reason in the English Renaissance* (Cambridge, Mass., 1962), introduction.

In opposing an encroachment on democratic liberties Wise projected his image of man. Two tracts, written in 1713 and 1717, convey that image—his conception of what are the relatively enduring human traits and needs. These he deduced, through the use of reason, from a priori principles—the laws of nature as discovered by Ulpian and by such contemporaries as Puffendorf. Though not altogether clear on the point, John Wise believed that all people in all times and places shared inborn traits or inherent needs and tendencies to action. These included, first, a need for liberty and a capacity for rational methods of thought in making decisions and conducting affairs; second, a tendency toward self-love and self-interest, which made man prone to take advantage of his fellows; third, and of great importance, "a Sociableness with others, agreeable with the main end and disposition of human nature in general"[6]; and fourth, a desire for equality. Since these traits and needs were found in the state of nature, they were presumably hereditary rather than the result of experience. Thus they seemed to be changeless. Moreover, these original endowments or "immunities" were all interrelated and carried far-reaching implications for human relations.

Possessed of an ability to use reason for discovering the basis of moral conduct in the natural law, man could appreciate his original propensity to both good and evil conduct, to selfishness and altruism. In rejecting the Hobbesian idea that everyone was engaged in a ceaseless war against everyone else, Wise made much of the human capacity to act for the common good in sociable conduct and affection for others. "From the principles of sociableness it follows as a fundamental law of nature, that man is not so wedded to his own Interest, but that he can make the common good the mark of his aim; and hence he becomes capacitated to enter into a Civill State by the Law of Nature; for without this property in Nature, viz. Sociableness, which is for cementing of parts, every Government would soon moulder and dissolve."[7] Wise did not explicitly define the line separating the innate tendencies toward self-love and sociability, nor did he assume that any one group of people had more or less of either quality than any other group.

Man's love of liberty, instamped on his rational nature, was not, as John Winthrop had held some three-quarters of a century earlier, a mere animal-like liberty, or as Hobbes believed, a liberty with which to annihilate others. It was rather a rational liberty to prevent anyone from exercising authority over others without their free assent.

In Wise's view this innate love of and gift for rational liberty accounted for another "immunity" or inborn trait, equality. He did not,

6. John Wise, A Vindication of the Government of the New-England Churches (Boston, 1772), p. 25.
7. Wise, A Vindication, p. 37.

any more than his Puritan predecessors, suppose that all were born in every way equal. Equality consisted rather in the fact that every man was the son of God, "that we all owe our existence to the same method of propagation, . . . death observes no ceremony, but knocks as loud at the barriers of the Court, as at the door of the Cottage."[8] But he knew that some excelled in "understanding and Prudence," that some were stronger, some weaker. He also knew that when men entered into civil life, "many great disproportions appeared," as society recognized special ability and conferred various honors. Yet these inequalities did not, in his eyes, justify the rule of the strong and more capable without the consent of the ruled.[9] This was the more obvious, since everyone had in greater or lesser degree some capacity for government.

Wise's underlying presupposition concerning the nature of man appeared in his argument for paper currency. Though sharing in some part the Puritan distrust of this world, he recognized the secular thrust of society and assumed that worldly activity was not unworthy of human nature. He also assumed that a single institutional change (in this case, the monetary system) could benefit the whole of human life. Thus while Wise had not arrived at the idea of progress, he thought human nature plastic enough to allow great improvement in man's condition. In other words, a good measure of happiness was possible in this life.[10]

Wise's image of man served him reasonably well in arguing for democratic principles and procedures in church government, economic policy, and political theory. In holding to the essential equality of men, in believing in their capacity to find the law of nature by reason and to shape their conduct toward the moral standard that the law of nature required, and in thinking both of man's selfishness and his love of others as original endowments impelling him to certain kinds of conduct, he developed an image of man markedly different from that of John Cotton, John Winthrop, and William Bradford. Wise's views reflected the transition from Puritanism to the early Enlightenment, incorporating aspects of both movements of thought.

In the second half of the eighteenth century other New England ministers skewed away from the old orthodoxy, and in doing so some became in a true sense Wise's successors in looking across the threshold to the Enlightenment. The next generation, in its struggle against what it

8. *A Vindication*, p. 28; John Wise, *The Churches Quarrel Espoused* (Boston, 1772), pp. 34 ff., 37, 74.

9. Wise, *A Vindication*, pp. 29 ff.

10. John Wise, *A Word of Comfort to a Melancholy Country* (Boston, 1721); also in *Colonial Currency Reprints 1682–1751*, ed. Andrew McFarland Davis, 4 vols. (1910–11; New York, 1964), with an introduction on the origins of monetary controversy in the United States, by Joseph Dorfman.

considered encroachments of king and parliament, swung wide open the door which Wise, in invoking natural law and the natural rights of man, had kept open.

In this transition, a notable figure among Wise's successors was the brave and controversial Reverend Jonathan Mayhew of Boston's West Church.[11] Like others who shared his general views, Mayhew held that men, while inherently neither good nor evil, were endowed however unequally with enough reason to grasp the universal rights to life, liberty, and the search for happiness. Most people, he felt, were capable of using a natural disposition toward mutual sympathy and kindness. He recognized evil in those who in their own interest usurped the rights of others. When such men thwarted the natural rights of their fellows to be governed only by consent, and failed further to regard office as a public test, it was a sin to acquiesce. Such subjection to tyranny could only dampen the human spirit and degrade men from their "just rank, into the class of brutes." In his celebrated sermon A Discourse Concerning Unlimited Submission and Non-Resistance to the Higher Powers, Mayhew developed these ideas and invoked the right of revolution when constituted authority defied the natural rights that gave men their human character.[12] There was, to be sure, nothing original in the sermon. Its basic ideas had been expressed by Algernon Sidney, Milton, Harrington, and Locke. But Mayhew put his ideas to work in vigorously opposing the Stamp Act.

Mayhew's belief in the crucial role of reason in man's makeup also largely explained his controversial religious position. Like the Anglican Arminians Dr. Samuel Clarke and Bishop Benjamin Hoadly, whom he read, he rejected the doctrine of total corruption and man's virtual helplessness in the search for salvation. While holding to the sanctity of Holy Scripture, Mayhew believed that every Christian must use his reason to test the meaning of biblical passages. To be sure, reason must be tempered by a warm, living emotion: he did not forget his early admiration for this aspect of the Great Awakening. His heterodoxy, which also included doubts about the doctrine of the Trinity, isolated him from all but a handful of like-minded ministers. He did not live to see these views cautiously accepted by an increasing number of

11. The biography of Charles W. Akers, Called unto Liberty: A Life of Jonathan Mayhew 1729–1766 (Cambridge, Mass., 1964), is well documented and sympathetic.

12. Jonathan Mayhew, A Discourse Concerning Unlimited Submission and Non-Resistance to the Higher Powers: With Some Reflections on the Resistance Made to King Charles I (Boston, 1750). The pamphlet was reissued in 1775 and evoked the enthusiastic commendation of John Adams and other Patriots. See also Mayhew's The Snare Broke: A Thanksgiving-Discourse Preached at the Desire of the West Church in Boston, N.E., Friday, May 23, 1766: Occasioned by the Repeal of the Stamp Act (Boston, 1766).

clergymen. For all that, Mayhew was a significant figure in trying to couple traditional Puritan piety with "enlightened" ideas in both the secular and religious sphere.[13]

One of Mayhew's close friends, Charles Chauncy of the First Church in Boston, had come to public attention in opposing the emotionalism of the Great Awakening.[14] Although Chauncy denied that reason alone could reveal the great religious truths, he went further than the early Puritans in emphasizing the rational component in man's nature. ". . . the human passions," he declared, "are capable of serving many valuable purposes in religion, and may to good advantage be excited and warmed: always provided, that they are kept under the restraints of *reason*; for otherwise they will soon run wild, and may make those in whom they reign to do so too."[15] Under the influence of the English Arminians and Latitudinarians, Chauncy gradually drifted to a position, first publicly stated in a sermon preached before 1751 but published only in 1784, that separated him even further from the old order. For he found it impossible to believe that a wise, loving, and beneficent Creator would condemn his children to eternal punishment. The human constitution itself proved God's beneficence: man's natural endowments, both material and rational, were designed to enable him to enjoy the sensible pleasures suitable to a creature of moral endowment, self-determination, and conscience.[16] In holding that everyone was destined for salvation, Chauncy further contended that God had created his children in his image that they might at last enjoy eternal happiness. "It appears to me a great reflection on that Being, who is infinitely perfect, to suppose him *unable finally to counteract*, and in a *moral* way too, the weakness, and folly, and obstinacy, of such poor inferior creatures as men are. And if he is able, in consistency with men's makeup, as *moral and intelligent agents*, to effect their *salvation*, I see not, I own, when it is said, *he desires that they should be saved*, but that such a declaration virtually and constructively amounts to the same thing as if it had been said, *he would save them in event and fact.*"[17] Thus in addition to relying

13. Clinton Rossiter, "The Life and Mind of Jonathan Mayhew," *William and Mary Quarterly*, 3d ser. 7 (1950): 531–58.

14. Charles Chauncy, *Seasonable Thoughts on the State of Religion in New-England* (Boston, 1743), pp. 3–37, 314, 424.

15. Charles Chauncy, *The Gifts of the Spirits to Ministers* (Boston, 1742), p. 8; also *Seasonable Thoughts*, pp. 418–19.

16. Charles Chauncy, *The Benevolence of the Deity* (Boston, 1784), pp. 162–63.

17. Charles Chauncy, *The Mystery Hid from Ages and Generations, and Made Manifest by the Gospel-Revelation; or, The Salvation of all Men the Grand Thing Aimed At in the Scheme of God*, 2d ed. (London, 1747), pp. 167, 359. See also Chauncy's *Twelve Sermons on the Following Seasonable Subjects* (Boston, 1765), pp. 193, 203, 214, 337–38; and the

on reason, Chauncy accepted the authority of the Bible, reasonably interpreted.

Others, too, began to speak in like vein. In 1790, only a few years after the publication of Chauncy's *The Benevolence of the Deity*, the scholarly William Bentley of the Salem church, preaching in the Stone Chapel of Boston, held that God had created his children to be happy, and that by developing this inherent social principle through education, man would find ways of overcoming evil, including the evils of society.[18]

Several factors accounted for the new stress on the reasonableness, efficacy, and even power of the human being. The temperaments of Wise, Mayhew, Chauncy, Bentley, and their kind made them hospitable to these views. A reconsideration of the emphasis in the ancient classics on Right Reason also played a part. Of special importance, too, was the influence of rising currents of thought in Great Britain, particularly those represented by Wollaston, Hoadly, Shaftesbury, Hutcheson, and Ferguson. Changes within the social structure of the New England seacoast towns also made the new outlook more appealing. Social mobility at the time was marked, and men were shifting their status and roles as they prospered in maritime commerce and in other enterprises. The doctrine of a fixed order, with the elect irrevocably on one level and everyone else on another, hardly fitted the temper of a society in which individual initiative, industry, skill, and drive paid off. Was it not sensible to assume that even salvation was largely in one's own hands? When the "river lords" of the Connecticut Valley began to show mild sympathy with the ideas of seacoast merchants and their Arminian teachers, the breach between prominent parishioners of the First Church in Northampton and their minister, Jonathan Edwards, was tellingly widened.

It is true, of course, that the role which New England liberals ascribed to reason found spokesmen in colonies where social conditions were quite different. Landon Carter, a Virginia planter, was a case in point. Like Malebranche, Mandeville, Pope, Dr. Johnson, and Bishop Butler, Carter was convinced of the power of the passions or emotions in human nature. He found men intoxicated with ambition, pride, and malice, prone to corruption less from innate evil than from frailty and weakness. Yet it was well to try to master the emotions. In this struggle the best weapon was reason, a faculty, impressed by nature on everybody, that

---

discussion in Conrad Wright, *The Beginnings of Unitarianism in America* (Boston, 1955), pp. 167–69, 171–76, 187–99.

18. William Bentley, *A Sermon Preached at the Stone Chapel, Sept. 12, 1790* (Boston, 1790); *The Diary of William Bentley, D.D.*, 4 vols. (Salem, Mass., 1905–14), 1:194, 205.

permitted man alone among all creatures to "govern" his instincts, to employ "the knowledge and experience and hopes and fears of Effects and consequences . . . to promote or avoid . . . causes according as they are known or Suspected to be advantageous or detrimental to us."[19] However limited reason might be in this contest with human passions, prejudices, vanities, and interests, and with the "constraint of tradition," people need not always submit to the tendencies, arguments, and practices that were "vastly against all or any spark of reason."[20] Accepting the Christian doctrine that men were at God's mercy, Carter, like some Puritans, felt that God favored those who tried to help themselves. "Perhaps," he wrote, "it is like other things, the Vitium Commune, that attends human nature, a sort of degenerating into indolence when there is not a visible necessity to be otherwise."[21] In any case, "man, the creature of Divine Power, must only complain according to his natural feeling, and as such, to be sure, the being that imprised him with that nature, can only look upon such a complaint as offensive, provided his reason is not disposed to comfort him through a religious hope."[22]

The image of man congenial to Wise, Chauncy, Mayhew, and Carter in many ways resembled that of Jefferson. Like them, he did not work out a systematic theory of human nature. Yet despite inconsistencies and shifts in emphasis with the years, Jefferson's image of man reflected both the moderate tenets of the Enlightenment and the influence of America.

To begin with, in Jefferson's scheme man acquired knowledge by observation and reason. He did not always distinguish between the views he owed to his own observations and those that came from reading and reflecting. Each, of course, reenforced and modified the other.

Unlike the early Puritans, Jefferson ruled out the intervening hand of God as an explanation of human behavior. He placed this within the sphere of nature, and in so doing was a true exponent of the Enlightenment. Thus in *Notes on the State of Virginia* he devoted much space to topography, geology, climate, and ecology, and made it clear that a human drama was being enacted in his native state. The stage was so bountiful that it could, and he believed would, further the expression of man's best potentialities. This was significant, since he also believed

19. Jack P. Greene, ed., *The Diary of Colonel Landon Carter of Sabine Hall, 1752–1779*, 2 vols. (Charlottesville, Va., 1965), 1:16.

20. Greene, ed., *The Diary*, 1:16.

21. *The Diary*, 2:626.

22. *The Diary*, 2:621.

that "human nature is the same on every side of the Atlantic, and will be alike influenced by the same causes."[23] After empirically refuting the notion, widespread among European savants, that America's environment stunted man and beast, Jefferson discussed the relation between environment and the distinctively human makeup.

Of man's essential traits, reason or intelligence was of course fundamental. Here Jefferson was not only thinking in terms of classical and Christian views of man as a reasonable creature but was, more specifically, taking his ideas from Locke, the Scottish philosophers of common sense, and the French philosophers, particularly Helvétius and D'Holbach. He also expressed a high regard for Pierre Georges Cabanis's *Rapports du physique et du moral de l'homme* (1802), which viewed psychology in physiological terms completely divorced from metaphysics. With these French thinkers, Jefferson was anticipating a major concept of twentieth-century functional behaviorism—the concept that, to quote his own words, thinking was "an action" of "particular organization of matter" rather than an intangible supersensation or manifestation of the supernatural through mystical intuition or insight.[24] Jefferson further noted, with a shrewdness reflecting the use of both reason and observation, that "all know the influence of interest on the mind of man, and how unconsciously his judgment is warped by that influence."[25]

Intelligence, Jefferson readily granted, was unequally distributed. Some had more, others less. But superior powers of reasoning and of judgment were not confined to any one class, however wealthy and socially prominent. His thought turned rather to a natural aristocracy based on virtue and talent. Many who had these nature-given potentialities failed to realize them because of conditions or circumstances over which they had no control. Jefferson's faith in the ability of the majority, given some education and a free press, to choose as their governors the wise, the good, and the competent was basic to his social philosophy.[26] His view of human nature was the cornerstone of a political theory that embraced popular sovereignty.

In taking stock of the differences in human intelligence, Jefferson

23. Thomas Jefferson, *Notes on the State of Virginia* (1787), ed. William Peden (Chapel Hill, 1955), p. 121.

24. Thomas Jefferson, *The Writings of Thomas Jefferson*, 20 vols. (Washington, D.C., 1903–4), 6:257; Jefferson to John Adams, August 15, 1820, 15:274. The best brief account of Jefferson's indebtedness to European thought is Robert G. Weyant, "Helvétius and Jefferson: Studies of Human Nature and Government in the Eighteenth Century," *Journal of the History of the Behavioral Sciences* 9 (1973): 29–41.

25. Jefferson, "Autobiography," in *Writings*, 1:1–164.

26. Jefferson, *Writings*, 1:121; 2:283; 13:396–97; 15:166, 196.

concluded that women as a group possessed less reasoning power than men. Here he sided with the Puritans and St. Paul rather than with such Old World contemporaries as Mary Wollstonecraft, William Godwin, and Helvétius. He was also reflecting a view common in the planting society of which he was a part, as well as one to which his observations of the women of his class lent support. Thus he felt that the education of girls should encourage the growth of their esthetic and moral gifts, which he valued highly.[27]

Jefferson also doubted the innate reasoning power of the Negro. He saw in these people no shortcoming in imagination or in the gifts of the heart. What he observed as moral deficiencies, such as proneness to theft, could, he believed, be easily explained in terms of the extreme poverty of the race and of faulty ethical training. On at least one occasion Jefferson even expressed reluctance to judge the native capacity of Negroes for reasoning. As an empiricist he knew that his own opportunities as an observer were limited to a slaveholding society. He also recognized the difficulties of making valid empirical judgments of such intangible factors as abstract reasoning. "Let me add too," he continued, "as a circumstance of great tenderness, where our conclusion would degrade a whole race of men from the rank in the scale of beings which their Creator may perhaps have given them."[28]

Recognition that blacks differed markedly from whites raised the question whether such differences were innate and immutable or the result of time and circumstance. Jefferson's attention was brought to the essay of the Reverend Samuel Stanhope Smith of Princeton, who in an effort to refute Lord Kames's theory of the diversity of races, argued for corporal plasticity and held that the climate and the "state of society" explained differences in skin color, hair, facial angle, and bone structure. Since mind and body influenced each other, it followed that climatic differences and contrasts in the manner of living explained the gulf in mental achievement. "Even minute differences in the power of the cause often become perceptible in the variety of the effect."[29] In the manner of the Scottish common sense philosophy, Smith held that if from the fact of diversity separate species were assumed, then the unity of mankind was destroyed and "no certain and universal principles of human nature

27. Jefferson to his daughter Martha, March 28, 1787, in *The Papers of Thomas Jefferson*, ed. Julian Boyd, 20 vols. (Princeton, 1950–), 11:250–52.

28. Jefferson, *Notes on the State of Virginia*, p. 143.

29. Samuel Stanhope Smith, *An Essay on the Causes of the Variety of Complexion and Figure in the Human Species* (Philadelphia, 1787). The enlarged 1810 edition has been edited by Winthrop D. Jordan (Cambridge, Mass., 1965), with a scholarly introduction that relates Smith's ideas to his time and to later thinking. See also Smith's *The Lectures . . . on the Subjects of Moral and Political Philosophy*, 2 vols. (New York, 1812), 1:17–18.

remain." His argument squared with the widely accepted idea of the inheritance of acquired characteristics which the French naturalist Lamarck (1744–1829) sponsored. Jefferson did not deny that distinctive characteristics of Negroes might be the result of climate and the special state of the society in which they lived. In a letter to Chastellux, Jefferson said that though the black man, in his present state, might not be equal in body and mind to the white, "it would be hazardous to affirm that, equally cultivated for a few generations, he might not become so."

In view of this, of his dislike of slavery and his recognition of its inconsistency with the natural rights philosophy he professed, the question arises why Jefferson did nothing after the Revolution to encourage the active opposition to slavery. Several factors explain his negativism and inaction: a growing sense of detachment, political expediency, and his assumption that slaveholders, sharing mankind's innate moral sense, would free their slaves once they understood the evil of slavery. There was something else, too, in his ambivalence about the blacks. In *Notes on the State of Virginia*, he voiced the suspicion that the poor showing the Negro made in reasoning power resulted from an innate and immutable deficiency. He thus questioned whether freedom, which he favored in theory, could improve the Negro enough to make him a neighbor on terms of equality.[30]

On the other hand, Jefferson affirmed, on the basis of his own observations and of those of men whom he trusted, the equal abilities of Indians and whites in "the same uncultivated state." After admitting that muscles used in toil were inferior in Indians to those of white working men, he explained the difference as the result of the red man's conviction that it was disgraceful to labor. "I believe the Indian then to be in body and mind equal to the white man."[31]

In a thoughtful study of Jeffersonian philosophy and the American Indian, Bernard W. Sheehan has identified a rough consensus in the combined admiration of certain Indian virtues, and an underlying view resting largely on a somewhat mechanistic environmental determinism qualified by the state-of-society thesis. With reference to assumptions about human nature, such a position failed to provide an adequate instrument for assessing the conflict between the persisting aspects of the white man's ways and values, on the one hand, and those of the tribal cultures, on the other. It failed, in other words, to understand concretely

30. Jefferson, *Notes on the State of Virginia*, p. 143. For keen insight into Jefferson's refusal to involve himself in the rising antislavery movement see David Brion Davis, *The Problem of Slavery in the Age of Revolution 1770–1823* (Ithaca, 1975), pp. 169 ff.; and John C. Miller, *Thomas Jefferson and Slavery* (New York, 1977).

31. Jefferson to Chastellux, June 7, 1785, in Boyd, ed., *Papers of Thomas Jefferson*, 8:186.

the basic realities by assuming that environment and a providential cosmic force could ultimately transform Indian cultures into the white man's superior ways. In so doing, the Jeffersonian formula carried the "seeds of destruction" by paving the way for the ultimate reliance on force in the resolution of conflicts between the two races.[32] Despite the pious rhetoric about Indian rights and the need for compassion and justice, Jefferson took steps that led to the removal of the trans-appalachian tribes.

Jefferson believed with the Scottish realists or common sense philosophers that all human beings—Indians and blacks as well as whites—possessed an innate moral sense. The Creator, Jefferson wrote to Thomas Law[33] in 1814, made the moral principle "so much a part of our constitution as that no errors of reasoning or of speculation might lead us astray from its observance in practice."[34] This moral principle expressed itself in man's innate impulse to be kind and helpful to his fellows. It was not enough to say with Helvétius that the good we did to others was done merely to give us pleasure. The question was, Why did it give us pleasure? The answer was that "nature hath implanted in our breasts, a love of others, a sense of duty to them, a moral instinct, in short, which prompts us irresistibly to feel and to succor their distresses. . . . The Creator would indeed have been a bungling artist, had he intended man for a social animal, without planting in him social dispositions."[35]

The innate and commonly shared sense of morality gave weight and worth to the collective opinion of mankind, to which Jefferson so ringingly appealed in the memorable first sentence of the Declaration of Independence. Men the world over, having an innate moral sense, could appreciate as self-evident truths the king's flagrant violations of the law of nature and the rights of man.

Jefferson conceded that the moral sense was not planted in every single man, for there was no rule without its exception. Just as some began life without organs of sight, or hearing, or hand, and were still men, so some were born without the moral propensity which still characterized the general definition of man. Even in those cases where it was lacking, it could in some part be supplied by training, by "appeals to reason and calculation," by emphasizing the rewards and penalties established by the laws and "ultimately the prospects of a future state of retribution for

32. Bernard W. Sheehan, *Seeds of Extinction: Jeffersonian Philanthropy and the American Indian* (Chapel Hill, 1973), pp. ix–5, 8–9, 278–79.

33. See Thomas Law's *Second Thoughts on Instinctive Impulses* (Philadelphia, 1810), pp. 10, 11, 18, 21, 71–73, 88–89.

34. Jefferson, *Writings*, 14:139. Also, the letter to John Adams, November 15, 1813, 14:1–8.

35. *Writings*, 14:141–42.

the evil as well as the good done while here."[36] It was no more to be expected that every man would be made virtuous "than that every tree shall be made to bear fruit, and every plant nourishment. The brier and bramble can never become the vine and olive; but their asperities may be softened by culture, and their properties improved to usefulness in the order and economy of the world."[37]

Jefferson's words about the improvement of the human being born with a deficient moral sense raised the larger question, could human nature be changed? This could not be answered simply, in part because, as we have seen, he did not work out his ideas in a logical way.

Thus some remarks suggested that in his view human nature had never really changed and never could change, whatever improvements in the conduct of individuals might be possible. At least on one occasion Jefferson wrote, we may recall, that he thought human nature was the same on both sides of the Atlantic and at all times contained elements of strength and weakness. Nor did he agree with the extreme French environmentalists who proclaimed the doctrine of human perfectibility. Then too, the eternal values in the Greek and Roman classics implied a universal and unchanging human nature.[38] Moreover, his views about the fixity of two main personality types suggested ineradicable traits. "As the division into whig and tory," he wrote to Joel Barlow in 1802, "is founded in the nature of man; the weakly and nerveless, the rich and the corrupt, seeing more safety and accessibility in a strong executive; the healthy, firm, and virtuous, feeling confidence in their physical and moral resources, are willing to part with only so much power as is necessary for their good government."[39]

But there was another side of the coin. Jefferson sensed a distinction between original endowment and traits formed by social experience. In his eyes, weakness, corruption, venality, and the boisterous passions on the one hand and reasonableness, morality, and dignity on the other were governed by the institutions, the situations, and the general environment that formed personality in infancy and childhood. The same actions were called virtuous in some countries, vicious in others. The explanation, he argued, was that "nature has constituted *utility* to man, the standard and test of virtue."[40] To be sure, human operations and justifications were sometimes, in the long run, deceptive. The Jacobin

36. *Writings*, 14:142–43.
37. Jefferson to Cornelius Camden Blatchly, October 21, 1822, *Writings*, 15:399–400.
38. Adrienne Koch, *The Philosophy of Thomas Jefferson* (New York, 1943), pp. 115–16.
39. Jefferson, *Writings*, 8:150. See also Lester J. Cappon, ed., *The Adams-Jefferson Letters: The Complete Correspondence between Thomas Jefferson and Abigail and John Adams*, 2 vols. (Chapel Hill, 1959), 2:332, 335.
40. Jefferson to Thomas Law, June 13, 1814, *Writings*, 15:143.

clubs in the French Revolution, for example, beginning as virtuous and patriotic organizations, degenerated to sad depths. We must, Jefferson said, guard against ourselves, not as we are, but as we may be.[41]

To Jefferson, a striking example of the role of environment or situation in bringing to the fore one set of potentialities rather than another was the part he believed that slavery played in the formation of the personality and character of the white child reared in its midst. Being imitative—one of the basic human characteristics present from birth to old age—the child, he asserted, learned from the cradle to model his conduct on the intemperance, passion, and tyranny that all too often marked the attitude of masters toward slaves. "The parent storms, the child looks on, catches the lineaments of wrath, puts on the same airs in the circle of smaller slaves, gives loose to the worst of passions, and thus nursed, educated, and daily exercised in tyranny, cannot but be stamped by it with odious peculiarities."[42] In much the same way, Jefferson thought, the impact of the monarchical environment in Europe on the young personality and character was so great that it was open to question whether most immigrants could throw it off, or if they did, whether they would not exchange it for "an unbounded licentiousness, passing, as is usual, from one extreme to another."[43]

But Jefferson's view of the role of the environment, including education, also led him to believe in the possibility of improvement in conduct. To appreciate his thinking on this point, account should be taken of the two basic human needs that he regarded as not only inborn but central: the need to be free and the need to try to be happy.

The most formidable barriers to the realization of these needs, he felt, lay in certain inborn propensities and in certain institutional and social arrangements which were not a necessary concomitant of these innate drives.[44] Specifically, man's native selfishness, especially when linked with a high degree of intelligence or cunning and a low endowment of moral sense, led him, whether merely a member of society or an officer of government, to exploit others and thus to interfere with their freedom and happiness.[45] The environmental factors that encouraged an innate selfishness and exploitative tendency included widespread though unnecessary ignorance, constraints on individual freedom inherent in nonrepublican governments, poverty, and economic dependence of the many on the few, especially in large cities and in prolonged war.

Since Jefferson did not believe that complete freedom and happiness

41. Jefferson to Jedidiah Morse, March 6, 1822, Writings, 15:356.
42. Jefferson, Notes on the State of Virginia, p. 162.
43. Notes on the State of Virginia, pp. 84–85.
44. Jefferson to Mann Page, August 30, 1795, Writings, 9:306–7.
45. Jefferson to Mann Page, 9:306; also 14:140–41.

were attainable, the problem was to try for as much as possible for everyone by following two main courses of action. One was the institution of a universal education, including child-rearing in the home and continuous learning thereafter. The aim throughout should be to balance reason and emotion, so that each, supplementing the other, might promote human good, individually and collectively. The limits to the improvement of reason through effort and practice could be determined empirically by sustained efforts over time. Likewise, experience could determine the extent to which the emotions of love and kindness might be nourished through exercise and social approval, and reciprocally, the selfish emotions leading to the exploitation of others restrained by strong disapproval.

But Jefferson did not stop here. If it were possible to uproot institutions that fettered human needs for freedom and happiness, he favored such a course. If this could not be, the ill effects of such institutions could be minimized.[46] Thus he wanted to abolish the remnants of feudal institutions and to develop self-government within the republican frame. Nor did he accept the argument that the great mass of people lacked the rational and moral endowments to govern themselves. "The sheep," he wrote, "are happier of themselves than under the care of wolves." This pointed, he felt, to a government too weak to help the wolves but strong enough to protect the sheep. Given the fact of innate thrusts for power and greed, given the fact that while not all men were rogues, most rogues managed to acquire power, Jefferson stressed the need for "eternal vigilance." This, he thought, could work best in the small community where truly representative institutions prevailed. Since there was some human weakness, some germ of corruption in all who were entrusted with government, a system of checks and balances was necessary in any constitution. This anticipated the point later made again and again in *The Federalist* papers.

Jefferson's feeling about human nature's plasticity was also illustrated by his comments on war, for which he had little heart. He believed that Americans might avoid the ruthless jockeying for position and power that had led to so much bloodshed in the Old World. The hope lay in the abundance of natural resources in America. Yet he recognized the deep commitment of many of his countrymen to commerce, a commitment which in his view invited wars. Even so, the incidence of war might be reduced by avoiding injustice toward others and by making the economy as self-sufficient as possible.

Making the economy as self-sufficient as possible involved, obviously, the encouragement of industry through tariffs and subsidies. But Jef-

46. Jefferson to James Madison, September 6, 1789, in Boyd, ed., *Papers of Thomas Jefferson*, 15:392–98.

ferson was also convinced that the essential goodness in man might best be approximated in an open society of independent freehold farmers, "God's chosen people, if he ever had a chosen people." Only the future could reveal how long abundant space and resources would permit this kind of society to prevail, particularly if, in developing an economy of self-sufficiency, the industry and commerce in growing cities became strong enough to bend government to their ends.

Thus Jefferson did not resolve the paradoxes implicit in his belief in the possibility of change, not of man's basic inheritance but of individual and social conduct—the possibility of greater freedom and happiness for everyone. What made his view of human nature distinctive was the role he gave to the American environment, actual and potential, an idea destined to have a long career. In providing a base for individual economic independence, for widespread participation in the decision-making functions of government, and for the training of mind and feelings for social as well as individual improvement, he believed America was man's best hope.

But neither Jefferson's temperament nor his response to American environment entirely explained his concept of human nature. It drew from the ancient classics. It owed a great debt to the seventeenth- and eighteenth-century thinkers who regarded themselves as breaking new paths, as freeing men from binding superstitions and irrational beliefs, and as showing how reason, the scientific spirit, and the knowledge of man and his environment might enhance control of the conditions under which he lived and thus of himself. In an age when many able and brilliant writers belittled and even scorned human nature, the men of the Enlightenment who influenced Jefferson insisted on giving it a new dignity. Jefferson did much to disseminate the ideas and values of the Enlightenment. His unique contribution, however, was to show by example how thought could inform action, how enlightened ideas might shape new and better institutions for the improvement of the human condition and the realization of human potentialities.

As President of the American Philosophical Society Jefferson was thrown with a group of scientifically disposed men bent on increasing useful knowledge. Among its best-known members was Dr. Benjamin Rush of Philadelphia, a man whose relation to the Enlightenment and to ideas about human nature was complex and notable.[47] Like others of his

47. I have drawn on Rush's writings, including his *Autobiography*, ed. George W. Corner (Princeton, 1948); his *Essays, Literary, Moral and Philosophical* (Philadelphia, 1806); *The Letters of Benjamin Rush*, 2 vols., ed. Lyman H. Butterfield (Princeton, 1951);

time Rush used the phrase *human nature* very loosely. Sometimes he spoke of it as "the earthly frame, a minute fabric, a center of wonders . . . forever subject to Diseases and Death."[48] At other times he thought of it as the total personality. Elsewhere he identified it with the human condition. At least until his later years, he believed that humanity was "not totally depraved and that benevolence is a leading feature of human nature."[49]

While Rush repudiated Deism and was nominally a Presbyterian and then an Episcopalian, his conception of human nature had much in common with that of many Enlightened philosophers. He too believed in a Natural Creator whose handiwork, Nature, was all-inclusive. Thus mind, the most elusive as well as the most distinctive mark of man, was as much a part of nature as the body. In stressing the power of education to mold character and personality, especially in childhood, he cherished a conviction dear to the Enlightenment. His active sympathy with humanitarianism, as well as his anti-elitism, owed much to his early involvement with the New Side branch of the revival movement, but it also reflected a prominent strand in Enlightenment thought. He opposed capital punishment. He was against slavery, a vice which "degrades human nature, and dissolves that universal tie of benevolence which should connect all the children of men in one great family."[50] While he shared the prejudice of his time and place against "blackness," Rush came to believe that the Negro's color resulted from leprosy and that science might some day restore it to normal whiteness.

Rush's approach to psychology, in his eyes the queen of the sciences, was both rationalistic and empirical, in spite of dogmatic statements and oversimplifications. He preached, if he did not always practice, careful observation, classification, and the formation and testing of hypotheses. His devotion to empiricism was, for example, illustrated when he rejected Thomas Reid's doctrine of an innate common sense. Judgments based on common sense, Rush pointed out, might support prejudices

---

and Rush's *Medical Inquiries and Observations upon the Diseases of the Mind* (Philadelphia, 1812). I am also indebted to David Hawke's *Benjamin Rush, Revolutionary Gadfly* (Indianapolis, 1971); to Norman Dain, *Concepts of Insanity in the United States 1789–1865* (New Brunswick, N.J., 1964); to Howard Feinstein's "Benjamin Rush: A Child of Light for the Children of Darkness," *Psychoanalytical Review* 18 (1971): 209–22; to Richard Shryock's "Eighteenth-Century Medicine in America," *American Antiquarian Society Proceedings* 59 (1950): 275–92; and especially, to J. D'Elia, *Benjamin Rush: Philosopher of the Revolution, Transactions of the American Philosophical Society*, n.s., vol. 64, pt. 5 (Philadelphia, 1974).

48. Butterfield, ed., *Letters*, 1:3.

49. *Letters*, 1:585. See also Rush's prediction of 1776 that the Continental Congress "that will sit in the year 1780 will be the history of the dignity of human nature," p. 108.

50. D. H. Runes, ed., *Selected Writings of Benjamin Rush* (New York, 1947), p. 17.

dominant at any given time; so-called common sense judgments always needed to be tested by experience. In his attitude toward science Rush was, at least for much of his life, a true son of the Enlightenment. He believed that by ultimately revealing the laws of nature, science could conquer all diseases and most human wrongs.

Rush's contribution to the discussion of human nature rested largely on the writings and clinical practice that won him the title Father of American Psychiatry, and on the Lectures upon the Mind given to medical students in Philadelphia between 1791 and his death in 1813.[51]

In his concept of the unity of nature, upon which he based his rationalistic approach to psychology, Rush owed a good deal to contemporary British scientists and philosophers. While he did not follow Thomas Reid and the other Scottish moral philosophers at all points, he went along with much of their position, which held that inasmuch as feelings and actions took place within the individual, they were "real" and thus nondeceptive. He borrowed from his medical preceptor in Edinburgh, the great Dr. William Cullen, the theory that various stimuli led to a reaction in the nervous system in the form of sensations or motions. To David Hartley, Rush also acknowledged his deep debt. Hartley's psychoparallelism held that mental operations and behavior reflected the association of ideas that in turn derived from vibrations set off by physical stimuli. Choices, including moral choices, were, Hartley insisted, made with reference to associations with pleasurable and painful sensations. Unable to accept the deterministic implications of this concept, Rush fell back on a faculty psychology that assumed morality to be, as the Scottish philosophers taught, an innate endowment of the mind. In the phrenological faculty psychology of two German physicians, Franz Joseph Gall and Johann Gaspar Spurzheim, Rush found corroboration for his belief in cerebral localization. This implied that the weakness of a given cerebrally based faculty could be corrected by sustained exercise. Such a view was compatible with Rush's emphasis on morality and a free will.

Rush listed nine faculties, some intellectual, others moral. All of these, but particularly memory, imagination, and the crucial moral faculty, were influenced by the physical condition of the brain.[52] In the normal functioning of healthy minds, the intellectual and the moral faculties operated properly, the intellectual responding to stimuli transmitted to

51. My discussion of Rush's psychology is indebted to Patricia S. Noel and Eric T. Carlson, "The Faculty Psychology of Benjamin Rush," *Journal of the History of the Behavioral Sciences* 9 (1973): 369–77.

52. Benjamin Rush, *An Inquiry into the Influence of Physical Causes upon the Moral Faculty* (Philadelphia, 1786), pp. 16 ff.

the brain and then becoming associated with ideas, the moral functioning more or less spontaneously.

Dreams also intrigued Rush. He held them to be the consequence of morbid and irregular action in the blood vessels of the brain, resulting from increased stimuli, both corporeal, such as overeating before bedtime, and mental, such as disquieting passions, difficult studies begun before sleep, and an undue weight of business.[53] In sleep, these dislocations or irregular actions of the blood vessels concentrated activity in the particular faculties that were affected, especially memory, imagination, will, and the passions and appetites. Rush's naturalistic and somatic explanation of dreams was in marked contrast with the still widely held supernatural explanations.[54]

Rush's psychiatry rested on his psychology. Madness, being a disease, was explained in naturalistic terms. It was thus wrong to attach the customary moral stigma to it. In derangement, the mind's perceptions, judgment, and reasoning broke away from the natural and habitual order. Rejecting as the primary seats of madness the mind, the nerves, and the abdominal viscera, Rush located the cause in the blood vessels of the brain. It was thus related to the same kind of morbid and irregular actions that explained other arterial diseases.[55] Deficient action in the blood vessels might result from accident and shock or from hereditary factors.

It followed that treatment was to be in the main physical: bloodletting, purges, medication, and a sparse diet. Since, however, Rush admitted that anxiety and melancholy might impair the nervous system and induce "vascular tension," he also favored moral or psychological supplements to physical treatment. These moral or psychological aids included music, occupational therapy, and the example of patience, compassion, and firmness on the part of attendants. Such procedures, Rush felt, could strengthen the dislocated and impaired faculties, the moral faculty in particular.

In 1812, when Rush's naturalistic and forward-looking views about mental derangement appeared, one of his pupils, Dr. Joseph Buchanan of Kentucky, published a much less influential but significant book. *The Philosophy of Human Nature* posited a monistic materialism in which body and mind were looked on as two aspects of a single organism. "If it be proven," Buchanan wrote, "as it now seems to be, that the intellectual

53. Rush, *An Inquiry*, pp. 10–11; *Medical Inquiries*, chap. 14.

54. Carl A. L. Binger, in his essay "The Dreams of Benjamin Rush," *American Journal of Psychiatry* 125 (1969): 1653–59, notes that Rush sensed that a dream might indicate personality characteristics the dreamer wished to avoid.

55. Rush, *Medical Inquiries*, pp. 17 ff.

transactions of feeling, thought, volition, made known to us by consciousness, correspond as their shadows to the physical transactions of
the brain discovered by our senses; may we not conclude, that they are
identically the same things perceived by us in different ways, and thence
thought different? We are authorized at least to prosecute the study of
human nature as a physical science, confining our metaphysical
inquiries to the vital organization of the brain; for what is true of this
cannot be false concerning mind, of which it is the archetype."[56] In
explaining emotion, Buchanan stressed the predominance of sensations
from the viscera and stomach. Thus a frontier doctor anticipated a much
later idea of William James. We know little about the reception of the
book, though Jefferson called it to the attention of John Adams.

Ideas related to Buchanan's found other exponents. Jefferson, had he
been living, would have been interested in a similar view held by his
friend Dr. Thomas Cooper. In 1831 Cooper, in an appendix to his
translation of a psychiatric exposition of Broussais, identified mental
processes with the motions of a glandular fluid in the nervous system.
His essay was, in effect, little more than a belated version of the
physiological psychology elaborated in L'Homme machine (1748). This
treatise by Julien Offray de La Mettrie, a French physician, held that
correlations between mental and physiological states warranted
regarding man as a machine.[57] American discussions of human nature
were not much influenced by Buchanan and Cooper. This seems also to
have been true of Dr. Joseph Priestley, Cooper's father-in-law, a friend of
Jefferson, and a leading chemist and Unitarian minister. Having sought
refuge in Pennsylvania from British harassment at the turn of the
century, Priestley tried to harmonize, with the aid of David Hartley's
psychology, his own theories of philosophical necessity, materialism,
and millenarian perfectionism.[58]

56. Joseph Buchanan, The Philosophy of Human Nature (Richmond, Ky., 1812), pp.
13–14.
57. Aram Vartanian, La Mettrie's L'Homme Machine: A Study in the Origin of an Idea
(Princeton, 1960), pp. 14 ff. For this incident in Cooper's American career see Maurice
Kelley, Additional Chapters on Thomas Cooper (Orono, Me., 1930), pp. 8–9, 40 ff.
58. The Theological and Miscellaneous Works of Joseph Priestley L.L.D., F.R.S., ed.
John T. Ritt, 25 vols. (London, 1817–32), 2:231 ff.; Priestley's Writings on Philosophy,
Science, and Politics, ed. John A. Passmore, 6 vols. (New York, 1964), 1:9–10;
Autobiography of Joseph Priestley, ed. Jack Lindsay (Bath, England, 1970), pp. 12, 23,
133; and Mary C. Park, Joseph Priestley and the Problem of Pantisocracy (Philadelphia,
1947), p. 47, for the contemplated community of English liberals near Priestley's retreat.
The Temple of Reason, a Philadelphia weekly paper, included in its pages in 1802 a serial,
"Equality: A History of Lithconia," which reflected many enlightened ideas about human
nature, including its perfectibility. This utopia was first published in book form in
Philadelphia in 1873. See Equality: A History of Lithconia, with a Bibliographical Note
(Philadelphia, 1947). The author seems to have been Dr. James Reynolds, who in 1799 was
involved in a riot over petitions for the repeal of the Alien Act.

The perfectibility of human nature, an idea espoused not only by Priestley but by such secular philosophers as Condorcet and William Godwin, found some favor among American intellectuals. Its adherents accepted the idea with and without qualifications and for varying reasons. Dr. Elihu Hubbard Smith was a case in point. A deist and an admirer of Condorcet, Volney, and Godwin, Smith, unlike most of their American disciples, did not accept Jefferson's political principles. If allowed to define perfectionism, Smith found the idea acceptable. Being human, man did not indeed have unlimited capacities, but these were improvable both by culture and "hereditary propagation." The history of mankind showed that the human race had gradually developed a refinement of manners and acquired a "fund of reasoning powers" that it certainly had not always possessed. "This capacity for progressive advancement toward excellence, is denominated *perfectibility* which . . . neither implies that man will ever become perfect, nor that he is not vicious and weak, & imperfect, *now*." Man, in short, was "an animal susceptible of all the improvement consistent with human nature."[59]

More doctrinaire champions of perfectibility held that two great obstacles kept human nature from realizing its full potentialities. One was religious superstition and ecclesiastical hierarchies; the other was the power and authority of the privileged orders that stymied democratic equality.

"The organic constitution of man," wrote Elihu Palmer, a one-time blind preacher who had become a deist, "induces a strong conclusion that no limits can justly be assigned to his moral and scientific improvements. . . . The strength of human understanding, its keenness of discernment would ultimately penetrate into every part of nature, were it permitted to operate with uncontrouled and unqualified freedom." Alas, religious superstition had buried man's moral existence in a gulf of ignorance and fanaticism. Orthodox creeds had blinded man to the dignity of his nature, stunted his reason, atrophied his capacity for moral and truly social behavior. "The period is at hand," Palmer went on, "in which kings and thrones, priests and hierarchies, and the long catalogue of mischiefs which they have produced, shall be swept away from the face of the earth. . . . Then will arrive the era of human felicity. . . . then will appear . . . the empire of reason, of science, and of virtue."[60]

Others, emphasizing the plasticity of human nature, argued that tyrants and the privileged classes had, for their own purposes, inculcated the idea that the innate evil and inequality of mankind closed the door to democratic hopes. Tunis Wortman, a New York democrat, made this

59. *The Diary of Elihu Hubbard Smith*, ed. James E. Cronin (Philadelphia, 1973), p. 151.

60. Elihu Palmer, *Principles of Nature; or, a Development of the Moral Causes of Happiness and Misery in the Human Species* (New York, 1801), pp. 24, 59–60, 143 ff., 243–44.

point in a pamphlet published in 1796. In describing the components of human nature, he claimed that Locke had wisely observed that "nine parts out of ten are what they are, good or evil, useful or not, by their education. 'Tis that which makes the great differences in mankind." Further buttressing his position by citing as authorities Hartley, Priestley, and William Godwin, and drawing on history for illustrations, Wortman argued that social and political institutions, not, as some thought, climate, explained human behavior. If properly safeguarded against reaction, American republican and democratic institutions were bound to usher in a new era in the history of human nature.[61]

Joel Barlow, Jeffersonian pamphleteer and poet, believed with Wortman and Thomas Paine that the discovery of truth depended on the use of reason by the masses as well as by the educated few. Barlow, who had not yet ventured into money-making, deprecated the "inordinate passion for wealth." The source of so much unhappiness, this passion, he insisted, was rooted, not in the "natural propensities of the human heart" but in the social habit that associated wealth with respect, "the desire of which is doubtless among the strongest passions of our nature." Well-meaning men, in calling on individuals to reform themselves, overlooked the role of habit, which arose out of the "unnatural and degrading system of government." True reformation, Barlow went on, could be expected only by "referring back to nature for change of these systems."[62]

Philip Freneau, like Barlow a poet and a Jeffersonian journalist, proclaimed that both poverty and war could be uprooted if human nature approached its potentiality—perfectibility—through laws and institutions consonant with reason:

> Let laws revive, by heaven designed
> To tame the tiger in the mind
> And drive from human hearts
> That love of wealth, that love of sway
> Which leads the world too much astray,
> Which points envenomed darts;

61. Tunis Wortman, *An Oration on the Influence of Social Institutions on Human Morals* (New York, 1796). In an eloquent passage (p. 9) Wortman deplored the tendency to identify thirst for gain and the allurements of luxury with national well-being. Wortman also understood the psychological mechanism now known as rationalization, though the authorities he quoted did not include some of its notable early exponents such as Malebranche, Pascal, La Rochefoucauld, La Bruyère, and Soame Jenyns. For these writers see Lovejoy, *Reflections on Human Nature*, pp. 24 ff. Wortman also gave some attention to human nature in *A Solemn Address to Christians and Patriots, upon the Approaching Election of a President of the United States* (New York, 1800).

62. Joel Barlow, *The Works of Joel Barlow*, 2 vols. (Gainesville, Fla., 1970), 1:273–75.

And men will rise from what they are;
Sublimer, and superior, far,
Than Solomon guessed, or Plato saw;
All will be just, all will be good—
That harmony, "not understood,"
Will reign the general law.[63]

Like these fellow writers, Charles Brockden Brown of Philadelphia reflected in his pioneer fiction the influence of William Godwin and Mary Wollstonecraft. He wanted his novels to serve social ends. Thus he made environmental influence account for what he regarded as the deficiencies in women's reasoning powers, to which the record of their slender achievements in literature, science, and public affairs testified. Yet his novels raised doubt about reliance on sense experience and rational interpretations of it. Neither, he came to believe, could be relied on to avoid error and evil in the dark and deep inner nature of the heart. It is, as we shall see, warrantable to regard Brown's view of human nature as a phase of the reaction against the moral radical Enlightenment.[64]

An Enlightenment image of man was never fully achieved in historical writing about the Revolution in the full-blown way that Joel Barlow, with Jefferson's encouragement, planned.[65] But David Ramsay[66] and Samuel Williams,[67] each influenced by the Enlightenment, did write

63. *The Poems of Philip Freneau: Poet of the American Revolution*, 3 vols., ed. Fred L. Pattee (Princeton, 1902–7), 3:223.

64. See p. 151.

65. The nearest approach to what Barlow and Jefferson had in mind was Mercy Otis Warren's *History of the Rise, Progress and Termination of the American Revolution*, 3 vols. (Boston, 1805). For discussions of Mrs. Warren's work see Merle Curti, *Human Nature in American Historical Thought* (Columbia, Mo., 1968), pp. 52–54; William Raymond Smith, *History as Argument: Three Patriot Historians of the American Revolution* (The Hague, Paris, 1966), chap. 3; and Maude Macdonald Hutcheson, "Mercy Warren, 1728–1814," *William and Mary Quarterly*, 3d ser. 10 (1953): 378–402.

66. Carnes Weeks's "David Ramsay, Physician, Patriot and Historian," *Annals of Medical History*, n.s. 1 (1929): 600–607, and Robert L. Meriwether's sketch in the *Dictionary of American Biography*, 15:338–39, give the essential biographical information. For analyses of Ramsay's historical ideas see Curti, *Human Nature in American Historical Thought*, pp. 46–52; William Raymond Smith, *History as Argument*, chap. 3; and Page Smith, "David Ramsay and the Causes of the American Revolution," *William and Mary Quarterly*, 2d ser. 17 (1960): 51–57.

67. For Williams see Ralph N. Miller, "Samuel Williams 'History of Vermont,'" *New England Quarterly* 22 (1949): 73–85; "Samuel Williams," in John L. Sibley, *Sketches of Graduates of Harvard University*, 3 vols. (Cambridge, 1873–85), continued by Clifford K. Shipton in vols. 4–18 (Cambridge, 1933–75), 15:134–46; and Merle Curti and William

histories of that great event which added new dimensions to the discussion of human nature. Both men were trained in natural science. Both had religious commitments. Both took part in public affairs; both were moderate Federalists in their political preferences. Each was well known abroad as well as at home.

Samuel Williams, a liberal Congregational minister and the Hollis Professor of Natural Philosophy at Harvard, the recipient of international honors for his scientific work, fled from Cambridge to Vermont because of a serious charge against his financial integrity. A pioneer of culture in the Green Mountain State, he wrote *The Natural and Civil History of Vermont* (1794), one of the best of the early state histories.

In holding that man's actions were subject to regular and uniform laws, Williams expressed a basic tenet of the Enlightenment. The corollary was the assumption that "the same state of society" would produce the same forms of government, the same manners, customs, and habits among different nations, in whatever part of the earth. Thus, while human nature remained unaltered, its manifestations differed with changes in the state of society, effecting the degradation or the improvement of man, as the case might be. Williams, then, modified the static view of human nature characteristic of much Enlightenment thought. The social state, changing at different rates in various places and at different times, produced significant differences in the people influenced by it. Williams further assumed that the "peculiar and distinguishing features" of society in the federal union had created a new type of man, or at least new values and kinds of conduct. To understand this, he thought, was the most important function of historical study.

This, then, was the frame for Williams's discussion of the soil, mountains, climate, flora and fauna, Indians,[68] the first settlements, and the distinctive institutions and customs of his adopted state. He found a high degree of individuality and freedom, and relative immunity from corruption and venality. These he ascribed to the rural character of Vermont, to an early sense of responsibility on the part of the young, and, above all, to an equality of condition, employment, and interest. This equality did not mean an equality of "power, capacity, and advantages. . . . To some, the Author of Nature has assigned superior

---

Tillman, eds., *Philosophical Lectures by Samuel Williams, L.L.D., on the Constitution, Duty, and Religion of Man, Transactions of the American Philosophical Society*, n.s. 60, pt. 3 (Philadelphia, 1970), pp. 5–12.

68. Samuel Williams, *The Natural and Civil History of Vermont* (Walpole, N.H., 1794), pp. xi ff., 163, 246 ff., 258. Williams argued that if men are to be truly free, if they are to realize their potentialities, they must relate themselves to nature in an appropriately functional way. This, he felt, the Indians had done.

powers of the mind, a strength of reason and discernment, a capacity of judging, and a genius for invention, which are not given to others."[69]

But in such a pioneer society little heed was paid to any differences based on the inheritance of wealth or position. Recognizing unequal endowments, men united to preserve nature's equalities. By contrast, European society degraded the people, corrupted those who had power and those who did not, and gave the most unfavorable view of the capacity of the latter and of the disposition of the former.

"In America," Williams wrote, "everything had assumed a different tendency and operation. The first settlers of the colonies had suffered severly under bigotry and intolerance and ecclesiastical power. . . . They had not at first, any more knowledge of the rights of human nature than their neighbors and they were as far from the spirit of candour and toleration."[70] When they were thrown into a similar and perilous situation, false notions of inequality had no meaning. In fact, the plain farmer often had a better idea of his rights and privileges than any European philosopher. "The one was in a situation, where the language, dictates, and designs of nature, were perpetually occurring to his views: the other was in a situation, where everything in society had deviated from nature; and with infinite labour and study, the first principles must be induced from theory and reasoning."[71] Williams concluded by emphasizing the necessity of safeguarding the freedom born of social conditions.

Dr. David Ramsay's histories[72] resembled those of Williams in stressing the influence of the American physical and social environment in bringing to the fore the best in man's varied and complex makeup. In Ramsay's eyes man was characterized by "the fierceness and rudeness of human passions," which fully aroused, blinded him to a reasonable assessment of his own interests. Human nature also expressed itself in conduct marked by "vices and follies." These included a desire for approbation and an ambition often incompatible with the inherent desire of all men for happiness. Another seeming paradox was that both habit and plasticity played large parts in the varied expressions of human nature. Thus in commenting on slavery, Ramsay wrote that "such is the force of habit, and the pliancy of human nature" that while

69. Williams, *Natural and Civil History*, p. 329.

70. *Natural and Civil History*, p. 371.

71. *Natural and Civil History*, p. 372.

72. Ramsay's books include *The History of the American Revolution*, 2 vols. (Philadelphia, 1789); *The History of South-Carolina from Its First Settlement in 1607 to the Year 1808*, 2 vols. (Charleston, S.C., 1800); and *The History of the United States from Their First Settlement as English Colonies in 1607 to the Year 1808*, 3 vols. (Philadelphia, 1818).

a free man prefers death to slavery, the Negro born and bred in it finds it quite satisfactory and in some cases expresses his preference by rejecting offers of freedom. Human nature was also marked by "elasticity of the human mind" and by its rationality. Though limited by passion, such a mind could provide an understanding of the general will of Providence. It could also shape decisions, with the help of trial and error, that were compatible with the special designs of Providence. The dignity of human nature was, unfortunately, often defiled by arbitrary authority and institutions incongruous with the inherent desire of all men for their natural rights to life, liberty, property, and happiness.[73]

In Ramsay's eyes the American Revolution illuminated the interplay of the components of human nature. He spelled this out both in delineating specific events and in considering its causes. Broadly speaking, the Revolution was rooted in the ardent commitment of the first colonists to the seventeenth-century English love of freedom and the defiance of arbitrary authority, an idea relevant to the circumstances of colonial life. The great distance from the mother country, the prevalence of independent freeholders, and the elbow room provided by the abundance of the New World, all enhanced freedom.[74] These special circumstances also explained why the ambition that all men shared found outlet in more honest conduct than in Europe. Again, the British heritage of freedom and American conditions explained the extent to which "the vices and follies in human nature," the "ferocity in man," and universal self-interest were checked when experience proved the need to unite in defense of liberties threatened by king and parliament. The successful outcome might point to ways by which men in the rest of the world could more fully realize human capacities and the inherent desire for freedom and happiness.

Ramsay probed other motives. Why did some take the Tory side and others the Patriot? He emphasized the role of age, place in society, personal interest, and constitution or temperament, including the intensity of the desire for approbation. Whereas those who had or hoped for royal favor wanted to keep the old tie, the young, the ardent, the ambitious and the enterprising were more apt to become Patriots. Those who were timid by temperament, or wanting in decision, were likely to be lukewarm if they chose either side. Ramsay thought that some degree of education also affected a man's decision. He claimed, not altogether correctly, that those whose minds had been warmed by the rays of

73. Ramsay, *History of the American Revolution*, 1:24, 53; William Raymond Smith, *History as Argument*, p. 51.
74. Ramsay, *History of the American Revolution*, 1:32 ff.

science took the Patriot side, while those uninformed or misinformed preferred the leading strings of the parent state.[75]

On the other hand, the war also encouraged those making common cause, at least for a time, to lay aside the selfish passions that in varying degrees marked all members of the human race. Even more striking, the war called forth talents in men who previously had been entirely unaware of having them. While Americans were guided by the mother country, Ramsay wrote, they had little scope or encouragement for exertion. British officials took the responsibility and acted for them. But with the Revolution, many discovered that they could speak and write in the public interest and, above all, act with "an energy far surpassing all expectations which could be reasonably founded on their previous requirements." It seemed "as if the war not only required, but created talents."[76]

But Ramsay also knew a darker side. The war brought out some of men's worst potentialities. Moreover, when the great expectations about personal fortunes, once independence was won, failed to materialize quickly, many felt bitter. Experiencing new suffering and not knowing its source or how to remedy things, they fell into an irritable, baffled mood and, as in Shays's Rebellion, turned against their own free government as ambitious demagogues induced them to close courthouses by mob threats and otherwise to interfere with the execution of the law.[77]

Neither Ramsay nor Williams had any hope for man's perfection. Each knew the depths of human weakness. Yet neither doubted that American environment and experience had enabled their country to surpass Europe in providing human nature with more freedom, individual responsibility, mutual association for common ends, and opportunities for talents likely to have lain dormant in the Old World.

Benjamin Franklin's career seemed to vindicate such a contention. His comments on human nature, over a long and full life, indicated a wider range of enlightened ideas than did those of Williams and Ramsay. His views of man also reflected his temperament and his conception of himself as an American highly honored by the enlightened community of two continents.

In becoming a deist early in life Franklin rejected the Puritan dogmas of total depravity and predestination. Though he later renounced his

75. *History of the American Revolution*, 2:314–21.
76. *History of the American Revolution*, 2:316.
77. *History of the American Revolution*, 2:340.

youthful philosophical materialism, he always held that physical health and the bodily condition influenced mind and conduct.[78] He practiced as well as professed humanitarianism. He unceasingly searched for political, social, and moral order that squared with the regularity and harmony of the physical universe.[79] Thomas Paine, whom he befriended, once said of him that no one was a better judge of human nature. The fiery author of *The Age of Reason* would, though, have been less at home in discussing human nature with the witty creator of *Poor Richard* than with Joel Barlow, Philip Freneau, and Tunis Wortman.

Franklin's image of man, insofar as it reflected concepts common to the Enlightenment, owed a good deal to his own place in the social structure and to his several social roles. The son of a candle and soap maker, Franklin illustrated the social mobility of the up-and-coming middle class. Being a self-made man, he took pride and pleasure in publicizing this role. He relished laying down rules of thumb to help other lowly young men realize their potentialities in the American milieu of generous opportunities for almost any white male who was industrious, frugal, amiable, modest, and civic-minded. He exemplified the idea that man had powers that could be realized by putting himself in the right relation to his environment in particular and to the orderly universe in general. In so doing he spelled out a major concept of the Enlightenment. Closely related to this idea was the equalitarianism that was congenial to Franklin's temperament and that guided so many of his activities. He not only gave lip service to the doctrine of natural rights, but in a common sense way implemented its egalitarian values in his personal relations, in his ultimate, if belated, opposition to slavery,[80] and in the part he took in revolution and constitution-making.

In still other ways Franklin's place in the social structure and the social roles he played explained his sympathy with cardinal ideas of the Enlightenment. He believed with his friend David Hume and with some of his acquaintances among the French philosophers that in the last analysis power rested on opinion. As editor and publisher, as the author

78. For Franklin's position on the influence of physical and physiological conditions on mental life, see "The Art of Procuring Pleasant Dreams," *The Writings of Benjamin Franklin*, ed. Albert H. Smyth, 10 vols. (New York, 1905–7), 10:131–37.

79. This point is brilliantly developed in Paul W. Conner's *Poor Richard's Politics: Benjamin Franklin and His New American Order* (New York, 1963).

80. Though an owner of household slaves, Franklin criticized the slave trade and the institution itself as unprofitable. Not until late in life did he respond to the influence of the British abolitionist Granville Sharp, as well as to that of the Quakers, in petitioning Congress for the abolition of slavery. For evidence that even before this he had come to doubt his ideas about innate Negro inferiority see Maurice J. Quinland, "Dr. Franklin Meets Dr. Johnson," *Pennsylvania Magazine of History* 73 (1949): 39.

of persuasive pamphlets and satirical essays, and as the deceptively modest commoner who stood before kings, Franklin helped shape public opinion. He turned his back—with notable exceptions—on the ancient idea that power must, in the main, rest on force. Much that he did showed his faith in the influence of opinion-making on the outcome of conflicts, a faith that American society nourished. And so he tried with zigzag pragmatism to bring about adjustments in the conflicts between Pennsylvania's embittered advocates and opponents of colonial defense, between the claims of aggressive frontiersmen and harassed Indians, and between British claims and American conceptions of colonial rights. In his later life, observing that there never was a good war or a bad peace, he tried to limit the inhuman effects of war on neutrals. Thus Franklin enacted his advocacy of tempered reason and a tolerant readiness to give and to take in responding to the need of mutual adjustments between conflicting interests. Here Franklin's commitments reflected the Enlightenment's belief in the efficacy of reason.

Franklin differed from the out-and-out exponents of the perfectibility of human nature in giving weight to the frequently intractable passions and emotions. These included avarice or thirst for gain, the thrust for power over others, self-esteem, pride, and vanity.[81] He candidly admitted the force of these passions and emotions in life, including his own.[82] Like Diderot, he did not regard the sex impulse, the power of which he knew, as in itself an evil to be largely repressed. He realized that reason was often a frail gift. He knew it was not always possible effectively to appeal to it or to guard its integrity against the deceptive role of the emotions. "So convenient a thing is it to be a *reasonable* Creature, since it enables one to find or make a Reason for every thing one has a mind to do."[83] In sum, Franklin realized the difficulty of controlling the emotions by reason, a difficulty that militated against any perfectibility of human nature and society.

Within limits, however, much could and should be done. Self-discipline and the deliberate cultivation of benevolence or altruism, of which man was also capable, were telling means to this end. Here he was by his own account indebted to Cotton Mather's preaching on the im-

81. For Franklin's occasional doubts about the efficacy of reason and for his views on its limitations in human relations and social policy see his letters to Dr. John Frothergill, March 14, 1764, *The Papers of Benjamin Franklin*, ed. Leonard W. Labaree and others (New Haven, 1959–), 11:101; and to his sister, Jane Mecom, September 29, 1769, *The Papers of Benjamin Franklin*, 16:210–11.

82. Nowhere did Franklin analyze vanity better than in his letter to Jared Eliot, September 12, 1751, *The Papers of Benjamin Franklin*, 4:194.

83. *The Autobiography of Benjamin Franklin*, ed. Leonard W. Labaree and others (New Haven, 1964), p. 88.

portance of good works, to Quaker example, and to the humanitarianism which Shaftesbury advocated and which the zealous English abolitionist Granville Sharp implemented. On another level, he
held that the technological improvements of his age also betokened the
likely expansion of human imagination, reason, and ingenuity.

Franklin also saw in religion no less than in self-restraint and
voluntary cooperation in good works a means of regulating the emotions
and passions.[84] In his effort in 1787 to dissuade a correspondent from
publishing a work on natural religion, he spelled out his pragmatic
views. "You yourself," he wrote, "may find it easy to live a virtuous life,
without the Assistance offered by Religion; you having a clear Perception of the Advantages of Virtue, and the Disadvantages of Vice, and
possessing a Strength of Resolution sufficient to enable you to resist
common Temptations. But think how great a Proportion of Mankind
consists of weak and ignorant Men and Women, and of inexperienc'd,
and inconsiderate Youth of both Sexes, who have need of the Motives of
Religion to restrain them from vice, to support their Virtue, and retain
them in the Practice of it till it becomes *habitual*, which is the great Point
for its Security." Continuing, he summed up his distrust both of abstract
reason and of the ability of the average man to exercise self-discipline
without religious faith: "If men are so wicked as we now see them *with
religion*, what would they be *if without it?*"[85]

In discussing Franklin's concept of human nature, Gerald Stourzh[86]
has held that his image of man midway between the pessimism of total
depravity and perfectibility rested on three factors. The first was
Franklin's own "happy constitution"—a condition he himself thought
necessary for anyone's well-being. The second, his own success in life,
taught him that man, whatever his limitations, could achieve certain
values and goals. The third was his sustained commitment to the Great
Chain of Being idea, which he early came by from reading Addison's
Spectator and Pope's *Essay on Man*. It will be recalled that this idea
assumed that every being in the universe occupied by the nature of things
a fixed position on a hierarchical ladder. Man stood above the lower
creatures but beneath the higher ones. Thus being neither condemned to
the lowest depths by total depravity nor raised to the ultimate heights,
man did not need to suffer either the anguish of total sinfulness or
frustration from pursuing a hopeless struggle for perfection.

Franklin's belief in the Great Chain of Being indeed explained a good

84. *A Dissertation on Liberty and Necessity, Pleasure and Pain* (1725), in *Papers of Benjamin Franklin*, 1:57–71. In the early years of the Junto in Philadelphia Franklin explicitly
repudiated this position as a youthful indiscretion.

85. *Writings of Benjamin Franklin*, 9:521–22; also, 2:293, 393.

86. Gerald Stourzh, *Benjamin Franklin and Foreign Policy* (Chicago, 1954), pp. 7 ff.

deal in his neither wholly pessimistic nor wholly optimistic view of man. But he did not merely borrow this ancient idea and fit it into his whole image of man. In the first place, if man stood on one rung of the ladder, he could improve his lot by effort, self-discipline, mutual helpfulness, by developing his toolmaking gifts and his capacity for reason, and by learning from experience. Moreover, Franklin emphasized in far greater degree than did most European exponents of the Great Chain of Being the basic equality of man and man, and even man and woman, for he stood with Helvétius and Godwin rather than with Jefferson in holding that the female sex was no weaker than the male in reasoning ability. Thus in his discussion of human nature Franklin modified the Great Chain of Being concept with a meliorism related to social environment. American experience suggested that man could improve his condition and that of his fellows through social effort, even if he could not reach utopia.

With some exceptions the ideas of the Enlightenment with the greatest appeal to Americans were modified by and assimilated into the traditional heritage of thought about human nature. As a result, the human constitution was now seen to be endowed with a comfortable combination of sense, reason, morality, and capacity for improvement in the favoring American environment. The Great Chain of Being idea was overshadowed by the belief in the emancipation of everyone, save blacks, from the fixed authority of traditions and institutional restrictions. An enjoyable autonomy with fluid ends was thus not beyond reach. The evil in man could not be eradicated. The tragic flaw in human nature, however, need not, at least in America, bar man from making great strides toward the realization of his legitimate desires and potentialities. The new light of science, aiding and abetting man's natural gifts and abilities, could broaden not only his private but his social vision. What man could conceive, he might achieve, especially in a land where the endowments of nature and the presence of fewer burdens of the past gave him advantage over his fellows in the Old World.

The techniques for making headway in the journey needed to be explored, improved, and put to work in practical ways. To be sure, in the rapid changes in the old order a new sense of community, if not brotherhood, was necessary to answer man's affectional needs and endowments.[87] Despite honest doubts about self-interest, desire for

87. This idea has been thoughtfully probed by William Carey McWilliams in *The Idea of Fraternity in the United States* (Berkeley and Los Angeles, 1973), esp. pp. 171–84.

prestige, and lust for power, those most hospitable to the American Enlightenment cherished faith in the better potentialities of human nature. With one eye on yesterday's experience and the other on the hope of tomorrow, such Americans believed that the best aspirations of the past and the most inviting promises of the future might be realized within the limitations of human nature. The immediate task was that of restraining human lust for power and dominion over others for selfish ends by instituting an orderly system of governmental checks and balances that might insure the supremacy of the law over men.

4
Searching for Balance

Let it be remembered finally that it has ever been the pride the boast of America, that the rights she contended were the rights of human nature. . . . If . . . our governments should unfortunately be blotted out with the reverse of these cardinal and essential virtues, the great cause which we have engaged to vindicate, will be dishonored and betrayed: the last and fairest experiment in favor of the rights of human nature will be turned against them; and their patrons and friends exposed and insulted and silenced by the votaries of tyranny and usurpation.

JAMES MADISON, 1783

Take mankind in general, they are vicious. . . . One great error is that we suppose mankind more honest than they are. . . . Men will pursue their interest. It is as easy to change human nature as to oppose the strong current of selfish passions. A wise legislator will greatly divert the channels, and direct it, if possible, to the public good.

ALEXANDER HAMILTON, 1788

The adoption of the Constitution was a triumph of virtue and good sense, over the vices and follies of human nature.

DAVID RAMSAY, 1808

Inequality of Mind and Body are so established by God Almighty in his Constitution of Human Nature that no art or policy can ever plain them down to a level. . . . Human Reason and human conscience though I believe there are such things, are not a match, for human passions, human Imaginations, and human Enthusiasm.

JOHN ADAMS, 1813, 1816

THOUGH AT times Franklin and Jefferson questioned the cheery view of human nature that some enlightened thinkers celebrated, many contemporaries forthrightly underlined the dark side of man's constitution. Such men scorned any effort to enthrone reason and made much of the influence of passion and prejudice on conduct. They looked on environmental meliorism as utopian. Skepticism seemed to them a denial of deep-rooted emotional needs. In their eyes only chaos could result from any view of human nature that questioned the experience of the past, established institutions, whether religious or economic, and an elite leadership.

Many, though by no means all, who thus questioned the high estimate of human nature cast their lot with the Federalists. Not all Federalists, however, looked at human nature in the same way. Some gave at least lip service to the Unitarian emphasis on reason and the moral sense. Others often phrased their ideas in secular terms, citing Machiavelli and Mandeville more often than Calvin and Edwards. On the other hand, many, like the esteemed President Theodore Dwight of Yale, preached the need of supplementing a limited reason with biblical revelation in the interest of truth and social order. A good number of younger Federalists also supported evangelical Christianity. Both the older and the younger generations denounced democracy on the grounds of human shortcomings, the one with vitriolic rhetoric, the other with more circumspection. All agreed that some kind of an elite was necessitated by human nature.

These ideas influenced the discussion of the best ways of insuring the permanence and success of the republic that the Revolution had established. As Arthur O. Lovejoy has shown, in such discussions the idea of counterpoise played a major role.[1] This assumed with Newton that the Creator had arranged an order in the universe by balancing opposition forces. Just as the centrifugal and centripetal forces, by neutralizing each other, kept the planets in their proper orbits, so the principle of counterpoise, operating in human nature, harmonized conflicting motives and competing egotisms. If balance was not effected by natural means, as it often was, government might, through the exercise of restraint, bring about the desired harmony. Such reasoning by analogy informed the writings of Pascal, Hooker, Mandeville, Pope, and other intellectuals well known to the framers of the Constitution.

In the Constitutional Convention it was often assumed that the principle of counterpoise offered ways of balancing antagonistic interests in society and the related prejudices and emotions in human nature. When representatives of the smaller states expressed fear of domination by the larger ones if these had a greater representation in the Senate, Madison countered by pointing out that Massachusetts, Pennsylvania, and Virginia, differing in "custom, manner and religion" as well as in economic interest, could not by any stretch of the imagination succeed in combining against the smaller states.[2] If such a natural counterpoise did not exist, he advocated well-devised checks to keep in balance the competing interests of northern and southern states so that neither region could dominate the other.[3]

The authors of *The Federalist* (1787–88), John Jay, James Madison, and Alexander Hamilton, argued that the strength of the Constitution lay in its effective use of counterpoise.[4] If at times these essayists expressed varying views about human nature,[5] they saw eye to eye when

1. Arthur O. Lovejoy, *Reflections on Human Nature* (Baltimore, 1961), chap. 2.

2. Max Farrand, ed., *The Records of the Federal Convention of 1787*, rev. ed., 4 vols. (New Haven, 1937), 1:447–48.

3. Farrand, ed., *Records of the Federal Convention*, 1:456 ff.

4. Gottfried Dietsze, in *The Federalist: A Classic on Federalism and Freedom* (Baltimore, 1960), documents this point in detail.

5. On the eve of the Revolution, for example, Hamilton rejected Hobbes's image of man which he later, at least in part, favored. See "The Farmer Refuted" (February 23, 1775). On this occasion Hamilton expressed a cheery view of human capacities. His essay is in *The*

discussing the relation of counterpoise to man's conflicting endowments.[6] This took on the more importance because the essayists assumed that the passions or emotions dominated the much feebler endowments of reason, altruism, and the ability to rise above self-interest.[7]

Thus when anyone asked why government had been instituted at all, Hamilton replied that it was "because the passions of man will not conform to the dictates of reason and justice, without constraint."[8] In meeting the argument that in a loosely bound union the states could be trusted to settle disputes amicably, he insisted that this overlooked the fact that "men are ambitious, vindictive, and rapacious."[9] Madison, in upholding the need for balancing the departments of government, warned that "Ambition must be made to counteract ambition. . . . It may be a reflection on human nature, that such devices should be necessary to controul the abuses of government." But, alas, internal and external controls could be dispensed with only if angels sat in the seats of government.[10] In arguing for the eligibility of the president for reelection, Hamilton noted that a one-term limitation might tempt a chief magistrate to make the most of his opportunities for self-advancement: if he knew a second administration was possible, he would make his honor the prime consideration.[11]

The authors of *The Federalist* assigned a limited role to reason.[12] "As long," Madison wrote, "as the reason of man continues fallible . . . his self-love, his opinions and his passions will have a reciprocal influence on each other."[13] In discussing the danger of executive influence on Congress, Madison observed that "the reason of man, like man himself is timid and cautious, when left alone; and acquires firmness and confidence, in proportion to the number with which it is associated."[14] This,

Papers of Alexander Hamilton, ed. Harold C. Syratt and Jacob E. Cooke (New York, 1961–), 1:82, 86–87.

6. I am indebted to Benjamin F. Wright, "*The Federalist* on the Nature of Political Man," *Ethics* 61 (1959): 656–77; James P. Scanlan, "*The Federalist* and Human Nature," *Review of Politics* 21 (1959): 657–77; Alpheus T. Mason, "The Federalist—A Split Personality," *American Historical Review* 57 (1952): 625–43; Cecilia M. Kenyon, "Conceptions of Human Nature in American Political Thought" (Ph.D. diss., Radcliffe College, 1949), pp. 355 ff.; and Lovejoy, *Reflections on Human Nature*, chap. 2.

7. *The Federalist*, ed. Jacob E. Cooke (Middletown, Conn., 1961), pp. 29, 31, 58, 59, 94–99, 107, 173–74, 195, 212, 340, 342, 346, 349, 374, 378, 488, 499, 505, 506, 511, 529.

8. *The Federalist*, no. 15, p. 96.

9. *The Federalist*, no. 6, p. 28. See also no. 34, p. 212.

10. *The Federalist*, no. 55, p. 349.

11. *The Federalist*, no. 72, pp. 488–89.

12. *The Federalist*, no. 15, p. 96; no. 50, p. 346; no. 58, p. 396; no. 70, pp. 474–75.

13. *The Federalist*, no. 10, p. 58.

14. *The Federalist*, no. 59, p. 340.

he thought, justified a sizeable House of Representatives. Commenting on the need for a well-defined mode of submitting policies to the people for public judgment, Madison reminded his readers that otherwise "the *passions* . . . not *the reason*, of the public would sit in judgment," even though its reason ought to control and regulate government.[15] Hamilton, in subscribing to the Lockean principle that ideas were formed only in relation to sensation, concluded that this set limits to the capacity for abstract reasoning.[16] Being very much creatures of habit, and subject to passions and prejudices, men were thus even further limited in the ability to make reasonable judgments.[17] In refuting the idea that unrestricted taxation led to despotism, Hamilton claimed that in matters of moral and political knowledge "the obscurity is much oftener in the passions and prejudices of the reasoner than in the subject."[18] Worse, in yielding to bias, many did not give even such understanding as they had to fair play.

All this, however, was only one side of the matter. Despite the doctrinaire way in which the term *human nature* was often used in support of this or that part of the Constitution, Madison, at least, realized that very little was actually known about man's nature. "The faculties of the mind itself have never yet been distinguished and defined, with satisfactory precision, by all the efforts of the most acute and metaphysical Philosophers. Sense, perception, judgment, desire, volition, memory, imagination, are found to be separated by such delicate shades, and minute gradations, that their boundaries have eluded the most subtle investigations, and remain a pregnant source of an ingenious disquisition and controversy."[19]

Nevertheless, since the Constitution projected a republican government resting on the direct or indirect action of qualified voters, it was inexpedient to concede the complete dominance of passion and self-interest. In particular, exceptional men of wisdom, virtue, and a knowledge of government might, in a crisis, display "exemption from the pestilential influence of party animosities."[20] Hamilton conceded that the framers of the Constitution, while fallible, had on the whole shown that reason, not passion, could guide the ship.[21]

Nor did the essayists hold that human nature among those less gifted

15. *The Federalist*, no. 49, p. 343.
16. *The Federalist*, no. 27, p. 173.
17. *The Federalist*, no. 27, p. 173.
18. *The Federalist*, no. 31, p. 195.
19. *The Federalist*, no. 37, p. 235.
20. *The Federalist*, no. 37, p. 239.
21. *The Federalist*, no. 37, pp. 222–33. Martin Diamond has developed this point in a discriminating essay, "Democracy and *The Federalist*: A Reconsideration of the Founders' Intent," *American Political Science Review* 53 (1959): 67 ff.

or less wise was always degraded. Thus Hamilton declared that "the supposition of universal venality in human nature is little less an error in political reasoning than the supposition of universal rectitude. The institution of delegated powers implies that there is a portion of virtue and honor among mankind, which may be a reasonable foundation of confidence."[22] He thought that if one were disposed "to view human nature as it is, without either flattering its virtues or exaggerating its vices," the Senate could be counted on to resist executive encroachments on its integrity.[23]

Madison was no less outspoken. "As there is a degree of depravity in mankind which requires a certain degree of circumspection and distrust: So there are other qualities in human nature, which justify a certain portion of esteem and confidence." Or, again, "There is in every breast a sensibility to marks of honor, of favor, of esteem, and of confidence, which, apart from all considerations of interest, is some pledge for grateful and benevolent returns." The wrath that ingratitude inspired proved the energy and prevalence of the contrary sentiment.[24]

Whatever the limits of reason, it could be assumed that, called on to accept or reject the work of the Constitutional Convention, a large body of people would make their judgments either with respect to the general good or in response to "sentiment" or "moral feeling." Thus Madison spoke of the "manly spirit which actuates the people of America, a spirit which nourishes freedom, and in return is nourished by it."[25] It was as if America provided a rare moment in history when "the prejudices of the community" were on the side of wisdom. Further, "it is impossible for any man of pious reflection not to perceive in it, a finger of that Almighty hand which has been so frequently and signally extended to our relief in the critical stages of the revolution."[26]

The use made of this view of human nature was summed up in Madison's admonition, "You must first enable the government to controul the governed; and in the next place, oblige it to controul itself."[27] He repeated the point in writing that "the aim of every political Constitution is, or ought to be, first to obtain for rulers, men who possess most wisdom to discern, and most virtue to pursue the common good of the society; and in the next place, to take the most effectual precautions for keeping them virtuous, whilst they continue to hold their public trust."[28]

22. *The Federalist*, no. 76, pp. 513–14.
23. *The Federalist*, no. 76, p. 514.
24. *The Federalist*, no. 56, p. 378; no. 57, pp. 385–86.
25. *The Federalist*, no. 57, p. 387.
26. *The Federalist*, no. 37, p. 238.
27. *The Federalist*, no. 51, p. 349.
28. *The Federalist*, no. 57, p. 384.

James Scanlan has clarified the role of interest and motive in *The Federalist*'s picture of human nature.[29] In his view the weight given to interest and motivation elevated the discussion of human nature into "one of the most comprehensive treatments of political motivation in existence." In his reading of *The Federalist*, behavior stemmed from three kinds of motives—motives of passion (amicable in evoking affection and confidence, antagonistic in evoking envy and jealousy), motives of reason and virtue, and motives of interest. Motives of interest might either be for immediate advantage or be true interests, which objectively and in the long run were of much more importance. Often, though not always, true interests conflicted with immediate interests, whether related to individual well-being or to that of the agricultural, commercial, and financial classes or to the community or nation. Immediate and personal interest were related to possessions or potential possessions, whether of goods or of privileges and emblems of status.[30] Such considerations led Hamilton to observe that "in the main it will be found, that a power over a man's support is a power over his will."[31]

The essayists maintained that the specific provisions of the Constitution took into account the interplay and relative force of such motives in human nature. In Hamilton's words, "momentary passions and immediate interests have a more active and imperious controul over human conduct than general or remote considerations of policy, utility, or justice."[32] Further, antagonistic passions were in the main more influential than amicable passions, common interests, and motives of reason and virtue.[33] In view of individual differences, some men were more susceptible than others to the various kinds of motives and interests.[34]

The operation of these competing and variously weighted motives and interests figured in the arguments for and against a stronger Union, separation of powers, and checks and balances. In upholding those provisions in the Constitution that gave the central government a direct and immediate relation to all individual citizens. Hamilton claimed that it was a "known fact in human nature that its affections are commonly weak in proportion to the distance or diffusiveness of the

29. Scanlan, "*The Federalist* and Human Nature."
30. *The Federalist*, no. 10, p. 59.
31. *The Federalist*, no. 73, p. 493; no. 79, p. 531.
32. *The Federalist*, no. 6, p. 31. Hamilton put this in the form of a question, but his intent seems unmistakable.
33. *The Federalist*, no. 15, p. 96; no. 5, p. 24; no. 15, p. 94.
34. *The Federalist*, no. 10, p. 62; the delegation of government to chosen representatives "whose wisdom may best discern the true interest of their country, and whose patriotism and love of justice, will be least likely to sacrifice it to temporary or partial considerations." See also no. 24, p. 165; no. 57, p. 384; no. 58, p. 396; no. 72, p. 497; no. 75, p. 405.

object"—as in the case of a man's greater affection for his family than for his neighborhood, for his neighborhood than for the community or nation.[35] Likewise, the strength of an individual motive stemming from possessions was greater in proportion to the security in which the possession was held—an argument Hamilton used in supporting the provision for the independence and durability of the judicial office.[36] Further, the Constitution encouraged the selection for office of the relatively small number of men in whom the motives of reason and virtue were evident. The authors also appealed both to the motives activating the immediate behavior of the commercial, agricultural, and financial classes and to those related to long-term self-interest and to a consideration for the common good. In so doing, the Constitution opened the road to solutions of the political problems of the American people. In short, it would check the powers and opportunities of those who might act from motives provocative to conflict and to the oppression of others.

The use of motivation was further illustrated in Madison's famous tenth essay on the origin of factions in unequal individual endowments and the corresponding inequality of possessions and achievements.[37] By insuring a strong Union, separation of powers, checks and balances, all spelled out in detail, the Constitution promised to prevent any one faction, whether representing a minority or a majority, from imposing its will on others.

Thus *The Federalist* transcended its immediate purposes. It did this by explaining how a government, taking account of and balancing motives, could promote individual and collective well-being and happiness.

The Antifederalists,[38] as the foes of the Constitution were known, produced no document as rich and far-ranging as the essays of Madison, Hamilton, and Jay. Nevertheless the arguments of leading Antifederalists, for the most part men of substance and position, were by no

35. *The Federalist*, no. 17, p. 107.

36. *The Federalist*, no. 78, pp. 521 ff.

37. Madison also included, as factors promoting faction, religious convictions, loyalty to leaders, and the whimsical love of contention over frivolous matters. Nevertheless, as Roy Branson has shown in his essay "James Madison and the Scottish Enlightenment," (*Journal of the History of Ideas* 11 [1979]: 235–40), Madison synthesized Locke's rationalistic understanding of contractual majorities with the emphasis of the Scottish philosophers on a moral-historical view of reform-minded occupational, political, and commercial groups.

38. For varying interpretations and emphases see Jackson Turner Main, *The Antifederalists: Critics of the Constitution, 1781–1788* (Chapel Hill, 1961); and Cecilia M. Kenyon, "Men of Little Faith: The Antifederalists and the Nature of Representative Government," *William and Mary Quarterly*, 3d ser. 12 (1955): 3–43.

means shallow or without merit. These arguments appeared in pamphlets, pieces in the public press, and speeches in the state conventions.[39] While often admitting the need for improving the Confederation, they attacked the Constitution for allegedly projecting a national, centralized government that jeopardized both the rights of the states and the interests and hard-won liberties of the people. Though some Antifederalists favored democracy, a term used loosely and in different ways, most stressed the fear of tyranny, whether exercised by the representatives of the rich and powerful or by dominant geographical or economic interests, or even by a deluded majority. The prevention of tyranny could best be secured if the power vested in government rested in the states. Given these convictions, the Antifederalists insisted that the Constitution should have gone much further in separating the powers of the executive, legislative, and judicial branches, in extending and strengthening checks and balances, and in insuring, by a Bill of Rights, the liberties of individuals against the use of arbitrary power by the new government.[40]

These contentions rested on arguments from both experience and human nature. In emphasizing the lust for dominion and the predominance of self-interest in human behavior, most Antifederalists expressed a view of human nature no less bleak and uncomplimentary than that in *The Federalist*. It is of course possible that appeals to the same image of man to justify conflicting positions robbed the arguments from human nature of any real meaning. In view, however, of the frequency of such citations and of the context in which they appeared, it seems likely that so widely held a view of man's limitations was thought worth calling attention to in the pro and con arguments about the Constitution.

The Antifederalists were also calling attention to man's limitations when they objected to a centralized government and a dangerous allocation of power to Congress and the President. The one would be more powerful than Parliament, whose tyranny Americans had known

39. Two convenient collections of contemporary discussions are easily accessible, each with useful introductory essays: John D. Lewis, *Anti-Federalists versus Federalists* (San Francisco, 1961); and Cecilia M. Kenyon, *The Antifederalists* (Indianapolis, 1966). My citations are to Jonathan Elliott, ed., *The Debates in the Several State Conventions, on the Adoption of the Constitution . . .* , 5 vols. (Washington, D.C., 1854); Paul Leicester Ford, ed., *Pamphlets on the Constitution of the United States Published during Its Discussion by the People, 1787–88* (Brooklyn, N.Y., 1888); and *Essays on the Constitution of the United States Published during Its Discussion by the People, 1787–1788* (Brooklyn, N.Y., 1892).

40. The idea that the love of power is a natural endowment of man and one to be distrusted was, as Main has noted (*The Antifederalists*, pp. 8–9), familiar to Americans throughout much of the eighteenth century, in part because of the popularity of *Cato's Letters* (London, 1748) and of James Burgh's *Political Disquisitions*, 3 vols. (Philadelphia, 1775).

only too well, the other more powerful than most European kings. The federal judiciary, named by the executive and holding office indefinitely, would be apt to interpret such ambiguous terms as "general welfare" and "necessary and proper" in the interest of the President, at the expense of both the states and the interests and rights of citizens. Even worse, such concentration of power in the central government would need to be enforced by a standing army—a "nursery of vice"—over which the public had no direct control. Many other examples could be cited of ways in which specific provisions of the Constitution, as well as its general thrust, were linked with the argument from human nature.

Two Virginians, speaking in the state's ratifying convention, held that the weakness of human nature argued against the great power the Constitution put in the hands of Congress. Patrick Henry contended that "the depraved nature of man is well known. He has a natural bias toward his own interest, which will prevail over every consideration, unless it is checked."[41] Nothing, he went on, should be trusted to accident or chance. "Will not the members of Congress have the same passions which other rulers have had? They will not be superior to the frailties of human nature. However cautious you may be in the selection of your representatives, it will be dangerous to trust them with unbounded powers."[42] Henry's colleague George Mason insisted that it was nonsense to claim that the House of Representatives would consist of the "most virtuous men on the continent, and that in their hands we may trust our dearest rights." It would in fact be made up of some good, some bad men, and "considering the natural lust of power so inherent in man, I fear the thirst for power will prevail to oppress the people." Elsewhere Mason prophesied gloomily that the new government, beginning "in a moderate aristocracy," was likely to end either as a monarchy or "a corrupt and oppressive aristocracy."[43]

A no-less-striking example of Antifederalist distrust of human nature was expressed in a speech of Melanchton Smith, a substantial New York lawyer. He contended that since the Author of Nature bestowed on some greater capacities than on others, and that since talents, birth, education, and wealth created distinctions among men, there would always be an elite to command superior respect in every society. If government was so

41. Elliott, ed., *Debates*, 3:326.

42. *Debates*, 3:437.

43. *Debates*, 3:32; Ford, ed., *Pamphlets*, p. 332. See also the position of another prominent Virginian, Richard Henry Lee (Ford, ed., *Pamphlets*, pp. 281–85), who declared that every part of the Constitution shows "a tendency toward aristocracy." While deliberate and thinking men must establish and secure governments in free principles, Lee believed "the great body of our people to be virtuous and friendly to good government, to the protection of liberty and property."

constituted as to admit but few to the exercise of power, it would, according to "the natural course of things," be in their hands. It might thus become an instrument of oppression, inasmuch as "the few and the great" were no more free from passions and prejudices than other men. Substantial yeomen of sense and discernment would seldom be chosen to office, even though they might be less subject to temptation: they were used by habit and company to set bounds to their passions and appetites. The Constitution should have provided for the participation in government of this worthy class.[44]

Ignoring a leading point in *The Federalist*, John Lansing, a New York jurist, opposed ratification on the grounds that the framers had seemingly set aside all experience in considering Americans as exempt from "the common vices and frailties of human nature. . . . Scruples would be impertinent, arguments would be in vain, checks would be useless, if we were certain our rulers would be good men; but for the virtuous government is not instituted; its object is to restrain and punish vice; and all free constitutions are formed with two views—to deter the governed from crime, and the governors from tyranny."[45] This the new Constitution failed to do.

Leading Antifederalists in Massachusetts also objected to inadequate checks on the lust for power and on other weaknesses of mankind.[46] "It is vain," declared one member of the ratifying convention, "to say that rulers are not subject to passions and prejudices." In an essay "Observations on the New Constitution"[47] the writer, probably Mercy Otis Warren, criticized the infrequency of elections. "Man is not immediately corrupted, but power without limitation, or amenability, may endanger the brightest virtue—whereas a frequent return to the bar of their Constituents is the strongest check against the corruptions to which men are liable, either from the intrigues of others of more subtle genius or the propensities of their own hearts." Since "passion, prejudice, and error are characteristics of human nature," it was foolish to invest rulers with discretional power which might, or might not, be abused.[48]

44. Elliott, ed., *Debates*, 2:246. On another occasion Smith wrote that "it is natural to expect, that selfish motives will have too powerful an influence on men's minds, and that too often, they will shut the eyes of a people to their best and true interest." *An Address to the People of the State of New York . . . by a Plebeian* (1788), in Ford, ed., *Pamphlets*, pp. 105–6.

45. Elliott, ed., *Debates*, 2:295–96.

46. For an interesting example see Elliott, ed., *Debates*, 2:159.

47. *Debates*, 2:28.

48. Ford, ed., *Pamphlets*, pp. 8, 17. Ford attributed the authorship to Elbridge Gerry. See, however, James Warren, "Mercy Warren and the Ratification of the Federal Constitution in Massachusetts," *Proceedings of the Massachusetts Historical Society* 64 (1932): 143–64.

Objections in Massachusetts to the Constitution did not rest solely on distrust of rulers. An able writer in the *Massachusetts Gazette* (1788), using the pen name "Agrippa," held that the Constitution did not adequately protect individuals against majorities. "The experience of all mankind," so Agrippa claimed, "has proved the prevalence of a disposition to use power wantonly. It is therefore as necessary to defend an individual against the majority in a republick as against a king in a monarchy." The proposed Constitution, Agrippa insisted, fell short of this.[49]

In the years following the ratification of the Constitution, many of those who had criticized it or insisted on substantial changes opposed the Federalists' domestic program and handling of relations with other countries. In this opposition, the emerging Republicans downgraded or ignored the unflattering view of human nature that had been expressed in opposing the Constitution. It now seemed expedient to emphasize man's capacity for sound judgment and for self-government. Some went even further in underlining the capacity of the common man to transcend personal and class interests should these conflict with the common good, a highly unlikely situation, since the interest of the great majority was, after all, the interest of the public weal.

On their side, the Federalists, in attacking the Republicans, ignored the well-publicized views about human limitations that the Antifederalists had advanced in opposing the Constitution. Federalist spokesmen indiscriminately identified the whole Republican cause with the doctrinaire minority that proclaimed man's rationality, essential equality, and even perfectibility. Such false and pernicious ideas, the charge went, stemmed from Jacobin philosophers and from perpetrators of the most heinous crimes committed in the French Revolution in the name of liberty, fraternity, and equality.

Thus Fisher Ames wrote to Timothy Pickering—high Federalists both—that only fools could indulge in the nonsensical view that the people were angels, the rulers devils, that "man is a perfectible animal, and all governments . . . obstacles to his apotheosis."[50] To believe, as Jefferson did, in the good sense of the people and to hold that they could be governed and improved by reason was rank and mischievous folly.

49. Ford, ed., *Essays*, p. 117.
50. Fisher Ames to Timothy Pickering, November 5, 1799, cited by Norman Jacobsen in "Political Realism and the Age of Reason: The Anti-Rationalist Heritage in America," *The Review of Politics*, 15 (1953): 456.

Unless checked, Ames concluded, such dangerous views about human nature were bound to subvert property rights, order, deference to superiors, decency, and religion itself. Federalist ministers, Fourth of July orators, and newspaper writers used similar rhetoric. The Reverend Solomon Williams of Northampton assailed the deluded "theorists" for spreading the view that "human nature is capable here of what modern philosophers call perfectibility . . . that nearly all opinions are wrong; that our ancestors were, for the most part, fools or knaves; . . . that innovations are always preferable to long established usages and habits; that restraints are abusive; that order is hurtful; that subordination is foolish."[51]

In attacking the Republican opposition, the Federalists drew on a concept of man suited to the taut situation. A case in point was Robert Goodloe Harper, who had launched his political career in South Carolina by taking up the cause of the French Jacobins. Elected to Congress as a Republican, he became a high Federalist. The Alien and Sedition Acts, which he helped engineer, rested on the assumption that, human nature being what it was, controversies could sometimes be managed, not by persuasion in the free interplay of ideas and prejudices, but by the compulsive isolation of dangerous doctrines. The radical philosophers, Harper declared, were the pioneers of revolution, setting themselves the task of seducing "the visionary, the superficial, and the unthinking part of mankind." Such dangerous theoreticians assumed that man actually was what he ought to be. Thus they were blind to the fact that in the social interest the people must be kept in tether by the force of authority and law.[52]

Without being entirely inconsistent, Fisher Ames shifted gears after the defeat of the Federalists in 1800. His party, he said, had appealed too much to the reason of the people, too little to their emotions. In so doing it had assumed that men had more reason and more virtue than was actually the case. "The truth is, and let it humble our pride," he insisted, "the most ferocious of all animals, when his passions are aroused to fury and are uncontrolled, is man; and of all governments, the worst is that which never fails to excite, but was never found to restrain those passions, that is, democracy. It is an illuminated hell, that in the midst of remorse, horrour, and torture, rings with festivity; for experience shows,

---

51. Cited in Jacobsen, "Political Realism and the Age of Reason," p. 462.
52. John C. Miller, *Crisis in Freedom: The Alien and Sedition Acts* (Boston, 1951), p. 74. See also Harper's speech, "On the Motion to Continue in Force the Sedition Law, Delivered to the House of Representatives," January 1, 1801, in *Selected Works of Robert Goodloe Harper* (Baltimore, 1814), pp. 375–84.

that one joy remains to this most malignant description of the dammed, the power to make others wretched."[53]

Such appeals to human nature in support of a given position have been largely forgotten. Only the work of John Adams matched *The Federalist* in applying to government an analysis of the human character. His image of man, expressed in letters to Benjamin Rush,[54] John Taylor,[55] and Jefferson,[56] and more systematically in a *Defence of the Constitutions of Government in the United States* (1787)[57] and *Discourses on Davila* (1790–91),[58] reflected the books he read, particularly those by Machiavelli, Mandeville, Harrington, Adam Smith, Bolingbroke, and Adam Ferguson.[59] Like them, he believed that presupposition about man's nature influenced one's position on religion, politics, and economics. Thus Adams agreed with them on the importance of a correct understanding of human nature in all speculations about social relations and government.

Adams's heritage, his family relationships, and his somewhat secularized "Yankee" version of Puritanism also influenced his ideas about human nature. These were confirmed when he examined his own motives, anxieties, doubts, and conduct and when he observed, as he thought, empirically, the behavior of those with whom he was thrown.

Adams's commitment to empiricism and rational analysis did not

53. "The Dangers of American Liberty" (1805), in *Works of Fisher Ames*, ed. Seth Ames, 2 vols. (Boston, 1854; rept. ed., New York, 1969), 2:394.

54. John A. Schutz and Douglass Adair, eds., *The Spur of Fame: Dialogues of John Adams and Benjamin Rush, 1805–1813* (San Marino, Cal., 1966), pp. 54, 65–66, 68, 70–72, 74–75, 158, 222.

55. John Adams, *The Works of John Adams*, ed. Charles Francis Adams, 10 vols. (Boston, 1856), 6:447–521.

56. *The Adams-Jefferson Letters*, ed. Lester J. Cappon, 2 vols. (Chapel Hill, 1959), esp. chap. 2.

57. The *Defence* was written in reply to an attack of Turgot in a letter to Dr. Price. The first volume was reprinted in New York and Philadelphia in 1787. The treatise is included in Adams's *Works*, vols. 4, 5, and 6.

58. Adams, *Works*, 6:232–81. These "letters" consist of translations of Enrico Caterino Davila's *History of the Civil Wars of France* and "useful reflections," based largely on Adam Smith's chapter "The Origin of Ambition, and of the Distinction of Ranks" in his *Theory of Moral Sentiments* (London, 1759).

59. Correa M. Walsh discusses the intellectual influences on Adams in *The Political Science of John Adams* (New York, 1915), esp. pp. 40–41, 248. Adams's marginal comments on the writings of leading eighteenth-century philosophers provide additional understanding of his reactions to currents of thought of his time. These have been made available by Zoltan Haraszti in *John Adams and the Prophets of Progress* (Cambridge, Mass., 1952).

always keep his remarks about human nature from contradicting each other. This was the case, for example, in his ambiguous discussion of equality and inequality. A cause of such inconsistencies was, as Cecilia Kenyon has noted, his frequent failure to distinguish closely between human nature in its descriptive and in its normative sense. Then, too, he stubbornly, if unconsciously, stuck to his a priori assumptions even when his empirical observations pointed in another direction.[60]

John Adams believed that most men possessed an innate moral capacity for virtuous behavior as well as an inborn ability to think rationally. In his view, reason consisted of an ability "to find out the Truth," to shape environment to human needs, and to foresee the consequences of a given action.

But an inborn moral sense and capacity for reason were only a part of human nature. All men, being of common clay, were also born with certain drives, such as hunger and sex ("the first want of man is his dinner, and the second his girl"). Fighting, too, was an innate disposition. Moreover, Adams had no doubt that an anti-authoritarian desire for "liberty is interwoven in the soul of man." But, hunger and sex apart, none of man's endowments was so powerful as self-love. Its corollaries included lust for power and distinction or "honor." This explained jealousy, envy, ambition, emulation (the desire for appreciation and praise), and proneness to self-deceit or the ability to use reason to justify desires and passions. Though men never lived in a purely natural state, in precivilized societies these drives, passions, and emotions expressed themselves in unrestrained selfish and evil conduct.[61] It was certainly known by "the constitution of human nature, by the experience of the world" that laws would be violated if man's passions were not restrained.[62] Education and religion encouraged a willingness, in the interest of order, to obey the laws needed to keep the powerful from exploiting the weak and the weak from jeopardizing the rights of the strong. Thus, under proper direction and regulation, the human proclivity to ambition, achievement, and power might, as nature intended, stimulate men to work for worthy and socially useful goals.[63]

60. Kenyon, "Human Nature in American Political Thought," pp. 213 ff. For examples see Works, 4:307, 392–97, and 5:185, 232, 278–80, 451–52, 502–3.

61. Adams, Works, 3:427; 4:259, 407; 5:9–10, 39; 6:182, 243, 262, 417, 424, 484, 516; Adams-Jefferson Letters, vol. 2 (to Jefferson, July 9, 1813), p. 351; (to Jefferson, July 13, 1813), pp. 355–56; (to Jefferson, July 14, 1813), pp. 357–58; (to Jefferson, August 14, 1813), pp. 364–66; John Adams, The Diary and Autobiography of John Adams, ed. Lyman C. Butterfield, 4 vols. (Cambridge, Mass., 1961), 2:22, 54, 335.

62. Adams, Works, 6:64.

63. Works, 3:429, 435; 5:40, 488; 6:271–73, 297–98; 8:560; Adams, Diary and Autobiography, 1:133.

The chances for this had seemed to Adams fairly good in the 1770s, when in his recollection a relatively virtuous people had united in a struggle for republican institutions.

Adams admitted that "benevolence and genuine affections" existed in some measure in the human breast and further held that the moral sense was related to the fact that man was a religious animal.[64] Yet he increasingly came to feel that these endowments did not adequately check the selfish passions which, normally at least, held sway. By the 1780s the evidence of dissension, disorder, selfish materialism, and corruption seemed to have overcome a one-time American simplicity, virtue, and general concern for stability and the common interest.[65] His view of human nature as exemplified in both America and Europe became more pessimistic, a pessimism enhanced by his critical reaction to the French Revolution.

In the context of constitution-making on both state and federal levels, Adams explored the dimensions of equalitarianism. "I believe that none but Helvétius would affirm, that all children are born with equal genius."[66] This inequality, together with the dominance of self-love, convinced him that the moral sense did not include a desire for equality. "No lover of equality, at least since Adam's fall, ever existed in human nature, any otherwise than as a desire for bringing others down to our own level, which implies a desire of raising ourselves above them, or depressing them below us."[67] Thus Adams, like some Puritans and several philosophers in the Enlightenment, thought of original nature as fixed and changeless.

Being unequal at birth in intelligence and the moral sense, men on the whole fell into two classes. Like Bolingbroke and Dugald Stewart, Adams spoke of the great mass of "simplemen" on the one hand, and on the other, of a natural aristocracy having those "superiorities of influence in society which grew out of the constitution of human nature." This seemed to mean "the rich, the well-born, and the able," that is, those superior in intelligence, wisdom, virtue, and governing skill, qualities generally linked with family background and means. Adams

64. "A Defense of the Constitutions of Government," in Adams, *Works*, 6:57; "Discourses of Davila," in Adams, *Works*, 4:232; Haraszti, *John Adams and the Prophets of Progress*, p. 243.

65. This point is well made by John R. Howe, Jr., in his psychological analysis *The Changing Thought of John Adams* (Princeton, 1966), pp. 88 ff. See also Gordon Wood, *The Creation of the American Republic 1776–1787* (Chapel Hill, 1969), chap. 14, for contemporary criticisms of Adams's writing, and for Wood's contention that Adams failed to understand the new, essentially federalist (not nationalist) aspects of the rising constitutional trend.

66. Adams, *Works*, 6:452.

67. *Works*, 6:210.

distinguished between the natural and the artificial aristocracies: the latter he defined as "those inequalities of weight and superiorities of influence which are created and established by civil laws."[68] Not all its members handed on their gifts to their children. If the hereditary aristocracy of Europe was once a natural aristocracy, it had failed to transmit its own wisdom and virtue to its offspring.[69] It was certain, he felt, that government would always be dominated by an aristocracy, whether hereditary or natural. The great problem of statesmanship was to insure, as far as possible, good management by the natural aristocracy.

In upholding the propriety of rule by the natural aristocracy, Adams spared no words in denouncing democracy. "No democracy," he wrote, "ever did or can exist . . . no such passion as a love of democracy, stronger than self-love, or superior to the love of private interest, ever did, or ever can, prevail in the minds of the citizens in general or of a majority of them, or in any party or individual of them . . . the democracy of Montesquieu, and its principal virtue, equality, frugality, etc. . . . are all mere figments of the brain, and delusive imaginations."[70]

Adams did not clearly explain just how republican citizens could be counted on to choose members of the natural aristocracy as governors. Even so, safeguards were possible. He believed, with Polybius, Harrington, Montesquieu, and Bolingbroke, and the authors of *The Federalist*, that a mixed constitution of checks and balances promised to protect the governors against the selfish ambition and passions of the masses, and in turn to shield the common people against the temptations that even a natural aristocracy was subject to.[71]

Like most celebrants of an elite based on unchanging aspects of human nature, Adams did not attach very much importance to the role of environment in nourishing the traits credited to a natural aristocracy. His image of man set more store on the principle of counterpoise in the search for order, stability, and compromise between extremes. The new American constitutions, he felt, brought these ends at least within sight.[72]

68. *Works*, 6:451–53.
69. *Works*, 6:498 ff.
70. *Works*, 6:210 ff.
71. *Works*, 4:290. This seems, on the whole, to represent the considered view of Adams, though it is worth noting that according to Jefferson, he declared in 1793 that "men could never be governed but by force, that neither virtue, prudence, wisdom, nor anything else sufficed to restrain their passions." Adrienne Koch, *Jefferson and Madison, the Great Collaboration* (New York, 1950), pp. 138–39. Miss Koch noted that this memorandum of a conversation with Adams was not included in any edition of Jefferson's writings available in 1950.
72. David Spitz has noted similarities between the thought of Adams and other conservatives. *Patterns of Anti-Democratic Thought* (New York, 1949), pp. 193–94.

Meantime, in Philadelphia, James Wilson was trying to show in a somewhat different way how the conflicting aspects of human nature might be reconciled. This well-educated Scot, who had migrated to Pennsylvania in 1765, joined Madison in the Constitutional Convention in urging that federal laws act directly on individuals in order to encourage a needed sense of national citizenship. Wilson took a leading part in securing Pennsylvania's ratification of the Constitution. In 1789 Washington appointed him to the Supreme Court. In his teaching, juridical writing, and decisions, Wilson insisted that society required the supremacy of law for insuring both order and freedom. He found the root of this need and requirement in human nature.

In lectures given in 1790 and 1791 at the College of Pennsylvania, Wilson admitted that he could not offer an adequate exposition of human nature. Nevertheless he held that without a knowledge of man's constitution and disposition, it was impossible to understand him as the author and subject of law. In his view, too many who held forth on human nature mistakenly based their position on analogy and hypothesis rather than on observation, experience, accurate reflection, and the precise analysis of language. Too many held an oversimplified view of man as either altogether selfish or completely benevolent: actually human nature was far more complicated.[73] Still others pictured it "as in a state of hostility endless and uninterrupted, internal as well as external . . . at war with all the world" as well as with man himself.[74]

Wilson went on to say that man was made up of a body and a soul, the interrelations of which were not well understood: the soul possessed faculties, intellectual and moral, which should not be thought of as discrete and passive but as interrelated and active. Here he was on familiar ground, as he was in two other positions that called for consideration. One was that the senses, another component of human nature, were useful and pleasing ministers of the higher powers. The second was that "man . . . finds or makes a system of regulations, by which his various and important nature, in every period of his existence, and in every situation, in which he is placed, may be preserved, improved, and perfected." That is, without law and the order it assured, man's potentialities would be sunk in licentiousness and chaos. "The more ingenious and artful the two-legged animal, man, is, the more dangerous he would be to his equals: his ingenuity would be employed for the purposes of malice."[75] On the other hand, it was equally true that

73. James Wilson, *The Works of James Wilson*, ed. Robert Green McCloskey, 2 vols. (Cambridge, Mass., 1967), 1:197 ff.

74. Wilson, *Works*, 1:200.

75. *Works*, 1:204.

the inherent need for self-exploration and growth would be stymied in submission to arbitrary and unwarranted authority and oppression.[76]

Wilson found support for his views and for their implications in a wide range of authorities. As became a Scottish Presbyterian and a convert to Episcopalianism, he gave weight to revelation in Holy Scriptures. He treasured the ancient classics, especially Aristotle and Cicero, and the Roman jurists. Wilson also cherished what his biographer has called the Anglo-Scholastic tradition of structure and hierarchy in which natural law provided security against tyranny.[77] Blackstone, Pufendorf, and Grotius also contributed to his thinking. In his emphasis on man's potential for improvement and on happiness as an end of earthly life, Wilson was a true son of the Scottish Enlightenment.[78] Its philosophers, as we shall see, were to have a prolonged influence on American views of human nature.[79]

In the lectures given shortly before he joined the Supreme Court, Wilson developed his ideas on the relation between law and human nature. He put natural law in the foreground as the context within which common law was to be sifted to meet American needs and conditions.[80] These needs included the right of revolution as an ultimate means of securing man's natural rights to freedom and to an orderly security based on law and necessary for human happiness. Such freedom and security were, in Wilson's view, grounded in popular sovereignty and an equality of contractual rights and obligations. In turn, these rested on mutual trust and conscience operating in relatively democratic channels.

Wilson distinguished between divine law and human law. The first included that made by God for man in his existing state. It was communicated by reason and by conscience, "the divine monitors within us, and by the sacred oracles, the divine monitors without us."[81] Whether addressed to men or to nations, whether communicated by nature or by revelation, it was equally the source of all law.

76. *Works*, 1:97, 130, 204.

77. Wilson did not, however, think it necessary to include a Bill of Rights in the Constitution: he believed that national energy and checks and balances were a sufficient guarantee of civil liberties. David G. Smith, *The Convention and the Constitution: The Political Ideas of the Founding Fathers* (New York, 1965), pp. 79–80.

78. Charles Page Smith, *James Wilson, Founding Father, 1742–1789* (Chapel Hill, 1956), pp. 328 ff.

79. See pp. 130–33.

80. Morton White, in *Science and Sentiment in America* (New York, 1972), chap. 2, spells out the similarities and differences between Hume and Locke on the one hand and Wilson on the other.

81. Benjamin F. Wright, *American Interpretations of Natural Law* (Cambridge, Mass., 1931).

Wilson rejected the hypothesis that the sanction of human law rested on sheer strength and power or on the superior excellence of rulers. Who, after all, could rightfully be compelled to obey mere strength, and who could be sure of just how those recognized as having excellence might be disposed toward the ruled in specific instances?[82]

Here Wilson fell back on his conception of human nature. In the first place, "to be without law is not agreeable to our nature: because, if it were without law, we should find many of our talents and powers hanging upon us like useless incumbrances. Why should we be illuminated by reason, were we only made to obey the impulse of irrational instinct? Why should we have the power of deliberating, and of balancing our determinations, if we were made to yield implicitly and unavoidably to the influence of the first impressions? Of what service to us would reflection be, if, after reflecting, we were to be carried away irresistibly by the force of blind and impetuous appetites?"[83]

Wilson next turned to the diversity of sentiments on the meaning and cause of obligation to law. He did not doubt "that there is, in human nature, such a moral principle [that] has been acknowledged in all ages and nations." While in particular cases Holy Scripture contributed to the distinction between right and wrong, "the power of moral perception is, indeed, a most important part of our constitution. It is an original power—a power of its own kind; and totally distinct from the idea of utility and agreeableness" to which some philosophers had wrongly attributed it.[84]

That the innate moral sense was a reality seemed clear from the fact that "the inclination appears very early in children."[85] In the second place, "the universality of an opinion or sentiment may be evinced by the structure of languages." Being pictures of human thought, "all languages speak of a beautiful and a deformed, a right and a wrong, an agreeable and a disagreeable, a good and ill, in actions, affections and characters. All languages, therefore, suppose a moral sense, by which these qualities are perceived and distinguished."[86] Fortunately the moral sense was capable of culture and improvement by habit, and by frequent and extensive exercise, as the results of education testified.

In sum, "this moral sense, from its very nature, is intended to regulate and control all our other powers. It governs our passions as well as our actions." Without it "we should not be moral and accountable beings." We would be torn by a variety of senses and interfering desires.[87]

82. Wilson, *Works*, 1:124.
83. *Works*, 1:127.
84. *Works*, 1:130.
85. *Works*, 1:132–33.
86. *Works*, 1:132–33.
87. *Works*, 1:135.

Like other enlightened thinkers, Wilson held that reason, in assessing the operations of the moral sense, often strengthened and extended its influence. It also served "to illustrate, to prove, to extend, and to apply what our moral sense had already suggested to us." Nevertheless, reason, even without experience, was "too often overpowered by passion; to restrain whose impetuosity, nothing less is requisite than the vigorous and commanding principle of duty."[88]

Wilson admitted that some able philosophers held that training and expediency explained the moral sense, that it differed in various ages and lands, and that the obvious lack of it among savages proved that it was the mere product of civilization. He insisted, nevertheless, that even the most uninformed savages manifested "common notions and practical principles of virtue." Nor was he impressed by the argument of Epicurus and some moderns who formed their estimate of human nature from "its meanest and most degrading exhibitions." In effect they failed to distinguish between man and man and between man and beast.[89]

From the obvious inequality of men in reason, the moral sense, talents, capacities, virtues, tastes, and achievements, Wilson drew three con-clusions.[90] First, the management of public affairs should be entrusted by popular choice to the "wisest and best" of the citizens. Next, however unequal men were in native reason and moral sense, they were all by nature equal in rights before the law. They were equal, too, in their obligations not to harm the innocent and to put trust in the good will of their fellows to keep contractual obligations incorporated in laws to which common consent had been given. Third, if few had adequate reasoning ability or the means of cultivating it, then it became all the more important that the common sense of every humble son of toil be recognized as indispensable in making and accepting decisions for the general good. This conclusion supported Wilson's conviction that sovereignty was vested in the people.[91]

Finally, man's makeup required social intercourse. "Human nature is so constituted, as to be incapable of solitary satisfactions."[92] Moreover, "of one blood all nations are made: from one source the whole human race was sprung."[93] This, together with the fact of individual differences and talents, implied "natural services and sympathetic pleasures." Frail and imperfect, man, in his own interest, had to take satisfaction from

88. *Works*, 1:136.
89. *Works*, 1:137–39.
90. *Works*, 1:139–40.
91. *Works*, 1:240.
92. *Works*, 1:241–43.
93. *Works*, 1:237. This idea was commonly held at this time. It was, for example, pivotal in the thought of Nathaniel Chipmen, a federal judge in Vermont. See his *Sketches of the Principles of Government* (Rutland, Vt., 1793).

acts of beneficence, since these added up to the good of the whole. In other words, man's constitution was such that in seeking his own advantages in his search for happiness, he was, as a social being, expressing his affections for human kind.[94]

Wilson did not live to see the development of an American jurisprudence, though the idea that this must be linked to a theory of human nature did not die.[95] Despite his many contributions to his adopted country, he was distrusted by the Democratic Republicans and never fully appreciated by the Federalists with whom he worked. To later Americans he was lost in obscurity. Robert McCloskey has suggested that his ambition for status, wealth, and reputation, his tendency to compromise, and his associations with the rich and the powerful blurred his contributions to political democracy. His reckless speculations led to bankruptcy, imprisonment for debt, and tragedy. Yet Wilson, more than any other Founding Father, conceptually anticipated the main current of American development in assuming the basis in human nature for a natural partnership between popular sovereignty, national power, and the rule of law. In effect he cut through the competing Federalist and Antifederalist ideologies of the time by offering a synthesis which in large part the future was to realize.[96]

Meantime, able jurists buttressed their views about law, power, and property by implied or explicit reference to a view of human nature. In his *Commentaries on American Law*, Chancellor James Kent of New York declared that "the sense of property is graciously implanted in the human breast, for the purpose of rousing us from sloth, and stimulating us to action; and so long as the right of acquisition is exercised in conformity to the social relations, and the moral obligations which spring from them, it ought to be sacredly protected." So keen was the appetite for property, and so impressive its blessings, that the passion to acquire it was "incessantly busy and active." Thus a state of equality in property was out of the question: "It is against the laws of our nature; and if it could be reduced to practice, it would place the human race in a state of tasteless enjoyment and stupid inactivity, which would degrade the mind, and destroy the happiness of social life."[97] Joseph Story, an even

94. Wilson, *Works*, 1:240.
95. *Works*, 1:234–38.
96. *Works*, introduction, pp. 6–7, 16, 48.
97. James Kent, *Commentaries on American Law*, 4 vols. (New York, 1825–30), vol. 2, pt. 5, lecture no. 34, pp. 257 ff., 265–66. Kent also believed that education of the masses would only "enlarge their capacity for mischief and add a fresh stimulus to delinquents and

more influential jurist, shared Kent's ideas about human nature and property as well as his distrust of democracy.[98]

For Story's great associate on the Supreme Court, Chief Justice Marshall, the dominant trait of human nature was self-interest—the wish to act according to one's will, to be secure, and to enjoy the liberty necessary for adding to one's possessions.[99] Determined by reason and emotion, self-interest often led men to take advantage of their fellows. Hence the need for national defense. Marshall challenged Patrick Henry's claim that there was no need for standing armies. "Look at history, which has been so often quoted. Look at the great volume of human nature. They will foretell you that a defenseless country cannot be secure. The passions of men stimulate them to avail themselves of the weakness of others."[100] Since self-interest was the main factor in conduct, "those who know human nature, black as it is, must know that mankind are too well attached to their interest" to risk any threat to it.[101]

To be sure, in Marshall's eyes self-interest was not the only aspect of human nature that influenced conduct. Prejudice occasionally overruled self-interest, as, for example, when Virginia forbade intermarriage between whites and Indians.[102] "Enthusiasms," whether religious, patriotic, or egalitarian,[103] also led men to disregard their own interests.[104]

Since it remained to be proved whether government and law could

---

to novelties, to change and revolution and contempt for ordinary restraints of law, morality and religion." John T. Horton, *James Kent: A Study in Conservatism* (New York, 1939), p. 321.

98. *The Miscellaneous Writings of Joseph Story*, ed. William W. Story (Boston, 1852; rept. ed., New York, 1972), pp. 183, 527–35, 657. As a Unitarian, Story repudiated the doctrine of total depravity and insisted that "no man is in another's way," since by God's law there was no collision between the various interests of men. William W. Story, *Life and Letters of Joseph Story*, 2 vols. (Boston, 1851), 1:409. For Story's defense of property rights see James McClellan, *Joseph Story and the American Constitution* (Norman, Okla., 1971), pp. 194 ff.

99. Robert K. Faulkner, *The Jurisprudence of John Marshall* (Princeton, 1963), p. 8.

100. John Marshall, *The Political and Economic Doctrines of John Marshall*, ed. John E. Oster (New York, 1914), p. 258.

101. Marshall, *Political and Economic Doctrines*, p. 277.

102. Marshall to James Monroe, November 7, 1834, in *Political and Economic Doctrines*, p. 58.

103. In a letter to Charles Cotesworth Pinckney, November 21, 1802 (*William and Mary Quarterly*, 3d. ser. 12 [1955]: 646), Marshall wrote: "This new doctrine of the perfectibility of man . . . begins to exhibit him I think as an animal much less respectable than he has hitherto been thought." On the fluctuating sentiment of patriotism see John Marshall, *The Life of George Washington*, 5 vols. (Philadelphia, 1807), 2:220.

104. John Marshall, *A History of the Colonies planted by the English on the continent of North America . . .* (Philadelphia, 1824), pp. 419–20; *Life of George Washington*, 1:104–5.

effectively check self-interest, Marshall expressed deep pessimism about the future. Even before the defeat of the Federalists in 1800 he questioned the human capacity for self-government: ". . . with many men the judgment is completely controlled by the passions."[105] On another occasion his despair went even deeper: "Seriously, there appears to me every day to be more folly, envy, malice, and damned rascality in the world than there was the day before; and I do verily begin to think that plain, downright honesty and unintriguing integrity will be kicked out of doors."[106]

Yet men did have some inclination toward peaceableness, humanity, and toleration. Admittedly, in case of conflict these values for the most part gave way to self-interest. Even so, the picture was not altogether hopeless. If guided by habits of industry, division of labor, and technological enterprise and if operative within the limits of law, self-interest might, by increasing wealth and power, benefit all citizens. Moreover, man need not rely solely on reason, fallible as it so often was. The human being, endowed with a troublesome conscience, could find happiness, less in the abodes of palace and cottage than in turning "his thoughts frequently to an omnipotent and all perfect being," on whom he depended and to whom he was "infinitely obligated."[107] Hardly less important was the fact that "the more excellent citizens," that is, "the thinking part," those graced with virtue, could and did rise above their own interests. Marshall's great hero, George Washington, was the most notable but by no means the only example. By and large, a judiciary free from the pressure of having to bow to popular passions could also transcend personal interest in deciding what the law was and how it applied in given situations.

In his Court opinions Marshall not only relied on the great jurists and *The Federalist* as guides in the reasoning process but also invoked the law of nature which influenced the Anglo-American search for justice. The Creator of all things, Marshall wrote, had endowed man with "principles of abstract justice." These regulated, in great degree, both the rights of civilized nations and the actions of the American government in particular cases.[108] Although he did not refer explicitly to the Scottish philosophers, Marshall believed that common sense was also an

---

105. Marshall to General James Wilkinson, January 5, 1787, in *Political and Economic Doctrines*, p. 90; Marshall to Mr. Justice Story, July 13, 1821, in *Political and Economic Doctrines*, p. 113.

106. Marshall to Judge Archibald Stuart, undated, in *Political and Economic Doctrines*, p. 64.

107. Marshall to his grandson, November 7, 1834, in *Political and Economic Doctrines*, p. 57.

108. Johnson and Graham's *Lessee* v. *William M'Intosh*, 3 Wheat. (U.S.), 543, 572 (1823).

important guide. Thus men whose intentions required no concealment generally used words that most aptly expressed the ideas they meant to convey. And thus the framers of the Constitution and the people who adopted it must be understood to have used words in their natural sense. "If, from the imperfections of human language, there should be serious doubts respecting the extent of any given power, it is a well settled rule that the objects for which it was given, especially when those objects are expressed in the instrument itself, should have great influence in the construction."[109] In a similar appeal to an innate universal common sense Marshall argued in the Dartmouth College case that every man found in his own bosom strong evidence of a donor's desire to have his gift to charity flow immutably and forever in the channel marked for it. Surely the framers of the Constitution were no strangers to such a sentiment. Hence they felt the need to give permanence and security to contracts by withdrawing them from the push and pull of legislative bodies.[110] Thus Marshall's image of man buttressed interpretations of the Constitution that modified and extended traditional views of human nature in the interest of balancing order with development.

The ideas about man drawn on during the conflicts over the Constitution and later over its meaning, provided a main strand in the emerging widely accepted views about human nature in the half century ahead. Such a philosophy was needed to defend the classical-Christian values, doctrines, and morals that had come under attack in the Enlightenment. Two interpretations of the widely proclaimed psychology of Locke seemed markedly subversive. Bishop Berkeley contended that the only realities existed as ideas in the mind, since there was no assurance of the reality of anything else. On the other hand Hume argued that if, as Locke said, the sensations provided the first and prime source of knowledge, there could be no assurance that the images of them in the mind were reliable. Relativism or skepticism was thus the only tenable position. If this was true, what happened to Christian doctrine?

Such eighteenth-century English masterpieces as Bishop Joseph Butler's *Analogy of Religion* (1736) and William Paley's *Evidences of Christianity* (1794) vindicated religious truths by analogistic and utilitarian reasoning. Now, however, new empirical challenges to religious orthodoxy required a more comprehensive, hard-hitting defense based on indisputable empirical authority. The upsetting anxieties bred by the French Revolution and its American repercussions,

109. *Gibbons* v. *Ogden*, 9 Wheat. (U.S.), 1, 188–89 (1824).
110. *Dartmouth College* v. *Woodward*, 4 Wheat. (U.S.), 518 (1819).

together with backsliding from the bursts of religious enthusiasm, and with heightened worldliness, seemed to threaten the influence of the clergy if not Christian faith itself. The apprehensive orthodox felt that no matter what empiricism might bring to light, the validity of the eternal verities must be somehow insured.

At the same time, the speed of economic growth, the disrupting effects on older areas of the westward movement and incoming immigrants from Europe, the welcome if disjunctive impact of the new technology, and the beginnings of divisive Jacksonian democracy also called for a fresh view of human nature. It needed to be more cheery than that of high Calvinism or the low estimate of human ability that skepticism and materialism often implied. The new way of looking at man's makeup and functioning also needed to be one that minimized conflicts between the old and the new and promised balance, order, and indisputable proof of the true and the false.

The common sense or realistic philosophy, a leading aspect of the Scottish Enlightenment, seemed to meet these needs.[111] While its exponents differed on several points, as in the emphasis given to reason and benevolence in moral judgments, they all held that their philosophy refuted the "false" idealism that Berkeley and the skepticism that Hume derived from Locke's empiricism.

The Scottish writers were read in America not only by intellectuals in public life, including Jefferson, John Adams, James Wilson, and John Marshall, but by professors and students as well. The most-favored writers were Francis Hutcheson, Thomas Reid and his pupil Dugald Stewart, a friend of Jefferson, and to a lesser extent the more controversial Dr. Thomas Brown. Hutcheson agreed with Locke in rejecting innate ideas, but insisted that people were born with capacities for moral and esthetic judgments spontaneously rooted in the emotions and free from selfish considerations. Such a gift, and the proper use of it, rather than hedonism, as the sensational philosophy implied, was the key to happiness. In his *Inquiry into the Human Mind: Principles of Common Sense* (1764), Reid accepted the empirical and rational approach in epistemology. Every discovery, so often looked on as the result of reason alone, rested on the active cooperation of all the faculties. The mechanical ones, like knee jerks, acted automatically. Ranking above these in the hierarchy were the animal impulses—the appetites, desires,

111. Gladys Bryson's still-useful *Man and Society: The Scottish Inquiry of the Eighteenth Century* (Princeton, 1945) can be supplemented by S. A. Grave, *The Scottish Philosophy of Common Sense* (Oxford, 1960); Louis Schneider, ed., *The Scottish Philosophers on Human Nature and Society* (Chicago, 1967), with introductory essay; and Douglas Sloan's *The Scottish Enlightenment and the American College Ideal* (New York, 1971), chaps. 1–3.

and affections. In some part these were subject to will. The rational powers stood first in rank. These included prudence and conscience, or the moral sense, the true queen. Inborn in all human beings, it revealed as axioms truthful propositions that, being a very part of man's constitutional essence, "make up what is called *the common sense of mankind.*"[112] Even more than language, reason, memory, and foresight, it differentiated man from all other creatures. The moral sense affirmed the reliability of Scripture, long since demonstrated by natural religion, with the self-evident axiom that "the interests of truth and virtue can never be found in opposition." In short, since the perceptions of phenomena and activities were valid and since the moral sense was the most distinctive part of human nature, absolute, objective truth was accessible. Reid would have been on more solid ground had he defined his key words, for his critics pointed out that common sense itself meant different things. Nor did he always scrutinize his axioms with enough critical insight.

Notwithstanding limitations, the Scottish philosophy appealed to a great many Americans of varying views. It offered a way of rejecting, on empirical grounds, the "errors" of "enlightened" radicals who fostered deism, materialism, the relativism of truth and knowledge, and human perfectibility: all of these were held to be meaningless to "common sense" perceptions. At the same time, the Scottish philosophy lifted the reputation of human nature by affirming man's ability to achieve valid, objective truth by empirical, intuitive, and rational methods. To those of whatsoever denomination who sought to preserve Christian faith and morals, it was highly useful and important. It opened the road to new knowledge when empirically or critically demonstrated without surrendering the eternal truths revealed by the moral sense through conscience. These endowments allegedly afforded individuals and thus society the opportunity to act with conscience as the guide and in accord with universal moral law, the certainty of which could no longer be questioned.[113] The new philosophy also had a democratic attraction, since it rested on everybody's common perceptions and presented no great metaphysical difficulties to the non-expert. It further appealed to Americans because of its possibilities for concrete everyday application, which proved to be even greater than the Scots themselves had shown— applications in mutually responsible relations between members of the family and community, between men in trade and finance, and between governors and governed. In doing all this, the Scottish common sense

112. Thomas Reid, *Inquiry into the Human Mind*, ed., with an introduction, by Timothy Duggan (Chicago, 1970), p. 268.
113. Reid, *Inquiry*, pp. 268 ff.

"realism" has rightly been thought of as the protean forerunner of the later specialized social sciences.

No one did so much in introducing the Scottish position to America as John Witherspoon, an orthodox Presbyterian professor of moral philosophy at Glasgow. He came to America as President of the College of New Jersey in 1768.[114] A moderate Calvinist, he recognized man's limitations, as his remark on the controversy over Independence showed: "What we have to fear and what you have to grapple with, is the ignorance, prejudice, particularly the injustice of human nature."[115] To the young men in his classes who would presently champion independence and the adoption of the Constitution, Witherspoon began his lectures by saying that knowledge of human nature as the work of God was hard to come by either because it was "perplexed or difficult in itself or because it was made so. . . . The truth is, the immaterial system," he warned in speaking of Berkeley, "is a wild and ridiculous attempt to unsettle the principle of common sense by metaphysical reasoning."[116] After dealing with the reality of perceptions as truths derived from the moral sense, Witherspoon spoke on the everyday uses of his theories. He verified the truth of the conventional Christian faith and doctrines, middle-class values, the responsibilities of husbands, wives, children, masters, and servants to each other and to public officials, the duties of elected representatives, and the rights of property. He made much of the need in an untried republic for a widespread knowledge of the moral sense in human nature and its application in conduct. In sum, in his teaching, writing, and patriotic services to the new nation, Witherspoon affirmed the empirical validity of high moral principles and the possibility of generally good behavior. In boldly asserting the independence of moral philosophy and conduct from theology, he gave powerful support to the idea that if the Bible was true, then no advance in knowledge could undermine its moral precepts.

The spread and prevalence of the common sense philosophy was a fascinating story. Witherspoon's successors at Princeton carried it on, while his students and theirs taught similar courses at the newer colleges in the South and West. Textbooks on moral philosophy, sometimes by well-known educators and sometimes by the local professors themselves

114. James P. Butterfield, ed., *John Witherspoon Comes to America: A Documentary Account Based Largely on New Material* (Princeton, 1953); and Sloan, *The Scottish Enlightenment*, chap. 4.

115. *The Miscellaneous Works of the Rev. John Witherspoon* (Philadelphia, 1803), p. 206.

116. The Rev. John Witherspoon, *Lectures on Moral Philosophy*, ed., with notes, by V. L. Collins (Princeton, 1912), p. 5. The first edition appeared in his *Works*, published in Philadelphia in 1800 four years after his death.

who gave the instruction, became the capstone of the curriculum.[117] The common sense philosophy was also influential at such orthodox seats as Andover Theological Seminary. At the Yale Divinity School Nathaniel William Taylor, one of the most eminent and influential theologians of the mid-century, stressed the evangelical need of a "common-sense philosophy such as all the world can understand if we would defend orthodox theology" against Unitarians and ironclad "Consistent Calvinists." The position he developed adroitly exempted God from all responsibility for man's sin and freed human beings from the binding "doctrine of necessity." The sovereignty of God, he argued, made room for free agency through the faculties of understanding, conscience, and will, "those powers, capacities, or qualities of the soul of man by which he is enabled to see the difference between good and evil. Give these faculties to the stones of the street and they become at once a free agent; take them from angels and their accountability ceases."[118] The path his theology cleared, in which revivalism was also useful, helped make it possible for such a younger man as Horace Bushnell to move still further toward "progressive orthodoxy" and thus guide the Congregational churches into the modern age. We shall see that Bushnell's emphasis on Christian nurture in home and community, while by no means as new as many have supposed, was a foundation stone in modern religious education and can be appropriately discussed in relation to the revivalism for which it was in part a substitute.[119]

In a way it seems surprising that a philosophy so useful in vindicating and thus making more widely acceptable the truths of orthodoxy proved no less helpful to Unitarianism and liberal religion. Unitarianism's

117. The role and importance of these professors and textbooks have been documented by George P. Schmidt, *The Old Time College President* (New York, 1930); Wilson Smith, *Professors and Public Ethics* (Ithaca, 1956); Daniel Walker Howe, *The Unitarian Conscience: Harvard Moral Philosophy, 1805–1861* (Cambridge, Mass., 1970); and D. H. Meyer, *The Instructed Conscience: The Shaping of the American National Ethic* (Philadelphia, 1972).

118. Sidney E. Mead, *Nathaniel William Taylor, 1786–1858: A Connecticut Liberal* (Chicago, 1942), 3:63–65, 124 ff. At the Yale Divinity School Taylor taught a course "steeped in Scottish thought." Terrence Martin, *The Instructed Vision: Scottish Common Sense Philosophy and the Origins of American Fiction* (Bloomington, Ind., 1961), p. 20; Sydney Ahlstrom, "The Scottish Philosophy and American Theology," *Church History* 24 (1955): 267. See, for Taylor, his *Lectures on the Moral Government of God*, 2 vols. (New York, 1859), vol. 1, chap. 13, and vol. 2, chap. 7; and H. Shelton Smith's *Changing Conceptions of Original Sin* (New York, 1955), chap. 5.

119. See p. 177. Philip Greven, in his richly documented *The Protestant Temperament* (New York, 1977), has shown that the child-rearing methods of "moderates" were in many ways like those later published by Bushnell.

formal beginnings in the early nineteenth century have been traced to the growth in the previous fifty years of the Arminian doctrine of man's free ability to take an active part in his own conversion, and to the erosion under various influences of belief in an angry and capricious deity. The Socinian denial of the Trinity, for which Unitarians found authority in neither natural religion nor Scripture, crept in more slowly. So did the view of the half-divine, half-human character of Jesus, which was taken to prove the possibility of human perfection or at least an approach to the divine. With the naming in 1805 of Henry Ware, Sr., as Hollis Professor of Divinity at Harvard, "the Unitarian Controversy" was under way. Another turning point came with the great sermons of William Ellery Channing in the 1820s. The congregations that chose Unitarianism consisted chiefly of the New England mercantile class and its allies at Harvard. Influential professors of theology, logic, rhetoric, and moral philosophy, all of whom owed much to the Scottish common sense persuasion, made this philosophy central in the instruction of future ministers and of the community of business elite and its associates.

Unitarians demonstrated the existence of God not only by the rational proofs of natural religion, especially the argument from design and analogy, but also from the conviction of man's universal feeling for religion and consciousness of moral sense. In combining Puritan piety and religious affections of moral sense with empiricism, the Harvard Unitarians also brought into convergence such doctrines of the Enlightenment as the importance of reason, belief in man's better nature and capacity, and the doctrine of gradual social progress. At its main intellectual center and elsewhere, Unitarianism also reflected the intuitive impulse of the Cambridge Platonists and a belief in the importance of balance and order as the appropriate symmetry in conduct.

The moral philosophy figured in the teachings of such Harvard philosophers as James Walker, who later became a president of the University. Walker assumed that the consciousness of the spiritual faculties and capacities warranted regarding them "*as much objective fact as by the same ontological principle of the foundation of religion in the soul of man.*" Conscious awareness of the spiritual faculties, especially veneration, conscience, and the conception of perfection, implied man's duty for moral conduct and piety. Thus followed the acknowledged existence of the capacity of man for perfection.[120]

In the popular mind, William Ellery Channing, minister of the Federal Street Church in Boston and a great leader and preacher, represented Unitarianism far more meaningfully than did the Harvard professors. Channing made human nature one of the two main aspects of his

120. James Walker, "Foundations of Faith," *Christian Examiner* 8 (1835): 2–3.

message. Not only had men and women the capacity for coming to just ideas of God, but there was also "a foundation in our nature for feeling and loving, as well as discerning, his character." The heart of every man and woman had at some time or other been moved on hearing of "the pure exalted, disinterested goodness of an enlarged and vigorous mind employed in vast and noble designs." Therefore it was man's duty to esteem highly the nature God has given him—"his range of intellect, his powers of thought and action, his tenderness of feeling and sensitivity to what is right."[121] In spite of all doubts and scoffs, "human nature is still most dear to me. When I behold it manifested in its perfect proportions in Jesus Christ, I cannot but revere it as the true temple of the Divinity."[122] Though Channing's views on this theme and his aspiration for man's perfect union to the divine seemed to some Unitarians more mystical than rational, his defense of the dignity of human nature and of freedom of thought and expression cut a deep mark, as did his belief in salvation by character or continuing moral and spiritual growth. For Channing was convinced that human nature was no lawless tiger that had to be bound in chains. It was rather prejudice and a religion based on lack of confidence in human nature that oppressed men and thus made them "fit only for a yoke."[123]

In agreeing that history and experience testified to a widespread taint of selfishness and injustice in the race, Channing declared that "our whole social fabric needs thorough searching, complete reform."[124] This was certainly evident to sensitive Unitarians when they compared their view of human nature with life around them. Channing himself set an example, forthrightly supporting antislavery, women's rights, public education, the relief of the needy and handicapped, and the cause of world peace. Many others, influenced by Channing, either supported or led social reforms according to their image of what man could be. Charles Sumner and Samuel J. May became militant abolitionists. Samuel Gridley Howe pioneered in helping the blind. Dorothea Dix initiated single-handedly a crusade for the humane treatment of the indigent insane. Joseph Tuckerman broke new ground in his ministry to Boston's poor. Horace Mann became a leader in the movement for

121. William Ellery Channing, "The Principle of Religion in Human Nature," in *The Life of William Ellery Channing*, ed. William Henry Channing 2d ed. (Boston, 1887), p. 144.

122. William Ellery Channing, "The Virtues of Human Nature Revealed by Jesus Christ," in Channing, *William Ellery Channing*, p. 249. For similar statements see William Ellery Channing, *The Works of William Ellery Channing, D.D.* (Boston, 1886), pp. 12–13, 36, 48, 945–46.

123. Channing, *Works*, p. 66.

124. *Works*, p. 167.

publicly supported universal schools. Back of his unstinting labor in this cause was his conviction that social order and the success of self-government depended upon the training of the moral as well as the mental faculties of the whole people. He also felt that the gap between poverty and wealth could be narrowed as the disadvantaged obtained educational opportunities, and that social tensions would thus be relaxed. As both a Unitarian and a disciple of the Scottish phrenologist George Combe, Mann believed that every individual needed encouragement for self-effort in developing moral faculties, character, and conduct.[125]

Considering the fact that the Unitarians remained a small minority save in eastern Massachusetts, this was not a bad showing in social reform. Yet it fell short of Channing's goal when he called for a full commitment, since he confessed that he was acclaiming human nature not as it actually was but as it might become. Inasmuch as the Unitarians and evangelical churches subscribed to the common sense philosophy, the remarkable contribution of some of the evangelical churches to social reform must have rested on other factors. One such factor, of course, was the much greater emotional appeal of the churches that favored revivals, to be considered in a later examination of religious aspects of the stress on the primacy of the emotions in human nature.[126] The rational emphasis of Unitarians and the stress on salvation by character pitched their reform interest in a lower key than that of religious bodies preaching religion of the heart and often favoring efforts to hasten the millennium. Also, the Unitarians, largely well-to-do merchants and socially prominent as well as Whig in politics, were as a group critical of the more radical expressions of democracy and of the expansive and emotional tendencies of the time. In addition to a commitment to middle-class respectability and self-help, some felt a Burkean respect for continuity with the past and even an incipient organic view of society rather than a contractual one. Great emphasis on education, cultural improvement, literature, and the related arts seemed desirable expressions of the esthetic aspect of human nature, and useful in the interest of balance and order as well as truth and beauty.[127]

No one in the academic Scottish school of realism who sought to reenforce Christian doctrine with empirical axioms of common sense,

---

125. Merle Curti, *The Social Ideas of American Educators* (Paterson, N.J., 1959), chap. 3.

126. See pp. 176–77.

127. Howe, *The Unitarian Conscience*, chaps. 6 and 7.

order and progress, and equality and freedom could represent the whole group. Besides theoretical and denominational differences, the philosophers did not, in meeting concrete problems of everyday life, see eye to eye in interpreting the intuitive, axiomatic truths of moral law conveyed by individual conscience. Yet it may not be misleading to take as an illustration Francis Wayland,[128] son of a Baptist minister, who studied his Scottish philosophy at Union College before trying medicine and then settling on theological training at Andover. A Jeffersonian Democrat, Wayland became a Baptist minister in Boston, where unlike many of his denomination, he combined emotional fervor with rational values and learning. Majestic in presence, and to some, imperial in spirit, he is best known in American educational history as a celebrated teacher and successful president of Brown University from 1829 to 1857,[129] as the author of the most widely used textbook in moral philosophy (a sale of over 200,000 copies in a sixty-year stretch), and as an innovator. He advocated the elective system and more emphasis on the social and applied natural sciences, with the purpose of training laymen as well as clergymen and making Brown a model for the social usefulness of universities in growing industrial communities.[130]

Yet in helping formulate widely accepted views based on moral philosophy, Wayland also warrants a considerable place in a discussion of the history of human nature in American thought.

In *The Elements of Intellectual Philosophy* (1854), Wayland, with some sophistication, accepted faculty psychology and offered interesting insight into the faculties of imagination, taste, and abstraction. A confirmed dualist, he all but passed over the nervous system and dodged questions about the connection between mental and physical organization. He stressed temperamental distinctions between individuals as well as differences in mental ability: conceding the importance of training and education, he thought that native equipment accounted for the greatest differences.[131]

In moral philosophy Wayland acknowledged his indebtedness to Bishop Butler and downgraded Paley's philosophical utilitarianism.

128. The biographies, Francis Wayland, Jr. and H. L. Wayland, A *Memoir of the Life and Labors of Francis Wayland*, 2 vols. (New York, 1867), and James O. Murray, *Francis Wayland* (Boston, 1891), may be supplemented by the discussion in Joseph L. Blau, *Men and Movements in American Philosophy* (New York, 1952), pp. 82–92, and by the introduction to his edition of Wayland's *The Elements of Moral Science* (Cambridge, Mass., 1963).

129. Francis Wayland, *University Sermons*, 2d ed. (Boston, 1849), pp. 62, 96.

130. Francis Wayland, *Thoughts on the Present Collegiate System of the United States* (Providence, 1842).

131. Francis Wayland, *The Elements of Intellectual Philosophy* (Boston, 1835), pp. 13, 25, 218–31.

Professing to use inductive, deductive, and analogistic reasoning, he ingeniously contended that scientists of Christian faith were more likely than atheists to make advances in their fields.[132] His most important book, *The Elements of Moral Science* (1835), made no effort to conceal the influence of the Scottish common sense philosophy on his thinking. He believed, with it, that human nature comprised a moral quality related to God's moral law which men had mistakenly supposed could be violated without payment of consequences. Though God had designed man for virtue, Wayland was convinced that "there is in the heart of man a moral temper averse to the character of God; that he naturally strives to substitute a fiction of his own as the object of worship in the place of the true God; that, this having been done all safeguards of virtue are removed, man is given over to a reprobate mind, and becomes the willing slave of passions and sensuality."[133] Thus sin was not an accident to which part of mankind was exposed but a universal fact of human nature.

Having thus squarely faced the problem of evil, Wayland struck a more hopeful note. The chief purpose of education was to cultivate the moral sense toward righteous character and conduct, for which the basis was at hand in human nature. After all, God was the moral governor of the universe. Designed for happiness, man could achieve this only by obeying the moral law as an actuality, communicated to him by conscience, which corresponded to perceptions of objective reality.

In opposing philosophical utilitarianism, Wayland insisted that results must be judged by intentions, not by whether intentions succeeded in bringing happiness or by any other end. If intentions even resulted oppositely from what an individual had in mind, he was still blameless, just as he had no responsibility if evil intentions led to good. The problem this posed was illustrated by his position on slavery. Holding that the institution "violates the personal liberty of man as a physical, intellectual, and moral being,"[134] he also regarded it as unscriptural. In opposing the abolitionists, he insisted that no individual was responsible for the sins of the society he lived in; and that the slaveholder bore the burden of inheritance and could well be right in holding that the slave was not fit for freedom. In that case he should, of course, take steps to prepare the blacks for ultimate emancipation.[135] Such a position, which

132. Francis Wayland, "The Philosophy of Analogy," in Joseph L. Blau, ed., *American Philosophic Addresses 1700–1900* (New York, 1940), pp. 344–63. Without yielding any commitment to inductive empiricism Wayland tried to bring natural philosophy and teleology together.

133. Wayland, *University Sermons*, p. 62.

134. Wayland, *The Elements of Moral Science*, p. 188.

135. Francis Wayland, *Limitations of Human Responsibility* (Boston, 1838), pp. 85–86, 119–20; *Sermons Delivered in the Chapel of Brown University* (Boston, 1849), p. 282; and

informed all but the last edition of *The Elements of Moral Science*, offended southerners for regarding slavery as immoral and contrary to the Bible. It displeased radical antislavery men by offering what they regarded as a compromise with moral law and by indicating a deficient conscience. Wayland, in his concern for individual judgment and intention, denounced the tyranny of public opinion and even disparaged the voluntary societies organized to get all sorts of good things done besides the abolition of slavery: he felt that the individual's personality and responsible conscience were merged in a collective corporation.

Yet Wayland's conscience, responding to perceptions of changing realities more certainly within the moral law, opposed the Mexican War, supported Frémont's Free Soil movement in 1848, and even admired the courage and dedication of John Brown, whose use of violence alone he could not condone. As the Civil War neared, Wayland, who had long been a friend of peace, saw moral reality in fighting an evil he had always opposed.

On other public issues, which he discussed in *The Elements of Political Economy* as well as in *The Elements of Moral Science*, Wayland's use of the Scottish philosophy was evident in his contention that the wealth and happiness of a country would reflect the moral and intellectual level of its people. Though he patriotically implied the superiority of the American government, he knew that in the long run its well-being depended on its acting in accordance with the precepts of Jesus.[136] The explosive Dorr Rebellion of the prosuffrage party in Rhode Island against the elite government posed a dilemma, for he saw that citizens could not be expected to give allegiance to a government in whose affairs they had no voice. Yet his distaste for the use of violence, his respect for property and social order, and his fear that the upheaval might work against the continued growth of Rhode Island's boom industry led him, when the chips were down, to oppose methods of the reformers.[137]

Wayland's economic views reflected the British classical school and served as a defense of the northern producing and financial class.[138] Assuming man to be a free agent, he felt that charity, which discouraged incentive and undermined self-help, was more harmful than beneficial save in rare exceptions. He could, to be sure, break with the forces dominating the state and the university in opposing tariffs and

---

Edward H. Madden, *Civil Disobedience and Moral Law in Nineteenth-Century Philosophy* (Seattle, 1963), chap. 3.

136. Francis Wayland, *Elements of Political Economy* (Boston, 1837), pp. 131, 137, 186; Wayland and Wayland, *A Memoir*, 2:313.

137. Francis Wayland, *The Affairs of Rhode Island* (Providence, R.I., 1842), p. 28; Smith, *Professors and Public Ethics*, pp. 136–42.

138. Joseph Dorfman, *The Economic Mind in American Civilization, 1806–1865*, 2 vols. (New York, 1946), vol. 2, chap. 27.

probanking laws, and his humanitarian sentiments led him to favor a constructive reform of the penal institutions and the extension of educational opportunities as well as world peace. Still, on the whole, his sensitivity to the mischievous restlessness of human emotions made him feel the need of institutional as well as moral restraints, if law were to be sustained in the interest of middle-class values of piety, production, and progress. It is obvious that Wayland's view of human nature, insofar as his version of the common sense philosophy shaped it, was an ambiguous mentor. It made individual good intentions and the degree of individual morality the criterion and safeguard of both public and private freedom. The common sense philosophy was more successful in providing a rationale for the reconciliation of a modified Christian orthodoxy with empiricism, and social order with economic and social change. Wayland continued to recognize the dependence of science on religion: he could see no possible conflict between them. The more thoroughgoing scientific effort to study human nature that would dominate later in the century had to wait for the high tide of another protest against the Christian classical synthesis to lose its force. Yet in the discussion of human nature and religion, the common sense philosophy was an indispensable intermediate step that anticipated and prepared for the further accommodating liberalism of Horace Bushnell, Henry Ward Beecher, and Washington Gladden.

The esthetic principles of Scottish realism, particularly in reference to literature, carried great weight, just as they did in jurisprudence, psychology, and religion. Its principal rhetoricians and literary critics, Lord Kames, Hugh Blair, and Archibald Alison, agreed that the esthetic impulse was a faculty closely related to that of morality and thus found in the common experience of mankind. Yet none of the leading authorities on Scottish realism assumed that it existed in equal endowments in various individuals, even though, like other faculties, it was susceptible to cultivation. This implied that there would be an elite especially qualified and entrusted with the maintenance of standards, a position which in general owed much to neoclassical literary principles as well as to Scottish realism.

American professors of moral philosophy and specialists who subscribed to it taught rhetoric to many of America's future editors and writers, including Emerson, Thoreau, and Lowell.[139] Like their Scottish

139. William Charvat's *The Origins of American Critical Thought 1810–1835* (Philadelphia, 1936; rept. ed., New York, 1968) and Martin's *Scottish Common Sense Philosophy and the Origins of American Fiction* are well-documented and illuminating studies that make clear the great influence of the Scottish philosophy on American literary culture in the early national period.

mentors, the professors assumed that literary style and substance should reenforce morality and the reality of perceptions. Thus the basic principle in criticism was analysis rather than appreciation. Precision, order, the sense of reliability and security discouraged the free play of imagination and unrestrained emotions.

Besides the general influence of these precepts on American writers in the first decades of the nineteenth century, two aspects of the philosophy played a special role, one relatively short-lived, one lasting. Scottish literary criticism, while making some concessions to historical novels, took a dim view of fiction. Novels violated the principle of the validity of perceptions and were thus misleading in conjuring up imaginary and hence false plots and characters that violated the truths of human nature. Besides, most novels, trivial if not flashy, discouraged solid, informative, didactic reading and often led young people astray. More lasting was the influence of Alison's application of Hartley's principle of the association of ideas. Among other things, this encouraged writers to develop a truly national literature corresponding to the unique realities of American life. The Hartford Wits were only one of the better-known examples of writers reflecting the Scottish principles of literary form. Their message stressed Federalist nationalism and an affirmation of the importance of a continuing social order.

A rising generation of writers represented a transition from the emphasis on preserving the heritage of the Revolution within a frame of orderly development to a new emphasis on revolt and demand for drastic changes. This included a fresh look at human nature. Of these writers James Fenimore Cooper towered far above others in craftsmanship and originality.[140] Whether expressed in romantic novels or in controversial tracts on national character, Cooper's attitudes toward human nature and behavior reflected his heritage, his crusty individualism, sturdy patriotism, and patrician bias, as well as the rapid changes in American life. If he listened to the lectures on moral philosophy during his brief stay at Yale, they seem at most to have had a mixed effect.

Like his father, the proprietary squire of a border community in upstate New York, Cooper shared the Federalists' distrust and dark

---

140. I am indebted to James Grossman, *James Fenimore Cooper* (Stanford, Calif., 1949); Warren S. Walker, *James Fenimore Cooper: An Introduction and an Interpretation* (New York, 1962); Edwin Harrison Cady, *The Gentleman in America* (Syracuse, N.Y., 1949); Frank McDonald Collins, "The Religious and Ethical Ideas of James Fenimore Cooper" (Ph.D. diss., University of Wisconsin, 1953), pt. 3; Robert E. Spiller, *Fenimore Cooper, Critic of His Times* (New York, 1931); and John P. McWilliams, Jr., *Political Justice in a Republic: James Fenimore Cooper's America* (Berkeley and Los Angeles, 1972).

vision of a human nature that everywhere and always was wayward and frail. "We are all so selfish," Cooper had one of his heroes remark, "that it is hard to say how far even our most innocent longings are free from the trait of this feature of our nature."[141] Selfishness infused even what appeared to be the generous feeling of patriotism. "One of the strongest of all the weaknesses of our very weak human nature" was "the vulgar prejudice of national superiority."[142] With such an image of man, Cooper was convinced that society imperatively needed institutional checks and Christian restraint on man's weaknesses, greed, and yearning for power. It also needed recognition of distinction based on the unequal endowment of talent with the resulting disparity of manners, education, and wealth. In assessing the part played by heredity and environment, Cooper let one of his characters speak for him in declaring that gentility was in part "obtained from education, but far more from the inscrutable gifts of nature."[143] He shared the Federalists' enthusiasm for the stake-in-society theory which held that property was the foundation of moral independence and the means of improving the faculties. These two attributes distinguished civilized men from savages.[144]

In his early career Cooper applauded the Jeffersonian ideal of a constitutional republic based on equal political rights. He viewed a virtuous yeomanry as a natural aristocracy of merit, talent, common sense, and public service. To deprive an unknown number of "natural born gentlemen" of the associations and education necessary to develop their talents was to impoverish society.

Yet Cooper's sympathy with democratic republicanism tapered off, even though he saw in Andrew Jackson a representative of his nostalgic idealization of American government and society. He shrank from the pettiness and acrimony of party politics and partisan journalism and from the increasing vulgarity, pushiness, arrogance, and greed of the "middling" people, especially the rising commercial class. He scorned their demand for social equality with their betters, their way of making heroes of demagogues who manipulated them, and their acceptance of the tyranny of public opinion. No less dreadful was the decline of privacy and the freedom to choose associates of like breeding and taste. The point was, as Cooper saw it, that the least desirable predispositions

141. *Miles Wallingford* (1844), p. 116. In James Fenimore Cooper, *The Complete Works of James Fenimore Cooper*, Leatherstocking ed., 32 vols. (New York, 1892). All citations to Cooper's writings are to this edition, unless otherwise stated.

142. Cooper, *Miles Wallingford*, p. 235.

143. *Miles Wallingford*, p. 328, cited by Edwin H. Cady in *The Gentleman in America*, p. 124. See also Cooper, *Home as Found* (1838), p. 36, and *Satanstoe* (1845), p. 486.

144. James Fenimore Cooper, *The American Democrat*, ed. H. L. Mencken (New York, 1931), pp. 85–87, 132.

of human nature flourished with egalitarian democracy. He turned against the humble farmers once so dear to him, when, in his view, they undermined moral choice by using violence to protect their interests in the antirent war. He slowly came to realize the difficulty, if not the impossibility, of reconciling equality of political rights with equality of condition.[145] After all, the root of the problem was man's limitations: "However repugnant it may be to the pride of human nature . . . the greatest sources of apprehension of future evil to the people of this country are to be looked for in the abuses which have their origin in the infirmities and characteristics of human nature. In a word, the people have great cause to distrust themselves."[146] Thus in his last years Cooper frankly encouraged institutional and religious restraints on democratic tendencies.

Some code of behavior, Cooper believed, was necessary to keep in tow man's anarchistic lawlessness, whether he lived in civilized society or in a savage state of nature. Thus the codes of the Indians, varying greatly from tribe to tribe, emphasized freedom and a rough equality, courage, and respect for the natural environment so sadly lacking in the American woodsman, trader, developer, and exploiter. On the whole, Cooper felt that the Indians—"good" ones such as the Delawares and Mohegans and "bad" ones such as the Iroquois—respected their codes of behavior far better than did white men theirs. "As human nature is every-where the same, it is not to be supposed that pure justice prevails even among savages; but one thing would seem to be certain, that, all over the world, man in his simplest and wildest state is more apt to respect his own ordinances than when living in what is deemed a con-dition of high civilization."[147] In either case, human nature might sometimes express itself in decent conduct under a "wrong" or "in-ferior" code or in malevolent behavior under a "good" or "superior" code.[148]

In delineating Indian character and behavior, Cooper accepted both the sentimental notion of the Noble Savage and the dominant view of the red man as the embodiment of vice and cruelty. His great hero, the hunter and pathfinder Leather-Stocking (Natty Bumppo), united the best qualities of the two races, thanks to the influence of the Moravian missionaries and the "good" Indians among whom he was reared and to

145. Marvin Meyers, *The Jacksonian Persuasion: Politics and Belief* (Stanford, Calif., 1957), chap. 4.

146. James Fenimore Cooper, *New York* (New York, 1930), Cooper's introduction to his unpublished history cited by McWilliams, *Political Justice in a Republic*, p. 393.

147. Cooper, *The Oak Openings* (1848), p. 112; also pp. 108, 110, 143, 150.

148. Grossman in his *James Fenimore Cooper*, p. 6, makes this point in analyzing Cooper's *The-Wing-and-the-Wing* (1848).

the stimulus of the wilderness in which he lived.[149] "The idea of delineating a character that possessed little of civilization but its highest principles as they are exhibited in the uneducated, and all of savage life that is not incompatible with these great rules of conduct, is perhaps natural to the situation in which Natty [Bumppo] was placed. He is too proud of his origin," Cooper wrote, "to sink into the condition of the wild Indian, and too much a man of the woods not to imbibe as much as was at all desirable, from his friends and companions. . . ." His hero, "removed from nearly all the temptations of civilized life, placed in the best associations of that which is deemed savage, and favorably disposed by nature to improve such advantages," was "a fit subject to represent the better qualities of both conditions, without pushing either to extremes."[150] In the dichotomy of good and evil in Indian conduct and in the white man's civilized code Cooper leaned both ways. With his commitment to class distinction he could not, for example, permit his virtuous and untutored Leather-Stocking to become a full-blown hero in romantic love: his awareness of his own social inferiority to the lady he loved led him to withdraw in favor of his more cultured, and he supposed superior, rival.[151] Cooper's stronger commitment to civilization was also evident in his emphasis on the need for control over the darker aspects of human nature through law based on reason, justice, and institutional checks.

Leather-Stocking also probably spoke for Cooper in his verdict on the unity of human nature and on the factors which differentiated the races. God made all three races, white, black, and red, and "no doubt had his own wise intentions in coloring us differently. Still, he made us, in the main, much the same in feelin's, though I'll not deny that he gave each race its gifts. A white man's gifts are Christianized, while a redskin's are more for the wilderness. Thus, it would be a great offense for a white man to scalp the dead; whereas it's a signal vartue in an Indian. Then ag'in, a white man cannot amboosh women and children in war, while a redskin may. 'Tis *cruel* work, I'll allow; but for them it's *lawful* work; while for *us*, it would be grievous work."[152] Thus the basic human nature which all men shared included a capacity for acquiring "gifts" or cultural traits which rested on traditions that fitted men for their roles in particular environments.

The idea of gifts, with the implication of moral as well as cultural relativism, was perhaps Cooper's most original contribution to the

149. Henry Nash Smith, *Virgin Land* (New York, 1957), pp. 60 ff. Walker, *James Fenimore Cooper*, pp. 49–50.
150. Cooper, preface to *The Deerslayer*, p. v.
151. *The Deerslayer*, pp. 438–39; Cooper, *The Pathfinder*, p. 154.
152. *The Deerslayer*, p. 36.

discussion of human nature. It provided an answer, not altogether satisfactory, to the white man's consciousness of guilt in his treatment of the aborigines. Cooper endowed Leather-Stocking with the qualities and role of the redemptive Messiah figure.[153] In his later and markedly pessimistic years, he attached less importance to the concept of gifts and redemption than to institutional religion. This was more satisfying than an inscrutable Providence or Divine Will which had once seemed to explain why things were what they were. A theistic God of love and justice with an ordered worship appeared to be the necessary guide for man. "We should all endeavor—so far as imperfect nature will enable us, and at a humble distance—to imitate this love of justice" which characterizes the Deity.[154] But neither reliance on institutional religion nor on the idea of gifts and the redemptive Messiah figure of Leather-Stocking entirely resolved the conflicts in Cooper's view of human nature. There remained the tension between the Federalist and Jeffersonian stresses in the image of man, between the romantic fondness for the "good" Indian and the candid portrayal of the "bad" Indian, and in the failure of the white man to use his ability to distinguish between right and wrong. The dangling antithesis between what man was and what he might become was one of Cooper's major contributions to the Romantic impulse that he heralded.

The heroic effort to balance the more and the less desirable aspects of human nature by institutionalizing the principle of counterpoise in government was significant not alone because the experiment was inaugurated on a vast terrain inhabited by people with different and often conflicting values and interests. Even more striking was the fact that for the first time in modern history, thoughtful men familiar with the great classics in political and social theory and aware of historical experience sought consciously to apply a more or less agreed upon view of the complexity and immutability of human nature to future conduct in the interest of preserving the heritage of the Revolution and of insuring orderly change in the future Republic. In doing this they did not depend on the supernatural sanctions invoked by the Puritans in small communities. With trust in Providence, they tried to make the best possible use of man's endowments by means within their own admittedly limited powers. Nor did the fact that competing groups appealed to what was, after all, pretty much the same view of human nature cancel the

153. Walker, *James Fenimore Cooper*, pp. 36–37.
154. Cooper to William Cullen Bryant and Parke Godwin, August 6, 1842, in James Franklin Beard, ed., *The Letters and Journals of James Fenimore Cooper*, 5 vols. (Cambridge, Mass., 1960–68), 4:303.

importance of involving it in demarking different roads to common ends. Here the public uses of varying conceptions of man were more important than the actual differences in such views.

In good part, the ideas about human nature used during the institutionalization of the Revolution in the Constitution continued to find expression in the high court and the scholarly literature of jurisprudence. The Scottish moral philosophy, which had been favorably known by some of the founding fathers, proved to be of great help in blending the heritage with new emphases in an evolving image of man. Though, as we shall see, it was challenged, it served many purposes as an unofficial, dominant view of human nature well into mid-century. Its assumption of the validity of sense perceptions, including above all mankind's common consciousness of a moral sense, elevated man's dignity in giving him an empirical key to truth. The eternal verities were authenticated, and yet a door was opened to new, though not unacceptably incompatible, ones. Common sense moral philosophy paved the way from the views of man current in traditional religious orthodoxy to a more liberal and brighter conception of man's nature and destiny. It also provided esthetic standards whose proponents claimed for them universal validity, standards important in the literary culture of the early Republic.

In searching to balance the conflicting aspects of human nature, one writer in this literary culture, James Fenimore Cooper, shared the traditional but by no means unchallenged emphasis on a static human nature, torn between good and evil impulses and thus in need of orderly institutional and religious restraint. He defied the common sense philosophers' objection to fiction by showing that it could be moral as well as entertaining. To be sure, he struggled somewhat unsuccessfully with the bearings of social change on human nature and with the problems focused by the movement of population into the Indian-inhabited West. At the most, he was a transitional herald of a view of man already being nourished by rising movements of thought and feeling in the Old World as well as by many rapidly changing social conditions at home.

5

The Romantic Impulse

The indigenous population of America offers no new obstacle to faith in the unity of the human race.

GEORGE BANCROFT, 1854

Human nature occupies the vast intermediate space between the angels and the demon. It may ascend to the one; it may fall to the other. It may select and occupy any spot in this immense ascending and descending scale.

HORACE MANN, 1842

The strife of the election is but human nature practically applied to the facts of the case. What has occurred in this case, must ever recur in similar cases. Human nature will not change. In any future great national trial, compared with the men of this, we shall have as weak, and as strong; as silly and as wise; as bad and as good. Let us, therefore, study the incidents of this, as philosophy to learn wisdom from, and none of them as wrongs to be avenged.

ABRAHAM LINCOLN, 1864

THE IDEAS about human nature useful during the Revolution and the constitution-making years continued to hold the allegiance of many intellectuals well into the nineteenth century. A group of young men and women, however, boldly challenged these ideas. To them the Age of Reason overemphasized the role of the senses, the rational faculties, and empiricism in the search for the laws of the universe and human nature. Nor did they like the focus of the widely acclaimed Scottish philosophy on order, system, counterpoise, consensus, and the constancy of human nature. Though more or less at one in what they opposed, they differed, sometimes in contradictory ways, in what they affirmed. Nevertheless many thought of themselves as kindred expositors of a new revelation to which the term *romanticism* was often given.[1]

The views of the new intellectuals were of course greatly influenced by far-reaching European movements of thought. Kant, Herder, Goethe, Rousseau, Chateaubriand, Wordsworth, and Coleridge rejected the idea of static, mechanical laws of mind and nature; they thought of mind and nature as both organic and dynamic. They perceived human beings, not

1. A leading romantic, Frederick Hedge, discussed late in life the perception he and his friends had of *romantic*, in an essay in the *Atlantic Monthly* 58 (1885): 309–16. For the controversy about the validity and usefulness of the terms *romanticism* and *Romantic movement* see Arthur O. Lovejoy, *Essays in the History of Ideas* (Baltimore, 1948), chap. 12, and the essays by René Wellek and Franklin L. Baumer in the *Dictionary of the History of Ideas*, 5 vols. (New York, 1973), 4:187–204.

as miniscule machines modeled on a balanced, rationally comprehended universe, but rather as spiritual emanations of it. Many romantics further felt that the overemphasis on reason and the slighting of emotions had excluded a living God from the human heart, from nature, even from the universe itself.

Unlike the philosophers of the Enlightenment, who in emphasizing the importance of the emotions often denigrated them, romanticists stressed their force. Feelings, intuitions, or unconscious perceptions, the imagination, even dreams, surpassed reason and logical analysis as roads to truth. Some even rejected the very concept of an objective reality apart from a subjective, though highly active, perception of the elusive, mysterious universe. Thus experience itself was often of greater significance than the result or solution of vexing questions. The emotions also heightened sensitivity to beauty and to a benevolence that, contrary to dominant eighteenth-century contentions, was no mere byproduct of selfishness.

The romantic approach to human nature, like that of Renaissance humanism, shifted emphasis from general categories to the individual. An appreciation and understanding of the self involved recognition of the tension between benign and malignant feelings, the beauty and danger of sex, the similarities and dissimilarities between selves, as entities, in relation to sex, class, race, and nationality. Romanticists also felt that the emotions unmasked false adjustments to institutions and customs and revealed the shallowness of conduct imposed by the conventions of society.[2]

Such views presented problems and contradictions. If human nature was a "given" emanation of the universe, it could hardly be the product of individual or social experience. Yet somewhat illogically human nature was also regarded as the fruit of growth in the self-activating individual. Nor was this all. Intrigued by and enthusiastic about evidences of change and progress in the present and the anticipated future, many romantic souls nevertheless found nurture in the haunting gothic myths of the Middle Ages. A more important paradox stemmed from the struggle of the emotions with the will and reason to maintain their central role in human nature. The outcome differed, as everyday observations made very clear. For some, the tension ended in *Welt-*

2. I am indebted to Lester C. Crocker, *An Age of Crisis: Man and the World in Eighteenth-Century French Thought* (Baltimore, 1895); H. G. Schenk, *The Mind of the European Romantic* (New York, 1964); Bruce Wiltshire, ed., *Romanticism and Evolution: The Nineteenth Century, an Anthology* (New York, 1968), introduction, p. 24; Morse Peckham, *Romanticism: The Culture of the Nineteenth Century* (New York, 1963); and, already mentioned, Baumer's essay on romanticism in the *Dictionary of the History of Ideas.*

schmertz, alienation, nihilism, defeat, tragedy. To be sure, this was not viewed as an imperative let alone general outcome of the inherent struggle within human nature. Its high potential for good and happiness often triumphed over the "dark" or "night" side of disillusionment, despair, and defeat. The reasons given, if given at all, for such a contradictory outcome left many issues unresolved.

The new, stimulating, and sometimes disturbing currents of thought were not the only explanation for the romantic vogue. The whole of society in the first decades of the nineteenth century was rapidly changing. Intellectuals were not alone in sensing this in the growth of industrial urbanism, shifts in family organization, fresh waves of strange-speaking immigrants, the agitation over slavery, and the accelerated westward movement. Awareness of such social changes stimulated consideration of their bearing on traditional ideas of human nature.

In reacting to the unsettling aspects of social change, some found assurance in the traditional ideas, whether religious or secular. The latter included reassertions of the eighteenth-century enshrinement of reasonable selfishness as virtue. With insight, Tocqueville noted that in America the widely accepted Lockean principle of self-interest gave full freedom of action to individuals, while the caveat "interest rightly understood" offered scope for benevolent cooperation in the characteristically American voluntary associations.[3] On their part, American economists asserted an optimistic meliorism that comfortably qualified awareness of self-interest as the dominant trait in human nature. Henry Carey, prominent Philadelphia economist and publisher, claimed that the selfishness of savages, inherent in human nature, disappeared with the acquisition of the "habit of association of man with his fellowmen." Carey felt that in the United States a true harmony of interests between commerce, industry, and agriculture had achieved this.[4]

On the other hand, the sense of dynamic social change seems to have contributed in two quite different ways to the appeal of new ideas about human nature. Some intellectuals, in enthusiastically welcoming change as evidence of movement and vitality, found traditional ideas about man's makeup somewhat outdated. Yet others reacted with a sense of malaise and displacement. They deprecated the emphasis on material values that seemed to be associated with the changing order. Some of those who did not make or try to make the next rung of the economic

3. Alexis De Tocqueville, *Democracy in America*, ed. Phillips Bradley, 2 vols. (New York, 1945), vol. 2, book 2, chaps. 5, 8, and 9.

4. Henry C. Carey, *The Harmony of Interests . . .* , 2d ed. (New York, 1852), pp. 28, 41, 48, 204, 228.

ladder found the new ideas about human nature appealing. This was more likely for those who thought that the undue weight given to a calculating reason and an acquisitive instinct limited the expression of individuality and spiritual growth. It is at least reasonable to suggest that such considerations encouraged sympathy with the stress on feeling and sensitivity to the conflict between a renovating creativity and the pull of an encumbering past and an overmaterialistic present.

Transitional figures, aware of the limitations of rationalism and related "enlightened" ideas about man and intrigued by the new emphasis on feeling, served as bridges between the old and the new.

A case in point was Charles Brockden Brown.[5] For the most part the men and women in his fiction assumed that the mind's rational analysis of its sense impressions explained natural phenomena as well as human motives and conduct. But in acting on such a view, the characters came to grief, even disaster. Such an image of man was seen to be self-deceptive in ignoring emotions and passions. In *Wieland* (1799) it led to confusion, misapprehension, even madness. In later novels the author reflected dissatisfaction with the Enlightenment view of man for failing to take due account of the ever-changing self. On the other hand, mere reliance on the emotions led to violence and tragedy, as the actions of the villain Carwin and the fanatically religious Wieland made all too clear. The later novels also suggested the shortcomings of a simple trust in benevolence. A need for correcting a rational analysis of sensations by ethical and religious discipline seemed clear. Brown's views on women in relation to human nature also reflected the influence of both the Enlightenment and an often-favored romantic attitude. *Alcuin* proclaimed equality of endowments, including reason, between the sexes and advocated new spheres of activity for women. Brown shifted, however, to sentimentality when his emancipated women learned in the hard way the cost of denying nature's intended role of "femininity."

The restless, passionately democratic Philip Freneau was, like Brown, a transitional figure.[6] On the one hand, he assumed man's capacity to respond rationally to anti-British and anti-Federalist satires and to make

5. Arthur G. Kimball, *Rational Fictions: A Study of Charles Brockden Brown* (McMinnville, Ore., 1968), pp. 3 ff.; Donald A. Ringe, *Charles Brockden Brown* (New York, 1966); and Harry E. Warfel, ed., *The Rhapsodist and Other Uncollected Writings by Charles Brockden Brown* (New York, 1943), pp. xvi, 136.

6. Philip Freneau, *Poems*, ed. with critical introduction by Harry Hayden Clark (New York, 1969); Mary Austin, *Philip Freneau, Poet of the Revolution* (Detroit, 1968); Philip Marsh, *Philip Freneau, Poet and Journalist* (Minneapolis, 1967); and J. Axelrad, *Philip Freneau: Champion of Democracy* (Austin, Texas, 1967).

reason and benevolence triumph. On the other hand, his playful lyric "On a Honey Bee" (1807) celebrated the human capacity to find the whims and vagaries of nature emotionally satisfying without pretending to understand nature or attempting to subdue it. Freneau also responded to the turbulent and emotional aspects of human nature and to its capacity for playful enjoyment. The opening stanza of "The House of Night" (1799) set the mood:

> By some sad means, when Reason holds now sway,
> Lonely I rov'd at midnight o'er the plain
> Where murmuring streams and mingling rivers flow
> Far to their springs, or seek the sea again.

The meaning of life and death was discovered, not in rational analysis, which he found useful as a propagandist for the Revolution and for Jefferson, but in the lonely, melancholy, and infinite sense of timeless beginnings and endings, in emotional experiences bared in dreams and "fearful visions."

> For fancy gave to my enraptur'd soul
> An eagle's eye, with keenest glance to see
> And bade those distant sounds distinctly roll,
> which, waking, never had affected me.

And life, which was not to be experienced in fixed and regular order, was enmeshed with "death which is no more than one unceasing change."

Before we look at the use that later writers made of the emotions, the revolt against the rational conception of the mind needs to be illustrated and amplified. In a memorable statement, Margaret Fuller expressed the reaction of the romanticists against their view of the Age of Reason. "The Mephistopheles of the eighteenth century," she declared, "bade the finite strive to compass the infinite, and the intellectual attempt to solve all the problems of the soul."[7] Implicit in this statement was a view of man that differed considerably from that of the Enlightenment's emphasis on order, categories, empiricism, and science.

The structure and meaning of the American version of the romantic impulse can best be approached through an examination of its position

7. Margaret Fuller Ossoli, *Life Without and Life Within* . . . (Boston, 1855), p. 36. For a brilliant and informed analysis of philosophy and literature in the Transcendental movement consult Lawrence Buell, *Literary Transcendentalism: Style and Vision in the American Renaissance* (Ithaca, 1973).

on man's place in nature, the role of emotions, intuitions, and reason, and the self as it impinged on other selves in the whole social structure.

The key figure was James Marsh, a philosopher at the University of Vermont who was acquainted with the science of his time and who was a careful student of Aristotle, Plato, and the seventeenth-century Cambridge Platonists, as well as Kant. In commenting on the newer views of man, he wrote that "in the mind of a modern . . . his more serious thoughts are withdrawn from the living world around him, and turned inward upon himself."[8] The boundless and invisible world, he went on, encompassed all that was visible in a mere microcosm. He sought to weaken the support allegedly given by Locke, Hume, and the French philosophers to "Infidelity" and to radical attacks on established institutions. He meant to awaken in professing Christians a deeper spiritual life. Though no mere disciple of Coleridge, he felt that the poet's philosophy furthered a spiritual transcendence of the empirical psychology of Locke and the Scottish moralists.

To this end Marsh edited in 1829 Coleridge's *Aids to Reflection*. He added his own argument for the identification of true philosophy with true religion. This identification rested on a graded distinction between sense experience, Understanding (the conceptualization of sense impressions), and Reason, defined as an intuitive and transcendent thrust to a spiritual reality more profound than anything sense and Understanding could yield. John Dewey has pointed out that Marsh did not fully develop the social implications of his position, beyond launching educational reform designed to create a community of individuals with opportunity for realizing their full potentialities.[9] Some of the young men whom Marsh trained, however, did become ardent critics of the radical humanitarian and socialist movements of the mid-century.[10]

The Massachusetts group for whom Marsh opened the door to Coleridge accepted the reality of the subjective intuitions of truth that linked man intimately to the spiritual universe. Emerson, Alcott, Hedge, Margaret Fuller, and Theodore Parker, unlike Marsh, questioned whether Transcendentalism could infuse orthodox religion with true spirituality. And, save for Parker, they did not believe that it could

8. *North American Review* 15, n.s. 6 (1822): 107. See also J. Torrey, ed., *The Remains of the Rev. James Marsh, D.D.* (Boston, 1843), esp. "Remarks on Psychology," pp. 239–360. John J. Duffy's edition of *Coleridge's American Disciples: The Selected Correspondence of James Marsh* (Amherst, Mass., 1973), throws a good deal of light on the spread of Marsh's ideas.

9. John Dewey, "James Marsh and American Philosophy," *Journal of the History of Ideas* 2 (1941): 131 ff.

10. Lewis S. Feuer, "James Marsh and the Conservative Transcendentalist Philosophy," *New England Quarterly* 21 (1958): 3–31.

rescue Unitarianism from its "pale negations," based, as they thought, on a passive and lifeless view of human nature derived from Locke and other empiricists.

Before finding a harbor in the Catholic Church, Orestes A. Brownson spoke for the group in holding that "the sentiments, the feelings are entitled to a much higher rank than it has been customary to assign them for the last century. To us," he went on, "the sentiments seem to be peculiarly the human faculties. They give to man his distinctive character. They supply him with the energy to act, and prompt him to the performance of grand and noble deeds. We fear that their power is seldom suspected, that little attention is paid to the mission which is given them to accomplish."[11]

No part of that mission seemed so elevated as the opening of immediate and intimate communication with the whole universe. In the romantic view the dynamism of external nature surged through man's being: the old distinction between man and the natural world surrounding him was breaking down. The effort merely to understand nature rationally was abandoned for the impulse to accept it as an integrated process of change and growth. Therefore, as Emerson insisted, nature, not books and schools, was the great teacher. But nature taught man only when he opened his soul spontaneously to the whole universe. To put it differently, man could, by actively and intimately experiencing fields, streams, brooks, and mountains, grasp the total reality. And this was to be a continuing experience full of sustained ecstasy, wonder, and mystery. Best of all, in containing all nature man's soul was not, as in Buddhism, itself to be contained. Nor could his soul be conquered, if he did not try to conquer—and spoil—nature. The danger, Emerson warned, was that in conquering nature, one was overwhelmed by the material objects that conquest brought. In identifying himself with the whole universe and in enjoying ceaseless experience with ever greater insight and rapture, man was choosing the best of all possible ways of holding in check his lower passions and of realizing his highest potentialities.

In identifying human nature with the universe by way of the emotions, Emanuel Swedenborg was, for a time, a valued guide. A scientist become theologian and visionary, he held that "nature is the symbol of the spirit and that the universe is the externalization of the soul." An appreciation of this great truth opened the path to communion with all the souls and spirits that infused the universe. While demurring from some of Swedenborg's ideas, Emerson praised him for the centrality he gave to

11. Orestes O. Brownson, "Benjamin Constant and Religion," *Christian Examiner* 17 (1834): 73–74.

man in nature and for the related concept that the universal human body fed the soul and was in turn fed by it.[12] The Doctrine of Correspondence, which also intrigued Emerson, was summed up in a quotation from Swedenborg: "If we choose to express any natural truth in physical and definite vocal terms, and to convert these terms only into the corresponding and spiritual term, we shall by this means elicit a spiritual truth or theological dogma, in place of the physical truth and precept."[13]

One did not, of course, have to accept "spiritualism" in the sense of communication with "departed" souls to give priority to the higher feelings and insights. These depended, as Theodore Parker put it, on no logical process of demonstration: they were "facts of consciousness that there is a God, the sense of the just and the right, operating independently of the will, and the consciousness" that "the Essential Element of man, the principle of individuality, never dies."[14] Parker's younger disciple George Ripley stressed the unique faculty that enabled man to experience the power of a perfection higher than he had ever reached.[15]

Discussion of the relation between emotions and the arts marked a shift from classical tradition, which held that a rational approach to art intellectualized the sense impressions and purified the emotions.[16] The more truly romantic outlook of James Jarvis, a collector and critic, contended that art "borrows of Divinity a portion of its spirit to refresh the heart of sorrowing man."[17]

In the romantic canon, music outstripped the visual arts as the universal language of the emotions, subtly penetrating all the walls of

12. For Emerson's appreciation of Swedenborg's first important American interpreter see Carl F. Strauch's introduction to Sampson Reed's *Observations on the Growth of the Mind with Remarks on Some Other Subjects* (Boston, 1838; facsimile rpt., Gainesville, Fla., 1970), p. viii.

13. Ralph Waldo Emerson, *The Complete Works of Ralph Waldo Emerson*, 14 vols. (Boston, 1903–21), 4:116. Swedenborg's belief that the interdependence between the inborn emotions and the universe enabled men to communicate with the souls of the "departed" appealed to such well-read men as Theodore Parker, William Cullen Bryant, Horace Greeley, and even Robert Dale Owen, who was reared in the tradition of the Enlightenment. See, for Owen's position, *Footfalls on the Boundary of Another World* (Philadelphia, 1860).

14. Theodore Parker's farewell letter to his parish, published under the title *Theodore Parker's Experience as a Minister* (Boston, 1859), p. 42.

15. George Ripley, *Jesus Christ, the Same Yesterday, Today, and Forever*, a sermon delivered in 1834 and often repeated. It is included in *The Transcendentalists*, ed. Perry Miller (Cambridge, Mass., 1950), pp. 284–93.

16. See, for examples, essays in the *North American Review* 2 (1816): 153–65; and 31 (1830): 309–37.

17. James Jackson Jarvis, *Art Hints* (New York, 1853), p. 63.

time and space. It was, in the words of John Sullivan Dwight, a Transcendentalist, a resident at Brook Farm, and a pioneer in musical journalism, both "God's alphabet" and "the language of the heart, a natural, invariable pure type and correspondence" that related beauty to "our invisible and real self." Music thus bestowed "a foretaste of moods and states of feelings yet in reserve for the soul, of loves which have never yet met an object that could call them out." The truest possible mark of the inner life, a musical score enshrined immortally the passions and feelings that originally dictated the melodious harmonies.[18] Even before Dwight sketched the requisites for a music truly expressing the highest reaches of "the American genius" in human nature, Anthony Philip Heinrich, an immigrant from Bohemia living in Bardstown, published *The Dawning of Music in Kentucky; or, the Pleasures of Harmony in the Solitudes of Nature, Opera Prima* (1820). His bombastic, freakish score for instruments and voices used Indian themes in the New World setting to express the primitive emotional forces in human nature.[19]

The concept of man in nature and nature in man as an endless process of growth rather than as a perfected machine implied, in the context of emotion and esthetics, an imagination that could surmount the limitations of time and place. Even Emerson, who so dramatically turned his back on the past for the inspiration of the present, admitted that "the old ballads are bowers of joy . . . that catch us up into short heavens."[20] In the South the cult of chivalry caught the fancy of young blades and damsels.[21] Washington Irving recaptured the almost forgotten lore of the Hudson River Valley and Charles Godfrey Leland collected legends ranging in subject from Charlemagne and the troubadors to the ubiquitous gypsies and the ancient Algonquins nearer home.[22] For others, space as well as time could be transcended, as

18. Dwight's theoretical explanations of music, evident in some of his comments on musical events for *The Dial*, were more fully developed in an essay for Elizabeth Peabody's *Aesthetic Papers* (Boston, 1849), pp. 25–36.

19. The sketch in the *Dictionary of American Biography* cites bibliographical information about his major compositions. See also Lubov Keefer's informative essay, "The Beethovens of America," in George Boas, ed., *Romanticism in America* (Baltimore, 1940), pp. 138–43, in which Heinrich is discussed in the context of efforts to create a national and romantic music.

20. Ralph Waldo Emerson, *The Journals of Ralph Waldo Emerson*, ed. Edward Emerson and W. E. Forbes, 14 vols. (Boston, 1909–14), 5 (1838): 120.

21. Rollin G. Osterweis, *Romanticism and Nationalism in the Old South* (New Haven, 1949), pp. 55, 80–90, 169 ff.; and William R. Taylor, *Cavalier and Yankee* (New York, 1961), pp. 165 ff.

22. Charles Godfrey Leland, *Memoirs* (New York, 1893); Joseph Jackson, *A Bibliography of the Works of Charles Godfrey Leland* (Philadelphia, 1927).

preoccupation with the exotic Orient came within tenuous reach, thanks to new trade routes and European scholarship. Pseudoscientific tales of voyages to the moon replete with bastard astronomy also played their part: an example was the satirical romance of the Virginia economist George Tucker. Thus all in all, the discovery of the limitless powers of the imagination invited the romantic adventurer to feel at home in the whole universe. It was even possible, as Emerson said, to "soar into the heaven of invention, and coin fancies of our own . . . and learn by bold attempt our own riches."[23]

Indispensable though the self-activating emotions were for enhancing the power to enjoy beauty and to transcend earthly barriers, some admitted that the mysteries of the human heart and the limitless universe could never be fathomed. No one put this better than Walt Whitman. He had some knowledge, for the most part at second hand, of Lucretius, Epictetus, Hegel, and the science and pseudo-science of his day. Yet he could conclude,

> Oh I perceive I have not understood anything
> —not a single object—and that no man can.

Whatever the limitations of the emotional approach to truth, no one questioned the importance of the emotions for conduct. In some ways there was nothing new in this. Philosophers in the Enlightenment had, as we have seen, been concerned with it, and long before and since, Christian theologians and moralists probed the relationship even more relentlessly. In 1824 Asa Burton, a little-known Vermont clergyman, published a study of the emotions which tellingly set forth a unique function for each: pity led to the relief of suffering, "the relish" or "taste" for good led to regeneration.[24] The romantic writers treated the subject in both religious and secular terms. Emerson, for example, stressed an innate emotional disposition toward benevolence. "Man's natural goodness is to do good to others," he declared. "If the soul do not bear its good deed, it will wither & die. It is made stronger, like the animal muscles, by use."[25]

Besides recognizing the power and on occasion the limits of the higher emotions, the romantic view did not deny the older emphasis on the

23. Emerson, *Journals*, 5 (1838): 120.

24. Asa Burton, *Essays on Some of the First Principles of Metaphysics, Ethicks, and Theology* (Portland, Me., 1824), pp. 275–76. Burton exempted the emotion of holiness from a specific behavioral counterpart.

25. Ralph Waldo Emerson, *The Journals and Miscellaneous Notebooks of Ralph Waldo Emerson*, ed. William Gilman and others, 19 vols. (Cambridge, Mass., 1964–73), 3 (1830): 174.

lower emotions, no less deeply encrusted in man's original nature. "Man has animal propensities as well as intellectual and moral powers," William Ellery Channing, a humanistic rationalist, warned. "He has passions to war with reason, and self-love with conscience. He is a free being, and a tempted being, and thus constituted he may and does sin, and often sins grievously." In most people, Channing admitted, the balance was on the side of the less-admirable propensities. Thus life was an endless conflict. Channing knew that man had "to summon to his aid all the powers of this world and the world to come" to communicate force and constancy to his will.[26]

This was the theme of some of the best creative writing of the romantic school, above all that of Hawthorne and Melville. Not without Puritan undertones, each probed the meaning of man's capacity and impulse for good and evil. Their tales and novels, often cast in the romantic mood of allegory, fantasy, and symbol, revealed the devastating spiritual annihilation resulting from conduct inspired by a self-centered, power-bent, iron will, or by intellect given to craft, fraudulent curiosity, or above all, stubborn pride. The tragedy was heightened by the alienation of its victims from a living sympathy of the heart, from communion with fellow beings.

Hawthorne's delicate and subdued treatment of sex can be understood if one understands the differing attitudes toward it in the first decades of the nineteenth century. Traditional views dominated references to this aspect of human nature. From the pulpit, ministers continued to storm against adultery. Apart from this, a veil of discreet silence generally marked the attitude of intellectuals. Sentimental novels, to be sure, didactically intoned the sorrows of pure maidens betrayed by unscrupulous suitors. Such novels did not get beneath the meretricious surface in relating sex to human nature.

A view seldom apparent in polite literature or even in serious writing reflected the naturalistic attitude of the Enlightenment. Diderot and Rousseau had claimed that sex morality had no existence in nature. French writers, inspired by the primitivism reported by visitors to the South Sea Islands, declared that violent passions sprang from the social and religious restraint on sex expression, and that civilized Europe, unlike Tahiti, wrongly linked promiscuity with shame, guilt, and vice. Although Tom Paine echoed this idea,[27] most American intellectuals

26. William Ellery Channing, "Likeness to God: Discourse at the Ordination of the Rev. F. A. Farley, Providence, R.I., 1828," *The Works of William Ellery Channing, D.D.* (Boston, 1899), p. 300.

27. Philip S. Foner, ed., *The Complete Writings of Thomas Paine*, 2 vols. (New York, 1945), 2:1118 ff.

either disapproved or remained silent. The tide turned somewhat in the 1820s when Robert Owen, who founded New Harmony in Indiana, claimed that celibacy was unnatural and often led to ailments of body and mind. On the other hand, he felt that marriage and family, like orthodox religion, worked against the communitarianism to which he was deeply committed. In any case, he looked upon marriage without love as prostitution warranting divorce. The sex act itself, while mainly meant for the propagation of the race, was justifiable if tempered with affection and common sense.[28] Robert Dale Owen worked out his father's ideas more fully. His little book on birth control emphasized the utilitarian need of checking the population growth which had alarmed many readers of Malthus.[29]

This argument also found a place in the first book on the matter to be written by an American, Charles Knowlton, a Massachusetts country doctor. His crudely printed little manual described techniques of contraception in greater detail than Owen's tract. It pulled no punches in discussing the personal suffering that resulted from repression of the sex drive and the happiness that a rational solution offered.[30] Circulated underground, the book did little to lift the taboo in genteel conversation and writing.

Thus it was something of a breakthrough when George Loring, a young Boston clergyman of transcendentalist leaning, testified publicly to the power and beauty of sex. In his review of Hawthorne's *Scarlet Letter* he asked, "who that has recognized the deep and holy meaning of the human affections, has not been frozen into demanding a warm-

28. Robert Owen, *The Book of the New Moral World* (London, 1842; rpt. ed., New York, 1970), pt. 3, chap. 4, p. 23. Owen's early writings were included in the *Life of Robert Owen Written by Himself*, 2 vols. (London, 1857–58). Of special relevance are his "Address." *New York Daily Tribune*, September 24, 1824; Arthur E. Bestor, Jr., *Backwoods Utopias* (Philadelphia, 1950; rev. ed., 1970), chap. 4; John F. C. Harrison, *Robert Owen and the Owenites in Britain and America: Quest for the New Moral World* (London, 1969), pp. 59–66; and Donald E. Pitzer, ed., *Robert Owen's American Legacy* (Indianapolis, 1972), pp. 56–57. For similarities and differences between the philosophy and psychology of Owen's "utopian socialism" and that of Charles Fourier, who stimulated the establishment of several communities a few years later, see Albert Brisbane, *The Social Destiny of Man* (New York, 1840; rpt. ed., Clifton, N.J., 1969).

29. Robert Dale Owen, *Moral Physiology; or, a Brief and Plain Treatise on the Population Question* (New York, 1832).

30. Charles Knowlton, *Fruits of Philosophy, or, The Private Companion of Young Married Couples* (Boston, 2d ed., 1833; 10th ed., 1877). Knowlton had earlier published *Elements of Modern Materialism* (Adams, Mass., 1828). This projected a materialistic philosophy that denied all spiritual and autonomous psychological concepts, including "soul" and "conscience," and which argued that definite, ascertainable forces operating in an orderly world explained all mental and physical behavior. Robert E. Riegel summarized both of Knowlton's books in "The American Father of Birth Control," *New England Quarterly* 6 (1933): 470–90. Norman Hines's *Medical History of Contraception* (Baltimore, 1936; rept. ed., New York, 1970) discussed both Owen and Knowlton.

hearted crime as a relief for the cold, false, vulgar, and cowardly asperity which is sometimes called chastity?"[31]

Loring's review suggested the paradoxical conflict between the beauty and the destructiveness of the erotic impulse that often characterized the romantic discussion of sex. This was illustrated in the many versions of the Kentucky Tragedy that had already inspired several novels and plays. The undisputed fact was that in 1825 Jereboam Beauchamp, an ambitious and disorganized lawyer of sorts, killed a well-known politician, Colonel Solomon Sharp, in cold blood. The Colonel had allegedly seduced Ann Cook, whose hand Beauchamp himself had sought unsuccessfully. The crime led to Beauchamp's trial, execution, and burial in the coffin with his beloved, who had killed herself as a way out of her trouble. Beauchamp's confession, the flaming letters of Ann Cook, and the reporters' account of the trial, published in 1826, were marked by unrestrained emotion and rank sentimentality: the erotic passion, inviting destructiveness, pathos, and potential beauty, was one expression of the romantic view of sex in human nature.[32]

The emotions bearing on sex, sometimes flamboyantly crushing as in the Kentucky Tragedy but more often subdued, flavored the increasing flow of sentimental novels of the 1830s and 1840s. This popular genre did, to be sure, display virtuous conduct presumably inherent in human impulses, however thwarted by circumstances, missteps, and uninhibited vanities. For the most part, however, the novels glorified the elegant, overdelicate emotions of soulful pity, dubious benevolence and tenderness, refined sympathy, and the false modesty that framed the glamor of sensuality with conventional proprieties and moralities. Human nature thus presented was also capable of finding outlet in emotional dissipation, tearful melancholy, and decadent gentility, all related covertly to sex.[33]

The discussion of sex nevertheless became more explicit, in part because of the naturalistic views of such innovators as Owen and Knowlton and the apparently widespread practice of birth control. The more outspoken discussion also owed something to the role given sex in new religious movements, to be discussed later. In literature, the

31. George Loring, "Hawthorne's Scarlet Letter," *Massachusetts Quarterly Review* 3 (1850): 497.

32. Loren J. Kallsen, *The Kentucky Tragedy: A Problem in Romantic Attitudes* (Indianapolis, 1963), gives the texts of the episode. Thomas Holley Chivers, Edgar Allan Poe, Charles Fenno Hoffman, William Gilmore Sims, and Robert Penn Warren made use of the events and its legend. David Brion Davis, in *Homicide in American Fiction 1798–1860* (Ithaca, 1957), pp. 22–29, has skillfully delineated the relationships between erotic impulse and suicide in pre-Civil War fiction.

33. I am deeply indebted here to Herbert Ross Brown's *The Sentimental Novel in America, 1789–1860* (Durham, N.C., 1940), chap. 3.

romantic impulse itself, as well as personal factors, explained Walt Whitman's remarkable emphasis on sex in human nature. In the case of Whitman, this was true even though his views to an extent reflected the naturalistic and hedonistic tone of such disciples of the Enlightenment as Frances Wright. Proclaiming himself the poet of procreation, Whitman insisted that "the animal fire" in men and women had been falsely and wrongly held back by social custom. That fire carried life-restoring powers. If rightly viewed and experienced, the sex drive could also lead to a deeply satisfying fusion of body and soul. By including the celebration of the comradely emotions or "manly love," Whitman gave sex a major part in promoting an inclusive fraternity of free and equal individuals which he saw as the essence of democracy. In his sublime moments, sex became the moving force in poetical fantasies that united man and man, woman and woman, and man and woman in a warm and exalted version of human nature that merged with eternity.[34]

The sentimental novelists, the religious leaders, and the joyous poet who celebrated the emotional power of sex did not define all the boundaries of the contemporary treatment of sex. Much of the discussion emphasized the distinctive characteristics and functions of the two sexes and the proper relations between them. Since this involved the interrelations of individuals it will be considered later.

Meantime, the varied recognition of the importance of sex in human nature that found expression in "materialistic" physiology, deviant religions, and romantic literature invited a reaction. This did not take the Shaker ground of denying the role of sexuality, but it did deprecate the weight given to the sex instinct in what seemed to be widening circles. In so doing, the reaction drew on religious and moral injunctions and appealed to natural science against any open conduct approaching indulgence. The gospel of restraint also found reenforcement in anxiety over the moral and utilitarian integrity of the family, as awareness of prostitution and venereal disease became more widespread. Self-defensive about middle-class values, spokesmen in the reaction associated indulgence and laxity with the French Revolution and the fall of the debauched aristocrats of the Old Regime. The reaction also took for granted an antipathy between sensual indulgence and achievement in the competitive struggle for material success and the rise in social standing it betokened. All these fears found their way into manuals of

34. Thoughtful discussions of the subject include those of Gay Wilson Allen, *The Solitary Singer: A Critical Biography of Walt Whitman* (New York, 1951); R. D. O'Leary, "Swift and Whitman as Exponents of Human Nature," *International Journal of Ethics* 24 (1914): 183–202; and Stephen Kern, *Anatomy and Destiny* (Indianapolis, 1974), chap. 8.

"advice" that warned against sex outside of, and if unduly indulged, within, marriage. The manuals denounced abortion and condemned the "secret vice" of masturbation, allegedly so terrible in its debilitating effects.

Sylvester Graham, a sometime minister and temperance reformer, had read French works on physiology which often assumed a limited amount of bodily vitality in great need of conservation. He may also have known Dr. Benjamin Rush's *Medical Inquiries and Observations*, which attributed several kinds of insanity to overindulgence. Graham argued that the dominant urges in human nature, the nutritional and reproductive, could and should be controlled by persistent restraint. A proper diet of bland nutriments insured not only health but also, with self-discipline, the control of the reproductive instinct. Overindulgence led, in Graham's view, to physical ailments, depressing dullness, and, in self-pollution, to shame, guilt, sickness, and even madness. Thus it was imperative for parents to teach the young the principles of physiology and to alert them to the awful effects of self-abuse, promiscuity, and sex-exciting books. Such a program would enable young and old alike to appreciate the fact that the human system was built on principles of benevolence and utility, principles ordained not only by biblical authority but by science itself.[35] Other sex manuals took no less firm a stand.[36] The reaction against sex, whether expressed in naturalistic, religious, or sentimental terms of purity and restraint, continued to play a part in estimates of human nature.

Meanwhile emotions and convictions associated with other aspects of the romantic impulse stirred lively and sometimes bitter discussion.

If the equality of condition that Tocqueville saw as the central fact of

35. Sylvester Graham, *A Lecture to Young Men on Chastity* (Boston, 1838), pp. 11, 15, 34, 119, 187. I am indebted to Stephen Nissenbaum's "Careful Love: Sylvester Graham and the Emergence of Victorian Sexual Theory in America" (Ph.D. diss., University of Wisconsin, 1968).

36. Ronald G. Walters, ed., *Primers for Prudery: Sexual Advice to Victorian America* (Englewood Cliffs, N.J., 1974); Lawrence J. Friedman, *Inventors of the Promised Land* (New York, 1975), chap. 4; G. J. Barker-Benfield, *The Horrors of the Half-Known Life: Male Attitudes toward Women and Sexuality in Nineteenth-Century America* (New York, 1976), pp. 135 ff.; Thomas Low Nichols and Mary Gove Nichols, *Marriage: Its History, Character, and Results* (Cincinnati, Oh. 1854); Thomas Low Nichols, *Forty Years of American Life*, 2 vols. (London, 1864), 2:17–47; and Mary Gove Nichols, *Lectures to Ladies on Anatomy and Physiology* (Boston, 1842). Henry Clarke Wright, who shared the fear of promiscuity and overindulgence, endowed the emotions surrounding sex in a good marriage with life-enhancing values. See his *Marriage and Parentage* (Boston, 1855; rept. ed., New York, 1974); and Merle Curti, "Non-Resistance in New England," *New England Quarterly* 2 (1929): 34–57.

American life had allowed most males to share in the political enterprise, it excluded the impoverished, women, Indians, and blacks. Such discriminations, in clear conflict with professed democracy, raised a fundamental question about human nature: was the equal or unequal spread of abilities in the human makeup inherent or the result of history and environment?

In the debate, the Christian doctrine of the brotherhood of man, the Enlightenment's emphasis on environment, and romantic views all played a part. Some of the arguments drawn from these movements contradicted each other. Thus Robert Owen founded his communal experiment at New Harmony on the conviction that whatever one's initial abilities or limitations, these could not keep him from "being formed into a *very inferior*, or a *very superior*, being, according to the qualities of the external circumstances allowed to influence that constitution from birth."[37] On the other hand Transcendentalists, in avowing equality, seemed to overlook environment in featuring the fullness as well as the uniqueness of every soul on entering the world. George Ripley, for example, rested his case for equality on an intuitive mysticism. "There is," he wrote in 1840, "a light . . . which enlighteneth every man that cometh into the world; there is a faculty in all . . . the most degraded, the most ignorant, the most obscure . . . to perceive spiritual truth when distinctly presented; and the ultimate appeal on all moral questions is not to a jury of scholars, a hierarchy of divines, or the prescriptions of a crowd, but to the common sense of the human race."[38]

Implicit contradictions often became explicit in much that Emerson wrote. In spite of an equalitarian commitment, he celebrated a natural aristocracy much like that of Jefferson and John Adams.[39] Though believing in a universal endowment of intuitional and moral qualities, Emerson, like his friend Carlyle, distinguished between the great man, the genius, and the common run. He liked to commune with persons of "commanding excellence," who alone could be relied on for defending the truth.[40] The thoughts of the mass of men, he observed elsewhere, "are ever in a crude, ungrown, unsteady state."[41] They obeyed example and surrendered to the judgment of others. Assuming that observable differences were in good part the result of native endowment, Emerson held that the evil "we would cure is out of reach of education viz. the original

37. Owen, *Book of the New Moral World*, p. 1; Merle Curti, "Robert Owen in American Thought," in Pitzer, ed., *Owen's American Legacy*, pp. 56–67.
38. Octavius B. Frothingham, *George Ripley* (Boston, 1888), p. 85.
39. *The Letters of Ralph Waldo Emerson*, ed. Ralph L. Rusk, 6 vols. (New York, 1939), 1:219–20.
40. Emerson, *Journals*, 7 (1851): 183.
41. *Journals*, 1 (1824): 316.

equality of the intellect."[42] Still, every man's character did depend in part on the scope given him for the development of his talents. Moreover, no great man could be sure that his offspring would inherit his gifts. Thus it was imperative to insure the widest opportunities for the growth of his endowments that, however limited, distinguished him from brutes.

Explanations of individual differences rested on various assumptions. It was generally believed that heredity explained disparities in talent and behavior.[43] A somewhat whimsical example was the effort of the romantic historian George Bancroft to refurbish the ancient doctrine of "humours" or "temperaments."[44]

In contrast to the elusiveness of these rather mystical explanations, the new phrenology rejected metaphysical presuppositions. It claimed scientific authority for identifying mind with brain and for explaining individual characteristics in terms of structural differences revealed by brain dissection. The founders of phrenology, Franz J. Gall and Johann Gaspar Spurzheim, identified cerebral localization with corresponding propensities—physical, mental, and moral. Phrenology met with a mixed reception when it was introduced to America in the 1830s and 1840s. While some physicians and scientists looked on it with open-minded sympathy, most religious leaders condemned its materialism and fatalism as incompatible with Christianity.[45] Such an indictment found support when a well-known opponent of capital punishment claimed that murderers responded unwittingly to an inborn super-abundance of the destructive propensity.[46]

The engaging, cultured, and idealistic George Combe, a Scot who developed an eclectic philosophy of human nature grounded in phrenology, answered the criticism of materialistic fatalism during his residence in the United States. Everyone, he contended, could strengthen

42. *Letters of Ralph Waldo Emerson*, 1:220. See also Emerson, "The Natural History of the Intellect," *Complete Works*, 12:1–90.

43. Charles E. Rosenberg, "The Bitter Fruit of Heredity: Heredity, Disease, and Social Thought in Nineteenth-Century America," *Perspectives in American History* 8 (1974): 189–90.

44. George Bancroft, *Literary and Historical Miscellanies* (New York, 1855), pp. 1–43.

45. The standard monograph, John D. Davies, *Phrenology Fad and Science: A Nineteenth-Century American Crusade* (New Haven, 1955), can profitably be sup-plemented by sampling contemporary materials that presented varying views; for example, H. W. Warner, *Autobiography of Charles Caldwell, M.D.* (Philadelphia, 1855); Thomas Sewall, M.D., *An Examination of Phrenology* (Boston, 1836); the review of George Combe's *Constitution of Man* by the distinguished psychiatrist Dr. Isaac Ray, in the *Christian Examiner* 16 (1834): 221–48; an anonymous review of Combe in the same periodical, 17 (1834): 249–69; and "Phrenology Vindicated," *New England Magazine* 7 (1834): 432–44.

46. Tobias Purington, *Report on Capital Punishment, Made to the Maine Legislature in 1836* (3d ed., Washington, D.C., 1852).

the higher and weaken the undesirable tendencies through sustained educational effort.[47] On such an exalted moral level, phrenology offered a bridge to narrow the gulf between doubt and insecurity on the one hand and noble aspirations on the other. When applied in this form to health, psychiatry, crime, humanitarian reform, and education, phrenology appealed to leading publicists, humanitarians, and educators.

The tide turned, however, with the vulgarization and commercialization of the cult by pretentious practitioners and itinerant lecturers.[48] After a superficial inspection of the skull's contours, these operators analyzed the customer's temperament and character by relating the brain structure to such attributes as reason, memory, will, amativeness, veneration, benevolence, and destructiveness. Advice on appropriate marriage partners and vocations followed as a matter of course. Moreover, phrenologists assured clients that inclinations could quickly and easily be changed by the force of will and by habit. In the test of experience, promises failed. Most intellectuals who had seen phrenology as the new science of individual differences and as a road to the improvement of human nature concluded that, after all, it was little more than a romanticized pseudo-science.

If individuals differed in endowment, difference between the sexes was even more of a reality, in the view of almost everyone. Virtually every discussion involved the emotional component of human nature, whether the argument rested on traditional or on new ideas.

On a level often remote from reality, the "innate" gifts of women for sensitivity, intuition, empathy, and wonderment inspired romantic love. Widely read novels and verse either endowed this with glorified sentimentality and ecstasy or shrouded broken trysts and broken hearts with a piercing inaccessibility and melancholy. Edgar Allan Poe's poems "To Helen" and "Annabel Lee" gossamered the image of fair maidens in a never-ending dream world, while Philip Pendleton Cooke poignantly wept from pain and sorrow at the death of the beautiful and haunting "Florence Vane."

In a different way, the genteel, middle-class version of the romantic impulse attributed to women a special inborn capacity for purity,

47. George Combe, *The Constitution of Man Considered in Relation to External Objects* (Boston, 1841), pp. 179–91, 351–80; and Nahum Capen, *Reminiscences of Dr. Spurzheim and George Combe* (New York, 1881).

48. Nelson Sizer's *Forty Years in Phrenology* (New York, 1882), an interesting and useful account, needs to be supplemented by Madeline B. Stern's *Heads and Headlines: The Phrenological Fowlers* (Norman, Okla., 1971).

submissiveness, piety, and domesticity.[49] In glorifying these traits, the devotees of True Womanhood largely ignored not only blacks but the countless wives and daughters who toiled long hours on farms or in mills and shops.[50] Nor did champions of the cult see any inconsistency between the submissive and domestic ideal and the courage, boldness, endurance, and vigor of the women whom Mrs. Elizabeth Ellet celebrated in *The Pioneer Women of the West*.[51]

Pauline Christianity lent authority to this version of women's relation to human nature. It taught that they were endowed with inferior ability for logical reasoning. Mrs. Sarah Josepha Hale, leading editor of ladies' magazines and an advocate of larger vocational and cultural opportunities for her sex, only slightly changed the stand she took in 1832. Woman was created, not inferior to man, she wrote, but dependent on him "because she was the first in transgression." For this she was subjected to him and thus "the government and the glory of the world, do in fact belong to him." At the same time, she added, "what men shall be, depends on the secret, silent, but sure influence of women."[52] The sentiment was endlessly echoed by self-made men who in paying tribute to their mothers—and wives—acknowledged the influence of feminine purity, piety, and domesticity on their achievements.

The science and pseudo-science of the day strengthened religious authority by also regarding women as the weaker sex. Dr. Charles Meigs, a well-known Philadelphia obstetrician, taught that woman's intellectual power differed from that of her Lord and Master.[53] Physiological and medical opinion generally held that the female brain was smaller than that of the male and implied that this signified mental inferiority. A more delicate and complex nervous system, functional to

49. I am indebted to Barbara Welter's brilliant discussion, "The Cult of True Womanhood," in *The American Quarterly* 18 (1966): 151–74, and to Nancy C. Cott's *The Bonds of Womanhood: "Women's Sphere" in New England, 1780–1835* (New Haven, 1977), for the analysis of the place of domesticity, religion, education, and sisterhood in a widely held image of the distinctive female aspects of human nature.

50. Gerder Lerner, "The Lady and the Mill Girl: Changes in the Status of Women in the Age of Jackson," *Mid-Continent American Studies Journal* 10 (1969): 5–15.

51. Elizabeth Ellet, *Pioneer Women of the West* (New York, 1852). Mrs. Ellet broke a new path in bringing attention to women's part in the western movement. Her *Domestic History of the American Revolution*, 2 vols. (New York, 1850), was also the first book to deal in detail with the contributions of women to Independence.

52. *Ladies Magazine* 5 (1832), cited in Isabelle Webb Entriken, *Sarah Josepha Hale and Godey's Lady's Book* (Philadelphia, 1946), p. 37. It is worth noting that in 1865 Mrs. Hale, writing to Dr. James Rush, took him to task for the inadequate treatment of women in his newly published magnum opus, *Brief Outline of an Analysis of the Human Intellect*. Mrs. Hale to Rush, October 24, 1865, Rush Papers, Library Company of Philadelphia.

53. Dr. Charles Meigs, *Females and Their Diseases* (Philadelphia, 1848), pp. 40 ff.; and *Lectures on Some of the Distinctive Characteristics of the Female* (Philadelphia, 1847).

child-bearing, accounted for both her proneness to ill health and insanity and her greater talents for love, affection, and tenderness. Woman's constitution also explained her sensitivity to religion, morality, purity, and beauty. Many medical writers held, long before Dr. William Acton, an English authority who gave his approval to the idea in 1857, that the baser passions, including the sex drive, were for the most part far less strong in women than in men. Nor were physicians alone among those in the scientific community in holding this vew. Phrenologists who, as we have seen, claimed scientific validity for their position, found in female skulls proof of superior Benevolence, Adoration, Veneration, Conscientiousness, and Ideality.[54]

The personal and social values of the image of female piety, virtue, and domesticity further reenforced its vogue. It gave many women a sense of self-esteem in the role of wife and mother by substituting dignity and uniqueness for what had often seemed to be fate or drudgery. It enhanced the sense of social importance by assuming that women, from their elevated pedestal, radiated piety, morality, and domestic virtues for the good of society. Promulgators of the image admonished mothers, uniquely fitted for child-rearing, to instill in children patriotic devotion to the Republic. Moreover, women, protected from the tumult of marketplace and forum could, thanks to their gift for compassion and understanding, cushion the harsh struggles of fathers and husbands by upholding moral and religious values and by making the home a sanctuary of beauty and comfort. Nor was this all. In the South, submission to male protection had a special meaning: it was necessary to insure the purity of the white race, which was seen to be endangered by the alleged sexual aggressiveness of the black male. Even so, a good many plantation wives, burdened with the demanding tasks of a complex household, the care of ailing slaves, and the demands of hospitality, chafed under the protective restrictions on self-expression and cultural improvement. Such a conflict between ideal and actuality only slightly dimmed the romanticized version of the southern lady.[55] The conflict was further implied in the sexual exploitation of female slaves and the burden for white women in the knowledge that husbands often had black mistresses.

Dissidents, in reacting against such a romanticized image, worked out several strategies, few of which themselves escaped the influence of romanticism.

Catharine Beecher, an extraordinary member of an extraordinary

54. J. G. Spurzheim, *Phrenology in Connection with the Study of Physiognomy* (Boston, 1836), pp. 216 ff.; Joseph A. Warne, *Phrenology in the Family* (Boston, 1839); and Lorenzo N. Fowler, *Marriage* (New York, 1846), p. 202.

55. Anne Firor Scott, *The Southern Lady: From Pedestal to Politics, 1830–1930* (Chicago, 1970), chaps. 1–3.

family, did not deny the innate gifts of her sex for piety, submissiveness, purity, and domesticity. On the other hand, she rejected the sentimentalized image of female delicacy and mystery. She offered in its place a utilitarian view of the nature and true functions of her sex. Through precept and example, she broadened the romantically defined role of women by capitalizing on their "inborn" capacities. Frowning on the "superficial ornaments" prized by female seminaries, Beecher founded schools that encouraged physical health, mental discipline, and efficient and enlightened teaching and homemaking. Her lectures and her books, including *A Treatise on Domestic Economy* (1841), admonished her sex to find satisfaction in developing its unique gifts for making life better for everyone.[56]

The small but determined band that rejected both the romantic view of Pure Womanhood and its utilitarian supplement launched its own crusade for equal rights and opportunities. The new militants were familiar in a general way with the pathbreaking ideas of Mary Wollstonecraft and such early nineteenth-century feminists as Frances Wright and Judith Sargent Murray.[57] Sensitive to the limitations imposed by law and custom on the activities of women and indignant at the refusal of leading abolitionists to allow them equal opportunities for opposing slavery and other social evils, Elizabeth Cady Stanton, Lucretia Mott, and like-minded friends organized the first woman's rights convention at Seneca Falls in 1848. Its now familiar resolutions invoked the Declaration of Independence by identifying universal rights with human nature. The right and duty of women, equally with men, to promote every righteous cause by word and deed in public as in private was elaborated in memorable rhetoric: ". . . this being a self-evident truth growing out of the divinely implanted principles of human nature, any custom or authority adverse to it, whether modern or wearing the hoary sanction of antiquity, is to be regarded as a self-evident falsehood, and at war with mankind."[58] Two years later a follow-up meeting in

56. Kathryn Kish Sklar's *Catharine E. Beecher: A Study in American Domesticity* (New Haven, 1973) emphasizes role analysis and psychological issues in a broadly informed, scholarly treatment.

57. Mary Wollstonecraft, *A Vindication of the Rights of Women* (London, 1792), esp. chaps. 8 and 9. For remarks on human nature, see pp. 51, 106, 168, and 295. In addition to A. J. G. Perkins and Theresa Wolfson, *Frances Wright, Free Inquirer* (New York, 1939), see Sidney Ditzion's account of the early crusaders in his *Marriage, Morals and Sex in America* (New York, 1953); and Linda K. Kerber, "Daughters of Columbia: Educating Women for the Republic, 1787–1805," in Stanley Elkins and Erick McKittrick, eds., *The Hofstadter Aegis: A Memorial* (New York, 1974), pp. 36–59.

58. "The Seneca Falls Declaration of Sentiments and Resolutions, July 19, 1848," Elizabeth Cady Stanton, Susan B. Anthony, and Matilda J. Gage, eds., *The History of Woman Suffrage*, 6 vols. (New York, 1881–1927), 1:70–73.

Ohio asserted that "rights are coeval with the human race, of univeral heritage and inalienable; that every human being, no matter of what color, sex, condition, or climate, possesses these rights upon perfect equality with all others."[59] But the trouble with this Enlightenment tenet was that it overlooked reality: the whole past, at least as it had been presented, denied any such equality.

The paradox did not go unchallenged. Lydia Maria Child, who had enjoyed literary success before becoming an abolitionist, brought to public attention the varied contributions of women in the past.[60] Elizabeth Oakes Smith, whose adventure stories and juveniles had won Poe's praise, went even further by insisting on the actual superiority of women. She claimed that the feminine gifts of intuition, flexibility, unselfishness, and love were of a higher order than masculine logic, hardness, and selfishness. "The angels," she somewhat pontifically announced, "recognize her as of nearer affinity."[61] Nor did she stand alone. Elizabeth Farnham, prison reformer, abolitionist, and feminist, boasted in *Woman and Her Era* (1864) that the reproductive function elevated the sex to a near God-like status. Supporting her thesis by arguments from physiology, religion, philosophy, literature, and art, Farnham insisted that this unrecognized and repressed inherent superiority explained discriminations against females, whether in lower wages in factories and shops or in limited opportunities for developing minds and personalities. Her bold thesis did not greatly appeal to women committed to equalitarianism. Such a contention may, however, have contributed to the sense of women's self-esteem. In any case, it broke new ground by viewing their innate characteristics as a superior expression of human nature.[62]

A better-known strategy on women's behalf identified natural rights with the whole living future by projecting a dynamic, organic concept of human nature. In this redefinition, the Transcendentalists could come to terms with the emphasis on the emotions that suffused the concept of

59. Stanton, Anthony, and Gage, eds., *History of Woman Suffrage*, 1:106.

60. Lydia Maria Child, *The History and Condition of Women, in Various Ages and Nations*, 2 vols. (New York, 1835).

61. Elizabeth Oakes Smith, *Woman and Her Needs* (New York, 1851); *Selections from the Autobiography of Elizabeth Oakes Smith*, ed. Mary Alice Wyman (Lewiston, Me., 1924), pp. 151–53.

62. Elizabeth Woodson Farnham, *Woman and Her Era*, 2 vols. (New York, 1864); see David Lewis's biographical sketch of Farnham in Edward T. James and Janet W. James, eds., *Notable American Women, 1607–1950: A Biographical Dictionary*, 3 vols. (Cambridge, Mass., 1971), 1:493–94. There is no evidence that Mrs. Farnham was familiar with a comparable view set forth three years earlier by the Swiss ethnologist Johann Jacob Bachofen.

pure womanhood more easily than could the rationalist heirs of the Enlightenment.

Theodore Parker was an ambivalent figure in this redefinition. The emphasis on development was clear in his sermon on the public role of women:

> If a woman is a human being, she has the nature of a human being; next, she has the right of a human being; third, she has the duty of a human being. The nature is the capacity to possess, to use, to develop, and to enjoy every human faculty; the right is the right to enjoy, develop, and use every human faculty; and the duty is to make use of the right, and make her human nature human history. She is here to develop her human nature, enjoy her human rights, perform her human duty. . . .[63]

Continuing, Parker held that just as each man had the natural right as a human being to develop his peculiar nature as a man, so "each woman has just the same natural and inalienable right to the normal development of her peculiar nature as woman, and not man." Had Parker stopped here, he might have rejected the static norm in the traditional natural rights image of man and undermined the romantic cult of womanhood as well. But he stopped short of this. "At present," he wrote, "mankind, as a whole, has the superiority over womankind, as a whole, in all that pertains to intellect, the higher and the lower. Man has knowledge, has ideas, has administrative skills: enacts the rules of conduct for the individual, the family, the community, the church, the state, and the world. He applies these rules of conduct to life, and so controls the great affairs of the human race. You see what a world he has made of it." Then he added: "I think man will always lead in affairs of intellect—of reason, imagination, understanding—he has a bigger brain; but that woman will always lead in affairs of emotion, moral, affectional, religious—she has the better heart, the truer intuition of the right, the lovely, the holy." Further, the function of woman was "to correct man's taste, mend his morals, excite his affections, inspire his religious faculties. Man is to quicken her intellect, to help her will, translate her sentiments to ideas, and enact them into righteous laws."[64]

Margaret Fuller was of a different mind about such distinctiveness as women might inherently have. It could be that the "especial genius of women" was "electrical movement, intuitive in function, spiritual in tendency. She is great, not so easily in classification, or re-creation, as in an instinctive seizure of causes, and a simple breathing out of what she

63. Theodore Parker, "A Sermon on the Public Function of Women," *The Works of Theodore Parker*, 15 vols. (Boston, 1907–11), 9:190.

64. Parker, *Works*, 9:202, 204–5.

receives that has the singleness of life, rather than the selecting or emerging art." But any such special endowments did not warrant the persistence of social customs that cramped the growth of a woman's capacities in whatever sphere. "I would have her free from compromise, from complaisance, from helplessness, because I would have her good enough to love one and all beings, from the fullness, not the poverty, of being." This was in effect the application of the Transcendentalist theme of the self-sufficiency of every soul in its meeting with the over-soul. The customary insistence of men on defining the limits of self-realization for women had actually made self-realization impossible for each sex. One example was the age-old admonition to women that men had stronger passions which women could not even understand. Thus she must submit to the male's will lest even the appearance of coldness or withdrawal "turn her husband's thoughts to illicit indulgence; for a man is so constituted that he must indulge his passions or die!"[65]

Emerson, at least in principle, also scorned masculine prescription of feminine duty. He argued that "woman only can tell the heights of feminine nature, and the only way in which man can help her, is by observing woman reverently, and whenever she speaks from herself, and catches him in inspired moments up to a heaven of honor and religion, to hold her to that point by reverential recognition of the divinity that speaks through her." Another corollary of the Transcendentalist assumption that every human being was natively endowed with divine intuitions and gifts suggested that sex, notwithstanding the innate differences between men and women, was relative rather than absolute. Emerson supposed that "Hermaphrodite is then the symbol of the finished soul."[66] Thus the Concord Seer, sometimes an uneasy friend of Margaret Fuller, reenforced her pronouncement that "Man partakes of the feminine in the Apollo, Woman of the masculine as Minerva."[67]

Assumptions about human nature also influenced much that was said about race. The constitution of the first antislavery society, founded in Philadelphia in 1775, asserted that the two sanctions on which its

---

65. Margaret Fuller, "The Great Lawsuit, Man *Versus* Men. Woman *Versus* Women," *The Dial* 4 (1843): 47; Margaret Fuller Ossoli, *Woman in the Nineteenth Century* (Boston, 1855), p. 150. The scholarly literature on Margaret Fuller is vast. For varying interpretations, see Barbara Welter's essay, "Mystical Feminist," in her *Dimity Convictions: The American Woman in the Nineteenth Century* (Columbus, Oh., 1976), chap. 9; and Susan Phinney Conrad, *Perish the Thought: Intellectual Women in Romantic America 1830–1860* (New York, 1976), which canvasses the relationship between intellectualism, feminism, and romanticism.

66. Emerson, *Journals*, 6 (1843): 369, 378, 405.

67. Ossoli, *Woman in the Nineteenth Century*, p. 116.

members relied were "the rights of human nature" and the "obligations of Christianity." Similarly, the memorial from Virginia to the House of Representatives in 1791 proclaimed that "slavery is not only odious degradation but an outrageous violation of one of the most essential rights of human nature."[68] This view was expressed again and again when antislavery became a lively issue a few decades later.

William Ellery Channing's *Slavery* (1835) yielded nothing in holding that the institution was a denial of human nature. He felt that what distinguished man as man was the common possession of attributes far more important than any differences. Thus it was right to speak of the equality of man. The shared attributes, innate in origin, were a rational nature, the power of conscience, and a capacity for the indefinite improvement of these faculties and for the happiness to be found in their virtuous use. Even the innumerable diversities among men were ordained to bind them together. From this it followed that no group had the right to subdue another. "Nature's seal is affixed to no instrument by which property in a single being is conveyed."[69]

On the issue of differences between races and nations, Emerson more or less spoke for his friends. In the spirit of primitivism, he professed sympathy with the wild man who might, along with the beast, enable civilized man to understand himself the better. It was an open question in such discourse whether the differences between wild and civilized men, and between races, resulted more from innate differences in endowment of reason, intuition and the sense of morality and beauty, or from environment and a particular stage of development. It was in any case generally assumed in circles given to romantic views that each race was to travel along its own road toward that growth which was the destiny of all peoples. Thus Emerson, who believed that the Negro, thanks to his temperament, appeared to make the greatest amount of happiness out of the smallest capital, could also write, "if the black man carries in his bosom an indispensable element of a new and coming civilization, for the sake of that element no wrong nor strength nor circumstances can hurt him, he will survive and play his part. . . . Here is Man; and if you have man, black or white is an insignificance. Why at night, all men are black!"[70]

Such an opinion ignored or denied the claims of empirical investigators of race differences. Dr. Samuel George Morton of Philadelphia reported measurable differences in the skull formation of

68. William F. Poole, *Anti-slavery Opinions before the Year 1800* (Cincinnati, Oh., 1873), pp. 42 ff.; *Annals of Congress* (December 8, 1791), p. 1239.

69. Channing, *Works*, p. 694.

70. Emerson, *Journals and Miscellaneous Notebooks*, 9 (1844): 125. For a criticism of the Transcendentalist position on slavery see Stanley Elkins, *Slavery: A Problem of Institutional Life* (New York, 1959), p. 169 ff.

Indians, Africans, and Caucasians. These were presumably responsible for character and conduct. "In disposition," he wrote, "the negro is joyous, flexible, and indolent; while the many nations which compose this race present a singular diversity of intellectual characters, of which the far extreme is the lowest grade of humanity."[71] The implication of inborn Negro inferiority confirmed the dominant view in both North and South that ineradicable shortcomings incapacitated blacks for freedom. Two statements may be taken to represent a wide spectrum. "I do not say," wrote Dr. Thomas Cooper, president of South Carolina College and a friend of Jefferson, "the blacks are a distinct species; but I have not the slightest doubt of their being an inferior variety of the human species; and not capable of the same improvement as the whites."[72] Nathan Appleton, a Boston merchant and philanthropist, expressed the common opinion in the North that it was impossible for the two races to have equal political and civil rights. "Without a change in *human nature*, the people most forceful will oppress the weaker."[73]

The full-blown southern proslavery argument cited, as evidence for innate racial inferiority of the blacks, not only skull measurements, but the record of history and the unquestionable need of the Negro for dependence, guidance, and control. These ideas, with appeals to Aristotle's argument of "born slaves" and the biblical justification for slavery, were systematically developed by President Thomas Dew of William and Mary College and Dr. Josiah Nott of Mobile. George Fitzhugh, a Virginia planter, made the added point that the benevolence, order, and good of a whole society, inherent in a non-competitive ordering of human nature, made slavery both necessary and desirable.[74] Albert Taylor Bledsoe of the University of Virginia went even further in his curious, involuted use of natural rights theory. He

71. Samuel George Morton, *Crania Americana* . . . (Philadelphia, 1839), p. 7; *Crania Egyptiaca* (Philadelphia, 1844). In the article "Hybridity of Animals," in the *American Journal of Science and Arts*, 2d ser. 3 (1847), Dr. Morton concluded that "the mere fact that the several races of mankind produce with each other, a more or less likely fertile progeny, constitutes, in itself, no proof of the unity of the human species" (p. 212). *Types of Mankind: or Ethnological Researches* . . . . , ed. Josiah Nott and George R. Gliddon (Philadelphia, 1854), stressed even more strongly than Morton the argument for the innate inferiority of the Negro race.

72. Dr. Thomas Cooper to Sen. Mahlon Dickerson, March 16, 1826, *American Historical Review* 6 (1901): 729.

73. Nathan Appleton to the Rev. I. N. Danforth, August 2, 1847, in Nathan Appleton Papers, Massachusetts Historical Society. See also John Campbell, *Negro-Mania* (Philadelphia, 1851).

74. For general exposition: William S. Jenkins, *Pro-Slavery Thought in the Old South* (Chapel Hill, 1935); and Eric L. McKittrick, ed., *Slavery Defended: The Views of the South* (Englewood Cliffs, N.J., 1963). Of special interest are George Fitzhugh's *Sociology for the South* (Richmond, Va., 1844); and Eugene Genovese's appreciative essay in his *The World the Slaveholder Made* (New York, 1969).

admitted that liberty was indeed an inalienable, natural right. Slavery did not deprive the slave of this. It insured the black, being "by nature a slave," his natural right to be owned and governed by his master. Moreover, the argument against slavery involved license, not liberty. Thus the institution gave the Negro the kind of liberty that conformed to his nature.[75]

Some white abolitionists and such bold Negro spokesmen as Dr. James McCune Smith,[76] Dr. Martin R. Delany,[77] and Frederick Douglass developed a counterargument.[78] They insisted that Africans had created great civilizations. The present degraded state of the race could only be laid at the door of the disrupting and corrupting slave trade and dehumanization of slavery. In their view the courageous struggles of slaves for freedom, whether in the West Indies or in the Gabriel, Vesey, and Nat Turner insurrections, or in the daring attempts to flee northward, proved that blacks shared with other races the common need and will of human nature to be free.

In challenging the proslavery doctrine, others made the democratic assumptions about human nature explicit.[79] George Sidney Camp, a Connecticut minister, argued that the same constitution that made men moral beings made them self-governing creatures. Freedom of the will insured the right to control one's own actions. Without this, the whole moral structure, an inherent part of human nature, was an awful mockery. Thus every step that society took to improve morality, Camp argued, was a step toward self-government. Moreover, the moral right of such freedom was equally true of every people in every age, for the principle was as fundamental, as permanent, as universal as human nature itself.[80]

The concern of many for the idea of freedom as an impulse of human nature was limited to the white people of Europe and America, however.

75. Jenkins, Pro-Slavery Thought, pp. 123–24.
76. Smith's essays appeared in The Anglo-African Magazine: "Citizenship," in 1 (May 1859): 144 ff.; and "On the Fourteenth Query of Thomas Jefferson's Notes on Virginia," in 1 (August 1859): 225–38.
77. Martin R. Delany, The Condition, Elevation, Emigration and Destiny of the Coloured People of the United States (Philadelphia, 1852; rept. ed., New York, 1968).
78. Philip S. Foner, ed., The Life and Writings of Frederick Douglass, 5 vols. (New York, 1950–55).
79. The anonymous essay, "The Absolute Equality of the Mind," in the United States Magazine and Democratic Review 24 (1848): 24–32 is, though abstract and over-argued, an arresting statement relating human nature and equality.
80. George Sidney Camp, Democracy (New York, 1841). Camp explicitly tried to refute Tocqueville's contention that democracy is apt to result in the tyranny of the majority (pp.

The United States, they contended, being more youthful and vigorous and in most ways a step ahead in the development of republican self-rule, should actively encourage others who were struggling for freedom. This might of course be just by shining example. More expansive and chauvinistic democrats held that the obligation ought to take the form of material aid. The point was pushed when Louis Kossuth came to America to beg help for a renewed Hungarian struggle against Hapsburg "tyranny."[81] The nationalistic concept of the mission of the United States in the world was not put to rest by the failure of the Young America interventionists of 1849–52. Moved by economic interest and romanticized patriotism, intellectuals issued countless statements on America's "manifest destiny" to spread abroad its superior civilization. This would not only give expression to the restlessly superior American temperament, but would also help less-favored peoples realize the potentialities which nature had bestowed on them. The concept of America as the redeemer was a powerful reenforcement for such urges; the new nation was destined to be the seat of the millennium and the agent for hastening it through evangelizing the world. America was imbued with high potential in its endowment of human nature.[82]

In the eyes of some, man's innate capacity for and right to freedom required that governmental action uproot props to artificial privileges. Andrew Jackson, in vetoing the Bank recharter bill in 1832, admitted that human institutions could not create equality of talents, of education, or of wealth, but he said, nevertheless, that "in the full enjoyment of the gifts of heaven and the fruits of superior industry, economy, and virtue, every man is equally entitled to protection by law." When laws undertook "to add to these natural and just advantages artificial distinctions . . . to make the rich richer and the potent more powerful, the humble members of society . . . have a right to complain of the injustice of their Government."[83]

102 ff., 160 ff.). For an interesting contemporary comment see the *United States Magazine and Democratic Review* 10 (1842): 122–28.

81. "Young America," in Merle Curti's *Probing Our Past* (New York, 1955), pp. 219–45, can be supplemented by Donald S. Spencer, *Louis Kossuth and Young America: A Study of Sectionalism and Foreign Policy* (Columbia, Mo., 1977).

82. Ernest Lee Tuveson, in *Redeemer Nation: The Idea of America's Millennial Role* (Chicago, 1968), relates the idea of the American mission to religious millenarianism. For secular contributions to the idea see Albert K. Weinberg, *Manifest Destiny: A Study of Nationalist Expansion in American History* (Baltimore, 1935; rpt. ed., Gloucester, Mass., 1958); Edward McNall Burns, *The American Idea of Mission: The Concept of National Purpose and Destiny* (New Brunswick, N.J., 1957); and Frederick Merk, *Manifest Destiny and Mission in American History: A Reinterpretation* (New York, 1963).

83. James Richardson, *Messages and Documents of the Presidency*, 12 vols. (Washington, D.C., 1896), 2:590.

The implications of the doctrine of innate capacities for an intuitional understanding of truth, for moral discrimination, for freedom, and for equality were even more far-reaching in religion than in secular affairs.[84] When applied to the saving of souls in revivals, the deeply entrenched and powerful emotions in human nature buttressed freedom and equality, since every sinner could become a "new man." To be sure, it could happen only through a benevolently bestowed grace. Yet both the wayward and the revivalist had to exert themselves to that end. This required first of all a communal atmosphere in which sinners on "the anxious seat" gave clear signs of "preparation" for receiving grace. Equally necessary was the talent of the skillful revivalist who understood human motives and emotions, especially the sense of guilt and the yearning for a share in the great experience. Eloquence was only a mainstay of the ladder, as the handsome and engaging Reverend John M. Maffit pointed out in his *Oratorical Dictionary* (1835):

> To avail ourselves of the full power of eloquence we must . . . respect and cherish the affections; we must deepen and verify them; we must cease to repress the intense aspirations of humanity after the great and the beautiful. . . . Truth must be planted in the hotbed of feeling if we would taste its richest fruits and please our senses with its flowery developments. . . . Man becomes like his God when he can by a word unchain the impulses of every deep, generous and rich feeling which ever throbbed in the bosom of humanity, and bring to earth the vast sweet thought of heaven.[85]

No revivalist, however, matched Charles G. Finney in skillful organization and clinical insight. Of the innumerable practical, down-to-earth suggestions and guidelines in his *Lectures on the Revivals of Religion*, none revealed more than the exhortation to regard religion as "something to *do*, not something to *wait for*"—something to be done now or risk eternal death.[86]

Criticisms of Finney's technique were in part based on the conviction that exaggerated emotions could not be maintained once the revival was over—as the subsequent "declension" of religion only too sadly proved. Unitarians and liturgical churchmen made much of this. So did the Old School Presbyterians in scholarly articles in the prestigious *Princeton*

84. Sydney Alstrom has delineated the wide-ranging religious responses to romanticism in *A Religious History of the American People* (New Haven, 1972), pp. 583–636.

85. Cited in Charles Cole, Jr., *The Social Ideas of the Northern Evangelists 1820–1860* (New York, 1954), pp. 234–35.

86. Charles G. Finney, *Lectures on Revivals of Religion* (New York, 1833), p. 181. See also William C. McLoughlin's excellent introduction to his edition of Finney's *Lectures* (Cambridge, Mass., 1960), pp. vii–lii.

Review. In terms of the discussion of human nature two leaders stood out because of the psychological insight that informed their criticism.

The Reverend John Nevin, an Old School Presbyterian who had become a force in the German Reformed Church, argued that Finney's great heresy lay in his claim that conversion was "the product of the sinner's own will, and not truly and strictly a new creation in Christ Jesus by the power of God." He denounced Finney's "anxious seat" as one of many "solemn tricks for effect." It was to be viewed, he went on, as a mechanical device for arousing "fanatical impressions." These misled sinners into thinking that justification could be experienced by feeling rather than by faith.[87]

The criticism offered by Horace Bushnell, a Congregational minister at Hartford, was more original, more controversial, and in the long run more influential than Nevin's. Bushnell's position has to be understood in terms of his role as mediator between the romantic, spontaneous intuitions and emotions that Coleridge emphasized and the modified Edwardianism of the New Divinity that Nathaniel Taylor expounded so ably at Yale. Recognizing the value of revivals, Bushnell also insisted that they obscured a fact of immense importance, one clearly upheld by Scripture and accepted in most churches of the Old World and within the tradition of some of the New. This was the importance of nurturing children in an "organic" Christian family in which distinctions between creed and conduct and between the natural and supernatural were minimized in daily life. When the developing nature of the child was thus nourished, he would feel no need of conversion, having always had the consciousness of being a Christian. In other words, revivals put too much emphasis on individualism and too little on the role of the "organic" Christian family, church, and community, all of which could nurture Christian faith, character, and conduct. Bushnell's conviction that language imperfectly conveyed meaning and truth also explained his reservations about catechetical drill and the rhetoric of the revivalist. Bushnell felt that his position pointed out ways of lessening the gulf between the potential goodness of human nature and the universal pull of the passions and appetites.[88]

Not only revivalism but two related movements also gave the heightened emotions an important place in human nature.

87. John Williamson Nevin, *The Anxious Bench* (Chambersburg, Pa., 1843), pp. 7–8, 14, 16. James Hastings Nichols has discussed Nevin in *Romanticism in American Theology: Nevin and Schaff at Mercersburg* (Chicago, 1961).

88. Horace Bushnell, *Christian Nurture*, centennial ed., with an introduction by Luther A. Weigle (New Haven, 1947), pp. 4 ff., 17 ff., and chap. 5. The most satisfactory biography is Barbara Cross's *Horace Bushnell: Minister to a Changing America* (Chicago, 1958). See also William A. Clebsch, *From Sacred to Profane: The Role of Religion in American History* (New York, 1968), pp. 33–35, 86–87, 164–65.

The ancient belief in millenarianism, revived in the Reformation, attracted the persistent interest of theologians.[89] Contradictions and figurative language in Scripture accounted for varied interpretations, but in general it was agreed that after a titanic conflict between good and evil Christ would return to earth to set up his kingdom, over which he would gloriously rule for a thousand years. The idea carried various implications for human nature. Samuel Hopkins in his *Treatise on the Millennium* (1793) thought that God's renovation of the hearts of men resulted in a "new creation," though this did not mean that man's fallen nature, his sinfulness, had been entirely snuffed out. It did mean, however, that with God's help, human beings had achieved a holiness and a disinterested or unselfish benevolence toward each other. It also meant that such human wants as harmony, peace, abundance, and comfort flowed from the enhanced intellectual ability insured by the total illumination of the soul. A universal language eased understanding, worked toward the abolition of war, and promoted the blessings of a true community.[90]

Others read the relevant biblical texts in their own way. Alexander Campbell, a lay preacher in the West in the early nineteenth century, believed that since ignorance rather than innate sinfulness was the root of evil in human nature, enlightenment before and during Christ's reign was an effective, if not all-sufficient, agency. On the other hand, as Mark Hopkins of Williams College warned, important though knowledge and social reforms were in preparing for "that triumph of Christianity in which the perfection of society is involved," they at the most helped human beings "receive those influences of Christianity through which alone our perfect manhood can now find its consummation."[91] The significance of millenarianism for human nature has often been obscured by the crisis drama of the Millerite movement. The confusing discussion of scriptural prophecy, the malaise and widespread aspiration of the 1840s, partly explained the frenzied expectations of thousands of followers of the charismatic leader William Miller.[92]

89. James W. Davidson's *The Logic of Millennial Thought: Eighteenth-Century New England* (New Haven, 1977) is the most useful approach. Also valuable are R. Richard Niebuhr, *The Kingdom of God in America* (New York, 1937); and Perry Miller, *Errand into the Wilderness* (New York, 1956), chap. 10.

90. Samuel Hopkins, D.D., *A Treatise on the Millennium* (Boston, 1793; rept. ed., New York, 1972), pp. 41, 48, 49, 55, 59 ff., 65 ff.

91. Cited in Tuveson, *Redeemer Nation*, p. 74.

92. Clara E. Sears, *Days of Delusion* (Boston, 1924), is largely outmoded. Leon Festinger and others, *When Prophecy Fails* (Minneapolis, 1956), esp. pp. 12–15, deserves note. The citations in David E. Smith, "Millenarian Scholarship in America," *American Quarterly* 17 (1965): 535–49, are indicative of what had been done at the date of publication.

Assumptions about human nature implicit in millenarianism were made explicit in perfectionism, a primitive Christian idea with secular counterparts. It set forth the mystical conviction that sufficient faith in Christ could infuse the believer with man's initial sinlessness. The fullness of Christ's love resulted in a holiness which insured consecration and confidence, though not complete freedom from error and carnal appetites. Notable exponents were Phoebe Palmer, a New York physician's wife who emphasized the Wesleyan version of holiness and whose influence reached far beyond Methodist circles.[93] Edward Beecher asked for *"the immediate production of the elevated standard of personal holiness throughout the universal church—such a standard of holiness as God requires, and the present exigencies of the world demand."*[94] Two Oberlin presidents, Charles G. Finney and Asa Mahan, offered distinctions in what came to be called Oberlin Perfectionism.[95] One of the most engaging members of the Perfectionist circle was Professor Thomas C. Upham, an active advocate of peace, abolition, and other reforms and a mystic who synthesized the Wesleyan view and the intuitive experiences of medieval saints.[96] Frederic Dan Huntington, a Unitarian minister and Harvard professor, was also influenced by Phoebe Palmer's doctrine of holiness. He came to believe that "the world's salvation consists in a spiritual redemption . . . and *not* in a mere natural development of the human powers according to natural laws." Converted to Episcopalianism, Huntington, as bishop of central New York, tried to promote the goal of a truly Christian community by actively championing the rights of workers, Indians, and other disadvantaged groups.[97]

For some years a very different kind of leader, John Humphrey Noyes, did institutionalize on a small scale another version of perfectionism in

93. The indispensable source is of course Phoebe Palmer's *The Way of Holiness, with Notes by the Way* (New York, 1845). The best brief account of her career is W. J. McCutcheon's article in *Notable American Women*, 3:12–14. See, again, Timothy L. Smith, *Revivalism and Social Reform in Mid-Nineteenth-Century America* (New York, 1957), esp. pp. 122–27, 140–46, 169–71.

94. Edward Beecher, "The Nature, Importance, and Means of Eminent Holiness Throughout the Church," *The American National Preacher* 10 (1835): 194.

95. Timothy L. Smith, *Revivalism and Social Reform*, pp. 104 ff.

96. Thomas C. Upham, *Principles of the Interior or Hidden Life . . .* (New York, 1843); *The Life of Faith . . .* (New York, 1845); *A Treatise on Divine Union* (Boston, 1852). For an interesting contemporary qualified commendation see George O. Peck, "Dr. Upham's Work," *Methodist Quarterly Review* 27 (1846): 250–65.

97. Frederic Dan Huntington, *Sermons for the People* (Boston, 1856), *Christian Believing and Living* (Boston, 1859), and *Human Society: Its Providential Structural Relations* (New York, 1860); and Arria S. Huntington, *Memoir and Letters of Frederic Dan Huntington* (Boston, 1906).

community life. Under the stimulus of revivalist enthusiasm, this young Congregational minister, who had been tormented by his sense of sin, became convinced that the truly redeemed could not sin. Alienated from his family, his church, and society, he perceived perfectionism as a return to primitive Christianity and as the herald of the promised redemption. The biblical picture of the patriarchal family and the communal experiments of his day intrigued him. He concluded that perfectionism could be realized only if attachment to property and persons were forbidden. In the communities he established—that at Oneida was the most successful—he sought to achieve cooperation, affection, and godliness by eliminating private property, traditional marriage, and a sense of sin. As the head and father he arranged, with nominal community assent, paired partnerships in place of monogamous marriage. The justification was that sex, if properly managed to prevent exclusive possessiveness and conception, was a necessary condition of true communitarianism. In 1869 Noyes took a bold step that emphasized the utilitarian rather than the emotional aspects of sex. He openly authorized unions for propagating physically, intellectually, and socially superior offspring with a perfectionist goal. This was a secular foretaste of the eugenics movement that one day would claim scientific sanction.[98]

The perfectionist and millenial influences on the image of man that Noyes tied to communitarianism played a role in the Church of Jesus Christ of the Latter Day Saints. Joseph Smith, its founder and charismatic leader, developed with the help of theologically minded converts an eclectic cosmology and ethnology with a distinctive concept of human nature. This assumed that emotional needs were best fulfilled by a religion that underlined familial fellowship, the work ethic, theocratic leadership, with the security it offered, social discipline and participation, wholesome recreation, and polygamy. Though strongly utilitarian and patriotic in social, economic, and political outlook, Mormonism was also related to the romantic view of man in its conviction that God continued to reveal his will through his prophets and

98. George W. Noyes, ed., *Religious Experiences of John Humphrey Noyes* (New York, 1932) and *John Humphrey Noyes: The Putney Community* (Oneida, N.Y., 1931); John Humphrey Noyes, *Male Continence* (Oneida, N.Y., 1872); Robert A. Parker, *A Yankee Saint: John Humphrey Noyes and the Oneida Community* (New York, 1935); Robert David Thomas, *The Man Who Would be Perfect: John Humphrey Noyes and the Utopian Impulse* (Philadelphia, 1977); and Constance Noyes Robertson, *Oneida Community Profiles* (Syracuse, 1977). For helpful discussions see Stow Persons, "Christian Communitarianism in America," in Stow Persons and Donald Drew Egbert, eds., *Socialism in American Life*, 2 vols. (Princeton, 1952), 1:140 ff.; Michael Fellman, *The Unbounded Frame* (Westport, Conn., 1974), chap. 3; and Raymond L. Muncy, *Sex and Marriage in Utopian Communities: Nineteenth-Century America* (Bloomington, Ind., 1973).

that human beings were mystically related to a universe of uncreated and eternal spirits.[99]

Secular efforts to improve the human condition owed a good deal to the religious impulse and like it occasioned diverse views about the nature and uses of the emotions.[100]

This was true, for example, in the movement for universal elementary education for white children. In urging support for tax-supported free public schools, leaders made full use of arguments based on human nature. With varying qualifications and degrees of enthusiasm, educational reformers assumed the importance of environment in nourishing mental potentialities, and no less important, in encouraging a vigorous expression of the moral impulse.

Horace Mann developed this argument in a social and national context. A new era in the world had begun, he insisted, with the founding of the colonies and more particularly with the Revolution and adoption of the Constitution. "These events, it is true, did not change human nature; but they placed that nature in circumstances so different from any it had ever before occupied, that we must exact a new series of development in human character and conduct."[101] The development of free institutions multiplied and intensified human energies and passions alike. Thus the moral faculties must be nourished from early childhood both at home and in schools. In the same way, antisocial propensities must be subordinated to both intelligence and the moral faculty. "The question then is, What measures shall be adopted to give scope, expansion, and supremacy to the better susceptibilities of human nature, and to clamp down, as with triple bands of iron and brass, the passions and propensities which heretofore have made such havoc of the world's affairs?"[102]

99. The obvious starting point is *The Book of Mormon* and commentaries and biographies by Mormons and Gentiles. One of the best accounts of the Mormon subculture is Thomas F. O'Dea, *The Mormons* (Chicago, 1957). Also useful for Mormon psychology are Sterling M. McMurrin, *The Theological Foundations of the Mormon Religion* (Salt Lake City, Utah, 1965); and the essays, especially those of David Brion Davis and Mario S. DePilis, in *Mormonism and American Culture*, ed. Marvin S. Hill and James B. Allen (New York, 1972).

100. Though the focus is not on ideas about human nature, John L. Thomas's "Romantic Reform in America, 1815–1865," *American Quarterly* 17 (1965): 656–62, is relevant.

101. Horace Mann in the 1845 report as Secretary of the Massachusetts State Board of Education, *Life and Works of Horace Mann*, 5 vols. (Boston, 1891), 4:7. Mann made human nature a central theme in a great deal of his writing and discussion, both before and especially after his interest in phrenology. See, for examples, *Life and Works of Horace Mann*, 2:6–7; 4:191 ff.; 5:32 ff., 64 ff.

102. Editorial in *Common School Journal* 4 (1842): 99.

Leading educational reformers, including Mann, linked the need for free universal schools with their fear of growing urban slums, class differences and tensions, and the increase of crime. It seemed to them that universal education was the best way of strengthening social order and a sense of community among very different kinds of people. The virtue of discipline, patriotism, frugality, and the blessings of capitalism were to be explicitly (in many cases) inculcated with sustained vigor. This was the most dependable means of preventing or decreasing crime, social discontent, mob action, and even revolution—all of them manifestations of insufficiently tutored passions.[103]

On the other hand, it must also be pointed out that reformers stressed the importance of universal education for developing the full capacities of every human being. "We should retain and develop all our faculties, each in its place," wrote Orestes A. Brownson, "so as to preserve unbroken harmony through the whole man."[104] Such a view inspired experiments with the aims and methods of Pestalozzi and Fellenberg—the education of body, mind, and emotions. Alcott's school,[105] that of George Bancroft at Northampton, Massachusetts,[106] and the program at New Harmony and Brook Farm testified to the revolt against the traditional emphasis on mental and moral discipline through mere teaching, as well as to the romantic conception of the purity of childhood. Though in his effort to establish and strengthen common schools Horace Mann was unable to implement the new approach to education, he viewed sympathetically its bearing on the democratic and romantic ideal of continuous personal growth.[107] A comparable belief in the capacity of adults for self-improvement (cultural or utilitarian) was, with the encourage-

103. Recent monographs tend to document this position, which was a leading emphasis in Merle Curti, *The Social Ideas of American Educators* (New York, 1935; rev. ed., Paterson, N.J., 1959), esp. chap. 4. See, for examples, Ruth Miller Elson, *Guardians of Tradition: American Schoolbooks in the Nineteenth Century* (Lincoln, Nebr., 1964); Michael B. Katz, *The Irony of Early School Reform* (Cambridge, Mass., 1968); and David B. Tyack, *The One Best System: A History of American Urban Education* (Cambridge, Mass., 1974).

104. Orestes A. Brownson, *Christian Examiner* 17 (1834): 73.

105. Elizabeth Peabody, *Record of a School: Exemplifying the General Principles of Spiritual Culture* (Boston, 1836); and Amos Bronson Alcott, *Records of Conversations on the Gospels Held in Mr. Alcott's School* (Boston, 1836).

106. M. A. DeWolfe Howe, *The Life and Letters of George Bancroft*, 2 vols. (New York, 1908), 1:167–79.

107. Bernard Wishy, *The Child and the Republic: The Dawn of Modern American Child Culture* (Philadelphia, 1968), pp. 21–22, 52; Robert H. Bremner and others, eds., *Children and Youth in America: A Documentary History*, 3 vols. (Cambridge, Mass., 1970), 1:343–560. An early study, Iris C. Mead's "Concepts of Child Nature in American Life and Education, 1800–1900" (Ph.D. diss., Columbia University, 1951), is still useful.

ment of Mann and other educational reformers, institutionalized in newly founded libraries and in the inspirational lyceum lecture.

Interest in the handicapped owed a good deal to the idea that all human beings had the capacity for loving others—an idea the romantic image of man shared, of course, with Christianity, and to a lesser extent, with some aspects of Enlightenment thought. In their concern for the poor and lowly, men and women inspired by romantic feelings felt that the rational approach lacked warm, emotional interest in individuals as individuals. Yet such feeling was needed if the criminal, the mentally ill, the delinquent, the blind, and the deaf were to be really helped. Dr. Samuel Gridley Howe, one among many with this outlook, not only preached the possibility of lifting up the unfortunate by changing the environment, but also amazed the world by defying the Lockean idea that all learning stemmed from sense impression. He did this by sympathetically stimulating the human capacities of young Laura Bridgman, who had neither sight nor hearing. In the rehabilitation, affection and appreciation, emotions much emphasized in the romantic canon, provided inspiration and incentive to the girl's own efforts. Her achievements and Dr. Howe's part in them were duly publicized and celebrated.[108]

The romantic convictions about human nature that influenced political life, education, religion, and humanitarianism also figured in the assessment of national character. Scholars have noted a tendency to think of America as a new Garden of Eden offering mankind a chance to regain lost purity and innocence.[109] At the same time, like-minded commentators also viewed America as a providential stage for the recovery of the whole man. New World followers of Goethe, Schiller, Herder, and Coleridge believed that the Enlightenment had blighted this possibility by overstressing harmony, restraint, and empiricism. The romantic imagery that pictured America as a new Garden of Eden enriched the thought and rhetoric of such theologians as Horace

108. "Laura Bridgman," *Common School Journal* 5 (1843): 145 ff.; Harold Schwartz, *Samuel Gridley Howe* (Cambridge, Mass., 1956), pp. 67–90; Samuel Gridley Howe, *The Letters and Journals of Samuel Gridley Howe*, ed. Laura E. Richards, 2 vols. (Boston, 1906–9), 2:51–95; and Maude Howe Elliott and Florence Howe Hall, *Laura Bridgman: Dr. Howe's Famous Pupil and What He Taught Her* (Boston, 1904).

109. Henry Nash Smith, *Virgin Land: The American West as Symbol and Myth* (Cambridge, Mass., 1950); R. W. B. Lewis, *The American Adam: Innocence, Tragedy and Tradition in the Nineteenth Century* (Chicago, 1953); David W. Noble, *The Eternal Adam and the New World Garden* (New York, 1968).

Bushnell and Theodore Parker and such novelists as Robert Montgomery Bird, Hawthorne, and Melville.

Related to the Garden of Eden metaphor was the conviction that America had created or was creating a new man. It was doing this in part by mixing peoples from many lands, a view Hector St. John de Crèvecoeur had voiced in 1782. Now, in mid-century, the creation of a new man seemed to owe more to the subordination of institutions to the individual and to testing the utility of the family, church, community, and state in terms of the contribution each made to the full and free development of all persons alike. In Theodore Parker's judgment, Emerson was the most American of writers because he best represented the new personality that America had molded and was still molding. "We mean," Parker went on, "the idea of personal freedom, of the dignity and value of human nature, the superiority of man to the accidents of a man. The results of human experience . . . the state, the church, society, the family, business, literature, science, art—all of these are subordinate to man; if they serve the individual, he is to foster them, if not, to abandon them and seek better things."[110]

Walt Whitman, if at times sentimental and chauvinistic, carried to majestic height the idea of the American as a new man. His prose and verse celebrated an America in the process of creating "a race of perfect men, women & children, grandly developt in body, emotions, heroism & intellect—not a select class—but the general population."[111] In time, he hoped, the whole world would be united through love; in time all men were to live in free, ardent, and equal comradeship. But this romanticizing was tempered with more realistic insights, for Whitman had to confess a disappointment in "the shallowness and miserable selfishness of men and women en masse"—"flippant people with hearts of rags and souls of chalk."[112] Yet even this recognition only dimmed his hope, a hope reenforced by his discovery in Lincoln of the ideal American type.

Within the romantic view it was possible to question not only the American creation of a new man but even the possibility of any improvement. Edgar Allan Poe made this point forcefully.[113] Using the

110. Parker, *Works*, 8:62–63.

111. C. J. Furness, ed., *Walt Whitman's Workshop* (Cambridge, Mass., 1928), p. 56. See also Walt Whitman, *Complete Prose Works* (Boston, 1907), pp. 244, 269, 302, 313, 316, 326.

112. Furness, *Walt Whitman's Workshop*, p. 57.

113. Writing to Lowell on July 2, 1844, Poe declared that "man is only more active—not more happy—nor more wise, than he was 6000 years ago. The result will never vary, and to suppose that it will, is to suppose that the foregone time is not but the rudiment of the future—that the myriads who have perished have not been on an equal footing with ourselves—nor are we with posterity." Edgar Allan Poe, *The Letters of Edgar Allan Poe*, ed. John W. Ostrom, 2 vols. (Cambridge, Mass., 1948), 1:256.

literary hoax and the mystery tale, he depicted human nature with a penchant for crime, violence, and unfathomable riddles. In his prose cosmological poem *Eureka*, he found in both God and man a power of attraction, which he identified as matter, and a power of repulsion, which he associated with mind. Since everything was in a perpetual state of expansion and contraction and since there was no fundamental difference between divine and human, individual souls would cease to exist when cosmic history had run its course.[114] Although in *Eureka* as in other writings Poe reflected vivid traces of the Enlightenment, his rationalism, as Perry Miller has noted, was mixed with a sense of mystery "less clear and sunny than Transcendental mysticism." This was becoming to one who found life painfully turbulent and who made much of bafflement and of "detective" techniques in trying to come to terms with existence.

Romantic views of man, which did not sweep away the earlier images, looked, then, in different and even opposite directions. Still, the emphasis on the evocatively emotional and intuitive aspects of human nature often seemed to fit the changes in American life. Exponents consciously or unconsciously used the image for one purpose or another. Although the influence of these views continued, the years after mid-century were to see new and quite different approaches to the persisting problem of man's nature.

114. Boas, "Romantic Philosophy in America," in *Romanticism in America*, pp. 196 ff.

6

The Emerging Science of Human Nature

I see no reason why the application of systematized knowledge to the control of human nature may not in the course of the present century accomplish results commensurate with the nineteenth century applications of physical science to the natural world.

J. McKeen Cattell, 1904

It was the reductionist, Helmholtz and his kind who first caught James' interest for the "new science." He refused, however, to go along with these founders. His drive derived not from his concern with the processes of understanding, but from his concern with the mystery of human nature."

Edwin G. Boring, 1961

Never was there such a need and opportunity for developing the higher powers as now and in this land; never such need to go back to first principles and ask again what human nature, so vastly older than all its institutions, really is and means and needs.

G. Stanley Hall, 1923

DURING THE mid-nineteenth century, when romantic images of man ran high tide, what may be broadly thought of as a naturalistic and scientific conception of human nature gradually took shape. From this time on, the crucial roles in shaping views of human nature were to be played by new developments in the natural sciences, especially physics, physiology, and a good deal later, genetics; by the social studies, notably sociology and anthropology; by the organization of these fields of knowledge in ever-more-specialized academic disciplines within universities and professional associations; and indirectly, by such social, economic, and political forces as industrialism, imperialism, "racism," and social protests, including Progressivism and socialism. Every such movement and countermovement appealed to some view of human nature for justification.

In a less-broad context, the rising image of man was the offspring of interactions between three intellectual positions. The oldest derived from the Newtonian heritage of an abstract, generalized, static conception of mind, made up of particles (ideas and related actions) operating in accord with the laws of association and described by introspection and logic.[1] This tradition still dominated mental philosophy, even though it was challenged by the neo-Hegelian stress on the unity and activity of mind. The second position was grounded on new work in the physiology

1. R. B. MacLean, "Newtonian and Darwinian Conceptions of Man, and Some Alternatives," *Journal of the History of the Behavioral Sciences* 6 (1970): 207 ff.

of the nervous system, on physics, and on the application of mathematical tools for precise measurement and quantification. The third, of course, was the new speculative and inductive development of the fairly familiar concept of evolution.

Even before the publication of Darwin's *Descent of Man* (1871) and *The Expression of Emotions in Man and Animals* (1872) there had been a growing disposition to regard mental life as intimately connected with physiological processes subject to investigation by experimental methods.[2] Those who came to regard mental life as an organic, unitary process assumed that it developed according to the laws of all life: it was not merely a theater for the exhibition of independent, autonomous faculties, or a "rendezvous in which independent, atomic sensations and ideas . . . gather, hold external converse, and then forever part."[3]

Such a view was slow in taking form. In 1863 Dr. Isaac Ray, a leading American authority on mental health and illness, expressed the opinion that "the most prevalent belief, both among the wise and the simple, is that the mind is an independent essence or principle requiring the brain, not for its existence, but only for the mode of its manifestation." Such a view, he suggested, was congenial to, if indeed not necessary for, the belief in the immortality of mind and spirit.[4] In holding a dualistic conception of body and mind, some assumed a Cartesian interaction between the material body and an essentially immaterial consciousness. Others assumed a parallelism that, in the tradition of Leibniz, implied that each order of events, mental and physical, operated independently according to identical laws.

Some Americans, of course, had long recognized the influence of physiology on mental phenomena, a doctrine favored by many philosophers in the Enlightenment. Writers in the magazines of the late eighteenth and early nineteenth centuries expressed enthusiasm for it.[5] So did such leading educators as Francis Wayland and Mark Hopkins. Horace Mann felt that it was not "extravagant to say, that if, amongst those who lead sedentary lives, physical power could be doubled, their

2. James Rowland Angell, "The Influence of Darwin on Psychology," *Psychological Review* 16 (1909): 152 ff.

3. John Dewey, "The New Psychology," *Andover Review* 2 (1884): 285.

4. Isaac Ray, M.D., *Mental Hygiene* (New York, 1863), p. 4. Dr. Frank J. Curran has written an introduction to a facsimile edition published in New York in 1968.

5. Typical examples can be found in Henry Rose, *An Inaugural Dissertation on the Effects of the Passions upon the Body* (Philadelphia, 1794); *The Columbia Magazine* 1 (1787): 480–81; *New York Weekly Magazine* 1 (1795): 143; and *The Literary Magazine and American Register* 2 (1804): 195–96. See also *The Diary of George Templeton Strong*, 4 vols. (New York, 1952), 1:308.

mental powers could be doubled also."[6] The vaguely dualistic conception of body and mind of these leaders stopped short of defining the nature of the interaction between the two entities.

Such dualism stood in marked contrast to the largely submerged materialistic monism that had informed the thought of a few late eighteenth- and early nineteenth-century writers.[7] Admitting the scanty state of knowledge about the nature of the connection between body and mind, Dr. Isaac Ray leaned toward the view that the mind was entirely the function of the brain, that every individual was "endowed with various powers which, though serving each a special purpose, form an harmonious whole." Such a position provided a rationale for holding that systematic and proper exercise of each function or constituent resulted in the increased vigor, capacity, and power of endurance of the others.[8] Two years later, in 1865, Dr. James Rush, a son of Benjamin Rush, published a *Brief Outline of an Analysis of the Human Intellect.* "The mind," Rush wrote in the preface of his long, wordy, and badly put together book, "has been and still is regarded as the working of a *spiritual something* in the brain, and therefore not to be investigated, as a physical function of the senses and the brain conjoined. This appears," he continued, "to be the principal cause why the problem of the mind has not been finally solved, on the clear and assignable data of observation and experiment: for who has ever experimented upon Spirit?"[9]

Ray and Rush were not altogether alone in questioning the prevailing dualistic mental philosophy. Four years after Rush's book appeared, Dr. Christopher Columbus Graham, an eccentric Kentucky explorer and health expert, attacked faculty psychology, especially for the support it gave to the doctrines of free will and an innate moral intuitionalism. He advocated a biological and naturalistic approach to the study of mental and emotional phenomena.[10] Like Rush, however, he looked backward to the materialism of such classical writers as Democritus and Epictetus, to Bacon's homily on the inductive method, to Hobbes's mechanistic materialism, and to the associationism and sensationalism of Locke, Hartley, and Mill. Though Graham mentioned Darwin, to whom he

6. Horace Mann, "Prospectus," *Common School Journal* 1 (1838): 11. See also Mark Hopkins, *An Inaugural Address, Delivered at Williams College* (Troy, N.Y., 1836), pp. 13–19.

7. Hopkins, *Inaugural Address.*

8. Ray, *Mental Hygiene,* p. 6.

9. James Rush (1786–1869), studied medicine in Edinburgh and was best known for *The Philosophy of the Human Voice,* first published in Philadelphia in 1827 and reissued in five successive editions by 1867.

10. Christopher Graham, *The True Philosophy of Mind* (Louisville, Ky., 1869), p. 34.

even sent a copy of his book, he was, like Rush, apparently unacquainted with the scientific procedures for and the results of the study of body-mind relationships that had been under way for some time in Britain and on the Continent.

The challenge that the rising view of body-mind relationships offered to dualism rested in the first place on far-reaching investigations of the physiology of the nervous system, in which Europeans took the lead.[11] Sir Charles Bell and François Magendie discovered the differences between motor and sensory nerves—that is, between the two great systems of nerves performing different functions, the one carrying impressions from the surface of the body to the centers, the other sending impulses from the centers to muscles. No less momentous was Dr. Marshall Hall's discovery of the independent action of the spinal cord, the basis in the nervous system of the principle of reflex action which Descartes had foreseen. This was held to demark the scope and limits of voluntary activity, to check impulsive tendencies, and to direct bodily movements to various ends. It followed that voluntary actions constantly became reflex actions, as in the case of walking, which at first required deliberate effort and then became automatic and unconscious. The implication seemed to be that only a small part of our knowledge was at any time in our consciousness but that all of it was in our mind.

Growing knowledge of the physiology of the nervous system, strengthening the idea of the correlation of motion and sensation with the structure and operations of the brain, supported a mechanistic and monistic image of man.[12] Claude Bernard's discovery of the sugar-storing function of the liver demonstrated the influence of the internal body's environment and thus laid the foundations of modern endocrinology. Albrecht von Haller, working with animals, advanced his famous theory of the irritability or contractibility of muscle tissue. Of importance, too, was Pierre Flourens's method of extirpation of parts of

11. In this development Joseph Jastrow's "A New Science of the Mind," *Science* 11 (1888): 256 ff., is worthy of note. Detailed discussions are accessible in Edward B. Tichener, *Experimental Psychology*, 2 vols. (New York, 1905); and Clifford Morgan, *Physiological Psychology* (New York, 1943), esp. chap. 1.

12. One group sought to explain all phenomena in physiochemical terms, with the end result of an all-inclusive monistic materialism. Another group did not deny vitalistic principles in some aspects of existence. The great pathologist and social activist Rudolph Virchow, while sharing the antivitalistic principles of the so-called medical materialists, stopped short of carrying mechanical materialism to its all-encompassing finality. See, for a significant discussion, Walther Riese and E. C. Hoff, "A History of the Doctrine of Cerebral Localization," *Journal of the History of Medicine and the Allied Sciences* 5 (1950): 50–71; 6 (1951): 439–70.

the nervous system as a means of studying the physiological mechanism of behavior. Dubois Reymond and Alessandro Volta demonstrated the electrical stimulation of nerve centers. New knowledge of cerebral localization, building on the work of Gall, included Hermann Munck's evidence for the localization of sight-memory in the posterior parts of a dog's brain and Paul Broca's proof that an injury to the third frontal convolution seemed to make the victim mute. Hughlings Jackson, in his studies of the neurological basis of speech disorders and epilepsy, showed that sensations and movements were represented in the nervous system at several levels of complexity. His work supported the idea that cerebral functions could be explained exclusively in physiological terms.

Deeply influenced by these developments, pioneer American neurologists also contributed to the nineteenth-century sensorimotor model of the nervous system and the somatic explanation of mental behavior. In cooperation with others, Dr. S. Weir Mitchell, in *Gunshot Wounds and Other Injuries to the Nerves* (1864), anticipated the discovery in Europe of the presence of motor areas in the forebrain that controlled muscles on the opposite side of the body. Mitchell was also among the first to describe distinctly psychic phenomena in postsurgical cases.[13] Dr. William A. Hammond, an authority on the physiology of sleep, contributed to the theory that the evolution of the mind was the result not alone of the brain but of the sympathetic nervous system. His work also enlarged knowledge of the localization of certain mental operations of the spinal cord.[14] The clinical and laboratory work of Edward C. Spitzka made him a respected authority.[15] Perhaps the most impressive laboratory work in the 1880s was that of Dr. Moses A. Starr, who had studied with leading German and Austrian neurologists as well as with Helmholtz and Charcot. His work on the physiology of memory and on the localization of visual functions, the sense of touch, pain, and temperature in the parietal region, and the nature and effects of brain

13. Ernest Earnest, *S. Weir Mitchell, Novelist and Physician* (Philadelphia, 1950), pp. 50, 51, 177. In 1869 Mitchell's study of the physiology of the cerebellum, based on experiments on pigeons, concluded, on the basis of the effects of various types of injuries to the brain, that the "cerebellum functions as an augmenting organ to the cerebrospinal motor system." Cecilia C. Mettler, *History of Medicine* (Philadelphia, 1947), p. 159.

14. William A. Hammond, "The Relations between Mind and the Nervous System," *Lehigh University Exercises . . . Oct. 9, 1884* (Bethlehem, Pa., 1884); *Sleep and Its Derangement* (Philadelphia, 1869); C. L. Dana, "Early Neurology in the United States," *Journal of the American Medical Association* 90 (1928): 1421–24.

15. Edward C. Spitzka, "The Architecture and Mechanism of the Brain," *Journal of Nervous and Mental Diseases* 6 (1879): 613–53; 7 (1880): 208–49. In holding Garfield's assassin, Guiteau, insane and irresponsible, Spitzka took the unpopular but sound view. See Charles E. Rosenberg, *The Trial of the Assassin Guiteau: Psychiatry and Law in the Gilded Age* (Chicago, 1968), pp. 206–7, 248–50, 255–56.

tumor threw new light on the relations between the nervous system and mental phenomena. Starr summed up his work and that of colleagues in his internationally respected *Atlas of the Nerve Cells* (1896).[16]

Such new knowledge greatly enriched physiological psychology and provided foundations for psychophysics, whose prime mover, Gustav Fechner, defined it as "an exact science of the functional relations of dependency between mind and body."[17] Its methodological procedures, controlled experiments, and statistical measurements rested on the assumption that mental life was always and everywhere accompanied by a nervous change. Moreover, this connection between mind and body was uniform, whether the nervous changes and mental concomitants were coincidental or causative. With these assumptions, Ernst Heinrich Weber, Hermann Lotze, and Hermann von Helmholtz, along with Fechner, described and measured the velocity of nervous impulses, memory span, association of ideas, space perception and rhythm, and time sense. Their work was carried further and systematized by Wilhelm Wundt, whose psychophysical model hypothesized an organic connection of nerve fibers and nerve cells associated with mental elements. His *Physiological Psychology* (1879) offered both experimental and introspective support for the theory that interconnections of tracts and centers were determined by experience and environment. Assuming a universal human nature, Wundt was less interested in individual differences than in relating associationism to physiology. In so doing he verged toward mechanism. This was illustrated by his use of the clockwork analogy in the operation of mental phenomena. Although Wundt was skeptical of the view that the nervous system could explain all of mental life, he still believed that the mind was a logical, law-abiding structure that could be described if not fully understood.[18]

Meantime, in Great Britain, Alexander Bain, Dr. Henry Maudsley, and Dr. Thomas Laycock were relating what was known about association of ideas to the new physiology of the nervous system and to

16. Of Starr's many scientific papers, that in the *Journal of Nervous and Mental Disease* 10 (1884): 327–407 was especially notable. His contributions included *Brain Surgery* (London, 1893) and his pioneer study, with Charles MacBurney, of fifty brain tumors. For evaluations see Frederick Tilley, *Journal of Nervous and Mental Disease* 77 (1933): 226–31; and Frederick Peterson, *Bulletin of the New York Academy of Medicine* 8 (1932): 677–80.

17. Every modern history of psychology gives the substantive details, but special note may be taken of Edwin G. Boring, *A History of Experimental Psychology* (New York, 1950); Gardner Murphy, *Historical Introduction to Modern Psychology* (New York, 1951; 3d ed., written with Joseph K. Kovach, New York, 1972); and Henry Misiak and Virginia Staudt Sexton, *History of Psychology: An Overview* (New York, 1966).

18. John C. Burnham, "Historical Background for the Study of Personality," in Edgar F. Borgatta and William W. Lambert, *Handbook of Personality Theory and Research* (Chicago, 1968), pp. 52–53.

psychophysics. As early as 1855 Bain had put into a distinctively physiological setting the doctrine of psychophysical parallelism earlier advocated in one form or other by Leibniz, Malebranche, and Hartley.[19] Maudsley's *Physiology and Pathology of the Mind*, first published in 1867, also strengthened the claim that nothing could be known about mental action except through the nervous system. Dr. Thomas Laycock made a distinctive contribution to the same general view in holding that every state of consciousness coincided with and depended on molecular changes in the encephelon.[20]

The theory of evolution was perhaps even more far-reaching in its significance for concepts of human nature than were physiological psychology and psychophysics. First developed, in relation to mental life, by Herbert Spencer in his *Principles of Psychology* (1855), the theory was amplified by Darwin in *Expression of the Emotions in Man and Animals* (1872), and somewhat later, by the French physiological psychologist Théodule Ribot.

Evolution offered an explanation of the gradual development of man's mental life within and as a part of the whole natural order. In its effort to survive, the human organism, like all forms of life, had to adjust itself to its environment. This was achieved thanks to inherited instincts and drives. The adjustments thus made to environmental conditions explained behavior. In adapting itself to its environment, the human organism developed a greater functional complexity than its nearest animal kindred. Thus in emphasizing the integrated unity and relationships of all adaptive organisms and in rejecting the idea of mind as a largely independent and unique entity with discrete faculties, evolution cast doubt on the duality of human nature. Further, its assumption that every holistic organism had developed by adaptations from predecessors implied a less-sharp distinction between the mental equipment of animals and men than had been assumed.[21] No wonder

19. Alexander Bain, *The Senses and the Intellect* (London, 1855), *The Emotions and the Will* (London, 1859), and *Mental and Moral Science* (London, 1868–72). Bain's *Autobiography* (London, 1904) supplements our knowledge of his work. For the relation between his idea of fixation of belief and that of Charles S. Peirce, see Max H. Fisch, "Alexander Bain and the Genealogy of Pragmatism," *Journal of the History of Ideas* 15 (1954): 441.

20. Dr. Thomas Laycock, *Mind and Brain: or the Correlations of Consciousness and Organization* (Edinburgh, 1860). The second edition was published by D. Appleton and Co. in New York in 1869.

21. Edwin G. Boring, "The Influence of Evolutionary Theory upon Psychological Thought," in Stow Persons, ed., *Evolutionary Thought in America* (New Haven, 1950), pp. 268–98.

that the new theory raised uncomfortable questions for advocates of established religious, philosophical, and psychological ideas about a human nature that had been explained in supernatural or in the static naturalistic terms of the Newtonian universe.

Since the bitter controversy in religion consciously or unconsciously affected psychologists in their attitude toward evolution, a notable point was reached in 1885 when the best-known Protestant minister publicly accepted Darwinism as a highly probable hypothesis. Having begun in the early 1840s as a disciple of the neo-Edwardianism of his father, Lyman Beecher, Henry Ward Beecher had kept abreast of many important religious developments. His experience with revivals convinced him that religion was fundamentally a matter of the heart rather than the head. He accepted the romantic aspects of Transcendentalism in emphasizing the interdependency of man, nature, and God, and Horace Bushnell's view of the importance of Christian nurture. His well-edited magazine carried to the nation the social, ethical, and religious ideas he eloquently preached from the pulpit of his fashionable Plymouth Congregational Church in Brooklyn. In *Evolution and Religion* (1885), he pictured scientists as unraveling God's laws of beginnings and development. Human nature, with all its blemishes, was pictured as a grand and glorious development destined to reach yet higher levels. Beecher's reconciliation of the conflict between spirit and matter appealed to a larger number of orthodox Christians than John Fiske's earlier synthesis of Spencer's evolutionary theory and religious faith. This was partly because of advances in science, partly because of Beecher's eloquence and prestige, and partly because his extrapolations, whether savoring of Social Darwinism or buoyant optimism, met with middle-class approval or at least acceptance. Thus, as William G. McLoughlin has so well shown in his biography, Beecher takes high rank among the creators of modern liberal evangelical Protestantism.

The first American to present a comprehensive synthesis of the new biophysics, physiology, and evolutionary theory in the context of an emerging view of human nature was Edward Livingston Youmans, a self-trained chemist and author of scientific textbooks. A disciple of Herbert Spencer, he imported, with some difficulty, a copy of *The Principles of Psychology*, and was deeply impressed by its view of mental phenomena as a continuous process of adjustment to and an integral aspect of life. After successfully soliciting essays from leading European scientists for an anthology, Youmans could find no one to report on the new work in psychology. Undaunted, he did this himself, broadening its scope to embrace a consideration of human nature. While in England looking out for the publication of his book, he read his essay "Observations on the Scientific Study of Human Nature" at a meeting of the College of Preceptors. John Tyndall wrote him the next day that the lecture was "very strong meat" and that it had surprised and delighted him. The essay was included in the anthology that bore the title *The Culture Demanded by Modern Life* (1867).[22]

Youmans contrasted older ideas about the body and mind with new ones, whose predecessors in the Enlightenment he overlooked. The ignorant and educated alike, he asserted, shared the traditional idea that the scientific method of inquiry was inapplicable to the study of the higher processes of human life. From time immemorial the prevailing position had been to cleave man asunder by assuming the separate, independent existence of mind and body. The body had been handed to medical doctors for study, the mind, assumed to be pure, aspiring and immaterial, to doctors of divinity and philosophy. In their view, not man, but mind, was the object of inquiry. With the rejection of the actual human organism there was left only *mind as abstraction*, viewed as if the material universe had never existed. The nature of mind thus perceived had been the object of endless logical and metaphysical speculation, limited to its manifestation in consciousness. In pointed contrast, Youmans said, modern science rejected as erroneous the idea of duality, and reconstituted the individual in thought as he existed in life— a concrete, thinking, acting being encountering daily experiences. "It is now established," Youmans boldly claimed, "that the dependence of thought upon the organic conditions is so intimate and absolute, that they can no longer be considered except as a unity." As a problem of inquiry, man was simply "an organism of varied powers and activities, to be studied scientifically in an effort to determine its mechanism, modes, and laws of action."[23]

Youmans summed up the achievements of some of the pioneers in physiology of the brain and nervous system and noted their significance for an understanding of human nature. With his deep commitment to the social and human usefulness of science, he related the basic implications of the new knowledge to education and mental illness. Without citing the findings of European and American pioneers, Youmans asserted that it had become patently clear that insanity could no longer be regarded as the work of the devil, to be exorcised: it was just a disease to be cured.

22. Elizabeth Youmans's account of the lecture is in *Popular Science Monthly* 30 (1887): 688–91. See also H. G. Good, "Edward Livingston Youmans, a National Teacher of Science, 1821–1887," *Scientific Monthly* 18 (1924): 306–17; and John Fiske, *Edward Livingston Youmans* (New York, 1894), and *A Century of Science and Other Essays* (Boston, 1899), pp. 61–95.

23. Edward Livingston Youmans, *The Culture Demanded by Modern Life* (New York, 1867), p. 377.

This was only one of the bright promises of the "new science of human nature."

Youmans's essay inaugurated a campaign to spread knowledge basic to the emerging psychology. His new International Science Series published, among other books by leading authorities, Alexander Bain's *Mind and Body*. Youmans did not stop here. In 1872 he founded the *Popular Science Monthly*, which introduced the new science to a wide audience of the well-informed.[24] It reported summaries of articles in the British journal *Mind*. Contributors discussed the pros and cons of Darwinism for an understanding of body-mind relationships and for the role of instincts in adapting the human organism to its environment.[25] The *Monthly* opened its pages to Francis Galton's early work on heredity and environment and published William James's critique of the British associationists.[26] Other original contributions included Moses Starr's analysis of the physiology of memory[27] and Joseph Le Conte's brief for comparative psychology and for relating mental phenomena to physiology without metaphysical connotations.[28]

Youmans also suggested the broader implications of the new learning for the idea of human nature. He repeatedly emphasized the point that the nature of man could be understood only if it was viewed as a product of an evolutionary process. Such a position required an understanding of the characteristically emotional basis of human beliefs and behavior. "That which lies beyond the reason and the will in the mental constitution, and gets vent continually under the pressure of sentiment, impulse, passion, love, hate, habit and prejudice, is of immensely greater volume and moment than all that is said or done under the influence of intelligent volition."[29] Youmans was apparently unaware of the em-

24. William Edward Leverette, Jr., gives a good summary of the content of the magazine in his essay "E. L. Youmans' Crusade for Scientific Autonomy and Respectability," *American Quarterly* 17 (1965): 12–32, and a more detailed account in his "Science and Values: A Study of Edward L. Youmans' *Popular Science Monthly, 1872–1887*," *Dissertation Abstracts*, 24 (1963), 5:2000 (Vanderbilt).

25. Joseph Le Conte, "Instincts and Intelligence," *Popular Science Monthly* 7 (1875): 653–64; Dr. R. Osgood Mason, "Evolution and After-Life," *Popular Science Monthly* 7 (1875): 46–72. Dr. Mason, a well-known New York physician, wrote extensively on psychic phenomena.

26. Francis Galton, "The History of Twins as a Criterion of the Relative Powers of *Nature and Nurture*," *Popular Science Monthly* 8 (1875–76): 345–57; William James, "The Association of Ideas," *Popular Science Monthly* 16 (1879–80): 577–93.

27. M. Allen Starr, M.D., "Where and How We Remember," *Popular Science Monthly* 25 (1884): 609–20.

28. "Instincts and Intelligence," *Popular Science Monthly* 7: 653 ff.

29. Edward Livingston Youmans, "Editor's Table: A Social Experiment," *Popular Science Monthly* 7 (1875): 620. For the history of thought on the emotions see H. M.

phasis in much seventeenth- and eighteenth-century thought on the predominance of self-serving and self-deceiving passions. Nor did he refer to Ribot's thesis that emotions were to be understood in physiological rather than in intellectualist terms. But he did emphasize Darwin's contention in *The Descent of Man* (1871) that there was no basic difference in either the mental or emotional faculties and drives in men and other mammals. Youmans also maintained that if man were to be understood in all his aspects, it was necessary not only to take account of biology but to study human beings in their social relationships, exactly as scientists investigated minerals and plants. Such studies were the more imperative because it was the "gross and widespread ignorance of human nature" that made possible the "quackeries of the platform, the bar, the state-house, and the pulpit, the gigantic swindles of speculators, and the frauds of petty traders, the omnipresent overreachings and deceptions by which people are victimized in the intercourse of life."[30] Youmans's utilitarian justification of the new science of man was clearly designed to appeal to the American sense of practicality. It thus heralded what was to become a characteristically American emphasis.

Meantime the New Psychology was only slowly making itself known in college classrooms. John Bascom of the University of Wisconsin represented the established teachers of and writers on mental philosophy in holding that the new empiricism, however useful in bettering knowledge of "sensuous fact," failed to illuminate the deepest problems of mental life.[31] President James McCosh of Princeton was almost alone among mental philosophers in sheltering physiological psychology, experimental psychology, and evolutionary theory. This he skillfully did under the cloak of the still-dominant Scottish common sense philosophy and religious orthodoxy.[32]

In academic circles Chauncey Wright was the first striking example of hospitality to the embryonic New Psychology in its evolutionary frame.

Gardiner, Ruth Clark Metcalf, and Jon Beeve-Center, *Feelings and Emotions: A History of Theories* (Boston, 1937).

30. Edward Livingston Youmans, "Editor's Table: Man as an Object of Scientific Study," *Popular Science Monthly* 1 (1872): 368, and "The Study of the Brain," *Popular Science Monthly* 13 (1877): 238.

31. John Bascom, *Things Learned by Living* (New York, 1913), pp. 161–62.

32. J. McKeen Cattell, "The Advance of Psychology," *Proceedings of the American Association for the Advancement of Science* 47 (1898): 446. One of McCosh's students, Moses Allen Starr, recalled that in McCosh's classes he was introduced to the newest European work in physiological psychology and psychodynamics.

When President Eliot asked him to lecture on psychology at Harvard in 1870, Wright reread Spencer, reviewed Darwin, and took another look at Alexander Bain, whom he used as a text.[33] More than this, he wrote an original essay, "The Evolution of Self-Consciousness."[34] The essay was important philosophically in criticizing both realism and idealism and in projecting a "neutral monism." It was important psychologically because it put the body-mind problem on new ground by offering in place of dualism a Darwinian orientation toward stimulus and response as variables. Wright rejected the dualism of the British associationists and the Wundtian structuralists, both of which seemed to reflect the Newtonian scheme of a static universe rather than the organic, dynamic Darwinian view. Further, he had no use for teleology. Within this context, he pondered the development of self-consciousness by comparing and contrasting human and other animals. Each, he held, developed a reasoning ability from a commonly shared, though differently accented, memory and attention. What differentiated the mental behavior of man was the capacity to use and manipulate signs, understood as both internal images and outward perceptions. Language, the most important of signs, enabled men to think scientifically, that is, reflectively and critically with reference to what the sign signified in terms of both past experience and future or "voluntary" uses. Often cited as a telling influence on William James's concept of reasoning and a herald of functional psychology, Wright certainly took a big step toward explaining the similarities and differences between human behavior and that of other creatures, and toward giving psychology an evolutionary and scientific as opposed to a metaphysical underlying structure.[35]

By 1876 Wright's friend and successor, William James, was working in his improvised laboratory, still using Bain as a text for his course, and familiarizing himself with leading European investigators.[36]

One of James's early students, G. Stanley Hall, adopted the new techniques of sensory and perceptual measurement in studying the aging and almost forgotten, but once-celebrated, Laura Bridgman. As we have seen, this blind, deaf, and mute child had, thanks to the patient and sympathetic care of her philanthropic mentor, Dr. Samuel Gridley

33. Fisch, "Bain and the Genealogy of Pragmatism."

34. Wright's essay was published in the *North American Review* 116 (1873): 245–310. It was included in his *Philosophical Discussions*, edited by his friend Charles Eliot Norton (New York, 1877).

35. This summary is indebted to Edward H. Madden's excellent biography, *Chauncey Wright and the Foundations of Pragmatism* (Seattle, 1963), esp. pp. 123–33.

36. See pp. 203–5.

Howe, made extraordinary progress in ability to communicate.[37] Hall's very different interest, characteristic of the new science, tested her sensory perception by tuning forks and rotary whirlings. These investigations were supplemented at her death by an examination of her brain. Hall's Laura Bridgman studies found their way into the canon of leading psychologists, European and American.[38]

Hall also set up at the new Johns Hopkins University a laboratory,[39] where his pupil Joseph Jastrow, working with Charles S. Peirce, carried out the pioneer American experimental measurements of the slightest noticeable differences in the perception of sensory experience. The findings were in themselves notable, and the improved pressure balance developed for the work became standard equipment of all psychological laboratories.[40] In a sense, too, the results of such experiments on reaction times indicated, in the words of a later psychologist, that "human nature was thus shown to be a measurable thing."[41]

But Hall was to become best known as the champion of an evolutionary, genetic psychology, a significant and in considerable part an American development.[42] This included comparative studies of animal behavior, a field in which Americans were to achieve far-reaching results. When Hall began his work in genetic psychology, a debate had developed between those who, like Paul Chadbourne of Williams College and the University of Wisconsin, held that animal behavior was almost exclusively instinctive, and those who were impressed by the contrary view of the ethnologist Lewis Henry Morgan.[43] In his path-breaking book *The American Beaver and His Works* (1868), Morgan argued, in a manner similar to that of Chauncey Wright a few

37. See above, p. 183.

38. For Laura Bridgman's early career see Maude Howe Elliott, *Laura Bridgman, Dr. Howe's Famous Pupil and What He Taught Her* (Boston, 1903). Hall's investigations were reported in *The Nation* 27 (1878), in *Mind* 4 (1879), and in his *Aspects of German Culture* (Boston, 1881), pp. 237–76. See also William James's essay "Laura Bridgman," in his *Collected Essays and Reviews* (New York, 1920), pp. 455 ff.

39. In the development of experimental laboratories, so fundamental in the New Psychology, see William O. Krohn, "Facilities in Experimental Laboratories in the Colleges of the United States," *Report of the Commissioner of Education for the Year 1890–1891* (Washington, D.C., 1894), pt. 2, pp. 1139–50.

40. C. S. Peirce and Joseph Jastrow, "On Small Differences of Sensation," *Memoirs of the National Academy of Sciences*, 23 vols. (Washington, D.C., 1866–1941), vol. 3 (1884), pt. 1, pp. 75–83; and Jastrow's account in his autobiography in Carl Murchison, ed., *A History of Psychology in Autobiography* (Worcester, Mass., 1930), 1:135–36.

41. John F. Dashiell, *Fundamentals of Objective Psychology* (Boston, 1928), pp. 4–5.

42. Robert Grinder, *A History of Genetic Psychology* (New York, 1967), pt. 5.

43. Paul Chadbourne, *Instinct, Its Office in the Animal Kingdom and Its Relation to the Higher Powers in Man* (New York, 1872); and Morgan's review, *The Nation* 14 (1872): 291–92.

years later, that men and mute animals were endowed with the same faculties, in varying proportions and with different potential rates of development.[44] Without resolving the issue, experimental work under Hall's stimulus at Clark University advanced knowledge of the sensory and perceptual aspects of the behavior of birds, rodents, and primates.[45] These beginnings were important. They were overshadowed when, in the late 1890s, Edward Lee Thorndike began his well-controlled experiments on animal learning at Columbia.[46]

The new interest in child psychology at home and abroad found in Hall its most important leader.[47] John Fiske had applied the evolutionary theory in an effort to explain the growth of altruism in human behavior—the principle of natural selection alone was, he argued, inadequate. The prolonged infant dependency on the mother provided the key to the growth of the finer human values.[48] But Hall broadened the evolutionary foundations of child study by exploring, through the questionnaire method, the content of children's minds and the values present at different stages.[49] Convinced of the importance of feelings and emotions, including the sex urge, Hall was critical of the emphasis in academic psychology on states of consciousness and, as we shall see, welcomed Freud's stress on unconscious drives as explanatory of much child and adult behavior. Hall's *Adolescence: Its Psychology and Its Relations to Physiology, Anthropology, Sociology, Sex, Crime, Religion and Education* (1904) was a landmark in the recognition of this stage of human development. Its shortcomings included a romantic overemphasis on the storm and stress of adolescence and on the idealism and perhaps the gregariousness of adolescent youth; a conventional

44. For contemporary reactions to Morgan's book and its later reputation see Bernhard J. Stern, *Lewis Henry Morgan, Social Evolutionist* (Chicago, 1931), pp. 102 ff.; and Carl Resek, *Lewis Henry Morgan, American Scholar* (Chicago, 1960), pp. 100–102.

45. Robert M. Yerkes, "Early Days of Comparative Psychology," *Psychological Review* 50 (1943): 74–76. Chicago, like Columbia, was to become an important research center in this field.

46. Joseph Jastrow, "Infant Psychology," *Science* 6 (1885): 435. Jastrow called attention to the importance of Alice M. Christie's translation of Bernard Perez, *The First Three Years of Childhood* (Syracuse, N.Y., 1889).

47. See, first of all, G. Stanley Hall's *Life and Confessions of a Psychologist* (New York, 1923), p. 397. Dorothy Ross's *G. Stanley Hall, the Psychologist as Prophet* (Chicago, 1972), chap. 15, provides an excellent discussion and evaluation.

48. John Fiske, "The Part Played by Infancy in the Evolution of Man," in *A Century of Science and Other Essays* (New York, 1899), pp. 96–116.

49. Merle Curti, *The Social Ideas of American Educators* (New York, 1935; rev. ed., Paterson, N.J., 1959), chap. 12. Iris Meadows traces the shift from faculty psychology to the total development of the child's nature in her "Concepts of Child Nature in American Life and Education 1800–1900" (Ph.D. diss., University of Missouri, 1951).

glorification of the female role; and the failure satisfactorily to reconcile the advocacy of freedom of self-expression with the religious and ethical discipline that Hall thought was imperative. Also questionable was the extent to which he carried the theory that the child recapitulated the cultural stages in the development of races. This did, though, reorient child psychology toward biology and culture. As a result, the school curricula were enriched by a new recognition of the importance of the social studies for children who were to make their way in a complex and expanding urban-industrial life.

Although the importance that James Mark Baldwin attached to development in human nature made him a leading figure in evolutionary psychology, his contribution to social psychology warrants detailed consideration of his work in the discussion of the emergence of a social view of human nature.[50]

The Wundtian insistence that experimental psychology confine itself to the structure of consciousness as this was revealed by controlled experiments and introspection reflected a Newtonian rather than a Darwinian view of the universe. It characterized much of the early work in the growing number of American laboratories. At Yale, for example, E. W. Scripture followed this pattern in his experiments on memory, and summed up his own and comparable work in *The New Psychology* (1897). E. B. Titchener, a British psychologist trained in Wundt's laboratory, made Cornell the stronghold of an experimental psychology that aimed to describe the structure of consciousness through the introspective analysis of immediate experience into its elements and attributes.[51]

Critics claimed that the New Psychology endangered religious and spiritual values by assuming that mental phenomena could be explained in terms of the nervous system. Joseph Jastrow, a pioneer in popularizing the New Psychology, insisted that such fears reflected misunderstanding, since great European figures in the movement were anything but materialists.[52] It was George Trumbull Ladd of Yale rather than Jastrow, however, who played the leading role of mediator between these critics and the New Psychology. His *Elements of Physiological Psychology* (1887) was the first comprehensive treatment of the field. Accepting the usefulness of physiological psychology for explaining a part of mental life, Ladd believed it could do little to clarify the rational and spiritual component. This he tried to do, somewhat in the manner of

50. See pp. 239–40.
51. Edward B. Titchener, *Experimental Psychology*, 2 vols. (New York, 1901–5); and Edwin G. Boring, *Psychologist at Large* (New York, 1961), p. 22.
52. Joseph Jastrow, "A New Science of the Mind," *Science* 11 (1888): 257.

his beloved Lotze. His suggested compromise satisfied neither the new psychologists nor the philosophical idealists.[53]

Far more characteristic of the course psychology in America took than either the structuralism of Titchener or the mediating role of Ladd was the claim made for its usefulness in education, and later, in business, law, and life. J. McKeen Cattell, a student in Wundt's laboratory, had also worked with Francis Galton, who by 1869 was using statistical techniques to measure individual differences. Cattell laid the American foundations for the psychology of capacity or individual differences. His contributions and those of such coworkers as E. L. Thorndike, Helen Thompson, Henry H. Goddard, and Lewis M. Terman made the measurement and application of individual differences to classroom procedures an earmark of the new science in the United States. What explained the preponderant interest in the application of the results of individual measurements? Obviously the traditional emphasis on individualism was a factor. Moreover, when the New Psychology made its first impact, it was no longer as easy as it had once been to satisfy needs by manipulating the natural environment through exploitation and the development of seemingly inexhaustible resources. In the future, more heed would have to be paid to adjusting people to their environment, and in this the measurement of individual differences seemed appropriate and even necessary.[54]

Another way in which the New Psychology in its American career differed from the dominant European pattern was its challenge to the thesis that consciousness was the only valid mental activity for experimental investigation. The challenge was, of course, functionalism. Though not unique to the United States,[55] it became most widely known and most influential in its American form. Based on biological evolutionary theory, functionalism regarded mental activities, conscious and unconscious alike, as a continuing, dynamic adjustment on the part of the organism to the demands of life. With the assumption that the

53. Ladd's major writings, in addition to *Elements of Physiological Psychology* (New York, 1887), included *Psychology Descriptive and Explanatory* (New York, 1894) and *Philosophy of the Mind* (New York, 1895). Eugene S. Mills, *George Trumbull Ladd, Pioneer American Psychologist* (Cleveland, Oh., 1969), relates Ladd to his times and judiciously evaluates his contributions.

54. In his retrospective essay "Psychology in America," Cattell found this circumstance, along with the lagging developments in the related and necessary supporting basic sciences, and the ease with which Americans would depend on European pioneers, the explanation of the tardy appearance of the New Psychology. *Scientific Monthly* 30 (1930): 115–26.

55. A purposeful emphasis in the work of some British psychologists, the role which Külpe gave to volition as adjustment, the functional conception of memory in the psychology of Ebbinghaus and Brentano, the monism of Höffding, and the functional role Claparède ascribed to language and play, are examples.

needs of the organism were met by sense perception, mental images, emotions, and thinking, functionalists tried to find at what stage in human development the need for each became sufficiently pressing to account for the appearance of a partial process or function.[56] Functionalism thus emphasized motor activity in the ongoing search for adjustment to changing situations as opposed to the structuralists' concern with describing a cross section of sensation, perception, and consciousness.

The first explicit emphasis on functionalism seems to have been John Dewey's article of 1884. In stressing the relation of human beings to their fellows in society, and in showing the bearing of the social and human disciplines, including language and folklore, he gave functionalism a social base entirely absent in structuralism. In 1896 Dewey suggested, in his article on the reflex-arc concept, a theoretical formulation of functionalism.[57] In all his early work he acknowledged his debt to William James, the towering figure whose formulation of problems and whose original insights made him a great leader.

William James was both an effective champion of the New Psychology and a trenchant critic. His ambivalent and contradictory positions did not greatly trouble him. He preferred to leave paradoxes dangling rather than to resolve them in misleading oversimplifications.

As early as 1867 James thought that perhaps the time had come for psychology to be a science in a descriptive and explanatory sense. Measurements had already been made, he went on, in the region lying between the physical changes in the nerves and the appearance of consciousness in the shape of sense perceptions.[58] His hope of studying with Helmholtz and Wundt did not materialize, but he kept up his interest. In 1875 he wrote to President Eliot of Harvard, where he was teaching physiological psychology and investigating problems in the little laboratory he had set up, that "a real science of man is now being built up out of the theory of evolution and the facts of archaeology, the nervous system and the senses."[59] He kept abreast of new work in psychophysics and physiological psychology, thanking George

56. Robert S. Woodworth, *Contemporary Schools of Psychology* (New York, 1931), p. 46.

57. John Dewey, "The Reflex-Arc Concept in Psychology," *Psychological Review* 3 (1896): 357–70.

58. James to Thomas Ward, November 1867, *The Letters of William James*, 2 vols. (Boston, 1920), 1:118–19.

59. James to Charles W. Eliot, December 2, 1875, in Ralph Barton Perry, *The Thought and Character of William James*, 2 vols. (Boston, 1935), 2:11.

Trumbull Ladd on the publication in 1887 of *Physiological Psychology* for providing him with a shortcut to much of the material he had been struggling with in preparing his own forthcoming work.[60]

In advancing the New Psychology, James's role in the first place was negative. Problems, he insisted, must be attacked "as if there were no official answers preoccupying the field." He thus helped clear the way for new positions by showing why so much that had been accepted as explaining mental phenomena was actually inadequate, in view of validated knowledge and inferences from that knowledge. Thus, for example, he criticized the associationist pain-pleasure psychology in the form in which Alexander Bain, a British leader, had partially assimilated it to a physiological psychology. He offered in place of a simple associationist pleasure-pain theory of decision one in which conflicting choices were resolved in any of five main ways. Or again, in his essay on memory, James explained the inadequacy of faculty and associationist psychology. He suggested a theory supported by his only important experiments. These showed that while training did not improve general retentiveness, as faculty psychology held, practice in memorizing one kind of material was in some measure effective for retaining a similar kind.

The long-awaited *Principles of Psychology* set forth as its main purpose the description, and insofar as possible, the explanation, of mental phenomena without reference to transcendentalism and metaphysics.[61] To this end James reported the new work in physiological psychology and experimental psychology in Britain, France, and Germany. He gave less space to it than seemed to many desirable, however, in view of the importance of physiology and experimentation in the New Psychology.[62]

James accepted with qualifications and modifications many tenets of the New Psychology. Thus in trying to offer a nondualistic view of the body-mind problem, he dismissed straight off the notion of "mind-stuff," which held that ideas resulted from a fusion of nonmaterial particles or "atoms." He accepted with an important modification the reflex-arc theory. This held that a stimulus was carried as an electrical impulse by the nerves to some part of the brain, which in turn sent some part of the impulse to the muscles, glands, and blood vessels. James was not happy with this position, which he felt implied the "conscious automation" theory—that the psychic chain was without any causal efficacy. In other

---

60. *The Nation* 44 (1887): 473.

61. William James, *The Principles of Psychology*, 2 vols. (New York, 1890), 1:v–vi.

62. In *Psychology: Briefer Course* (New York, 1894), frankly designed as a textbook, James did put more emphasis proportionally on physiological psychology.

words, feelings were mere correlates of some nerve movements, the cause of which lay in some previous nerve movement. James contended that the stimulus-response process was saved from being entirely automatic by the function of a "thought or idea" in the brain which could, in choosing which muscles to activate, keep outgoing impulses from following a predetermined path. This was even more the case since interest and attention influenced the response of the brain to the stimuli by suppressing or recognizing the immediate or delayed response of a given behavioral act. In other words, without solving the historical body-mind problem, James assumed at least the causal efficacy of ideas or purposefulness in the conscious selection of responses or energies for which a sheer mechanical conception of interactionism found no place.[63] He was, in fact, anticipating Dewey's famous conception of the non-mechanistic character of the reflex-arc theory, the position that the interaction between stimulus and response was reciprocal and continuing rather than mechanical and static.[64]

Again, in accepting the position that it was possible, at least in the sphere of sensation, to measure the relation of nerve changes to stimuli, James found no evidence for holding that every emotion or idea had a *necessary* physical concomitant. The nervous system was too complex, the environment too unstable, for any such reductionist, mechanistic relationship. While in effect rejecting the theory of psychophysical parallelism, James did not commit himself unreservedly to the interactionism which informed much of the New Psychology. Either of these views of the relation of the physical and mental order of events seemed to him too monistic and thus deterministic. Influenced by the French philosopher Charles Renouvier, James favored a pluralistic view that allowed for contingency, indeterminacy, flexibility, and by inference, the effective role of free will, faith, values, and purposefulness. Any other hypothesis seemed to concede that the perceptive state of mind was a compound, atomistic and reductionist (the reduction of all mental events to neural events). In insisting on the reality of values and purposes, James seemed, like George Trumbull Ladd, for all the latter's clearcut dualism which James tried to avoid, to have more sympathy with traditional and spiritual than with modern, scientific ideas.

In still other ways, James modified and expanded the boundaries of the New Psychology as its European founders formulated it and its orthodox American disciples promoted it.

The one overarching concept in James's work was his popularization

63. I am indebted here to Milic Capek's essay "James' Early Criticism of the Automaton Theory," *The Journal of the History of Ideas* 15 (1954): 260–79.

64. Dewey, "The Reflex-Arc Concept in Psychology," pp. 357 ff.

of the cerebral hypothesis of the conditions of thought as they related to instinct, emotion, active selectivity, and habit, and the constitution, state of health, and interests of the "thinker." All this was without any tight-water mechanism. Here again the key was the evolutionary, organic, functional view of the body-mind problem. That is, mind was thought of as a function of living, a function in which perception and thinking existed only for the sake of behavior, thought action being that which gave the adapting organism the greatest subjective satisfaction. The view of Peirce and Dewey that James thus admitted too much subjectivity into his concept of thinking found confirmation in an analysis of his social ideas.[65]

Yet James in some part sensed the limitations of subjectivism. He recognized that thinking could not be separated from the thinker, including his instincts, emotions, and habits, and from the action or behavior to which all of these, operating independently, led. This pointed to the conclusion that an idea was not an abstraction but rather a self-conscious, animated part of a functional process of adaptation. Put still differently, mind was to be regarded not as the sum of sensations, feelings, and conations, not as an atomistic melange, but as a dynamic, organic, purposeful, and above all selective process *engaging* the whole being. In other words, thinking was the ability of the organism to select from consciousness[66]; mind was a function rather than a thing. It was to be looked at much as breathing was a function rather than a thing. On this cornerstone Mead, Dewey, and Angell were to build, with refinements and greater social emphasis, functional psychology and instrumentalism.

Within the functional psychology whose foundations he laid, James developed several notable ideas expressed in brilliant and dramatic language. A thoroughgoing evolutionist, he believed that in man's struggle for survival, reflexes which proved useful became deeply rooted and in some cases immutable. Having a great number of instincts or impulses to act in a particular way in response to determinate sensory stimuli, men often found themselves frustrated and hesitant because one instinct interfered with the expression of another. While some instincts appeared to be transitory, even these might, during their primacy, establish important, lasting habits. In addition to many complex learned social modes of response, the "intense" or enduring instincts included anger, appropriation, acquisitiveness, emulation, rivalry, and pugnacity. Despite the fact that "the instinct of pugnacity" was so deeply ingrained as never to be eliminated, James argued that it might be

65. Curti, *Social Ideas of American Educators*, chap. 13.
66. William James, "Are We Automata?" *Mind* 4 (1879): 3 ff.

expressed in attacking formidable obstacles for socially useful purposes.[67] The great emphasis on the instincts of acquisition and rivalry
and the important place James gave them in education probably confirmed many readers in their belief that an acquisitive economic system
was inevitable. In his later life, however, James's tender concern for the
down-and-out led him to express some interest in socialism.

Habits developed from instincts. The physiological basis of the doctrine owed much to Theodor Meynert, whose *Psychiatry: A Clinical
Treatise on the Diseases of the Forebrain* stressed the interconnections of
brain areas or neurons. From a functional point of view, habit provided
both individuals and society with a balance wheel conservative in
nature. "It alone is what keeps us all within the bounds of ordinance, and
saves the children of fortune from the envious uprisings of the poor. It
alone prevents the hardest and most repulsive walks of life from being
deserted by those brought up to tread therein. . . . It dooms us all to fight
out the battle of life upon the lines of our nurture or our early choice,
and to make the best of the pursuit that disagrees, because there is no
other for which we are fitted, and it is too late to begin again."[68] Yet at
the same time habit could open the door to possible changes of conduct
and social relations. In connection with selected teachings of
associationists, his theory enabled James to stress the binding character
of habits while opening the way to the possibility of developing new ones
by the exercise of attention, choice, will, and persistent repetition.
Though all this lacked the precision and experimental support of the
later conditioned-reflex concept of Pavlov and Bekhterev, James drove
home the point with telling effect in his widely read psychological texts
and educational essays.

The theory of the emotions, associated with the independent discovery
by the Dane Carl Lange,[69] held that "the bodily changes follow directly
the perception of the existing fact, and that our feeling of the same
changes as they occur *is* the emotion." Thus, to recall a famous example,
one did not run because he was afraid: one was afraid because he ran.
The James-Lange theory was often called the peripheral theory of
emotions, because of the emphasis on peripheral activity as the initiator
of the emotions. More than one writer had anticipated it, but James's
forthright assertion helped reverse the common sense belief that the
stimulus led to the feeling and the feeling in turn to motor and visceral

67. William James, "The Moral Equivalent of War," *Essays on Faith and Morals* (New
York, 1947), pp. 320 ff.
68. James, *Principles of Psychology*, 2:121.
69. Carl George Lange and William James, *The Emotions*, ed. Knight Dunlap (Baltimore, 1922).

accompaniments. It aroused much criticism, which James did not entirely meet in his later effort at clarification and elaboration. But the idea of the physiological base for emotions was of major importance. It stimulated many later and qualifying investigations. These, in shifting the emphasis from the peripheral to the role of the central nervous system and in showing the dependence of both emotional experience and bodily change on thalmic discharge, kept the physiological base for which James pioneered.[70]

Equally memorable was James's theory of consciousness. This rested in part on the work of the older Mill and of Spencer and Bain, all of whom had emphasized the constant flux of consciousness. James elaborated this suggestion, developing more fully and explicitly the idea that consciousness was not a specific static state or series of isolated ideas associated by mental bands, but rather was present only when change was sensed. It was thus comparable, not to the successive tickings of a clock, but to a moving, flowing, shifting stream. Associated with, perhaps even the result of, "currents and vibrations of the nerve cells of the human brain," consciousness performed the useful, indeed necessary function of rejecting or choosing from the flowing objects of attention that characterized it. Conceived of as involving *transitive* rather than *substantive* states, consciousness, James held, was so vague, indefinite, and fleeting that it often escaped introspection. In a later essay "Does Consciousness Exist?" James suggested that if the term meant anything substantive, the question must be answered in the negative. Consciousness was rather a name for the fact that events were related not merely to time and space but to the life of the experiencing organism.[71]

James's stream-of-consciousness theory bore on his psychology of the self. Like Lotze, he emphasized the idea of relatedness. The self was related to other selves, inasmuch as "every thought you now have and every act and intention owes its complexion to the acts of your dead and

70. James, *Principles of Psychology*, vol. 2, chap. 25. For anticipations of the theory see James McCosh, *The Emotions* (New York, 1880), pp. 102–3; Edward Titchener in *The American Journal of Psychology* 25 (1914): 427–47; C. A. Ruckmick in *The American Journal of Psychology* 46 (1934): 506–9. See also Gardiner, Metcalf, and Beebe-Center, *Feeling and Emotion: A History*, pp. 334–35; Dashiell, *A History of Psychology in Autobiography*, 4:313; and Walter B. Cannon, *Bodily Changes in Pain, Hunger, Fear and Rage* (New York, 1915).

71. William James, "Does Consciousness Exist?" *Journal of Philosophy, Psychology and Scientific Methods* 1 (1904): 477–91. See also Murphy and Kovach, *Historical Introduction to Modern Psychology*, pp. 194, 196–97. Knight Dunlap (*Scientific Monthly* 11 [1920]: 507) claims that James discarded this brilliant idea because he subsequently realized that he had omitted the empirical basis and thus had constructed a theory of the "mind" for which there was no evidence that such a mind ever existed.

living brothers." Moreover, "all *personal* relation is finite, conditional, mixed." With much insight he wrote in 1868 that "the closest love" enclosed a germ of estrangement or hatred.[72] Along with the unity of the self, there were as many "social selves" as there were individuals who recognized a person. This idea was developed later by Cooley and Mead in their social psychologies.[73] James also related his idea of the self to human instincts, including gregariousness and the desire for esteem, traits widely emphasized in the seventeenth and eighteenth centuries as both inborn and immensely powerful.

James's psychological synthesis of older work and the new European contributions, if so unsystematic a treatise as *The Principles* could be called a synthesis, was thus full of ideas and hypotheses, biologically oriented and broadly conceived to include much more than his coworkers here or abroad regarded as the proper domain of the New Psychology. This became even more markedly the case when he applied his psychology to the problems of everyday life in *Talks to Teachers on Psychology* (1897), and above all, to religious faith and mystical experience, which he did superbly in *The Varieties of Religious Experience* (1902). Combining psychology and physiology in an organic, evolutionary way did not mean divorcing it from philosophy—at least from the pragmatic philosophy he was helping to launch. So broad a stage, so catholic an approach, so marked an emphasis on relating what he wrote and taught to the whole of man's experience, to the totality of life, warranted regarding James, in much greater degree than his contemporaries, as the psychologist of human nature.

Beyond the area for which a scientific approach seemed suitable lay the wide-ranging, open-ended mysteries of human motives and conduct. And so, after recognizing awareness or consciousness as the centrality of experience, James agreed with F. H. W. Myers in holding that there was, in addition, a subliminal or twilight zone of inestimable importance in explaining both abnormal and normal mental phenomena.[74] And so, too, he viewed with earnest interest the discovery by Janet, Charcot, and other French investigators of the existence of parts of the personality functioning in ways unknown to introspective consciousness. Given such a predisposition, it was natural for him in his later years to express the hope that Freud and his disciples would push to the limit their insight into the unconscious and thus open new scientific vistas for understanding motives and conduct.

72. James to Thomas W. Ward, January 1868, *Letters of William James*, 1:131.
73. See pp. 243, 246.
74. James, *Principles of Psychology*, 1:400; 2:133; *The Varieties of Religious Experience: A Study in Human Nature* (New York, 1958), pp. 128, 148, 153.

In view of James's strictures of many tenets of the New Psychology and his extension of psychological boundaries beyond those deemed proper by its orthodox champions, his distinguished pupil James R. Angell may have overstated the case in holding that his mentor was more responsible for the development of the New Psychology than anyone else.[75] This judgment also overlooked the impressive contributions of other early pioneers, especially G. Stanley Hall, James Mark Baldwin, and J. McK. Cattell. Nor did other eminent figures in the new movement accept Angell's view. Wundt saw beauty in *The Principles*, which he recognized as "literature" but not as psychology. George Trumbull Ladd, who shared James's indebtedness to Lotze for an insistence on the validity of values and ideals, felt that James, despite his disclaimer, actually introduced a good deal of metaphysics in a backhand fashion, some of which he misused in paradoxical and contradictory ways.[76] G. Stanley Hall, while recognizing great merit in *The Principles of Psychology*, held that the hypotheses were too broad to permit experimentation in the manner of the New Psychology.[77] Charles S. Peirce objected to James's uncritical acceptance of the data of science, and at the same time to his reversal of the conclusions of science on many important points in deciding by negative means the character of its data. "The one thing upon which Professor James seems to pin his faith is in the general incomprehensibility of things," a method hardly consonant with the tenets of the New Psychology.[78] To cite still another verdict, Lightner Witmer of Pennsylvania concluded that James's two volumes partook more of the "old" than of the "new" psychology. He repeated the earlier charges that it was based, not on the author's own experimental investigations, but on the work of others and on his speculation about this, on imaginative inferences from such work, and on fragmentary handouts of plain common sense.[79] Finally, James himself at least privately shared some of the points of his critics when he wrote to his brother in 1890 that in his view, psychology had as yet reached only the prescientific stage. It was but "a very *small* part" of the larger science of living human beings.[80]

No doubt can exist that James, more than his contemporaries, advanced and deepened the concept of human nature. In truth, he nowhere gave a formal or systematic definition of the term. His references to it

75. James R. Angell, "William James," *Psychological Review* 18 (1910): 79.

76. George Trumbull Ladd, "Psychology as a So-called 'Natural Science,'" *Philosophical Review* 1 (1892): 24–53. James's reply appeared in the March issue of the *Review*, 146–53.

77. *The American Journal of Psychology* 3 (1890): 551–52.

78. *The Nation* 53 (1891): 15.

79. *The Psychological Clinic* 2 (1908–9): 284–99.

80. William James to Henry James, June 4, 1890, *Letters of William James* 2:296.

were casual and incidental, as if of course everyone understood what was meant.[81] Yet the context in which this time-worn, celebrated phrase was used threw some light on his understanding of it. On the most general level he saw it as extraordinarily complex and full of contradictions: he spoke of the natural inheritance of "deadness and blindness" of men toward each other, but also of action-provoking anger, lust, and fear—three of the most dominant emotions in human behavior and human relations.

However much James regarded men's makeup as complex, contradictory, voluntaristic, and "self-made," he had no doubt that basic universalities gave the concept of human nature validity. In his view the most eloquent testimony to a common human nature was the plain fact that all men and women alike shared in experiencing consciousness of pain and joy. Less familiar for the time (1903), even quite novel, was his view that the average churchgoer failed to recognize "the aboriginal capacity for murderous excitement which lies sleeping in the human bosom"—a capacity that, breaking through inhibitions, responded to the stimuli of mass excitement and found outlet in lynching and mob rule.[82] The persistence of war, with all its atrocities and horrors, testified to the survival of man's brute past, a phenomenon that might not have endured in his long evolutionary history had it not been socially useful. Men's insistent unwillingness to contemplate an order without war must, James felt, be listened to and respected. "One cannot meet them effectively by mere counter-insistency on war's expensiveness and horror. The horror makes the thrill; and when the question is of getting the extremest and supremest out of human nature, talk of expense sounds ignominious."[83] Notwithstanding such impulses, the murderous excitement lurking in the often unaware human breast, the impulse to mob excitement, bestiality, and violence should not overshadow man's commonly shared strengths: "However mean a man may be, man is *the best we know.*"[84]

James's idea of human nature was further clarified by his views on the differences he thought he saw between man and his kin in the animal world.[85] It is true that human beings shared with their brute relatives

81. For illustrations see James, *Principles of Psychology,* 1:202, 215, 294; 2:436, 436–7; *Talks to Teachers on Psychology; and to Students of Some of Life's Ideals* (New York, 1901), pp. 274–75; Perry, *The Thought and Character of William James,* 1:709; 2:121.

82. Interview in the *Boston Journal,* July 29, 1903, cited in Perry in *The Thought and Character of William James,* 2:317.

83. James, "The Moral Equivalent of War," p. 320.

84. James to Thomas W. Ward, January 1868, *Letters of William James,* 1:131.

85. In holding that the human animal possesses a much greater number of instincts than other animals, James was responding to biological naturalism and making the instinctive equipment of man a central feature of his conception of human nature. See James, *Principles of Psychology,* 2:390–93, 441.

certain reflex instincts such as aggressiveness and brutality, as well as anger, lust, and fear, but in the course of man's evolution, increased security had inhibited many fears that he had originally had and that still prevailed among animals. Most significant of all, man, unlike his less-developed kin, had the power of memory, reflection, and inference. Thus he could *feel* in a self-conscious way his numerous instincts or impulses and could forecast the result of yielding to them. Perhaps man was less well endowed with reason than tradition and authority asserted, perhaps even all but lacking in abstract reason. Yet he was able, through his ability to remember, reflect, infer, compare, and select, to set loose an imagination, and thus an impulse, leading to a course of action different from and even opposed to the one initially stimulated. This, it appeared, other animals could not do. Though reason, so understood, was the feeblest of Nature's forces, it had the unique advantage over prejudice, partiality, and excitement of pressing in one direction and thus, like a sandbank, gradually expanding.

Further light on the meaning of the term for James is shed by his adoption of it as the subtitle for *The Varieties of Religious Experience: A Study of Human Nature* (1902). As in *The Principles of Psychology*, the phrase was still undefined, and James's remark about the book, "There is a good deal of human nature in it," did not help. But James made it clear that the term implied the meaningfulness of exceptional experiences, whether pathological or normal or both.[86] This conviction he owed to his early medical studies and to the influence of his father, who was immensely and indefatigably intrigued by and hospitable toward the unusual, the exceptional, the wide and even pluralistic range of possibilities and contingencies. This, then, was the key to *The Varieties of Religious Experience*, which in the opinion of Charles S. Peirce penetrated into "the hearts of people" and was thus "the best of his books."

The importance attached to the exceptional and unusual as an earmark of a universal human nature was also seen in James's belief in man's ability, in times of stress and emergency, to summon hitherto unknown, unrealized sources of energy for doing what had to be done. That ability was most clearly evident in the highly visible and dramatic

86. See also *Principles of Psychology*, 1:201–2. A not-unrelated instance of this meaning is evident in James's remark that in spite of his dislike of the semi-pessimism and fatalism in the novels of Tolstoy, the Russian's "infallible veracity concerning human nature" together with his "absolute simplicity of method" make all other writers of novels and plays "seem like children." James to Renouvier, August 4, 1896, cited in Perry, *The Thought and Character of William James*, 1:709. See also James, *Varieties of Religious Experience*, pp. 128, 148, 153.

performances of the recognized hero. But in everyday life, it also had the broadest possible and generally unacknowledged, even unobserved, base. Thus in the daily existence of the laboring classes "every day of the year somewhere, is human nature *in extremis* for you. And whenever a scythe, an axe, a pick or shovel is wielded, you have it sweating and aching and with its powers of patient endurance racked to the utmost under the length of hours of strain."[87]

If there was a common humanity, this did not mean for James that all human beings were alike or equal. The contrary was clear, for example, in his verdict that differences in individual intelligence, character, and worth, resting as they did on physical and psychological bases, were as yet unanalyzed. The rule of the more intelligent and educated man was thus "to offset to the best of his powers both the self-seeking of the ambitious and the blind passions of the crowd."[88] Such efforts alone gave life and vitality to the community, but only when the community appreciated and sympathized with individual effort.

Another striking difference in the distribution of intelligence, James felt, was that between the sexes. In the main, girls, maturing earlier than boys, did not reach the level of intelligent capacity achieved by them. Hence the masculine brain, he thought, could deal with new and complex matter more effectively and over a longer period than the more limited and intuitive feminine mind. Further, women were weaker than men in the hunting instinct, a basic factor in the evolution of mankind. Quicker to anger, women were more prone to conceal this because of "other principles in their nature."[89] Here James was, of course, reflecting attitudes characteristic of both Victorian England and the America of the Gilded Age.

Besides individual and sex differences James believed that personality types, however derived, ranged over a spectrum from the "resolute" to the "irresolute," from the "tough-minded" with a respect for facts to the "tender-minded" with a dedication to principles,[90] from the dare-devil, mercurial, spontaneous (so common among the Latins) to the more cautious and sober (more frequent among the northern "races").[91] In making such judgments James was untroubled by the contradiction it presented to his frequently expressed suspicion of the abstract and the personal.

87. James, *Essays on Faith and Morals*, pp. 291–92.
88. Perry, *The Thought and Character of William James*, 2:290.
89. James, *Principles of Psychology*, 2:368–69, 415.
90. *Principles of Psychology*, 2:530.
91. *Principles of Psychology*, 2:537–38.

No less suspicious of the absolute and of bigness and greatness in all its forms, James in the main emphasized the situational and the concrete in applying to human problems his psychological principles and vivid insights. This he did in a way that most of his contemporary psychologists looked on as outside the proper sphere of experimental and introspective investigation (or what James called "the official psychology"). It was his conviction that everyone needed to have, with all moral earnestness, commitment—to a cause or value—and in so having to make never-ending choices. Only in this way could one discover and realize his self-identity. James's zest for spontaneity was no less than that for commitment. Adhering to his early contribution to the psychobiology of voluntary movements,[92] he rejected every mechanistic interpretation of human behavior. This was evident in his discussion of the possibility of forming new habits, of the constructive role of education, of the ecstasies as well as the torments of religious experience. It was also reflected in his interest, late in life, in a recurrent dream that suggested his own early identity confusion in the matter of choosing a career.[93] Thus in the limited but real freedom open to everyone inhered an invigorating if painfully ambiguous emotional experience.

In the later 1960s, several scholars held that in all this James anticipated movements of thought to become important long after his death—the gestalt psychology with its emphasis on the totality of relationships in perception, the psychology of personality and human relations, existentialism and phenomenology with their emphasis on active participation rather than contentment with the role of the onlooker.[94] Whatever subsequent scholarly opinion on these contentions may be, it is fairly clear that James has a rightful claim to having anticipated Freud in thinking of psychology in terms of a human nature

92. James, "The Feeling of Effort," *Principles of Psychology*, 2:533, 562, 578–79. Ash Gohar, in "The Phenomenology of William James," *Proceedings of the American Philosophical Society* 114 (1970), has explicated this important essay of James. In brief, the volitional idea "can excite only that sensory sector which 'corresponds' to it and none other; and the excitatory strength of the idea is inversely proportional to the resistance potential of the 'neural path' (connecting the sensory center and the effector organ) and the inhibitory reaction of the 'neural field' (corresponding to the aggregate of conflicting ideas). And since ideas, as *Effektsbilder*, are capable of originating the causal concatenation of ideo-motor action, given the selective function of consciousness which attends to a given idea among others at any given time, to that extent the freedom of the will is grounded in human nature" (pp. 296–97).

93. Saul Rosenzweig, "Erik Erikson on William James' Dream," *Journal of the History of the Behavioral Sciences* 6 (1970): 258 ff.

94. William James, "A Suggestion about Mysticism," *Journal of Philosophy, Psychology and Scientific Method* 7 (1910): 85–92, included in *Collected Essays and Reviews* (New York, 1920), 500–513.

embracing much more than measurable sensations and an introspective awareness of conscious acts.[95]

In view of the contributions of other Americans to the emerging "science of human nature" it is easy to overemphasize James's role. But if "the course of history is nothing but the story of man's struggle to find the more and more inclusive order," then James's place in the discussion of human nature is secure and impressive.

95. Gordon W. Allport, "William James and the Behavioral Sciences," *Journal of the History of the Behavioral Sciences* 2 (1966): 145–47; John Wild, *The Radical Empiricism of William James* (New York, 1963); John K. Roth, *Freedom and the Moral Life: The Ethics of William James* (Philadelphia, 1969); Ash Gobar, "The Phenomenology of William James."

7

Toward
a Social Interpretation

This social self comes into being when through imitation, the child begins to understand the inner life of others in terms of his own and, by a return process, to understand his own life in terms of theirs.

JAMES MARK BALDWIN, 1894

It will be a long step in the direction of the scientific explanation of human nature when the introspective evaluation of emotion is superseded by a recognition of the fact that the psychological environment outside of the individual is quite as important in guiding human action as are the internal tendencies which were born with the Individual.

CHARLES H. JUDD, 1926

IN THE last decades of the nineteenth century, when the New Psychology claimed scientific authority for its explanation of the individual psyche, a quite different conception of human nature emerged. It viewed man's makeup in terms of the social forces and interpersonal relationships that molded both individual and social behavior. The new view may be thought of as a reaction against or supplement to the stress on a self-sufficient individual, whether derived from Emersonian idealism, the frontier heritage, the competitive economic system, or the dearth of self-sufficiency in urban life. The view of human nature that recognized the interdependency of individuals may also have owed something to the need of social coherence in a nation fragmented by regional and class conflicts. To some, the new view seemed to offer a realistic explanation of political corruption, crime, poverty, hazards to public health and welfare, and the tensions associated with little wanted but much needed ethnic minorities.

New movements of thought and new approaches to social problems, as well as the requirements of a changing social scene, also contributed to the emerging social image of man. To be sure, it owed little, at least at first, to the New Psychology, which in stressing the individual character of the mind largely ignored public issues. On the other hand, evolutionary theory, a cornerstone of the New Psychology, played an important part in its rise. So too did the professionalization of concern with social issues.

Yet the social image of man by no means put to rest the traditional view that inner drives, instincts, motives, and values largely explained human behavior. Although the timeworn individualistic view could claim validation from evolutionary theory and particularly from Social Darwinism, it also cherished the support of older movements of thought and traditional attitudes.

These included classical economics and its identification with common sense and folk wisdom. Its central emphasis on a utilitarian, hedonistic, and rational self-interest combined desire and calculation.

Writing in *The New Englander* in 1877, John Bates Clark, on his way to becoming a leading economist, noted the prevailing acceptance in his field of a selfish, mechanistic, and in his eyes erroneous view of human nature.[1] But a recognition of cooperative predispositions, which he was to develop guardedly,[2] and a similar emphasis in the Social Gospel,[3] only dimmed the dominant image. This was well represented by the influential Boston entrepreneur, economist, and publicist Edward Atkinson, who held that "it might be said by the prophets of present that the Lord maketh the selfishness of man to work for the material benefit of his kind." Hence, he added, unwise laws that interfered with this process, not men's selfishness, threatened society.[4] A contemporary, Arthur Latham Perry, professor of economics at Williams College, declared that the right to trade freely "rests on the same ultimate principle in the constitution of man and in the providential arrangements of nature."[5] In the view of E. L. Godkin, captious editor of the elite journal *The Nation*, the rules of trade or political economy were in reality the laws of human nature, notably the accumulation of property, the fear of losing it, and the related law of competition.[6]

Of the far-reaching implications of this image of man none was more important than the conviction that the functions of government must be limited to the protection of life and property against possible excesses of unrestrained individualism. The need for education was conceded if people were to understand their true interests and responsibilities. Thus enlightened, men could rightly claim a large field for individual liberty. It followed that everyone must be allowed to accumulate and use his capital as he saw fit. All this echoed Manchesterian liberalism buttressed by associationist psychology.

1. John Bates Clark, "Unrecognized Forces in Political Economy," *The New Englander* 36 (1877): 712.
2. John Bates Clark, *The Philosophy of Wealth* (Boston, 1886), pp. 48–49, 151.
3. Henry F. May's *Protestant Churches and Industrial America* (New York, 1949) still provides the best introduction to Social Christianity in this period.
4. Edward Atkinson, *The Industrial Progress of the Nation* (New York, 1890), p. 208.
5. Arthur Latham Perry, *Elements of Political Economy* (New York, 1866), pp. 386–87.
6. E. L. Godkin, "Cooperation," *North American Review* 106 (1868): 174.

According to this frame of thought, individual endowment explained success and failure. Poverty had nothing to do with the prevailing order of laissez faire. It resulted rather from the deficient native talents and character of those who experienced such degradation. Moreover, poverty served as a beneficial stimulus to effort. It warned everyone of the penalty for sloth, failure of will, inebriation, and other violations of the middle-class Christian code.[7] On the other hand, the successful man owed everything to his superior endowment, including character, to his superior effort, or to both. This message, reenforced by biblical authority, was the dominant note in the literature of the self-made man, even though some exponents conceded the contributing role of chance or even of the unwholesome environment of wayward city urchins.[8]

Such an emphasis on individual autonomy and inner drives, derived in part from classical economics and identified with common sense realism, found advocates well into the twentieth century. During a congressional investigation in 1912, J. Pierpont Morgan maintained that he and his kind should be allowed to exercise their great power as they saw fit, without any check whatsoever. *The Nation*, in reporting his remarks, wryly noted that "human nature may too much respect finance; but finance may expect too much of human nature."[9] As late as the 1920s, James Warren Prothro, in an analysis of business ideology of the time, found that the traditional view of human nature was held to be eminently realistic in emphasizing, above all, inner native endowment and springs of action. Such a view ignored the effect of the social environment as a handicap to the poor and unsuccessful. On the other hand, writers favorable to business applauded American society for uniquely opening to all men the road to self-fulfillment. In the main this was achieved through the egotistical selfishness that provided the common core in the human makeup. It was this drive that had conquered the American wilderness and built a great industrial civilization. Since capacities for fulfilling the drive for economic aggrandizement differed greatly among individuals, those who best realized their natural gifts made up the business elite. Like other elites, business leaders professed a sense of noblesse oblige—"service." This might take the form of giving the masses what they thought they wanted or what was actually best for them to have. In brief, to quote Prothro,

7. Robert H. Bremner, *From the Depths: The Discovery of Poverty in the United States* (New York, 1964), is the best discussion of the subject.

8. Secondary authorities include Irvin G. Wyllie, *The Self-Made Man in America* (New Brunswick, N.J., 1954), Kenneth S. Lynn, *The Dream of Success: A Study of the Modern American Imagination* (Boston, 1955), John G. Cawelti, *Apostles of the Self-Made Man* (Chicago, 1965), and Richard Weiss, *The American Myth of Success: From Horatio Alger to Norman Vincent Peale* (New York, 1969).

9. *The Nation* 95 (1912): 604–5.

"the leaders of the most vocal segments of American business took an understandable pride in the rigorous realism of the theory of human motivations as the internal force for molding man."[10]

Conservative foes of the New Deal would appeal to a similar idea of human nature, and insist that since men were unequal in their innate capacities to-do things, their immediate problems could not be dealt with in a centralized, standardized way. The Depression itself was the result, not of a faulty economic system, but of human nature.[11]

In politics as in economics, such an allegedly realistic view was often called on to sanction the status quo. Roy N. Peel has summarized the view of human nature held by a typical ward boss, Plunkitt of Tammany Hall. He was sure that "every man has his price, never too high if you study him carefully. . . . You are selfish, cold, calculating, and corrupt, but you maintain constantly the illusion that you are generous, warm, informal, and honest. 'To hold your district, study human nature and act accordin'.' " Human nature, Plunkitt went on, was to be studied, not in books and libraries, but rather in the rough and tumble of politics and in day-by-day experience.[12] In due course a student of political psychology provided a gloss, observing that the secret of victory was in making the correct inferences from all the little clues of personality and behavior.[13] Lincoln Steffens, onetime student of the New Psychology in Wundt's laboratory in Leipzig, later a muckraker and the confidant of city bosses, was no less cynical. "You must not trust human nature; it will always go back on you, and if you have learned as a child to put faith in it, you will suffer what human nature calls a disillusionment, which is the Main Street slang for getting rid of bunk."[14] The identification of politics with the mutual trading of self-interest jarred Professor Wilbur Cross of Yale when he became a candidate for the governorship of Connecticut and was taunted with having no practical knowledge of human nature. He recalled Henry Adams's observation that "knowledge of human nature is

10. James Warren Prothro, *The Dollar Decade: Business Ideas in the 1920s* (Baton Rouge, 1954), p. 58. For a more complex view of the image of man in business thought see Merle Curti, "The Changing Concept of 'Human Nature' in the Literature of American Advertising," *Business History Review* 41 (1967): 335–57; and Merle Curti and Peter Karsten, "Man and Businessman: Changing Concepts of Human Nature as Reflected in the Writing of American Business History," *Journal of the History of the Behavioral Sciences* 4 (1968): 3–17. See also Thomas C. Cochran, *Business in American Life* (New York, 1972), chap. 18.

11. George Robinson, "Right of Center: Conservative Critics of the New Deal, 1933–1939" (Ph.D. diss., University of Wisconsin, 1956), chap. 7.

12. William L. Riordan, *Plunkitt of Tammany Hall* (New York, 1948), pp. xvii–xviii, 33–34.

13. Harold D. Lasswell, *The Analysis of Political Behavior* (London, 1948), pp. 102–3.

14. *The Letters of Lincoln Steffens*, 2 vols. (New York, 1938), 2:726.

the beginning and end of political education."[15] A persistent student of boss politics summed up this view: "The pattern of politics has an inner core that is human nature and is more or less constant. Its fashion and outer manifestations change . . . but in a large sense the basic pattern of politics in a democracy remains the same from generation to generation."[16]

It is true that some who stressed the inner impulses and ideas of the individual as the springs of human nature drew conclusions somewhat at odds with the "realistic" emphasis that informed such writers as Godkin, such practical politicians as Plunkitt, such reporters as Steffens, and such champions of the established economy as J. Pierpont Morgan and the critics of the New Deal. Self-activating individual freedom was seen as the key to the highest values of personality, and hence the best means of securing the highest public good.[17] Thus Charles W. Eliot associated manhood suffrage with the individual's freedom of the will, in his eyes a basic actuality of human nature.[18] In the same key William James held that meliorism was a necessary implication of the varied and often conflicting inner drives and instincts of all human beings.

Social Darwinism lent support to classical economics and common sense realism by arguing that an innate selfishness explained motives and behavior and somehow worked for the public good. Andrew Carnegie attributed the accumulation of his fabulous fortune to the strength of his instinct to survive in the struggle with his kind. To be sure, he thought that it would insult human nature and civilization to permit the unfit to be completely annihilated. According to his Gospel of Wealth, the fittest who survived should devote their talents, in some part at least, to the general welfare and the public interest. Carnegie's philanthropies stimulated other men of wealth to follow his example.[19]

William Graham Sumner did not share Carnegie's enthusiasm for

15. Wilbur Cross, *Connecticut Yankee* (New Haven, 1943), p. 247.

16. J. T. Salter, *The Pattern of Politics: The Folkways of a Democratic People* (New York, 1940), p. 114.

17. William E. Hocking, *The Lasting Elements of Individualism* (New Haven, 1937), p. 51; A. C. Garnett, "Liberalism as a Theory of Human Nature," *Journal of Social Philosophy and Jurisprudence* 7 (1942): 127–41.

18. Charles W. Eliot, *American Contributions to Civilization* (New York, 1897), p. 22.

19. Andrew Carnegie, "Wealth," *North American Review* 148 (1889): 655–57, included in Carnegie's *The Gospel of Wealth, and other timely essays* (Garden City, N.Y., 1903). For varying views on the importance of Social Darwinism in the defense of competitive big business see Richard Hofstadter, *Social Darwinism in American Thought 1860–1915*, rev. ed. (New York, 1955); and Irvin G. Wyllie, "Social Darwinism and the Business Man," *Proceedings of the American Philosophical Society* 103 (1959): 629–35.

widespread philanthropy. A popular teacher of economics and sociology at Yale and a crusading, hard-headed writer, he bleakly contended that in the struggle for survival each must eat the fruit of his endowment and his effort: the fittest survived in the social as in the biological order. Talent, effort, work, and frugality bore rewards, just as inferior endowment and sloth brought their penalties. According to this view, interference with the natural order by social planning and sentimental reform was irrational, pernicious, and in the end fruitless, except for penalizing the hard-working and the frugal by burdening them with the support of the meritless unfit and the drones. To his credit, Sumner was no less harsh in condemning interference with the natural order when it took the form of monopolistic thwarting of competition, political corruption, imperialistic adventures, and war in the interest of plutocrats. Yet he doubted that war would ever be given up: it was a function of competitive struggle and of the enduring brute in human nature.[20]

In view of his stress on individual effort and merit in the competition for survival, Sumner might be thought somewhat inconsistent in suggesting in his later work something like a social conception of human nature. In his eyes men, like other animals, were activated by powerful innate drives—hunger, love (including sex), fear, and vanity. The first three led to the growth of such institutions as a labor force, capital, the market, marriage, religion, and the state. Such basic drives also required continuing struggle for survival in an economy of scarcity and, for securing that survival, an "antagonistic cooperation." This was bound to increase with the ever-more-specialized functions of society that the interdependence of its members forced on it. "Antagonistic cooperation" took shape unconsciously, without rational thought, in fact, instinctively, as the pressure of population on limited resources determined social patterns and all-embracing habits—the folkways. In time the folkways that took on normative status became mores: these influenced individual behavior as much as and often more than folkways themselves. Neither bore any relation to the absurd fiction of natural rights as an inherent implication of man's nature. Only a small, talented minority of superior intelligence and creativity now and then broke custom and institutions by engineering better ways of meeting new economic and

20. William Graham Sumner, *What Social Classes Owe to Each Other* (New Haven, 1925), chaps. 9 and 10; *Folkways* (1906; New York, 1959), p. 181; *War and Other Essays* (New Haven, 1911), pp. 3–4, 285–334; *Essays of William Graham Sumner*, 2 vols. (New Haven, 1935), 1:107–11, 460–65; 2:87–149, 205–6, 154. For a brief statement and interpretation of Sumner's position on a major tendency in American economic life, see Bruce Curtis, "William Graham Sumner on the Concentration of Wealth," *Journal of American History* 55 (1969): 823–32.

technological realities. Thus human nature was incapable of real improvement, despite the possibility of limited betterment.[21] In holding, with reservations, to the supremacy of unconscious, binding nonpersonal forces over presumably autonomous individuals, Sumner seemed to be paradoxically edging toward a qualified social interpretation of human nature.

The social orientation in the discussion of human nature challenged the traditional emphasis on the inner drives of the self-directing individual. In the new approach one emphasis was pragmatic, operational, and melioristic, the other theoretical or "philosophical." The interrelatedness of the two approaches was clear from the fact that writers in each camp shared many views about the meaning of human nature: the recognition of the impulses, motives, and ideas of the individual, though downgraded in relation to the older view; stress on the social environment to which the organism was exposed; and a search for some kind of balance between external and internal forces. Notwithstanding the impossibility of differentiating sharply between the pragmatic and operational approach and the more theoretical, it seems warranted to discuss them separately.

The assumption that human nature was relevant, if not the key, to such issues as political corruption, poverty, crime, health, welfare, education, and the plight of ethnic minorities underlay the ideas and activities of many voluntary groups and associations. Of these the most broadly representative was the American Social Science Association, organized in 1865 on the model of a similar British institution.[22] One of its founders, Franklin B. Sanborn, a liberty-loving classical scholar, former abolitionist, and Transcendentalist, was at the time the efficient secretary of the Massachusetts State Board of Charities. Sanborn proved to be a devoted officer of the American Social Science Association for thirty-three years, and served as the editor of the *Journal of Social Science* for much of that time.[23]

21. Sumner, *Folkways*, chap. 1 and following chapters; *Social Darwinism: Selected Essays*, with an introduction by Stow Persons (Englewood Cliffs, N.J., 1963), chaps. 6–8; and *Earth Hunger and Other Essays* (New Haven, 1913), pp. 31–64; and Sumner and Albert G. Keller, *The Science of Society*, 4 vols. (New Haven, 1923–33). Of special interest: Robert G. McCloskey, *American Conservatism in the Age of Enterprise* (Cambridge, Mass., 1951), chap. 2.

22. Philip Abrams, *The Origins of British Sociology, 1834–1914* (Chicago, 1968), pp. 44–53.

23. Alexander Johnson, "An Appreciation of Frank Sanborn," *Survey* 37 (1917): 656–57.

The American Social Science Association[24] was made up of some three hundred men and women, largely New Englanders prominent in charity, public service, and education. Only a few could claim professional status as social scientists, but many might be thought of as amateur predecessors of those who later organized specialized, professional associations for the several social disciplines. Members differed about the causes and methods of ameliorating urban and industrial problems. A good many manifested a traditional sense of noblesse oblige and goodwill in their attitudes toward the new immigrant, the criminal, the mentally ill, the poor, orphans, and dependents generally. In stressing self-help with guidance from voluntary organizations, many members implied a belief in the autonomous individual, and thus failed to understand the fact of interdependency in the changing American scene. As the years passed, however, an increasing number moved toward what might be thought of as a social view of human nature.

When E. L. Godkin declared in 1871 that human nature was the main component of all social and political problems,[25] he expressed a view common to many who took part in the Association's programs. Neither Godkin nor anyone else who invoked human nature to support or oppose a specific issue defined the term. Explicit references to the Christian image of man seldom informed the secular rhetoric of the discourse. To be sure, the ethical tenets of Christian tradition persisted in the assumption of the worthiness of each individual as an object of concern.[26] Nor were Transcendentalist and other forms of mid-nineteenth-century romanticism generally apparent, despite the active part of two prominent members, Sanborn and William T. Harris, in the Concord School of Philosophy. Some papers suggested the influence of Comtean Positivism.

24. Thomas L. Haskell, in *The Emergence of Professional Social Science: The American Social Science Association and the Nineteenth-Century Crisis of Authority* (Urbana, Ill., 1976), emphasizes as an objective the legitimization of the expertise of the participants. Anthony Oberschall, in his essay "The Institutionalization of Empirical Sociology" (Oberschall, ed., *The Establishment of Empirical Sociology* [New York, 1972], pp. 206 ff.), stresses the influence of the ASSA in fathering such reform organizations as the National Prison Association, the Civil Service Reform Association, and the National Conference for Charities and Correction, as well as its influence on the reform orientation of the early American Economics Association and the first outstanding Department of Sociology at the new University of Chicago.

25. E. L. Godkin, "Legislation and Social Science," *Journal of Social Science*, no. 3 (1871): 115–32, esp. 122–23 and 129. (References to the *Journal of Social Science* are abbreviated to *Journal* for remainder of chapter.)

26. For examples: the Rev. J. H. Jones, "Ten Hours," *Journal* 16 (1882): 149–64; and Washington Gladden, "The Arbitration of Labor Disputes," *Journal* 21 (1886): 147–58.

A larger number reflected the post-Enlightenment image of man. This, it will be recalled, offered a hypothetical model or archetype that assumed the existence of a mind influenced only by experience: human nature was understood in terms of individual entities beneath the accretions of environmental and institutional experience. The laws of human nature, rational in character, operated as certainly as those of Newton. "God's laws of human progress," declared Professor Benjamin Peirce of Harvard in 1878, "are more indelibly engraved upon each man's nature than were those of the great lawgiver in the tablets of stone. They cannot be ground out by despotism, nor burned out by communism, nor voted out by the ballot-box. Violate them, and they dash to stones you and all your idols: obey them, and they will be one of your ministering angels."[27] In other words, the light of reason and the dissemination of scientific knowledge provided guides for adjusting institutions to these laws.

Many papers reflected such a view of natural law. It was to be discovered empirically by observation and especially by the statistical methods pioneered by British, European, and American practitioners. Two papers, offered at early meetings of the Association, staked out the promise of this relatively new tool. John Stanton Gould maintained that the statistical method showed the precise relationship between not only the prices of wheat and cattle but also the proportions of marriages, illegitimate births, and crime.[28] In commenting on the census of 1870, James A. Garfield claimed that statistical sequences in mass data indicated that society was "an organism, whose elements and forces conform to laws as constant and pervasive as those which govern the universe." The statistical tool enabled man "to ameliorate his condition, to emancipate himself from the cruel dominion of superstition, and from the countless evils which were once thought beyond his control, and will make him the master rather than the slave of nature."[29] Statistical method was thus hailed as a major scientific tool for discovering the laws of social behavior—the prerequisite for guiding and controlling human nature.

While some discussions continued to identify classical economics with human nature,[30] many rejected the relevancy of laissez faire and

27. Benjamin Peirce, "The National Importance of Social Science in the United States," *Journal* 12 (1880): xxi.

28. James Stanton Gould, "The Texas Cattle Disease," *Journal* 1 (1869): 70.

29. James A. Garfield, "The American Census," *Journal* 2 (1870): 31–32.

30. Examples: William Graham Sumner, "Finance," *Journal* 2 (1870): 31–32; Gamaliel Bradford, "Financial Administration," *Journal* 6 (1874): 51–56; Charles Dudley Warner, "The American Newspaper," *Journal* 14 (1881): 52–70; David A. Wells, "Rational Principles of Taxation," *Journal* 6 (1874): 131; F. H. Betts, "The Policy of Patent Laws," *Journal* 10 (1879): 158–71.

competition to current issues. Several participants suggested the unfortunate effects of competition in augmenting mental disease[31] and in stifling marital affection in the relentless drive for creature comforts and middle-class standards.[32] Convinced of the inadequacy of the competitive drive to protect the general interest, some urged government supervision of public carriers, food processors, and sanitation.[33] On the whole, the participating membership, in relying on obedience to the laws of social science to release man from a supine acceptance of oppressive social evils, repudiated the idea of helplessness before the powerful forces of nature and human nature.

Such a rudimentary approach to the social foundations of human nature found virtually no support in Social Darwinism[34] or even in more than an occasional reference to Darwin himself. Evolution in its idealistic version did, however, inform some discussions. William T. Harris, America's leading Hegelian and a major figure in education, claimed that man existed in a series of ascending selves each one of which was realized through such social institutions as the family, civil society, the state, the church, and education. These social institutions enabled men to become conscious of their ascending selves and to find true being in the consummate Ideal.[35] Julia Ward Howe struck a more naturalistic note in holding that the inborn progressive desire in human nature, "deeper and stronger than mere love of change, pushes the whole heterogeneous mass of humanity onward in a way from which there is no return."[36]

In spite of the recognition of the importance of heredity, many believed that the varied expressions of an innate human nature were greatly influenced by social environment. Thus, having the power to shape environment and institutions, men could modify, indeed change, the expressions of human nature. This conviction was evident, for

31. Dr. Walter Channing, "The Treatment of Insanity in Its Economic Aspects," *Journal* 13 (1881): 89–98; D. F. Lincoln, M.D., "The Nervous System as Affected by School Life," *Journal* 8 (1876): 88–90.

32. Prof. W. C. Robinson, "Divorce Laws," *Journal* 14 (1881): 136–51.

33. Gardner G. Hubbard, "American Railroads," *Journal* 5 (1874): 137; Joseph D. Pott, "The Science of Transportation," *Journal* 2 (1870): 115 ff.; Elisha Harris, "Health Laws and Their Administration," *Journal* 2 (1870): 186–87.

34. Godkin's contributions at meetings of the Association did not include any remark comparable to his contention, in an article "The Great Economical Difficulty of the Day," that "the great capitalist is, in other words, generally a man who has been appointed by natural selection to take charge of a portion of the savings of the community and use them to the best advantage in producing and exchanging." *The Nation* 27 (1878): 78.

35. William T. Harris, "The Method of Study in Social Science," *Journal* 10 (1879): 30–31.

36. Julia Ward Howe, "Changes in American Society," *Journal* 13 (1881): 170.

example, in attitudes expressed about corruption. Many argued that civil service could undermine the spoils system, which brought out the worst in human nature.[37] In attacking political corruption Charles Francis Adams, Jr., urged that laws would be as unnecessary as they were useless if the down-and-out did not have to sell their votes to city bosses in return for the bare essentials of life.[38] Again, an authority on immigration held that municipal and federal supervision of entering aliens could undercut exploitation by unscrupulous hustlers, even though it might be as impossible entirely "to cure the evil as it is to put an end to human depravity in general."[39]

Several papers ascribed crime and poverty in the growing cities to an unfavorable environment rather than to some inborn incapacity or innate proneness to evil. The specific proposals—the elimination of tenements, home-owning, and a wisely administered system of public and private charity,[40] however lacking in realism, nevertheless suggested the role of social factors in deviant behavior. In the words of Dr. Elisha Mosher of the Sherborn Reformatory Prison, "wherever men and women are herded together as in the poor and squalid portions of large cities, or great numbers are employed at special work, as in our manufacturing towns, there will be found these influences which make criminals of men and even more surely of women. Morbid conditions of the body," he went on, "react upon the moral nature, increasing and perpetuating the tendency to criminality."[41]

Others spoke in much the same voice. William C. Eliot, a Unitarian minister in St. Louis, founder of Washington University and a leader in reform movements, argued, in an article entitled "Treatment of the Guilty," that however aggravated the guilt of a wrongdoer, he had been led into such conduct by "the ordinary motives, under like temptations, through the same errors and mistakes, which are common to us all. . . . He retains the same necessity of self-respect, love of approval, and

37. Samuel Eliot, "Civil Service Reform," *Journal* 1 (1869): 116; Dorman Eaton, "The Experiment in Civil Service Reform," *Journal* 8 (1876): 76–77.

38. Charles Francis Adams, Jr., "The Election of Presidents," *Journal* 2 (1870): 148–58; "The Protection of the Ballot in National Elections," *Journal* 1 (1869): 101 ff.

39. Frederick Knapp, "Immigration," *Journal* 2 (1870): 27–29.

40. Robert Treat Paine, Jr., "Homes for the People," *Journal* 15 (1882): 104–20; Frederick J. Kingsbury, "Debate on Factory Labor," *Journal* 16 (1882): 148; and, especially, Franklin B. Sanborn, "The Supervision of Public Charities," *Journal* 1 (1869): 76.

41. Dr. Elisha M. Mosher, "The Health of Criminal Women," *Journal* 16 (1882): 46–51. Carrol D. Wright, in a paper entitled "The Factory System as an Element in Civilization," took exception to Mosher's remarks on factories, maintaining their superiority to the putting-out system in terms of the earnings, conditions of work, and hours. *Journal* 16 (1882): 102.

consciousness of right, the same feelings of remorse and self-reproach, the same inward protest against injustice and wrong." The only hope of restoring wrongdoers, Eliot felt, was "skillful and judicious treatment to stimulate the good that is left in them, and thereby to drive out the bad."[42] Some, in arguing that repressive treatment only deepened the passion that led to crime in the first place, advocated a reform in the whole system of criminal justice.[43] While recognizing inborn predispositions as causes of physical, mental, and moral degeneracy, Zebulon R. Brockway of the Elmira State Reformatory urged the need of training the whole man, his capacity, habits, and tastes, especially under the discipline of industrial efficiency.[44] Another proposal, that of Frederick Kingsbury, aroused less interest than it merited: in his view economic security, in the form of guaranteed pensions, would stimulate incentive and reinforce the courage needed to cope with the harsh struggles of daily life.[45]

The importance of a good environment also showed up in discussions of public health. Its leading exponents urged greater government responsibility and control. This, to be sure, could not prevent the nervous degeneracy and insanity resulting from excessive ambition to make money quickly, to rise on the social scale, and to push children beyond their strength. But contributing factors, such as poor diet and slum conditions, could be controlled. Dr. D. F. Lincoln, for one, argued that since man was an organism with functions clearly related to his surroundings, society had an obligation to improve such social environment.[46]

Emphasis on the need for bettering the environment and on the formative importance of childhood testified to the indirect influence of the new biology and the new psychology. Three influential figures in the child-study movement, William T. Harris,[47] G. Stanley Hall, and Emily Talbot, sponsored programs for moral training for infants and young

42. *Journal* 8 (1876): 80.

43. George C. Barrett, "The Administration of Criminal Justice," *Journal* 2 (1870): 170–75.

44. Zebulon R. Brockway, "Reformation of Prisoners," *Journal* 6 (1874): 144–59. See also Brockway's *Fifty Years of Prison Service* (New York, 1912); and "The Ideal of a True System for a State," *Transactions of the National Congress on Penitentiary and Reformatory Discipline* (Albany, N.Y., 1871), pp. 38–65.

45. Frederick J. Kingsbury, "Pensions in a Republic," *Journal* 13 (1882): 1–11.

46. D. F. Lincoln, "The Nervous System as Affected by School Life," *Journal* 8 (1876): 88–93.

47. William T. Harris, Henry Barnard, and Emily Talbot, "Report from a Department Subcommittee on Kindergarten," *Journal* 12 (1880): 9–12.

children.[48] Others saw salvation in a healthy environment for disadvantaged children in foster homes that were thought to be better suited than custodial institutions for overcoming hereditary weaknesses.[49] Charles Loring Brace outdid everyone in working for the removal of unprotected orphans from institutions to a favorable environment in western farm homes.[50] The assumed influence of environment on social behavior also played a part in the movement for public parks. These were thought to encourage the virtues associated with country living and to lessen deviancy by providing wholesome programs for underprivileged children.[51]

Nor did child welfare exhaust the Association's interest in encouraging middle-class virtues. Many felt that the best man was capable of could be forwarded by multiplying agencies for developing self-respect and moral growth, such as the YMCA and the public library.[52] Measures recommended for decreasing dependency also included people's savings banks, vocational training, and job placement.[53]

In view of the interest in child welfare, a reflection of both the environmental and evolutionary assumptions of so many participants, it seems strange that racial issues got so little attention. In 1874 Dr. Edward Jarvis, an authority on insanity, statistics, and anthropology, modestly admitted that the puzzling differences in race were inadequately explained by statistical variations in vitality, the

48. G. Stanley Hall, "Moral and Religious Training," *Journal* 15 (1882). This issue of the *Journal* included Darwin's observations on infants, republished from *Mind* (1877), Darwin's response to Mrs. Talbot's request for cooperation, and Dr. William Preyer's "Observations on Children."

49. Anna Hallowell, "The Care and Saving of Neglected Children," *Journal* 12 (1880): 117.

50. Charles Loring Brace, "What Is the Best Method for the Care of Poor and Vicious Children?" *Journal* 11 (1880): 94. See also Miriam Z. Langsam, *Children West* (Madison, Wis., 1964). Bernard Wishy's *The Child and the Republic: The Dawn of American Child Welfare* (Philadelphia, 1968) is a useful study.

51. Frederick Law Olmstead, "The Justifying Value of a Public Park," *Journal* 12 (1880): 163–64. The discussion of the city park was widespread in the periodical literature of the last decades of the century.

52. Willliam Greenough, "Some Conclusions Relative to Public Libraries," *Journal* 7 (1874): 329–32; Ainsworth Spofford, "The Public Libraries of the United States," *Journal* 2 (1870): 113; Cephas Brainerd, "The Social Science Work of the Young Men's Christian Associations," *Journal* 7 (1874): 334.

53. Henry Villard, "People's Savings Banks in Germany," *Journal* 1 (1869): 127–28; Robert Treat Paine, Jr., "The Work of Volunteer Visitors of the Associated Charities among the Poor," *Journal* 12 (1880): 101–16; the Rev. Dr. Kellogg, "The Principle and Advantage of Association in Charities," *Journal* 12 (1880): 90; Mrs. Florence Lockwood, "The Principle of Volunteer Service," *Journal* 12 (1880): 125–34.

proportion of births to marriages, and life expectancy.[54] President Merrill E. Gates of Rutgers University, in one of the few papers on the Indian, assumed the validity of the "civilizing" and "Americanizing" objectives of the Dawes Act.[55] The well-known Sinologist and missionary S. Wells Williams, in criticizing the treatment of Chinese on the West Coast, insisted that these immigrants were not "held back" by any innate racial characteristics and that they could be assimilated to the Christian-American way of life.[56]

The dearth of discussion of the Negro probably reflected the tacit decision of the northern middle class to leave the black man in southern hands. In 1880 Frederick Douglass did hold that the migration of Negroes to Kansas and to northern cities proved that the blacks were by no means too indolent and stupid to better their condition. On the other hand, he deplored the migration. These Negroes, being products of southern life, could best forge ahead in a familiar environment. By having to compete with white labor in the North they found themselves shoved into alleys, cellars, and garrets without adequate food and means of self-advancement.[57] A few papers discussed other aspects of the "Negro problem." General Thomas Logan felt that however inferior the black was in native capacity, education would enable him to improve his lot and thus benefit society.[58] A former Virginian woman slaveholder, in expressing warm appreciation of the progress blacks had made, urged that with sympathetic understanding they would develop the full potentialities of human beings.[59] Negro crime, like education, occasioned varying judgments. Professor Walter F. Willcox of Cornell presented statistics purporting to show that Negroes were several times as liable to commit crimes as whites.[60] A paper that deplored lynching

54. Edward Jarvis, "Vital Statistics of Different Races," *Journal* 7 (1874): 233–34. Jarvis's manuscript autobiography is in the Houghton Library at Harvard. See also *Proceedings of the American Antiquarian Society*, n.s. 3 (1885): 484–87; and *Proceedings of the American Academy of Arts and Sciences*, n.s. 20 (1885): 519–22. Cf. Jarvis's discussion with that of Professor C. A. Gardner, "The Race Problem in the United States," *Journal* 18 (1884): 266–75.

55. Merrill E. Gates, "Land and Law Agents in Educating Indians," *Journal* 12 (1885): 113–46.

56. S. Wells Williams, "Chinese Immigration," *Journal* 10 (1879): 121–22.

57. Frederick Douglass, "The Negro Exodus from the Gulf States," *Journal* 10 (1880): 1–21.

58. Gen. T. M. Logan, "The Opposition in the South to the Free School System," *Journal* 9 (1878): 92–100.

59. Mrs. Ora Langhorne, "Colored Schools in Virginia," *Journal* 11 (1888): 44–45.

60. Walter F. Willcox, "Negro Criminality," in Alfred Holt Stone, *Studies in the American Race Problem*, introduction and three papers by Walter F. Willcox (New York, 1908), pp. 443–44.

thought that it was widely tolerated because of delays in the administration of justice.[61] None of the discussions got very far with the problem of asking whether the lag of blacks in property-owning, education, and other accomplishments important on the middle-class scale of values resulted from innate racial characteristics or unfavorable background and opportunities.

Ten years after the founding of the Association, Sanborn admitted that reform had proved more stubborn and complex than he had once supposed. He saw no reason, though, to doubt man's ability to control institutions and the environment—the most important influences on human behavior.[62] Yet at the twenty-fifth anniversary his caution had become more explicit. "Whoever expects to see human nature greatly changed by any constitution or social reform, or by anything except inward regeneration," Sanborn wrote, "will probably be disappointed; and whoever has ventured much in the experiment of setting right the disjointed times in which he was born, with the hope that he would receive even thanks for his pains, will certainly be disappointed, as he deserves to be."[63] He did not question the assumption that if existing institutions and the material conditions on which the social order rested were changed, human nature and the moral order would respond. It remained for later social scientists to test the assumption of individual autonomy and inner regeneration and to offer better evidence for the belief that a shift from free enterprise, the profit system, and competition to social planning and cooperation would result in a change of human nature.[64]

The limitations imposed by middle-class values, by amateur incompetence, and by the failure to embark on interdisciplinary research with adequate methods now seem obvious. Nevertheless, the Association's members raised serious doubts about a view of human nature that ignored or downgraded social factors in behavior and in the possibility of its substantial improvement.

Not until 1890 did the Association give any real consideration to Henry George. Such well-known figures as Samuel B. Clark, Thomas Davidson, William Lloyd Garrison, John Bates Clark, E. Benjamin Andrews, E. R. Seligman, Louis F. Post, Edward Atkinson, William T.

61. George C. Holt, "Lynching and Mobs," *Journal* 32 (1894): 67–81.

62. Franklin B. Sanborn, "The Work of Social Science, Past and Present," *Journal* 8 (1876): 23–24.

63. Sanborn, "The Work of Twenty-Five Years," *Journal* 27 (1890): xlviii.

64. For example, see the article by Robert E. Park, "Social Planning and Human Nature," *Publications of the American Sociological Society* 26 (1935): 19–28.

Harris, and George himself took part in the discussion of *Progress and Poverty*.[65]

Henry George's social conscience had been stirred by the startling contrasts he saw in California and in New York between poverty, wealth, and economic development. After several years of mulling over causes for such a paradox, he diagnosed them in *Progress and Poverty* (1879) and prescribed the single tax as the remedy. The arguments in all his writings owed a good deal to his view of human nature, which reflected the natural rights philosophy, Christian ethics, and evolutionary assumptions. "There is a stage in the growth of every organism," he wrote, "in which it cannot be told except by environment, whether the animal that is to be will be fish or reptile, man or monkey. And so with the new-born infant: whether the mind that is yet to awake to consciousness and power is to be English or German, American or Chinese—the mind of a civilized man or the mind of a savage—depends entirely on the social environment in which it is placed."[66] The narrow and seemingly unconscious "intelligence" called instinct in animals became, almost by a sudden, qualitative leap, conscious reason in man.[67] Unlike any other animal, man set no limit to his desires. "To arouse his ambition, to educate him to new wants, is as certain to make him discontented with his lot as to make that lot harder."[68] Again, the savage still lurked in the breast of civilized man even though civilization, as it advanced, required a higher conscience, a wider public spirit.[69] Finally, men not only had the power to adapt in higher degree than other animals but also the unique power to create.[70] This creativity was enhanced by equal association for the common good. The apparent stupidity of the masses was like that of a tethered bull whose own binding stymied his action when green grass was within easy reach. Cooperative intelligence, by changing the conditions that shaped human nature, could enable people to observe the Golden Rule—God's words and Nature's laws.

Henry George's conviction that human beings could develop a more socially motivated human nature also found reenforcement in his acceptance and rejection of certain eighteenth-century ideas. On the one

65. "The Single Tax Discussion at Saratoga, September 5, 1890," *Journal* 27 (1890): 1–124.

66. Henry George, *Progress and Poverty*, 4th ed. (New York, 1880), pp. 493–94. The literature about George is extensive; Charles A. Barker's *Henry George* (New York, 1955) is the definitive biography.

67. Henry George, *Social Problems* (New York, 1883), p. 2.

68. George, *Social Problems*, p. 33.

69. *Social Problems*, p. 241.

70. *Social Problems*, pp. 57, 216–17.

hand, he denounced the classical economists' attribution of "deep wrongs in the present constitution of society . . . to wrongs inherent in the constitution of man."[71] On the other hand, he accepted the Lockean tenet of *tabula rasa* in declaring, "We come into the world with minds ready to receive any impression." Due weight was given to the great power of habit stemming from the social environment. Thus "human nature is human nature the world over." This lesson was to be learned in any library containing the mementoes of life of other times and other peoples which, "translated into the language of today, are like glimpses of our lives and gleams of our own thought. The feeling they inspire is that of the essential similarity of men."[72]

Though Henry George shared the equalitarianism implicit in the natural rights philosophy and the Christian tradition, he did not claim that all men possessed the same capacities. He admitted that there had probably never been two human beings who were exact mental and physical counterparts. Nor did he deny that there might well be inherent mental as well as physical race differences. Nevertheless, he thought that there was a "common standard and natural symmetry of mind, as there is of body, toward which all deviations tend to return . . . the differences between the people of communities in different places and at different times, which we call differences of civilization, are not differences which inhere in individuals, but differences which adhere in society."[73]

Such were the underpinnings of Henry George's distinctive economic analysis and program—the message was equally valid for all peoples since every man and woman shared a common human nature. But he did not rely solely on man's intelligence, social cooperativeness, creative powers, and sense of fairness and right. If men were to change the social environment that caused injustice and dereliction, they must feel a true and deep religious commitment. Fortunately, all men, George believed, had such a capacity. Its full expression would give the needed incentive and provide the dynamic force for social and institutional change.[74]

George's contemporary critics held that he took the perfectibility of the social order too much for granted and paid too little heed to the evil inherent in man.[75] He tried to meet the criticism not only in argumentative lectures and writing but in seeking political office and en-

---

71. *Social Problems*, pp. 57, 71, 77, 244. George also emphasized the desire for the esteem of one's fellows as a powerful motive in behavior.

72. George, *Progress and Poverty*, pp. 494–95.

73. *Progress and Poverty*, pp. 494–95.

74. George, *Social Problems*, p. 9.

75. Reuben C. Rutherford, *Henry George versus Henry George* (New York, 1882).

couraging experimental single-tax communities. The considerable attraction of his gospel during two decades of widespread social discontent
owed a good deal to the fact that it rested on a well-understood and
engaging view of human nature.

Edward Bellamy, whose social conscience was stirred at the same
time, developed a social view of human nature that in some ways
resembled and in others differed from that of Henry George. "Few men
of his day," wrote his biographer, "had more penetratingly observed or
more acutely thought upon the springs of human action. His assumption
that 'human nature' is but the raw material out of which culture and
purposes may form motives, events, habits and desires—this was the
deliberate conclusion of one who had thought long and incisively upon
the matter."[76] A close examination of *Looking Backward* (1888),
Bellamy's widely read fanciful account of a socialist America in the year
2000, shows that the theme of human nature was central to his whole
discussion.

Several influences, together with his distaste for the ugliness of the new
industrialism, the horror of poverty, and his personal insecurity, shaped
his ideas. There can be little doubt that the rationalism and environmental relativism of such eighteenth-century thinkers as Condorcet
appealed to him.[77] His concept of human nature also reflected his
sympathy with the utopian tradition and its resurgence in his day. He
found in Auguste Comte, in Plutarch's *Lycurgus*, and in accounts of the
Incas confirmation of his conviction that happiness and well-being were
most likely to be found in societies where the individual subordinated his
own interests to the public weal. At the same time, he saw great shortcomings in the lack of democracy in Sparta and ancient Peru.[78] Late in
life he said that an unfinished essay he had written in 1874 summed up
the view of man and his relation to the universe that he had never
questioned. The essay, "The Religion of Human Solidarity," reflected
the influence of the Judeo-Christian vision of the brotherhood of man to
be achieved within historical time, the Sermon on the Mount, Emersonian Transcendentalism, the philosophy of Henry James, Sr., and neo-
Platonism, Hegelianism, and the religions of India.

Although Bellamy expressed sympathy with some of Darwin's
writings, his essay regarded man as a duality. On the one hand the

76. Arthur E. Morgan, *Edward Bellamy* (New York, 1944), p. 414.

77. Joseph Schiffman, "Edward Bellamy's Altruistic Man," *American Quarterly* 6
(1954): 205.

78. Edward Bellamy, "What Nationalism Means," *The Contemporary Review*, July
1890, reprinted in *Edward Bellamy Speaks Again* (Kansas City, 1937), p. 87.

human being was a well-defined personality, and on the other an impersonal yet very real alien to this personality. It relentlessly reached out toward eternal nature, toward all other souls, and though he did not use the word, toward the Oversoul. "This dual life of man, personal and impersonal, as an individual and as a universal goes far to explain the riddle of human nature and of human destiny."[79] It was this "instinct" of mutual love for everyone, this identity of the individual life with all lives, this universal solidarity that explained man's unceasing, restless aspiration to transcend time and place and the limitations of his concrete and parochial personality. To be sure, the instinct of universal solidarity was thwarted by social conventions, the egotistical urge, and the limited view commonly taken of human nature as unworthy if not downright evil. Nevertheless, this impersonal consciousness of solidarity within each human being would evolve over time into fullness, just as existing mental faculties had slowly and painfully evolved from the savage state.

The natural desire of the soul to fuse with others and with the "all" might find fuller expression in love of humanity than in the passion, beauty, and spirituality of sexual union.[80] Bellamy made it clear, however, that the search for fusion of the personality with the universe was not to be a Buddhist-like escape from tangible reality. In short, Bellamy's conception of the self reflected the more social aspects of Transcendentalism and resembled Whitman's fraternal, mystical urge for perfect comradeship as the basis for endless spiritual growth as well as a democracy of the present. In combination with social utopianism and responsiveness to some aspects of the emerging psychology, it also opened the door to *Looking Backward.*

Bellamy was sensitive to the revolutionary implications of the new science for theories of human nature. Although vigorously repudiating Social Darwinism, he greatly admired Darwin, as his review of *Expressions of the Emotions in Man and Animals* indicated. He was also acquainted with Dr. Oliver Wendell Holmes's "Mechanism in Thought and Morals," and other current medical psychology.[81] These led him to suggest a physiological interpretation of thinking and versification that anticipated later behaviorist theory.[82] The naturalistic concept of a plastic human nature expressed in several of Bellamy's reviews was not,

79. Edward Bellamy, *The Religion of Solidarity, with a Discussion of Edward Bellamy's Philosophy,* ed. Arthur E. Morgan (Yellow Springs, Oh., 1940), p. 16. The essay is included in Joseph Schiffman, ed., *Edward Bellamy: Selected Writings on Religion and Society* (New York, 1955). I am indebted to Professor Schiffman's introduction.

80. Bellamy, *The Religion of Solidarity,* pp. 32–33.

81. Charles Bowe, "Reflex Action in the Novels of Oliver Wendell Holmes," *American Literature* 26 (1954): 303–19.

82. Morgan, *Edward Bellamy,* pp. 163–65.

in his mind, incompatible with "The Religion of Humanity." It was in any case indispensable to his melioristic view of man the altruist.

Dr. Heidenhoff's Process, a "daringly original" little novel that appeared serially in the Springfield, Massachusetts *Union*, represented the scientific aspect of Bellamy's view of human nature.[83] In the story, a winsome young village woman, after involvement in a scandal, fell into a deep depression as the result of a devastating sense of guilt. Her inability to forgive herself reflected both an unreasonable moral code and the sense of unworthiness related to the Calvinism against which Bellamy had rebelled. Dr. Heidenhoff, who believed in the physiological nature of the mind, was experimenting with a therapy for depression that subjected the patient to galvanic shock. It succeeded marvelously in the case of the guilt-ridden protagonist; but in the end the whole episode turned out, ironically, to be a dream of the devoted lover, who was awakened by news of the suicide of his beloved.[84]

An interesting example of Bellamy's use of his view of human nature in *Looking Backward* was his handling of the relationship between environment and motivation. A given environmental situation evoked one kind of motive, such as the selfish exploitation of others, unworthy emulation, or belligerency, while another situation brought into play very different motives. Thus Dr. Leete, in explaining socialist America in the year 2000 to Julian West, his visitor from the Boston of 1887, observed that there were no parties or politicians, no demagoguery or corruption. Whereupon Julian West exclaimed, "Human nature itself must have changed very much." On the contrary, his host replied, only "the conditions of life have changed, and with them the motives of human action." Since an official could not possibly use ill-gotten gain for himself or others, there was thus no motive for trying to do so.[85] In reply to Julian West's amazement on hearing that a worker in the America of 2000 put forth his best efforts without expecting an added reward, Dr. Leete returned, "Does it then really seem to you . . . that human nature is insensible to any motives save those of fear of want and love of luxury? Even in your America of 1887," he went on, "though it was pretended that only motive for economic gain actuated endeavor," soldiers died for their country because of their devoted patriotism. Now,

83. The novel was published in New York in 1880 and later in Edinburgh and London. Among others, William Dean Howells expressed appreciation of it.

84. Joseph Schiffman, "Edward Bellamy's Altruistic Man," *American Quarterly* 6 (1954): 198–202. Schiffman's comparisons of *Dr. Heidenhoff's Process* with the psychological and psychiatric novels of Oliver Wendell Holmes and S. Weir Mitchell and his discussion of the ways in which Bellamy anticipated Dr. Harry Stack Sullivan and other later social psychiatrists are noteworthy.

85. Edward Bellamy, *Looking Backward* (Boston, 1926), pp. 60, 61.

in the America of 2000, poverty and the fear of it having been abolished, "the coarser motives, which no longer move us, have been replaced by higher motives wholly unknown to the wage-earners of your age. Now that industry of whatever sort is no longer self-service, but the service of the nation, the motives of patriotism and passion for humanity impel the worker as in your day they did the soldier."[86] The motives of appropriation and emulation, expressed so largely in the traditional America by the struggle for gain and status, found, in "the fraternal society" of 2000, outlets in rewards and in honorable recognition for work well done in the service of the commonweal.

Nor, in the America of 2000, were laws any longer necessary, since voluntary action was "the logical outcome of the operation of human nature under rational conditions."[87] With no private property and no competition, with security and opportunity for everyone, crimes had almost disappeared: the small number that turned up were atavistic throwbacks to some earlier flaw in racial antecedents. Equally impressive, war was only a remote memory, there being no longer competition between nations, most of which had followed America on the cooperative path.

In owning the whole system of production, the nation did not enforce a deadly conformity. As a result, Dr. Leete explained, the social order was now "elastic enough to give free play to every instinct of human nature which does not aim at dominating others or living on the fruit of others' labor."[88] Differences in natural and mental endowment, capacities, and tastes were now fully recognized: children were early exposed to all sorts of activities, closely watched and classified; but they were given a choice of the type of national service they were to perform, and if they found themselves unsuited or the work distasteful, they might make another choice. Differences between the sexes were also to be taken into account. Women no longer competed with men, but worked with them in roles suitable to their gifts and training, as companions and equals. Tender love between human beings had increased, to fill the vacuum left by the old emphasis on competition with its resulting inequality and insecurity.

Thus Julian West came to see that the system of his day was less congruous with human nature than the new order, in part because, as Dr. Leete put it, private property and the resulting inequality had forced society to stand, as a pyramid, poised on its apex. "All the gravitations of human nature were constantly tending to topple it over, and it could be maintained upright, or rather upwrong . . . by an elaborate system of

86. Bellamy, *Looking Backward*, pp. 96–97.
87. *Looking Backward*, p. 116.
88. *Looking Backward*, p. 169.

constantly renewed props and buttresses and guyropes in the form of laws.''[89] Dr. Leete summed things up by observing that "the solidarity of the race and the brotherhood of man" were mere fine phrases a hundred years ago. But they had now become in everyday thinking and feeling "ties as real and as vital as physical fraternity."[90] Gradually, under the stimulus of the fraternal order, West himself began to feel its values and to be transformed into a personality with the same social motivation as those he met and saw.

Shortly after the longest discussion about human nature[91] Julian West woke up from his strange dream—for of course his experience in a utopian America in the year 2000 was only a dream. He woke up to the irrational and inhuman realities of his own day: political corruption, labor turmoil, the ugliness of industrial cities, poverty, crime, social callousness, and ruthless competition. But the waking turned out actually to be a nightmare. Julian West was not dreaming—he was actually experiencing a society based on the Golden Rule.[92]

Generally speaking, most reviewers of Looking Backward took vigorous exception to Bellamy's view of human nature. The psychological portrait that had eliminated individual antagonism and implemented in everyday life the sense of solidarity and love seemed to many simplistic, optimistic, and unrealistic in its blindness to the selfishness and evil in man as he always had been and always must be. Others questioned whether in such a hierarchical bureaucracy human beings, largely subordinate to the managerial authority of the few, could realize the initiative and freedom so necessary if human nature was to realize its best potential. Again, to those used to continual movement and change, personalities in a static equilibrium seemed likely to stagnate. Moreover, many thought that Bellamy failed to give due weight to the enduring role of political, religious, esthetic, and other factors in man's thinking and values.[93]

Undeterred by such criticisms and determined to implement his vision by social action, Bellamy encouraged the 165 "nationalist" societies founded to spread his belief in the compatibility of human nature with

89. Looking Backward, p. 209.
90. Looking Backward, p. 134.
91. Looking Backward, p. 276.
92. Looking Backward, pp. 307–52.
93. Edward Bellamy, Looking Backward, foreword by Eric Fromm (New York, 1960), pp. xi–xiv. In a stimulating and original interpretation of Bellamy, R. Jackson Wilson ("Experience and Utopia: The Making of Edward Bellamy's Looking Backward," Journal of American Studies 2 [1977]: 45–60) suggests that the emphasis in Equality, a sequel to Looking Backward, on pastoral values reflected both a response to such critics as William Morris of the mechanized industrialism of Looking Backward and to Bellamy's own deep-seated dislike of modern industrialism itself.

the rational and benevolent organization of society. His image of man, in assuming the efficacy of education for such ends, eliminated the need for the Marxist doctrine of class conflict and violent revolution he had known and disliked as a student in Germany. His faith in human plasticity, in the ability of the finite personality to solve its creature problems as the necessary preliminary to still further progress toward a religion of humanity, rested on his social view of human nature.

Obviously the millions who read *Looking Backward* were not sufficiently moved to act or felt unable to do so. At the same time many, including John Dewey, Charles A. Beard, William Allen White, Thorstein Veblen, Eugene V. Debs, and Norman Thomas, testified to Bellamy's influence on their thinking and careers.

Before Henry George's death in 1897 and Bellamy's the next year, the development of a social interpretation of human nature shifted from the popular to the academic forum. With greater concreteness and increasing sophistication pioneer social psychologists added new dimensions and depth to the idea of human nature as an essentially social concept and reality.

Notwithstanding the stress on cognition and individual differences in the New Psychology, one of its American "fathers," James Mark Baldwin, a progressive conservative who taught at Princeton and the Johns Hopkins, developed a noteworthy social view of human nature. Baldwin's position took into account the Scottish philosophy's commitment to the individual's moral responsibility, the experimental psychology of Wundt's laboratory, and Tarde's sociology of imitation. Above all, Baldwin realized the importance of evolution. For him this leaned toward the nondeterministic Lamarckian version and, like that of Hall, held that the growth of the child recapitulated the evolution of the race. His unique contribution also owed a good deal to watching his children learn and play.

The self, Baldwin believed, was a social product, the result of give-and-take between a human being and his fellows. What man is or can become depends upon his social relations with others. Social suggestion accounted for much in the development of self-consciousness and personality. Sin was a function of the social situation. Capacity for sympathy, "one of the strongest and most saving elements in human nature," resulted from this ability to put oneself in the place of another.[94] "It is," Baldwin wrote, "impossible for anyone to begin life as an individual in

94. James Mark Baldwin, *Social and Ethical Interpretations of Mental Development* (New York, 1897), p. 223.

the sense of radically separating himself from his social fellows. The social bond is instituted and rooted in the very growth of self-consciousness. Each individual's apprehension of his own personal self and its interests involves the recognition of others and their interests; and his pursuit of one type of purpose, generous or selfish, is insofar the pursuit of others also."[95] Searching for scientific support for ethical morality, he faulted the excesses of both psychological individualism and "sociological collectivism." In the turgid prose of *Mental Development of the Child and the Race* (1895) and *Social and Ethical Interpretations of Mental Development* (1897) Baldwin reinterpreted in the dialectical terms of "self-other" such phrases as social heredity, social intelligence, social sanctions, social accommodation, and social environment. His later metaphysical view of logic and esthetics, deeply tinged with philosophical idealism, also reflected his perception of evolving stages of interaction between individuals in a true moral community.

What Baldwin did in outlining a social view of human nature in psychological terms Charles Horton Cooley, a sociologist at the University of Michigan, also did, but with greater influence on con-temporary discussion. His image of man can be understood only in the light of his whole social philosophy, which was indebted to Emerson's insistence on the dignity and all-pervasiveness of mind ever in process and to Goethe's idea of the mental life as a work of art. From the Ger-man social idealist Albert Eberhard Friedrich Schäffe he took the idea that society could be free from deterministic control by an external environment while it was at the same time the formative setting for human nature. Cooley was also indebted to Darwin, and to the func-tional and genetic psychologies that James and Baldwin derived largely from evolutionary theory. In spite of finding a distinct role for each person, Cooley had little interest in the individual biological organism, which he assumed to have great plasticity and teachability. He also thought of it, like every other unit of social existence, as a product of an all-encompassing but effective process impelled by a continuing thrust into unexplored territory. In the end, the pragmatic test spelled success or failure, and conflict led to a higher social synthesis.[96]

95. James Mark Baldwin, *The Individual and Society* (New York, 1911), p. 26. See also Baldwin's own account in Carl Muchison, ed., *The History of Psychology in Autobiography*, 6 vols. (Worcester, Mass., 1930–74), 1:1–30; Fay Berger Karpf, *American Social Psychology* (New York, 1932), pp. 279–91; and the brilliant assessment in R. Jackson Wilson's *The Quest of Community, 1860–1968* (New York, 1968), pp. 60–96.

96. Charles Horton Cooley, *Human Nature and the Social Order* (New York, 1902), p. 174. The standard biography is Edward C. Jandy, *Charles Horton Cooley* (New York, 1942).

In the first edition of *Human Nature and the Social Order* (1902) Cooley used the term *human nature* in an offhand way. Introspective in his approach, he spoke of the need of insight if "the clandestine impulses of human nature were to be understood and shared." Elsewhere he suggested that the self and self-seeking sprang from human nature as respectable and healthy traits.[97] Human nature and human ideals developed together. A reasonable idealism must look to the organization and control of all passions with reference to some socially conditioned conception of right, rather than to the expulsion of some passions by others.[98] This reflected the importance he gave to man's emotive character and to the possibility of controlling the less-desirable emotions through social organization. Cooley's casual references showed that whatever he had in mind when he used the term human nature, he did not mean mere native biological equipment.

In *Social Organization* (1909) Cooley amplified his idea of human nature. He insisted that "it is not something existing separately in the individual, but a *group-nature* or *primary phase* of society, a relatively simple and general condition of the social mind." It was, he went on, "the nature which is developed and expressed in those simple, face-to-face groups that are somewhat alike in all societies: groups of the family, the playground, and the neighborhood. In the essential similarity of these is to be found the basis, in experience, for similar ideas and sentiments in the human mind"—ideas and instincts ranging from cooperative and friendly to antagonistic and hostile. The latter were checked by the sentiments of sympathy and the development of agreed-on rules. In other words, "by human nature, I suppose, we may understand those sentiments and impulses that are human in being superior to those of lower animals, and also in the sense that they belong to mankind at large, not to any particular race or time. It means, particularly, sympathy and the innumerable sentiments into which sympathy enters, such as love, resentment, ambition, vanity, hero-worship, and the feeling of social right or wrong. Human nature in this sense is justly regarded as a comparatively permanent element in society."[99] Here Cooley broke unplowed ground in specifically explaining human nature in terms of the human organization that developed only in the experience of the individual in primary groups.

In 1922, in a revision of *Human Nature and the Social Order*, Cooley added a chapter on the relation between hereditary instincts and environment. He had insisted, as early as 1896, on their complementary

97. Cooley, *Human Nature and the Social Order*, pp. 205, 211.
98. *Human Nature and the Social Order*, p. 280.
99. Charles Horton Cooley, *Social Organization: A Study of the Larger Mind* (New York, 1909), p. 28.

and inseparable character.[100] He now spelled out three common uses of the phrase human nature. The first identified it with "the strictly hereditary nature of man, borne by the germ plasm, the formless impulses and capacities that we infer to exist at birth." No one knew much about these capacities, as they became manifest only in social development. There was little reason to think that contemporary man's equipment at birth differed much from that of his ancestors a thousand years back. A second meaning of the term identified it with specific types of behavior, such as pecuniary selfishness or generosity, belligerency or peacefulness, conservatism or radicalism, all of which arose from particular institutions and situations. Contrary to common opinion, human nature in this view was subject to changes, since the traits associated with it changed with institutions and situations. The third meaning of the term implied "a social nature developed in man by simple forms of intimate association or primary groups. These worked upon the individual everywhere in somewhat the same way. This nature, Cooley continued, "consists chiefly of certain primary social sentiments and attitudes, such as consciousness of oneself in relation to others, love of approbation, resentment of censure, emulation and a sense of social right and wrong formed by the standards of the group." It meant, that is, "something much more definite than hereditary disposition . . . and yet something fundamental and widespread if not universal in the life of man found in ancient history, and in accounts of remote nations, as well as now and here." In this sense, which was that in which Cooley used the term, human nature changed, but only as the primary groups in which it took form changed.[101] Let us see how he developed this image of man.

The superiority of the human being to the rest of animal life consisted in the essential character of his mind. This was the process by which thought, ideas, and imagination were communicated through distinctively human symbols developed in the evolutionary process. Here Cooley spoke of an all-pervasive mind, the instrumentality in the social process which gave the individual's mind its human distinctiveness. The self developed through social or face-to-face communication in primary groups and provided the entire theater for every distinctively human action: hence the priority of mind in the whole organic process of which the individual and society were merely different aspects. Cooley illustrated his point—that persons and groups existed for each other only in their own and in the minds of others—in a striking example of child development. At first a child experienced a growing sense of self in

100. See the discussion in chap. 9, "Nature versus Nurture."
101. Cooley, *Human Nature and the Social Order*, pp. 31–32.

relation to primary groups. In play he became able to cast himself in the role of father, mother, policeman, Indian, or whatsoever. In games he became aware that interpersonal relationships were governed by rules. He then became able to imagine through gestures, especially through language, what went on in the minds of others and what they might be thinking of him. Thus, also, meaning was attached to the retroactive or retroflexive symbols *I, you, we, ours,* and *us*—the "looking-glass" or reflective self.[102] Personality was thus the subjective aspect of the social process. In the course of these interpersonal experiences, the reality was the image projected in the minds of the participants.

With a wealth of examples based on observations of his own children and drawn from literary sources, Cooley used reference groups and the interplay of imaginations to explain the appearance of such distinctively human traits or concepts as self, self-respect, pride, vanity, fame, and consequence. Thus society shaped human nature from the biological unit and in turn partook of the impact of every individual whose life process was another aspect of it. This let Cooley substitute for an atomistic non-person a human being endowed with a freedom to influence, more or less, social life in his own unique ways.

Though heredity might account for many differences in individuals and races, the particular form of social organization, simple or complex, existing in time and place, seemed the more important explanation. Commonly shared traits, emerging from the interactive process of interpersonal relations, made all individuals and peoples more alike than different.

Cooley's sociology suffered from its rudimentary conception of social structure and the problem of power. He did, though, note the curtailment of the universal need of self-expression, appreciation, and a reasonable security in the currently dominant American attitudes toward domestic servants, immigrants, and most of all, Negroes. An Emersonian idealist, he held that the democratic vision might yet be more fully realized with an imaginative approach toward effective interpersonal and intergroup understanding.

Crime, pauperism, idiocy, insanity, and drunkenness, Cooley thought, all reflected personal degeneracy. This could be laid at the doors of heredity and environment in unknown, if not unknowable, measures. Yet at bottom, personal degeneracy must be thought of as a social

102. Cooley noted that Dr. Oliver Wendell Holmes in *Autocrat of the Breakfast Table* had observed that in every conversation between John and Thomas six persons took part— what John thought of himself and of Thomas and what he imagined Thomas thought of him, and in turn, the same sequence in the case of Thomas. Cooley, *Life and the Student: Roadside Notes on Human Nature, Society, and Letters* (New York, 1931), p. 200.

matter, since it existed only in a certain relation between a person and the rest of the group.[103] He knew that social conflict was necessary both for the solution of such social problems and for the maintenance of the active soul. Having a personal distaste for conflict, he largely left to others whatever action might be necessary to change the character of human nature through the realization of a fuller measure of interpersonal and group understanding in the ongoing process of life.

George Herbert Mead,[104] a key figure in the University of Chicago's version of pragmatism, acknowledged his indebtedness to Cooley's conception of the uniquely social character of human development. He shared his Michigan colleague's conception of an emergent evolution, both individual and social. He agreed that this found expression in a distinctive capacity for interpersonal and intergroup communication and interaction in social organizations that led either to cooperative and friendly or to hostile and antagonistic attitude and behavior. Nevertheless, as a pragmatist and social behaviorist, Mead noted the limiting factors in Cooley's introspective method and approach. He also rejected the mentalistic concept of society which denied its objective reality by placing it altogether in the minds and imaginations of interacting individuals.[105] In refining and amplifying the social conception of human nature, Mead contributed a new depth of understanding and a subtlety of analysis.

Man, he observed in emphasizing the impact of the organism on its environment, shared with other animals an ability, on the lower levels of behavior, to manipulate the environment by trial and error. When confronted by ambiguities, obstacles, and problems, the human being, having a unique power to analyze the field of stimulation, was thus capable of dominating it in a way unknown to other higher primates. This ability involved the selection, holding, breaking down, and recombination of the components of stimuli. Thus the human being, as

103. Cooley, *Human Nature and the Social Order*, p. 406.

104. Mead's major writings appeared after his death in 1931: *The Philosophy of the Present*, the Paul Carus Lectures, 3d ser. (Chicago, 1932); *Mind, Self and Society*, ed. with an introduction by Charles W. Morris (Chicago, 1934); *Movements of Thought in the Nineteenth Century*, ed. with an introduction by Merritt H. Moore (Chicago, 1936); and *The Philosophy of the Act* (Chicago, 1938). For interpretive evaluations see Grace Chin Lee, *George Herbert Mead, Philosopher of the Social Individual* (New York, 1945); *The Social Psychology of George Herbert Mead*, ed. Anselm Strauss (Chicago, 1956); and Paul Pfuetze, *Self, Society, Existence, Human Nature in the Thought of George Herbert Mead and Martin Buber* (New York, 1961).

105. George Herbert Mead, "Cooley's Contribution to American Social Thought," *American Journal of Sociology* 35 (1929–30): 693–706.

actor, could mediate the environment in a purposeful way. A distinctive central nervous system, at once sensitive and discriminatory, enabled humans to give meaning to stimuli in terms of memory, present conflict, and a projected future (perception) and gave them a related ability to choose conditioning responses to stimuli. Such a conscious, problem-solving, and reflecting "act" was Mead's definition of intelligence. In this way mind was teleologically creative without having a metaphysical character. The whole mechanism, on becoming truly self-conscious, found expression in scientific method. Once understood it enabled man, if he chose, to control his social no less than his physical environment.

In contrast with most individualistic psychologists, Mead did not think that this capacity existed at birth. The organism that was to become human became so by virtue of a unique capacity to use the conversation of gestures with the group. It was true that other animals responded to each other's gesture-stimuli, as when dog meeting dog barked or bees performed patterned responses. But human "conversation in gestures" was far more complex, thanks to language and an ability to attach to these gestures commonly accepted meanings not present in the im-mediate environment.[106] That is, what were at first spontaneous gestures became, through group experience, "identical gestures" or "significant symbols" when they were internalized, and they affected ongoing wants of those in the group. Nor was "conversation in gestures" limited to communication in interpersonal experience. Such conversations also took place "within" a single person—that is, in reflective thought. In giving reality to such covert behavior, in regarding mental activity as necessarily within the orbit of the social act or unit of human existence, and in stressing the nonmechanistic character of "the act," Mead felt that his social behaviorism had the advantages of the generally objective behaviorism without its cramping limitations.[107]

Both self and personality, thus developed by significant symbols in group experience, became objective realities in a self-conscious sense when an individual, invoking a gift for histrionic behavior, learned in group experience to take the role of the other and to play the roles ex-pected of him in different group relationships. A crucial stage in this development was the experience of a child in games. This enabled him to assume many positions toward himself and the others and to organize and generalize the positions taken. Such an organization Mead called

106. Adam Smith, among others, called attention to the importance of language behavior as a possible matrix of all social behavior (C. E. Ayres, "Fifty Years' Development in Ideas of Human Nature and Motivation," *American Economic Review* 26, Supplement, March 1936).

107. See chap. 12.

"the generalized other"—society's representative, so to speak, in an individual. Though anticipated by Cooley, role-playing, as Mead developed it, explained how man as a gesture-maker and symbol-user could identify "outside himself." He could in this way realize his human potentialities, take part in interpersonal and group behavior and understanding, and, if he would, reconstruct in terms of both change and order the relations that made up the social environment.

Mead's contributions to the discussion of human nature have been widely recognized as original and enduring. In the words of Anselm Strauss, he challenged both mechanistic and mystical conceptions of human action by restating the problems of autonomy, freedom, and innovation in an evolutionary and functional matrix. In doing this he came to terms with some of the doubts about human capacity to effect social reconstruction.

Mead's critics have felt that he was overly optimistic, however, in stressing the cognitive at the expense of the emotive aspects of human impulses and behavior. Moreover, some have held that he never faced up to the limitations of his image of man. He seemed unaware of the fact that men and women could and did use their unique symbol-making capacity, formalized in the scientific method, for antisocial pursuits of power and profit. He seemed to forget people's use of distinctive human gifts for enhancing rather than controlling the capacity for antagonistic behavior. Still others claimed that, generally speaking, he did not state his ideas in testable ways.[108]

Whatever the validity of these criticisms, Mead offered a frame of reference that helped make possible the contributions of Harry Stack Sullivan and Kenneth Burke in the field of symbolic meaning, personality development, and social behavior. All in all, his contributions to a more precise, a fuller and deeper understanding of human nature entitled him to a major place in the history of its American exploration.

At the very time that a social interpretation of human nature took clearer shape in the work of its pioneers, a more sharply focused and even more far-reaching view was well underway.

108. *Social Psychology of George Herbert Mead*, ed. Strauss, p. vii; Pfuetze, *Self, Society, Existence*, pp. 267–71.

8

A Cultural View
Takes Shape

Not only have the habits of men changed with the changing exigencies of the situation, but these changing exigencies have also brought about a correlative change in human nature. The human material of society itself varies with the changing conditions of life. This variation in human nature is held by the later ethnologists to be a process of selection between relatively stable and persistent ethnic types or elements.

THORSTEIN VEBLEN, 1899

The early evolutionistic anthropologists failed because they possessed no analyzed and classical corpus of comparative knowledge of culture similar to that which biology had accumulated ready for reinterpretation by 1859.

A. L. KROEBER, 1955

. . . a culture that hampers realization of certain of the psychic and social needs of all human beings will have difficulty in surviving when faced by competition of cultures better adapted to human nature.

QUINCY WRIGHT, 1955

As cultures evolved, men were tailored by natural selection to fit them, and as men evolved, they were altering cultures to fit themselves.

GERALD E. McCLEARN, 1968

THE IMAGES of man that owed so much to the evolutionary impact on the New Psychology and on the emerging social view of human nature were supplemented by a cultural explanation of man's constitution and conduct. Generally, though not always, the cultural concept was viewed in evolutionary terms. Thus all in all the influence of evolutionary theory on ideas about man constituted the great achievement of the nineteenth century in explanations of human nature.

Among the leaders who used evolution to explain the interaction of man's original endowment with the various stages of cultural development, Lester Frank Ward merits a special place. A largely self-trained government geologist and paleobotanist, a social philosopher, and in some eyes the American "father" of the emerging sociology, he was a transitional figure in the interpretation of human nature from the standpoint of cultural evolution.

Like Spencer and Comte, Ward was a law-seeking and law-proclaiming system builder, who took little interest in the new rigid methodology of field studies, quantification, and the controlled investigation of social behavior in specific situations. Like most members of the American Social Science Association, he believed that meliorism was the great justification of social inquiry. On the other hand, in emphasizing the overarching importance of an evolutionary social experience in forming human nature, he belonged with an upcoming group of social scientists. His influence on this group has been debated. It

248

was in any case limited both by reason of his isolation from academic circles, at least until late in life, and because of his essentially philosophical outlook.[1] At the same time, his stress on social meliorism was not alien to all of the younger social scientists. His theories in the end were to be partly justified by the mounting attack on laissez faire and Social Darwinism, by the growing prestige of science in American education and the gradual growth of a social conscience on the part of some scientists, and in the claims of a growing number of women for equality of opportunity in every sphere of life.

The idea of human nature held a large place in Ward's evolutionary "cosmic monism," a theory which owed a good deal to Lamarckianism. In Ward's view the transmission of acquired characteristics included social ethics. The related theory of synergy held that throughout the whole universe antithetical conflict and cooperation of units of energy interacted with a continuously creative thrust to form physical, social, and psychological phenomena. Ward thought that the same laws governed the makeup and functioning of the human mind.

Ward defined man as an animal that had come to have unique qualities but that nevertheless was still very much an animal, in the sense that emotions constituted the dynamic agent that guided him to action. He identified emotions as wants, desires, anger, hate, jealousy, love, and somewhat inconsistently, lofty and refined sentiments. Yet unlike other animals, man had acquired intelligence, or the power of judgment and reason. Similar in some ways to animal sagacity, these nevertheless differed both quantitatively and qualitatively in their more complex character. Ward denied a dichotomy between mind and matter. Somewhat like the functional psychologists, he viewed man's character and conduct as the outcome of the adaptive function of that part of the nervous system called the brain.[2] He also viewed adaptation as an inventive function. It enabled the human organism to free itself from

1. This view has been ably advanced by John C. Burnham in his essay "Lester Frank Ward in American Thought," *Annals of American Sociology* (Washington, D.C., 1956). For the defense of Ward's importance in American social science see Samuel Chugerman, *Lester Frank Ward: The American Aristotle* (New York, 1939; rpt. ed., 1965); James Q. Dealey, "Lester Frank Ward," in Howard W. Odum, ed., *American Masters of Social Science* (New York, 1927), pp. 79–88; Charles A. Beard and Mary R. Beard, *The American Spirit* (New York, 1942), pp. 405 ff.; Ralph Gabriel, *The Course of American Democratic Thought* (New York, 1940; 2d ed., 1956), pp. 207–9; and Henry S. Commager, *The American Mind* (New Haven, 1950), chap. 10. Clifford H. Scott's *Lester Frank Ward* (Boston, 1976) is a judicious evaluation.

2. John Dewey nevertheless thought that Ward accepted uncritically the pain-pleasure pre-Darwinian psychology: John Dewey, "Social Psychology," *Psychological Review* 1 (1894): 400–411. See also Herbert W. Schneider, *A History of American Philosophy* (New York, 1944), p. 389.

helpless domination by the physical environment and to substitute conscious (telic) action for that of the blind forces of trial and error in the evolutionary process. In any case, a gradually growing intelligence, itself the result of social experience, had channeled much but by no means all of these catabolic tendencies into cooperative and creative achievements. Besides language, he included institutions such as marriage, law, the state and ethical codes, all of which curbed the selfish egoism of tooth-and-claw struggle that had once exclusively governed behavior in the fight for survival.

Thus civilization, a human achievement, resulted from an accumulation of psychologically initiated creative and artificial checks on the self-centered impulses that all men and women shared with the whole animal kingdom. In the making of civilization, the needs and desires of the group in its struggle for survival and development comprised dynamic social forces. The civilization that distinguished the human condition was, therefore, a psychic rather than a purely biological phenomenon. Economic development, an important part of civilization, was, for example, far from being a blind response to instinct. It resulted rather from creative psychic forces that included "saving" with an eye to the future, calculating probable effects of one course of action against another, and inventing and using material products.

What was to be thought of as human nature, though based upon biological, indeed cosmic, evolution, was thus itself a psychological development of interpersonal, social experiences marked by a growing mutuality and cooperation.[3] On the negative side, it was not an independent attribute or entity, nor a faculty, nor a mere biological heritage.[4] To be sure, at one point Ward did with some inconsistency speak of human nature as man's "natural animal constitution."[5] From the positive standpoint, human nature, in the commonly understood sense of the term, comprised the motives that explained behavior as these had come to be classified in folk wisdom, and gradually and as yet incompletely, in scientific terms. Being the product of ongoing human contacts and experiences, the motives making up human nature were neither a "given" nor an "end" product. Human nature was rather a function of ever-changing social conditions and needs, an interaction of intellect with desire, or what Schopenhauer, to whom Ward was in-

3. Lester Frank Ward, *Dynamic Sociology*, 2 vols. (New York, 1883; rept. ed., 1968), 2:332–36; "Ethical Aspects of Social Science," *International Journal of Ethics* (1896), included in *Glimpses of the Cosmos*, 6 vols. (New York, 1913–16), 5:275–81.

4. Ward, *Dynamic Sociology*, 2:335.

5. Lester Frank Ward, *Pure Sociology* (New York, 1903), p. 276.

debted for this point, thought of as social will. Thus human nature had long been developing as a result of the changing social environments in their creative and dynamic role. "The group habits and social attitudes of human beings," Ward held, "are no more external nor unchanging than are animals or plants."[6] Such a position left no valid place for the use of "human nature" as a convenient escape for hiding errors and prejudices—a use familiar in the justification of slavery, the exploitation of the producing classes, and the subordination of women.[7]

One of the principal branches of sociology, Ward thought, was to be the science of human nature. This might be thought of as the logical and scientific classification of the laws of human action with a view to referring all the most prominent actions which man performed to their appropriate categories. The science of human nature, he went on, was already in its empirical stage; considerable accuracy in its application had been achieved. "All the dealings of man with man are based on certain intuitive predictions of how men will act under certain circumstances."[8] As yet, to be sure, this was the case only with the more simple and superficial human motives. About the deeper and more involved ones much was yet to be learned. Ignorance of these laws might justifiably be regarded as the main cause of human failures. If most human failures resulted from such lack of knowledge, it might nevertheless be assumed that an acceleration of social progress would follow the reduction of the laws to a tangible science similar to the reduction of physical phenomena to laws and scientific principles. As an example of the sort of knowledge to be authenticated, Ward cited the possibly unfortunate effects over a long period of time of the suppression of the strong natural appetite imposed by the celibacy of the clergy. Sex and other appetites—fear, hatred, jealousy, and the like—could and should be channeled into constructive social achievement.[9]

Ward's rejection of Spencerian determinism and his commitment to a democratic, nonpaternalistic version of Comtean positivism cleared the path. He held that thanks to the telic power of ideas, values, and in-

6. Chugerman, *Lester Frank Ward*, p. 228.

7. Ward, *Dynamic Sociology*, 2:335. The identification of economic distress with worthlessness, resulting in the detestable human trait of refusing to give to those who let it be known that they were in deep need, stood in contrast with the tendency to give to those who made it appear that they had no need. Ward, *Pure Sociology*, p. 257.

8. Ward, *Dynamic Sociology*, 2:335.

9. *Dynamic Sociology*, 2:336. *Young Ward's Diary*, ed. Bernhard J. Stern (New York, 1935), makes it clear that Ward and his wife, in regarding sexual expression as not only natural but pleasurable, did not share the widespread opposition of many contemporary authorities in the 1860s to the use of various methods of birth control.

telligence, man could consciously modify the evolutionary process. He could do this to effect a more rapid and a greater measure of cooperation to satisfy expanding wants, above all the basic human desire for happiness. With the conscious use of the telic principle, man could end the unnecessary burdens of poverty, mass ignorance, and injustice toward women and disadvantaged classes and races. He could even end war, an institution that had once served a useful purpose in welding together races and nations.[10] All this was to be done by equalizing opportunities for acquiring knowledge and then putting that knowledge to work in the interest of equality, security, justice, and an enhanced life of the mind for everyone. In such social engineering government was to play the major role, using its power purposely to curtail inequality of opportunity, to advance cooperation, and to make and execute social plans in the general interest. Sociocracy, as Ward cumbersomely called his version of meliorism, was in his view superior to socialism. Socialism, he felt, glorified the idea of conflict between the classes. Its paternalistic authority, by attempting to prevent the exploitation of the producing classes, for whom he had deep concern and sympathy, hampered individual fulfillment.

Admitting individual differences, Ward insisted that these were far less telling than human similarities. Moreover, no matter how gifted an individual in any stage of evolutionary development might be, he could use his superior gifts only through such social creations as language, material goods, institutions, and values. No ground was left for the assumptions about the "self-made man" so widely cherished in the Gilded Age.

On race and sex differences Ward took no less firm a stand. To be sure, no reliable scientific evidence existed to prove the equality of races in intellectual endowment. Such a hypothesis, however, was reasonable, and future investigation, anthropological and psychological, might very well demonstrate it. He also projected the priority and superiority of the female throughout nature, and the central role of women in the development of civilization. This was evident, he thought, in their gifts of insight and intuition. Flatly repudiating a widely held belief about women's inherent intellectual inferiority,[11] he urged the equalization of opportunities in every sphere, not only to promote the happiness of women as individuals, but also as a means of advancing and accelerating social progress. Charlotte Perkins Gilman, a leading feminist,

10. Bernhard J. Stern, ed., *The Letters of Ludwig Gumplowicz to Lester Frank Ward* (Leipzig, 1933).

11. Ward, *Pure Sociology*, chap. 14.

publicized these ideas in *Women and Economics* (1898) and in her hard-hitting and readable *The Man-Made World* (1911), which she appropriately dedicated to Ward.

Thorstein Veblen, one of the twentieth century's most original economists and a disturbing social critic, also acknowledged his debt to Ward, whom he excelled in sophistication and influence as a major exponent of the cultural-evolutionary view of human nature.[12]

Personal background and experience helped shape Veblen's ideas. A satirical and ironical rhetoric that expressed his often mystifying and alluring thought reflected the alienation of a second-generation immigrant who felt uncomfortable in the "Yankee"-dominated environments of his boyhood and of the college and universities in which he studied and taught.

His reading also counted. Ward and the German institutional economists appealed to him. He owed a good deal to the early ethnologists, especially John Ferguson McLennan, a Scot who wrote on primitive marriage, and above all Lewis Henry Morgan, an exponent of the cultural-epoch theory of evolution. Veblen's somewhat fanciful, Rousseauistic idealization of the savage stage in man's development explained his leaning toward an anti-institutional utopian anarchism. Marxism, which he criticized for its Benthamite calculus and overrationalism, as well as for its downgrading of gradual cumulative changes, nevertheless also contributed to his conviction that in every cultural stage technology largely shaped institutions, values, and ideas.[13] Above all, Darwinism, especially its concept of natural selection, was basic in Veblen's evolutionary thought. Related to this was the appeal of

12. The Veblen scholarship is far-ranging. Joseph Dorfman's *Thorstein Veblen and His America* (New York, 1934) is still the standard biography. Special note should be taken of David Riesman, *Thorstein Veblen* (New York, 1953); Douglas F. Dowd, ed., *Thorstein Veblen: A Critical Reappraisal* (Ithaca, 1958); David Seckler, *Thorstein Veblen and the Institutionalists: A Study in the Social Philosophy of Economics* (London, 1975); Leonard A. Dental, *Veblen's Theory of Social Change* (New York, 1977); and three easily overlooked essays: Daniel Aaron, *Men of Good Hope* (New York, 1951; rept. ed., 1961), pp. 208–43; Arthur K. Davis, "Thorstein Veblen Reconsidered," *Science and Society* 21 (1957): 52–85; and Thomas C. Mayberry, "Thorstein Veblen on Human Nature," *American Journal of Economics and Sociology* 28 (1969): 315–23. While working on Veblen I did not have access to the excellent account of his ideas about human nature in John P. Diggins's *The Bard of Savagery: Thorstein Veblen and Modern Social Theory* (New York, 1978), pp. 69–77, 81–84.

13. Thorstein Veblen, "The Socialist Economics of Karl Marx and His Followers," *Quarterly Journal of Economics* 20 (1907): 575–95, reprinted in *The Place of Science in Modern Civilization and Other Essays* (New York, 1919), pp. 409–56.

William James's functional psychology. (Wesley C. Mitchell has emphasized the importance of this for Veblen's theory of human nature.)[14]

In Veblen's writing the term *human nature* occurred again and again but never with definition.[15] His criticisms of classical economics, to be sure, clearly showed that he rejected its assumptions of a human nature that was passive, inert, and responsive only to a hedonistic calculation of pleasure and pain in terms of pecuniary stimuli in the market place.[16] In other contexts, the term was used in several sometimes contradictory senses. On occasion Veblen seemed to have meant the enduring and distinctive propensities and the "tropismatic" aptitudes with which the species was endowed and that determined the routine and details of life in every cultural stage. These innate and persistent propensities, as they functioned in the give and take of adjustment to cultural change, Veblen called instincts.[17] Thus he wrote that human nature was "substantially uniform, passive and unalterable in respect to man's capacity for sensuous affection."[18] Again, he referred to emulation as a propensity of "ancient growth" and as "a pervading trait of human nature."[19]

But Veblen also spoke of "the barbarian type of human nature," of "archaic, predatory human nature," and of "the human nature of the hereditary present."[20] The traits that differentiated man from the rest of the animal world took shape very early in the evolutionary process. They were developed by natural selection, as were the traits in those stages to which the preceding ones were transmitted. Of the several phases of human culture, savagery exercised the most influence in shaping man's abiding traits. On the other hand, "for the greater part of the race, at least for the greater part of civilized mankind, the regime of the mature barbarian culture has been of relatively short duration, and has had a correspondingly superficial and transient selective effect. It has not had

14. Wesley C. Mitchell, *Lecture Notes on Types of Economic Theory*, ed. August Kelley, 2 vols. (New York, 1949; rept. ed., 1969), 2:254 ff., 599 ff.

15. A possible exception is a remark in "The Limitations of Marginal Utility," *Journal of Political Economy* 17 (1909): 620–36, reprinted in *The Place of Science in Modern Civilization*, p. 242. Referring to "the underlying traits of human nature," Veblen added, in parentheses, "Propensities, aptitudes, and whatnot."

16. Thorstein Veblen, "Why Is Economics Not an Evolutionary Science?" *Quarterly Journal of Economics* 12 (1898): 373–97; and "The Preconceptions of Economic Science," *Quarterly Journal of Economics* 13 (1899): 121–50, 396–426. Both articles reprinted in *The Place of Science in Modern Civilization*, pp. 56–81, 82–179.

17. Thorstein Veblen, *The Instinct of Workmanship and the State of the Industrial Arts* (New York, 1914), pp. 1–3.

18. Veblen, *The Place of Science in Modern Civilization*, p. 134.

19. Thorstein Veblen, *The Theory of the Leisure Class* (New York, 1899; New American Library ed., 1959), p. 109.

20. Veblen, *Theory of the Leisure Class*, pp. 219, 246–47, 262; *The Place of Science in Modern Civilization*, p. 23.

the force and time to eliminate certain elements of human nature handed down from an earlier phase of life, which are not in full consonance with the barbarian animus or with the demands of the pragmatic scheme of thought."[21]

Elsewhere Veblen indicated that he thought of human nature in a relative, changing sense, as might be expected from the evolutionary concept that framed his thinking. In speaking of the "conservation of archaic traits" he wrote that changing exigencies of the situation effected changes in habit and a correlative change in human nature. Continuing, he introduced the idea of ethnic types or elements. "The human material of society itself varies with the changing conditions of life. This variation of human nature is held by the later ethnologists to be a process of selection between several relatively stable and persistent ethnic types or ethnic elements. Men tend to revert or to breed true, more or less closely, to one or another of certain types of human nature that have in their main features been fixed in approximate conformity to a situation in the past which differed from the situation of today."[22] Still another use of the term further clarified Veblen's attitude toward the problem of a static or a changing human nature. "Departures from the human nature of the hereditary present are most frequently of the nature of reversions to an earlier variant of the type. This earlier variant is represented by the temperament which characterizes the primitive stage of peaceable savagery. . . . And it is to these ancient, generic features that modern men are prone to take back in case of variation from the human nature of the hereditary present."[23]

What Veblen had in mind in using the term *human nature* with various connotative adjectives remained somewhat ambiguous. He certainly believed that over a long evolutionary development men had acquired an unrelenting drive toward a less immediately "personal" character. In other words, the nature of man was more objective than that of other animals. These activities, with the capacity for sensual affection, served as instruments or behavior patterns functional to the urge for survival and perpetuation. In other words, each cultural stage in man's evolutionary career had developed special traits functional to the maintenance of life, some of which were transmitted to succeeding cultural ages.

Thus with the prehistorical epoch which Veblen thought of as savagery, man had acquired, among other traits, three basic, tenacious,

21. Thorstein Veblen, "The Place of Science in Modern Civilization," *American Journal of Sociology* 15 (1906), reprinted in *The Place of Science in Modern Civilization*, pp. 23–24.

22. Veblen, *Theory of the Leisure Class*, pp. 213–14.

23. *Theory of the Leisure Class*, pp. 218–19.

teleological instincts, regulatory rather than substantive, and conceivably made up of even more elemental constituents. These were the parental instinct, the instinct of workmanship, and the instinct of idle curiosity. It was these closely intertwined instincts that helped explain man's capacity for more-or-less-objective activity, that constituted, together with the sex drive, a generic human nature. The paternal instinct, which Veblen differentiated from procreation, expressed itself in the sense of conserving resources for future use, in improving the conditions of life for offspring, and in a benevolent feeling toward kin and fellow men. The instinct of curiosity contributed substantially to the development of technologies in each cultural stage, including, relatively late, the discovery of scientific ways of controlling the environment. Closely connected with this was the instinct of workmanship—the desire to produce as much as possible in the approved manner and with an esthetic sense of the importance of the job for its own sake. In addition to these instincts, Veblen sometimes spoke of emulation or the desire to excel. Emulation, to which, it will be recalled, eighteenth-century thinkers attached great weight, has come to be thought of by most contemporary psychologists as a cultural norm.[24]

Though taking account of the rising criticisms of the instinct theory, including the implications of Mendelian genetics, Veblen concluded that the term was valid and useful in the limited sense in which he used it. Despite such qualifications, his essentially reductionist view did not meet the objections to the instinct theory that some psychologists had begun to advance and that were later developed more fully.

Veblen held, with James, that habituation could modify instincts. This was particularly true of the accumulated social instincts or institutions. As men's way of life changed, so their thinking and manner of using resources to make a living changed. Changing institutions and manners of thinking in turn altered the role and operation of the basic instincts— but not always in functionally desirable ways. Thus modern pecuniary or business institutions, in separating industrial production (workers and engineers) from profit-motivated management (businessmen), contaminated the instinct of workmanship by subordinating it to the profit motive. Moreover, competition or emulation in matters of status was exemplified in modern industrial civilization by conspicuous waste and consumption, and by making upper-class women its idle votaries. This thwarted the parental or conserving instinct, as well as that of workmanship. Or again, the innate distaste for futility, related both to the

24. These ideas were developed in *The Theory of the Leisure Class* (1899), *The Theory of the Business Enterprise* (1904), *The Higher Learning in America* (1918), and the first essay in *The Place of Science in Modern Civilization and Other Essays* (1919), pp. 1–31.

parental and workmanship instincts, led men of wealth to find activities they could regard as serviceable and purposive, such as philanthropy. The subordination of so much of life to business values also contaminated the instinct of idle curiosity. "The higher learning" had come to be infused with the assumptions, discipline, and technology of the business culture. In brief, the dominant image of man, with the behavior it sanctioned, was obsolete in the contemporary business culture. It conflicted with basic urges and needs and with the demands of a machine economy which only engineers could manage in the social interest.[25]

Given the character of culture, it might be expected that an existing culture which thwarted the fundamental instincts would change. Science and its application in technology offered the best chance for modern men to shake off the dominating influence of business institutions that had so thoroughly thwarted and contaminated the fundamental instincts.[26] In the long run, social institutions must, in view of the principle of natural selection, serve the purposes of life. Yet when Veblen pondered the powerful influence of cultural lag, he was not sure that the modern age could or would revamp its institutions in the interest of better serving the basic instincts and of providing a new situation for further human development in a noncompetitive, constructive, and peaceful life.[27]

Veblen's ambivalence about the likelihood of cultural and institutional change in the direction of freeing machine production and its workers from the dominance of predatory business was illustrated in his discussion of war and peace. Man's propensity for fighting, closely related in the nontoiling class to the sporting instinct, had dominated the predatory barbarian culture. In modern times war was closely related to patriotism, defined as "a sense of partisan solidarity in respect to prestige." Patriotism appeared to be "an enduring trait of human nature, an ancient heritage that has stood ever unshorn from time immemorial, under the Mendelian rule of the stability of racial types. . . ."[28] Presumably patriotism in its earlier stages of evolution had served community purposes. It might still provide psychological and

25. Veblen, *The Instinct of Workmanship*, pp. 1–3.

26. Veblen, *The Place of Science in Modern Civilization*, p. 30.

27. Arthur K. Davis, in his essay in the *International Encyclopedia of the Social Sciences*, holds that Veblen did not recognize that "the concept of cultural lag may give undue weight to factors of ignorance and drift, at the expense of vested-interest rationality," or that technology may not always change in advance of established institutions.

28. Thorstein Veblen, *An Inquiry into the Nature of Peace and the Terms of Its Perpetuation* (New York, 1919), pp. 31, 41. See also pp. 42, 45–47, and 73–88.

esthetic satisfactions and on occasion serve materially the predatory interests of the business civilization. If in Western civilization patriotism was a necessary concomitant of war, it had not always and everywhere so expressed itself, as the record of ancient Iceland and traditional China proved. The peaceableness of these peoples was to be explained, presumably, by historical circumstances, including isolation, and by nonplundering institutional arrangements.

If modern war was an expression of patriotism and of the presumed interest of competing businessmen, it was far too wasteful of human and material resources to serve the parental instinct and the instinct of workmanship. It was also antithetical to the full realization of the potentialities of machine production for individual and social well-being. Veblen concluded that a league of nations which repudiated the outworn concept of national sovereignty might be a useful means of limiting war. Still, man's original peaceableness could not be fully recaptured or institutionalized as long as modern business dominated culture. It might be that the impact of transnational machine culture was eroding national sovereignty and directing an innate and enduring patriotism into expressions less disserviceable to public interest than in its tieup with war. The interplay between cultural lag and selective adaptation for survival concealed the answer to the question, at least in the foreseeable future.

It would, of course, be too much to claim that Veblen alone was responsible for the growing concern of economists with a corrective psychology of the productive and distributive processes in the industrial order. Simon N. Patten, John R. Commons, and Wesley C. Mitchell were also awake to pragmatism and the new psychology. Patten's *The Theory of Prosperity* reflected his interest in the psychology of James and Baldwin. He gropingly sought for the causes of poverty in an emerging economy of abundance. Rejecting the traditional idea that poverty was rooted in the inevitable laws of economics and human nature, Patten ascribed it in large part to excessive competition and inadequate cooperation. It could, he felt, be largely eliminated by an improvement in the techniques of production and by a redistribution of income— necessary adjustments to man's altered condition.[29] John R. Commons was also broadening the scope of economics by including the study of the behavior of such institutions as trade unions, consumers' organizations,

29. Simon N. Patten, *Theory of Prosperity* (New York, 1902). See also his *The New Basis of Civilization* (New York, 1907) and *The Social Basis of Religion* (New York, 1910). For assessments of Patten consult Daniel M. Fox, *The Discovery of Abundance: Simon N. Patten and the Transformation of Social Theory* (Ithaca, 1967), and David W. Noble, *The Paradox of Progressive Thought* (Minneapolis, 1958), chap. 8.

and courts of law.[30] As early as 1903 Wesley C. Mitchell had concluded that social reorganization must be based on the knowledge of how humans behaved. This could be accomplished by collecting a large body of scientific data on economic behavior and analyzing the relationship of the data by statistical methods.[31]

By the time of the First World War and the early 1920s, a whole spate of articles by economists emphasized the importance of current psychological findings, whether functional, behaviorist, or Freudian,[32] a vogue that remained as the years went by.[33]

Two disciples of Veblen oriented economics toward the newer psychology. Carlton Parker argued that in stifling basic impulses, the prevailing economic order provoked violent revolt on the part of such rootless wanderers as the "wobblies." Robert Frank Hoxie also found Veblen's ideas useful in explaining the psychology of trade unionists. When these economists read the new Freudian literature they found Veblen's theories less attractive, particularly the emphasis on unending social conflict between human nature and capitalism.[34]

Algie M. Simons, a leading Socialist, tried to acclimatize Marxism to the American scene by developing a broader and at the same time more explicit psychology. Marx and Engels had projected a somewhat ambivalent image of man. At times this emphasized the inherited inner

30. John R. Commons, *Legal Foundations of Capitalism* (New York, 1939), and *The Economics of Collective Action* (New York, 1950). See also Wesley C. Mitchell's comments on Commons in *The Backward Art of Spending Money and Other Essays* (New York, 1937), pp. 115–16; and Joseph Dorfman, *The Economic Mind in American Civilization*, 6 vols. (New York, 1946–59), 3:277–94; 4:377–95.

31. Lucy Sprague Mitchell, *Two Lives: The Story of Wesley Clair Mitchell and Myself* (New York, 1953), p. 93.

32. Examples are Wesley C. Mitchell, "The Rationality of Economic Activity," *Journal of Political Economy* 18 (1910): 97–113; and "Human Behavior and Economics," *Quarterly Journal of Economics* 29 (1914): 1–41; John M. Clark, "Economics and Modern Psychology," *Journal of Political Economy* 26 (1918): 1–31; Rexford Guy Tugwell, "Human Nature in Economic Theory," *Journal of Political Economy* 30 (1922): 316–45; C. E. Ayres, "Fifty Years' Developments in Ideas of Human Nature and Motivation," *American Economic Review* 26, Supplement (1936): 224–36, 250–54; Logan McPherson, *Human Effort and Human Wants* (New York, 1923); and Zenas Clark Dickinson, *Economic Motives* (Cambridge, Mass., 1922).

33. From many examples: George Katona, *Psychological Analysis of Economic Behavior* (New York, 1951), Harry K. Girvetz, *From Wealth to Welfare: The Evolution of Liberalism* (Stanford, 1950), and Albert Lauterbach, *Man, Motives and Money* (Ithaca, 1954).

34. Carlton Parker, *The Casual Laborer and Other Essays* (New York, 1920); Mark Perlman, *Labor Union Theories in America* (Evanston, Ill., 1958), pp. 37–39, 123–38; and Louis Schneider, *The Freudian Psychology and Veblen's Social Theory* (New York, 1948). See also Robert Frank Hoxie's piece on the psychology of socialism in the *Journal of Political Economy* 24 (1916): 394 ff.

psychic springs of individual action, but more often, the individual's class relations and role expectations.[35] Simons's revision of Marxism borrowed from Veblen the emphasis on the instinct of workmanship, in an effort to inject a humanistic and esthetic motive in man's economic behavior. He specifically pointed up, as Tocqueville had done almost a century earlier,[36] the deadening machine process under capitalism and the need of providing psychological satisfaction for the instinct of workmanship.[37] If Simons's effort failed, in time other Marxists, discovering the early humanistic writings of the founder, followed the path to which Simons pointed.[38] Such efforts met with the argument that whatever validity there might be in its humanistic aspects, Marxism ran counter to basic American psychological values.[39]

Even with allowances for his shortcomings, Veblen's contributions and influence have been telling. His criticism of psychological egotism and the hedonistic rationalizing aspects of traditional economics was a significant factor in the growing tendency to include contemporary psychology in economic discussion. No one was quite able to discount the conflict he pointed to between man's basic drives and needs and the prevailing economic institutions and operations. Nor could the effects of business processes on society, which he laid bare with irony and

35. M. M. Bober, *Karl Marx's Interpretation of History*, 2d ed. (Cambridge, Mass., 1962), chap. 4; Vernon Venable, *Human Nature, the Marxian View* (New York, 1945); Gary L. Chamberlain, "The Man Marx Made," *Science and Society* 27 (1963): 302–30. S. Cohen, R. Johnson, and R. West, in "Marxist Psychology in America: A Critique" (*Science and Society* 21 [1957]: 120–21), argued that in America "Marxists writing in the field of psychology have, we feel, overemphasized psychiatric, philosophic, and social approaches in psychology, to the exclusion of almost all other areas."

36. Tocqueville, as he surveyed the whole industrial process of America in the early 1830s, noted the increasing division of labor and contrasted the narrowing effect of machine routine on the worker, with the enlargement of the role of master-manager. "This man resembles more and more the administrator of a vast empire; that man, a brute. The master and the workman have then here no similarity, and their differences increase every day. They are connected only like the two rings at the extremities of a long chain." Alexis de Tocqueville, *Democracy in America*, ed. Phillips Bradley, 2 vols. (New York, 1945), 2:159.

37. Willam A. Glasser, "Algie M. Simons and Marxism in America," *Mississippi Valley Historical Review* 41 (1954): 426–28; and Kent Kreuter and Gretchen Kreuter, *The Life of Algie Martin Simons 1870–1950* (Lexington, Ky., 1969), p. 105.

38. Erich Fromm, *Marx's Concept of Man* (New York, 1961). Cf. J. F. Brown, *Psychology and the Social Order* (New York, 1936).

39. Clinton Rossiter, *Marxism: The View from America* (New York, 1960), pp. 77 ff., held that Marxism was antithetical psychologically to "the American tradition" in failing to recognize that there can be such a thing as "a good man" rather than simply a "good member of a social class," and further, in overemphasizing the plasticity of human nature, particularly because such an overemphasis implied a manipulability that could issue in dictatorship.

exaggeration, fail to invite continuing attention. His idea of the incompatibility of human nature with current institutional arrangements was not, of course, the first statement of the kind. Veblen, however, developed and ponderously argued the contention. Above all, his insistence that institutions must be judged in relation to a realistic image of man focused attention sharply on the consequences of such incongruities in human affairs.[40]

Veblen's use of the idea of cultural evolution should be considered in relation to the whole of developmental theory in its biological and biophilosophical frame. As embraced by ethnology and related disciplines in the mid-to-late decades of the century in England and America, cultural evolution bore directly on the discussion of man's nature. The new vistas thus opened included a fresh approach to the origin of races, the development over time of similarities and differences between them, and the role of heredity and environment in explaining them.

The concept of cultural evolution stemmed in good part from the new biology and its philosophical applications. Several other influences, however, contributed to its development. The humanistic idea of an evolving culture as a self-conscious, purposeful, perfectionist goal in a hierarchy of values played a part. So did the distinction Matthew Arnold made in the 1860s between culture in a normative, spiritual sense and civilization in its materialist manifestations. The idea of cultural evolution also owed something to newly discovered archaeological remains and to the Victorian doctrine of progress exemplified in industrial achievements and expansion overseas.

The early development of ethnology in Germany, which greatly influenced the American discussion, drew on eighteenth-century humanistic thinkers, on Comte's emphasis on the primacy of cultural phenomena, and on reports of primitive peoples that pioneer geographers and ethnologists had seen or read about. Franz Theodore Waitz (1813–86), an ethnologist and psychologist, brought out the first volume of his *Anthropologie der Naturvölker* in the year that Darwin's *Origin of Species* was published and shortly before Spencer's *First Principles* appeared. He postulated the unity of mankind and the development of racial differences through cultural evolution. According to Waitz, all human groups possessed a fundamental psychic unity, an idea anticipated by Plato, Descartes, Spinoza, Leibniz, and certain

40. Daniel Aaron's *Men of Good Hope*, pp. 211–13, gives an informed discussion of Veblen's later reputation.

eighteenth-century philosophers. Given psychic unity, races traveled the same course of cultural development though at different rates. Environment and history determined when a particular stage was reached by any given group.[41] A similar view developed independently by Adolph Bastian (1826–1904) also contributed to the incipient theory of cultural evolution.[42]

The assumption of the psychic unity of mankind met with early attack by such mid-nineteenth-century Americans as George R. Gliddon and Josiah C. Nott and by the French diplomat Count Joseph Arthur de Gobineau (1816–82). They denounced it in justifying slavery, the commercial and territorial expansion of Europe, and the concept of degeneracy.

Brushing such attacks aside, exponents of cultural evolution explained the similarities observed between all peoples as the result of the uniform operation of the human mind under similar circumstances. Psychic unity seemed to be confirmed by an inherent, universal capacity to develop languages, techniques, social institutions, and customs. Never very clearly defined, psychic unity was conceived in terms of a cluster of nonexperiential "elementary ideas" or the "principle of intelligence," or, in modern idiom, innate cultural patterns.[43] As a result of man's psychic unity, peoples over the world developed successive normative stages of culture in a universal or orthogenetic manner—broadly speaking, from the simple to the complex, from slavery to barbarism, from barbarism to civilization. Thus cultural evolution struck a blow both at the idea of separate origins of innately different peoples and at the gloomy theological notion of degeneration of primitive tribes from an assumed earlier apex.

41. Waitz accepted the hereditary differences between individuals and admitted that there is an anatomical gap between Caucasians and Negroes but held, to quote Robert Lowie, that in view of "the interracial variability no significant psychological differences existed." He also regarded the idea that there is some simple connection between native racial capacity and cultural achievement as an unsound abstraction. See the discussion in Robert H. Lowie, *The History of Ethnological Theory* (New York, 1937), pp. 16–18, 121, 137, 189; and Theodore Waitz, *Introduction to Anthropology*, ed. J. Frederick Collingwood (London, 1863), pp. 10–14, 67–80, 269 ff.; and *Die Indianer Nordamerica's: Eine Studie* (Leipzig, 1865; rpt. ed., 1974), pp. 83 ff.

42. Bastian believed that certain elemental ideas in the human species expressed themselves in folk ideas. These were tied to geographical provinces. Thus Bastian in a sense anticipated the idea of "the cultural area." T. K. Penniman, *A Hundred Years of Anthropology*, 3d ed. (London, 1965), pp. 111–15. For Bastian's emphasis on a geographical historical perspective and anticipation of Boas's culture-area position see Annemarie Fiedermutz-Laun, *Der Kulturhistorische Gedanke Bei Adolf Bastian* (Wiesbaden, 1970), pp. 272–73.

43. In some respects "elementary ideas" were roughly similar to the inborn instincts of William James, William McDougall, and Sigmund Freud.

Whatever the influence of the German pioneers on Edward Tylor, an English Quaker often called "the father of modern anthropology," he developed his own cautious but original exploration of the totality of man's history and experience. Tylor was by no means a doctrinaire exponent of the idea of unilateral or unilinear cultural evolution. He did, however, unite the humanistic idea of culture with progressive evolutionism. Moreover, he provided impressive support for the theory by his telling insights as well as his use of new methods of investigation. These included the statistical analysis of comparative ethnological data. Thoroughly committed to the doctrine of the psychic unity of mankind, he early attacked the theological dogma of degeneration of primitive peoples. In trying to explain universal human experiences in given environments, he found in the neglected area of body gestures, picture-writing, legends, and myths, as these survived in modern primitive cultures, evidence for the unity of mental processes. To his theory of "survivals" and his sense of cultural relativism, which was unusual for the time, Tylor added the concept of animism. This was the belief in spirits or ghosts, present originally in plants and animals as well as in human beings. These spirits were assumed to merge progressively into special spirits or "manes" and, at last, into the idea of a supreme being. Tylor's *Researches of the Early History of Mankind* (1865) and his *Primitive Culture* (1871) offered impressive evidence for a unifying, evolutionary, and normative view of the human mind as it was reflected in man's cultural history and in his nature.

Cultural evolution and psychic unity, then, presumably explained the similarities of peoples in particular stages of development. But this assumption left unsettled the reasons why different peoples advanced at different rates. Answers to this problem varied considerably. In some cases, notably that of Herbert Spencer and Lester Frank Ward, the different stages of development were related to the varying ways in which natural selection and adaptation evoked more cooperative behavior or less. Some fell back on the idea that despite the basic unity of human nature, distinctive races did exist and did explain, by reason of greater or lesser gifts, differences in the rates of evolution. Others explained the varying rates at which peoples moved through the progressive stages in terms of environmental factors, including climate, natural resources, and the degree of isolation from other groups.

If cultural evolutionists offered contradictory reasons for the varied rates at which peoples passed through the several progressive stages, virtually all took it for granted that the civilizations of western Europe marked the highest stage. The pioneer American ethnologists Lewis Henry Morgan and John Wesley Powell believed that the apex had been reached in the individualist democracy of the United States. This assumption reflected a commitment to the doctrine of inevitable progress. It could also justify the colonial conquests of less-advanced overseas peoples. In judging peoples and cultural stages by the criteria of their own societies, evolutionists were in effect culture-bound, to use the term of later anthropologists.

The methods of the cultural evolutionists included, in the first place, the comparison of archaeological remains and the similarities and differences between peoples of the contemporary world as these were reported by travelers, traders, and missionaries. It is true that something like a field study was not unknown on the part of such European pioneers as Waitz and Tylor and even more specifically and thoroughly by such Americans as Morgan and the scientists of the federal Bureau of Ethnology. Of special importance was the library study and textual analyses of the languages of American Indians. Here Daniel Brinton took high rank for both his competence and his insistence that the Indian languages, in differing so markedly from those of Europe and Asia, constituted a great separate family of languages. Brinton could thus plausibly assume the independent or parallel development of American aborigines, an assumption for which he found further confirmation in his comparative studies of Indian mythologies and religions. In the main, however, cultural evolutionists deduced differences and similarities among peoples from the "laws" of cultural evolutionism and psychic unity. The differences and similarities in environmental experiences which they observed derived, they believed, from these laws.[44]

Lewis Henry Morgan (1818–81), sometimes called the "father of American anthropology," studied at first hand the life of the Seneca and other Iroquois tribes and, later on, that of the Indians from the Northwest to the Southwest. His early studies of the Iroquois and his *Ancient Society* (1877) illustrated the relationships he believed to exist between cultural evolution and psychic unity on the one hand and the conception of human nature on the other. "The principle of intelligence, although conditioned in its powers within narrow limits of variation, seeks ideal standards invariably the same," Morgan wrote. "Its operations, consequently, have been uniform through all the stages of human progress. No argument for the unity of origin of mankind can be made, which, in its nature is more satisfactory. A common principle of intelligence meets us in the savage, in the barbarian, and in the civilized man. It was in virtue of this that mankind were able to produce in earlier conditions the same

44. This discussion is indebted to Robert H. Lowie's *The History of Ethnological Theory*; Marvin Harris, *The Rise of Anthropological Theory* (New York, 1968); and George W. Stocking, Jr., *Race, Culture, and Evolution: Essays in the History of Anthropology* (New York, 1968).

implements and the same utensils, the same inventions, and to develop similar institutions from the same original germs of thought."[45] Morgan illustrated his thesis in citing the development of the arrow by the savage, the smelting of iron by the barbarian, and the construction of the railway train as the triumph of civilization. "All these inventions represented the same thought in the same kind of brains, on different levels of complexity." In relating technology to man's psychic unity Morgan brought together a materialistic and a psychological principle. In a dynamic interplay each influenced the other, even in the social institutions distinctive to each cultural stage, a contention that appealed to Marx and Engels. In defending his theory of cultural evolutionism and psychic unity, Morgan also held that social evolution was illuminated, and indeed confirmed, by the similarity in terminology of kinship systems among some seventy Indian tribes. Closely related to his kinship theory was his thesis that the evolution of family proceeded from the promiscuous savage to the patriarchal family of early civilization.

Though less important in ethnology than Morgan, Major John Wesley Powell played a useful role in developing the implications of cultural evolution for the image of man. A geologist, a famed explorer of the Colorado River, and a champion of conservation and irrigation, he founded in 1879 the Smithsonian's Bureau of Ethnology, which he ably administered for many years. Powell insisted on the primacy of fact-finding in the study of Indian cultures: theoretical explanations and laws must await the accumulation and organization of data on tribal identities, nomenclatures, languages, beliefs, and achievements. He respected the dignity and worth of Indians as human beings. A truly scientific understanding of their cultures would, he hoped, overcome prevailing ignorance, fear, legend, sentimentality, white arrogance, and exploitation. It might also illuminate the role of the native Americans in the evolution of mankind.

Like such earlier explorers and geographers as George Gibbs and George Perkins Marsh, Powell placed human beings squarely in nature. He assumed a common biological heritage but envisioned the evolution of multiple cultures. In this evolution, each culture was influenced by geographical environment and above all by the way man's developing mind controlled and fashioned his surroundings. This took place as the result of purposeful, conscious mental efforts. Cultural evolution as Powell saw it owed something to Lamarck's emphasis on the inheritance of acquired characteristics. He was also impressed by Darwin's stress on social instinct and above all by Morgan's and Ward's theories of cultural

45. Lewis Henry Morgan, *Ancient Society* (1877), ed. Leslie A. White (Cambridge, Mass., 1964), p. 467.

stages. But Powell did much more than reflect the influence of others. He revamped Spencer's view of cultural evolution by denying the role of chance and determinism. He emphasized the universal replacement of natural selection by human selection, of biological evolution by cultural evolution. In his view, developing cultures did not completely transcend the biological heritage of competition and brutelike selfishness. These cultures moved forward by "emulative competition" and "reciprocal altruism." Having rejected Social Darwinism, he hoped that the trend toward homogeneity everywhere would recapture some of the interdependence and solidarity that had marked earlier stages of cultural evolution. Were this in the lap of the future, there might be brought to the foreground a democratic social conscience and a humane scientific culture.[46]

Otis T. Mason, Powell's associate in federally sponsored ethnology and director of the National Museum, also contributed to the doctrine of cultural evolution. Mason held that "men and women of all races and conditions, in all ages, were engaged in devising. In this respect there has been an inborn kinship of minds, savage and civilized, from first to last." Man lacked the anatomical advantages of certain animals in the struggle with environment for survival. He had, though, been endowed with a brain superior in size and intricacy. This had enabled him to meet the universal human wants with infinite inventions. These found expression in the activities based on the nature of man himself: languages, industries, esthetic arts, social arrangements, knowledge, and the explanation of things, creeds, cults, and mutual services.[47]

The first influential criticism of the theory of cultural evolution in the 1880s should be understood in terms of the whole development of the modern concept of culture. Hamilton Cravens has presented persuasive reasons for distinguishing, in this development, an initial emphasis on the divorce of biology and culture and on the autonomy of the latter, an

46. Key essays include John Wesley Powell's "Savagery to Barbarism," *Transactions of the American Anthropological Society of Washington* 3 (Washington, D.C., 1884); and "Competition as a Factor in Human Evolution," *American Anthropologist*, o.s. 1 (Washington, D.C., 1888). For biographical details see Wallace Stegner's *Beyond the Hundredth Meridian: John Wesley Powell and the Second Opening of the West* (Boston, 1954), including a brief discussion of Powell's contributions to ethnology. I am especially indebted to the excellent discussion of Powell in Curtis M. Hinsley, Jr., "The Development of a Profession: Anthropology in Washington, D.C., 1846–1903" (Ph.D. diss., University of Wisconsin, 1976), pt. 2, chap. 2.

47. Otis T. Mason, "Mind and Matter in Culture," *American Anthropologist*, n.s. 10 (New York, 1908), pp. 187 ff.

innovation that influenced anthropological thought through much of the second decade of the twentieth century; and the recognition, increasingly after 1925, of the interrelatedness of biology and culture.[48]

In a genuine sense, the leader in this development was Franz Boas, a German born and trained geographer, statistician, humanist, and ethnologist.[49] He was much indebted to Virchow, Wundt, and especially Waitz. His own geographical field studies in Baffinland in 1884 seem to have been influential in leading him to question the logical, progressive, and orthogenetic development of peoples from savagery through barbarism to civilization. In rejecting cultural evolutionism and in insisting on the distinctive history of every culture group, Boas did not suppose that the characteristic differences in each culture group wiped out a commonly shared humanity. "I had seen," he wrote after his first experience with Eskimos, "that they enjoyed life, and hard life, as we do; that nature is beautiful to them; that feelings of friendship also root in the Eskimo heart; that, although the character of their life is rude as compared to civilized life, the Eskimo is a man as we are; that his feelings, his virtues, and his shortcomings are based on human nature, like ours."[50] But despite such similarities, the Eskimos and the Bella Bella Coola Indians of the Pacific Northwest, whose language and folklore he studied at first hand a few years later, seemed to him in no way to resemble some earlier stage in the unitary culture which had reached its apex in western Europe. Thus he attacked the prevailing museum custom of displaying culture artifacts in progressive sequence to illustrate the historical development of human traits. He insisted, instead, on arranging these in terms of geographic provinces or culture areas. Such an arrangement might imply both the diffusion of culture traits and some measure of independent development.

In rejecting a unilinear cultural evolution through identical and in-

48. Hamilton Cravens, *The Triumph of Evolution: American Scientists and the Heredity-Environment Controversy 1900–1941* (Philadelphia, 1978), pp. 18–33, 57–71, 159–71, 192–201. With insight and thorough documentation Cravens emphasizes the roles of academic professionalization, social policy, and the influence of genetics, psychology, and sociology in the successive developments.

49. A good introduction to the work of Boas, with a bibliography of his writings, is Alexander Lesser's essay in the *International Encyclopedia of the Social Sciences* 2:99–109. Also valuable are Melville J. Herskovits, *Franz Boas: The Science of Man in the Making* (New York, 1953); Walter R. Goldschmidt, ed., *The Anthropology of Franz Boas: Essays on the Centennial of His Birth* (Menasha, Wis., 1959); George W. Stocking, Jr., "Franz Boas and the Culture Concept in Historical Pespective," *American Anthropologist*, n.s. 48 (1966): 867–82; and Leslie A. White, *The Ethnography and Ethnology of Franz Boas* (Austin, Tex., 1963).

50. Abram Kardiner and Edward Preble, *They Studied Man* (New York, 1961), p. 119.

variable stages, Boas seemed to overlook the fact that few champions of cultural evolution had insisted on an inevitable, unalterable, and completely rigid pattern of successive stages of development. Tylor, and indeed others, including American ethnologists, had in some sense anticipated such a culture concept, embracing the ideas of diffusion through contact, borrowing, and acculturation. But in general they had done so in terms of a unitary culture based on psychic unity, in one or another stage of development. Boas advanced, instead, the concept of many cultures which in spite of greater or fewer similarities to each other were nevertheless unique. Each presented a group organization, identity, and sense of continuity no less interesting and significant than the beliefs and behavior differing from or shared with those of others, particularly contiguous groups. The totality of learned behavior, or culture, seemed to him to reflect a good deal of independence from biology, in the sense that it was doubtful whether complex traits could have been transmitted through germ plasm. A culture, then, was the environment of both biological and behavioral life. Heredity by family strain might be influential. But the members of the group, being plastic organisms, realized some of their potentialities in unconscious ways as specified by the particular culture that gave them identity as human beings.

As Boas never tired of pointing out, the theory of cultural evolution rested in part on deductive methods and in part on unproven generalization. Moreover, the concept was culture-bound in that it projected the assumed stages of Western culture on all other cultures. In his own field studies, Boas found that sequential developments of the components of culture did not always move from the simple to the complex. Instead, they appeared to develop as a totality in large part as the result of their own distinctive histories. The office of the anthropologist was thus to reconstruct, as best he could, these histories, not in terms of the values of his own culture but in accordance with the values of the culture being studied. That is, he was to try to understand a culture in terms of those who had been formed by it and whose life and character could not be separated from it. Such an approach of course implied cultural relativism.

Boas contributed further to the cultural interpretation of human nature by directly confronting the problem of the stability of races or ethnic groups and the influence of culture on physical structure. It was, he held, warrantable to assume that environment had an important effect on the structure and physiological functions of plastic human beings. It also seemed warrantable to assume that differences between primitive or preliterate peoples might be expected. But he found no evidence of the existence of pure races in historical Europe nor of deleterious effects of race mixture. Measurable differences between races seemed less significant than differences within a race, which in part might be laid at the door of specific family strains.

This led Boas to an early interest in the statistical analysis of somatological measurements in growing children. Here he was responding to the new view of physical nature that derived from scientific and statistical rather than from typological models. Using biometric methods, he investigated immigrants and their American-born children as part of the program of the United States Commission on Immigration, set up to make recommendations on admission policy. Boas found various changes, particularly in head forms, in American-born children of immigrants. The changes were the more marked the longer the migrant had lived in the United States. Such changes might be attributed in some part to differences in infant care in an urban environment. Though Boas's views on heredity and environment were complex, and shifted over time, he felt that physical changes argued against a conception of an absolute, fixed ethnic type and gave a place to cultural factors in physical changes.[51] We shall see that the controversy over the relative roles of "nature" and "nurture," which was well under way when Boas made his report, was a tangled and heated aspect of the discussion of man's makeup and behavior.

In the larger issue of the cultural interpretation of human nature it is not easy to assess the significance of what Boas did. He limited his field investigations to a small number of neighboring tribes. He paid less attention to social and economic structure than to the expressive aspects of culture such as language, mythology, art, folklore, and religion, which he viewed as objective manifestations of inner feelings and thoughts. This emphasis gave depth and psychological dimension to his work. He also shifted the prevailing emphasis by asking, in view of the widespread existence of diffusion, why people accepted some elements rather than others in the process of cultural diffusion. A logical answer seemed to be that the values in a culture and the needs of those shaped by it largely influenced the process of selection by conscious and especially unconscious choices. It is still open to question whether Boas created a new intellectual tradition, as some of his disciples claimed. He certainly contributed to the reshaping of anthropology by challenging unilateral culture evolution and psychic unity and by reformulating existing ideas and approaches.[52]

51. Franz Boas, "Changes in Bodily Form of Descendants of Immigrants," *American Anthropologist*, n.s. 14 (1912): 530–62.

52. Ronald P. Rohner, ed., *The Ethnography of Franz Boas* (Chicago, 1969), p. xvii. In his essay "Horatio Hale and the Development of American Anthropology" (*Proceedings of the American Philosophical Society* 111 [1967]: 30 ff.), Jacob Gruber has noted some of the influences of Hale on Boas.

Boas seldom used the term *human nature* and never, apparently, defined it in so many words. Some have assumed that he rejected the concept itself, in holding that the human being could not be conceived of without culture, and that if human nature was knowable, it could be known only in many kinds of complex and varying cultures. The human nature often described as an assumed generalized universal entity could be better thought of in terms of learned behavior or culture. Thus it might be supposed that Boas's emphasis on cultures as immensely influential factors in explaining differences between groups in effect made the idea of human nature, as a universal inborn attribute explaining all behavior, a useless and invalid inferential generalization, a kind of primitivistic dream or a statistical shadow.

But this was not quite the case. In *The Mind of Primitive Man* (1911) and in early papers anticipating the leading ideas in this classic, Boas identified all human beings as culture-creating and culture-transmitting creatures. He clearly stated that all domesticated men—savage, barbarian, civilized—alike shared inherent capacities distinguishing them from other domesticated primates. These included the use of articulate, structured language that influenced ways in which experience was conceptualized, the ability to reason, and the capacity to control impulses. In asking why cultures changed, Boas found a partial answer in the creativity of the individual which resulted in tensions, conflicts, and readjustments. He compared the innovative proclivities of a few men and women in preliterate societies with the philosophers and scientists of civilization. He found, further, evidence for some definite act of creativity at least once in the life of everyone, no matter where, no matter how humble. If creativity in primitive cultures tended to challenge deeply habituated behavior and associated values, this was also true in civilized societies. Thus in finding in primitive groups no less than in civilized societies unique and universal capacities, including an essential creativity and dignity, Boas in effect projected a concept of human nature understandable in large part in cultural terms.

Yet Boas did not see all the implications of the concept of culture as a distinct, autonomous actuality. It remained for other anthropologists, notably Robert H. Lowie, Alexander Goldenweiser, Alfred L. Kroeber, George P. Murdock, and especially Leslie A. White to do that. The idea of cultural evolution,[53] long held in disfavor by Boas and his students, was reasserted by Professor White and figured explicitly in his discussion

---

53. White found support for cultural evolution in the discoveries over time of new sources of energy. These explained the development of new technologies. In turn these, by reciprocal, dialectic interaction, changed the related social structures, values, and ideologies.

of human nature. In 1939 he first used the term culturology to denote the "science of culture," a phrase Tylor had used in 1871. White admitted that, of course, culture could not exist without human beings. But, he insisted, the concept of culture made traditional ideas about human nature obsolete. What was taken to be human nature was not *natural* in the biological sense, but cultural. "The tendencies, emphases and content that one sees in the overt behavior of human beings are often not due to innate biological determination—though such determinations do of course exist—but to the stimulation of external cultural elements. Much of what is commonly called 'human nature' is merely *culture* thrown against a screen of nerves, glands, sense organs, muscles, etc."[54]

As we shall see, however, in the 1950s several prominent anthropologists, reacting to new social situations, began to argue for the validity and usefulness of the idea of human nature in its traditional verbal designation.[55]

All in all, the cultural theorists, in studying the similarities and differences between groups, raised basic problems involving the idea of human nature. On the one hand, they cast further doubt on the theological and supernatural explanations of man's origins, development, and destiny. In rejecting the theory of multiple racial origins, cultural anthropologists undermined arguments often used after as well as before the Civil War to justify white supremacy.[56] The discussion of culture also stressed the unique human role of communication between groups as well as individuals, a position ardently supported by the diffusionists. The idea of a common human nature derived support from the anthropologists who emphasized man's unique gift of originality in independently creating institutions and technologies everywhere at a given stage of culture. On the other hand, even advocates of the idea that culture created culture, that everything came from it, struck a blow at traditional ideas about human nature and at the validity of the idea itself. Without settling some problems and in raising others, the whole cultural concept opened a highly significant chapter in the history of the reputation of human nature.

54. Leslie A. White, *The Science of Culture: A Study of Man and Civilization* (New York, 1949; rev. ed., 1969), pp. 149–50, 158–61.

55. See pp. 298, 354, 368–69, 386, 406.

56. For a well-documented discussion of this phase of "racism" consult George H. Frederickson's *The Black Image in the White Mind: The Debate on Afro-American Character and Destiny, 1817–1914* (New York, 1971), chap. 9.

9

Nature versus Nurture

The Negro . . . is, by nature, incapable of creating societies of an order above barbarism, and this . . . feature of his nature, depending as it does upon the lack of certain qualities in his mind, is irremediable.

NATHANIEL S. SHALER, 1904

The union of nature and nurture is not one of addition or mixture but of growth, whereby the elements are altogether transformed into a new organic whole.

CHARLES H. COOLEY, 1896

The question of questions in eugenics is this: How shall the inroads of degeneracy be prevented, and the best of our human qualities preserved and disseminated among all the people.

CHARLES B. DAVENPORT, 1909

If the thousand babies born this week in New York City were given equal opportunities they would still differ in much the same way and to much the same extent as they will in fact differ.

EDWARD LEE THORNDIKE, 1913

The genes have *determined* the intelligence (or stature or weight) of a person only in the particular sequence of environments to which that person has been exposed in his upbringing and life experience. What actually develops is *conditioned* by the interplay of the genes with the environments.

THEODOSIUS DOBZHANSKY, 1973

LONG BEFORE the first two decades of the twentieth century, when the nature-nurture controversy pinpointed more sharply than ever before the relative roles of heredity and environment in human nature, the problem had been confronted in one form or another. It would, in fact, be possible to see forerunners of the dispute in the literature of classical Chinese wisdom—Mencius emphasized a widely spread or even universal endowment of native ability and Hsün Tzu attributed supreme importance to training.[1] Ulysses implied the formative role of environment in early Greek thought when he proclaimed "I am a part of all I have met," while Theognis, a sixth-century B.C. poet, in anticipation of Plato, held that a superior human stock could be achieved by foresightful breeding. Central to all later discussion in Western civilization, however, was the Hebraic-Christian belief that the iniquities of the fathers tainted the sons unto the fourth and fifth generations.

We have also seen that in the seventeenth and eighteenth centuries such environmentalist thinkers as Locke, Bodin, Montesquieu, Helvétius, and Godwin challenged traditional, scholastic, and Calvinist portraits of man's immutably low estate, and that these writers attracted some disciples in America. It may also be recalled that in the 1830s and 1840s William Ellery Channing, the Transcendentalists, and the communitarians held that human nature could be bettered or even perfected

1. Donald J. Munro, *The Concept of Man in Early China* (Stanford, 1969), pp. 4, 12 ff., 51–52, 72, 82, 128 ff., 159, 182.

by improvements in the social environment. On the other side, the slavery controversy inspired in both North and South the almost universal conviction of Negro inferiority. The conviction rested in part on evidence of anatomical differences. Few questioned the transmission of these "inferiorities" to posterity.[2]

Much that happened in the last two-thirds of the century confirmed the belief, on the one hand, in an unchangeable human nature, and on the other hand, in its malleability.

The first discussion of note concerned the Negro. Drawing on the physical measurements of black, white, and mulatto soldiers made during the war by the United States Sanitary Commission and the Bureau of the Provost Marshal General, statisticians and scientists in the postwar decades claimed that anatomical and anthropometric differences confirmed the historical record of black inferiority. Southern doctors conducting autopsies on Negroes reported brains of smaller dimension among blacks—an assumed added proof of innate Afro-American inferiority.[3] These investigations, buttressed by citations of higher mortality rates among blacks and mulattoes than among whites, seemed to confirm the pre-Civil War doctrine of the inborn and immutable inferiority of the darker people. Seldom challenged, these widely publicized claims strengthened a climate of opinion slanted toward dominance of heredity in the human makeup.

Nor were such claims, based on the murky and ill-understood nature of heredity, confined to the question of racial differences. Most penologists held to the biological transmission of criminality or at least the proclivity to crime. The statement in the Forty-Ninth Annual Report of the Board of Inspectors of the Eastern State Penitentiary of Pennsylvania represented the typical position: ". . . there is an inherited trait or taint in many, which may possibly lead to the commission of crime, a motor, as it were, that unconsciously impels those who suffer from this hereditary taint, to become criminals."[4] Even when penologists ad-

2. This is well documented in William Stanton's *The Leopard's Spots: Scientific Attitudes toward Race in America 1815–1859* (Chicago, 1960).

3. Benjamin A. Gould, *Investigations in the Military and Anthropological Statistics of American Soldiers* (New York, 1869). Gould cautiously admonished against making sweeping racial generalizations, pp. 297, 315, 347, 379. Also J. H. Baxter's *Statistics, Medical and Anthropological of the Provost-Marshal-General's Bureau . . .* , 2 vols. (Washington, D.C., 1875); John S. Haller, Jr., *Outcasts from Evolution: Scientific Attitudes of Racial Inferiority 1859–1900* (Urbana, Ill., 1971), chaps. 1–3; and George H. Frederickson, *The Black Image in the White Mind: The Debate on Afro-American Character and Destiny, 1817–1914* (New York, 1971), chap. 6.

4. Quoted in Arthur E. Fink, *Causes of Crime: Biological Theories in the United States 1800–1915* (Philadelphia, 1938), p. 153.

mitted that no one cause explained crime, they stressed the theory of degeneration and the criminal type. At least one unhesitatingly urged society to make it impossible for criminals to reproduce themselves.[5]

Worsening conditions in the city slums strengthened the claims of the hereditarians. Even before the Civil War, but more strikingly in the decades following it, the social conflicts and the social costs incidental to the quickening pace of urban industrialism focused attention on the relative roles of heredity and environment in human nature. The early efforts of many taxpayers to stymie the public school movement found a parallel in hard-headed objections to the expanding public expense of caring for the feeble-minded, the mentally ill, the criminals and impecunious immigrants in mill towns and city slums. Men and women professionally concerned with such matters took conflicting stands on both the causes of crime and poverty and what should be done. A sizeable group, discouraged by the complexity of the problems and the ineffectiveness of remedial measures, as well as by the cost of public charity and private philanthropy, held that such derelictions and the inability to climb the social ladder demonstrated inborn weakness and incapacity. Transmitted to offspring, this could only multiply the number of paupers and criminals. Yet hereditarians, in denying the operation of free will in certain cases, did not always blame criminals for heinous offenses. Some alienists, for example, in testifying at trials of murderers and assassins, contended that unsavory crimes often resulted from inherited pathological defects. Society should not hold such criminals morally responsible for their acts.[6]

On the other side, some concessions were made to the role of environment in shaping behavior. Until the last decades of the century, the scientific community and those directly in touch with it accepted the validity of the Lamarckian theory, which held that environmentally acquired characteristics were in varying degrees transmitted to offspring. Thus the next generation inherited desirable traits acquired in a favorable environment. In view of this, the meliorists in the American Social Science Association, like the more doctrinaire Henry George and Edward Bellamy, took heart from the belief that if the environment could be improved, the socially inept who acquired habits of restraint, frugality, and self-respect would transmit these virtues to their descendants.

Richard Dugdale, a New York prison reformer, provided an influential example of the use of Lamarckianism in discussions of the roles of heredity and environment in human nature. In 1877 he reported the

5. Henry M. Boies, *Prisoners and Paupers* (New York, 1893), pp. 206–8, 270, 292.

6. Charles E. Rosenberg, *The Trial of the Assassin Guiteau: Psychiatry and Law in the Gilded Age* (Chicago, 1968), chaps. 5–8.

results of his investigations of the pauperism, crime, prostitution, and feeble-mindedness in a family to which the name Jukes was given. He laid these derelictions at the door of heredity. As a Lamarckian, however, he noted that "environment tends to produce habits which may become hereditary, especially in pauperism and licentiousness if it should be sufficiently constant to produce modifications of cerebral tissue. If these conclusions be correct," he went on, "then the whole question of the control of crime and pauperism becomes possible, within wide limits, if the necessary training can be made to reach over two or three generations." Thus the logical deduction seemed to be "that environment is the ultimate controlling factor in determining careers, placing heredity itself as an organized result of invariable environment."[7]

Even in the hereditarian stronghold of racial theory some conceded a limited role to environment. Advocates of white supremacy claimed that after emancipation blacks and mulattoes had, as health and mortality records showed, become prone to increasing illness and to early death. Without paternalistic supervision, Negroes were thus destined to become, by reason of the unfavorable environment of freedom, extinct or at least a marginal fragment.[8]

Just when social problems were sharpening opposite views on heredity and environment, a new theory raised basic questions about the immutability of human nature save for the Lamarckian concession to improvability under favorable conditions or degeneration under adverse ones. This new challenge, of course, was the Darwinian theory of the development of species by natural and sexual selection: it turned out to be the nineteenth century's major contribution in shifting the character of the discussion of human nature.

In some ways Darwinism could be thought of as neutral in relation to the heredity-environment controversy. Part of the trouble lay in the

7. R. L. Dugdale, "The Jukes": A Study in Crime, Pauperism, Disease and Heredity, with an introduction by Elisha Harris, M.D., 4th ed. (New York, 1910), p. 66. Dugdale's emphasis on environment as a contributing causal factor in the record of social dereliction was overlooked, and his book was generally, and in the main rightly, cited as providing evidence of the relation between heredity and mental and moral shortcomings. In his essay "Origins of Crime in Society" Dugdale, while emphasizing the importance of environment for crime, also stated that there was the hereditary criminal whom civilization so far had failed to improve. Atlantic Monthly 48 (1881): 452–53.

8. The literature is extensive: examples are Frederick L. Hoffman, "Race Traits and Tendencies in the American Negro," American Economic Association Publications, 1st ser. 11 (1896); and Nathaniel Shaler, "Science and the African Problem," Atlantic Monthly 66 (1890): 42–43.

uncertainty about the nature of heredity, the definition of a species, and the confusion of the individual and the species in both biological and psychological thought. A no less important problem stemmed from the nature and role of instincts. Darwin believed that instincts, a term he used in various ways, evolved by natural selection and could be assumed to be hereditary. At the same time, it seemed to him possible that something could be inherited and yet depend on a sort of experience: intelligence was inherited and yet relied on environment and experience for its expression. Yet it also appeared that something in the whole picture might be developed independent of experience and yet inherited. In the words of C. C. Beer, an authority on the discussion and nature of instincts, Darwin "anticipated most of the questions and confusions associated with the term 'instinct' in the writings of students of behavior who followed him."[9]

The confusion was evident, for instance, in the uses to which psychologists put the hereditarian aspect of Darwin's conception of instincts. Without any experimental evidence, William James identified a great number of complex behavioral characteristics as inherited instincts. James also, however, staunchly held that the human nervous system, being more complex than that of other organisms, enabled man to modify instincts by the development of automatic habits and to solve some problems by rational processes. William McDougall, the British psychologist who came to Harvard a decade after James's death, emphasized, on the other hand, the deterministic aspects of the doctrine of instincts. He had long maintained that all human behavior directly or indirectly expressed one of the instincts with which people were born. In circular reasoning, he explained social as well as individual behavior by identifying a large number of specific instincts with specific motives and conduct. Thus thought itself became merely a kind of mental palliative, freedom a mere illusion. Only in the second decade of the twentieth century did the gloomy instinct theory, which many sociologists as well as psychologists adopted, meet with serious and widespread criticism.[10]

Meantime, without addressing himself directly to the doctrine of instincts, Francis Galton, a cousin of Darwin, had given what many intellectuals regarded as firm scientific support to the overweening importance of heredity. On the basis of biostatistical studies of

9. C. C. Beer, "Instinct," *International Encyclopedia of the Social Sciences*, 7:364–65.

10. William McDougall, *An Introduction to Social Psychology* (London, 1908), pp. 19–44. Leonard Carmichael's Harvard doctoral dissertation summarized the history of technical thought about human and animal instincts. For a review, see *The Journal of Abnormal and Social Psychology* 20 (1925): 245–60. Also important are Luther Lee Barnard, *Instinct: A Study in Social Psychology* (New York, 1924), and the excellent recent treatment by Hamilton Cravens, *The Triumph of Evolution: American Scientists and the Heredity-Environment Controversy 1900–1941* (Philadelphia, 1978), pp. 191–223.

genealogies Galton, in his major book, *Hereditary Genius* (1869), concluded that man's mental as well as his physical abilities and even his traits of character derived from inheritance.[11] He held that no one could achieve a very high reputation without superior native abilities and that few who had these failed to win eminence. In 1874 he offered further pedigree evidence for his thesis. *English Men of Science* carried the subtitle "Their Nature and Nurture." The phrase came to represent the central issue in the controversy about the immutability or mutability of human nature. Moreover, Galton's conviction that heredity was the decisive factor in ability did not rest solely on pedigree data. In 1875–76 the *Popular Science Monthly* presented to American readers the results of his pioneer study of identical twins. He concluded that such twins reared separately resembled each other more than did fraternal twins brought up together. In his view, the inquiry confirmed his belief that nature, not nurture, was the dominant force.[12] His study inspired many later American investigations of twins.

Galton did not convince everyone. A conventionally religious reviewer felt that the emphasis on heredity as an iron chain binding human fate robbed men and women of the Christian obligation to care for the needy and weak with compassion.[13] The criticism offered by Chauncey Wright, whose original thinking about evolution had impressed Darwin, represented a very different approach. Wright sensed Galton's mistake in presupposing that the differences he might find in the twins would be a sufficient proof of native ability: he had not established his thesis. Since the evidence in respect to the heritability of mental and moral peculiarities was much less clear than that of physical peculiarities, Wright felt that education must be regarded as an influence of great importance in shaping mental and moral character.[14] Wright's friend William James shared his doubt. Though respecting Galton's laborious investigations, he questioned whether intellectual genius, like murder, "will out." James properly noted that Galton failed to take into account

11. Francis Galton, *Hereditary Genius: An Inquiry into Its Laws and Consequences* (London, 1869), pp. 1, 49. For the follow-up work of the British biostatisticians, which affirmed Galton's hereditarian thesis, see the jointly published reports, Ethel M. Elderton, *The Relative Strength of Nature and Nurture*, and Karl Pearson, *Some Recent Misinterpretations of the Problem of Nature and Nurture* (Cambridge, 1915).

12. Francis Galton, "The History of Twins, as a Criterion of the Relative Powers of Nature and Nurture," *Popular Science Monthly* 8 (1875–76): 345–57.

13. Henry W. Holland, "Heredity," *Atlantic Monthly* 52 (1883): 447–52.

14. Wright's principal scientific and other writings were collected and edited in Charles Eliot Norton, *Philosophical Discussions by Chauncey Wright* (Cambridge, Mass., 1877), and by James Bradley Thayer, *Letters of Chauncey Wright* (Cambridge, 1878).

the great complexity of the social conditions that affected the realization of potential greatness.[15]

Using Galton's own material, Charles H. Cooley, a sociologist at the University of Michigan, showed that in each case of genius, opportunity for education played a part in the fulfillment of its promise. Cooley asked how any potential genius could possibly have emerged from the illiterate, inarticulate mass of mid-nineteenth-century England. After carefully criticizing Galton's methods, he faulted the hereditarian thesis as unproved. Invoking a metaphor, he suggested that with the knowledge at hand it might be said that the relation between genius and fame could be compared with what happened when a farmer planted mixed seeds in a furrow traversing a great variety of soils. "Here many come up and flourish, there none, and there again, only those of a certain sort. The seedbag is the race, the soil, historical conditions other than race, the seeds, genius, and the crop, fame."[16]

But Galton and his more doctrinaire disciple Karl Pearson[17] enlisted much support among the rising generation of biologists, psychologists, and sociologists, as well as among well-established men of prominence. These included Dr. Oliver Wendell Holmes,[18] President Charles W. Eliot of Harvard,[19] David Starr Jordan of Stanford,[20] and the vigorous genetic psychologist G. Stanley Hall.[21]

The hereditarian position drew support from genealogical studies

15. William James, "Great Men, Great Thoughts, and Great Environment," *Atlantic Monthly* 46 (1880): 453.

16. Charles H. Cooley, "Genius, Fame and the Comparison of Races," *Annals of the American Academy of Political and Social Science* 2 (1897): 317–58, esp. p. 342; "Nature versus Nurture in the Making of Social Careers," *Proceedings of the National Conference of Charities and Corrections* 22 (1896): 397 ff.

17. Pearson, who claimed that heredity accounts for nine-tenths of a person's capacity, expounded a harsh social philosophy. Richard Hofstadter, *Social Darwinism in American Thought* (Philadelphia, 1944; rev. ed., New York, 1955), p. 164.

18. *The Works of Oliver Wendell Holmes*, 12 vols. (Boston, 1892), 3:303; 5:238. For a good discussion of Holmes, see E. M. Tilton, *Amiable Autocrat* (New York, 1947), pp. 314–15.

19. Charles W. Eliot, *American Contributions to Civilization and Other Essays* (New York, 1897), pp. 93–96.

20. David Starr Jordan, *Days of a Man*, 2 vols. (Yonkers-on-Hudson, N.Y., 1922), 1:132; *Care and Culture of Men* (San Francisco, 1896), pp. 209 ff.; *The Human Harvest* (Boston, 1907), p. 46; *The Heredity of Richard R. Roe* (Boston, 1910), pp. 31 ff. Jordan was much concerned over what he regarded as the disastrous effects of wars in eliminating the physically and mentally "most fit" young men.

21. G. Stanley Hall, "Galton's Philosophy," *The Nation* 36 (1883): 512–13; Merle Curti, *The Social Ideas of American Educators* (New York, 1935; rev. ed., Paterson, N.J., 1959), pp. 404 ff.; Dorothy Ross, *G. Stanley Hall* (Chicago, 1972), pp. 354–55, 378–79.

inspired by those of Galton.[22] The most celebrated was, as we have seen, Richard Dugdale's *The Jukes* (1877). Dugdale's popularizers and imitators argued the claims of heredity with few or no qualifications. This was true in the studies that compared the Jukes with the distinguished descendants of Jonathan Edwards,[23] that surveyed the Jukes in 1915,[24] or that considered the forebears of "the tribe of Ishmael in Indiana."[25] Naive in statistical theory and messy in genealogical scholarship, the reports, though challenged again and again, continued to provide support for the hereditarian thesis that nurture counted for little.

Dr. Henry H. Goddard, who had taken his doctorate under G. Stanley Hall, directed a school for the feeble-minded in New Jersey. In many eyes this gave credence to his study of the family histories of the institution's inmates. *The Kallikak Family* was a report on the genealogy of a feeble-minded eight-year-old girl, descended from a Revolutionary soldier and his mentally defective sex partner. Of the 480 identified offspring, Goddard labeled 143 feeble-minded and 46 normal. The mental state of the rest was unknown or in doubt. The incidence of alcoholism, prostitution, and crime in this branch of the family seemed as disturbing as that of feeble-mindedness. On the other hand, descendants of the same forefather and the worthy woman he married succeeded as honored citizens in their community. Goddard viewed the evidence for the primacy of heredity as overwhelming. No amount of environmental improvement, he concluded, could have changed the record of the offspring of that feeble-minded ancestor.[26]

The theory of evolution and its implications played a major part in assessments of human nature in other ways. Hamilton Cravens has shown the central and misleading importance of the identification of

22. Dr. Frederick Adams Woods, *Mental and Moral Heredity in Royalty* (New York, 1906), and *The Influence of Monarchs: Steps in a New Science of History* (New York, 1913).

23. Dr. Albert E. Winship, *Jukes-Edwards: A Study in Education and Heredity* (Harrisburg, Pa., 1900); see also Edith A. Winship, "The Human Legacy of Jonathan Edwards," *World's Work* 6 (1903): 3081–84.

24. Arthur H. Estabrook, *The Jukes in 1915* (Washington, D.C., 1916).

25. The Rev. Oscar C. McCulloch, "The Tribe of Ishmael: A Study in Social Degradation," *Proceedings of the National Conference of Charities and Correction* 15 (1888): 154–59.

26. Dr. Henry Goddard, *The Kallikak Family: A Study in the Heredity of Feeble-mindedness* (New York, 1912), p. 116.

biological and cultural evolution.[27] The theories of Darwin and Spencer were made to explain, by analogy, social evolution. The explanation rested on the assumption that physical and mental kinship of animals and human beings was the basis for the development of character and conduct, that is, human nature. This was evident, for example, in the discussion of race. The general acceptance of the monogenetic origin of races made champions of the polygenetic theory seem somewhat antiquated in academic circles even though evolutionary theory was accommodated to the assumption that some races were inferior to others by reason of innate characteristics. As long as biology and race were identified, however, the white, Anglo-Saxon, Protestant scientists chiefly concerned with racial theory unconsciously accepted the hierarchy of races as scientifically valid. Only after the separation of biology and culture, which the nature-nurture controvery in the end furthered, did the commitment to science transcend the pull of ethnoculture.[28]

Evolutionary theory, when it identified biology and culture, suggested to many commentators that human nature had not changed very much in the course of its development from an animal past. This was clear from most discussions of war. To cite just one example, at the time of the Franco-Prussian conflict in 1870, Henry Ward Beecher, the most glamorous Protestant preacher, described war as "the remnant in man of that old fighting animal from which Mr. Darwin says we sprang." War, he went on, could not be regarded as an acute disease to be cured by specific remedies. As "a constitutional disorder" it "belongs to human nature." A presumption in favor of Darwin's theory, Beecher concluded, lay in the fact that "there is so much of the animal left in us yet."[29]

On the other hand, the dynamic view of man that evolutionary theory substituted for the traditionally static one suggested that human nature had not been frozen. It might degenerate. Indeed, it had degenerated in the minds of many who no longer found any charm in the doctrine of progress. Yet the inevitable change in human nature was generally

27. Hamilton Cravens, "The Discovery of Man: The Heredity-Environment Controversy and the Divorce of Biological and Social Theory in the Twentieth Century," paper read at a meeting of the American Historical Association in Boston, December 29, 1970.

28. Hamilton Cravens, "Race or Culture: American Scientists, the Problem of Race Theory, and the Invention of Cultural Pluralism, 1900–1930," paper read at the Chicago meeting of the Organization of American Historians, April 12, 1973.

29. Henry Ward Beecher, "War," July 17, 1870, *Plymouth Pulpit*, 19 vols. (New York, 1868–84), 4:341. See also Beecher's "The Study of Human Nature," *Popular Science Monthly* 1 (1872): 327–35; and *Evolution and Religion* (New York, 1885), pp. 83 ff.

thought to be an improvement, in view of the survival of the fittest and the inheritance of slowly evolving superior characteristics.[30]

John Fiske, a devoted exponent of Herbert Spencer's evolutionary naturalism and an effective writer and platform speaker, popularized an optimistic interpretation of this position. Since the first appearance of human beings, he wrote in *The Destiny of Man Viewed in the Light of His Origin* (1884), enormous changes had taken place through natural selection and adaptation. Fiske regarded improvability as the most characteristic, indeed the most essential, feature of human nature. Inasmuch as civilization thus far had advanced largely through fighting and the deadly struggle of competition, quick-wittedness had developed as a mental trait faster than compassion and kindness. Even so, over the past centuries, strife had gradually lessened. Cooperation, so necessary to the emerging industrial civilization, must become the dominant trait, since it would, like all traits when put to use, be strengthened and transmitted through heredity. In sum, Fiske concluded: "Man is slowly passing from a primitive social state in which his character shall become so transformed that nothing of the brute can be detected in it. The ape and the tiger in human nature will become extinct."[31] In developing the optimistic interpretation of evolution Fiske, though the most effective popularizer, did not stand alone.[32]

Such interpretations met with a serious challenge when scientists advanced new theories of inheritance based on experimental evidence in cytology and laboratory breeding. In 1882 August Weismann's *Studies of the Theory of Descent* reached the English-speaking world. He persuasively argued that characteristics were transmitted entirely independently of environment through a biochemical carrier in an immutable germ plasm. Though able neo-Lamarckians insisted on the speculative character of the theory, it won general acceptance in America as it did abroad. Its implications for the discussion of human nature were far-reaching. In view of the independence of heredity and environment, the Weismann position brought into question the assumption that the evolutionary process was generally, if not necessarily, "progressive." By raising doubts about the variability of organisms, the theory also implied the reality of universal and im-

30. On Lamarckianism in the United States see George W. Stocking, Jr., "Lamarckianism in American Social Science, 1890–1915," *Journal of the History of Ideas* 23 (1962): 239–56; and *Race, Culture and Evolution* (New York, 1968), chap. 10.

31. John Fiske, "Improvableness of Man," in *The Destiny of Man Viewed in the Light of His Origin* (Boston, 1886), pp. 102–3. For a discussion of Fiske's evolutionary philosophy see Milton Berman, *John Fiske: The Evolution of a Popularizer* (Cambridge, Mass., 1961), chaps. 7–8.

32. See pp. 252–53 for the similar view of Lester Frank Ward.

mutable human nature that did not change as groups adjusted themselves to different environments. Thus Weismann raised uncomfortable problems for such social meliorists as John Fiske, Lester Frank Ward, and William James.

Varying strategies developed in response to the issue. James Mark Baldwin, a leading psychologist, grasped the implications of Weismann's theory of heredity far better than William James did. He concluded that since biological heredity could not be invoked to explain human development, the concept of "social heredity" or "culture" was necessary.[33] If Weismann was correct, wrote Henry Fairfield Osborn, a geologist and paleontologist, then fatalism must triumph. Environment might be improved and such improvement might produce better individuals in each generation. The result, though, could not be cumulative for individuals through transmission to offspring.[34] Amos Warner, America's principal authority on charities and correction, approached the problem in pragmatic terms. On the one hand, he observed, the new theory "does not limit our efforts to improve environment, while, on the other hand, it gives to us a sharp realization of the importance of selection, a factor which we are otherwise prone to forget or undervalue."[35]

In 1900 three European biologists independently discovered the work of an Austrian monk, Gregor Mendel. Though published in 1866, his paper had been unknown to the scientific community. Counting color and other traits of peas of different types that were bred under controlled conditions, Mendel formulated ratios of inheritance of specific traits.[36] In varying combinations the carriers of hereditary traits (genes) explained diversities in bodily structure. Biologists on both sides of the Atlantic undertook breeding experiments to test Mendel's laws, the results of which seemed to support the formulae. It appeared at first that

33. Hamilton Cravens and John C. Burnham, "Psychology and Evolutionary Naturalism in American Thought, 1890–1940," *American Quarterly* 23 (1971): 635–57.

34. Henry Fairfield Osborn, "The Present Problem of Heredity," *Atlantic Monthly* 67 (1891): 353–54.

35. Amos G. Warner, *American Charities* (New York, 1908), p. 21. The book, first published in 1894, became a classic in the field.

36. According to Mendel, one gene in each pair derives from each parent. When an organism received a different gene from each parent, one of the genes might become dominant, reappearing, the other, recessive, remaining submerged until such time as both parents transmitted to offspring the same gene. New species, according to Mendel's laws, did not develop by accumulated changes; the units of heredity (genes and chromosomes) remained constant, recurring in fixed patterns. For details consult Leslie C. Dunn, *A Short History of Genetics* (New York, 1965), and the readable essays by outstanding authorities on the history, nature, and subsequent reputation of Mendelianism, in the *Proceedings of the American Philosophical Society* 109 (1965): 189–248.

every conceivable trait was transmitted according to the Mendelian ratios. Some of the experiments suggested that all traits were determined by single genes acting independently with a one-to-one correspondence between genes and observed traits.[37] The new work in experimental heredity caught hold because it could be verified by controlled methods. Obviously Mendelianism, like the theory of Weismann, lent strong support to the belief in heredity as the dominant factor in human nature. Such belief found added support when, in the course of Mendelian breeding experiments, Hugo De Vries, a Dutch botanist, advanced his mutation theory. New species of plants and animals often arose, he claimed, from sudden "leaps" or mutations. Appearing at any time, these might be continued from generation to generation.

Concerned in the main with Mendelian theory, several American geneticists helped to substantiate it. No one was as influential as Charles B. Davenport in its application to the nature-nurture controversy. A Harvard-trained biologist, a leading exponent of Pearson's biostatistical methods, and an able organizer, Davenport was unquestionably a major figure in his field. Thus it was of importance when he turned from useful experiments in plant and animal breeding to human genetics, obviously less suited to laboratory techniques. As director of the Cold Spring Harbor Station for Experimental Evolution and later of the Eugenics Record Office, Davenport and his coworkers published findings on heredity in the eyes, skin, and hair color of human beings.[38] Though his controls were not always adequate and though he did not make the most effective use of the Galton-Pearson correlations and standard deviations, Davenport concluded that virtually every human trait was recessive or dominant and governed by a single gene uninfluenced by other genes or by internal physical conditions in the organism. The presence or absence of one or more genes, he held, determined not only physical traits but behavior. People, in other words, reacted to a given stimulus largely in terms of genetic antecedents. Davenport also contended that genes determined mental deficiency, criminality, shiftlessness, poverty, and even an inborn love of the sea.[39] Convinced that genes explained dif-

37. Kenneth M. Ludmerer, *Genetics and American Society* (Baltimore, 1972), pp. 13 ff.

38. Charles E. Rosenberg, "Factors in the Development of Genetics in the United States: Some Suggestions," *Journal of the History of Medicine and Allied Sciences* 22 (1967): 27–46.

39. Charles B. Davenport, "The Influence of Heredity in Human Society," *Annals of the American Academy of Political and Social Science* 24 (1909): 16, 21; and *Heredity in Relation to Genetics* (New York, 1911), chap. 8, p. 262. The best brief discussions are Charles E. Rosenberg's "Charles Benedict Davenport and the Beginnings of Human Genetics," *Bulletin of History of Medicine* 35 (1961): 266–76; and his "Charles Benedict Davenport and the Irony of American Genetics," in *No Other Gods: On Science and Social*

ferences in racial traits, Davenport offered flimsy proof for his belief that racial mixture, whether between blacks, whites, and browns in Jamaica or between ethnic populations in the United States, brought out in offspring the least-desirable traits in the "inferior" group.[40]

At first, Davenport's application of Mendelian principles, as currently understood, to human beings did not lead to criticism by his fellow geneticists. With new evidence in hand, many became skeptical of the claim that Mendelianism explained complex mental and moral as well as physical traits. By 1913 leading geneticists and cytologists in the Old World and such outstanding Americans as E. B. Wilson and Thomas Hunt Morgan had disproved the idea that simple genes determined complex traits. Davenport, however, clung to the view he had taken in 1911 when he declared that heredity was sufficiently well understood to warrant the sterilization of the unfit and to encourage the genetically fit to have large families in order to safeguard desirable human qualities.[41] Nor did he give up his position when, years later, the distinguished Harvard geneticist William Castle admonished, "We are scarcely as yet in a position to do more than make ourselves ridiculous in this matter. We are no more in a position to control eugenics than the tides of the ocean."[42]

The story of the eugenics movement which Davenport led has been well told by Mark H. Haller and Kenneth M. Ludmerer.[43] Taking advantage of the rising middle-class feeling against open immigration, zealous propagandists[44] pushed for the restriction act of 1924. Almost unchallenged, they provided Congress with what they claimed to be

---

Thought (Baltimore, 1976), chap. 4. Oscar Riddle's obituary in the *Biographical Memoirs of the National Academy of Sciences* 25 (1949): 75–110, gives a judicious estimate of Davenport's career.

40. Charles B. Davenport and Morris Steggerda, *Race Crossing in Jamaica* (Washington, D.C., 1929), pp. 468 ff.

41. Davenport, *Heredity in Relation to Genetics*, chap. 8. Theodore Roosevelt popularized Davenport's ideas. See, for example, his essay "Birth Reform, from the Positive, Not the Negative, Side," *The Works of Theodore Roosevelt*, 24 vols. (New York, 1923–26), 12:158–60.

42. Cited in Rosenberg, "Factors in the Development of Genetics in the United States," pp. 36–37.

43. Mark H. Haller, *Eugenics: Hereditarian Attitudes in American Thought* (New Brunswick, N.J., 1963); and Ludmerer, *Genetics and American Society*.

44. These included Edward A. Ross, *The Old World and the New* (New York, 1914), Madison Grant, *The Passing of the Great Race* (New York, 1916), Michael Guyer, *Being Well-Born* (Indianapolis, 1916), Lothrop Stoddard, *The Rising Tide of Color* (New York, 1920), and William McDougall, *Is America Safe for Democracy?* (New York, 1921). In addition to Haller and Ludmerer, see the excellent discussion in John Higham, *Strangers in the Land* (New Brunswick, N.J., 1955), chaps. 8 and 9.

scientific evidence of the genetic inferiority of the peoples of southern and eastern Europe. Moreover, by 1930, eugenicists, with support from some progressives and some conservatives, induced thirty states to authorize the sterilization of the feeble-minded, and in some cases, the mentally ill. In 1927 the Supreme Court, with Justice Holmes writing the opinion, upheld the constitutionality of the Virginia law.[45] The point thus made was that the eugenicists assumed that human nature could be changed, not by anything that might be done to improve environmental conditions, but through a selective breeding that eliminated the inferior and increased the superior stock. Thus the eugenics movement, which reached its high tide in the 1920s, sharpened the nature-nurture controversy by claiming scientific proof for the complete dominance of heredity.

The prestige of the hereditarian thesis also owed a good deal to a developing movement in psychology. In 1905 the early interest in psychophysical measurement of individual differences took a new turn when Binet and Simon, wanting to separate normal and abnormal children in Paris schools, worked out measures of performance on an ascending scale of difficulty. Standardized on children identified by teachers as normal, the measurements came to be called intelligence tests. Though Binet assumed the inheritance of intelligence, or "practical sense, initiative, the faculty of adapting oneself to circumstances," he recognized that home, school, and personality could also influence the measure of intelligence so understood.[46]

Such caveats as Binet had suggested were largely ignored by the hereditarian-biased American psychologists who took leading parts in

45. The Supreme Court sustained the constitutionality of sterilization of mental defectives in *Buck* v. *Bell*, 274 (U.S.) 200 (1927). A good account is that of Rudolph J. Vecoli, "Sterilization: A Progressive Measure?" *Wisconsin Magazine of History* 42 (1960): 190–202. The exaggerated claims of the eugenicists, concern over the applications of the sterilizing program, and the withdrawal of such support as distinguished geneticists had given all contributed to the transformation of the movement when Nazi racism gave a frightening example of what might happen. See, in addition to Haller and Ludmerer, S. J. Holmes, *Studies in Evolution and Genetics* (Princeton, 1925); H. S. Jennings, *Prometheus: or Biology and the Advancement of Man* (New York, 1925); and the retreat that Carl Brigham made from his early overemphasis on heredity, "Intelligence Tests of Immigrant Groups," *Psychological Review* 37 (1930): 165.

46. For a discussion of the lagging relation between the psychological study of individual differences and genetics see Jerry Hirsh, "Individual Differences in Behavior and Their Genetic Basis," in E. L. Bliss, ed., *The Roots of Behavior* (New York, 1962), pp. 3–23. In an unpublished paper, "Intelligence Testing and the Heredity-Environment Controversy, 1910–1941," Thomas P. Weinland has put the American movement in a social context.

the first decades of the testing movement. Edwin L. Thorndike, well known for his experiments at Columbia with animal learning, tested the ability of fifty pairs of twins in learning skill and concluded that heredity shaped such capacity. Using arithmetical tests, he also found that adult groups from two social classes varied in learning ability, even after both had taken a special training course. It seemed plain to him that equal opportunity did not create equal ability, and that environmental advantages counted for little in relation to inherited ability.[47] Henry Goddard, who adapted the Binet tests, concluded that heredity explained both general intelligence and feeble-mindedness, which he regarded as a Mendelian unit character.[48] At Stanford, Lewis Terman, using a school population of advantaged children, standardized the Binet test for given age levels. In so doing he adjusted the difficulty of the question to the "right" number of children who passed in each age group, the number being determined by the Gaussian curve. Unaware of his circular reasoning and of the culture-bound character of his sample, he declared that "the results of five separate and distinct lines of inquiry based on the Stanford data agree in supporting the conclusion that the children of successful and cultured parents test higher than children from wretched and ignorant homes for the simple reason that their heredity is better."[49] Terman further regarded the IQ as stable and as incapable of improvement by environmental advantages.[50]

Sweeping claims were made for the reliability of the measurements, particularly after leading psychologists supervised the testing of Army recruits in World War I. The tests mainly measured competence in the use of the English language and familiarity with American middle-class environment. Yet despite these and other limitations, authorities interpreted the results as proof of the inborn inferiority of both Negroes and immigrants from southern and eastern Europe.[51] In the face of

47. E. L. Thorndike, *Educational Psychology*, 3 vols. (New York, 1914), 3:247–51; and "Eugenics: with Special Reference to Intellect and Character," *Popular Science Monthly* 83 (1913): 131.

48. Henry H. Goddard, *Feeble-Mindedness: Its Causes and Consequences* (New York, 1914).

49. Lewis M. Terman, *The Measurement of Intelligence* (Boston, 1916), p. 115. I am indebted to the papers by Cravens and Weinland, already cited, and to Joseph Peterson, *Early Conceptions and Tests of Intelligence* (Yonkers, N.Y., 1925), and Frank N. Freeman, *Mental Tests: Their History, Principles and Applications*, rev. ed. (Boston, 1939).

50. Terman's investigation of one thousand gifted California children led him, again, to conclude that heredity is the dominant factor in achievement—in short, that his work gave a good deal of support to Galton's theory of the hereditary nature of genius. Lewis Terman, *Genetic Studies of Genius*, 5 vols. (Palo Alto, Calif., 1925–59), 1:111.

51. Robert M. Yerkes, ed., *Psychological Examining in the United States Army: Memoirs of the National Academy of Sciences* 15 (Washington, D.C., 1921), chap. 6; Carl Brigham, *A Study of American Intelligence* (Princeton, 1923), sections 8–10, pp. 197 ff.

telling criticisms of the tests and the interpretations given them,[52] Terman linked the doubters with those who repudiated the efficacy of vaccination for smallpox. Professor McDougall lumped them with religious fundamentalists. Well-qualified psychologists nevertheless increasingly questioned the possibility of measuring precisely the exact role of heredity and training in mental and performance tests. Still, as late as 1940, Thorndike claimed that intelligence could be allocated, roughly, to genes in the proportion of 80 percent, to training in the proportion of 17 percent. He admitted that by 3 percent, accident might play a role.[53]

The near-dominance of the hereditarian theory in the first two decades of the twentieth century, buttressed as it seemed to be by genetics and by the intelligence test movement, did not silence the environmentalists. American faith in democracy had always leaned heavily on the assumed importance of equal environmental opportunities. If the concept of environmentalism be broadly understood, its adherents, though making some concessions to heredity, included such renowned authorities in the older disciplines as Frederick Jackson Turner and Ellsworth Huntington. Overbold in his generalizations about the influence of climatic energy and the selective role of the weather, and tending increasingly to emphasize heredity, Huntington nevertheless put environmental theory on a new footing. He did this by simply viewing heredity as the total result of environmental experience from the most remote geological age, and by anticipating some of the contentions of later ecologists.[54]

Critics of hereditarianism in related social disciplines also made impressive points. "The qualities and virtues the individual strives to attain, or the vices he attempts to avoid," wrote Simon N. Patten, a seminal thinker at the University of Pennsylvania, "are determined by

52. For examples: J. McKeen Cattell, "The Interpretation of Intelligence Tests," *Scientific Monthly* 18 (1924): 508–16; Frank N. Freeman, "A Referendum of Psychologists," *Century* 107 (1923): 237–47; Walter Lippmann, "The Reliability of Intelligence Tests," *New Republic* 32 (1922): 275; and "The Mystery of the 'A' Men," *New Republic* 32 (1922): 246. Franz Samelson, in a recent study, has contrasted the rather equivocal contributions of the program to the fighting efficiency of the Army and to the increase of scientific knowledge with the prestige the participation of psychologists in the war effort gave to the still somewhat struggling discipline. Samelson, "World War I Intelligence Testing and the Development of Psychology," *Journal of the History of the Behavioral Sciences* 13 (1977): 274–82.

53. E. L. Thorndike, *Human Nature and the Social Order* (New York, 1940), p. 320.

54. Ellsworth Huntington, *The Character of Races as Influenced by Physical Environment, Natural Selection and Historical Development* (New York, 1924), and *Season of Birth: Its Relation to Human Abilities* (New York, 1938).

the environment, and the values of any society are formulators of the character of man."[55] In like manner Herbert A. Miller, a student of psychology and sociology at Yale and Chicago and a socialist, argued that no germ plasm was needed to explain "the differences between 'the first families of Virginia' and the poor white trash." That was just what such environmental factors as mores, social classes, and psychological barriers made perfectly understandable.[56] The innovating, empirical investigations of the Chicago urban sociologists drew attention to the sudden exposure of rural peoples to complex, unfamiliar city surroundings, an exposure that explained much of the deviant behavior of immigrants that hereditarians laid at the door of innate "racial" differences.[57] In the not altogether unrelated field of ethnography Franz Boas, whom we have seen playing a notable part in the development of the culture concept, left little doubt about the role of a particular culture in explaining the level and character of the achievements of those molded by it. In showing that many traditional theories of "race" reduced culture to biology, Boas and his pupils went far toward weakening the props of a narrowly hereditarian explanation of race differences.[58]

Several factors accounted for the confusion, bitterness, and inconclusiveness of the great debate about nature and nurture. The problems were interdisciplinary and multidisciplinary, but most of the scientists involved were truly competent in only one discipline. Then, too, many partisans on each side made extreme claims. Too many insisted on an absolute dichotomy: heredity *or* environment. Few recognized the unconscious influence of a contestant's social and economic bias on his findings.[59] Few in either camp at first recognized

55. Simon N. Patten, "The Laws of Environmental Influence," *Popular Science Monthly* 79 (1911): 397–402. Daniel M. Fox, in *The Discovery of Abundance: Simon N. Patten and the Transformation of Social Theory* (Ithaca, 1967), gives a good account of Patten's social thinking.

56. Herbert A. Miller, "The Psychological Limits of Eugenics," *Popular Science Monthly* 84 (1914): 394.

57. Of special note was W. I. Thomas and Florian Znaniecki, *The Polish Peasant in Europe and America*, 2 vols. (New York, 1918–20). See also Robert E. Park and Herbert A. Miller, *Old World Traits Transplanted* (New York, 1921).

58. Boas's statements included those in such scholarly essays as *Race, Language, and Culture* (New York, 1940), pp. 76–81; and such popular articles as "The Problem of the American Negro," *Yale Review* 10 (1921): 384–95; "The Question of Racial Purity," *American Mercury* 3 (1924): 163–69; and "What is Race?" *The Nation* 120 (1925): 89–91.

59. Nicholas Pastore, *The Nature-Nurture Controversy* (New York, 1949), pp. 176–82. Professor Hamilton Cravens has suggested the need of qualifying Pastore's emphasis on the social "conservatism" of some hereditarians. He has found, for example, evidence in the papers of Yerkes and Terman of a "liberal" position on some public issues.

the inadequacy of the methods they used. Even more to the point, few understood that the issue actually involved many issues.

This aspect of the confusion and indeterminacy of the controversy was related to the common failure to define precisely the meaning of the terms *heredity* and *environment*. Hereditarians did not always use the crucial word *intelligence* with precision. Sometimes they identified it with achievement or adjustment, sometimes with a capacity to manipulate concepts and intellectual tools. On the other side, many also failed to appreciate the complex meanings of environment. Nor did they always see the difficulties involved in efforts to hold constant the variables in both the physical and social environments that they tried to measure. It took some time to sense the need for a shift from the concept of environment to that of social process. It also required much trial and error to discover that the more carefully heredity and environment were defined and broken into their constituent components, the more clear it became that what had been thought of as two discrete factors were inextricably interwoven. Thus a good deal of time passed before it became evident that environment as a whole and heredity as a whole could not be properly compared. Only gradually did it become clear that the relations between the two resembled those between the base and the altitude of a triangle, that the two factors were equally necessary.

All this was concretely illustrated by the way in which research in genetics only slowly undermined the misleading view that heredity operated independently as an inexorable force without reference to environment. The famous fruit-fly experiments of Thomas Hunt Morgan and his students showed that only a specific combination of genes under specific conditions of humidity and temperature produced abnormalities, and equally significant, that any one genetic factor operated differently under varied environmental conditions. Heredity and environment, while distinct factors, constantly interacted in the development of individuals and species. It will also be recalled that Morgan's work suggested that individual determiners for each trait did not exist in the germ plasm. All this weakened the strictly hereditarian interpretations of Mendelian laws that early geneticists fostered.[60]

Before considering further these general factors and the continuing advance of exact knowledge in the nature-nurture controversy, let us see

60. Thomas H. Morgan, *Evolution and Genetics* (Princeton, 1915; rev. ed., 1925); *The Scientific Basis of Evolution* (New York, 1922), chaps. 3, 9, and 10. Garland E. Allen's *Thomas Hunt Morgan: The Man and His Science* (Princeton, 1978) discusses Morgan's work clearly and authoritatively (chaps. 4–7).

how the conflict over heredity and environment affected positions taken on public issues, and how these reflected attitudes toward human nature.

Broadly speaking, leading intellectuals in the first decade and a half of the twentieth century looked on war as an inevitable outcome of the fact that human nature does not and cannot change. In 1903 William Graham Sumner saw no reason to believe that war could be abolished. "Since evil passions are a part of human nature and are in all societies all the time, a . . . war in the future will be the clash of policies of national vanity and selfishness when they cross each other's path."[61] Leading psychologists and biologists agreed. In his now famous "Moral Equivalent for War" essay[62] William James developed the idea that "a millenium of peace could not breed the fighting disposition out of our bone and marrow." If, as he thought, man's nature in this respect could not be changed, he nevertheless believed that the incidence of war might be reduced by fostering rival excitements and by devising new outlets for heroic energy similar, as so many have noted, to the modern Peace Corps. James's one-time pupil G. Stanley Hall identified the fighting instinct as a secondary sexual trait that in good part matured in adolescence. The instinct could be checked only at the risk of emotional disturbance. Physical and moral pedagogy might at the most temper and direct it. By 1915 Hall viewed war, at best, as a reversion to barbarism, however much it might encourage "togetherness" within the fighting group.[63]

When such authorities on the nature of man regarded war as a function of an unchanging human nature, it was no wonder that military figures like Hudson Maxim, General J. G. Harboard, and General J. R. Storey believed that civilization had not changed a human nature that made war inevitable.

In this discussion Hiram Martin Chittenden, a West Point-trained military engineer, a student of the topography of the Great West, and a historian of the fur trade, cleared up several points. Excluding from his analysis the evolutionary process, all of prehistory, anatomical changes

61. William Graham Sumner, *War and Other Essays* (New Haven, 1911), pp. 35–36.
62. William James, *Memories and Studies* (New York, 1911), pp. 299–305.
63. G. Stanley Hall, *Adolescence . . .* , 2 vols. (New York, 1904), 1:211 ff.; 2:367–68; "Some Educational Values of War," *Pedagogical Seminary* 25 (1918): 303–7; and "Practical Relations between Psychology and War," address before the American Psychological Association, *Journal of Applied Psychology* 1 (1917): 9–16. The distinguished psychopathologist Dr. Frederic Lyman Wells lent support to Hall's thesis by holding that the instinctive bases of pacifism were self-abasement, which inhibited the supreme combatic effort that war demands, and the pleasure-seeking instincts that conflicted with and blocked the instincts involving self-sacrifice for the group. "Instinctive Basis of Pacifism," *Atlantic Monthly* 118 (1916): 44–46.

as in the cephalic index, and everything embraced in the words *education* and *environment*, Chittenden concluded that human nature, or the innate passions of envy, hatred, pugnacity, love, and generosity, remained just as they were when St. Paul had dissected the workings of the human heart. But Chittenden held that if human nature as evidenced in an individual did not change, civilization, or the fund of human experience, had changed and could hold in check the cruelty, revenge, hatred, and corruption that lurked in man's inner depths. Since few doubted the waste and general ineffectiveness of war, he could believe in the restraining potentialities of civilization. These might include the development of cooperation between countries, the administration of justice among nations by a world agency, and the moral sanction for the laws governing the earth's peoples in their relation to each other.[64]

The new mechanistic biology, which projected man as an adaptive mechanism, reenforced Chittenden's argument that while the fighting response was functional to a changeless human nature, war might still be eliminated. Dr. George W. Crile, distinguished in both experimental and clinical medicine, held that man could so change the stimuli in his environment, to which the "kinetic system" reacted, that his responses would make peaceful living as natural and inevitable as fighting had been.[65]

During World War I, when Crile took his stand, the Russian Revolution startled the world. Such an event might be expected to test the arguments of those who had long held that socialism and human nature were incompatible and those who insisted that only under communism could the best potentialities of man's native endowment be realized.[66]

Some of the relatively few Americans who went to the Soviet Union in the 1920s spoke to the question.[67] John Dewey probed it with some

64. Hiram Martin Chittenden, "Does Human Nature Change?" *Atlantic Monthly* 109 (1912): 777–82; and *War or Peace* (Chicago, 1911), pp. 172, 196–97, 237–39.

65. George W. Crile, *A Mechanistic View of War and Peace* (New York, 1915). Crile had earlier developed many of the ideas in this book. Also relevant is the work of Jacques Loeb on tropisms and the place he found for ethical values. See Jacques Loeb, *The Mechanistic Conception of Life*, ed. Donald Fleming (Cambridge, Mass., 1964).

66. See, for example, Hugo Munsterberg, *Psychology and Social Sanity* (New York, 1915), pp. 73 ff.

67. Thomas Dickinson, who served with Hoover's relief mission in Russia, contended that socialism did not change human nature. "Russia and the Red Shadow," *New York Herald Tribune* (April 3–17, 1922). See also "American Educators in Russia," in *School and Society* 27 (1928): 779. Also the foreword of Adolph Meyer, a leading psychiatrist who worked for several years in the 1920s in medical and psychological laboratories in the USSR, in A. R. Luria, *The Nature of Human Conflicts; or Emotion, Conflict and Will, an Objective Study of Disorganization and Control of Human Behaviour* (New York, 1932), trans. Dr. W. Horsley Gantt.

perception. For him the revolution involved a "release of human powers on such an unprecedented scale" that the outcome of the experiment mattered less than the "liberation of a people to consciousness of themselves as a determining factor in the shaping of their ultimate fate."[68] The implications of the revolution for human nature became more explicit in the 1930s. In growing numbers psychiatrists, educators, and social scientists visited the USSR and brought back both favorable and critical impressions of the effort to socialize motives and behavior. In any case, the great depression at home raised in thoughtful minds the pros and cons for human nature of drastic modifications of the "free enterprise" system.[69] In the end, the discussion stimulated by the war, the Russian Revolution, and the Depression and New Deal by no means put the issue of immutability or plasticity of human nature to rest.

Meantime, the postwar years brought a new turn in the nature-nurture controversy. Several events and circumstances seemed to favor the hereditarian view of human nature, or at least to throw doubt on the likelihood that environmental factors could be counted on for a brighter future. In seeming to confirm the hereditarian view of the inferiority of certain races and classes, the Army Testing Program stimulated similar interpretations of new tests. Those undertaken at the University of Virginia and Columbia were, though culture-bound, often read as support for the innate inferiority of the Negro race.[70] Popular hysteria, fanned during the war by anti-German propaganda, was channeled into Ku Klux Klan fanaticism. Bitter feelings and violence in labor strife suggested deep-rooted irrational drives in human beings. Freud, in emphasizing ineradicable instincts, seemed to undermine any ex-

68. John Dewey, *Impressions of Soviet Russia and the Revolutionary World: Mexico—China—Turkey* (New York, 1929), pp. 8, 15, 58–59, 113.

69. Examples include E. C. Lindeman, "Is Human Nature Changing in Russia?" *New Republic* 74 (1933): 95–98; Frankwoode E. Williams, M.D., "Can Russia Change Human Nature?" *Survey Graphic* 22 (1933): 137–42; Dr. Ross A. McFarland, "Psychological Research in Soviet Russia," *Scientific Monthly* 40 (1935): 177 ff.; C. Dreher, "Collectivism and Human Nature," *Harper's Magazine* 169 (1934): 489–91; Herbert Hoover, *Addresses upon the American Road 1933–1938* (New York, 1939), pp. 55 ff.; and Max Eastman, "Socialism Doesn't Jibe with Human Nature," *Reader's Digest* 38 (1941): 41–49. See also Arnold Peterson, *Socialism and Human Nature* (New York, 1945); Vernon Venable, *Human Nature: The Marxist View* (New York, 1947); and Irving Fetscher, "Karl Marx on Human Nature," *Social Research* 40 (1973): 443–67.

70. George O. Ferguson, *The Psychology of the Negro: An Experimental Study* (New York, 1916), pp. 123 ff.; I. A. Newby, *Jim Crow's Defense: Anti-Negro Thought in America, 1900–1930* (Baton Rouge, 1970), pp. 41–42; and Morris S. Viteles, "The Mental Status of the Negro," *The Annals of the American Academy* 140 (1928): 166–67.

pectation of a change in human nature. In depicting the recent war, leading American novelists seldom celebrated the better aspects of men's conduct, let alone heroism. On the contrary, the portrait of man in war, if not one of hopeless boredom and brutality, hardly flattered human nature. In short, much that happened in the postwar years darkened hopes for the reconstruction of human nature through the environment.

Yet fatalistic dogmatism invited reaction; a quite different view of human nature insisted on a hearing. By a striking coincidence several books were published in 1921 and 1922 that made it henceforth hard to talk about the nature-nurture controversy in the old terms.

In *Human Nature and Conduct* John Dewey brought out the implications of the functional psychology he had helped launch. By holding that mind should be regarded not as an entity distinct from the body but rather as the totality of ways in which an organism adapted to and modified the environment, Dewey offered a new setting for the discussion. In this readable book he came to grips with the ambiguous term *human nature:* man's original or "native human nature supplies the raw materials but custom furnishes the machinery and the designs." Thus we might never know the true character of human nature beyond realizing that man's potentialities at birth were an indispensable ingredient in what he became and in what he might become. Since this original equipment was a bundle of potentialities, it was the culture that allowed some to find expression and others to be stunted. The kinds of behavior observed resulted largely from the way in which customs or social habits molded the potentialities. Behavior differed, as anthropologists had shown, in different cultures. Thus if the term human nature was used at all, Dewey insisted, it must be spoken of as a product of social experience. The limits and potentialities of plastic impulses could be tested only in social experience.[71]

Both reformers and conservatives, Dewey went on, had staked their case on the very factor that weakened their conclusions. "The radical reformer rests his contention in behalf of easy and rapid change upon the psychology of habits, of institutions in shaping raw nature, and the conservative grounds his counter-assertion upon the psychology of instincts." Actually, however, custom was the least susceptible to change, while so-called instincts lent themselves readily to modification through use and educative guidance.[72]

After noting that Aristotle had grounded slavery in human nature and that many now claimed the same sanction for the prevailing economic order, Dewey turned to war as an institution, "War would not be possible," he wrote, "without anger, pugnacity, rivalry, self-display and

71. John Dewey, *Human Nature and Conduct* (New York, 1922), p. 110.
72. Dewey, *Human Nature and Conduct*, p. 107.

such like native tendencies. . . ." But to fancy that these impulses must "eventuate in war is as if a savage were to believe that because he uses fibers having fixed natural properties in order to weave baskets, therefore his immemorial tribal patterns are also natural necessities and immutable forms."[73] Since pugnacity and fear were no more native to human nature than pity and sympathy, institutional forms of living could express either or both in greater or less degree as man used his intelligence or adaptive ability to reconstruct his experience and to act in accord with these redirected habits and institutional patterns.

No longer enjoying the prestige in his profession he once had, William McDougall could still muster his force in attacking Dewey. He claimed that his opponent's argument rested on "vague generalities" and that confusion resulted from his failure to reconcile the contradictions associated with his shift from defending to minimizing instincts. In discussing motives, McDougall thought that Dewey did not distinguish the quality of the emotional experiences that accompanied impulse actions or that evoked impulses. In short, Dewey's loose use of the term *habit* led him both to cover all mental structure built up through individual experience and to confound sentiments with simple motor habits.[74]

Feeling, perhaps, that the issue was still at sea, Dewey resumed the discussion. Asking, in 1938, "Does Human Nature Change?" he answered that if human nature meant the present residue of what civilization had done with man's raw potentialities, then human nature had changed, and could be further changed. "The assertion that a proposed change is impossible because of the fixed constitution of human nature diverts attention from the question of whether or not a change is desirable and from the other question of how it shall be brought about."[75]

Three other books by well-known scholars supported the general position taken in *Human Nature and Conduct*. Charles H. Cooley, who, we may recall, had in 1892 set forth a social interpretation of per-

73. *Human Nature and Conduct*, p. 110. My discussion is largely a paraphrase of Dewey. For a pungent use of his arguments see Arthur Bullard, "Arms and the Instincts," *Harper's Monthly Magazine* 144 (1922): 167–74. The sympathetic review of C. E. Ayres (*Journal of Philosophy* 19 [1922]: 469–75) elaborated and refined some of Dewey's arguments. Morris R. Cohen in his review (*American Review* 1 [1923]: 360–64), while generally sympathetic, felt that Dewey's natural zeal led him to make too sharp an antithesis "between the absence of any science of human nature in the past (to which all the ills of other worldliness are attributed) and contemporary achievement . . ." (p. 361). In "Dewey's Theory of Human Nature" (*Psychiatry* 12 [1949]: 77–85) Benjamin Wolstein related his ideas about human nature to those of Peirce, Mead, and other writers.

74. William McDougall, "Can Sociology and Social Psychology Dispense with Instincts?" *American Journal of Sociology* 29 (1924): 657–66.

75. John Dewey, "Does Human Nature Change?" *The Rotarian* 3 (1938): 59.

sonality, now brought out a revised edition of *Human Nature and the Social Order*. In a new chapter on heredity and instinct, Cooley wrote that if by human nature one meant the nature developed in intimate contacts with primary group life, it must be regarded as decidedly changeable. "We can make it work in about any way, if we understand it, as a clever mechanic can mould to his will the universal laws of man and motion."[76] In the same year William F. Ogburn, a member of the group of influential sociologists at the University of Chicago, saw through the press *Social Change with Respect to Culture and Original Nature*. This argued that the same human nature might seem very different in two dissimilar cultures and thus could change with the cultures: indeed, if human nature were defined in cultural terms, it could change, thanks to higher education, even in a lifetime.[77] James Harvey Robinson's *The Mind in the Making* optimistically lent support to all this by a striking if oversimplified view of the intellectual history of the Western world. To be sure, Carl Becker questioned his thesis by wondering just how the mind could free itself from the very conditions that had made it what it was, just how, in other words, an accumulation could throw itself on the scrap pile.[78] Finally, Vernon Kellogg, the well-known Stanford biologist, who had often sided with the hereditarians, also published his *Human Life as the Biologist Sees It* (1922). Distinguishing between the unchangeable biological heritage and the social heritage, Kellogg specifically applied this to the issue of war and human nature. The biological heritage, he insisted, included both combative instincts and impulses, and as Kropotkin had shown, impulses toward mutual aid. The latter favored man, unless he chose to be ruled by the combative components in his biological heritage. Kellogg summed the matter up as he saw it: "The protagonists of inevitable war declare that human nature does not change. The biologist declares that human nature does change both by virtue of the influence of strictly biological factors and especially, more rapidly, by reason of the influence of social inheritance."[79]

The fact that Dewey's image of man found such support did not settle the nature-nurture issue. That position, after all, was largely though not

76. Charles H. Cooley, *Human Nature and the Social Order* (New York, 1922), pp. 31–34.

77. William F. Ogburn, *Social Change, with Respect to Culture and Original Nature* (New York, 1922), pp. 297 ff.

78. James Harvey Robinson, *The Mind in the Making* (New York, 1921); Carl Becker's review in *The New Republic* 30 (1922): 175.

79. Vernon Kellogg, *Human Life as the Biologist Sees It* (New York, 1922), pp. 49 ff., 62. Kellogg's position resembled that of President David Starr Jordan of Stanford, who had long opposed war on biological grounds. For Jordan's views see Merle Curti, *War or Peace: The American Struggle* (Boston, 1959), pp. 213–14, 151–52, 255.

entirely based on inference and analysis rather than on experimental evidence. Nor did the seemingly conclusive summary of the biological and psychological literature that Leonard Carmichael made in 1925 end the discussion. Existing research and analysis, he wrote, indicated that after the fertilized egg had once begun to develop, no distinction could be explicitly made at any given moment between inherited and acquired behavior. The so-called hereditary factors, he went on, could only be acquired in response to an environment, and the so-called acquired factors could only be come by through a modification of an already existing structure, which in the last analysis was hereditary.[80]

Such a view fitted into the conceptual framework of the new "synthetic" theory of evolution, which assumed the interaction between heredity and environment and recognized the distinction between different levels of biological and cultural evolution.[81]

In the decades ahead, movements of thought, events, and achievements in science and other disciplines raised questions related to the debate over the plasticity or immutability of human nature. The implications of the relativity theory were a case in point. George Boas, a Johns Hopkins philosopher, noted that one of the most impressive evidences for the contention that human nature had changed was the revolution in the character of man's thinking. Statistical logic had largely replaced that of Aristotle and his successors. The latter, Boas observed, conceived of human qualities such as courage and justice as fixed, changeless, and absolute, while the former ranked measurable differences according to the degree of difference and thus established a type of thinking characterized in terms of probability.[82]

But traditional ideas persisted. Within the Church's tradition, Catholic writers held to an Aristotelian-Thomistic view of the immutability of human nature.[83] The New Humanists, finding continuity

80. Leonard Carmichael, "Heredity and Environment: Are They Antithetical?" *Journal of Abnormal and Social Psychology* 20 (1925): 245 ff. See also the statement from his autobiography in Carl Murchison, ed., *A History of Psychology in Autobiography* (New York, 1967), 5:34.

81. R. A. Fisher, *The Genetical Theory of Natural Selection* (Oxford, 1930); Julian Huxley, *Evolution: The Modern Synthesis* (New York, 1942); T. Dobzhansky and M. F. Montagu, "Natural Selection and the Mental Capacities of Mankind," *Science* 105 (1947): 587–90; William Provine, *Origins of Theoretical Population Genetics* (Chicago, 1971), chaps. 4 and 5; and G. E. Allen, *Life Sciences in the Twentieth Century* (New York, 1975), chap. 5.

82. George Boas, "From Truth to Relativity," *Harper's Magazine* 104 (1927): 516–22.

83. C. W. Thompson, "Unimportant Revolution," *Catholic World* 140 (1935): 392–97; Rudolf Allers in *Freedom and Authority in Our Time* (New York, 1953), pp. 550–70; and Gordon George, "Margaret Mead and Human Nature," *America* 93 (1955): 152–54.

in cultural tastes and ethical values over time, and in the East as well as the West, also insisted on the immutability of human nature.[84] In the same key Robert M. Hutchins, president of the University of Chicago, wrote that "human nature is, always has been, and always will be the same everywhere."[85] In defending the validity of a timeless human nature, an esteemed man of letters, Joseph Wood Krutch, took note of an inconsistency on the part of relativists. Many of those who had rejected the idea of an immutable human nature regarded Nazi genocide, including irreverence for the dead, as "repugnant not merely to 'prevalent ideas of right and wrong' but to the nature of man himself. Perhaps," he went on, "the fundamental horror of Nazism may be just that it follows further than we have yet followed the implications of the relativism we profess without yet having so consistently implemented them."[86] Though in discussions of war the majority of psychologists rejected the idea that human nature made it inevitable,[87] a leading historian of American foreign relations could write in 1951, "No institution is so deeply ingrained in human nature as war, and the attempt to flee from this fact is no solution to an age-old problem."[88] Without reference to war, a few anthropologists began to argue, in opposition to the long-accepted view in their profession, for the usefulness of the concept of a universal, timeless human nature. The idea found its validity in man's culture-making and culture-transmitting capacities and perhaps his basic common values, but certainly in the observed fact that similarities among all known culture groups surpassed differences.[89]

Such humanistic views of the immutability of man's nature, with the implied importance of some kind of heredity, were overshadowed by the

84. For example, Irving Babbitt, *Democracy and Leadership* (Boston, 1924). J. David Hoeveller, Jr.'s *The New Humanism: A Concept of Modern America, 1900–1940* (Charlottesville, Va., 1977) relates the "New Humanists" to other movements of thought and to the social situation at the time the movement enjoyed its widest hearing.

85. Robert M. Hutchins, "Toward a Durable Society," *Fortune* 27 (1943): 201.

86. Joseph Wood Krutch, *Human Nature and the Human Condition* (New York, 1953), p. 178. At about this time Walter Lippmann also subscribed to a similar view. See Lippmann's *An Inquiry into the Principles of a Good Society* (Boston, 1937), pp. 376–89; and *Essays in the Public Philosophy* (Boston, 1955).

87. John M. Fletcher, "The Verdict of Psychologists on War Instincts," *Scientific Monthly* 35 (1932): 142–45; "Human Nature and Enduring Peace," *Third Yearbook of the Society for the Psychological Study of Social Issues*, ed. Gardner Murphy (Boston, 1945).

88. Dexter Perkins, "American Wars and Critical Historians," *Yale Review* 40 (1951): 695.

89. For discussions of this point see David Bidney, "Human Nature and the Cultural Process," *American Anthropologist*, n.s. 49 (1947): 375–99; and *Theoretical Anthropology*

continuing experimental approach to the nature-nurture issue. For some time the psychologists held the field. At Stanford, Iowa, Minnesota, Chicago, and other centers, investigations of fraternal and identical twins reared by natural and foster parents in varying environments led to controversial and indeterminate results. This was also true when the test scores of children were related to those of natural and foster parents. Nor did all authorities retreat from their conviction about the priority of heredity when studies of preschool children in two groups indicated that superior advantages resulted in an improvement in test scores.[90]

Several factors explained differences in the interpretation of data. It was always possible, and often true, to maintain that neither the preschool children nor identical twins reared together or apart by natural or by foster parents were representative of the total population of their age group. Conflicting views about what the tests proved also resulted from the varied meanings attached to the term *intelligence*. Those who identified it with achievement could rightly claim that environmental influences counted for a great deal. On the other hand, those who thought of intelligence as the quality of mind that set limits to "achievement" could rightly claim support from the experimental evidence.[91] It also was clear that environmental conditions were too shifting, varied, and complex to be adequately measured.

Though the experiments and the conflicting interpretations of the data did not resolve the basic issue, the work did have positive effects. Psychologists increasingly agreed that heredity set limits to what an individual could achieve but that environmental conditions often worked against the realization of potential ability. In 1954 John Fuller observed that the nature-nurture issue excited less bitterness than it had

---

(New York, 1950), pp. 5–6, 112–12, 150 ff., 395 ff.; W. W. Howells, "Universality and Variation in Human Nature," *Yearbook of Anthropology* 1 (1955): 227 ff.; Melford Spiro, "Human Nature in Its Psychological Dimensions," *American Anthropologist*, n.s. 56 (1954): 19–30; Margaret Park Redfield, ed., *Human Nature and the Study of Society*, 2 vols. (Chicago, 1964), 1:489–90 and passim; and for a critical view, Clifford Geertz, *The Interpretation of Culture* (New York, 1973), chap. 2.

90. In addition to the *Yearbooks of the National Association for the Study of Education*, representative titles include T. L. Kelley, *Crossroads in the Mind of Man: A Study of Differentiable Mental Abilities* (Stanford, 1928); S. J. Holmes, "Nature versus Nurture in the Development of the Mind," *Scientific Monthly* 31 (1930): 245 ff.; H. S. Jennings, *The Biological Basis of Human Nature* (New York, 1930); F. N. Freeman, *Mental Tests: Their History, Principles, and Application*, 2d ed. (Boston, 1939); R. S. Woodworth, "Heredity and Environment: A Critical Survey of Recently Published Material on Twins and Foster Children," *Social Science Research Council Bulletin* no. 47 (New York, 1941); and George D. Stoddard, *The Meaning of Intelligence* (New York, 1943).

91. Florence Goodenough's summation in *Intelligence: Its Nature and Nurture*, National Society for the Study of Education, Yearbook no. 39 (Bloomington, Ill., 1940), p. 451.

two decades earlier. "Insofar as it still exists," he went on, "it will be resolved by careful longitudinal studies at the genetic, psychological and physiological levels and by new theoretical formulations rather than by any further gathering and analyzing of statistics."[92]

Several factors explained the later resurgence of interest in the roles of nature and nurture. The extraordinary developments in genetics included the uncovering of the structure of deoxyribonucleic acid (DNA). Its molecules seemingly contained the blueprints governing the myriad manifestations of life's architecture, the alteration of genes through radioactivity, and the chemical synthesis of copying genes. In short, the genetic factor appeared to be less fixed and determined than many assumed. Laymen understandably expressed anxiety over the power such discoveries might give scientists, power to control heredity and the social composition and direction of society itself.[93] The Nobel laureate Theodosius Dobzhansky, writing in 1964, held that the day was still far off when genetic chemists could at will change the "ladder" which encoded genetic instructions. Yet he warned of the prospect of genetic twilight if society permitted the weak and deformed to propagate and of moral twilight if it allowed these unfortunates to suffer or die when help was within reach. Meantime the best course might be the wisest possible counseling that carefully avoided the eugenicists' misuse of genetics.[94]

No comparable breakthrough took place in psychology. But greater precision and clarity marked much of the new work. Investigators defined the concept of intelligence more carefully, drawing a distinction between fluid intelligence (a general "brightness" independent of education and experience) and crystallized intelligence (acquired knowledge and intellectual skills).[95] In devising new tests, psychologists aimed to make them culture and status fair. Many felt that the increasing use of multiple abstract variance analysis (MAVA) insured reliable measurements of the relative strength of innate and acquired factors in specific behavior.[96]

Interest in the nature of human nature has often increased in times of

92. John Fuller, *Nature and Nurture: A Modern Synthesis* (Garden City, N.Y., 1954), p. 32.

93. For examples: *New York Times*, September 12, 1963; S. E. Luria, "Modern Biology: A Terrifying Power," *The Nation* 209 (1969): 406–9.

94. Theodosius Dobzhansky, *Heredity and the Nature of Man* (New York, 1963), pp. 161–63; and *Genetic Diversity and Human Equality* (New York, 1973), pp. 112 ff.

95. Raymond Catell, "The Structure of Intelligence in Relation to the Nature-Nurture Controversy," in Robert Cancro, ed., *Intelligence: Genetic and Environmental Influences* (New York, 1971), pp. 3–30.

96. Jane Loevinger, "On the Proportional Contributions of Differences in Nature and Nurture to Differences in Intelligence," *Psychological Bulletin* 40 (1943): 205–6; L. Erlenmeyer-Kimling and L. F. Jarvik, "Genetics and Intelligence: A Review," *Science* 142 (1963): 1477–79; and Edward W. Gordon, "Methodological Problems and Pseudo-Issues in the Nature-Nurture Controversy," in Cancro, ed., *Intelligence*, p. 240.

marked social malaise and tension. Thus the racial revolution of the 1950s and 1960s stimulated a renewed interest in the psychology of racial differences within the context of the whole question of nature versus nurture. In preparing briefs for the 1954 Supreme Court case of *Brown* v. *The Board of Education of Topeka*, psychologists presented evidence for the claim that segregation of school children by race had deleteriously affected both the learning achievements and the personalities of the blacks. Prosegregationists scoffed at such testimony. They argued that races, considered as peoples with gene pools differing in statistically significant ways from those of other peoples, varied in innate endowment, including intelligence. They argued further that many clinical studies showed that the personalities of black children suffered far more from integrated school experience than from segregation.[97]

That the old controversy about nature and nurture had by no means been shelved was clear from the heated and often bitter debate provoked by a long article in the *Harvard Educational Review* in 1969 entitled "How Much Can We Boost IQ and Scholastic Achievement?" The author, Arthur R. Jensen, a leading educational psychologist at Berkeley, showed competence in multiple abstract variance analysis but offered little new experimental evidence. He pointed out that in averaging all the results of the twin studies, two authorities had found that in the variance of measured intelligence heredity counted four times as much as environment.[98] Jensen concluded that in American white populations inheritance must therefore be credited for 80 percent of IQ scores. Though admitting that intelligence tests often measured performance in tasks culturally defined by Western civilization, he suggested that the ability to perform such tasks might itself be largely if not altogether genetic. Apparently attaching little importance to the fact that many children had been known to show an improvement in IQ scores from childhood to adulthood, he made much of the evidence for the stability of the IQ, which he felt to be largely fixed by the age of eight. To be sure,

97. *Brown* v. *the Board of Education of Topeka*, 347 (U.S.) 483 (1954); I. A. Newby, *Jim Crow's Defense* (Baton Rouge, 1965), pp. 41 ff.; and *Challenge to the Court: Social Scientists and Defense of Segregation* (Baton Rouge, 1969), chap. 6. See also the volume edited by Newby, *The Development of Segregationist Thought* (Homewood, Ill., 1968), for some of the appropriate historical background, and especially, Richard Kluger's detailed and readable *Simple Justice* (New York, 1976).

98. Arthur R. Jensen, "How Much Can We Boost IQ and Scholastic Achievement?" *Harvard Educational Review* 39 (1969): 48. In commenting on the claim of critics that similar values could just as well be expected on the basis of the degrees of environment shared, Steven G. Vandenberg wrote, "The only serious difficulties for the environmental point of view are presented by the *absence* of large differences between the median value for siblings and one-egg twins reared apart versus together and the *presence* of a difference of about 0.25 between the parent-child and foster-parent-child correlation." Cancro, ed., *Intelligence*, p. 186.

Jensen granted that environmental factors, working at the prenatal level and at that of later deprivation, might have harmful effects in keeping a child from performing up to his genetic potential.

Since individual IQ differences within the white population as a whole could be largely attributed to heredity, one might, Jensen went on, reasonably assume that the average differences between social-class groups and between racial groups were apt to reflect genetic differences. On the average, black Americans scored 15 points lower than white Americans. Jensen, using the heritability of IQ concept,[99] held that undefined environmental differences could not be accepted as valid explanations of IQ averages. Citing studies that aimed to equate the environments of blacks and whites by comparing population samples of equal socioeconomic status (SES) he observed that the IQ differences of the blacks in the upper socioeconomic groups, while diminishing, did not disappear. This he held to be strong support for a genetic explanation in the differences between the IQ measures of blacks and whites. "If environmental factors were mainly responsible for producing such differences, one would expect a lesser Negro-white discrepancy at the upper SES. Other lines of evidence also show that this is not the case."[100] As Lewontin observed, Jensen, while admitting that his thesis was not absolutely proved, believed that it was fairly clear that most of the differences in IQ between whites and blacks were genetic. If heredity outranked environmental factors in explaining differences, then compensatory education, Jansen concluded, had failed to change IQs and could not reasonably be expected, save in the case of individuals, to shift the status roles of the genetically inferior.

The article created a furor in the popular press and the intellectual community. The *Harvard Educational Review* devoted its spring issue to comments by leading geneticists, psychologists, and educators. Some accepted the estimate of the high heritability of intelligence and the educational implications that Jensen had made explicit. Others entered qualifications. Still others rejected his whole position.[101]

99. Arthur R. Jensen, in *Genetics and Education* (New York, 1972), p. 114, defined heritability estimate as a technical term in genetics meaning specifically the proportion of phenotypic variance due to genotypes. Theodosius Dobzhansky, in *Genetic Diversity and Human Equality* (New York, 1973), p. 16, defines heritability as a "statistic computed as a ratio (or percentage) of the genetic to total observed variance." Variance is an index of the total amount of variation among scores.

100. Arthur R. Jensen, *Environment, Heredity, and Intelligence*, Reprint Series no. 2 (Cambridge, Mass., 1969), p. 83. I owe the statement summing up Jensen's position to Richard C. Lewontin, "Race and Intelligence," in N. J. Block and Gerald Dworkin, eds., *The IQ Controversy: Readings* (New York, 1976), p. 89.

101. In 1969 the *Harvard Educational Review* reprinted the original Jensen article together with some of the leading criticisms under the title *Environment, Heredity, and*

Dr. Richard Herrnstein, a Harvard psychologist of the "new behavioral" school, made claims even more controversial than Jensen's. Writing in the *Atlantic Monthly* in 1971, he concluded that IQ was approximately 85 percent a product of heredity. He admitted that success, whether in scholastic performance or in status roles in everyday life, involved energy and motivation as well as a high IQ. These alone, however, were not enough. People with low IQs could not achieve successful careers and high earning power. Those with such a genetic handicap must be consigned to low-paying jobs, if they were to have any jobs at all. He believed that better and largely equal educational opportunities opened the gate to upward mobility for all children with high intelligence.[102] Thus he projected a future, described as a meritocracy, in which a caste system rested on high IQ. "The correlation between IQ and social class (usually defined in terms of occupation, income, and patterns of personal association) is undeniable, substantial, and worth noting."[103] Since IQ affected one's occupation, since occupation affected one's social standing, it followed logically, Herrnstein went on, that IQ affected social standing. Not unexpectedly his position, so disturbing to democratic commitments and values, met with sharp dissent. As *The Economist* observed, Herrnstein was using strong words in a country dedicated to the belief that with the aid of technology man could master his destiny by education and hard work.

The criticisms of Jensen, Herrnstein, and others with similar views[104] involved, of course, more than ideological shock. Some of the problems in the controversy stemmed, once more, from confusion and misunderstanding about basic terms. Thus it was common but unwarranted to identify *genetic* with *deterministic*. Much uncertainty remained, even when the social-cultural aspects of ethnic groups were subordinated to or replaced by the genetic definition of race as a population with different

---

Intelligence. In *Genetics and Education* (New York, 1972) Jensen discussed the background of his famous article and gave his interpretations of the criticisms it had met. *Educability and Group Differences* (New York, 1973) amplified his position. No one has so well and in so brief a space put Jensen's contributions and limitations in the whole perspective of the intelligence-testing movement as Lee J. Cronbach in "Five Decades of Public Controversy over Mental Testing," *American Psychologist* 30 (1975): 1–14.

102. For documentation on the inequality of educational opportunities see James S. Coleman and others, *Equality of Educational Opportunity*, 2 vols. (Washington, D.C., 1966).

103. Richard J. Herrnstein, "IQ," *Atlantic Monthly* 228 (1971): 50. Herrnstein developed his ideas in *IQ in the Meritocracy* (Boston, 1973).

104. These included H. J. Eysenck, *The IQ Argument: Race, Intelligence, and Education* (New York, 1971); and especially, William Shockley, "Negro IQ Deficit: Failure of a 'Malicious Coincidence Model' Warrants New Research Proposals," *Review of Educational Research* 41 (1971); and "A Debate Challenge: Geneticity Is 80 Percent for White Identical Twins' IQ," *Phi Delta Kappan* 53 (1972): 415–19.

frequencies of genes relating to ambivalent skin color, the commonly accepted criterion of difference.[105] Notwithstanding efforts to define intelligence more precisely, no consensus existed.[106] Jensen and Herrnstein seemed to equate it with scores in various types of IQ and achievement tests. Many regarded their value doubtful when cultural and subcultural or clearly defined class boundaries were crossed. The tests measured, some insisted, not innate intelligence but the ability to perform in a middle-class educational system oriented to a competitive, acquisitive society. Even so, despite the statistical predictive value of the tests in school achievements, IQ did not reliably forecast every individual's achievement, since correlations were by no means perfect. Several writers pointed out that intelligence, however understood, could not be thought of as a simple, homogeneous factor. If intelligence was a product of a particular set of psychological structures interacting with particular environments to produce certain kinds of behavior, it could not be inherited as a unit.[107] The growing emphasis in the 1960s on the idea of special separable abilities was reenforced when R. C. Nichols found that "specific abilities may have a higher heritableness than does general ability."[108] Further, in the large context of human values and purposes, whatever IQ measured, no competent scientist, as Theodosius Dobzhansky noted, could take "the IQ as a measure of overall quality or worth of human beings, although a part of the public has been misled into believing this."[109]

Some felt sure that with existing techniques various genotypes could not be randomly assigned to designated environments inasmuch as, to quote Dobzhansky again, "similar genes may have different effects in dissimilar environments, and so may dissimilar genes in similar environments." Richard C. Lewontin, also a distinguished geneticist,

105. Bruce E. Eckland, "Genetics and Sociology: A Reconsideration," *American Sociological Review* 32 (1967): 173–74; Newby, ed., *The Development of Segregationist Thought*, p. 2; M. Mead, T. Dobzhansky, E. Tolbach, and R. E. Light, eds., *Science and the Concept of Race* (New York, 1968).

106. For examples see the articles in Cancro, ed., *Intelligence*, pp. 11–12, 17–31 ff., 51 ff., 59 ff., 237 ff.

107. Erlenmeyer-Kimling and Jarvik, "Genetics and Intelligence: A Review," pp. 1477–79; David Wechsler, "Intelligence, Definition, Theory and the IQ," in Cancro, ed., *Intelligence*, pp. 51–52; Robert Cancro, "Genetic Contributions to Individual Differences in Intelligence," in Cancro, ed., *Intelligence*, p. 61; Steven G. Vandenberg, "The Nature of Nurture and Intelligence," in David C. Glass, ed., *Biology and Behavior Genetics* (New York, 1968), pp. 18, 32–38, 40 ff.; and Gerald E. McClearn, "Social Implications of Behavioral Genetics," in Glass, ed., *Genetics*, p. 166.

108. Steven G. Vandenberg, "The Nature and Nurture of Intelligence" in Glass, ed., *Genetics*, p. 28.

109. Dobzhansky, *Genetic Diversity and Human Equality*, p. 11. See also Gerald E. McClearn, "The Inheritance of Behavior," in Leo Postman, ed., *Psychology in the Making* (New York, 1962), p. 210.

pointed out that factor analysis did not give a unique result for any given set of data. Rather, "it gives an infinity of possible results among which the investigator chooses according to tastes and preconceptions of the model he is fitting. One strategy in factor analysis is to pack as much weight as possible into one factor, while another is to distribute the weights over as many factors as equally as possible. Whether one chooses one of these or some other aspects depends on one's model, the numerical analysis only providing the weights appropriate for each model. Thus, the impression left by Jensen that factor analysis somehow naturally or ineluctably isolates one factor with high weight is wrong."[110] In much the same vein, James F. Crow, although inclined to favor the Jensen position, suggested qualifications in drawing inferences from existing studies in biometrical genetics and in assuming the reality of mathematical assumptions implicit in the analysis of variance models. That is, predictive models had inherent limits when newer, qualitatively different treatments were introduced into the environment.[111]

Some authorities noted still other limitations. Steven Vandenberg found good evidence for the thesis that "the ratio between hereditary potential and realized potential was generally lower for Negroes than for whites."[112] In sum, he held that "estimates of heredity-environment variance ratios take place in the narrow confines of the intersection of a normal environment with a normal genetic makeup. The permissible variation in genetic makeup is just as small as that for the environmental. A little extra genetic material or even a simple mutated gene may be lethal or cause some gross abnormality."[113]

If the influence of each factor depended on the contribution of the other, the proportional contribution of heredity and environment to a given behavioral trait would vary under different hereditary and environmental conditions.[114] If a population was examined at a given moment in time, could methods be devised to determine whether the genes or the environmental experience figured the more in the variation of a measured trait?[115] The problem was complicated by the fact that

110. Dobzhansky, *Genetic Diversity and Human Equality*, p. 8; Richard C. Lewontin, "Race and Intelligence," in Carl Senna, ed., *The Fallacy of IQ* (New York, 1973), p. 5.

111. James F. Crow, "Genetic Theories and Influences," *Harvard Educational Review* 39 (1969): 301–9.

112. Steven Vandenberg, "A Comparison of Heritability Estimates of U.S. Negro and White High School Students," *Acta Geneticase Medical et Gemellogiae* 19 (1970): 280–84.

113. Steven Vandenberg, "The Nature and Nurture of Intelligence," in Glass, ed., *Genetics*, p. 23.

114. Anne Anastasi, "Heredity, Environment and the Question of 'How'?" *Psychological Review* 65 (1958): 198; Robert Cattell, "Structure of Intelligence," in Cancro, ed., *Intelligence*, pp. 24–25.

115. McClearn, "The Inheritance of Behavior," in Postman, ed., *Psychology in the Making*, p. 210.

any measure of heritability would be reliable only as long as the environment remained relatively constant. This was no easy condition, in view of the fact that its wide range of variables could be controlled only by methods used in several disciplines. Thus, headway in determining the genetic basis of behavior could be made only with concurrent progress in understanding the complex and shifting environmental base by holding its constituents constant.[116]

Leon J. Kamin, a Princeton psychologist, raised further questions. He analyzed in detail the four major European and American investigations of separated identical twins and adopted children, work basic to Jensen's thesis. Kamin pointed out inconsistencies, contradictions in the reports, failures to use adequately standardized tests, and the likelihood that general population norms did not apply to twins. Neither the twins nor the foster children studies seemed "to offer evidence to reject the hypothesis of zero heritability of IQ scores."[117]

Some questioned the claims of the hereditarians on grounds other than those of method. Dobzhansky noted that in modern India, despite centuries of rigid caste segregation, low castes contained "at least some individuals capable of performing quite creditably the functions heretofore reserved for the higher ones; and," he added, "it has also been discovered that the converse is true."[118] Assorted mating and a unitary reward system could explain, according to Robert C. Tyron, why the elites reaching certain economic levels tended to come out ahead in conventional tests and in factor analysis procedures.[119] John Fuller and William Thompson noted that "in all societies there is a selection for plasticity or general intelligence and that consequently one should not expect to find biologically determined differences in intelligence between races or societies."[120]

Empirical investigations not easily ignored pointed in much the same direction. In 1949 Marie Skodak and Harold Skeels had found that correlations between the IQs of adopted children were higher by 20 points than those of their biological mothers.[121] The work of Rick F.

116. Cattell in Cancro, ed., *Intelligence*, pp. 25–26.

117. Leon J. Kamin, "Heredity, Intelligence and Psychology," unpublished paper. In Professor Kamin's view, "since its introduction to America the intelligence test has been used more or less consciously as an instrument of oppression against the underprivileged—the poor, the foreign-born, and racial minorities." Professor Kamin has elaborated his position in *The Science and Politics of IQ* (New York, 1974).

118. Theodosius Dobzhansky, "Genetics and Equality," *Science* 137 (1962): 113.

119. Robert C. Tryon, "Behavior Genetics in Social Psychology," *American Psychologist* 12 (1957): 453.

120. Gardner Lindzey, "Genetics and the Social Sciences," *Social Science Research Council Items* 18 (1964): 34.

121. Marie Skodak and Harold Skeels, "A Final Followup Study of One Hundred Adopted Children," *Journal of Genetic Psychology* 75 (1949): 85–128.

Heber with Milwaukee ghetto children whose mothers had IQs of 70 or less showed that intensive nurture of one group of disadvantaged children over a four-year period resulted in significant improvements not evident in the nonstimulated control group.[122] Sandra Scarr-Salapatek, in a study of IQ heritability in various racial and social class groups, including 2,042 pairs of Philadelphia twins, black and white, found a much lower proportion of genetic variation among lower-class than among middle-class children in both black and white groups. This suggested that the "greater the environmental equality, the greater the hereditary differences between levels in the social structure." In other words the percentage of genetic variance and mean scores seemed to be a function of the rearing conditions of the population.[123]

Geneticists, in the main regarding the basis of intelligence as polygenetic, held that it was impossible to identify many polygenes in man. As a result, precise information about inherited "racial" differences in general intelligence was not accessible. In the words of J. N. Spuhler, since "it seems clear that if differences between major races exist in general intellectual abilities, these differences are small in magnitude compared with the range of genetic variation within all major groups."[124] Richard Lewontin insisted on the lack of conclusive evidence about the genetic factor in interracial differences. Thus he felt that Jensen, Herrnstein, and others, despite the qualifications they made, in effect confused heritability of a character within a population with heritability of the difference between two populations.[125] The evidence of considerable variation within groups further complicated the problem.

Moreover, even if genetics entirely explained the differences between the IQs of the races, this provided no genetically sound reason for assuming the fixity of genetically conditioned traits. It was once thought that because certain disorders were genetic in character, no cure could be found. But if the biochemistry of inborn errors of metabolism were well understood, and if deficient metabolic products were supplied, many inborn errors could be corrected. Moreover, as Lewontin pointed out, "in the normal range of environments, these inborn errors manifest themselves irrespective of the usual environmental variables. . . . Even though no environment in the normal range has an effect on character,

122. Rick F. Heber, *Rehabilitation of Families at Risk for Mental Retardation* (Madison, Wis., 1972).

123. Sandra Scarr-Salapatek, "Race, Social Class and IQ," *Science* 174 (1971): 1285–95. See also Scarr-Salapatek's informative and balanced review article, "Unknowns in the IQ Equation," *Science* 174 (1971): 1223–28.

124. J. N. Spuhler, "Race and Genetics," *International Encyclopedia of the Social Sciences*, 6:112; J. N. Spuhler and Gardner Lindzey, "Racial Differences in Behavior," in Jerry Hirsch, ed., *Behavior-Genetics Analysis* (New York, 1967), p. 19.

125. Lewontin, "Race and Intelligence," in Senna, ed., *The Fallacy of IQ*, p. 13.

there may be special environments created in response to our knowledge of the underlying biology of a character, which are effective in altering it."[126]

Critics also challenged the educational implications that Jensen and Herrnstein spelled out. Compensatory education had not, as Jensen claimed, been tried and failed; it had been tried only in limited areas and ways.[127] Moreover, who could say what genetically derived traits society might value in the future? In addition, as David Z. Robinson of the Carnegie Corporation observed, "the racial problem in our society is not that blacks have lower IQs than whites. It is that we do not treat blacks equally. We must treat people as individuals, and not according to the average IQ of their group."[128] Economically disadvantaged blacks with high IQs, in their relations with police and landlords, often came out no better than those handicapped by both poverty and low IQs. As Christopher Jenckes wrote, "low IQs are not the cause of American racial problems and higher IQs could not solve these problems. Any white reader who doubts this should simply ask himself whether he would trade the genes which make his skin white for genes which would raise his IQ 15 points."[129]

The Society for the Psychological Study of Social Issues took an even more extreme stance. It held that an accurate understanding of the role of genetic and cultural factors in the average IQs of whites and blacks could be achieved only when social conditions for both races had been equal for several generations. More realistically, some insisted that in view of the indeterminate evidence at hand and of the problems in designing a study fully able to resolve existing confusion, the sensible thing, given the democratic values in American society, was to provide the disadvantaged with every opportunity within the power of society. Admittedly, many influences, political, economic, social, and psychological, militated against efforts to implement such a policy fully.[130]

Dr. Edward Zigler of Yale, an able student of retardation, contended that many environmentally oriented investigations reflected "a profound disrespect for the biological, constitutional and/or genetic

126. Lewontin, "Race and Intelligence," p. 16.

127. The arguments for and against the thesis that compensatory education had succeeded in raising IQ and scholastic achievements were presented by several authorities in Jerome Hellmuth, ed., *Disadvantaged Child*, 2 vols. (New York, 1970).

128. David E. Robinson, "If You're So Rich, You Must Be Smart," in Senna, ed., *The Fallacy of IQ*, p. 30.

129. Christopher Jenckes, "What Is the IQ?" in Senna, ed., *The Fallacy of IQ*, p. 41.

130. William Buchanan and Hadley Cantril, *How Nations See Each Other* (Urbana, Ill., 1953; rpt. ed., Westport, Conn., 1972), p. 83; "The SPSSI Statement," *Harvard Educational Review* 39 (1969): 625–27.

integrity of the human organism." He pointed to various shortcomings of investigators who in effect ignored genetic factors. In stressing the capacity of environment to mold a virtually unlimited plasticity of behavior, many failed to isolate "the particular environmental factors which affect intelligence" and to designate the "exact process through which all components of intelligent behavior are equally affected by these, as yet unspecified, factors." By no means excluding the influence of environmental factors, Zigler found little convincing evidence for the sweeping assumption that environmental manipulations had substantially improved the achievements of defective genetic endowment.

On the positive side, Zigler pointed out that all environmental influences did not have the same behavioral effects on different individuals. Citing experimental evidence, he specified a genetic influence on early infant behavior in such sensory areas as motility and sleeping and feeding patterns. Moreover, genetically determined characters might, in evoking distinctive responses from others, help create a special environment. An individual's genetic endowment might also lead him to create a particular environment for himself, as, for example, in the relation between esthetic sensibility and relative social isolation. Though Zigler's critique was related specifically to mental retardation and was partly speculative, it had important implications for the more comprehensive controversy over heredity and environment.[131]

As Zigler noted, the nature-nurture controversy clarified many issues and left others in doubt. Investigation had shown that IQ is an empirically significant variable and that average differences at the present time did exist between ethnic and social-economic groups. Yet "differences among individuals *within* racial-ethnic (and socioeconomic) groups greatly exceed in magnitude the average differences between such groups." Beyond this, as John C. Loehin, Gardner Lindzey, and J. N. Spuhler observed, the bias of investigators, the inadequacy of tests, the varying environmental conditions, made it possible to give different weights to genetic differences. While IQ was indicative of future achievements in certain fields, it was by no means a determining factor

131. Zigler's essay was first presented at a symposium on mental retardation, as a criticism of Ina C. Uzgiris's paper, "Socio-Cultural Aspects of Mental Retardation." The papers were printed in H. Carl Haygood, ed., *Social-Cultural Aspects of Mental Retardation* (New York, 1970). For examples and further illustration, see Gerard Piel, "The New Hereditarians," *The Nation* 220 (1975): 455–59; J. C. Loehlin and R. C. Nichols, *Heredity, Environment, and Personality* (Austin, Tex., 1976); the pro and con statements by eight well-known leaders on both sides of the controversy in "I.Q. and Race," *The Humanist* 33 (1972): 5–18, and (1972): 4–8; Donald M. Levine and Mary Jo Bane, eds., *The "Inequality" Controversy: Schooling and Distributive Justice* (New York, 1975); and Ned J. Block and Gerald Dworkin, eds., *The IQ Controversy: Critical Readings* (New York, 1976).

in shaping the future lives of most Americans. Such an assumption left out the roles of motivation, personality, and the shifting importance in a changing environment of particular abilities and values. Thus the limitations of what was known about the relation between IQ findings and ethnic and socioeconomic groups did not justify slanting social policy, including education, toward a "meritocracy."[132]

Muted insofar as it related to the nature-nurture controversy, the revival of the instinct theory, with new supporting evidence, attracted a good deal of attention in the violent atmosphere of the 1960s. The instinct theory was now applied to man's assumed innate predatory, aggressive, and killing behavior. Ethologists claimed that observations under natural conditions of insects, birds, and animals revealed "inborn schemata" that programmed compulsive behavior without any aid from imitation or learning. American and British ethologists largely took their cue from Konrad Lorenz, an engaging and respected figure in the study of animal life and codirector of the Max Planck Institute for Behavioral Research in Bavaria. Lorenz held that inborn schemata released mechanisms for such phylogenically programmed behavior as imprinting, male bonding, mating patterns, and predatory aggression. Fighting and killing, he believed, provided the indispensable means for survival in the evolutionary process of both nonhuman and human species. Moreover, these inborn compulsions had been functionally necessary for bringing about a more or less even distribution of populations in life-sustaining geographical areas. This was true in the world of insects, birds, and animals and seemed also largely to hold for man.[133]

Not all ethologists accepted sweeping extrapolations from subhuman to human behavior. The Americans and British who reached the largest popular audiences, however, did.[134] Robert Ardrey, a playwright with academic credentials, was an outstanding example. Citing a long list of

132. John C. Loehlin, Gardner Lindzey, and J. N. Spuhler, *Race Differences in Intelligence* (San Francisco, 1975), 238–39.

133. Konrad Lorenz, *On Aggression* (New York, 1966). By 1974 Lorenz had come to concede the effects of learning and habit in behavior, which, he insisted, had an inherited base in the genomes of the species. See Robert J. Richards, "The Innate and the Learned: The Evolution of Konrad Lorenz's Theory of Instinct," *Philosophy of the Social Sciences* 4 (1974), 111–33.

134. British writers include the zoologist Desmond Morris, *The Naked Ape* (New York, 1968), and *The Human Zoo* (New York, 1969); and the psychologist Anthony Storr, *Human Aggression* (New York, 1968). The Americans include Robert Ardrey, *African Genesis* (New York, 1961), and *The Territorial Imperative* (New York, 1966); and Lionel Tiger, *Men in Groups* (New York, 1969), and *The Imperial Animal* (New York, 1971), written with Robin Fox.

authorities, particularly paleo-anthropologists, and extrapolating from reports of nonhuman behavior, Ardrey emphasized as functional byproducts of the evolutionary process deference, submissiveness, dominance, and above all the inborn proclivity to kill with weapons in the predatory, aggressive defense of territoriality. He even ventured to suggest the operation of these instincts in current conflicts in Israel and Vietnam.

Unlike many lay readers and commentators in popular and semipopular magazines, the scientific community found serious short-comings in the field reports and especially in transpositions to human behavior. The most unsparing critic turned out to be the British-born anthropologist Ashley Montagu, professor of anthropology at Rutgers University. To be sure, Montagu did not speak for all his colleagues. He insisted, however, that anthropological evidence on the whole indicated that nonviolent cooperation had been the necessary requirement for group survival, nonhuman and human. Man killed in order to eat rather than to satisfy a killer-instinct. His nearest subhuman kin, moreover, assimilated opposing groups in a competitive-cooperative process rather than by violent destruction.[135]

Another critic pointed out that Lorenz's work showed little or no familiarity with Mendelian and post-Mendelian genetics, or with verified knowledge of the biochemical aspects of appetite and emotion that led to aggression. Lorenz also left out evidence of learning as a factor in aggression: training, for example, could lead mice to attack females and infants of their own species. Moreover, man had bred or trained most of the "killing aggressiveness" out of his domesticated animals. Nor did Lorenz cite examples of work that showed that animals were not born with, but developed, social organization. Only when conditions disturbed this did normally cooperative baboons become violent.[136]

Leon Eisenberg of Harvard University contended that the trans-position from animal to human behavior had no scientific standing unless based on careful, controlled studies of the precise conditions, situational and biochemical, that evoked the governing mechanism. Bird behavior illustrated the point. On the one hand genes explained oriole nest-building, and young sparrows isolated from conspecies and fostered by canaries did indeed sing their own songs. On the other hand meadow

135. Ashley Montagu, *The Human Revolution* (Cleveland, 1965), pp. 115–20; and the volume of essays by several authorities and edited by him, *Man and Aggression* (New York, 1973).

136. John Paul Scott, "That Old-Time Aggression," *The Nation* 204 (1967); and *Aggression* (Chicago, 1958).

larks, similarly isolated from infancy, acquired the songs of the particular foster-parent species.[137]

As for territoriality or the aggressive defense of familiar living space, critics noted that if many animal and human populations displayed what seemed to be an inborn fighting behavior, others just as "naturally" indulged in trial and error roaming and adventuring in search of food. Moreover, ethologists failed to take into account distinctively human behavior which coexisted with aggression. The prime example was facility in the use of language, symbolization, and the creation of cultures. In some of these, behavior was clearly non-violent.[138] Nor did ethologists give much attention to the human capacity for loosening or broadening genetic controls.[139]

Loren Eiseley summed matters up with his usual insight and thoughtfulness. Man had "conditioned himself readily to complex institutional forms of order he did not once possess." Old though man is, he had, even in living memory, risked northern snows "to ease the souls of slain animals and reduce his own blood guilt—a strange act for an 'instinctive hunter.' " Such writers as Ardrey should be read "with an eye to man's infinite variety, dynamism, and, dare I say it, educability. For of this latter, in its true form, man knows as yet but little." In an evolving future, vast and uncertain, in which humanity might or might not survive, it was worth favoring his seed with great nurture.[140]

137. Leon Eisenberg, "The Human Nature of Human Nature," *Science* 176 (1972): 125.

138. Noam Chomsky, review of B. F. Skinner's *Verbal Learning*, in *Language* 25 (1959): 26–27; and *Language and Mind* (New York, 1968), pp. 75–85.

139. George Gaylord Simpson, review of Desmond Morris's *The Naked Ape*, in the *New York Times Book Review*, February 4, 1968, p. 14. Of special interest, on a broad scale, is Edward O. Wilson, *On Human Nature* (Cambridge, 1978), pp. 232–33 and passim.

140. Loren Eiseley, review of Ardrey's *The Territorial Imperative*, in the *New York Times Book Review*, September 11, 1966, p. 6.

10

Exploring
the Unconscious

. . . we recognize our spiritual natures as having only incidental and temporary relations with the material substance and general forces of the universe. But we may concede that, the farther our examination extends, the more completely the organic or simply vital forces appear to resolve themselves into manifestations of those closely related or mutually convertible principles which gave activity to the unconscious portion of the universe. We have no experimental evidence that these physical agencies can form any living person by their action on matter; nor can we prove the contrary. . . . We are obliged to recognize a special intervention of creative power in the introduction of spiritual existence in the midst of the pre-existing unconscious creation.

OLIVER WENDELL HOLMES, 1857

AT THE very time that the issue of nature v. nurture stirred the intellectual community and that the New Psychology, with the conscious mind as the focus of interest, was forging ahead, a different image of man was taking form. A dualistic model of mind was projected, in which unconscious psychic activities, mental operations without awareness, were assumed to explain many perplexing problems and a good deal of everyday behavior as well. Despite the investigations of a few leaders of the New Psychology, its practitioners tended to hold that unconscious mental life was largely inaccessible to introspection, controlled observation, and especially experimentation and quantification, the key methods of scientific psychology.

Three main influences largely accounted for the early explorations of unconscious mental life: philosophic thought, empirically derived mental therapies, and the changing society of the late nineteenth and early twentieth centuries. The international concern with the unconscious sphere followed no regular, progressive course. Reactions took place and rediscoveries were sometimes made by investigators unfamiliar with the work of their predecessors.[1]

On the philosophical level the recognition of an unconscious mental life had a long history.[2] The ancient Hindus, Buddhists, Plato, Plotinus,

1. Henri F. Ellenberger, *The Discovery of the Unconscious* (New York, 1970), pp. vi, 53 ff., 192 ff.
2. Lancelot L. Whyte's *The Unconscious before Freud* (New York, 1960) is useful for its discussion of the concept in technical philosophy. Also useful is James G. Miller's *Un-*

and Augustine took it into account, as did theologians, mystics, and philosophically inclined medical writers in the Middle Ages.[3] The modern concern began when Leibniz pictured ordinary perceptions as the sum of countless small ones which operated chiefly below the level of awareness, and when Kant discussed perceptions of which the perceiver was unaware. Sir William Hamilton, an early nineteenth-century Scottish philosopher, argued on one occasion that "the mind may, and does, contain far more latent furniture than consciousness informs us it possesses. . . . What we are conscious of is constructed out of what we are not conscious of—our whole knowledge, in fact, is made up of the unknown and the unrecognizable."[4]

American college teachers of philosophy were aware of the problem, but influenced by Locke and the early Scottish school, gave little attention to it.[5] The general indifference of collegians to unconscious factors largely remained, even when post-Kantian "romantic" philosophers regarded these factors as of great if not paramount importance.

The post-Kantian Germans, distrusting reason and probing the inner unrest of the mind, found in multiple personalities, dreams, and symbols a key to unconscious forces. Some even projected the unconscious as a highly creative connecting link between individual and universal powers. Arthur Schopenhauer in *The World as Will and Idea* (1818) held that reality, a blind, impelling force, was manifest in individuals as the will to live. It conflicted with other wills and often operated below the level of consciousness. Thus impulses, wants, and desires, including sex, were repressed. It was the inability of the restless will to find satisfaction

consciousness (New York, 1942), for its identification of sixteen different meanings in the discussion of the idea and for its summary of efforts to further knowledge of unconscious mental activities through laboratory experimentation. For later experimentation see Charles W. Ericksen, "Unconscious Perception," _International Encyclopedia of the Social Sciences_, 11:575–81.

3. Edward L. Margetts, "The Concept of the Unconscious in the History of Medical Psychology," _Psychoanalytical Quarterly_ 22 (1953): 610–11.

4. Sir William Hamilton, _Lectures on Metaphysics and Logic_, 2 vols. (Boston, 1874), 1:153, 235, 241.

5. Thomas C. Upham of Bowdoin College, an opponent of war and slavery, in discussing the suppression of desires and the resulting outburst of perverted behavior, wrote: "By a thousand circumstances, and in thousands of instances, the feelings are wrenched from their natural position, and shoot forth and show themselves in misplaced and disproportionate forms. Casual associations, in the shape of antipathies, fears, aversions, prepossessions, remorse, etc. are found seated in many a mind, which is otherwise unembarrassed and unexceptionable in its actions; they have established their empire on immovable foundations, and are incorporated with the whole mental nature." _Outline of Imperfect and Disordered Mental Action_ (New York, 1840), p. 365. For Upham's recognition of unconscious factors in "rationalization" see _Elements of Mental Philosophy_ (New York, 1845), pp. 440–41.

for these wants that was the basis of Schopenhauer's pessimism. In a less-well-known but notable study, *Psyche* (1846, 1869), Carl Gustav Carus developed a theory of the movement from the unconscious to the conscious and back again. A universal unconscious achieved awareness through conscious individuals. Schelling's interest in the problem of the unconscious was related to his attempt to explain the origin of different degrees or levels within the ultimate unity of mind and matter in the Absolute.

Emerson followed these developments with some eye to conceptions of human nature. His insight into the thrust and mystery of unconscious-conscious mental relationships did not, to be sure, add up to an integrated whole. What he said was scattered and disjointed.[6]

Although Emerson, getting on in years, paid little if any attention to Eduard von Hartmann's *Theory of the Unconscious* (1869), some of the younger men in his onetime circle took some interest in it.[7] This much-discussed treatise, which aimed to present a systematic account, was based in part on the work of such forerunners as Leibniz, Schopenhauer, and Schelling. It also used data provided by the natural and historical sciences. Considerable confusion among American readers resulted from the various ways in which Hartmann used the term *unconscious*. At times he meant the united unconscious will, and at others, an unconscious idea. Again, the substance of the universe was the cosmic Unconscious, which was the source of other levels of the unconscious in living human beings. The whole complicated philosophy was used to justify a pantheistic pessimism. Suffering and evil advanced with the increase of consciousness, and unhappiness could be eliminated only with the total annihilation of being.[8]

With some exceptions, Hartmann's *Theory of the Unconscious* met with qualified respect. The most critical reaction appeared in the

6. For examples: *The Letters of Ralph Waldo Emerson*, ed. Ralph L. Rusk, 6 vols. (New York, 1939), 3:76–77; *The Complete Works of Ralph Waldo Emerson*, 14 vols. (Boston and New York, 1883, 1904), 12:65 and 10:9; William Gilman and others, eds., *Journals and Miscellaneous Notebooks of Ralph Waldo Emerson*, 19 vols. (Cambridge, Mass., 1964–73), 7:307, 8:10, 344. See also L. E. Emerson, "Emerson and Freud: A Study in Contrasts," *Psychoanalytical Review* 20 (1933): 208–14.

7. Christopher Cranch, "The Unconscious Life," *Unitarian Review* 33 (1890): 97–122. George Ripley, though he disliked cosmic pessimism, found much to attract him in Schopenhauer and Von Hartmann, especially the interplay between the conscious and unconscious in man. See Octavius Brooks Frothingham, *George Ripley* (Boston, 1888), p. 228; and Charles Crowe, *George Ripley: Transcendentalist and Utopian Socialist* (Athens, Ga., 1967), pp. 259–60.

8. Miller, *Unconsciousness*, p. 189; Dennis N. Kenedy Darnoi, *The Unconscious and Eduard von Hartmann* (The Hague, 1967), esp. p. 174; and Ellenberger, *The Discovery of the Unconscious*, p. 210.

Popular Science Monthly—a translation of an article by Léon Dumont, best known for his *Théories scientifiques de la sensibilité: Le plaisir et la peine.* Dumont, noting Hartmann's metaphysical commitment to the superiority of the psychic over the material, felt that reflex action, to take a single example, could be better understood in terms of physiology and Darwinism than by "an unconscious manipulation of unconscious volition." Nor did it seem justifiable to invoke, in a priori fashion, the idea of an unconscious intelligence, in order to justify the thesis that evil ruled the world relentlessly, fatalistically, and interminably.[9]

Paul Shorey, the University of Chicago's noted authority on Plato, granted the usefulness of Hartmann's suggestion of unconscious factors in latent memory, subtle associations of ideas, the dexterous role of habits, and the relation of all this to uncontemplated and unanticipated expressions in sexual love, the formation of language, and the movements of history. On the other hand, he regarded the effort to correlate unconscious ideas with physical expressions as only an imaginary and convenient formula. Above all, he objected to the negative and sorry, if ingenious, patchwork of nihilism that failed to do justice to man's noble, if limited, achievements.[10]

Francis H. Johnson, a liberal theologian of the Andover Theological Seminary, commended the view that consciousness extended to only a small part of the field of intelligent operation. Hartmann's illustrations of the role of the unconscious in reasoning and in much daily behavior seemed impressive, as did his unifying principle that "an intelligence which is not the intelligence of the creature is everywhere at work in the world." Johnson could not accept the argument set forth to prove the unconscious operation of the Author of all the wonderful illustrations Hartmann offered, however. He nevertheless felt that the German philosopher had contributed significantly to an understanding of human nature in relation to the cosmos.[11]

The American most competent to evaluate the *Philosophy of the Unconscious* was G. Stanley Hall, who had become acquainted with its author during his student days in Germany and who was a leader of the new school of academic psychology. A notice in *The Nation* of the most

9. Léon Dumont, "A New Phase of German Thought: Hartmann's *Philosophy of the Unconscious*," *Popular Science Monthly* 2 (1872): 152–58; and Dr. William B. Carpenter, "On the Hereditary Transmission of Acquired Psychical Habits," *Popular Science Monthly* 3 (1873): 303–20.

10. Paul Shorey, "Hartmann's *Philosophy of the Unconscious*," *The Dial* 5 (1885): 237–40.

11. "What Is Reality," *The Andover Review* 15 (1891): 613–30. For Johnson's "personalism" see Daniel D. Williams, *The Andover Liberals* (New York, 1941), pp. 34–36, 40–42, 58–59.

recent Hartmann volume published in German indicated its importance, from the point of view of the question "Is there in consciousness a spontaneous ethical estimate of human actions apart from all conformity to outer authority or influence?"[12] Hall's almost equally brief notice of the English translation of the ninth German edition of the *Philosophy of the Unconscious* neither answered this question nor did much more than inform the reader of the scope of the book.[13] In 1912, however, after Hall had become aware of the Freudian movement, he included Hartmann in the *Founders of Modern Psychology*.[14] Though critical of his violations of logic and the pessimistic directions of his thought, Hall concluded that Hartmann's "proof of the eccentric . . . marginal nature of consciousness makes him a modern Copernicus. The erection of the Unconscious as a world principle marks the great revolution of views since the Renaissance, which was its prelude, in emancipating the world from the views of the past." Hall went on somewhat dubiously to claim that Hartmann's sense of sadness and suffering did not lead to quietism and oriental resignation, and that if ever there was to be a new idealism in the world, it "would be somewhat along the lines of Hartmann's Unconscious."[15]

Such a conclusion contrasted with the position of Henry Adams. Having also read Hartmann, as well as Schopenhauer, Ernest Haeckle, Wilhelm Ostwald, and Lord Kelvin, Adams professed the feeling that "chaos was the law of nature, and order the dream of man." The "mind could gain nothing by flight or by fight" but must "merge in its supersensual multiverse, or succumb to it."[16]

In view of the technical difficulties of the *Philosophy of the Unconscious* and the American optimistic belief in progress, it seemed unlikely that Hartmann's ideas would find any considerable audience at all. That a distorted, oversimplified version of some of his ideas did so was the result of the efforts of Edgar Saltus, who had studied with the master in Germany. *The Philosophy of Disenchantment* (1885) and *The Anatomy of Negation* (1886) put his skeptical and pessimistic doctrines in a longer historical perspective. A series of flashy, melodramatic, "decadent" novels of murder, suicide, eroticism, and psychic emptiness crudely implied some of Hartmann's ideas about the unconscious. These

12. *The Nation* 28 (1879): 103.
13. *The Nation* 38 (1884): 553–54.
14. G. Stanley Hall, *Founders of Modern Psychology* (New York, 1912), pp. 181–243.
15. Hall, *Founders of Modern Psychology*, pp. 228, 237–39.
16. Henry Pochmann, *German Culture in America 1600–1900* (Madison, Wis., 1957), p. 483. For Adams's reference to Hartmann see *The Letters of Henry Adams*, ed. Worthington C. Ford (Boston, 1938), p. 524.

books suggested an inchoate and superficial view of human nature, the upshot of which was that men and women should be emancipated from their futile and conscious love of life.[17]

On another stage, the educational psychology of Johann Friedrich Herbart attracted some attention. His metaphysics, psychology, and pedagogy stressed the importance of conscious and unconscious forces in the mind and indeed in the whole universe. Rejecting innate ideas, Herbart assumed the existence of an infinite unconscious realm in which permanent entities (derived from experience) at times combined harmoniously and at other times competed with each other for a place in consciousness. To find out the speed and favorable-unfavorable conditions governing these operations or "presentations," Herbart experimented with mathematical formulae, time and force being the variables. When something new in experience was perceived, past experience in its totality (the apperceptive mass or mind) must be invoked if the new ideas were to be assimilated into consciousness.[18]

Although Herbart received little attention from American writers on mental philosophy,[19] the German revival of interest in his work in the 1870s and 1880s was reflected in American periodicals.[20] Educators, notably Charles De Garmo and Frank and Charles McMurry, disseminated with great enthusiasm the interpretations of Herbart's new German disciples. The American Herbartians,[21] while giving some emphasis to unconscious factors in learning, were influential mainly in emphasizing literature and the social studies and in stressing the interests

17. *Edgar Saltus, the Man* (Chicago, 1925), a biography by Marie Saltus, his third wife, has been supplemented by the excellent essay of Eric McKitrick, "Edgar Saltus of the Obsolete," *American Quarterly* 3 (1951): 22–35; and Ruth E. Stevenson's doctoral dissertation, "Literary Techniques, Background, and Ideas of Edgar Saltus" (University of Wisconsin, 1953). The few writers of short stories of this period who made explicit use of the unconscious showed no evidence of familiarity with Hartmann: for example, John E. Wilkie, "An Unconscious Crime," *Cosmopolitan* 27 (1899): 478–83; and Eugene R. White, "A Subconscious Courtship," *Atlantic Monthly* 88 (1901): 502–10.

18. The best brief introductions to Herbart's metaphysics, psychology, and pedagogy are James Mark Baldwin's essay in the *Dictionary of Philosophy and Psychology,* 2 vols. (New York, 1901), 1:469 ff.; and Harold B. Dunkel's *Herbart and Education* (New York, 1969).

19. For example, Noah Porter, *The Human Intellect* (New York, 1869), pp. 92–95, 245, 412; and John Dewey, *Psychology* (New York, 1891), esp. appendix A. In *The Principles of Psychology* (2 vols. [New York, 1890]) William James referred to Herbart several times but found "something hideous in the glib Herbartian jargon . . ." (1:603).

20. *Journal of Speculative Philosophy* 10 (1867): 166–94; and *American Journal of Education* 28 (1877): 45–49. See also Harold Dunkel, "Herbartianism Comes to America," in the *History of Education Quarterly* 9 (1969): 202–33.

21. Harold Dunkel, *Herbart and Herbartianism: An Educational Ghost Story* (Chicago, 1969), chap. 14.

of the individual child, based on previous experience, as the basis for social values and moral character.[22]

Building on the early German romantic philosophers, Nietzsche, toward the end of the nineteenth century, advanced a more comprehensive and subtle conception of conscious and subconscious activity. This emphasized its relation to nonrational and irrational components of human nature, the role of civilization in repression, sublimation, self-deception, destructive and self-destructive motives, and symbolism.

H. L. Mencken's *The Philosophy of Friedrich Nietzsche* (1908), the first American exposition of Nietzsche's philosophy, barely touched on the concept of the unconscious. The iconoclastic critic from Baltimore, like most Nietzsche admirers among the American intelligentsia, was intrigued by the master's emphasis on the will to power, the Superman, and the bankruptcy of nineteenth-century scientific and moral progress. Eugene O'Neill's early plays, especially *Lazarus Laughed*, showed some understanding of Nietzsche's unconscious; Robinson Jeffers's poems owed something to the philosopher's *The Birth of Tragedy*; and possibly Theodore Dreiser, who read Nietzsche, took over the will-to-power idea so evident in *The Titan* and other novels. But most writers who professed admiration for Nietzsche distorted his paradoxical ideas in support of their own prejudices without familiarizing their readers with his philosophy of the unconscious.[23]

Philosophical interest in the exploration of the unconscious or subconscious also included speculation about dreams. To be sure, mental philosophers of the Lockean and "common sense" persuasions in general agreed with physiologists in regarding dreams as byproducts of automatic activities somatic in nature and unrelated, except insofar as associationist psychology might reveal cause-effect relationships.[24] On

22. Charles De Garmo, *Herbart and the Herbartians* (New York, 1895); Charles A. McMurry, *The Elements of General Method* (Bloomington, Ill., 1892); and the *Yearbooks of the National Herbart Society* (Bloomington, Ill., 1895–99; reprinted in one vol., New York, 1969).

23. *The Complete Works of Friedrich Nietzsche*, ed. Oscar Levy, 18 vols. (Edinburgh, 1909–11; ltd. ed., New York, 1964), 10:44, 47–48, 296–97; 14:64; 16:141; Benjamin de Casseres, *The Superman in America*, University of Washington Chapbooks, no. 30 (Seattle, 1920); Oscar Cargill, *Intellectual America: Ideas on the March* (New York, 1941), pp. 487 ff., 705 ff.; Frederick J. Hoffman, *The Twenties: American Writing in the Postwar Decade* (New York, 1955), pp. 304–6; Henry F. May, *The End of Innocence* (New York, 1959), pp. 206–7.

24. In the later nineteenth century several inquirers conducted investigations of dreams based on careful observations and experimentation with sensory stimuli. Merle Curti, "The American Exploration of Dreams and Dreamers," *Journal of the History of Ideas* 27 (1966): 405 ff., reports these investigations and efforts to direct dreams at will.

the other hand, baffling nocturnal phenomena were viewed by Romantic philosophers as creative processes and as significant indicators of unconscious forces in mental life. Gotthilf von Schubert, in *The Symbolism of Dreams* (1814, 1836), described them as a picture language that combined fleeting, unconscious images. In his opinion dreams, whether poetic or ironic, were distinctive and meaningful, if deceptive, expressions. Like similar-minded writers,[25] he thought they were to be read in terms of universal symbols of sex objects and organs, of forgotten childhood memories, of creative fantasies, including imaginative performances and insight into motives perceived only dimly if at all. Further, dreams unconsciously concealed conflicts, shame, and guilt, often expressed in seemingly nonsensical images. They were also a means of relieving the dreamer of mental burdens that would otherwise become overwhelmingly oppressive. A contemporary authority has possibly gone a bit too far in concluding that these investigations and musings projected almost all the concepts that were to be synthesized by Freud and Jung.[26]

Men and women of letters of the Romantic school interested in unconscious mental and emotional life included notable figures on both sides of the Atlantic.[27] Modern critics have shown that unconscious factors were present not only in the creation of much outstanding fiction but also in the emotional satisfaction its readers derived from it. An early example from the American side of the use of this concept in literary criticism was an essay of Julia Gulliver. A graduate of the first class at Smith College, she had studied with Wilhelm Wundt, translated some of his work, and taught literature at Rockford College before becoming its president.[28] In an analysis of the motive of a leading character in George Eliot's *Middlemarch*, she raised the question of the influence of the "so-

25. In addition to Von Schubert, important writers include Karl Albert Scherner, *Das Leben des Traumes* (Berlin, 1861); L. F. Alfred Maury, *Le Sommeil et les rêves* (Paris, 1861; 2d ed., 1878); Marie-Jean-Léon Hervey de Saint-Denis, *Les Rêves et les moyens de les diriger* (Paris, 1867); W. Robert, *Der Traum als Naturnothwendigkeit erklärt* (Hamburg, 1886); and Yves Delage, "Essai sur la théorie du rêve," *Revue scientifique* 48 (1891): 40–48. Two important recent historical accounts are Ludwig Binswanger, *Wandlungen in der Auffassung und Deutung des Traumers, von den Griechen bis zur Gegebwart* (Berlin, 1928); and Norman MacKenzie, *Dreams and Dreaming* (New York, 1965).

26. Ellenberger, *The Discovery of the Unconscious*, p. 311.

27. Robert Lee Wolff's *Strange Stories and Other Explorations in Victorian Fiction* (Boston, 1971); and Simon Lesser, *Fiction and the Unconscious* (New York, 1951), esp. pp. 49 ff. and 67 ff.

28. For Gulliver's training and career see the sketch in *Notable American Women, 1607–1950: A Biographical Dictionary,* ed. Edward T. James and Janet W. James, 3 vols. (Cambridge, Mass., 1971), 2:104–5.

called secondary, reflex, sub-waking consciousness on the waking, voluntary, primary self." Her handling of the problem reflected original insight based on her knowledge of theories of unconscious motives.[29]

Interest in unconscious mental life was not confined to philosophical and literary circles. Belief in it was implicit in the therapeutic use of suggestion in both preliterate and more-sophisticated cultures. The power of the exorcisor to "cleanse" body and spirit of pain and torment rested on the manipulation of unconscious forces through suggestion. In some cases this was used to discover and remove unconscious sources of anxiety, in others to aid in the cultivation of detachment.[30]

Despite some interest in seventeenth-century England, modern therapeutic concern with suggestion as the royal road to the unconscious really began in the late eighteenth century. Johann Joseph Glassner, a Swabian priest and popular exorcisor, attracted attention, and Franz Anton Mesmer, a Vienna physician, enjoyed a brief but spectacular career in Paris. Mesmer's belief in the special role of a magnetic fluid in his own body and channeled into his patients was repudiated by a royal commission of scientists that included Benjamin Franklin. Mesmer's belief was nevertheless developed and modified by his successors. Dr. James Braid, a Scottish surgeon, rejected the magnetic fluid theory, and was the first to use the term *hypnosis* in his *Neurypnology* (1843). He offered a scientific explanation of the phenomenon, presenting commendable if crude demonstrations that attracted wide interest.[31] Popular misuse of hypnotism by itinerants, however, led most medical practitioners to associate it with charlatanism.

Meantime in America as in Europe, mesmerism had provided a backdrop of interest in unconscious phenomena. Charles Poyen, a French visitor, proved to be an important agent of transmission. By the late 1830s he was lecturing in New England.[32] Demonstrations given in Belfast, Maine, intrigued Phineas Quimby, a clockmaker of sorts. In his

29. Julia Gulliver, "The Temptation of Mr. Bulstrode: A Study of the Subconscious Self," *The New World* 9 (1900): 503–17.

30. Some authorities hold that certain features of Stoicism resembled the Adlerian and existentialist schools of our time, that Plato's Academy anticipated some of the concepts of the Jungian school, and that the Epicureans, who aimed at the removal of unconscious sources of anxiety, foreshadowed Freud. For a brief discussion, see Ellenberger, *The Discovery of the Unconscious*, p. 648.

31. An early but reliable account by Joseph Jastrow, *Fact and Fable in Psychology* (Boston, 1900), pp. 170 ff., should not be overlooked. For more recent accounts see Ilza Veith, *Hysteria: The History of a Disease* (Chicago, 1965), chap. 10; and Clark L. Hull, *Hypnosis and Suggestibility: An Experimental Approach* (New York, 1933), pp. 3–14.

32. Charles Poyen, *Progress of Animal Magnetism in New England* (Boston, 1837).

view, successful exhibitions of mental healing issued entirely from susceptibility. Unconventionally religious and a sincere idealist, Quimby held that all disease resulted from erroneous thinking and was subject to control by the proper use of occult powers of subconscious realities. Quimby influenced one of his patients, Mary Baker Glover (Eddy), as well as the exponents of the mental cure known as New Thought.[33]

James Stanley Grimes and Andrew Jackson Davis, two mesmerists well known in their own day, were less influential than Quimby. Grimes was an untutored but honest practitioner, Davis an impecunious "failure" in shoemaking and merchandising. Davis used mesmerism as a technique for clairvoyant prescriptions for various and sundry diseases amply described in his twenty-six curious volumes that mixed trances, transcendentalism, Swedenborgianism, Fourierist socialism, and spiritualism.[34]

In 1848, the Fox sisters in upstate New York attracted widespread interest in spiritualist feats, thanks to their apparent sincerity and to the excitement of religious ferment and social dislocation. Prominent literary and public figures were impressed, until one of the sisters confessed that the whole thing was a hoax.[35] Though popular spiritualism stimulated the scientific study of unconscious mental phenomena only indirectly, William James, as we have seen, felt that all claimants, no matter how untutored and dubious, might have something to teach academic psychologists.[36]

The view of mesmerism and related phenomena as charlatanry was

33. Of note in this connection is Stephen Gottschalk's *The Emergence of Christian Science in American Religious Life* (Berkeley, 1973). The Emmanuel Movement, which developed in Episcopal circles in Boston in the early 1900s, occasionally used hypnotism in treating emotional disturbances identified with unconscious conflicts. For an interesting treatment of all these movements consult Donald Meyer, *The Positive Thinkers: A Study of the American Quest for Health, Wealth, and Personal Power* (Garden City, N.Y., 1965), Gail T. Parker, *Mind Cure in New England from the Civil War to World War I* (Hanover, N.Y., 1973), and Ellwood Worcester, Samuel McComb, and Dr. Isidor H. Coriat, *Religion and Medicine: The Moral Control of Nervous Disorders* (New York, 1908).

34. Grimes's writings included *Phreno-Geology* (Boston, 1851), in which he supported a naturalistic theory of evolution. He came to oppose spiritualism, dramatically, in a debate with Leo Miller: *The Great Discussion of Modern Spiritualism* (Boston, 1860). Davis's autobiography, *The Magic Staff* (New York, 1857), is an interesting book, not written in trance. See Frank Podmore, *From Mesmerism to Christian Science* (New York, 1963). Edward Bellamy's later use of mesmerism as a literary device in *Looking Backward* (Boston, 1887) indicates continuing familiarity with the phenomenon.

35. Ernest Isaacs, "A History of Spiritualism: The Beginnings, 1845–1855" (Master's Essay, University of Wisconsin, 1958); and his biography of the Fox sisters in *Notable American Women*, 1:655–57, with bibliography.

36. Frank Podmore, *Modern Spiritualism: A History and a Criticism*, 2 vols. (London, 1901), 1:197, 200, 210; and Gardner Murphy and Robert D. Ballou, eds., *William James on Psychical Research* (New York, 1960).

challenged in the 1870s and 1880s by Jean-Martin Charcot, an eminent neurologist at the Salpêtrière hospital in Paris. Charcot felt that hypnotism illuminated unconscious mental life by readjusting the states of consciousness and the authority governing the hierarchy of nervous centers. This pioneer demonstrated that the hysterical crisis constituted the same sort of alteration of personality. His position on many points was challenged by a rival school at Nancy where, as early as 1866, Dr. A. A. Liebeault described his method of putting subjects to sleep by verbal command and suggesting to them the relief of pain and illness. Liebeault and his more-renowned successor, Dr. Hippolyte Bernheim, emphasized a psychological interpretation and provided evidence for unconscious motivation by demonstrating that subjects, without knowing the reasons for their act, carried out posthypnotic suggestions.

Whatever Charcot's limitations, he was on sound ground in showing that forgotten memories, including those associated with sexual difficulties, could be recaptured by hypnosis. His work was carried further by Pierre Janet, whose dissertation *The Mental State of Hystericals* (1892) argued that hysteria was a form of mental disintegration in which the field of consciousness was contracted and personality divided. In his preface to Janet's dissertation, Charcot accepted the argument that hysteria was essentially a mental rather than a physical phenomenon.[37] At about the same time a student of his, Eugen Bleuer, showed how hysteria was often related to disturbed but dynamic subconscious mental life, and he demonstrated the effectiveness of hypnosis in therapy.

Meanwhile a group of scholarly inquirers and would-be believers advanced a different concept of unconscious mental activity in efforts to explain clairvoyant foresight, trances, and the possibility of communication with the dead. Under the auspices of the British Society for Psychical Research, Frederic W. H. Myers sought to study these questions in a scientific manner. The subconscious was thought of not only as a metaphysical personality or "subliminal self" but also as a transcendental reservoir which controlled the physical processes of the body even though the conscious mind was aware of only a small part of the great storage tank. Challenged by the findings and interpretations of this group, Theodore Flournoy in Geneva tried to find a naturalistic explanation for phenomena previously regarded as occult. He concluded after long and painstaking investigations that the revelations of a

37. In addition to the articles on Charcot and Janet by Robert I. Watson in the *International Encyclopedia of the Social Sciences* (8:234–35) see Pierre Janet, *The Major Symptoms of Hysteria* (New York, 1907; 2d ed., 1920). In some of his work Janet was influenced by the Americans Josiah Royce, George M. Beard, James Mark Baldwin, and George Herbert Mead.

medium could be "romances of the subliminal imagination," based on forgotten memories (cryptomesias) and on unconscious wishes. In effect, he postulated the existence of an unconscious personality that functioned in a compensating and protective capacity. In France, Dr. Charles Richet also systematically gathered data, thus likewise opening the door to a scientific investigation of claims that in time would be known as parapsychology.[38]

The clinical approach was not the only evidence of a growing scientific interest. Even before the peak of somatic explanations of these psychological phenomena was reached in nineteenth-century Germany, Robert Wyatt had described involuntary actions as a function of unconscious mental life. New avenues to an understanding of unconscious mental activity were opened by Charles Bell, Marshall Hall, Johannes Muller, William Griesinger, and Thomas Laycock. In 1852, Dr. William B. Carpenter coined the term "unconscious cerebration" to connote a storing up of impressions that could be brought to consciousness only by association. In other words, neural processes operated without any mentation whatever.[39] Yet in denying that the human being was a mere automaton and in clinging to a belief in a divine plan in the creation of the universe, Carpenter differed from doctrinaire exponents of materialism. Thus he remarked, in a lecture in Boston, that his concept of human nature was very much like that of William Ellery Channing. On the other hand, Jacobus Moleschott (1822-93) and Ludwig Büchner, for example, held that the so-called psychical phenomena were "unreal," being actually only epiphenomenal products of the physical, while Karl Lange insisted that all psychological definitions should be replaced by physiological ones.[40]

The investigations of these and other physiologists, neurologists, and psychiatrists were extended by pioneers in the emerging fields of

38. Edmund Gurney, Frederic W. H. Myers, and Frank Podmore, *Phantasms of the Living*, 2 vols. (London, 1886); Frederic W. H. Myers, *Human Personality and Its Survival of Bodily Death*, 2 vols. (London, 1903); Theodore Flournoy, *From India to the Planet Mars: A Case Study in Somnambulism* (London, 1900); Ellenberger, *The Discovery of the Unconscious*, p. 85. For William James's early and continuing interest see, again, Murphy and Ballou, eds., *William James on Psychical Research*, esp. pp. 327–32.

39. Carpenter's *Nature and Man, Essays Scientific and Philosophical* (New York, 1889) includes some earlier papers, among which special importance attaches to "On the Influence of Suggestion in Modifying and Directing Muscular Movement," pp. 168–72; and "On the Doctrine of Human Automism," pp. 261–83. See also Carpenter, "On the Unconscious Activity of the Brain," *Proceedings of the Royal Institute* 5 (1868).

40. Bernard Hart, "The Conception of the Subconscious," in Morton Prince, ed., *Subconscious Phenomena* (Boston, 1910), p. 109.

physiological psychology and biostatistics. Among these, Helmholtz, Oswald Külpe, and Francis Galton attempted, in limited ways, to encompass segments of unconscious mental operations empirically and quantitatively.[41]

In the international exploration of unconscious mental life, Americans were at first primarily receivers. In philosophic discussion, no one offered a systematic analysis of the unconscious mind comparable to those produced in Europe. Nevertheless, however derivative American contributions were, those that stemmed collaterally from therapeutic concerns deserve notice, although they have often been overlooked. Throughout much of the nineteenth century, the focus of interest of psychiatrists in America, as in Europe, was largely but not exclusively somatic. In the etiology of mental illness, the recognition of American environmental as well as personal factors operating on unconscious mental life began with Dr. Benjamin Rush. He suggested an inverse relation between the incidence of neuroses and social crises. Many persons of "infirm and delicate habits," Rush wrote shortly after the American Revolution, "were restored to perfect health, by the changes of place, or occupation, to which the war exposed them. This was the case in a more especial manner with hysterical women, who were much interested in the successful issue of the contest. . . . It may," he continued, "perhaps help to extend our ideas of the influence of the passions upon the disease, to add, that when either love, jealousy, grief or even devotion, wholly engrosses the female mind, they seldom fail, in like manner, to cure or to suspend hysterical complaints." This was also a comment on the effect of women's "place" on the feminine aspect of human nature, and on the influence of changes in women's roles (if only partial) in times of crisis. On the other hand, in some persons the terror and distress of the Revolution brought on a true melancholia.[42]

Rush's suggestion that the interaction of environmental and emotional factors unconsciously affected mental health and illness was not altogether forgotten. In a remarkable address given before the New York Academy of Medicine in 1847, Dr. John W. Francis, an eminent obstetrician and man of wide-ranging cultural interests, ascribed many nervous diseases to environmental or intrapersonal factors of which the

41. See above, pp. 190–93.
42. Benjamin Rush, "The Influence of the American Revolution . . . Oct. 1, 1788," in *The Selected Writings of Benjamin Rush*, ed. Dagobert D. Runes (New York, 1947), p. 330. The ideas of Rush's European contemporaries are well discussed in M. Foucault, *Madness and Civilization: A History of Insanity in the Age of Reason* (New York, 1965).

patient was unaware. What were called nervous diseases, Dr. Francis claimed, had increased in the ratio of civilization. "In proportion as mankind have been freed from physical toil and intellectual resources have been developed, a new sensitiveness of the brain and nervous system has betrayed itself. . . . We need a hygiene which will bring about harmony between the animal and the moral natures, which will reconcile the conflict between cerebral activity and the functions of life. Thousands die every day from over-wrought minds and baffled emotions. Leisure induces crime, and ennui breeds hypochondria." Dr. Francis further ascribed such illnesses not only to "ill-regulated, overtasked, or inactive mental and moral energies" but also to "unsatisfied sympathies, harassing domestic cares, and especially the almost rabid ambition for gain or distinction which creates so much of the insanity and invalidism of this country." Warning that prevention was better than cure, Francis prescribed, as therapy, bathing, proper food, and exercise, together with "cultivation of self-understanding of the operation of the different passions on the heart, and a deliberate commitment to cheerfulness."[43]

Nor was Dr. Francis alone in emphasizing environmental factors in the etiology of nervous disorders. Dr. William Sweetser, a professor of medicine at Bowdoin College and other places, noted the role of modern civilization in intensifying and modifying the emotions, and of American society in bringing on nervous ailments by subjecting men to "frequent and painful vicissitudes of fortune" and the pressures stemming from ambition.[44] In articles entitled "Mental Hygiene" published in 1859, Dr. George M. Cook of Canandaigua, New York, stressed as causes of insanity in later life unconsciously unwise child-rearing, including lack of affection, and the reckless ambition of many youths.[45] Dr. Isaac Ray also believed that the tensions resulting from the complexities associated with social progress contributed to mental illness, and that needed reform of the social environment might reduce its incidence.[46]

Later psychiatrists also stressed the influence of American social environment on nervous depletion and other disorders of which patients

43. Dr. John W. Francis, *Anniversary Address before the New York Academy of Medicine* (New York, 1847), pp. 101–3. See also Dr. Francis's *Old New York, or, Reminiscences of the Past Sixty Years* (New York, 1858).

44. Dr. William Sweetser, *Mental Hygiene*, 2d ed. (New York, 1850), pp. 55, 105, 327.

45. Dr. George M. Cook, "Mental Hygiene," *American Journal of Insanity* 15 (1859): 272–82, 353 ff.

46. *Butler Hospital Annual Report* (1859), cited by Norman Dain in *Concepts of Insanity in the United States 1789–1865* (New Brunswick, N.J., 1964), p. 95. See also Dr. Isaac Ray's *Mental Hygiene* (Boston, 1863; rpt. ed., New York, 1968).

were unaware. Dr. George M. Beard of New York, a class-conscious Spencerian evolutionist and Social Darwinist, felt that competition and pressure, necessary for progress and lacking among primitive and even Latin peoples, stimulated an excessive though desirable mental activity which, without immediate physical warning, found expression in the unconscious, nonvolitional side of human nature.[47] Dr. S. Weir Mitchell of Philadelphia, a prestigious practitioner as well as a poet and novelist, also ascribed mental malaise and related functional disorders of the heart and stomach, presumably increasingly widespread in American cities, to the anxiety and worry stemming from the cruel competition for the dollar. Great fortunes had come to possess new value as a means toward social advancement. Like many other authorities, Dr. Mitchell held that overrigorous intellectual discipline in schools, especially in the case of girls, resulted in mental troubles.[48] In also emphasizing the extremes of temperature and the dryness of the air as factors in mental depletion or neurasthenia, Mitchell, like Beard, reflected the influence of such environmentalists as Thomas Buckle, John W. Draper, and Herbert Spencer. Thus in the discussion of the bearing of social and physical environment on mental problems, Beard and Mitchell skirted, without making central or sometimes even explicit, the concept of unconscious psychic influences on motives and behavior.

Dr. Oliver Wendell Holmes, who was neither psychologist, psychiatrist, or experimental neurologist but rather a clinician, teacher, and homespun philosopher, contributed explicitly to an understanding of unconscious mental life in a justly famous address before the Harvard Phi Beta Kappa Society in 1870. Holmes admitted indebtedness to Leibniz, Hartley, and the nineteenth-century neurologists, especially Marshall Hall, whose treatise on medicine he edited and enlarged. Holmes was deeply impressed by Hall's description of reflex action in terms of a neural arc that functioned independently of the brain. For Holmes, this meant that action could sidestep volition and consciousness. Aside from immediate sense impression and that which was mainly

47. Dr. George M. Beard, *American Nervousness: Its Causes and Consequences* (New York, 1881), pp. vi–ix, 126 ff. See also Philip P. Wiener, "G. M. Beard and Freud on 'American Nervousness,' " *Journal of the History of Ideas* 17 (1956): 269–74; and Charles Rosenberg, "The Place of George M. Beard in Nineteenth-Century Psychiatry," *Bulletin of the History of Medicine* 36 (1962): 245–59. John S. Haller, Jr., and Robin M. Haller, in *The Physician and Sexuality in Victorian America* (Urbana, Ill., 1974), emphasize the "racist" implications, as well as those of class, in Beard's thinking, pp. 6–7, 9–11.

48. S. Weir Mitchell, *Wear and Tear, or Hints for the Overworked* (Philadelphia, 1871), pp. 7 ff., 17, 31, 41–42, 52. For Mitchell's fiction see David M. Rein, *S. Weir Mitchell as a Psychiatric Novelist* (New York, 1952); and Joseph P. Lovering, *S. Weir Mitchell* (New York, 1971). John Duffy has an excellent discussion of this widely held idea in his "Mental Strain and 'Overpressure' in the Schools: A Nineteenth-Century Viewpoint," *Journal of the History of Medicine* 23 (1968): 63–79.

pictured, worded, or modulated, as in remembered music, mental activity was largely unconscious. It was "the rule with the actions most
important in life." A great deal of behavior was to be explained in
relation to reflex action. The sudden reappearance of forgotten ideas
was, for instance, a common example of unconscious cerebration.
Holmes also cited cases indicating that questions had been answered or
problems solved in dreams or during deep sleep. Unconscious action was
also to be found in what were called "absent" persons, those who, while
awake, acted from apparent purpose without really knowing what they
were doing. Again, many movements were performed with perfect
regularity while conscious thought was focused on something else.
Moreover, the results of unperceived mental processes constantly appeared in consciousness. Holmes noted examples of thoughts that never
emerged into consciousness at all, yet made their influence felt among
perceptible mental currents. Thus "old prejudices, that are ashamed to
confess themselves, nudge our talking thought to utter their magisterial
veto." Moreover, personality was often doubled in dreams battling with
the dreamer, even though he was unconscious that he was his own an-
tagonist. In short, "the more we examine the mechanism of thought, the
more we shall see that the automatic, unconscious action of the mind
enters largely into all its processes." This was true even though no
microscope could find the table "inscribed with the names of early loves,
the stains left by tears or sorrow or contrition, the rent where the
thunderbolt of passion has fallen, or any legible token that such experiences have formed part of the life of the mortal, the vacant temple of
whose thought it is exploring."[49]

The burden of the address was to suggest the mechanism of free unconscious association in thinking and its relation to forgotten memories
and experiences. It also suggested the unconscious role of wish
fulfillment in dreams. In sum, the address clarified and reenforced by a
wealth of examples the major tenets about unconscious mental life as
they were understood in 1870 and as they were to be corroborated by
research.[50]

Holmes's understanding of unconscious factors in mental life also

49. Dr. Oliver Wendell Holmes, *Mechanism in Thought and Morals: An Address Delivered before the Phi Beta Kappa Society of Harvard University, June 29, 1870* (Boston,
1872), pp. 35, 44, 48, 71. The address is included in *The Works of Oliver Wendell Holmes*,
13 vols. (Boston, 1892), 8:260–314.

50. Clarence P. Oberndorf, M.D., *A History of Psychoanalysis in America* (New York,
1953), pp. 30–33; Van Wyck Brooks, "Dr. Holmes: Forerunner of the Moderns," *Saturday
Review of Literature* 14 (June 27, 1936): 3–4, 13–14; M. A. DeW. Howe, *Holmes of the
Breakfast Table* (New York, 1939), p. 146; S. I. Hayakawa and Howard Mumford Jones,
Oliver Wendell Holmes: Representative Selections . . . (New York, 1939), p. xlix; Eleanor
Tilton, *Amiable Autocrat: A Biography* (New York, 1947), pp. 260, 353.

found expression in his fiction, written in large part to show that whatever moral responsibility a person might have for his or her actions, it did not include responsibility for the blight of heredity and forgotten experience. Elsie Venner, whose pregnant mother had been bitten by a rattlesnake, behaved unconsciously, because of reflex action, in some ways like a rattlesnake. In *The Guardian Angel*, inherited reflexes operating unconsciously explained adolescent hysteria. In *A Mortal Antipathy*, reflexes of which the victim was unaware accounted for a neurosis labeled Gynophobia, fear of women. In this case the phobia stemmed from physical and psychic shock experienced by a handsome and otherwise healthy young man in early childhood; it was rooted in the "primacy over the heart" of the nerve center controlling inhibition. The phobia was cured by a combination of psychic and physical shock that broke the chain of inhibition and effected a rebirth after a loss of consciousness. In this novel Holmes also described what has come to be known as the conditioned reflex, a mechanism operating on the level of unawareness.[51]

In the Old World, as in America, the discussion of sex on the intellectual level had traditionally been the domain of men of letters and moral theologians. As we have seen, in early nineteenth-century Europe the power of the sexual impulse was now and then recognized by philosophical explorers of the unconscious, a few of whom linked repression with dreams and unusual behavior. In medical circles, the interest in sex was largely somatic, however, until at least the mid-century. In emphasizing its psychic aspects, including repression as the effective agent in producing hysteria, Ernst von Feuchtersleben (1845) and Robert C. Carter (1853) were pioneers.[52] Later on, sexual psychopathology, or sexology, emerged from the growing interest in the physiology of sex and the recognition of its role in the etiology of disease and in abnormal behavior and dreams. The mounting incidence of syphilis and the advance of the woman's rights movement were also contributing factors. Richard von Krafft-Ebing's *Psychopathis Sexualis* (1886) classified case histories of sexual abnormalities and claimed that

51. *A Mortal Antipathy* in *The Works of Oliver Wendell Holmes*, esp. chaps. 17-20. See also Clarence P. Oberndorf, *The Psychiatric Novels of Oliver Wendell Holmes* (New York, 1943). I am indebted to Charles Boewe's "Reflex Action in the Novels of Oliver Wendell Holmes," *American Literature* 26 (1954): 303-19; and to his doctoral dissertation, "Heredity in the Writings of Hawthorne, Holmes, and Howells" (University of Wisconsin, 1955).

52. Veith, *Hysteria: The History of a Disease*, pp. 184-85, 199-216.

disguised sexual instincts found outlet in various deviations and acts of crime.

Though Krafft-Ebing attributed sexual abnormalities to constitutional and degenerative tendencies, other sexologists ascribed these deviations to psychological factors. Theodore Meynert, a leading psychiatrist, held that sexual abnormalities resulted from infantile or youthful interpersonal experiences that were often pushed into the unconscious realm. Clinicians suggested that ungratified or inadequately gratified sex drives led to neuroses and psychoses, and that sexual and aggressive instincts could be and often were diverted into acceptable channels.

In American discussions of sex as a component of human nature, the predominant emphasis was on somatic aspects of normal and abnormal behavior. Experts generally held that anatomy and physiology not only explained women's lesser intelligence but also the "weakness" of their sex drive and their susceptibility to "female complaints" as a result of too much or too little coition.[53] Such views reenforced traditional ideas about the damaging mental and emotional effects of overintellectual stimulation of women in higher education and the unsuitability of any career save childbearing and homemaking.[54] To be sure, Dr. Elizabeth Blackwell was not alone in taking exception to these views, in holding that in general women had as much native intelligence as men, a similar endowment of sex drive, and, like men, an ability to be healthy in continence provided "accumulative force" found wholesome outlets in other activities.[55] The dominant emphasis on somatic aspects of sex was

53. A good introduction to the whole problem of the "nature" of female sexuality is Nancy Cott, ed., *Root of Bitterness: Documents of the Social History of American Women* (New York, 1972). See also Haller and Haller, *The Physician and Sexuality in Victorian America*, chap. 2; Dr. Charles Meigs, "Sexual Peculiarities," in *Females and Their Diseases* (Philadelphia, 1848), pp. 40 ff.; Nathan Allen, *Physiological Laws of Human Increase* (Philadelphia, 1870); Carl N. Degler, "What Ought to Be and What Was: Women's Sexuality in the Nineteenth Century," *American Historical Review* 79 (1974): 1467–90; and Carol Smith-Rosenberg and Charles Rosenberg, "The Female Animal: Medical and Biological Views of Woman and Her Role in Nineteenth-Century America," *The Journal of American History* 60 (1973): 332–56.

54. Edward H. Clarke, M.D., *Sex in Education; or a Fair Chance for Girls* (Boston, 1873), pp. 180–81; Dr. George L. Austin, *Perils of American Women* (Boston, 1883); Meigs, "Sexual Peculiarities" (Letter IV), in *Females and Their Diseases*, pp. 40 ff.; Allen, *Physiological Laws of Human Increase*. For the other side: Anna C. Brackett, ed., *Education of American Girls* (New York, 1874), pp. 151 ff., 175 ff.

55. Dr. Elizabeth Blackwell, *The Human Element in Sex*, new ed. (London, 1894); Alice Stockham, *Tokology: A Book for Every Woman* (Chicago, 1886); Antoinette Brown Blackwell, *The Sexes throughout Nature* (New York, 1875), p. xix; and Charles F. Taylor, M.D., "Effects on Women of Imperfect Hygiene of the Sexual Function," *American Journal of Obstetrics* 15 (1882): 161–77.

also reflected in medical treatises and in "advice manuals" which, like their Civil War predecessors, warned against the dangers of "self-abuse" and "undue" indulgence in intercourse.[56] Toward the turn of the century and for some years later, the Purity Crusade, which reflected these views, also derived strength from the increasing influence of organized middle-class Christian women, from fears for the integrity of the family, and from moral revulsion against the "dens of iniquity" in the city slums that exploited wayward or impoverished girls.[57] The Purity Crusaders, like most authors of sex manuals, acted on a view of human nature that stressed the possibility and desirability of controlling a fundamental impulse through sustained, organized appeals to will power, fear, reason, and emotional persuasion.

Whatever their views on the physiological and mental differences of the sexes and on the virtues of continence or moderation, most authorities showed little interest in the unconscious aspects of sex behavior. As we have seen, some medical spokesmen did appreciate the role of sex in physical and mental ailments and still others developed this position in interesting ways.

Dr. Edward J. Ingersoll, a general practitioner in Corning, New York, probably worked out his ideas pretty much by himself. He held that man's "affectional" nature was his highest faculty and claim to distinctive individuality. In fact, sexual force suffused the whole body, not merely the reproductive organs alone. On the basis of forty-five years of experience, Ingersoll viewed sexual repression as a major cause of hysteria and declared that "the unconscious action of the will occasioned by fear seems to take possession of the body." Thus the paralysis of one woman was traced to dread of sexual relations and childbirth. The fear once removed, the paralysis disappeared. Another woman's hysteria was traced to her more or less unconscious desire to be a man. The therapy was psychological, that is to say, religious. "We should not seek to *suppress* sexual life, but should desire Christ to *redeem* it. The more we are in harmony with Christ's spirit and subject to His will, the greater power will the life of the body, which is sexual, have for its sustenance, and for the overcoming of disease."[58]

56. The most widely read manual was John H. Kellogg's *Plain Facts for Old and Young* (Buffalo, 1882). Kellogg deprecated the emphasis on sex as detrimental to physical and mental health, denounced masturbation as a prime cause of physical and mental ailments, and urged the importance of physical activity, a special diet, and will power. Richard W. Schwartz has given the main facts in his biography, *John Henry Kellogg, M.D.* (Nashville, 1970).

57. The movement is well discussed in David J. Pivar's *Purity Crusade: Sexuality and Social Control 1868–1900* (Westport, Conn., 1973).

58. Andrew J. Ingersoll, M.D., *In Health* (Corning, N.Y., 1877; 4th rev. ed., Boston, 1892), pp. 21, 55. See also A. A. Brill, "An American Precursor of Freud," *Bulletin of the New York Academy of Medicine* 16 (1940): 631–41.

Like Ingersoll, Dr. Alexander J. C. Skene was also concerned with unconscious factors relating to sex and behavior. He felt that women were in a special sense the creatures of their internal sex organs, which generated tidal forces that they could not consciously control. The hysterical and emotional changes of pregnancy, like sexual desire itself, were determined by internal physiological processes beyond the awareness of conscious volition.[59]

Dr. George Beard ascribed a good deal of mental distress and illness not only, as we have seen, to American social and physical environment, but also to worries related to unhappiness in love. Beard did not explicitly relate sexual neuresthenia to unconscious factors, though he implied that some of the anxieties were not consciously formulated. In reporting the case histories of forty-three males, he attributed many of their physical ailments to sexual fears and worries. Though Beard was deeply committed to somatic factors in the etiology of such ailments, and recommended physical treatment, he also insisted on the patient's proper use of his own mental forces. This was spelled out somewhat blandly in terms of what he called mental and sexual hygiene.[60]

Dr. Albert Freeman Africanus King, a Washington obstetrician, attracted some note by claiming that hysteria occurred most often in women whose sexual wants were ungratified. The "reproduction government" overruled the "government by volition," inasmuch as women's hysterical behavior was in the main an unconscious approach to the other sex or an automatic action of the nervous system. The conflict between the emotions of the reproductive ego and the volition of the personal, self-preserving ego resulted, for the moment, in a dual personality. Since in civilized societies the sexual purpose of the hysterical state was not recognized, the hysteria became chronic phenomena that, taken alone, "appear to conceal, cover up, or even antagonize any idea of functional utility." For such hysteria King advised intellectual and muscular exercises, valerian extract, narcotics, oophorectomy, and a satisfying marriage.[61]

A year later, in 1892, Dr. Charles Page, superintendent of the

59. Alexander J. C. Skene, *Education and Culture as Related to the Health and Diseases of Women* (Detroit, 1889), pp. 22–23.

60. George M. Beard, *Sexual Neurasthenia: Its Hygiene, Causes, Symptoms and Treatment*, ed. A. D. Rockewell, M.D. (New York, 1884), p. 245. For an interesting interpretation in terms of the history of psychiatry see Rosenberg, "The Place of George M. Beard in Nineteenth-Century Psychiatry," *Bulletin of the History of Medicine* 36. Freud took note of Beard in his *Collected Papers*, ed. John Strachey, 5 vols. (New York, 1959), 1:76.

61. A. F. A. King, M.D., "Hysteria," a paper read before the Washington Obstetrical and Gynecological Society, April 25, 1891, *American Journal of Obstetrics* 24 (1891): 513–32. Ellenberger, *The Discovery of the Unconscious*, p. 144, notes that King's position was "remarkably similar" to that which Moritz Benedict was formulating in Vienna at the same time.

Massachusetts State Hospital at Danvers, explained the profanity of a patient whose character had been exemplary before her mental breakdown. Dr. Page ascribed the irrepressible exhibitions of the language of the slums to a chance experience that resulted in anxiety and conflict between religious duty, shame, and guilt.[62] In quoting a passage from Hawthorne's "Haunted Mind," Page further illustrated his understanding of the relation between repression, unconscious psychic conflicts, and behavioral disorders.[63] If, as a modern psychoanalyst noted, Page was somewhat vague in his conception of repression, he exhibited a psychological approach to psychiatric phenomena unusual in his day. He sensed, "however dimly and falteringly, the operation of a mental mechanism which Freud was on the eve of subjecting to scientific demonstration. With all due reservations, Dr. Page stood, in this respect at least, well in the vanguard of his American contemporaries."[64]

The direct association of the unconscious life and abnormal behavior owed a good deal to Dr. Morton Prince, a student of William James. Prince transmitted to America the work of Charcot, Bernheim, and Janet, with whom he also studied, and in addition made impressive clinical and theoretical contributions to an understanding of the subconscious. His first book tried to solve the body-mind problem by restating the materialist position in acceptable psychological terms and by finding a valid role for purposive action.[65] In 1890, at a meeting of the Boston Society for Medical Improvement, he presented patients he had cured of functional ailments through hypnosis and related techniques involving suggestion and association. He also offered what Nathan G. Hale, Jr., has described as "a rudimentary conception of the subconscious." This, Prince felt, explained how suggestion and association operated "deep down in the lower strata of consciousness" or in what Dr. Oliver Wendell Holmes had called the "second self" or "the other fellow." In 1891, Prince, following James on the importance of habit, took a forward step in devising an "essentially behavioristic

62. Charles W. Page, "The Adverse Consequences of Repression," *American Journal of Insanity* 49 (1892–93): 382 ff.; E. E. Southard, "The Laboratory Work of the Danvers State Hospital, Hathorn, Mass., with special relation to the policy formulated by Dr. Page," *Boston Medical and Surgical Journal* 163 (1919): 150–52. See also Merle Curti, "The American Exploration of Dreams and Dreamers," pp. 391–416.

63. "The Haunted Mind" (1835) is included in *Twice-Told Tales* in the Centenary Edition of *The Works of Hawthorne*, 12 vols. (Columbus, Oh., 1962–77), 9:306–7.

64. Herbert A. Bunker, "Repression in Pre-Freudian Psychiatry," *Psychoanalytic Quarterly* 14 (1945): 477.

65. Morton Prince, *The Nature of Mind and Automatism* (Philadelphia, 1885). Prince's position resembled that of the English philosopher Professor W. K. Clifford, which he discovered only after his book had been completed.

theory of neurosis." According to his hypothesis, many neuroses, expressed in pain, limping, and paralysis, originated involuntarily in unconscious attempts to deceive, but moving beyond "control of will," persisted as genuine pathological processes. In this way mental states might become linked with physiological functions, or visual images might become associated with horrifying experiences, with the result that "learned" neuroses became, in fact, "independent neuroses."[66] A few years later he applied this general position in explaining deviant behavior.

In 1898 Prince rejected the widely held idea that sexual perversions arose from organic or constitutional tendencies toward degeneration. Such phenomena were to be explained in terms of "nervous reflexes" influenced by education, environment, and personal experience. Thus homosexuality, though related to inherent tendencies in the human makeup, resulted from the failure to suppress the tendency and to "learn" how to express the sex drive in heterosexual relationships.[67] Prince held that nature had drawn no hard and fast line between the sexes in their normal characteristics—that male and female personality characteristics shaded imperceptibly the one into the other, with environmental factors largely determining the strength of the socially acceptable sex roles. Here was scientific support for the intuitively derived idea Margaret Fuller had expressed more than half a century earlier.[68]

Prince's The Dissociation of Personality (1905) became a classic. The book described the case of a young college student to whom the name "Miss Beauchamp" was given. She unconsciously played the roles of three contradictory personalities. "Now these three personalities," Prince wrote, "had very sharply defined traits which gave a very distinctive individuality to each. One might say," he continued, "that each represented certain characteristic elements of human nature, and that the three might serve as an allegorical picture of the tendencies of man." These Prince labeled The Saint, The Woman, and The Devil.[69] The dissociation of personality resulted from confused meanings associated with motivational conflicts stemming from "a psychical

66. This summary is based on the account in Nathan G. Hale, Jr., Freud and the Americans: The Beginnings of Psychoanalysis in the United States, 1876–1917 (New York, 1971), pp. 128–30.

67. Morton Prince, "Sexual Perversion or Vice: A Pathological and Therapeutic Inquiry," Journal of Nervous and Mental Diseases 25 (1898): 237–56.

68. See above, p. 171.

69. Morton Prince, The Dissociation of a Personality: A Biographical Study in Abnormal Psychology (New York, 1906), p. 16.

catastrophe." Through analytic reduction, including hypnotic states and dream interpretation, the disorder proved susceptible to a reintegration of the personality. In this and later work, including *The Unconscious* (1914), Prince also emphasized the value of bringing into the patient's consciousness "exalting ideas and memories." By integrating psychology, psychiatry, and neurology and by advancing useful concepts couched in scientifically acceptable language, Prince contributed richly to the development of abnormal psychology, to mental hygiene, and to the exploration and therapeutic use of the unconscious psychic life.[70]

Boris Sidis was less well known than Prince. A refugee from tsarist Russia, he made sensitivity to poverty and social injustice in America a part of his therapeutic doctrine. He was, like Prince, a student of William James and a graduate of the Harvard Medical School, first becoming generally known through his *Psychology of Suggestion* (1902), an effort to explain the dissociation of personality in relation to unconscious mental life. Sidis used hypnosis to uncover forgotten traumatic experiences in childhood, and investigated dreams in terms of split-off subconscious memories that provided cues to therapeutic synthesis of the disordered personality. Although his studies of multiple personality[71] were of clinical and theoretical importance, Sidis was especially notable for his therapeutic use of William James's theory of unconscious reserves of energy. As director of a private institution at Portsmouth, he reported impressive achievements from inducing patients to become conscious, in a semihypnotic state, of the "stores of potential subconscious energy" that could be "trapped" and effectively used.[72]

In 1906 Joseph Jastrow of the University of Wisconsin, in his book *The Subconscious*, evaluated current theories of unconscious mental life. He contended that the position upheld by the majority of psychologists—which differed very little from the "old-fashioned unconscious cerebration" purged of its mystical elements—needed to be modified by greater emphasis on the functional continuity of the conscious and unconscious. Believing, as did most of his colleagues, that all mental processes were accompanied by neural processes, Jastrow rejected the idea that a secondary personality, severed in some basic way from the self of the familiar sort, explained phenomena commonly attributed to such a secondary self. His balanced treatment was illustrated by a

70. William S. Taylor, *Morton Prince and Abnormal Psychology* (New York, 1928), chap. 12.

71. Boris Sidis and S. P. Goodhart, *Multiple Personality: An Experimental Investigation into the Nature of Human Individuality* (New York, 1904).

72. Hale, *Freud and the Americans*, pp. 141–42; Addington Bruce, "Boris Sidis—An Appreciation," *Journal of Abnormal and Social Psychology* 18 (1923): 274–76.

wealth of material and flavored with picturesque metaphors.[73] In reviewing the book, James B. Angell of the University of Chicago observed that the whole subject illustrated the "psychological paradox of sincere and vital concern for the deep and baffling problems of life combined with an indisposition to submit to rigorous discipline." Angell commended Jastrow for bringing that discipline to bear on his discussion.[74]

At the same time that neurotherapy deepened the understanding of the unconscious aspects of sex as a part of human nature, a few representatives of the New Psychology made some contributions of their own. These in the main used the questionnaire method, which rested on introspection.[75] At Clark University, G. Stanley Hall initiated the best-known inquiry at this level. Sanford Bell, one of his students, beginning his study about 1890, noted in his report (1902) that psychologists had generally neglected sex, particularly adolescent sex. On the basis of data on 1700 cases Bell concluded, much as Morton Prince had four years before, that even the most repulsive perversions were "but exaggerations of instincts and emotions that are germinal in normal human beings."[76] He felt that inhibition imposed unconsciously by civilization increased such substitutes for normal sex expression as masturbation, onanism, and pederasty. Like Hall, and in anticipation of Freud, Bell envisioned the development of the emotion of sex love through various states in the same way that other instincts evolved over time. The emotions of sex love sometimes appeared as early as the middle of the third year, and moved thereafter through five well-defined states duly described. His data indicated the frequently unconscious use by adults of the love of a child as an escape for their own repressed love. President Hall, in his voluminous *Adolescence* (1904), made use of this investigation.[77]

The wide range of speculation about unconscious factors in thinking, dreaming, and sex reached creative philosophical, psychological, and

---

73. Joseph Jastrow, *The Subconscious* (Boston, 1906), esp. pp. 530 ff.

74. *Dial* 41 (1906): 106–9.

75. It is true that both G. Stanley Hall and William James regarded dreams as worthy of study and that in his later life James analyzed one of his own dreams with great insight; but the bearings of dreams on sex were only slightly sensed. See G. Stanley Hall, *Adolescence*, 2 vols. (New York, 1917), 1:262, 454, 502.

76. Sanford Bell, "A Preliminary Study of the Emotion of Love between the Sexes," *American Journal of Psychology* 13 (1902): 326.

77. A study of middle-class college women begun by Clelia D. Mosher in the 1890s was later resumed at Stanford. It indicated that there was little support for the widely held view that women were deficient in sexuality, and suggested further that the stereotypes and hortatory advice of a great many marriage manuals for restraint had little effect. Carl N. Degler, "What Ought to Be and What Was," pp. 1467–90.

esthetic dimensions in the writings of George Santayana and Henry James.

In *The Sense of Beauty* (1896) the young Harvard philosopher George Santayana argued that had nature solved the problem of reproduction without sex differentiation, "our emotional life would have been radically different. So profound and, especially in woman, so pervasive an influence does this function exert, that we should betray an entirely unreal view of human nature if we did not inquire into the relations of sex with our esthetic susceptibilities."[78] Santayana went on to emphasize the importance of secondary sex characteristics in men and women. "It is precisely from the waste, and from the radiation of the sexual passion, that beauty borrows warmth. . . . the whole sentimental side of our esthetic sensibility—without which it would be perceptive and mathematical rather than esthetic—is due to our sexual organization remotely stirred." Before sex found expression, the senses had to be stimulated—the eye and ear in particular. Hence both senses developed secondary characteristics, and the sexual emotions were simultaneously extended to various secondary objects, including some of the most conspicuous elements of beauty. "If anyone were desirous to produce a being with a great susceptibility to beauty, he could not invent an instrument better designed for that object than sex. . . . We may say, then, that for man all nature is a secondary object of sexual passion, and that to this fact the beauty of nature is largely due."[79] This conception of the unconscious relation of sex and beauty differed markedly from the traditional view that art consciously fulfilled an ennobling and divine function in the expressions of human nature.

Among the men of letters in the post-Civil War decades who wrote pointedly, if somewhat off-handedly, about human nature, James Russell Lowell[80] and William Dean Howells[81] made some shrewd and varied

78. George Santayana, *The Sense of Beauty: Being the Outline of Esthetic Theory* (New York, 1896), pp. 38, 39, 40.

79. Santayana, *Sense of Beauty*, pp. 38, 39, 40.

80. Lowell once gave as a reason why Americans could not develop a distinctive literature the "fact" that human nature, the center of creative writing, is without time or place. On another occasion, in reviewing Harriet Beecher Stowe's *The Minister's Wooing*, he agreed with the proverb that there is a good deal of human nature in men but amazingly little in books. Charles Edward Stowe, *Life of Harriet Beecher Stowe* (Boston, 1889), p. 328.

81. In an essay entitled "Equality as the Basis of Good Society" Howells wrote: "I am a great friend of human nature, and I like it all the better because it has had to suffer so much unjust reproach. It seems to me that we are always mistaking our conditions for our natures, and saying that human nature is greedy and mean and false and cruel, when only its conditions are so. We say you must change human nature if you wish to have human

comments, without explicitly recognizing the significance of either unconscious mental life or sex as a major force in man's makeup. As we have seen, this was not entirely true of Walt Whitman. Mark Twain's sense of the bitter irony in much of life was most explicitly expressed in an essay *What Is Man?* (1906). In later essays, often unfinished, he sensed the power of unconscious forces in symbols that inextricably fused realities and dreams.[82] Henry James, however, was the most notable exception. Whether or not he remarked that the unconscious was whatever was in man's mind when he was not thinking about sex, he displayed great skill and subtlety in depicting the unconscious wishes and mechanisms that explained the characters and motives of those he wrote about. Indeed, in the words of Leo Levy, "the substance of James's fiction is in its representation of moral and psychological relations as they are refracted upon surface awareness and within the subterranean levels which shape awareness."[83] While James had not developed a clear theory of how unconscious determinants emerge, he had by 1880 constructed a working hypothesis about the reasons why and the ways in which unconscious motives operated in conventional society. In his novel *Confidence* (1880) he did not approach the unconscious through "emblematic forms of the supernatural and the apparitional." *Confidence*, Levy wrote, stood up "as a study in the difficulties which arise from our failure to know ourselves in love, it establishes the thesis that 'confidence'—in the extended, nearly allegorical sense of self-knowledge—must draw upon the self that is unconscious and make it accessible to awareness. It is, accordingly, a landmark in the history of James's long and rewarding study of human consciousness."[84] In his

---

brotherhood, but we really mean that you must change human conditions, and this is quite feasible. It has always been better than its conditions, and ready for newer and fitter conditions." *Century Magazine* 51 (1895): 67. See also his "True Talk of Dreams," *Harper's Magazine* 15 (1895): 836–45.

82. Mark Twain, *Autobiography*, 2 vols. (New York, 1924), 2:248. ". . . human nature is all alike. . . . we like to know what the big people are doing, so that we can envy them. . . . Conspicuousness is the only thing in a person to command our interest and, in a larger or smaller sense, our worship." *Autobiography*, 2:37–38, 248–49. Also relevant: Mark Twain's *Innocents Abroad*, 2 vols. (New York, 1911), 1:297 and 2:18; *The Mysterious Stranger and Other Stories* (New York, 1922), p. 195; *What Is Man?* (New York, 1906); *What Is Man? and Other Essays* (New York, 1917); and *What Is Man?* ed. S. K. Ratcliffe (London, 1936). For the later essays special account needs to be given to John S. Tuckey, ed., *Mark Twain's "Which Was the Dream?" and Other Symbolical Writings of the Later Years* (Berkeley, 1967).

83. Leo B. Levy, "Henry James' *Confidence* and the Development of the Idea of the Unconscious," *American Literature* 28 (1956): 347.

84. Levy, "Henry James' *Confidence*," pp. 353, 358.

great biography as well as in other comments, Leon Edel has further shown the techniques by which James "makes the reader aware of how the unconscious motives are formed and how they affect conscious personality and behavior."[85]

Thus in America, as in Europe, explorations of the unconscious, in philosophy, medicine, and literature, contributed to a new understanding of a crucial component of human nature. This achievement heralded still further explorations and the rise of an organized cult attractive to increasing numbers of American intellectuals.

85. Leon Edel, *The Psychological Novel 1900–1950* (New York, 1955), p. 359.

11

Searches for Greater Understanding

If someone had asked Freud about the nature of human culture, he would probably have answered as follows: Human nature is the basis of culture. Culture is the product of human nature, and psychology of the individual is the key that opens the door to the study of culture.

If someone should ask Fromm, Horney, or Sullivan what the nature of human nature is, they would probably answer: Culture is the determinant of personality. Human nature is a product of culture, and interpersonal relations are the key to the interpretation of the riddle of human nature.

BENJAMIN B. WOLMAN, 1960

THE FAMOUS visit of Freud, Jung, and Ferenczi to Clark University in 1908 launched the psychoanalytic movement in America, the basic ideas of which, as we have seen, had been anticipated on both sides of the Atlantic. Freud had already made well-known contributions to neurology and physiology and had begun to formulate a view of human nature to which the name *psychoanalysis* was given in 1896. It was distinctive in its sharp focus on unconscious mental and emotional life and in the ways advocated for understanding and coping with it. Psychoanalysis favored the use of free association and the interpretation of dreams as more effective methods than hypnosis for getting at the conditions that kept repressed and trouble-making wishes from crossing the threshold of consciousness.

Freud had not yet fully come to the biological or instinctual image of man that he had been forging. At first, in stressing sex trauma as the underlying factor in mental illness and neuroses, he seemed to deny the prevailing focus on inborn factors. Between 1900 and his visit to Clark University in 1908 he had decided that human nature was basically made up of instincts or psychic energies that he called libido (sexual energy) and self-preservation. In its tidal thrust for realization the former led to conflicts with the norms of society. The repression of the libido, particularly as the result of traumatic sex experience in very early childhood, led to neurotic behavior. The conflict between the endless urge for expressing libido and the set patterns of adjustment to community life also explained the forgetting of unpleasant memories, slips of the tongue, unconscious body movements, and above all, the seemingly absurd dream experience, a disguised fulfillment of hidden wishes and fears. Freud's largely deterministic view of behavior was modified by his conviction that dream analysis and free association could bring the true character of troublesome wishes into consciousness. But he did not expect miraculous cures. At most, a useful but limited reason might help clarify the effect of repression, conflict, and "resistance." This in turn could lessen the inevitable and enduring tension between pleasurable instincts and the demands of life in civilized society.[1]

Freud's views in part reflected, as so many have said, the patriarchal and structured Viennese society of the 1890s and the dominating "Victorian" attitudes toward women and sex. At the same time, his great concern with the primitive was a legacy from both the Romantic impulse and Darwin's theory of evolution. It also reflected his interest in the ethnology of Fraser, Tylor, and Robertson-Smith. The Greek tragedies, too, impressed on him the basic, primitive drives in human nature, an impression evident in his classical rhetoric and in his concept of an Oedipus complex—a persisting and perplexing love-hate relationship between child and parents. Since Freud took the Oedipus complex to be both innate and universal,[2] he ascribed what he observed in the personality and behavior of his patients to a universal, biologically based human nature.

During the First World War and in the following years, Freud expanded and modified his image of man. He now sensed that the self-preservation instinct as well as the sexual could, when held back, give birth to neurotic anxieties. Expressed in aggression and lust for power, that instinct was associated with feelings of guilt and shame, whether outlet was found in sadism or in destructive war. Since any adequate image of man had to account for the dynamic development of personality, Freud elaborated, in the 1920s, his stages of personality development (oral, anal, genital). He further complemented his first theory of anxiety, identified with the reemergence of repressed libido, with his second theory, the ego's response to the threat of the loss of a loved object. Freud also consolidated his structural psychology in terms

1. When Freud came to America in 1908, his principal writings, as yet untranslated into English, included *Studies in Hysteria* (with Breuer), 1895; *The Interpretation of Dreams*, 1900; *On Dreams*, 1901; *Three Contributions to Sexual Theory*, 1905; and *Jokes and Their Relation to the Unconscious*, 1905.

2. For a searching discussion of the Oedipus complex in relation to anthropology see A. L. Kroeber, "Totem and Taboo in Retrospect," *American Journal of Sociology* 45 (1939): 446–51.

of the classic formulation of id, ego, and superego, giving to ego a somewhat larger organizing and integrating function in relation to id and superego than he had done in his earlier writing. Although in effect he rejected the culture concept which contradicted his instinctual or biological view of man, he did develop a culture theory of his own. In his view, human nature created culture and civilization through conflict between the pleasure-giving instincts and the reality principle, the necessity of work and of the restraint imposed by living in society.

The sublimation process accounted not only for the creative arts but for religion. Freud touched on this in *Totem and Taboo* (1913) and elaborated his views in *The Future of an Illusion* (1927) and *Moses and Monotheism* (1939). Faced by the unending conflict between impulses and necessary restraints, man developed religion to explain his tortured fate. The omnipotent gods became the substitute for the necessary but rejected authority of the father figure. In further meeting the emotional requirements of punishment for aggression (sin), religion rationalized the need of sanctioned communal restraints on instinct and thus offered man a welcome crutch. Freud failed to sense that religion might give creative and self-fulfilling meaning to life. Thus he could feel that human beings might not and should not always have to use religion—a "compulsive neurosis"—as the means of reconciling the conflict between wayward and destructive impulses with necessary social restraints.

Neither *Civilization and Its Discontents* nor his other later books, written while suffering from a jaw cancer, lessened this essentially dark and grim view of human nature. He stressed increasingly the never-ending conflict between the life-love instinct and the concomitant thrust toward death and destruction, ordained by the inevitable destruction of organic into inorganic. At best, the human fate was precarious.[3] The alarming upsurge of Nazism could only confirm his pessimism, as he found refuge in England from the anti-Semitism that swept over Austria.[4]

3. Sigmund Freud, *Civilization and Its Discontents* (New York, 1930), pp. 25, 28. In addition to this and *New Lectures on Psychoanalysis* (New York, 1933), and to earlier writings by Freud, I am indebted, for this bare outline of his concept of human nature, to Ernest Jones, *The Life and Work of Sigmund Freud*, 3 vols. (New York, 1953–57); Clara Thompson, *Psychoanalysis: Evolution and Development* (New York, 1950); Philip Rieff, *Freud: The Mind of a Moralist* (New York, 1959); H. Stuart Hughes, *Consciousness and Society* (New York, 1958), chap. 4; Paul Roazen, *Freud: Political and Social Thought* (New York, 1968); Daniel Yankelovich and William Barrett, *Ego and Instinct: The Psychoanalytic View of Human Nature* (New York, 1970); and Steven Kern, *Anatomy and Destiny* (Indianapolis, 1975), chap. 4.

4. In his correspondence with Einstein, Freud took a somewhat less grim view of war than might have been expected. See the *Standard Edition of the Complete Psychological Works of Sigmund Freud*, 24 vols. (London, 1953–74), 22:197–215.

In addition to Freud's own accounts of the initial American reaction to his ideas, a good deal of information is at hand.[5] He was surprised, in view of the hostility he had met professionally in Europe, to find on his American visit that such "important" men as William James, G. Stanley Hall, and Dr. James Putnam, a noted Harvard neurologist, knew his work and viewed it open-mindedly. He was to be deeply indebted to Dr. Putnam, whose influence in persuading leading neurologists and psychiatrists to take Freud's work seriously could hardly be overemphasized. He also owed a good deal to the pioneer American analysts Isador Coriat of Boston, William A. White, the progressive humanitarian who administered St. Elizabeth's hospital for the mentally ill in Washington, and Smith Ely Jelliffe, a stimulating pioneer in psychosomatic medicine. Dr. Abraham A. Brill, a Jewish immigrant from Austria-Hungary who was the first practitioner in New York, translated his works and popularized his theories. Freud was also indebted to Dr. Ernest Jones, who from his chair at the University of Toronto found opportunities to address psychiatric meetings in the United States. Despite his indebtedness to all these and others, Freud never overcame his contempt for what he regarded as the hypocrisy, materialism, and superficiality of American civilization.

John C. Burnham's thorough study of American medicine and psychoanalysis before 1918 has shown that, despite opposition, the reception by psychiatrists of the teachings of Freud and his group was on the whole favorable.[6] This resulted in part from the already keenly felt dissatisfaction with the somatic explanation of mental and emotional problems, and from the eclectic and generally hospitable attitude of the profession. Moreover, even those who understood psychoanalysis best

5. Sigmund Freud, *The History of the Psycho-analytic Movement* (New York, 1917), pp. 22–39; and *An Autobiographical Study* (New York, 1927), pp. 102 ff.; John Chynowith Burnham, "The Beginnings of Psychoanalysis in the United States," *The American Imago* 13 (1956): 65–68; "The New Psychology: From Narcissism to Social Control," in John Braeman, Robert Bremner, and David Brody, eds., *Change and Continuity in Twentieth-Century America: The 1920s* (Columbus, Oh., 1968), pp. 351–98; and *Psychoanalysis and American Medicine, 1894–1918: Medicine, Science and Culture* (New York, 1967), monograph 20 (vol. 5) of *Psychological Issues*; A. A. Brill, "The Introduction and Development of Freud's Work in the United States," *American Journal of Sociology* 45 (1939): 318 ff.; William A. Koelsch, "Freud Discovers America," *Virginia Quarterly Review* 46 (1970): 115–32; John R. Seeley, *The Americanization of the Unconscious* (New York, 1967); Hendrick M. Ruitenbeek, *Freud and America* (New York, 1966); Frederick J. Hoffman, *Freudianism and the Literary Mind* (Baton Rouge, 1945; 2d ed., 1957); F. H. Matthews, "The Americanization of Sigmund Freud," *Journal of American Studies* 1 (1967): 39–62; Paul Roazen, "Freud and America," *Social Research* 39 (1972): 720–32; and above all else, a high-water mark in scholarship, Nathan G. Hale, Jr., *Freud and the Americans: The Beginnings of Psychoanalysis in the United States, 1876–1917* (New York, 1971).

6. John C. Burnham, *Psychoanalysis and American Medicine, 1894–1918*, pp. 196–97.

presented it in modified terms, some deemphasizing the importance
Freud gave to sex.[7] Dr. James Putnam linked psychoanalysis with ethical
idealism, in the hope that it might be developed within a context of
community service.[8] That psychoanalysis made the headway in the
profession that it did was also related to the way in which Americans
featured its melioristic implications in the reformist climate of opinion
of the Progressive era, implications hardly in line with Freud's own
reservations.

Though Dr. Jelliffe concluded in 1939, the year of Freud's death, that
psychoanalysis had beneficially penetrated American psychiatry,[9] the
attitudes of practitioners varied from outright rejection to enthusiastic
acceptance and moderate affirmation.

The moderate position found a spokesman in Dr. Adolph Meyer, a
Swiss immigrant psychiatrist and clinical director of the Worcester,
Massachusetts, Insane Asylum, and later, of the Pathological Institute of
the New York State Hospitals. Meyer was a major force in moulding the
psychoanalytic stress on early childhood experience and on the role of
symbols. In the context of his own psychobiology, which William James
and Charles S. Peirce had influenced, he also believed that
psychoanalysis, in giving undue weight to instinctual vicissitudes and
unconscious motivations, neglected the total personality.[10]

Objections to Freudian theory and therapy in psychiatry found their
most original and in the long run influential critic in Harry Stack
Sullivan (1892-1949). Notwithstanding, perhaps in part because of,
inadequate early professional training and his own persistent emotional
problems that analysts failed to resolve, Sullivan approached even the
severest mental disturbances empirically and pragmatically. Though

7. This was not the case with Dr. Horace W. Frink, professor of neurology at Cornell
University Medical College, who thought that analysis should help patients accept sexuality
and who emphasized its potentialities for happiness. His *Morbid Fears and Compulsions*
(London, 1921), which reflected the influence of Dewey and the environmentalists, was
nevertheless an able exposition of psychoanalysis. Paul Roazen in *Freud and His Followers*
(New York, 1975), pp. 378–80, offers interesting insight.

8. Dr. James Jackson Putnam, "Personal Impressions of Sigmund Freud and His Work,"
Journal of Abnormal Psychology 4 (1909–10): 293–310, 372–79; *Human Motives* (Boston,
1915); *Scientific American* 78, Supplement (1914); *Addresses on Psychoanalysis* (Vienna,
1921); and Nathan G. Hale, Jr., ed., *James Jackson Putnam and Psychoanalysis: Letters between Putnam and Sigmund Freud* (Cambridge, Mass., 1971).

9. Dr. Smith Ely Jelliffe, "Sigmund Freud and Psychiatry: A Partial Appraisal,"
American Journal of Sociology 45 (1939): 326–40.

10. For brief accounts of Meyer see Theodore Lidz's essay in the *International Encyclopedia of the Social Sciences*, and Alfred Lief's *The Commonsense Psychiatry of Dr.
Adolph Meyer* (New York, 1948). Eunice Winters has edited Meyer's *Collected Papers*, 4
vols. (Baltimore, 1950–52).

influenced by the ideas of such distinguished psychiatrists as Dr. William Alanson White and Dr. Adolph Meyer and by Edwin Sapir, Charles Cooley, George Herbert Mead, and the indeterminist principle of Werner Heisenberg, Sullivan looked upon his substitute for Freudianism as derived largely from his own insight and experience as a teacher and clinician.

Sullivan felt that the basic theories of Freud were essentially metaphors which could neither be seen, heard, and felt nor scientifically validated. This was notably true of the idea of unconscious as a "thing" (for which he substituted the concept of awareness and unawareness), of the theory of infant sexuality and its bearing on the formation of a fixed personality, and of the therapeutic methods of free association, dream analysis, and introspection. He was convinced that emotional problems resulted from maladjustments in interpersonal relations from infancy to death, and that emotional well-being resulted when such relations were wholesome. Sullivan taught that interpersonally derived anxieties and insecurities blocked unnecessarily the full use of human powers and restricted the natural tendency toward emotional well-being. In his later life he also emphasized the idea of the one-genus postulate: "We are all much more simply human than otherwise"—similarities between human beings, regardless of differences in culture, environment, and mental health, that is, are much greater than differences. Sullivan never fully developed the implications of this conviction for relations between races and generations, though he suggested ways for spelling out his position. In short, Sullivan's theory of the basic role of interpersonal relations in personality formation, together with his distinctive therapy of participant-observer dialogue, offered an alternative to the Freudian theory and practice he largely rejected. In some respects, perhaps, his teaching penetrated American psychiatry to an equal or even greater extent than orthodox and variant psychoanalytic schools of thought and therapy.[11]

The objections to the new search for depth at the time of Freud's death were best summed up by Dr. Abraham Myerson. A distinguished neurologist and psychiatrist, he was widely known for his telling attacks on the doctrine of the heritability of mental illness. Myerson polled the American Neurological Association and the American Psychiatric

11. Most of Sullivan's principal work was brought together and published after his death: *The Interpersonal Theory of Psychiatry* (New York, 1953), *The Psychiatric Interview* (New York, 1954), *Schizophrenia as a Human Process* (New York, 1962), and *The Fusion of Psychiatry and Social Science* (New York, 1964). Commentators include Dorothy Blitstein, *The Social Theories of Harry Stack Sullivan* (New York, 1953), Helen Swick Perry, "Harry Stack Sullivan," *Dictionary of American Biography*, Supplement 4 (New York, 1974), and Arthur H. Chapman, *Harry Stack Sullivan, His Life and Works* (New York, 1976).

Association to find out just how their members stood. He himself viewed Freud as a man who, more than any forerunner, had realized the importance of sex and of inner psychic struggles. He also conceded the usefulness of certain Freudian concepts, the validity of which had not been clearly shown—the sharp separation of conscious from unconscious processes, for example, and the belief that the unconscious was an organized personality or place where complexes and forgotten experiences roamed looking for a chance to find expression. Myerson thought, however, that psychoanalysis, while giving lip service to the idea of the human being as a unified entity, helped keep alive the ancient body-mind dilemma. Nor did he approve what he considered the Freudian assumption that patients' complexes existed in an economic as well as a physiological vacuum. And finally, Freud's theorizing, to him, seemed rigid, overdone, and premature.[12]

It was hardly to be expected that academic psychologists would look on psychoanalysis with as much favor as psychiatrists on the whole did. The exploration of unconscious mental activity was alien to their commitment to laboratory experiment, measurement, and control. William James, notwithstanding his early encouragement to Freud and his associates and his insight into the importance of the fleeting, hazy, and devious in his "stream of thought" idea, objected to what seemed to him Freud's dogmatism and oversimplified, monistic reductionism.[13] Other psychologists also felt that Freud vastly overemphasized sex and its bearing on neuroses, dreams, sublimation, and creativity. To some it seemed that he generalized from observations of neurotic patients and thus left no real distinction between normality and abnormality. Still others, claiming that he had little or no sense of the basic principles of inductive and deductive logic, characterized his theories as highly speculative and cloaked in vague, metaphorical, even mystical terminology.[14] Several circumstances widened the gulf between what Freud

12. Abraham Myerson, "The Attitude of Neurologists, Psychiatrists and Psychologists toward Psychoanalysis," *American Journal of Psychiatry* 96 (1939): 636–41.

13. *Letters of William James*, ed. Henry James, 2 vols. (Boston, 1920), 2:327–28; Ralph Barton Perry, *The Thought and Character of William James*, 2 vols. (Boston, 1934), 2:123; Robert C. Le Clair, ed., *The Letters of William James and Theodore Flournoy* (Madison, Wis., 1966), p. 224.

14. Christine Ladd-Franklin, "Freudian Doctrines," *The Nation* 103 (1916): 373–74; R. S. Woodworth, "Followers of Freud and Jung," *The Nation* 103 (1916): 396; W. B. Pillsbury, "New Developments in Psychology," *Philosophical Review* 26 (1917): 56–69; Knight Dunlap, "The Social Need for Scientific Psychology," *Scientific Monthly* 11 (1920): 502–17; and *Mysticism, Freudianism and Scientific Psychology* (St. Louis, 1920). See also

was saying and what psychologists assumed that he was saying: only part of his writing was at hand in faulty translations; most psychologists depended on not always accurate second-hand accounts; and Freud's shifts in emphasis and his amendments to his early theories made it hard to keep abreast of his thinking.

Then why did a few psychologists favor the new movement?[15] One possible explanation was the perception of some kinship between psychoanalysis and the dynamic character of functional psychology. In his early writing John Dewey, notwithstanding grave differences, agreed with Freud that human beings were governed by memories rather than by actual facts and that, in turn, association, suggestion, and dramatic fantasy governed memory.[16] A more striking example was Edwin B. Holt, a student of James. In *The Freudian Wish* (1915) he interpreted a leading Freudian concept in psychological, behaviorist, and pragmatic terms as a simple but universal technique for the release of instinctive energies. He suggested that psychoanalysis might provide the solution of conflicts in such a way that in the satisfaction of any one wish, all other wishes would be ethically satisfied.[17] Even John B. Watson, once a functionalist and later a behaviorist who rejected the concept of consciousness, wrote appreciatively in 1916 of Freud's emphasis on sex.[18]

In the view of G. Stanley Hall, the leading psychologist to champion psychoanalysis, Freudianism marked the greatest epoch in the history of psychology. It brought to the fore the neglected element of feeling and of sex. To be sure, Hall did not accept the view that sex was all-dominant, nor did he regard all dreams as wish fulfillment or the Oedipus complex as more than a doubtful notion. Yet the "immense fruitfulness" of the Freudian methods of exploring the unconscious and the fundamen-

---

Edna Heidbreder, "Freud and Psychology," *Psychological Review* 47 (1940): 185–95; and the thorough study of David Shakow and David Rapaport, *The Influence of Freud on American Psychology* (Cleveland, 1968).

15. E. W. Scripture, writing in the *New York Medical Record*, presented a not unsympathetic account of Jung's free-association techniques. See *Current Literature* 50 (1911): 167–69.

16. Shakow and Rapaport, *The Influence of Freud on American Psychology*, pp. 8, 73–74; Morton Levitt, *Freud and Dewey on the Nature of Man* (New York, 1960), pp. 113–16. While not minimizing differences, Leavitt notes several other similar concepts.

17. For comments on Holt: William E. Hocking, *Human Nature and Its Remaking* (New Haven, 1918), p. 19; James Gibson, in Carl A. Murchison, ed., *A History of Psychology in Autobiography*, 6 vols. (Worcester, Mass., and New York, 1930–74), 5:129; Daniel Katz, "Edwin B. Holt," *Science* 103 (1946): 612; and Herbert S. Langfeld, "E. B. Holt," *Psychological Review* 53 (1946): 251–58.

18. John B. Watson, "The Psychology of Wish Fulfillment," *Scientific Monthly* 3 (1916): 479–87. See also Watson's essay in Ethel S. Dummer, ed., *The Unconscious: A Symposium*, (New York, 1928), pp. 91–113.

tal importance assigned to the first four years of childhood seemed to Hall to overshadow Freud's limitations. By 1914 he found much to commend in Adler's "individual psychology." In his autobiography (1924), he praised the Freudian school for its influence on the study of history, biography, esthetics, and medicine. He again declared that the unconscious, with Freud as its pioneer explorer, "marks more than anything else, the belated advent of evolution into the study of man's psychic nature."[19] At least one other leading psychologist, William McDougall, took a comparably favorable view. Despite their differences he wrote, in 1926, that Freud had done more to advance the understanding of the mind than anyone since Aristotle.[20]

In the 1920s, and more particularly in the next decade, an increasing number of psychologists recognized the relevance of many Freudian concepts to the study of abnormal behavior, child psychology, and the personality.[21] Yet a survey in 1940 showed that experimentalists had only recently come to view the psychoanalytical ideas with any favor, and that this was by no means overwhelming.[22] According to Professor Ernest H. Hilgard, the more or less unconscious rapprochement that did take place hinged on the mechanism of adjustment, including the role of conflict, repression, rationalization, and indirect fulfillment. Motivation psychology, which with some exceptions academic psychologists had bypassed, profited from the Freudian encouragement of projective tests and from the emphasis on "goal directedness." At Yale, Clark L. Hull and his group related the conditioned reflex to psychoanalytical concepts. The drive-reduction theory of learning, as Hull developed it, corresponded in some sense to Freud's concept of pleasure as the goal of behavior. In each case the emphasis was on the reduction of stimuli. The puzzle of subconscious mental activity also encouraged new experiments on the reaction of subjects to stimuli below the threshold. Still, Professor Hilgard, assessing the evidence in 1958, attributed less importance to the results than some.[23]

19. G. Stanley Hall, *Life and Confessions of a Psychologist* (New York, 1923), pp. 410 ff., 414.

20. William McDougall, *Psychoanalysis and Social Psychology* (London, 1936), p. 17.

21. Robert R. Sears, *Survey of Objective Studies of Psychoanalytic Concepts*, Social Science Research Council Bulletin no. 51 (New York, 1953), chap. 8; Shakow and Rapaport, *The Influence of Freud on American Psychology*, pp. 62 ff., 191 ff.; John Dollard and Neal Miller, *Personality and Psychotherapy* (New York, 1950); Rollo May, ed., *Existential Psychology* (New York, 1969), p. 29.

22. J. F. Brown, "Freud's Influence on American Psychology," *Psychoanalytic Quarterly* 9 (1940): 283–92.

23. Ernest R. Hilgard, *Unconscious Processes and Man's Rationality* (Urbana, Ill., 1958), pp. 9 ff. See also Ernest R. Hilgard, "Experimental Approaches to Psychoanalysis," in E. Pumpian-Mindlin, ed., *Psychoanalysis as Science* (Stanford, 1952), pp. 44–45; and *Theories of Learning* (New York, 1956), chap. 9.

Despite all this, many psychologists would have accepted the judgment of E. G. Boring in 1950 that the founder of psychoanalysis had awakened the profession's interest in human nature.[24] What Boring had in mind was in part spelled out by Edward S. Robinson, a functionalist who pioneered in bringing psychology to bear upon an understanding of law and legal thinking. He noted that one of the strongest tendencies in human nature led man to hide motives unacceptable to prevailing social customs, a tendency observed long before Freud. Despite the knowledge of this, psychology had continued to err in its overly moral and intellectual view of human nature. "The Freudian theory," Robinson wrote, "has shown us how to look behind rationalizations that men give of their own conduct and to view candidly any motive whatever that may be discovered there. Sex desire, personal ambition, feelings of insecurity, from which even men of science used to turn away, have become admitted normal ingredients of human life."[25]

Most philosophers shared the largely negative reaction of psychologists to psychoanalysis as the key to depth and inner truth. Warner Fite of Princeton felt that it distorted the ancient and respectable conscious self into foolish obscenity.[26] Mortimer Adler, a neo-Thomist, acknowledged some truth in some Freudian ideas but regarded psychoanalysts as "uncritical speculators, as bad philosophers."[27] Paul Carus and Ralph Barton Perry also deplored the seeming denigration of reason and the elevation of instinct and emotion.[28] In his willingness to submit Freudian doctrines to clinical, instrumental tests, Horace Kallen, a Jamesian pragmatist, stood somewhat alone in philosophical circles.[29]

Notwithstanding the ultimate rapprochement of religion and psychoanalysis, the first reactions of the cloth were hostile. To some churchmen, Freud made no proper distinction between normal and abnormal personalities in matters of sex, and encouraged the analyst to

24. Edwin G. Boring, *A History of Experimental Psychology* (New York, 1950), p. 713. In *Psychologist at Large* (New York, 1961) Boring says that at the age of forty-eight he had been analyzed and was "wiser about human nature for having been analyzed, and wiser for finding the analysts human and without a magic to dispense" (p. 55).

25. Edward S. Robinson, *Law and Lawyers* (New York, 1937), p. 60. See also Jerome Frank's *Law and the Modern Mind* (New York, 1930), a brilliant interpretation of law in psychoanalytical terms.

26. Warren Fite, "Psychoanalysis and Sex Theory," *The Nation* 103 (1916): 127–29.

27. Mortimer Adler, *What Man Has Made of Man* (New York, 1937), p. 118.

28. Paul Carus, "Wrong Generalizations in Philosophy," *The Monist* 23 (1913): 150–51; Ralph Barton Perry, *A Modernist View of National Ideals* (Berkeley, 1926), p. 190.

29. Horace Kallen, "The Mystery of Dreams," *Dial* 55 (1913): 79–80. For a comparison of the ideas of John Dewey and Freud see Morton Levitt, *Freud and Dewey on the Nature of Man*, chap. 7.

usurp the function of parson and priest. Others felt that psychoanalysts denied the autonomy of spiritual values by identifying them with compensations for frustrated primary needs. At the core of such criticism was the inadmissibility of free will if, as Freud insisted, motives were in large part unconscious.[30] By the time of the Second World War, however, many religious leaders had accepted psychotherapy as a useful technique pointing toward religion in the sense of "the goal and meaning of life." According to Rollo May, a leader in the alliance, therapists such as Dr. Karl Menninger realized "that they overburden their knowledge when they require it to serve as a religion too, and religious thinkers are now seeing that they rob themselves chiefly if they do not make use of the techniques of those who endeavor to be scientific in their understanding of the human soul."[31] Psychoanalysis and religion, "fundamentalism" and the pentecostal sects apart, had indeed become in large part collaborators rather than competitors.[32]

Most social scientists were at first as skeptical of Freud as religious leaders and philosophers were—or they were indifferent. Economists felt that Freud gave little or no place in his picture of patriarchal tyranny and revolt against it to bread-and-butter factors. Moreover, neoclassical economists still clung to logic and a rational calculus. By the 1920s, however, Elton Mayo and a few others, chiefly in schools of business administration, recognized the bearing of certain Freudian ideas on the increase of output and consumption and on smoothing labor-management relations.[33] Advertising authorities began the shift from the

30. For an early Catholic criticism see Charles Bruehl, "Psychoanalysis," *Catholic World* 116 (1923): 577–89. Contrast this with Gregory Zilboorg, *Psychoanalysis and Religion* (New York, 1962), the testament of a Catholic convert who had long been a practicing analyst. Paul W. West and Charles Edward Skinner, *Psychology for Religious and Social Workers* (New York, 1939), pp. 195 ff., saw some merit in Freudian therapy but felt that it overstressed sex and the death instinct and that its theory was largely hypothetical.

31. Rollo May, *The Springs of Creative Living: A Study in Human Nature and God* (New York, 1944), pp. 24–25.

32. The dimensions of the problem are discussed with special insight in Anton Boisen, *Out of the Depths: An Autobiographical Study of Mental Disorder and Religious Experience* (New York, 1960); and Paul Tillich, "Psychotherapy and a Christian Interpretation of Human Nature," *The Review of Religion* 13 (1949): 264–68.

33. Elton Mayo, *Human Problems of an Industrial Civilization* (New York, 1933), pp. 131 ff.; Calvin Hall and Gardner Lindzey, "Psychoanalytic Theory and Its Application in the Social Sciences," in Gardner Lindzey and Elliott Aronson, eds., *Handbook of Social Psychology*, 2 vols. (Reading, Mass., 1954), vol. 1, chap. 4. Lorenz Baritz, *The Servants of Power: A History of the Use of Social Science in American Industry* (Middletown, Conn., 1960), is a stimulating, pioneer study.

old emphasis on human rationality as an effective way of producing desired results to one that stressed egocentricity and unconscious motives. Edward L. Bernays, a nephew of Freud and a prominent figure in public relations, reported that Dr. A. A. Brill explained in Freudian terms the strength and weakness of advertisements for cigars.[34] By the 1950s, *Printers' Ink*, a leading trade journal, had shifted from its earlier skepticism about the usefulness of psychology. Its editor, J. George Frederick, was impressed by the Freudian emphasis on the unconscious and its implications for advertising. He also championed motivation research, which he defined as "an attempt to dredge up out of the hidden depths of human nature . . . some good practical hints as to how to sell a particular item of goods more readily and agreeably."[35] Others, in similar vein, emphasized the value of nonverbal symbols, including those associated with sex.

Nor did the first response of sociologists differ very much from that of economists. In retrospect, Ernest Burgess explained the negative attitude of his profession toward psychoanalysis during the first decade of its American career. Indifference or criticism owed much to "an aversion toward the explanation of human behavior in terms of sexual motivation, its particularistic emphasis, the simpler and apparently adequate cultural explanations of behavior, a predisposition against absolute interpretations as opposed to the relative, its apparently questionable technique, the rise of rival schools of psychoanalysts, its lack of integration with previous studies of instincts, and a preoccupation on the part of sociologists with their own problems."[36] It was nevertheless true that some sociologists fairly soon sensed the need for taking into account Freud's emphasis on the unconscious in behavior, the stress on the role of wish fulfillment, and the subtle analysis of cultural influences and personality development.[37] William G. Ogburn, Carlton Parker, Ernest Groves, Robert Park, and Ernest Burgess, in studying race relations, labor unrest, crime, and the family, used psychoanalytic concepts, notably compensation and sublimation. W. I. Thomas related the unconscious development of role and taste preferences in the personality to stimulus mechanisms, in the operation

34. Edward L. Bernays, *Biography of an Idea: Memoirs of a Public Relations Counsel* (New York, 1965), p. 395.

35. Merle Curti, "The Changing Concept of 'Human Nature' in the Literature of American Advertising," *Business History Review* 41 (1967): 356.

36. Ernest Burgess, "The Influence of Sigmund Freud upon Sociology in the United States," *American Journal of Sociology* 45 (1939): 356.

37. Manford H. Kuhn, "The Contributions of Sigmund Freud to Social Science" (Ph.D. diss., University of Wisconsin, 1941); Gisela Hinkle, "The Role of Freudianism in American Sociology" (Ph.D. diss., University of Wisconsin, 1950); Robert A. Jones, "Freud and American Sociology, 1909–1949," unpublished paper.

of the four famous "wishes," or partly inborn, partly learned impulses and values—the wishes for love, security, new experience, and recognition. Thomas, with his associate Znaniecki, also showed, in a famous study of the Polish immigrant, how unconscious factors affected the intricate interactions between the cultural values of the Old World and the expectations and requirements of living in a very different social order. Both the depression of the 1930s and the Second World War, in focusing attention on social disorganization or "pathology," invited greater consideration of Freud. By 1950 the structural-functional theory as developed by Talcott Parsons and others reflected the impact of psychoanalytical methods and theories.

At first, social work was mainly oriented toward sociology, but in the 1920s many of its leaders turned to an enthusiastic interest in psychoanalytic therapy. To critics at the time, within and outside the profession, this emphasis denigrated economic and social realities by overstressing personal psychological maladjustments.[38]

Anthropologists, while critical of the method Freud used and the oversimplification evident in *Totem and Taboo*, gradually discovered in psychoanalysis useful aids for understanding death beliefs, witchcraft anxieties, and other cultural puzzles. Edward Sapir explicated the historical and social patterning of linguistic behavior which to the speaker was more intuitive than consciously rational. Though seemingly self-evident in daily practice, in actual fact linguistic behavior was subtly involved with history and unconscious social experience. Moreover, "the average person unconsciously interprets the phonetic material of other languages in terms imposed upon him by the habits of his own language."[39] With Sapir and Alfred Kroeber breaking the path, anthropologists recognized that such concepts as ambivalence, projection, and compulsion neuroses clarified symbolic processes in language, religion, and art. Above all, the emphasis of psychoanalysis on child-rearing practices did much to focus anthropological interest on these and on culture and personality theory. In time some anthropologists, admitting an indebtedness to psychoanalysis for sharpening their awareness of universals in culture, rehabilitated the idea of a human nature that transcended cultural differences.[40]

38. Roy Lubove, *The Professional Altruist: The Emergence of Social Work as a Career, 1880–1930* (Cambridge, Mass., 1965), chap. 4.

39. In Ethel S. Dummer, ed., *The Unconscious: A Symposium* (New York, 1928), pp. 134, 136.

40. Clyde Kluckhohn, "The Influence of Psychiatry on Anthropology in America during the Past Hundred Years," in *One Hundred Years of American Psychiatry* (New York, 1944), pp. 589–617; "The Impact of Freud on Anthropology," in Aago Galston, M.D., ed., *Freud and Contemporary Culture* (New York, 1957), pp. 66–72; and Theodora Kroeber, *Alfred Kroeber, Personal Configuration* (Berkeley and Los Angeles, 1970), pp. 101 ff.

Students of politics also began to pay some heed to Freud and his followers, particularly to the emphasis on unconscious behavior, the role of wish fulfillment, and compensation. Walter Lippmann's *A Preface to Politics* (1914) held that the energy of original desires might be sublimated in socially useful ways, once people had learned not to impose artificial restrictions on natural wishes but to work out a political ethic consistent with their actual nature.[41]

Thoroughly at home with Freudian writing, Harold D. Lasswell published a pioneer study in 1930. He interviewed, using free association and dream analysis, such politically oriented persons as the agitator, the administrator, and the theorist. The assembled life histories pointed to connections between political role and personality structure in developmental sequences, and related these to social processes. The results explained ways in which, in Lasswell's terms, private motivations were more or less unconsciously and irrationally subsumed into such public causes as radicalism and military crusades, with moral rationalization in the name of patriotism, religion, class struggle, and race superiority. Conceiving of society as a patient, Lasswell suggested ways by which a psychoanalytically related political science might bring to bear preventive and curative therapy on a disordered society.[42] His methods and his evidence raised some eyebrows, even among friendly critics, nor were his models very well understood. But his later work, extended to world politics, the policy sciences, mass media, communication, and broadly conceived democratic values, suggested possibilities of understanding, predicting, and controlling political behavior. Though Lasswell was the outstanding example of Freudian influence on political science, Louis Hartz also reached a considerable audience, in an analysis of American political theory which made some use of Freudian theory.[43]

41. Walter Lippmann, "Freud and the Layman," *New Republic* 2 (1915), pt. 2, pp. 9–10; and *A Preface to Politics* (New York, 1913). Lippmann later revised his views. See, for example, his "Man's Image of Man," *Commonweal* 35 (1942): 406–9. In retreating from his early emphasis on the irrationality of man and from a humanism he had suggested as a modus vivendi, he advanced arguments stressing, not the "inherent rightness of the natural impulses of man's first nature," but "the second civilized nature which is the ruler within each man and is identified with the grand necessities of the commonwealth." See *The Public Philosophy* (New York, 1954), p. 64.

42. Harold D. Lasswell, *Psychopathology and Politics* (Chicago, 1931). The 1960 edition included an interesting essay "Afterthoughts: Thirty Years Later," pp. 269–319. See also Lasswell's *World Politics and Personal Insecurity* (New York, 1935), and "The Impact of Psychoanalytic Thinking on the Social Sciences," in Leonard D. White, ed., *The State of the Social Sciences* (Chicago, 1956), pp. 74–115.

43. Arnold A. Rogow, ed., *Politics, Personality and Social Science in the Twentieth Century* (Chicago, 1969), pp. 62, 120, 123 ff., 142; Louis Hartz, *The Liberal Tradition in America* (New York, 1955); Marvin Meyers, "An Appraisal," in *Comparative Studies in Society and History* 5 (1963): 264, 279.

Freudian and related ideas about human nature made an even more telling impact on literature than on the social studies. While a few younger writers such as Maxwell Bodenheim scorned the new creed, many poets, playwrights, and critics welcomed it as illuminating and emancipating. Already in revolt against philistinism and hypocritical attitudes toward sex, they ignored Freud's own prudishness and found in him a scientific justification for rejecting repression and for exploring the role of the unconscious in creativity.[44] The zest of such avant-garde literati and bohemians as Mable Dodge Luhan, James Oppenheim, Lincoln Steffens, and Max Eastman[45] spread quickly to others like Harvey O'Higgins, Floyd Dell, Sherwood Anderson, Conrad Aiken, Waldo Frank, Theodore Dreiser, Edgar Lee Masters, James Branch Cabell, and Eugene O'Neill. These writers, with or without firsthand knowledge of the master, exploited the repression of the sex drive by parental authority and social convention.[46]

Several critics followed Freud himself and some of his disciples in adopting psychoanalytical ideas as tools of literary analysis.[47] To be sure, Van Wyck Brooks and Joseph Wood Krutch used only partly grasped concepts in their studies of Mark Twain and Edgar Allan Poe.[48] Kenneth Burke, Lionel Trilling, Frederick Hoffman, and others demonstrated the dangers as well as the subtle rewards of the psychoanalytical interpretation of writers.[49] Increasingly, too, biographers and literary critics revealed new insights into the intricacies of personality as an

44. Oscar Cargill, *Intellectual America: The March of Ideas* (New York, 1941), chap. 6; Henry F. May, *The End of American Innocence* (New York, 1959), pp. 233–36, 260, 319–21; and Arthur Frank Wertheim, *The New York Little Renaissance* (New York, 1976), chap. 5. Wertheim notes that the first Bohemian group, unlike that of the 1920s, did not use Freudianism as a justification for promiscuity.

45. Mable Dodge Luhan, *Movers and Shakers* (New York, 1936), pp. 439 ff.; James Oppenheim, editorial, *Seven Arts* 2 (1917): 341; *The Autobiography of Lincoln Steffens* (New York, 1931), p. 655; Max Eastman, *Heroes I Have Known* (New York, 1942), p. 261.

46. Sherwood Anderson, *Sherwood Anderson's Memoirs* (New York, 1942), pp. 245, 284, 339–43; May, *The End of American Innocence*, pp. 233–63; Frederick Hoffman, *The Literary Mind* (Detroit, 1960); and Floyd Dell, *Homecoming* (New York, 1933).

47. Sigmund Freud, "The Relation of the Poet to Daydreaming" (1908), in *Collected Papers*, 5 vols. (New York, 1959), 4:173–83. See also the brilliant analysis of the unconscious in Shakespeare's *The Tempest* by Dr. Hanns Sachs, *The Creative Unconscious: Studies in the Psychoanalysis of Art*, ed. A. A. Roback (Cambridge, Mass., 1931). Sachs, a friend of Freud, practiced in Boston. Also pertinent: Lois Freiberg, *Psychoanalysis and American Criticism* (Detroit, 1960), and Claudia C. Morison, *Freud and the Critic* (Chapel Hill, 1968).

48. Marie Bonaparte, a student and friend of Freud, paid Krutch, however, a compliment for his use of psychoanalytic concepts in his *Life and Works of Edgar Allan Poe* (London, 1949), p. 20.

49. Kenneth Burke, *The Philosophy of Literary Form* (Baton Rouge, 1941; 2d ed., 1967); Lionel Trilling, *The Liberal Imagination* (New York, 1950); *The Opposing Self* (New York, 1955); Frederick Hoffman, *Freudianism and the Literary Mind*.

aspect of human nature. Newton Arvin's *Melville* (1950) depicted the interweaving of American middle-class morals and ideology with unconscious motivation, imagined sources of evil and suffering, deep instinctive impulses toward destruction, the conflict of these drives with life-asserting impulses, and the relation between irrational fears and desires with symbols and myths.[50] To take another example, Simon Lesser showed that Hawthorne's "My Kinsman, Major Mollineaux" would be in whole or in part meaningless on the basis alone of what the reader understood consciously. Indeed, Lesser went on, most fiction "says one thing to the conscious and whispers something quite different to the unconscious."[51]

Such examples from several fields, as well as the dissemination of ideas about psychoanalysis on a popular level,[52] aroused interest in the reasons for its American vogue. Doubtless the widespread general interest owed much to oversimplification and distortion. As a result, many failed to understand Freud's view of the ineluctable instinctual basis of human nature. In short, Freud's image of man failed for some time to be presented in anything like its complexity and subtlety.

Several writers suggested other explanations for the favor psychoanalysis enjoyed in many circles. It seemed somewhat far-fetched to assume that the appeal of analysis reflected the Puritan heritage of self-probing, concern with guilt and expiation, and the sanctification of achievement. Possibly the attrition of a traditional individualism and the readiness to accept the message of adjustment and manipulability provided a favorable context for some of Freud's teachings. Something might be said for the contention that psychoanalysis was less attractive as a psychological support in the Old World, with its greater social stability, than in an America of weakened middle-class family ties and uprootedness from settled communities. A more likely reason was that traditional American hospitality to messianic ideas corresponded with the optimistic mood of Progressivism.[53]

The impact of psychoanalysis on the American discussion of human nature became further complicated when such European dissenters as

50. Henry A. Murray, "In Nomine Diabole," *New England Quarterly* 24 (1951): 435–52.

51. Simon Lesser, *Fiction and the Unconscious* (New York, 1957), pp. 212–24.

52. The best account is Nathan G. Hale, Jr., *Freud and the Americans*, chap. 15.

53. Hendrick M. Ruitenbeek, *Freud and America*, pp. 14–23; John R. Seeley, *The Americanization of the Unconscious* (New York, 1967), esp. chap. 1; F. H. Matthews, "The Americanization of Sigmund Freud: Adaptations of Psychoanalysis before 1917," *Journal of American Studies* 1 (1967): 39–62; Paul Roazen, "Freud and America," *Social Research* 39 (1972): 720–32; and John C. Burnham, "Psychiatry, Psychology, and the Progressive Movement," *American Quarterly* 12 (1960): 464–65.

Carl Jung, Alfred Adler, and Wilhelm Reich won followers in the United States. The American disciples of these dissidents seldom offered a strikingly different image of man from that of their masters, but the influence of Jung, Adler, Reich, and others contributed to the growth of a "humanistic" psychology. This asserted the possibility of individual responsibility and the autonomy of the self in a balance between freedom and determinism. In addition to its indebtedness to the Freudian dissidents, the emerging position, sometimes spoken of as the third force, owed a good deal to the rediscovery of William James's psychology. It also owed something to Heidegger, Husserl, and Jaspers, exponents of phenomenology (understood as the acceptance of phenomena as given), and to the existentialisms of Kierkegaard, Sartre, Buber, Frankl, and Binswanger.

Generally speaking, in discussing human nature, the Americans responding to these movements emphasized not only the meaning of suffering but especially the concepts of responsibility, intentionality, choice, and futurity, all of which presumably defined the human condition. Yet more than their Old World mentors, the Americans managed to stress the optimistic implications of their teachings, which they sometimes tried to reshape into testable propositions.

Leading spokesmen for this new position included Rollo May, Abraham Maslow, Carl Rogers, Gordon W. Allport, and Hadley Cantril.[54] Dr. Rogers's client-oriented therapy assumed that the varying tendencies in every individual come to a continually changing balance in himself, though sometimes only with the help of an understanding therapist. More socially directed, Hadley Cantril, a psychologist at Princeton, maintained that every viable society "must satisfy basic survival needs, must provide security, must insure the repeatability of value-satisfactions already attained and must provide for new and emerging satisfactions." In Gordon Allport's more generalized words, phenomenology and existentialism invited an American psychology of mankind with due respect for the ideographic depiction of the unique individual and for the search for a world view as a central motive in

54. Representative writings are Rollo May's *Man's Search for Himself* (New York, 1953), and *Love and Will* (New York, 1969); Rollo May, Ernest Angel, and Henri Ellenberger, eds., *Existence: A New Dimension in Psychiatry* (New York, 1958); Rollo May, ed., *Existential Psychology* (New York, 1969); Carl Rogers, *On Becoming a Human Being: A Therapist's View of Psychotherapy* (Boston, 1961); Abraham H. Maslow, *Motivation and Personality* (New York, 1954), *New Knowledge and Human Values* (New York, 1959), *Religion, Values and Peak Experience* (Columbus, Oh., 1964), *Toward a Psychology of Being* (Princeton, 1968), and *The Farther Reaches of Human Nature* (New York, 1971); Gordon W. Allport, *Personality: A Psychological Interpretation* (New York, 1937), and *Becoming: Basic Considerations for a Psychology of Personality* (New York, 1961); and Hadley Cantril, *Human Nature and Political Systems* (New Brunswick, N.J., 1962).

living.[55] Meantime others, including Trigant Burrow, had helped reshape psychoanalytic ideas in roughly comparable directions.[56]

In the 1930s and 1940s, when economic insecurity, war, and the totalitarian test of democratic and humanistic traditions were shaking American society, a group of psychoanalysts worked out a distinctive view of human nature. Except for Abram Kardiner, everyone in the loosely affiliated group—Franz Alexander, Karen Horney, Erich Fromm, and Bruno Bettelheim—had migrated from Europe.[57] Though they accepted many of Freud's basic ideas, all of them responded to the new social setting. The crucial role assigned by Cooley, Mead, and other American social psychologists to very early interpersonal relations as shaped by the value system of primary institutions influenced their outlook, whether or not they knew at first hand the work of these pioneers. In further taking into account the anthropological discovery that the classic Oedipus complex and latency period did not exist in all cultures,[58] the neo-Freudians sensed the culture-bound limitations of many of Freud's generalizations. Dr. Adolph Meyer, Dr. William A. White, and Harry Stack Sullivan, who had long been stressing the role of environmental factors in mental illness, also influenced them.[59]

Whatever their differences, the neo-Freudians agreed that the individual must be seen, not as an isolated entity, but in terms of functional interaction with a particular social environment. In other words, man was in great part the product of the specific culture in which he lived; hence the learning experience necessarily bulked large in their image of man's nature. The deterministic centrality given to the libido and death wish were rejected, and the related never-ending conflict

55. Hadley Cantril, "The Human Design," *Journal of Individual Psychology* 20 (1964): 135–36; Gordon W. Allport, "Comment on Earlier Chapters," May, ed., *Existential Psychology*, pp. 93 ff.

56. Trigant Burrow, *The Social Basis of Consciousness* (New York, 1927), *The Biology of Human Conflict* (New York, 1937), and *A Search for Man's Sanity: The Selected Letters of Trigant Burrow* (New York, 1958).

57. Ruitenbeek has discussed the neo-Freudians in *Freud and America*, pp. 98 ff., as has Clara Thompson in *Psychoanalysis: Evolution and Development*, pp. 193 ff. For a more comprehensive treatment, see Martin Birnbach, *Neo-Freudian Social Philosophy* (Stanford, 1961), and Paul A. Robinson, *The Freudian Left: Wilhelm Reich, Géza Róheim, Herbert Marcuse* (New York, 1969). The revisionists tended to use a more informal, friendly relationship between analyst and patient than that in classical analysis.

58. Kenneth Burke, *Philosophy of Literary Form* (Berkeley and Los Angeles, 1973), pp. 272–73; Bronislaw Malinowski, *Sex and Repression in Savage Society* (New York, 1927). In some measure this view found support in the field work of Margaret Mead reported in *Coming of Age in Samoa* (New York, 1928).

59. See pp. 346–47.

between Eros and Thantos. Nor did they see personality as taking immutable shape in early childhood as the result of sexual trauma, conflict,
and fixation. They put much more emphasis on present and more
recently experienced interpersonal relations, including, to be sure,
relations with one's own unconscious in a disturbing social milieu. Such
relations helped form both the unique individual and the group-shared
social personality. This was so, since these interpersonal experiences
functioned in the familial acceptance of the value system of a given
social group. But personality and character were by no means forever
frozen, subject only, as Freud implied, to some lessening of conflict-
produced tensions through an understanding of them.

Though the group recognized the influence of the shaping characteristics of a particular culture and specific personal experiences on
behavior and personality, it had trouble in identifying these with a
universal human nature. Seeming at times to assume their own transcendence of such limitations, the neo-Freudians rejected the founder's
doctrine of a largely biologically determined personality and human
nature. They also rejected the view of the newly born as tabula rasa on
which any environment might impose its special characteristics.
Without denying the thrust of the sex drive, revisionists emphasized an
impulse toward psychic growth and maturity or the wholesome acceptance of "the true self," the need for and the capacity to give love,
and the ability to adjust to the requirements of changing interpersonal
relations and shifting social environments. These allegedly inherent
characteristics or drives, when properly implemented, added up to
mental health, freedom from slavery to the thwarting biologically and
socially imposed restrictions.

The neo-Freudians did not see eye to eye in assessing the social obstacles imposed on the drive for realizing mental health. Karen Horney,
who came to America in 1932 from the famous Berlin Psychoanalytic
Institute, claimed that the death-wish concept provided a dangerous
rationalization for destructiveness and discouraged effective therapeutic efforts to reduce it. In *New Ways of Psychoanalysis* (1939) she held
that the culture taught women to accept a masochistic role and subordination and service to and dependency on others. Horney also laid a
good deal of emotional distress at the door of such social pressures as
excessive competition, struggle for status, the resulting sense of failure
and insecurity, and the urge to accept a facade that repressed not only
egotistic "instinctive" drives but also spontaneous feelings and personal
judgments. All these social pressures aggravated the individual's
problem in handling the realities of his anxieties. Thus child-rearing, in
reflecting the dominant cultural conflict between the urge for success

and the sense of failure, stymied self-control, the ability to cope with life, and an inherent desire for joyful, life-giving psychic growth. Horney's critics, contending that she was substituting culture for the instincts that functionally shaped human nature in any social system, read her out of the psychoanalytic circle.[60]

Other neo-Freudians emphasized different factors in the development of neuroses. Kardiner and Fromm stressed social obstacles in terms of a long evolutionary past. Fromm, coming to psychoanalysis from a sociological and socialist background, projected the inborn longing and capacity of all men and women for life, liberty, and happiness, with a conflicting desire for dependence on authority. Human potentialities could not be realized, since capitalism imposed fratricidal competition, manipulativeness, overemphasis on adjustment and conformity, alienation (fragmented loneliness), and glorification of a marketplace personality. In Fromm's view modern society had all but repudiated the cooperative attributes of the great Western humanistic tradition and Marxist socialism. Such a repudiation made it all but impossible to meet the psychic need for love, self-realization, and emotional maturity in warm, understanding, and tolerant interpersonal relations in a lifelong process. Yet even Fromm did not give up hope that people could solve the dilemma in which they found themselves.[61]

In some ways Bruno Bettelheim's experiences in Europe and the uses he made of them after his arrival in the United States in 1939 gave him special distinction among the revisionist emigrés. Growing up in Vienna, he weighed both Marxism and psychoanalysis as ways of meeting the increasing social tension and chaos. Without great fervor or conviction he chose the latter, but presently found himself a prisoner in Nazi concentration camps. At the time he arrived in America he was almost alone in bringing to public attention the brutalizing and sadistic conditions in the camps and in interpreting in psychoanalytic and social terms the meaning of worthy and of unworthy survival. As clinical psychiatrist working

60. Karen Horney, *The Neurotic Personality of Our Time* (New York, 1937), pp. 188 ff. For a good brief discussion see Rona Cherry and Laurence Cherry, "The Horney Heresy," *New York Times Magazine*, August 26, 1973, pp. 12 ff. Also useful are Harold Kelman, *Advances in Psychoanalysis: Contributions to Karen Horney's Holistic Approach* (New York, 1964); Harold Kelman, ed., *New Perspectives in Psychoanalysis* (New York, 1965); and Jack L. Rubins, *Karen Horney, Gentle Rebel of Psychoanalysis* (New York, 1978).

61. Erich Fromm, *Escape from Freedom* (New York, 1961), p. 289 (in the 1941 ed., p. 276). Of special interest: Erich Fromm, *Marx's Concept of Man: With a Translation from Marx's Economic and Philosophic Manuscripts* (New York, 1961), and *Beyond the Chains of Illusion: My Encounter with Marx and Freud* (New York, 1962). For quite different evaluations of Fromm see Edward S. Tauber and Bernard Landis, eds., *In the Name of Life: Essays in Honor of Erich Fromm* (New York, 1971), and John H. Schaar, *Escape from Authority* (New York, 1961).

with psychotic, largely autistic children in the Orthogenic School at the University of Chicago, he also wrote such vigorous yet poignant and sensitive books as *The Informed Heart: Autonomy in a Mass Age* (1960), *The Empty Fortress* (1967), *The Children of the Dream* (1969), and *Surviving and Other Essays* (1979). Bettelheim emphasized the fundamental importance of an environment, whether in an American home or in a kibbutz in Israel, that would provide the child not only with love but with other conditions needed for maturing into a responsible, worthy, and happy human being. He believed, with some of the other European-trained revisionists, that such an environment could be compatible with legitimate demands of society.

Such culturally oriented views were more in tune with American optimism than were those of classical psychoanalysis. This optimism was evident in the conviction that a solution ought to exist for every problem that could be identified. It was also evident in the prevailing commitment to the plasticity of human nature: social environment and learning, rather than the unconscious thrust of biology and sublimation, were paramount in shaping motives and behavior.

Thus the revisionists' view of human nature could be seen as a working hypothesis, a yet-unfinished synthesis of psychoanalytic concepts, the democratic and humanistic values of a great Western tradition, and the contemporary social sciences. In other words, the chief contribution of the revisionists was to foresee and explain that human nature *could* be freed from the dogmatism of biological, psychological, and social "inevitabilities."[62]

Orthodox Freudians scorned the culture-minded dissidents for obscuring the founder's emphasis on the unconscious, on infant sexuality, and on the limitations of the rational component of human nature for remaking it and the social order.

Nonprofessionals, more or less influenced by orthodox psychoanalysis, criticized the cultural revisionists on several, often contradictory grounds. The neo-Freudians were, like the liberals, said to have universalized the optimistic mood of the 1920s and the New Deal just when the black clouds of fascism confirmed Freud's tragic view of an aggressive, destructive, and tragic human nature.[63] Others felt that the revisionists erred in too neatly oversimplifying the social environment and in undermining the need for coherence in theory and in discipline:

62. Karen Horney, *Self-Analysis* (New York, 1942), p. 10; and "Symposium: Human Nature Can Change," *American Journal of Psychoanalysis* 12 (1952): 68.

63. Lionel Trilling, *Freud and the Crisis of Our Culture* (Boston, 1955); and Floyd W. Matson, *The Idea of Man* (New York, 1976), pp. 41 ff.

even their relaxed view of child-rearing pointed in that direction.[64] Still others declared that in underestimating the sex drive, reformers cut short the life-giving pleasures of a basic instinct by trying to replace it with a sublimated religious internalization which in effect supported the status quo.[65] Neo-Freudian revisionists were also accused of substituting for the scientific criticism of society the doctrine of social adjustment, or of generalizing their private prejudices in favor of the "democratic" or the "self-actualizing personality."[66]

The so-called right-wing and left-wing critics of revisionism by no means exhausted the possible implications and emendations of Freudianism in the continuing exploration of human nature.

Ego psychology, founded by Freud's daughter Anna and by Heinz Hartmann, attributed an autonomy to the ego that Freud, except in his last years, had subordinated to the id and superego. During his New York years (1941–70), Hartmann quietly practiced clinical analysis and sought, without violating the core of orthodox Freudianism, to resolve some of its ambiguities, to seek cooperation with anthropology, and to construct a general psychology.

It remained, however, for the much better known Erik Erikson to develop and apply ego psychology. Though resembling some revisionists, he looked on himself as a classical Freudian who, in taking stock of new situations and new knowledge, further developed the master's theories and insights. Thus in many ways his work might be regarded as an original statement of the nature of man. Born of Danish parents living in Germany and trained in that country, Erikson began his career as an artist and teacher in Vienna. Working with Freud and his daughter, he brought to ego psychology a literary and urbane temperament as well as an acquaintance with new studies in child development, including those of Piaget. In time he took up anthropology. He also pondered the historian's view of time in its generational dimensions. Coming to the United States in 1933, he was intrigued by the ways in which American culture influenced the

64. Paul Roazen, *Freud: Political and Social Thought* (New York, 1968), chap. 4; also pp. 210, 268.

65. Herbert Marcuse, "The Social Implications of Freudian Revisionism," *Dissent* 2 (1955): 228; *Eros and Civilization: A Philosophical Inquiry into Freud* (Boston, 1955), pp. 19 ff., 238–74.

66. Norman O. Brown, *Life against Death: The Psychoanalytical Meaning of History* (Middletown, Conn., 1959), p. 144.

universal biopsychological and psychosocial development of human beings.[67]

In forming his view of human nature, Erikson focused on the universal needs of the growing ego as channeled by distinctive yet related experiences in all societies. Every infant's libidinal energies existed in a particular context of changing social customs. These were necessary for the growth to which the helplessness of the infant also contributed by posing, as John Fiske had argued earlier, parental responsibility. Erikson put the importance of parental relationships through adolescence into a larger frame than Freud had done.

Erikson postulated a polarity of conflicting forces in every human being at each of the eight stages of the universal life cycle. On the one hand, each person embraced inner forces which would enable him to achieve a necessary competence in his own culture; on the other, everyone also longed to revert to earlier and less-complex stages of existence. In each stage, conflict between the urge to meet the demands of growth and the urge to resist them resulted in a crisis distinctive for the particular phase. Every crisis readied the ego for further crises and thus, positively as well as negatively, affected the continuing formation of personality. In Erikson's words, the conflict-related crisis is so crucial that "human nature can best be studied in the state of conflict," whether clinically or historically. The role of the ego was central for integrating past and present, for coping with the demands for living, and for anticipating the future.

Recognizing in every culture distinctive patterns of expected behavior at each stage of the individual's development, Erikson emphasized the existence everywhere of common life processes, experiences, and related values. Newborn infants the world over needed a sense of basic trust in a mother or mother surrogate and at the same time needed to overcome a basic distrust. Many variables influenced successes and failures in achieving a ratio favorable to trust, and this pattern of trust-mistrust became a part of personality development. The way in which the crisis presented by this polarity was met affected the changing character of the struggle for identity in succeeding stages. As growth proceeded, the child in every culture had to achieve a sense of industry and fend off one of

67. Marie Jahoda, "The Migration of Psychoanalysis," in Donald Fleming and Bernard Bailyn, eds., *The Intellectual Migration: Europe and America, 1930–1960* (Cambridge, Mass., 1969), pp. 431, 440–41; H. Stuart Hughes, *The Sea of Change: The Migration of Social Thought 1931–65* (New York, 1975), pp. 217 ff.; Richard I. Evans, *Dialogue with Erik Erikson* (New York, 1967), pp. 9–10; Henry W. Maier, *Three Theories of Child Development: The Contributions of Erik H. Erikson, Jean Piaget, and Robert R. Seurs, and Their Applications* (New York, 1965), pp. x, 8, 12 ff.; Paul Roazen, *Erik H. Erikson: The Power and Limits of a Vision* (New York, 1976).

inferiority or ineffectiveness—with an impairment or a reenforcement of will. In all these early stages of infancy and childhood, play provided a tool for the ego's self-expression and self-exploration in a social context; play signaled, more than dreams, unconscious and preconscious wishes and conflicts.

As the growing child moved into adolescence, it became imperative to acquire a sense of identity—in relation to parents, peers, what was considered appropriate sexual behavior, vocation, and the whole relation of past, present, and future. The identity crisis of adolescence was more acute in some than in others. It was always responsive to the intensity and form of conflict between old and new. In the social, cultural context, the ego functioned in establishing a synthesis between past and future and between conflicting polarities. Elaborating on the nature of identity, Erikson showed how this was variously affected by the concept of time, by self-certainty versus apathy, role experimentation, anticipation of achievement versus work paralysis, sexual identity versus bisexual diffusion, leadership polarization versus authority diffusion, and ideological polarization versus diffusion of ideals.[68]

As the maturational process moved forward, new problems related to earlier ones arose. It was important for the young adult to acquire a sense of intimacy and solidarity. It also became important to avoid a feeling of isolation, to come to a sense of his relationship to his own and other generations, and to avoid self-absorption. In maturity, it was desirable to acquire a sense of integrity and to avoid one of despair: this was the integrity crisis.[69]

Erikson's theory inevitably met with criticism, even from those who acknowledged his contribution in bringing the problem of identity to the fore in psychoanalytical thinking. According to some authorities, ambiguities in his mental image of identity included the "sense of one's existence and continuity in time." Daniel Yankelovich and William Barrett saw Erikson's epigenetic identity as basically biological rather than "fully human." Thus it failed to exhibit the part played by freedom in human identity.[70]

The focus on conflict and crisis in each maturational stage should not obscure other aspects of Erikson's developmental biosocial psychology. For each stage he also set forth values or "virtues" such as faith, will,

68. Erik Erikson, "Autobiographical Notes on the Identity Crisis," *Daedalus* 99 (1970): 730–59.

69. Erikson's *Young Man Luther* (New York, 1958) was widely read as a concrete example of his theory of maturation and identity crisis. See also, of course, his *Childhood and Society* (New York, 1950; rev. ed., 1963).

70. Daniel Yankelovich and William Barrett, *Ego and Instinct: The Psychoanalytic View of Human Nature*, rev. ed. (New York, 1970), pp. 323, 435.

conscience, reason, and purpose or goal-directedness. These "virtues" transcended cultural differences by reason of a universal functional relation to the ways in which people surmounted or failed to surmount crises.

If all the challenges to maturation existed in every culture and provided a common human nature, each culture had its own variants. Fairly soon after coming to the United States, Erikson studied, hand in hand with anthropologists, the cultures of the Sioux and the Yurok. In *Childhood and Society* (1950), he reported what he saw in child-rearing that bore on his overall view of human nature.

As an immigrant to America and a social scientist, Erikson took stock of the ways in which the earmarks of the dominant culture were related to his whole image of man. Here he stressed the relevance of the rapid changes in American society to child-rearing and adolescent and adult experiences and expectations. He also emphasized the existence of polarities, notably the conflicting values in American culture. In stressing human potentialities, the growing individual as a creative enterprise, and the problems set by the hazards of living as these issued from instinctive, parental, communal, cultural, and environmental forces, Erikson worked out a comprehensive synthesis. It may be thought of as embracing variant images of man—Freudian, neo-Freudian, and that projected by the cultural orientation of the social sciences. In contrast to what have been called the darker and more perilous aspects of human nature, Erikson offered a model at once developmental and dynamic, biological and social. The model was also conditional, yet affirmative of individual freedom, of capacity for growth and maturity for "increased sanity and service to man." Had he given more consideration to Marxist views about the impact of economic forces and their related technologies on man's native endowment, his synthetic model might have been even more impressive.

Thus the gifted intellectual refugees from fascist Europe contributed to a fresh assessment of human nature. In holding that this was a more subtle and profound and thus truer view of man than any of its predecessors, its enthusiasts claimed too much. Still, depth psychology, as the broad movement came to be called, set great store on ego autonomy, on individual identity and its acceptance, on the priority and meaning of the feelings, and, in some cases, on the immediate and playful satisfaction of erotic urges as the key to individual well-being and social health. In some ways such emphases defied the authority of reason, the ties of family, established educational patterns, competition, status, technology, social engineering, and scientific materialism. Yet it would be hard to deny the importance of the ways post-Freudians handled the concepts of the unconscious and of sex in a dynamic social context. Their vogue continued into the post-1950s, when in the words of one student, fiction, drama, and philosophy "celebrated the life of the unconscious" and connected "political life not with the authority of reason but with that of sexuality."[71]

It would stretch more than a point to group Herbert Marcuse with the migrating European post-Freudians and their American colleagues.[72] Yet Freud played a large part in the thinking of this brilliant European-born and Hegelian-trained immigrant. He made his own interpretation of Marx, emphasizing the early humanistic writings that gave little support to the stereotype of one-dimensional economic, technological man. Marcuse in fact viewed Marx as less revolutionary than the founder of psychoanalysis. For Freud, as H. Stuart Hughes put it, set forth "a sense of cosmic injustice in the thwarting instinct—an injustice which cried out for radical, but unspecified, social changes."[73] Rejecting the pessimistic implications of Freud's *Civilization and Its Discontents,* Marcuse argued that man's capacity for love, hedonistic pleasure, and fulfillment could be realized here and now, without the slavery of toil or the tyrannies of bureaucracy.[74]

Paul Goodman, an educational rebel, a poet of some appeal, and a voluminous essayist, and O. Norman Brown, a classicist deeply impressed for a time by psychoanalysis, saw eye to eye with Marcuse on many points.[75] The flagging zest of the early brave crusaders for civil rights, the emptiness, horror, and pain of the Vietnam War, and the successes (mixed with failures) of guerrilla warfare provided a favorable atmosphere for the enthusiastic and youthful following that Marcuse, Goodman, and Brown for a time attracted. The mentors took their cue from the Freudian conviction that all cultures violated man's instinctive drives with neurotic damage to a heightened consciousness and to personality itself. They realized, of course, that people could not become

71. Ronald Berman, *America in the Sixties: An Intellectual History* (New York, 1968), p. 266.

72. Robinson, *The Freudian Left,* pp. 147 ff.

73. Hughes, *The Sea of Change,* p. 178.

74. See, primarily, Marcuse's *Eros and Civilization* (Boston, 1955, and later editions), and *One-Dimensional Man* (Boston, 1964). Robert Mark's *The Meaning of Marcuse* (New York, 1970) raises some thoughtful questions.

75. See especially Norman O. Brown, *Life against Death: The Psychological Meaning of History* (New York, 1959), and *Love's Body* (New York, 1966); and Paul Goodman, *Growing Up Absurd* (New York, 1960), *Compulsory Miseducation* (New York, 1964), and *Like a Conquered Province* (New York, 1967).

human nor live without culture. Nevertheless they protested against the life-defying restrictions of an "irrelevant" official educational and social establishment. They counseled the making of a counterculture to give maximum scope to the impulse for love and self-fulfillment. A note of defiant anarchism appeared in their writings. All tried to resolve the paradox in the Freudian view that the superego (conscience) strove to repress natural drives and thus kept mankind from becoming truly self-fulfilled. Put in another way, their message seemed to be a reply of sorts to the view that while man was necessarily a socialized being, he could never be a fully socialized creature and yet truly himself, at least in the dominant culture.

Thus on the American stage, in relation to American conditions, Freudianism, in its revisions and accretions, added up to a critique of the image of man dear to the Judeo-Christian tradition, to academic psychology, and to many middle-class values and goals. The views of the most-pronounced dissenters, in fusing Freud and Marx, tried also to fuse anarchism and community. In the eyes of their critics, the proclaimed new view of man was only another romanticized, utopian vision of individual freedom for self-realization and love, impossible of implementation save perhaps in isolated, fragmentary subcultures.[76]

Not all intellectual migrants from a Europe of fascist turmoil and war subscribed to the neo-Freudian and neo-Marxian views. Exponents of logical positivism and philosophic analysis insisted on precision and clarity of thought in operational definitions and explanations—an insistence that, if implemented scientifically, promised to be useful in the often loose discussion of human nature. Hannah Arendt, an existentialist[77] trained by Jaspers, repeatedly emphasized the error, indeed the evil, of all views of human nature that failed to endow men and women with an innate, unique, and ineluctable essence of freedom and responsibility, and that mistakenly accepted the universal malleability of instrumentalists and neo-Freudians.[78] Paul Tillich, a learned yet

76. My indebtedness here should be again expressed to Paul Robinson, *The Freudian Left*; to Yankelovich and Barrett, *Ego and Instinct*; to Dennis H. Wrong, "The Over-Socialized Conception of Man in Modern Sociology," *American Sociological Review* 26 (1961): 183–93; and to Richard King, *The Party of Eros: Radical Social Thought and the Realm of Freedom* (Chapel Hill, 1972), chaps. 3, 4, 5, and pp. 176 ff.

77. Professor William Barrett of New York University provides clear descriptions of the several kinds of existentialism, including that of the principal American exponents of existentialism. See his *Irrational Man: A Study in Existential Philosophy* (Garden City, N.Y., 1958).

78. Arendt's contributions to the literary press were extensive; her principal books include *The Human Heritage* (Chicago, 1958); *Utopian Essays and Practical Proposals* (New

worldly theologian, gave new meaning to the role of religious myths in meeting man's enduring emotional needs.[79]

Another intellectual migrant, Ernst Cassirer, did a good deal to direct along arresting lines the discussion of self-knowledge as a distinctive aspect of human nature. A leading revisionist of neo-Kantianism, Cassirer influenced a small but important group of American thinkers before, during, and after his professorships at Columbia and Yale. *The Philosophy of Symbolic Forms* provided a significant complement to such customary ways of exploring human nature as psychological introspection, biological observation and experiment, and historical investigation. More than that, symbolic forms added a new dimension to human reality. In turn, this deepened the understanding of a more comprehensively perceived human nature. Cassirer was not the first to take note of man's symbol-making capacity. But he insisted that what most distinguished man from all other creatures was his ability to create symbols and to use them dramatically and dynamically on every level of experience. Man, alone possessing a symbolic language, imagination, and intelligence, lived in a symbolic as well as a physical universe. In fact, his conceptualization of the physical universe depended not on a separate, objective reality but on his own rational, symbol-making gift. Cassirer assumed that humanity was not a monolithic unity but rather immensely rich, subtle, versatile, and complex in its use of symbols in myth, language, religion, art, history, logical thinking, and science. He held that only the human being could distinguish between the real and the possible and constantly reshape the human universe, as he had in the emergence of each level of symbols at the appropriate stage in the evolution of culture.[80]

Cassirer hoped that the recognition of man as the unique *animal symbolicum* might provide a bridge between profoundly different peoples in an age of conflict. Such a bridge, he felt, might result from an adequate understanding of the similarities as well as the diversities—the

York, 1962), *Eichmann in Jerusalem* (New York, 1963), *Men in Dark Times* (New York, 1968), *The Origins of Totalitarianism* (New York, 1951; new ed., 1973); and *The Life of the Mind,* 2 vols. (New York, 1978). For comment see Margaret Conovan, *The Political Thought of Hannah Arendt* (London, 1974); and George Kateb, "Freedom and Worldiness in the Thought of Hannah Arendt," *Political Theory* 5 (1977): 141–82.

79. Of special relevance are Paul Tillich's "Psychotherapy and a Christian Interpretation of Human Nature," *Review of Religion* 13 (1949): 264–68; *The New Being* (New York, 1955); *Systematic Theology,* 3 vols. (Chicago, 1951–65); *Morality and Beyond* (New York, 1963); and *My Search for Absolutes* (New York, 1967). For varying approaches consult Alfred R. Chandler, *Beauty and Human Nature: Elements of Psychological Esthetics* (New York, 1932).

80. Ernst Cassirer, *An Essay on Man: An Introduction to the Philosophy of Human Culture* (New Haven, 1944), pp. 24 ff.

common denominator that existed in the multiple forms of thought, value, conduct—all based on a synthesis of the sensory, the emotional, and the rational or logical as these found expression in symbolic forms. As Theodore Brameld has pointed out, Cassirer's hope would have been better grounded had he adequately recognized institutional, social, and economic forces and symbols as well as the political ones that provided centrality to his impressive *Myth of the State* (1946).[81] Even so, Cassirer must be credited with contributing to a deeper grasp of the meaning of human nature.

European-derived movements of thought thus influenced the search for an understanding of man, his constitution and his condition. Yet from time to time Americans looked to the Orient. This was true in the Transcendentalist years, as it was when religious leaders from Asia attended the Parliament of Religions at the Chicago Exposition in 1893. With the twentieth-century expansion of American interests in the Far East, the Pacific War of 1941–45, and later involvements in Southeast Asia, Taoism, Buddhism, and Hinduism interested a growing number of philosophers, literati, and laymen.

Though by no means the most scholarly of those who found truth and wisdom in Eastern thought, Alan Watts, born and reared in England and an Episcopal priest in Chicago, reached many would-be intellectuals in almost twenty books and in lectures on college campuses. As Watts put it, Western individualism drew false boundaries between the human being and even the immediate environment. Oriental philosophy perceived the harmful artificiality of any boundaries between the individual personality and the whole cosmos. Eastern awareness of the continuum between self and cosmos resulted, not in what Westerners wrongly misunderstood as mysticism, but in a direct sensation of man-and-the-universe as a single behavior pattern. This resulted in a deeper and truer reality. It was evident in the Eastern assumption that an intelligent humanity could develop only in an intelligent universe. It was evident in Western loneliness, alienation, dissatisfaction with the search for security in a conformist social structure that committed its victims to the capitalist-Marxist domination and exploitation of a living, life-giving nature. Watts tried to show that the two views of man, Eastern and Western, supplemented each other, and that a synthesis might be made of them. Consciousness-raising drugs, the Zen way in psychotherapy, and giving up rational efforts to solve problems offered some bridges. An open champion of freedom in life styles and in sex, of immediate sensory

---

81. Theodore Brameld, "The Educational Significance of Ernst Cassirer," in *Cultural Foundations of Education: An Interdisciplinary Exploration* (Westport, Conn., 1957; rpt. ed., New York, 1973), pp. 275–303.

satisfaction, Watts for a time symbolized the counterculture and served as a guru to disenchanted youth in the late 1960s.[82] Despite his efforts at popularization and synthesis, the Eastern views of man seemed to most intellectuals obscure, esoteric, escapist, and unscientific.

It was the task of another group, largely native-born, to show the possibility, desirability, and necessity of forging an image of man in which control of behavior reaffirmed the plasticity of human nature under the guiding hand of education, science, and power.

82. Alan Watts, "Oriental and Occidental Approaches to the Nature of Man," in John J. Mitchell, ed., *Human Nature: Theories, Conjectures, and Descriptions* (Metuchen, N.J., 1972), pp. 170–73. Among Watts's long list of books, *Does It Matter? Essays on Man's Relation to Materialism* (New York, 1968) and *Cloud-Ridden, Whereabouts Unknown* (New York, 1973) are good starting points. David Stuart's *Alan Watts* (Radnor, Pa., 1976) is a first-rate biography.

12

The Behavioral Movement

It is what happens to individuals after birth that makes one a hewer of wood and a drawer of water, another a diplomat, a thief, a successful business man or a far-famed scientist. What our advocates of freedom in 1776 took no account of is the fact that the Deity himself could not equalize the 40-year-old individuals who have had such different environmental trainings as the American people have had. . . . I have no venom to display against human nature. I am just trying to show you that our way of acting in certain situations is almost automatic.

JOHN B. WATSON, 1924

The defects of behaviorism . . . may be grouped under three heads: First, behavior is not explicable in reference solely to the objective situations physically present at the time of the observed response. Second, no motive for control is provided, and no method for the valuation of any proposed objective of the process which it sets up. . . . Third, it easily passes over into a materialistic philosophy which, while no proper part corollary of true behaviorism, often receives the same sanction of its spokesmen and the benefit of its prestige.

W. E. GARRISON, 1930

If Skinnerian psychology is taken as the model of the major inquiry of the future, then, once again, the thingness of humanity is affirmed. The supreme irony is that you can, by conditioning, transform a human being into everything except a human being. You can make him contented or wretched or docile or hard-working, but you cannot condition him into rationality.

GEORGE KATEB, 1973

The new field of behavioral sciences will in all probability be ranked among the important intellectual revolutions of the twentieth century.

BERNARD BERELSON, 1968

. . . we as Americans have motorized psychology. Our theories of human nature transform meditative functions into active functions. The success clearly reflects the demand of our culture that inner life issue quickly and visibly into tangible success: that closures be reached both overtly and swiftly.

GORDON W. ALLPORT, 1945

EXPONENTS OF behaviorism, which led to a view of human nature less comprehensive than Freudianism, claimed that it was the first really scientific view of man and that in origin and character it was truly American. It began as a revolt in professional psychology. It came to influence the social sciences, education, business, government, views about sex, and indirectly, religion and the humanities.

Boldly declaring that "psychology as the behaviorist views it is a purely objective experimental branch of natural science," John B. Watson, a well-known experimentalist, formally launched behaviorism in 1913. "Its theoretical goal," he continued, "is the prediction and control of behavior."[1] As it took form under Watson's leadership, behaviorism became a vigorous effort to explain human nature in terms of natural science.

Behaviorism owed much to the functionalism of William James and the Chicago group under whom Watson had studied before moving to the Johns Hopkins University. He nevertheless looked on functionalism as an obsolete hindrance to the development of scientific psychology. It refused forthrightly to deny a dualistic view of body and mind, and it relied on introspection as well as on objective experimentation. Even if functionalists did not reify consciousness, they used it to explain sen-

1. John B. Watson, "Psychology as the Behaviorist Views It," *Psychological Review* 20 (1913): 158.

sation, perception, image, memory, emotions, language, and thought.[2] At full tide the behaviorist rejected the functionalists' concern with individual differences, denied the reality of instincts, and conceded little importance to heredity as a factor in conduct. Watson was also unhappy with James's emphasis on contingency and indeterminism in behavior. Such a view, he felt, stemmed from the failure to put psychology on a par with the physical and biological sciences.

The matter of the derivative or original character of behaviorism has often been discussed.[3] At first Watson himself made no claim to having created behaviorism. He spoke of an indebtedness to colleagues at Columbia, Chicago, and the Johns Hopkins.[4] He denied, however, any association of behaviorism with earlier revolts in psychology such as German objectivism, or with the Russian reflexologists. Behaviorism was, he declared, a purely American phenomenon growing out of work in animal psychology.[5]

In any case, a climate of opinion within and without institutional psychology had developed that made behaviorism natural if not inevitable. Broadly speaking, factors in philosophy, psychology, and the American social, economic, and political situation pointed toward the position that Watson urged.

Its philosophical roots reached far back. They included the monistic, materialistic, and mechanistic conceptions of life advanced by Democritus and Epicurus which Hobbes, LaMettrie, and others revived in the seventeenth and eighteenth centuries. The atomistic empiricism and assumption of human plasticity of Locke and the associationists influenced the later mechanistic image of man. "Philosophical

2. Watson, "Psychology as the Behaviorist Views It," pp. 166 ff.; *Behaviorism: An Introduction to Comparative Psychology* (New York, 1914), pp. 8–9.

3. John B. Watson, *Psychology from the Standpoint of a Behaviorist* (Philadelphia, 1919), p. vii. Watson explicated the sequential phases of the development of his ideas in the second edition of this book (Philadelphia, 1924), pp. viii–ix. For fuller discussion see John C. Burnham, "On the Origins of Behaviorism," *Journal of the History of the Behavioral Sciences* 6 (1968): 143–51; and Lucille Birnbaum, "Behaviorism in the 1920's," *American Quarterly* 7 (1955): 15–30, together with her doctoral dissertation "Behaviorism: John Broadus Watson and American Social Thought" (University of California, Berkeley, 1964).

4. Watson, in Carl Murchison, ed., *A History of Psychology in Autobiography* (Worcester, Mass., 1936), 3:271–81; John B. Watson, "The Origin and Growth of Behaviorism," *Archiv für Systematische Philosophie und Sociologie* 30 (1927): 248 ff.

5. Watson, *Psychology from the Standpoint of a Behaviorist*, 2d ed. (Philadelphia, 1924), pp. xi–xii. See, for similarities between Watson's psychology and European counterparts, E. B. Titchener, "On 'Psychology as the Behaviorist Views It,'" *Proceedings of the American Philosophical Society* 53 (1914): 1–17; Cedric A. Larson and John J. Sullivan, "Watson's Relation to Titchener," *Journal of the History of the Behavioral Sciences* 1 (1965): 339–354; and Margaret Washburn, "Some Thoughts on the Last Quarter Century of Psychology," *Philosophical Review* 25 (1917): 46–55.

Radicals," Utilitarians, and Positivists more or less regarded any conception of mind as an illusion, unless it was identified as a clock-like machine automatically stimulated by outside and inside physical forces. In rejecting introspection and consciousness, Comte held that the phenomena of mind were accessible only through the observation of their "more or less durable results—that is, behavior." Others, including Ernst Mach, added scientific refinements to the broad mechanistic outlines of modern monistic materialism.[6]

By the turn of the century a few Americans responded favorably to these developments within the framework of the pragmatism of James and Peirce. Edgar A. Singer of the University of Pennsylvania held mind to be observable in terms of the behavior with which he identified it, defined consciousness as "an expectation of probable behavior based on an observation of actual behavior," and related thinking to observations of the organs of expression, chiefly the tongue and the eyes.[7] At Harvard Ralph Barton Perry, a leader in the neorealistic modification of pragmatism, expressed a similar view in 1909 in declaring that "the mind within" was an incomplete expression of mind. One had to look to the "mind without," or what Singer regarded as "mind as an observable object." Perry also presently interpreted purpose in a mechanistic and behaviorist way.[8]

Meantime, a mechanistic biology developed by German experimentalists and in harmony with the philosophical materialism of the later nineteenth century provided a related setting for behaviorism. Jacques Loeb, a philosopher and biologist who came to America in 1891, developed from the work of his mentors the concept of tropisms, or obligatory movements of living things evoked by such environmental factors as light, moisture, and gravity. Though some have seen Loeb as a major influence on Watson, this seems hardly likely.[9]

6. For competent discussions of these movements of thought consult Murphy and Kovach, *Historical Introduction to Modern Psychology* pp. 237–70; Floyd W. Matson's *The Broken Image: Man, Science and Society* (Garden City, N.Y., 1966), pp. 30–38; and Howard Rachlin's *Introduction to Modern Behaviorism* (San Francisco, 1970), pp. 4–19.

7. Edgar A. Singer, "On Mind as an Observable Object," *Journal of Philosophy, Psychology, and Scientific Method* 9 (1912): 206–14; "Consciousness and Behavior: A Reply," *Journal of Philosphy, Psychology, and Scientific Method* 9 (1912): 15–19; *Mind as Behavior* (Columbus, Oh., 1924), pp. 10–11.

8. Ralph Barton Perry, "The Mind Within and the Mind Without," *Journal of Philosophy, Psychology, and Scientific Method* 6 (1909): 169–75, and "Purpose as Tendency and Adaptation," *Psychological Review* 24 (1917): 477–95.

9. The best introduction to Loeb's work is Donald Fleming's essay in his edition of *The Mechanistic Conception of Life* (Cambridge, Mass., 1964). John C. Burnham in "On the Origins of Behaviorism" (p. 147) cites a letter from Watson to Loeb, Jan. 2, 1914, in which Watson pointed out that though they both believed that behavior could be analyzed into reflex action, Loeb's scheme seemed "a little too simple as it now stands."

The experimental work of the Russian physiologists Sechenov, Pavlov, and Bechterev was more far-reaching. Sechenov's experiments with reflexes showed that behavior seemingly voluntary was actually involuntary. Pavlov distinguished between simple, innate reflexes and those developed through experience—the conditioned reflexes. Thus behavior usually called mental was explicable in physiological terms. Pavlov did not develop a systematic human psychology. However, he held that objective research within the context of the conditioned reflex could lead to the prediction and control of behavior.[10]

Though a few Americans knew the work of the Russians,[11] Watson did not at first refer to the conditioned reflex. By 1915 it had become for him a crucial principle. True, he denied that behaviorism merely extended the Russian findings to human subjects. The Russian work implied an unacceptable psychoparallelism and dealt with units of physiological behavior rather than with that of the whole organism. Even so, in 1927, Watson wrote that Pavlov and Bechterev "must be looked upon as furnishing the keystone to the arch of behavior."[12]

Meantime, experimental, objective work of a nonintrospective character had made striking headway in Germany and the United States as well as in Russia. At the Congress of Arts and Sciences in St. Louis in 1904 J. McKeen Cattell, while recognizing the importance of introspection, noted that much of the laboratory work in his field was as nearly independent of it as reports in physics and zoology. He saw no reason why "the application of systematized knowledge to the control of human nature may not in the course of the present century accomplish results commensurate with the nineteenth century applications of physical science to the material world."[13] Four years earlier W. Stanton Small of Chicago had introduced the maze method of objectively studying animal behavior.[14] E. L. Thorndike at Columbia had reported on carefully controlled experiments with chickens, dogs, cats, and monkeys in an effort to find how they learned to reach food at the end of a complicated maze through the selective process in random trial and error movements. He assumed that specific "bonds," to be understood in the light of neural theory, explained the functional relationships between

10. Ivan Pavlov, *Lectures on Conditioned Reflexes*, trans. C. P. Ditt (London, 1927); Y. P. Frolov, *Pavlov and His School: The Theory of Conditioned Reflexes*, trans. C. V. Anrep (London, 1927); Gregory Razras, "I. Pavlov," *International Encyclopedia of the Social Sciences*, 11:486.

11. An article by Robert M. Yerkes and Sergius Morgulis, "The Method of Pavlov in Animal Psychology," appeared in the *Psychological Bulletin* 6 (1909): 257–73.

12. Watson, "The Origin and Growth of Behaviorism," p. 249.

13. J. McKeen Cattell, "The Conceptions and Methods of Psychology," *Popular Science Monthly* 66 (1904): 179, 186.

14. W. Stanton Small, "An Experiment with the Mental Processes of Rats," *American Journal of Psychology* 11 (1900): 133–65.

stimulus and response in the learning process, and that these "bonds" were altered when exercise and frequency of association resulted in successful and satisfying outcome. While recognizing, like his mentor William James, the role of ideas in some kinds of human learning,[15] Thorndike felt that these experiments, together with those he undertook with infants and children, warranted the hypothesis that "amongst the minds of animals that of man leads, not as a demigod from another planet, but as king from the same race."[16]

Others, too, anticipated Watson in working toward a nonintrospective explanation of behavior. At the Johns Hopkins, Knight Dunlap's motor theory, based on experiments relating kinesthetic movements of the eyeball with visual images, confirmed Watson's view of response or reaction as the basis of mental, including thought, processes. Consciousness, in short, was an abstract reference to an undeniable fact of responses.[17] Nor was he alone in such an orientation. Max F. Meyer, Carl Stumpf's pupil, who continued at the University of Missouri the studies he had begun in Germany on the psychology of hearing and musical sounds, argued in 1911 that human life could be described without any reference whatever to subjective factors or states of consciousness.[18]

In sum, the work of Thorndike, Dunlap, Meyer, and such physiologists as Jacques Loeb indicated that when behaviorism was launched by its chief promulgator, no sharp break took place with developments in biology and institutional psychology.

The American social and cultural situation also explained the rise of the behavioral movement and its later professional and popular vogue. In spite of some deterministic implications, behaviorism echoed the general tone of the Progressive movement by associating it with a revolt against a psychological status quo that preserved age-old superstitions identified with introspective dualism. The scientific claims of behaviorism and its presumable usefulness for social control and meliorism still further appealed to Progressive assumptions and goals.[19]

15. E. L. Thorndike, *The Human Nature Club: An Introduction to the Study of Mental Life* (New York, 1901), p. 33.

16. E. L. Thorndike, "The Evolution of the Human Intellect," *Popular Science Monthly* (1901), included in *Animal Intelligence: Experimental Studies* (New York, 1911), p. 294.

17. Knight Dunlap, "The Nature of Perceived Relations," *Psychological Review* 19 (1912): 415–46, and "Images and Ideas," *Johns Hopkins Circulars* 33 (1914): 25–41; Kate Gordon, "Knight Dunlap," *Psychological Review* 56 (1949): 309–10.

18. Carl Murchison, "Max F. Meyer," *Psychological Register* 3 (1932): 336; Max Meyer, "The Present Status of the Problem of the Relation between Mind and Body," *Journal of Philosophy, Psychology, and Scientific Method* 9 (1912): 365–71. For a fuller exposition of Meyer's ideas see his *The Psychology of the Other-One* (Columbia, Mo., 1921; rev. ed., 1922).

19. John C. Burnham, "Psychiatry, Psychology, and the Progressive Movement," *American Quarterly* 12 (1960): 464–65.

In a related view, David Bakan[20] suggested that behaviorism promised to meet the need for adjustment of interpersonal relations in a machine culture and in the heterogeneous urban subcultures associated with it. Watson himself explicitly noted the need of a mechanism for adjusting people to the machine and to each other. "Civilized nations," he wrote in a preface to the 1924 edition of *Psychology from the Standpoint of the Behaviorist*, "are rapidly becoming city dwellers. . . . If we are ever to learn to live together in the close relationships demanded by modern social and industrial life we shall have to leave behind for a time our interest in chemistry and physics and even physiology and medicine, and enter upon a study of modern psychology. . . . The past ten years," he continued, "have seen the development of new points of view in psychology—points of view that have grown up partly to meet our ever changing social needs and partly because the very existence of these needs has made a new viewpoint possible. . . . Behavioristic psychology . . . contends that the most fruitful starting point for psychology is the study not of our own self, but of our neighbor's behavior—in other words it assumes that the student should take the view that the most interesting and helpful method is the study of what other human beings do and why they do it. Only by so doing can we ever hope to understand our own behavior. Those who have any familiarity with the psychology current a few years ago will realize that this reverses the method of study recommended by Wundt and James and many of our other most prominent psychologists."[21]

The image of man that Watson, the crusading polemicist and social commentator, projected in the 1920s when he quit academic life for advertising, rested largely on experiments and on hypotheses that were often stated as established facts. In experimenting with infants[22] Watson excluded from innate emotional responses everything except fear, rage, and love (broadly conceived in the Freudian sense). These, he held, could be stated in terms of stimulus and response. While his experiments proved less conclusive than he supposed, he claimed that the physiological work of Walter B. Cannon and George Crile substantiated his findings. His theory of emotions held that many of the reactions James and Thorndike regarded as innate were actually the product of

20. David Bakan, "Behaviorism and American Urbanization," *Journal of the History of the Behavioral Sciences* 2 (1966): 5–28.

21. Watson, *Psychology from the Standpoint of a Behaviorist*, 2d ed., pp. xi–xii. This statement did not appear in all copies of the 1924 edition. See, for explanation, Bakan, "Behaviorism and American Urbanization," p. 12.

22. John B. Watson, *Psychological Care of Infant and Child* (New York, 1928). For Watson's experiments with infants consult R. Dale Nance, "G. Stanley Hall and John B. Watson as Child Psychologists," *Journal of the History of the Behavioral Sciences* 6 (1970): 309–16.

environmental experience and thus might be conditioned in such a way as to shape the habit systems and future behavior of the organism.[23]

More important from a theoretical and even substantive standpoint were Watson's ideas about language and thinking. These anticipated later psychological experimentation, theory, and generalization. Explicit and implicit language habits and thinking (subvocal talking to ourselves without words) could, he felt, be explained in terms of stimulus and response without the traditional conception of images. Stimuli evoked implicit mediating responses or events, which he identified as largely verbal but also visceral and muscular. With further stimuli, these mediating responses resulted in, for the moment, terminating responses.

In acquiring language habits, the child's motor responses to objects were at first strengthened. After this, stimuli called forth responses of labeling objects, and later, the motor responses as well. Thus the child learned to name both object and motor response aroused by it. Each object, Watson wrote, "now becomes a stimulus capable of releasing either the bodily habits or the word habit." Objects then evoked naming responses without the motor reactions, and subsequent verbal responses were initiated by appropriate stimuli at any point.[24]

The so-called higher thought-processes operated in terms of faint reinstatements of the original muscular act (including speech). Later Watson hypothesized that the interplay of kinesthetic, visceral, and laryngeal organization in thinking constituted implicit activity of the laryngeal musculature and explicit activity of manual gestures and other "word substitutes" involving the whole body. In such ways memory, meaning, concepts, and reasoning developed. Thus, in the words of Alfred E. Goss, Watson "provided an entirely stimulus-response paradigm for the 'higher thought' processes: initiating stimulus—primarily verbal (vocal, laryngeal), implicit responses, and consequent stimuli—overt terminating responses." Watson also formulated and used "more specific paradigms, equivalent to the basic variants of response mediated association and response mediated generalization." These appeared in his analyses of language and such thinking phenomena as

23. John B. Watson and J. J. B. Morgan, "Emotional Reactions and Psychological Experimentation," *American Journal of Psychology* 28 (1917): 163–74. See also George W. Crile, *Origin and Nature of the Emotions*, ed. Amy F. Rowland (Philadelphia, 1915); and Walter B. Cannon, *Bodily Changes in Pain, Hunger, Fear and Rage* (New York, 1915). In the 1929 revision of his book, Cannon clarified his emphasis on the usefulness of emotional response to stress. Anticipating psychosomatic medicine, Cannon also developed the concept of homeostasis or the tendency of the body to achieve stability, a concept that influenced later work in the behavioral sciences.

24. John B. Watson, *Behavior: An Introduction to Comparative Psychology* (New York, 1914), pp. 329–30, 332.

meaning, meaningfulness, concept formation, reasoning, repression, and "the unconscious." His substantive contributions to the role of verbal mediating responses in complex behavior could not, Goss concluded, be easily underestimated.[25]

Watson's conception of human nature involved his attitude toward Freudianism. In spite of an often-expressed disdain for its dogmatic cultism and lack of experimental evidence, Watson, writing in 1913, felt that the Freudians had "made good their main point concerning the sex reference of all behavior."[26] Elsewhere, too, he accepted a good part of the canon.[27] At the same time, he tried to state these ideas in terms consistent with his basic behaviorism. For example, "I would call that part of the individual's object world which he constantly manipulates with his hands, feet and body but does not name or attach a word to—his world of situations and his own responses to them which he does not name, his 'unconscious' world or, in my own terminology, his unverbalized world." Included were the "unverbalized world of the man who was trained to be a *silent* man . . . the unverbalized world of each of us made up of the activity of the unstriped muscular and glandular parts of our body and of the stimuli which call forth that activity in these parts. . . . This whole world we may call the unverbalized world of the emotions" and "the world of our infancy which is totally unverbalized for the first year and practically unverbalized until the end of the second year."[28]

Convinced that "an enormous number" of mental habits were formed both in infancy and throughout life without corresponding verbal habits, Watson associated the unverbalized organization with the Freudian "unconscious."[29] "Wishes" in the unverbalized organization (unconscious) might be repressed. In 1916 Watson wrote that even apart from sleep, many reasons suggested that so-called repressed wishes

25. Albert E. Goss, "Early Behaviorism and Verbal Mediating Responses," *American Psychologist* 16 (1961): 294–95.

26. John B. Watson, "Image and Affection in Behavior," *Journal of Philosophy, Psychology, and Scientific Method* 10 (1913): 426–27.

27. John B. Watson, "The Psychology of Wish Fulfillment," *Scientific Monthly* 3 (1916): 479–87; Watson and Morgan, "Emotional Reactions and Psychological Experimentation," p. 165. See also John B. Watson, "Does Holt Follow Freud?" *Journal of Philosophy, Psychology, and Scientific Method* 14 (1917): 85–92, and "The Origin and Growth of Behaviorism," pp. 248–49.

28. John B. Watson, "The Unconscious of the Behaviorist," in Ethel S. Summer, ed., *The Unconscious: A Symposium* (New York, 1928), pp. 96–99.

29. John B. Watson, "The Unverbalized in Human Behavior," *Psychological Review* 21 (1924): 273–80.

revealed themselves in behavioral responses. He noted that William James anticipated the "true doctrine" in emphasizing the point that the human organism was instinctively capable of developing along many different lines, some of which civilization thwarted in order to make one of an individual's selves "actual." The other "selves" thus had to be more or less repressed. Such wishes, Watson went on, need never have been conscious, particularly since a child under three years had no memory and no verbalization of his experiences. Finally, Watson agreed that dream analyses might, in the hands of experts, be of "almost unbelievable service in treating functional diseases."[30]

In discussing women's autobiographies, Watson further revamped Freudian views in behaviorist terms. The autobiographies, in blaming lack of achievement on socially imposed frustrations, failed to recognize that the very sorrow and tribulations were "the conditioning stimuli that passed them on their way." The accounts, he went on, strikingly confirmed the view that "militance passes as soon as the woman, by a trial-and-error process, finds sex adjustment. Then they cease to hunt for freedom and lose themselves in work." But women, untrained from infancy in incessant manipulative work, thus dropped out of the race on achieving comfort. If a girl were to succeed in the complex world of affairs, she must be taught from infancy the habit of manipulation, skillful techniques, and endurance, "as well as what to expect in the realm of sex."[31]

In no way, perhaps, did Watson's behaviorism differ so markedly from Freudianism as in its repudiation of the importance of individual differences and heredity. From the time when, just before World War I, he joined the growing number of psychologists and social scientists who denied the validity of the instinct theory, Watson moved steadily toward an almost unqualified environmentalism. In his most daring statements he declared it was possible and desirable to develop behavioral patterns which could shape the human organism as the potter shaped his clay.[32] Such a hyperbole reflected his faith in the possibility of training infants and children both emotionally and in aptitudes and skills. In *Psychological Care of Infant and Child*, written with the help of his wife Rosalie Rayner, Watson declared that "the vocation your child is to follow in later life is not determined from within, but from without—by you, by the kind of life you make him lead."[33]

30. Watson, "Psychology of Wish Fulfillment," pp. 484 ff.
31. John B. Watson, "The Weakness of Women," *The Nation* 125 (1927): 9–10.
32. John B. Watson vs. Will Durant, "Is Man a Machine? A Socratic Dialogue," *Forum* 82 (1929): 264 ff. For Watson's most frequently quoted hyperbole on the ability to fashion an infant for any desired vocation, see his *Behaviorism*, rev. ed. (New York, 1930), p. 104.
33. Watson, *Psychological Care of Infant and Child*, pp. 7, 15, 39.

Watson's extreme environmentalism in the stimulus-response frame also found expression in his view of the widespread twentieth-century transgression of conventional and religious mandates and the identification of business honesty with mere legal decisions. Men and women had become, as the stimulus-response and environmental theory implied, vulnerable when approached long and hard enough on the inherently weak side of human nature. Susceptibility to flattery, selfishness, and the inclination to avoid difficult situations or to confess weakness, hurling criticism on others to escape it oneself, and rationalizing proclivities were all a part of the human makeup, at least in its existing environment. "I have no venom to display here against human nature. I am just trying to show you that our way of acting in certain situations is almost automatic." At the same time psychological understanding in behaviorist terms might be applied advantageously in every phase of human relationship.[34]

Watson's early statements about the practical uses of behaviorist psychology in education, medicine, law, business, and life in general found implementation both in his career in advertising and in his exhortations to use the conditioned reflex, stimulus-response theory for "free and happy living within the predominant order." In advocating behaviorism as a foundation for saner living, Watson did not ask for free love, for revolution, or for a utopian community. "I am trying to dangle a stimulus in front of you, a verbal stimulus which, if acted upon, will gradually change this universe. For the universe will change if you bring up your children, not in the freedom of the libertine, but in behaviorist freedom—a freedom which we cannot even picture in words, so little do we know it."[35]

Watson admitted that too little was known about what is good or bad for the human organism to enable society to guide its conduct on experimentally sound lines. Thus he viewed Prohibition as "only a blind rearrangement of a situation." Society had indeed condemned much that was associated with the saloon. Yet champions of the Eighteenth Amendment could not reasonably predict what would occur. They thought crime and extramarital sex could be wiped out. "But any student of human nature or even of geography could have predicted that those results could not come although he might have been unable to predict what would occur." The overthrow of the Russian monarchy and the establishment of the Soviet regime offered another example of "blind manipulation of situations." Neither friend nor foe could predict what changes in behavior would occur. The change had led to isolation

34. Watson, *Behaviorism*, 1930 ed., p. 291.
35. Watson, *Behaviorism*, 1930 ed., p. 248.

and to intellectual and scientific retrogression. Without small scale experimentation, behavior often became moblike and reverted to infantilism.[36]

The indictment of behaviorism rested in part on its alleged technical errors and shortcomings. Critics claimed that both logic and experiment undermined Watson's theory that habit formation could largely be explained in terms of repetition. John Dewey, echoing William James, argued that such a mechanistic thesis ignored the foreseeing and construing role of creative invention, a position eloquently proclaimed by the Gestalt psychologists, who insisted on insight as well as foresight in learning. Later experiments lent support to early doubts about Watson's emphasis on contiguity as against reenforcement and deprivation in the learning process. On another level, the application of behaviorism to mental illness, Dr. S. E. Jelliffe, a leading psychiatrist, regarded Watson's position[37] as extremely naïve and simplistic, and in its own way mechanistic and materialistic.[38]

Other objections to behaviorism as a method and theory of human nature quickly appeared. Its wholesale rejection of introspection aroused sharp dissent. When Watson relaxed his early opposition to it and admitted "verbal report" as an auxiliary to observation and experimentation, leading authorities observed that behaviorists had made no serious, sustained effort to improve introspection as a method of investigation.[39] More significant was the point that behaviorism, in limiting psychology to observations of persons other than the observing scientist himself, excluded observations of the scientist's own internal activities.[40] Arthur O. Lovejoy argued that the behaviorist was unable, in terms of his own theory, to explain the fact that the behaviorist psychologist himself existed. If existence was "perceiving and thinking about external objects," the behaviorist who insisted that he was only a movement of muscles could not be aware of that movement. "If the behaviorist's description of thinking were accepted, it is, of course, equally true that he can profess a knowledge even of his own muscular movements, 'overt' or 'implicit,' only by claiming for himself a power

36. Watson, *Behaviorism*, 1930 ed., pp. 41–42.
37. John B. Watson, "Behavior and the Concept of Mental Disease," *Journal of Philosophy, Psychology, and Scientific Method* 13 (1916): 589–97.
38. Dr. S. E. Jelliffe, "Dr. Watson and the Concept of Mental Disease," *Journal of Philosophy, Psychology, and Scientific Method* 14 (1917): 267–75.
39. Robert S. Woodworth, "Four Varieties of Behaviorism," *Psychological Review* 31 (1924): 260.
40. Kenneth W. Spence, "Postulates and Methods of Behaviorism," *Psychological Review* 55 (1948): 68–69.

which he at the same time denies to all organisms including himself."[41] In somewhat the same vein George Santayana contended that private experience was necessary for insight into what went on when others were aware of and interpreted their experience.[42]

Technical criticisms emphasized other shortcomings inherent in the denial of consciousness. The fact that psychologists did not know precisely what consciousness was did not prove its nonexistence, since after all, physicists did not know the real nature of matter.[43] In either identifying what was commonly called consciousness with physical processes, or in conceding some difference while excluding the concept from the realm of science, the behaviorist was, Brand Blanshard insisted, on loose ground. Such an exclusion or such an assumption was untenable as a simple consideration of agreeable and disagreeable experiences showed. These experiences were forms of consciousness, not physical events or movements, because it was impossible to know precisely the direction and velocity of agreeable and disagreeable experiences.[44]

The repudiation of the traditional concept of mind, of which consciousness was a denotation, also led to other criticisms. In trying to prove the thesis that there were no interacting minds, Watson had falsely and foolishly felt that he had to prove there were no minds at all. As Gustav Bergmann, an admirer of Watson's contributions to methodology, observed, the Wundtians had long ago laid the ghost of the concept of substantive minds. But minds in the sense of awareness of phenomena, or precepts, memories, volitions, and thoughts, incontestably did exist and were real.[45]

Others objected to the exclusive reliance on the stimulus-response relationship as the explanation of behavior. Though John Dewey felt that "anything that tends to make psychology a theory of human nature as it concretely exists and human life as it is actually lived, can only be an instrument of emancipation of philosophy," he pointed out that a narrow view of stimulus-response was misleading because of the con-

41. Arthur O. Lovejoy, "The Paradox of the Thinking Behaviorist," *Philosophical Review* 31 (1922): 135–47, esp. p. 142.

42. George Santayana, "Living without Thinking," *The Forum* 68 (1922): 731–35. Santayana somewhat playfully argued that Watson implicitly subscribed to philosophical idealism, a "false philosophy," in that he fused "the light of thought and the actuality of experience with all the objects which he mentions and which he only *seems* to regard as existing materially. He does not need the human mind in his world because his world is already in the human mind" in much the same way as in a theater "the whole play is addressed to us from the beginning, and is only a play."

43. Edward Robinson, "Behaviorist: L'Enfant Terrible," *New Republic* 57 (1929): 181–82.

44. Brand Blanshard, "Critical Reflections on Behaviorism," *Proceedings of the American Philosophical Society* 109 (1965): 23.

45. Gustav Bergmann, "The Contribution of John B. Watson," *Psychological Review* 63 (1956): 265.

tinuity of experience. "In Watson's zeal to eliminate everything 'mental' from psychology," wrote Sidney W. Bijou, ". . . he was left without an objective way of accounting for the influence of past interactions on current interactions. Consequently, he had no way of showing in what he thought was an objective frame of reference, what a set of physically defined stimuli might 'mean' to the individual."[46]

Among the groups that indicted behaviorism in terms of its false concept of human nature were the New Humanists, literary critics rich in learning and deeply committed to classical dualism. To them, behaviorism was only an extreme example of the unfortunate victory of naturalism and materialism in American civilization in the 1920s and 1930s. In making man an automaton governed by his outer environment, behaviorism denied the validity of the "inner check" or disciplined self-restraint. This most human aspect of man enabled him to curb his brutal impulses and kept him from being the slave of his own feelings and of the relativistic and materialistic standards of modern culture.[47]

On philosophical, social, moral, and religious levels, the case against behaviorism informed the essays edited by the Reverend William P. King of the *Quarterly Review*, the organ of the Methodist Episcopal Church South. The contributors, who included leading intellectuals, viewed behaviorism as an inadequate, false, and in its implications dangerous image of man. According to these critics the shortcomings of behaviorism stemmed from several factors. It was self-limiting in assuming that the physical sciences were the only sciences, and that the tangible and visible were the only legitimate material of science. Were this true, what would become of mathematics, jurisprudence, and other fields of knowledge? In denigrating individual differences and their biological inheritance, behaviorism closed its eyes to modern genetics and well-established psychological findings. McDougall castigated behaviorism as a deduction from a false metaphysics that regarded the universe as a machine, a position at odds with the more plausible and in his opinion generally accepted theory of emergent evolution.[48] Moreover, behaviorism could predict reactions only on a rudimentary and simplistic level, nor had it proved its effectiveness in the control of behavior.

46. John Dewey, "Psychological Doctrine and Philosophical Teaching," *Journal of Philosophy, Psychology, and Scientific Method* 11 (1914): 511; Sidney W. Bijou, "Environment and Intelligence: A Behavioral Analysis," in Robert Cancro, ed., *Intelligence: Genetic and Environmental Influences* (New York, 1971), p. 228.

47. J. David Hoeveler, Jr., *The New Humanism: A Critique of Modern America, 1900–1940* (Charlottesville, Va., 1977), pp. 32, 47.

48. William McDougall, "The Psychology They Teach in New York," in William P. King, ed., *Behaviorism, a Battle Line* (Nashville, 1930), pp. 35–36.

Further, behaviorism ignored the findings of modern social science. Cooley had shown that human nature as manifested in adult behavior resulted from the interactions of the growing infant and child with primary groups. In neglecting social process and in emphasizing extreme individualism, behaviorism ignored the fact that "all sanity is a matter of social reference."[49] Nor did it take into account the fact that the culture, which played so striking a part in explaining behavior, was itself a product of such essentially human attributes as the powers of imagination, reason, and sympathy.[50]

Finally, the indictment held that the Gestalt psychologists and the experimental work of Hartshorne and May on deceit demonstrated that behavior was not merely the response to objective situations physically present at the time of the observed response, but was rather the reaction to a total situation which included the personality with its beliefs, attitudes, purposes, fears, hopes, and aspirations. "The concept of the psychological whole," wrote Charles C. Josey, "is valuable in directing our attention to the essential conditions for all human activity—namely, a self, which is a functional system in a larger functional whole."

In fact, uneasiness, even alarm, about what seemed to be the amoral and unethical implications of behaviorism dominated the volume. The emphasis on the automatic roles of the conditioned reflex and habit and on the shaping role of whoever controlled the stimuli overlooked the importance of values and robbed the individual of spontaneity and responsibility, debased the mind, dismissed personality, and brutalized the emotions. In the domestic circle, McDougall wrote, it boldly applied its deductions, regarding romantic life, marital fidelity, and premarital chastity as absurd survivals. If Watson's theory of human nature could be shown to be true, or if it continued to spread, his forecast about the obsoleteness of marriage would in truth be realized.[51] In denying an inner life, behaviorism stripped humanity of all its spiritual significance and left it in a world indifferent to human values and struggles.[52] It smeared religion as a delusive superstition. There could thus be no peace between religion and behaviorism.[53]

49. James S. Sonekar, "Behaviorism and Character," in King, ed., *Behaviorism*, p. 239.

50. Charles A. Ellwood, "The Uses and Limitations of Behaviorism in Social Science," in King, ed., *Behaviorism*, pp. 201 ff.; and Charles C. Josey, "Behaviorism and Behavior," in the same volume, pp. 66–67.

51. McDougall, "The Psychology They Teach in New York," p. 54.

52. Josey, "Behaviorism and Behavior," pp. 73–75.

53. Julius Mark, "Behaviorism and Religion," in King, ed., *Behaviorism*, p. 287. Harris F. Rall, in an essay in the same volume entitled "What Does Behaviorism Mean for Religion?" considered "radical behaviorism" as hostile, but conceded that in its moderate form, it might be an aid (pp. 300 ff.).

Critics of behaviorism attributed its appeal to its oversimplification, easy and naïve promises, alleged practicality, and denial of the importance of heredity. Watson himself admitted that some of his statements went beyond the facts.[54] Others contended that its appeal was related to its seeming rapport with the nation's engrossment in the production and use of machines. Thus McDougall viewed behaviorism as both a product and a prime agency of that mechanization of human life that all Europe recognized as the essence of Americanization.[55] Norbert Wiener, well known for his work in cybernetics, seemed to confirm this opinion in suggesting that the feedback principle in the nervous system explained operations once thought to be unique to human beings with immortal souls.[56]

However sound the explanations for the popularity of behaviorism at its height and however valid the criticisms, its contributions to ideas about human nature were substantial and impressive. In the words of Horace Kallen, a former student of James and a respected philosopher, it reoriented the mind with respect to the nature of man, making the world a simpler place in which to adjust and human nature a more hopeful matter to deal with.[57] In 1957 the American Psychological Association paid a high tribute to Watson in a resolution declaring that his "work has been one of the vital determinants of the form and substance of modern psychology. He initiated a revolution in psychological thought, and his writings have been the point of departure for continuing lines of fruitful research."[58]

Without Watson's dogmatism, other psychologists, using whatever method seemed appropriate, qualified and amplified early behaviorism

54. For additional criticisms see A. A. Roback, *Behaviorism and Psychology* (Cambridge, Mass., 1923), and *Behaviorism at Twenty-five* (Cambridge, Mass., 1937). Of more consequence: Jerry Hirsch, "Behavior—Genetic Analysis and Its Bio-social Consequences," in Cancro, ed., *Intelligence: Genetic and Environmental Influences*, pp. 89–90; Jacob R. Kantor, *The Scientific Evolution in Psychology*, 3 vols. (Chicago, 1963–69), 2:368; and Willard Harrell and Ross Harrison, "The Rise and Fall of Behaviorism," *The Journal of General Psychology* 18 (1938): 367–421.

55. Josiah Morse, "Introduction," in King, ed., *Behaviorism*, p. 12; McDougall, "The Psychology They Teach in New York," pp. 55–56.

56. Norbert Wiener, *Cybernetics, or Control and Communication in the Animal and the Machine* (New York, 1948); Norbert Wiener and J. P. Schade, *Cybernetics of the Nervous System* (Amsterdam, N.Y., 1965); and Norbert Wiener, *Ex-prodigy: My Childhood and Youth* (New York, 1953).

57. Horace Kallen, "Behaviorism," *Encyclopedia of the Social Sciences*, 2:495–98.

58. Cited in Watson, *Behaviorism*, rev. ed. (Chicago, 1958), front piece.

in trying to find out precisely how particular organisms acquired a distinctive behavior.[59] In 1937, John F. Dashiell noted that recently discovered complex neural functionings discredited the concept of neurons and reflex arcs as complete explanations of behavior. The idea of a motivated organism to be interpreted by the principles of life as well as those of mechanism largely pushed into the background the concept of "man the machine."[60]

Those who stressed action by the total organism sometimes spoke of themselves as molar behaviorists. In emphasizing a biosocial approach to behavior, two older pioneers might be thought of as transitional figures. Max Meyer, who in 1921 formulated laws of behavioristic mechanism in terms of a hypothetical nervous system, also took account of the social factor by insisting that private consciousness had no place unless it could be converted to public data.[61] His student Albert Paul Weiss assimilated psychological materials to a time-space frame of reference, with emphasis on social communication. "The factors which traditional psychology vaguely classified as conscious or mental elements merely *vanish* without a remainder into the biological and social components of the behavioristic analysis."[62]

The 1930s and 1940s witnessed a creative search for a methodological base for a general theory of behavior. Logical positivism and philosophical analysis clearly proved useful. Under the rubric *neobehaviorism* Clark Hull and his associates at Yale made the epistemological decision that sensory experiences of the observing scientist were the basic data of psychology, and that explanation was equated with theoretical deduction. At first using classical conditioning as the main source for theoretical assumptions, Hull worked out a "mathematico-deductive" theory of learning and habit formation. Convinced that all behavior, whether individual, social, moral, normal, or psychopathic, was "generated from the same primary laws," Hull

59. Rachlin, *Introduction to Modern Behaviorism*, p. 69. André Tilquin's *Le Behaviorisme: Origine et développement de la psychologie en Amérique* (Paris, 1950), gives a good discussion of the leading figures in the behaviorisms of the 1930s and 1940s.

60. John F. Dashiell, *Fundamentals of General Psychology* (New York, 1937), p. vii.

61. Meyer, *Psychology of the Other-One*, rev. ed. (Columbia, Mo., 1922), chaps. 19–20; Carl Murchison, "Max Meyer," *Psychological Register* 3 (1932): 336; Erwin A. Esper, "The Making of a Scientific Isolate," *Journal of the History of the Behavioral Sciences* 2 (1966): 341–56; and "Max Meyer in America," *Journal of the History of the Behavioral Sciences* 3 (1967): 107–31.

62. Albert P. Weiss, *A Theoretical Basis of Human Behavior* (Columbus, Oh., 1925; 2d ed. rev., 1929); R. M. Elliott, "Albion Paul Weiss, 1879-1931," *American Journal of Psychology* 43 (1931): 707–9; Edwin G. Boring, *A History of Experimental Psychology* (New York, 1950), pp. 648–49.

held that the differences in the objective behavioral manifestations were due to "the differing conditions under which habits are set up and function." His detailed diagrams of stimulus-response representations included the introduction of drives or persisting stimuli, goal stimuli, and resulting responses. This clarified the beginning and end of behavioral sequences, including intervening variables, and contributed to more precise predictions.[63] Despite progress, Hull concluded that the systematic development of the behavioral sciences must wait until the arduous and exacting task of thinking in terms of equations and higher mathematics was mastered.[64] Among those contributing to this end, Kenneth Spence of Iowa, Hull's close associate who had formulated the discrimination-learning theory, proved to be a driving force in the not altogether satisfactory effort to erect a theoretical structure with broad implications.[65]

Edward T. Tolman, whose work was once characterized as "behaviorism come of age," was another of the major figures in the revision of early behaviorism. His eclecticism reflected the influence of European phenomenology in its emphasis on perception and organization as well as methodological traditions of behaviorism.[66] The concept of consciousness could be accepted, Tolman thought, when viewed behavioristically as the "moment of readjusting" or "regestalting."[67] His psychology conceived of mental products as "functional variables intervening between stimuli, initiating physiological states, and the general heredity and past training of the organism, on the one hand, and the final resulting responses, on the other."[68] His work on learning held behavior to be purposive in the sense of "persisting until" a goal was reached. Purpose, in other words, was "that aspect of behavior which is present wherever merely to describe the behavior it is necessary to include a reference to the position or nature of the goal-object, as such."[69] Tolman thus met some of the harshest criticisms once leveled against Watson.

63. Albert E. Goss, "Early Behaviorism and Verbal Mediating Responses," *American Psychologist* 16 (1961): 294–95.

64. Clark L. Hull, *Principles of Behavior* (New York, 1943), p. 400.

65. Howard H. Kendler and Janet T. Spence, *Essays in Neobehaviorism: A Memorial Volume to Kenneth W. Spence* (New York, 1971), pp. 36–37.

66. Edward C. Tolman, *Purposive Behavior in Animals and Men*, introduction by Richard M. Elliott (New York, 1932), p. viii.

67. Edward C. Tolman, "A Behaviorist's Definition of Consciousness," *Psychological Review* 34 (1927): 433–39.

68. Tolman, *Purposive Behavior in Animals and Men*, p. 414.

69. Edward C. Tolman, "Behaviorism and Purpose," *Journal of Philosophy* 22 (1925): 36–41. See also "Purposive Behavior," *Psychological Review* 35 (1928): 524–30.

In terms of the discussion of human nature, B. F. Skinner at Harvard was the most publicized of the later behaviorists. His autobiography[70] spoke of such influences on his position as Baconian empiricism and "pragmatism," the epistemological scheme of the logical positivists and operationalists, Ernst Mach's identification of cause with correlation, Thorndike, Pavlov, and Watson, whom he never met. Skinner's experimental work seemed to Edwin G. Boring, the leading historian of psychology, to have changed the nature of behaviorism in its theoretical exposition, the application Skinner and others made of it in educational practice, in psychotherapy, and in other closed systems involving human populations.[71]

Ruling out the psychology of events in the nervous system as well as those laid at the door of consciousness, Skinner held that behavior was to be understood in terms of correlations between stimuli and responses without concern for any neural connections or for the unconditioned stimulus. His position, however, differed from reflexology in emphasizing the consequences of behavior rather than the conditions that led to it. "The word operant," he explained, "is used to emphasize the fact that behavior operates upon the environment to produce consequences, certain kinds of which 'reinforce' the behavior they are contingent upon, in the sense that they make it more likely to occur again. So-called contingencies of reinforcement," he continued, "represent subtle and complex relations among three things: the setting or occasion upon which behavior occurs, the behavior itself, and its reinforcing consequences."[72] In other words, the reinforcement by success shapes behavior into the pattern which by chance led to the reward. By arranging contingencies and controlling variables, Skinner's experiments with pigeons showed that their behavior could be programmed in such ways that the birds pecked at varied color spots and shapes on a wall and could even guide missiles. His experiments also demonstrated the greater effectiveness of positive reinforcements over negative, "punitive" ones or deprivations. Partly on the basis of these experiments Skinner concluded that in the family, the school, the job, the mental hospital ward—in short, in our whole society—human beings

70. B. F. Skinner, "An Autobiography," in P. B. Dews, *Festchrift for B. F. Skinner* (New York, 1970), pp. 1–21; B. F. Skinner, *Particulars of My Life* (New York, 1976), the first of two or more anticipated volumes. John A. Weigel's *B. F. Skinner* (Boston, 1977) is a well-balanced account of Skinner's work.

71. Edwin G. Boring, "The Trend toward Mechanism," in *Proceedings of the American Philosophical Society* 108 (1964): 451–54.

72. B. F. Skinner, "Answers to My Critics," in Harvey Wheeler, ed., *Beyond the Punitive Society: Operant Conditioning, Social and Political Aspects* (San Francisco, 1973), pp. 257–58.

had to operate in what was primarily an antipathetic system of conditioning and control.[73]

Skinner's behaviorism was nicely exemplified when he asked whether human nature was the same the world over. "This may mean," he wrote, "that behavioral processes are the same wherever they are encountered—that all behavior varies in the same way with changes in deprivation or reinforcement, that discriminations are formed in the same way, that estimation takes place at the same rate, and so on." Such a contention, he continued, might be as correct as the statement that human respiration, digestion, and reproduction are the same the world over. Undoubtedly there were personal differences in the rates at which various changes took places in all these areas, but the basic processes may have been relatively constant properties. The statement that human nature was the same everywhere might also mean that the independent variables that determined behavior were the same the world over. "Genetic endowments differ widely, and environments are likely to show more differences than similarities, a large number of which may be traced to cultural variables. The result is, of course, a high degree of individuality." The effect of social environment upon the behavior of the individual might be inferred point for point from an analysis of that environment.[74] In brief, Skinner held that the extension of behaviorism as a philosophy of science to the study of political and economic behavior was "the application of a tested formula to important parts of the field of human behavior."[75]

In *Walden Two* (1948), *Contingencies of Reinforcement* (1969), *Beyond Freedom and Dignity* (1971), and *About Behaviorism* (1974), Skinner developed the social and political implications of operant conditioning. Again and again he contrasted "the traditional view of man" as a creature with an inner capacity for self-control, decision-making, freedom, and responsibility for ethical or immoral behavior with the view of man as an organism whose behavior resulted from his genetic and environmental histories. The inclination to act in ways detrimental to the individual and society could best be controlled and

73. B. F. Skinner, "The Concept of the Reflex in the Description of Behavior," *Journal of General Psychology* 5 (1931): 427–58, *The Behavior of Organisms* (New York, 1938), *Science and Human Behavior* (New York, 1953), *Verbal Behavior* (New York, 1957), in which Skinner in effect negated the speaker as an autonomous agent, and *Contingencies of Reinforcement: A Theoretical Analysis* (New York, 1969). A good introduction is the dialogue between Skinner and Richard L. Evans in Evans, ed., *B. F. Skinner: The Man and His Ideas* (New York, 1968).

74. Skinner, *Science and Human Behavior*, pp. 421–22.

75. B. F. Skinner, "Behavior at Fifty," *Science* 140 (1963): 958; also included in *Contingencies of Reinforcement*, pp. 221–68.

even eliminated, Skinner argued, if the conditions that made such behavior were changed or eliminated. On behaviorist principles, a world could be built in which desirable conduct would be reinforced by careful management of causative stimuli and identified variables. The key was to deprive individuals of the opportunity and inducement for self-defeating and antisocial behavior, and to reinforce conduct conducive to personal happiness (effective adjustment free from struggle) and social harmony.[76] In *Walden Two* and elsewhere Skinner spelled out the kind of social engineering, including the necessary child-rearing, that he was convinced would promote a world of tranquility and creativity.

On almost every conceivable level *Walden Two*, and more particularly *Beyond Freedom and Dignity*, invited criticisms that cut deeper than those earlier made of Watson. These included Joseph Wood Krutch's *The Measure of Man* (1953), the contentions of Carl Rogers at a symposium in which Skinner took part at the 1956 meeting of the American Psychological Association,[77] C. S. Lewis's *The Abolition of Man* (1957), Abraham Maslow's *Toward a Psychology of Being* (1962), Noam Chomsky's essays (1971–72), and the papers presented at seminars at the Center for the Study of Democratic Institutions at Santa Barbara in which Skinner again took part.[78]

The technical criticisms held that the exclusive level of inquiry Skinner insisted on—a law-seeking and law-stating science of visible behavior as such—was a matter of principle rather than of fact, and thus unacceptable, in view of the legitimate claims of other levels of inquiry. Some critics pointed out that from what was known of biology, including genetics, it was doubtful whether an organism, especially man, could be treated as clay in the hands of a potter-conditioner. Others questioned whether Skinner or anyone else had provided warrantable scientific evidence of how behavior was actually determined. Still others felt that even if operant behavior were effective in the case of individuals, the behavior of human communities differed in important ways from that of individuals. The linguistic theorist Noam Chomsky held that vague and ambiguous terms such as control, responsibility, and environment deprived "mentalistic" psychology of whatever content its disciplined terminology had. Far from thus achieving a scientific analysis of behavior, Skinner failed to understand even the rudiments of scientific thinking, with the result that his claims faded into incoherence and

76. This summary is a paraphrase of Skinner's admirably clear and succinct essay "Man," in *Proceedings of the American Philosophical Society* 108 (1964): 482–85.

77. "Some Issues Concerning the Control of Human Behavior," *Science* 124 (1956): 1057–66.

78. Harvey Wheeler, ed., *Beyond the Punitive Society*, pp. 247–55.

triviality. Worse, his so-called science of human behavior, since it was vague and vacuous, was meaningless in being as congenial to libertarianism as to fascism.[79] Joseph J. Schwab, having summed up the criticisms made at the Santa Barbara seminars, viewed skeptically the extrapolation from knowledge of things *in vitro* to conclusions about things *in vivo*, that is, from the glassware of the laboratory to "life."

Criticisms relating to values emerged from several quarters. Carl Rogers, a leading exponent of a humanistic and personalistic psychology, characterized Skinner's position as weakened by ambiguities and misunderstandings in the face of crucial questions: "Who will be controlled? Who will exercise control? What type of control will be exercised? Most important of all, toward what end or what purpose, or in the pursuit of what value, will control be exercised?"[80] The veteran humanist Joseph Wood Krutch contended that such a behavioristically managed society as Skinner envisioned would rob men and women of their individuality, responsibility, and freedom for action in accord with an inner sense of justice and dignity. Some critics claimed scientific support for their criticism. The conception of indeterminacy, chance, and uncertainty in physics and other sciences suggested that in any science of behavior, freedom in some degree might well exist. Arnold Toynbee questioned whether either heredity or environment, or the two together, could fully account for the behavior of Hosea, Zarathustra, Jeremiah, the Buddha, Socrates, Jesus, Muhammad, and Saint Francis of Assisi. Several humanists and literary critics objected, not to Skinner's concept of "a design of culture," that is, the creation of social forms more conducive to the satisfaction of human needs, but rather to his dogmatic perception of these needs.

To all this Skinner replied that the conception of such motivations as freedom of action in accord with an inner sense of justice and dignity involved an unwarranted assumption in the traditional view of man. If this was true, then none of the characteristics attributed to men could be taken from them, since they existed only as assumptions. To the argument that a controlled or managed society would mean that some would control the actions of others, Skinner replied that this had always been the case, since people were controlled by those who controlled the environment in which life was lived, and might yet be further controlled by those who one day might control the genetic heritage as well. When some elites effected changes in the culture that changed the conduct of others, they controlled these others and reduced or eliminated their

79. Noam Chomsky, "Psychology and Ideology," in *For Reasons of State* (New York, 1970), pp. 318–69. This discussion expanded Chomsky's criticisms in his review of *Beyond Freedom and Dignity* in the *New York Review of Books*, December 30, 1971.

80. Rogers, "Some Issues Concerning the Control of Human Behavior," p. 1060.

"freedom" as much as those who might manage a society in which children were reared to behave in agreed-upon ways by reenforcement and deprivation. To the contention that those power-hungry to an excessive degree would control the variables and programmed behavior in their own interest, Skinner countered that a society could be designed to prevent such people from manipulating others. Finally, to the argument that a managed society based on operant conditioning would mean the end of individual differences, Skinner argued that the unique genetic and environmental experiences of every individual would always insure a unique personality.[81]

Skinner admitted that just as the physicist did not change the nature of the world he studied, so no science of behavior could change the essential nature of man, "even though both sciences yield technologies with a vast power to manipulate their subject matters. If we must have something to admire, let it be man's willingness to discard a flattering portrait of himself in favor of a more accurate and hence more useful picture. . . . The hard fact is that the culture which most readily acknowledges the validity of a scientific analysis is most likely to be successful in that competition between cultures which, whether we like it or not, will decide all such issues with finality."[82]

In view of the eventual impact of the behavioral movement, broadly considered, on the social disciplines, the cautious response of most academicians to Watson's formulation seems surprising. Movements of thought in some ways similar to behaviorism in their implications for society and human nature had begun, by the turn of the century, to interest a growing number of social scientists. These influences included the German historical school, empiricism, pragmatism, and the functional psychology of James and the Chicago group.

The American version of neoclassicism in economics, with its rationalistic, atomistic, and prudentially modified hedonistic image of economic man as he should be in terms of the prevailing order, met with challenge and erosion as leading practitioners realized the inadequacy of its underlying psychological abstractions.[83] A shift toward the "analysis

81. B. F. Skinner, "Answer to My Critics," in Wheeler, ed., *Beyond the Punitive Society*, pp. 256–66.

82. Skinner, "Man," p. 485.

83. Walter A. Weisskopf has succinctly summed up and thoughtfully explained the assumptions of classical and neoclassical economics in "The Image of Man in Economics," included in "Human Nature: A Reevaluation," *Social Research* 40 (1973): 547–63. See also his *Psychology of Economics* (Chicago, 1955) and *Alienation and Economics* (New York, 1971).

of working institutions and the motivation of behavior"[84] reflected, in addition to the influence of new currents of thought, the pressures of contentious social interests, inherent, apparently, in the swift changes in corporate capitalism, technological industrialism, and a heterogeneous urbanism.

The harbingers of something like a behavioral approach to economics included, as we have seen, Thorstein Veblen, Simon Patten, John R. Commons,[85] John Maurice Clark,[86] and Wesley C. Mitchell.[87] The difficulties of using behavioral concepts and methods did not go unnoticed. The whole stimulating situation and the total state of the organism might be ignored at hazard, when a single situation focused attention on reactions in behavior. Moreover, it was easy to force economic theory into psychological molds without due respect for the unique aspects of economic activity.[88] Nevertheless Zina Clark Dickinson of Michigan, in a study of the psychological foundations of economic theory (1925), flatly stated that "the economist is a behaviorist, trying to find out what people can be depended on to do in certain common situations."[89] That very year Jacob Viner of Chicago pointedly wrote that human behavior in the marketplace, as elsewhere, presumably [is] "not under the constant and detailed guidance of careful and accurate hedonistic calculations, but is the product of an unstable and unrational complex of reflex actions, impulses, instincts, habits, customs, fashions, and mob hysteria."[90]

In 1922 Rexford Tugwell, a one-time student of Simon Patten,

84. Mary O. Furner, *Advocacy and Objectivity: A Crisis in the Professionalization of American Social Science, 1865–1905* (Lexington, Ky., 1975), chaps. 12, 13.

85. John R. Commons, *Legal Foundations of Capitalism* (New York, 1939), *Institutional Economics: Its Place in Political Economy*, 2 vols. (Madison, 1934), and *Myself: The Autobiography of John R. Commons* (Madison, 1934); and Joseph Dorfman, *The Economic Mind in American Civilization*, 3 (New York, 1949): 276–94, and 4 (New York, 1959): 377–95.

86. John M. Clark, "Economics and Modern Psychology," *Journal of Political Economy* 26 (1918): 10, 12, 22–23, 29–30.

87. See Lucy Sprague Mitchell, *Two Lives: The Story of Wesley Clair Mitchell and Myself* (New York, 1953), p. 93; Wesley C. Mitchell, *Business Cycles and Their Causes* (Berkeley, 1941), pp. 190–91.

88. Adolf J. Snow, "Psychology in Economic Theory," *Journal of Political Economy* 32 (1924): 487–96. Snow, a psychologist, wrote extensively on the applications of psychology to economics. See, for examples, his *Psychology in Business Relations* (Chicago, 1925) and *Psychology in Personal Selling* (Chicago, 1926).

89. Zina C. Dickinson, *Economic Motives: A Study in the Psychological Foundation of Economic Theory, with some reference to the other social sciences* (Cambridge, Mass., 1922), p. 208.

90. Jacob Viner, "The Utility Concept in Value Theory and Its Critics," *Journal of Political Economy* 33 (1925): 373.

plumped for a full-fledged acceptance of the new psychology, especially in its behavioral dress. He anticipated his New Deal career by suggesting the relationship between stimulus-response and planned economic activity in the interest of the common welfare. His premises regarding the "true nature" of man derived from experimental behaviorism. The needed change in attitudes about human nature, still resting as of old on the concept of self-imposed controls, involved, of course, discarding most of the cherished preconceptions and assumptions by which neoclassicists justified free enterprise and laissez faire.[91] By 1936 a like-minded colleague, Clarence Ayres of the University of Texas, surveying the past half-century, concluded that institutional economists made little explicit use of any specific psychological discovery about behavior and that, rather, the two movements coincidentally paralleled each other. "In psychology the concept of behavior has been proposed as a substitute for the psyche, and in economics institutions and technology have been proposed to replace the price system conceived as a rebirth of wants and satisfactions."[92] The behavioral emphases quickened as economists found useful applications of their craft in time-motion studies, labor-management relations and other aspects of industrial production, and of course in advertising and related means of whetting consumers' appetites.[93]

Thus without always subscribing to behaviorism, the profession increasingly accepted the idea that psychological study of economic processes was possible because "human decisions, and human behavior in general, are governed by laws, that is, are not arbitrary, unpredictable, indeterminate. While human beings are not "marionettes pushed about by external forces," in the words of George Katona of the University of Michigan, "the latitude of their choice itself is subject to scientific analysis."[94] Katona's work reflected, to be sure, the influence of gestalt

91. Rexford Tugwell, "Human Nature in Economic Theory," *Journal of Political Economy* 30 (1922): 317–45.

92. Clarence E. Ayres, "Fifty Years' Development in Ideas of Human Nature and Motivation," *American Economic Review* 26 (1936): Supplement, 236.

93. Albert T. Lauterbach, *Man, Motives and Money: Psychological Frontiers of Economics* (Ithaca, 1954), pp. 83–89; John Ise, *Economics* (New York, 1946; rev. ed., 1950), p. 309; Thurman Arnold, *The Folklore of Capitalism* (New Haven, 1937); Frank Knight, *Risk, Uncertainty, and Profit* (Boston and New York, 1921; rev. ed., 1933), pp. 136, 167; and *On the History and Methods of Economics: Selected Essays* (Chicago, 1956), esp. pp. 96–97, 227 ff., and 479 ff. Alfred D. Chandler, *The Visible Man: The Managerial Revolution in American Business* (Cambridge, Mass., 1978), argues that managerial capitalism resulted from the refinement of industrial management or competitive efficiency rather than from "monopoly power."

94. George Katona, *Psychological Analysis of Economic Behavior* (New York, 1951), p. 8.

psychology and field theory in greater measure than the influence of strict behaviorism.

With the outstanding exception of the controversial and academically isolated Arthur F. Bentley, political scientists responded to behaviorism with more reservation than economists. Bentley, in *The Process of Government: A Study in Social Pressures* (1908), completely rejected the dominant view of feelings, faculties, and ideas as independent causes of political action, and focused on overt behavior—"the raw material of political process is the activity of human beings." *The Process of Government* was, among other things, concerned with the resolution of conflicts. Over the years, Bentley tried to improve the use of language as a tool for precise, objective descriptions of concepts and behavior.[95] In partership with John Dewey, he worked out a transactional view of behavior that went beyond Watson's emphasis on the datum of observation in postulating a nonmechanistic, nonspacial, and nontemporal model.[96]

The eclecticism of many political scientists[97] did not stem a growing interest in behavioral approaches. Walter Lippmann's *Public Opinion* (1922) did a good deal to direct academic attention to the behavioral aspects of politics. At the University of Chicago Charles E. Merriam, while disavowing behavioral determinism, analyzed political action in terms of what might be thought of as a stimulus-response relationship.[98] His students and those influenced by him published noteworthy studies that, generally speaking, met many of the canons of behaviorism broadly viewed.[99] Nor did the Chicago circle monopolize the behavioral approach. At Columbia, to be sure, European emigrés modified this with

95. Arthur F. Bentley, *Behavior, Knowledge, Fact* (Bloomington, Ind., 1935), pp. 55–56, 246, 337, 385–87.

96. Arthur F. Bentley, *A Philosophical Correspondence, 1932–1951* (New Brunswick, N.J., 1964); Arthur F. Bentley and John Dewey, *Knowing and the Known* (Boston, 1949); Richard W. Taylor, "Arthur F. Bentley," in *International Encyclopedia of the Social Sciences*, 2:58–62.

97. Seba Eldridge, while using behavioral techniques, also found a place for introspective and cognitive factors, for emotions and volitions, in his accounts of the interactions between political power and economic forces. In addition to *Political Action: A Naturalistic Interpretation of the Labor Movement in Relation to the State* (Philadelphia, 1924), see *The Organization of Life . . .* (New York, 1925), pp. 234–35.

98. Charles E. Merriam, *New Aspects of Politics* (Chicago, 1925), *Chicago: A More Intimate View of Urban Politics* (New York, 1929), and *The Making of Citizens* (Chicago, 1931); Barry Karl, *Charles E. Merriam and the Study of Politics* (Chicago, 1974), chap. 8.

99. For example, Harold F. Gosnell, *Getting Out the Vote: An Experiment in the Stimulation of Voting* (Chicago, 1927); Harold D. Lasswell, *Politics: Who Gets What, When, and How* (New York, 1936); Herbert A. Simon, *Administrative Behavior: A Study of Decision-Making Processes in Administrative Organizations* (New York, 1947); V. O. Key, Jr., *Politics, Parties, and Pressure Groups* (New York, 1942); Gabriel A. Almond, *The American People and Foreign Policy* (New York, 1950); David B. Truman, *The Govern-*

adaptations of the ideas of Marx, Durkheim, Freud, Mosca, Pareto, Michels, and Weber. Of special note was *The People's Choice* (1944) by Paul Lazarfeld, Bernard Berelson, and Hazel Gaudet. In due course, studies from several departments were published on behavior in the legislative, judicial, administrative, community, and international spheres. David Easton, summarizing in 1962 new trends in theory and methods, observed that these so linked the subject "to broader behavioral tendencies in the social sciences" that political science could be described as "political behavior."[100]

Behaviorist sociology owed much to Floyd H. Allport, a psychologist trained at Harvard by Hugo Munsterberg and Edwin A. Holt. His ground-breaking *Social Psychology* (1924) repudiated the prevailing idea, associated with Tarde, Le Bon, and Everett Dean Martin, of a group or collective mind, and firmly insisted that behavioristic or operational principles explained interactions between individuals in groups. Thus the problem of adjustment was the reconciliation of conflicts between the individual's social drives and his more primitive, unsocialized impulses. Allport also applied behavioral measurements to institutions. The highly abstract system he laid out in *Theories of Perception* (1955) strengthened his biographer's claim that "the concept of the behavioral sciences is the logical outcome of Allport's teachings."[101]

In sociology itself, behaviorism divided the profession as it did practitioners in other social disciplines.[102] A new chapter began with the work of the versatile, learned, and influential Luther L. Bernard. In his

mental Process: Political Interests and Public Opinion (New York, 1951); and Ithiel de Sela Pool, "The Mass Media and Politics in the Modernizational Process," in *Communications and Political Development* (Dobbs Ferry, N.Y., 1963), pp. 234–53.

100. David Easton, "The Current Meaning of 'Behavioralism' in Political Science," in James C. Charlesworth, ed., *The Limits of Behaviorism in Political Science* (Philadelphia, 1962), p. 25. See also Evron M. Kirkpatrick, "The Impact of the Behavioral Approach on the Traditional Study of Politics," in Austin Ranney, ed., *Essays on the Behavioral Study of Politics* (Urbana, Ill., 1962), pp. 14, 25; and Heinz Eulaw, Samuel J. Eldersveld, and Morris Janowitz, eds., *Political Behavior: A Reader in Theory and Research* (Glencoe, Ill., 1956).

101. Floyd H. Allport, *Social Psychology* (Boston, 1924), *Institutional Behavior* (Chapel Hill, 1933), and *Theories of Perception* (New York, 1955). See also the criticisms of *Social Psychology* in the generally appreciative review by A. B. Wolfe in the *Journal of Philosophy* 21 (1924): 538; and the judicious comments of Daniel Katz, "Floyd H. Allport," in the *International Encyclopedia of the Social Sciences*, 1:271–73.

102. Simon Patten, "The Failure of Biological Sociology," *Annals of the American Academy of Political and Social Science* 4 (1894): 919–47, cited by Furner in *Advocacy and Objectivity*, p. 300; Fred H. Mathews, in *Quest for an American Sociology: Robert E. Park and the Chicago School* (Montreal, 1977), emphasizes the influence of James, Dewey, Cooley, and Mead, rather than Watson, on Park's conception of human nature (pp. 148–49).

1911 Chicago dissertation, he declared that subjectivistic and idealistic views of personal liberty and individual wants could well be spared by substituting objective standards of social control.[103] *An Introduction to Social Psychology* unequivocally held that "behavior, the concern of social psychology is interested directly and primarily in human behavior in a social situation," and found in such behavior the key to social structure and interpersonal adjustments.[104] Perhaps Bernard's most distinctive contribution involved the concept of man's two-fold or two-way adaptation to the natural and cultural environment in which he functioned as a social being. Yet his position differed from Watson's in regarding value systems and ameliorative purposes as valid motives.[105] Bernard boldly proclaimed that the behaviorist concerned with social psychology must not stop with the process of conditioning individual behavior patterns in social situations. He must also contribute to the building up of social or collective patterns of behavior.[106]

Asserting that every mental phenomenon could best be studied with the same objective methods used in investigating other kinds of behavior, George A. Lundberg of the University of Washington applied this concept to the image of man.[107] Prevailing ideas about human nature, having derived from folklore and literature, could not be accepted until the maxims and pronouncements of poets, novelists, playwrights, preachers, journalists, and radio commentators were scientifically validated. "In that testing, a certain degree of validity will undoubtedly be found in Homer, Shakespeare, and others—perhaps about the same validity as has been found in the geographical and biological contributions of these authors."[108]

Such an uncompromising view found no favor with Charles A. Ellwood of the University of Missouri (later, of Duke). Ellwood outlined the main objections to the behaviorist interpretation of society. It failed to show the true nature of the human social process, which was essen-

103. Luther L. Bernard, *The Transition to an Objective Standard of Social Control* (Chicago, 1911).

104. Luther L. Bernard, *An Introduction to Social Psychology* (New York, 1926), p. 107.

105. Bernard, *Introduction to Social Psychology*, pp. 22, 425 ff.

106. Bernard, "Social Psychology Studies Adjustment Behavior," *American Journal of Sociology* 38 (1932): 1–9. See also Bernard's *Social Control in Its Sociological Aspects* (New York, 1939), for a thoughtful differentiation between exploitative and constructive aspects of social control.

107. George A. Lundberg, "Public Opinion from a Behavioristic Viewpoint," *American Journal of Sociology* 36 (1939): 387–403; and "Contemporary Positivism in Sociology," *American Sociological Review* 4 (1939): 42–55.

108. Lundberg, *Can Science Save Us?* (New York, 1961), p. 74. For a sociologically behaviorist comment on the old question "Can Human Nature Be Changed?" see Read Bain, "Sociology as a Natural Science," *American Journal of Sociology* 53 (1948): 9–16.

tially one of communication. It also failed to show the true nature of human institutions, "which are essentially based upon values and valuing processes." In favoring "a synthesis of behavioristic methods with methods of studying human desires, beliefs, emotions and imagination"[109] Ellwood probably represented a majority of his colleagues at mid-century.

Whatever the continuing influence of older educational psychologies, behaviorism, as Watson, Skinner, and their followers applied it to education, greatly affected thought and practice in home, preschool, classroom, and policy-making. Defenders of behaviorist education argued that since all learning consisted of the reactions built up to the many stimuli in the environment, "the learned man is the one who has built up the most varied and complete responses and is thus able to take advantage of a rich and varied environment."[110] Yet much that was done in applying behavioral theory seemed to limit experience or to control it in questionable ways. This seemed evident in programmed instruction, teaching machines, and in time, the management of recalcitrant or maladjusted youths by behavior modification techniques which sometimes included the use of drugs affecting body chemistry and the nervous system. Nor was this all. Emphasis on adjustment to the existing environment with little or no reference to other purposes or moral values and goals seemed to one more-or-less-sympathetic educator to be "the most sordid feature of behaviorism."[111] Another difficulty in the emphasis on adjustment was the stubborn fact of the swiftly changing character of the environment. This awareness led to a growing discussion, often vague and indeterminate, on conditioning or educating for adaptation to change itself as the only realistic procedure. Reliance on an increasingly refined measurement of variables did not, however,

109. Charles A. Ellwood, "The Uses and Limitations of Behaviorism in Sociology," *American Sociological Society Publications* 24 (1929): 74–82. See also Ellwood's *Sociology in Its Psychological Aspects* (New York, 1915), which reflected the influence of Darwin, Lloyd Morgan, Jacques Loeb, and E. L. Thorndike; and *Methods in Sociology: A Critical Study* (Durham, N.C., 1933), which warned against the dangers of excessive quantification and a repudiation of value judgments, including those associated with social amelioration and religion. For education in the broadest sense the indictment of Ward Cannel and June Macklin, *The Human Nature Industry: How Human Nature is Manufactured, Distributed, Advertised, and Consumed in This Part of the World* (Garden City, N.Y., 1973) was, though too sweeping, a criticism not without some point.

110. Otis E. Young, "Some Educational Implications of Behaviorism," *Education* 51 (1931): 352–53.

111. Frederick E. Bolton, "Behaviorism and Education," *School and Society* 30 (1939): 723 ff.

always explain the numerous, complex, and ever-shifting stimuli that affected individual, group, and institutional behavior.

Measuring with refined observation methods the growth, maturation, and behavior of thousands of infants through childhood, Dr. Arnold Gesell of the Yale Clinic of Child Development developed *An Atlas of Infant Behavior* (1934) and successive charts. He was criticized for underestimating the complex culture in which the child learned and grew and for consequently claiming too much for a fixed, genetic and constitutional "behavior profile" of successive stages of growth. His statement that science had dictated "an almost invariant, unchangeable and fatal outcome" hardly squared with the announcement that "the intrinsic charm and goodness of childhood still constitutes the best guarantee of the further perfectibility of mankind."[112] The model failed to establish Gesell's concept of universality in the early phases of a developing human nature.[113] Yet he was a pioneer in developing more precise techniques of observation, measurement, and control, and brought psychology and the medical sciences into closer cooperation in the effort to understand the complex process of growth and development.

In his approach to behavioral change, Kurt Lewin, a German refugee, seemed to have little in common either with Gesell's interest in physical growth and conduct or with the classical behaviorists. He emphasized the limitations of the conditioned reflex as either an explanation of behavior or a technique for modifying it. Still, he thought of behavior as a functional reaction to the total field of events and facts that determined what an individual did at a given time and in a given situation, and he used controlled group experiments for changing motivation and behavior.[114] Group dynamics, the term given to his theory and experiments, aimed to reduce group tensions and personal, ethnic, and class prejudices in behavior. If group dynamics did not always succeed on any considerable scale in these aims or in promoting the humane democratic values Lewin cherished,[115] it often helped people find an acceptable self in comfortable social relations. Thus in the larger

112. Arnold Gesell and Frances L. Ilg, *The Child from Five to Ten* (New York, 1946), p. 453.

113. In addition to *An Atlas of Infant Behavior* and *The Child from Five to Ten*, the best-known volumes in the voluminous output of Gesell and his associates included *Genes and Growth* (New York, 1934) and *Infant and Child in the Culture of Today* (New York, 1943). I am indebted to the estimate of Gesell's work in Walter S. Miles, "Arnold Lucia Gesell, 1880–1961," *National Academy of Science Biographical Memoirs*, 37:55–96.

114. Lewin was willing to regard his basic field theory as behaviorist "if this means the tendency to provide 'operational definitions' [testable assumptions] for the concepts used." Kurt Lewin, *Field Theory in Social Science: Selected and Theoretical Papers*, ed. Dorwin Cartwright (New York, 1951), pp. 61–62, 133.

115. For evaluations of the evangelical practitioners of sensitivity training and the encounter movement, derived in part from the experimental work of Lewin and his circle, see

behavioral movement, group dynamics pointed to feasible ways of realizing the tolerant, trusting, and cooperative potentialities of human nature.[116]

The main factor in shaping how and what men and women of letters wrote was of course their own personality and experience. Insofar as intellectual movements played a part in literary achievements, behaviorism was much less important than well-established traditions. A conventional dualism completely opposed to behaviorism partly explained the bright treatment of man's capacities in the novels of the reform-minded William Dean Howells and Winston Churchill.[117] Literary naturalism, which held that men and women could be studied much as their animal kin were, as well as mechanistic and materialistic philosophies such as Social Darwinism and nihilism, influenced the grim view of human nature in the later writing of Mark Twain. He relentlessly explored the dark recesses of man's frailties in elaborating his view that "by the law of his nature, he takes the color of his place of resort."[118] These influences also affected the fiction of Frank Norris and James T. Farrell. Theodore Dreiser did, to be sure, read Watson as well as the literary naturalists and materialist philosophers. He seemed, though, to have been little impressed by the door behaviorism opened to a more sunny view of human potential in denying the major influence of

Hubert Bonner, *Group Dynamics: Principles and Applications* (New York, 1959), and Kurt W. Back, *Beyond Words: The Story of Sensitivity Training and the Encounter Movement* (New York, 1973).

116. In addition to *Field Theory in Social Science*, Lewin's American writings included *A Dynamic Theory of Personality: Selected Papers* (New York, 1935), *Principles of Topological Psychology* (New York, 1936), and *Resolving Social Conflicts: Selected Papers on Group Dynamics* (New York, 1945). Useful comment includes Robert Leeper, *Lewin's Topological and Vector Psychology: A Digest and a Critique* (Eugene, Ore., 1943); Morton Deutsch, "Field Theory in Social Psychology," in Gardner Lindzey, ed., *Handbook of Social Psychology* (Cambridge, 1954), pp. 181–222; and Alfred J. Marrow, *Changing Patterns of Prejudice: A New Look at Today's Racial, Religious, and Cultural Tensions* (Philadelphia, 1962). Marrow has also written an appreciative biography, *The Practical Theorist: The Life and Work of Kurt Lewin* (New York, 1969). Special note should be made of the way in which Walter Coulter, a social psychologist at Pennsylvania State University, applied field theory explicitly to the concept of human nature in *Emergent Human Nature* (New York, 1949), pp. 62–67 ff.

117. Robert W. Schneider, *Five Novelists of the Progressive Period* (New York, 1965), esp. the introduction, and *Novelist to a Generation: The Life and Thought of Winston Churchill* (Bowling Green, Oh., 1976).

118. Samuel L. Clemens, *What Is Man? and Other Essays* (New York, 1917), pp. 43, 65 ff.; and *The Autobiography of Mark Twain*, 2 vols. (New York, 1924), 2:7–9. The most thoughtful analysis of Mark Twain's complex views of human nature is that of Don M. Wolfe, *The Image of Man in America*, 2d ed. (New York, 1970), chap. 9. Also admirable are his studies of the idea of human nature in Dreiser and other writers.

heredity and in stressing the role of the conditioned reflex in changing conduct for the better or for the worse.[119] It seems that behaviorism made its chief mark on the biographical sketches in some of the popular magazines.[120] In any case, it had slight influence on serious literature as a whole. This may have been because of its "arbitrary and narrow definition of human experience" and of the fact that it "stopped at the very threshold of moral significance," being a psychology, not of depth and understanding, but primarily of use to educators, businessmen, advertisers, and statisticians.[121] As we have seen, it was Freudianism that cast its spell on the most gifted writers of the second quarter of the century.

Although Dewey and Bentley in 1949 broke fresh ground in delineating the physical, physiological, and behavioral realms of science,[122] the point that they made probably played only a minor part in the general use of the term *behavioral sciences* in the 1950s. The phrase caught on in part because, with the ever-increasing specialization in each of the social sciences, the traditional and informal give and take between them lacked sufficient relevance to be very fruitful; in part because of the influence on many social scientists of logical positivism and operationalism, or the doctrine that scientific concepts have meaning only in the set of operations involved; and in part because of the Ford Foundation's promotion and generous support.

The behavioral sciences comprised the specifically identifiable behavioral aspects of biology, psychology, sociology, economics, political science, anthropology, and law. Eschewing all possible value assumptions, exponents emphasized the working out of new methods for understanding and predicting behavior, particularly quantification, mathematical symbolization, and model building.[123]

119. Oscar Cargill, *Intellectual America: Ideas on the March* (New York, 1941), pp. 154–58.

120. Leo Lowenthal, "Biographies in Popular Magazines," in Paul F. Lazarfeld, ed., *Radio Research* (New York, 1943), pp. 527 ff., 538, 551. Cf. David Riesman's *The Lonely Crowd: A Study of the Changing American Character* (New Haven, 1950), written in collaboration with Reuel Denney and Nathan Glazer; and *Faces in the Crowd: Individual Studies in Character and Politics* (New Haven, 1952).

121. Henry F. May, *The End of American Innocence* (New York, 1959), pp. 176–77; and Frederick J. Hoffman, *The Twenties: American Writing in the Postwar Decade* (New York, 1955), pp. 203–4. For an arresting and somewhat exaggerated criticism of applied psychology in the broad sense, see Cannel and Macklin, *Human Nature Industry.*

122. Dewey and Bentley, *Knowing and the Known*, pp. 65–66, 77.

123. Charles E. Osgood, "Behavior Theory and Social Science," *Behavioral Science* 1 (1956): 167–85; Peter R. Senn, "What Is 'Behavioral Science'?" *Journal of the History of*

Bernard Berelson, a leading early pioneer, thought that the behavioral movement would "in all probability be ranked among the important intellectual revolutions of the twentieth century." Such a judgment, though, came far from representing many social scientists. To critics in the older constituent fields, the new interdisciplinary movement seemed pretentious and absurdly empirical in deductive formulations applied to narrowly defined, trivial questions. In explaining its appeal, one early critic observed that "this transformation of social science from a field of knowledge into a bundle of research techniques is strictly in conformity with the structuring of behavior along procedural lines in all parts of American culture."[124] Indeed, some charged behavioral sciences with being a conscious or unconscious smokescreen for avoiding the investigation of such truly significant problems of our times as those related to the retreat of the capitalist order, the threats to constitutional democracy, and the colonial revolutions.[125]

However useful motivation and other studies were to advertising agencies and to the so-called military-industrial complex, no one could rightly claim that the behavioral sciences had, by the early 1960s, constructed "a science of man" or discovered "the laws of human behavior which could serve as a reliable means for prediction and control."[126] With refinements in methodology and cumulative investigations of issues bearing on some aspect of man's actions, the behavioral scientists might in time make significant contributions to the understanding of human nature to which earlier social scientists had given new dimensions and goals.

Man, having the most flexible genetic equipment known, had in his hands the means of substituting human selection for natural selection. The genetic code seemed to reach as far and as wide, in the directions it transmitted for one or another path of development, as the most optimis-

the Behavioral Sciences 2 (1966): 107–22. See also the early issues of the first periodicals devoted to the subject, Behavioral Science (1956) and The American Behavioral Scientist (1959). For a trenchant criticism of the behavioral emphasis in political science see Lewis Lipsitz, "Vulture, Mantis, and Seal: Proposals for Political Scientists," in George J. Graham, Jr., and George W. Carey, eds., The Post-Behavioral Era: Perspectives on Political Science (New York, 1972), pp. 171–91.

124. George Simpson, "The Assault on Social Science," American Sociological Review 14 (1949): 306.

125. Barrington Moore, Jr., "The New Scholasticism and the Study of Politics," World Politics 6 (1954): 137–39.

126. Evron Kirkpatrick, "The Impact of the Behavioral Approach on Traditional Political Science," in Ranney, ed., Essays on the Behavioral Study of Politics, p. 25.

tic prescientific utopians imagined. What could or could not be developed depended among other things on the variables of human values and social environment, including the possibility of catastrophe.

Behaviorial scientists recognized the importance of the genetic endowment and the promise of mathematical models in exploring its relation to behavior and culture. In the 1970s Edward O. Wilson, a distinguished Harvard authority on the social behavior of insects, went further in proposing a new science, sociobiology, which he defined as the systematic study of the biological basis of all social behavior. He regarded human nature as the product of its underlying biology and evolutionary history: these explained its fixities and its flexibilities. Wilson had no doubt that the fixities included a genetic thrust toward aggression, male dominance, altruism, and reverence for sacred things. Though he regarded the genetic endowment and behavior as more structured than it appeared to many social scientists, Wilson felt that Marxism, like Judeo-Christianity, thwarted human nature. Flexibility or variability (in human nature) stemmed from the genes that enabled man and man alone to create and modify cultures and thus to change the forms in which inherited traits must find expression. Wilson looked to sociobiology to build a common life which would coordinate the basic fixities with the still largely unmet fundamental needs of the human kind.

Sociobiology: The New Synthesis (1975), and more particularly *On Human Nature* (1978), an essay intended for the informed general reader (and awarded a Nobel prize), met with both praise and criticism.[127] Some insisted that no proof had been offered for most of Wilson's positions. Several behavioral scientists objected to allocating behavioral traits to biology when these seemed to them better explained in terms of

127. Reviews of *Sociobiology, the New Synthesis* written by scientists were generally favorable. Those in the publications of the social science associations were mixed. Edward Chapple (*American Anthropologist* 78 [1976]: 590–94) was unusually harsh, expressing doubt about many statements on the score of inadequate evidence or no evidence at all. Understandably, cultural anthropologists found unacceptable, in the main, the thesis that genes are the basic factor in the development of human nature and more determining than culture. The review in the *Political Science Review* (71 [1977]: 674–76) insisted that sociobiology is no solution for many problems facing the profession. The *American Journal of Sociology* devoted a review essay to which several sociologists contributed, the consensus seeming to be that Wilson made unjustifiable claims (82 [1976]: 692–701). See also *Contemporary Sociology: A Journal of Reviews* 5 (1975): 727 ff.; and the *American Psychologist* 31 (1976): 341–84. The verdict of professional social scientists about *On Human Nature* had not, in general, appeared by 1979. Two titles merit attention, though: Stuart Hampshire's critical assessment in the *New York Review of Books* 25 (1978): 64–69; and the debate between Edward O. Wilson and Marvin Harris, printed as "Heredity versus Culture: A Debate," Ann Carroll, moderator, in *Society* 15 (1978): 60–63. (The discussion originally appeared in a Radio Smithsonian debate of February 15, 1978.)

culture. A Sociobiology Study Group in Cambridge, which included well-known scientists and social scientists, feared that Wilson's high claims for the role of the genetic endowment would feed the springs of war, racism, male dominance, the whole established order.

Wilson dismissed such criticisms as unfounded. Aware that the science of today might be obsolete tomorrow, he muted his final chapter of *On Human Nature*, "Hope." By giving man some control over his physical endowment science might, on another level and in a new age, he said, construct "the mythology of scientific materialism, guided by the corrective devices of scientific method, addressed with precise and deliberately affective appeal to the deepest needs of human nature, and kept strong by the blind hopes that the journey on which we are now embarked will be farther and better than the one just completed."[128]

128. Edward O. Wilson, *On Human Nature* (Cambridge, Mass., 1978), p. 109.

13

Summing Up

Without a clear-cut map of man's present understanding of his own nature, no frontier of innovation is definable.

Joshua Lederberg, 1973

IN DISCUSSING man's nature American intellectuals drew on a heritage that reached back to the ancient Orient, classical Greece, medieval Christianity, and the threshold of the modern Western world. The underpinnings of this heritage were classical thought, biblical revelation and exegesis, theological disputations, philosophical speculation, the "lessons" of history, and random observation of human actions and inferences made from them. Such guides and methods influenced writing about human nature even after the great revolutions in the natural and social sciences from the seventeenth century through our own. In spite of some similarities in the discussion during the earlier and the later periods and the enduring questions about debatable aspects of man's nature, the two periods differed strikingly.

The boundaries of the idea of human nature, complex, vague, and amorphous, have been hard to define and contain. The use of the term *human nature*, though always present, increased during marked social and intellectual upheavals such as the American Revolution, the pre–Civil War tensions, and the social conflicts and intellectual controversies of the late nineteenth century. Yet even in these times the theme was elusive and one has trouble in clarifying and explaining it. Few who used the term defined it. To most seventeenth-century theologians human nature meant that span in the Great Chain of Being between animal and divine nature. Often it was not clear whether a writer was describing an example of observed human behavior or confusing his perception with a normative model. Some, particularly after the great scientific developments, refused to regard human nature as a substantive reality. It was, they held, a fictional generalization made up of traditional beliefs and inferences from random observations. Recent events and new knowledge, however, have led many to accept its reality.

The discussion of the heritage, its modification and accretions both religious and secular, was influenced by such Old World upheavals as revolutions in France and Russia. The discussion also owed a good deal to distinctively American conditions. These included the relatively late point at which colonization got under way and the circumstances under which the new land was settled by peoples of varied backgrounds. Its unique historical experiences created problems, institutions, fears, and values that further shaped the discussion. These varied experiences and conditions fell into two broad patterns.

One pattern contributed to what was for a long time most distinctive in the American discussion of human nature—the bright and hopeful view of what man might become and stood a good chance of becoming in his new home. From the start, newcomers believed or were encouraged to believe that America would undermine the burdensome Old World feudal heritage and open new paths for enhancing human resourcefulness, achievement, and power. To put it another way, America might create, if not a new man, at least a people of superior gifts and conduct. The Puritan belief that God had sent a chosen people to build a Zion in the wilderness and the secular counterpart of that belief seemed to stimulate performance in terms of rising expectations. With relatively little pressure of population on seemingly inexhaustible natural resources, America invited faith in the ability of men and women to overcome the limitations that history and environment had, under God, imposed on their forebears and on contemporaries in less-favored lands. Freedom from endless military threat of invasion and occupation further nourished this optimistic view of the new land and its happy implications for welfare, character, conduct, and fortune.

By contrast, a disparaging view of human nature, derived from the European heritage, also owed much in implementation to unique American conditions as well. Many feared the unknown wilderness and its threat to cherished institutions and human decencies. Decade after decade upstanding (and rascally) native Americans, as well as courageous but bewildered immigrants, met hardships, suffering, struggles, conflicts, defeat—tragedy. Much white and Indian blood was shed in the conquest of the frontier. Slavery rested on the threat of force and often on the use of violence. In the end, the terrible yoke was broken in four years of bloody civil war. Even the assumption of the redemptive virtue of violence evident in banal prose, great poems, and memorable songs ("Mine Eyes Have Seen the Glory . . .") did not blot out the memory of violence as a dynamic part of human nature. Nor did the industrial revolution in any country breed more ruthless and bloody conflict than it did here. No wonder that a sense of tragedy found expression in the great literary achievements of Hawthorne, Melville, Mark Twain, and Faulkner.

During the course of American history some view of human nature was generally invoked to defend the rightness and inevitability of such established institutions as private property, free enterprise, class structure, slavery, race superiority, sex identity and role, and the ultimate meaning of life and death. Paradoxically, these same institutions and values were also challenged on the grounds of violating the needs and requirements of human nature. Under such a sanction, some intellectuals upheld anarchism, socialism, communitarianism, and democratic decision-making. It might seem that the effectiveness of these appeals cannot be proved or disproved, but the partisan uses to which they were put undoubtedly illustrated and sharpened patterns of thought and the functional relationship of ideas and interests.

American life has not yet produced thinkers who can rank with the greatest commentators on human nature. Moreover, much that our intellectuals wrote was, as already noted, influenced by movements in the Old World. Yet American thought on this theme was neither insignificant nor lacking in originality. The contributions of scientists, social scientists, philosophers, theologians, and men and women of letters bore ample witness to this.

In America as elsewhere the truly big questions divided intellectuals. This was evident in the long disputes regarding the innate evil, goodness, or moral neutrality of the human being as such.

The dark view of human nature, which some aspects of American experience encouraged, was well known when the first settlers came to America. It was reenforced by both religious and secular authority. While Christianity taught the innate depravity, brutality, aggressiveness, vanity, lust, and selfishness of all mankind, Augustinianism and Calvinism seemed to make escape harder by questioning or denying the free will of those who sought escape from hell. Theologians in early New England contributed to the discussion of the means by which a sinner might or might not take an active and effective part in preparation for that Grace which God alone could bestow. Even though few received it, he did not in reality deny it to any of his sinful and wayward children. It was rather they who rejected grace by rejecting faith in him and obedience to his law. Many concluded that effort paid in any case, that the sinner was not wholly helpless in his fate, a view that the Great Awakening and later revivals spread.

The same distrust and dark view of human nature that marked all but a minority of Christians was echoed in the writings of American secular followers of Hobbes, the Machiavellian satirists and cynics, and Mandeville. This view would influence leading members of the Constitutional Convention of 1787 and some of the great jurists in later years, as well as Calhoun and his associates when they defended slavery in denouncing equality as impossible by the laws of human nature.

In another sphere, classical economists, reeforced by associationist psychology, endowed reason with the "calculating" or selfish thrust and in neat rationalizations identified private interest with public good. Such a view of man in general served the interests of the managers and promoters of the industrial revolution, who needed a stable social order, the security of profits, and the dominance of new elites that were replacing older ones.

The degree and scope of an innate depravity or capacity for beneficence was not the only major question dividing intellectuals in Europe and in early America. No issue was more persistent and troublesome than that of the immutability or plasticity of human nature. In this discussion intellectuals who regarded human nature as a substantive reality often thought of it as unchangeable. Both ancient philosophy and impregnable faith in the Newtonian model of the universe supported that view. To hold that the whole universe operated with precise regularity in accord with fixed laws seemed, when applied to human nature, to leave little room for change. The problem was met in several ways. On the secular side it was believed that nature was good and that if her laws were discovered and followed all would be well. The bright view of man's nature and the relevancy of effort to insure it received reenforcement from the eighteenth- and early nineteenth-century belief that inalienable rights to life, liberty, and property inhered in human nature itself. By the 1830s phrenology, which claimed scientific credentials, further encouraged the cult of intellectual and moral improvement by knowledge of one's innate strengths and weaknesses and by the cultivation of the desirable and the repression of the unworthy. The rising idea of a unique American progress and the awareness of social mobility and change further shook confidence in an absolute fixed human nature. On the religious side, the popular Scottish philosophy, which endowed every human being with an innate moral sense capable of improvement, opened another door to the possible improvement of human nature. The spread of evangelical revivals may well have been more important than anything else in bringing hope and cheer to those holding orthodox views of sin. A Christian idea of the perfectibility of human nature in this world also won adherents. Disciples of this view, with heirs of the Enlightenment and optimists among the Romantics, envisioned a human nature able to create a heaven on earth day after tomorrow if not today. Communitarians, religious and secular, sought to prove the contention. Melioristic reformers, acting on all these assumptions about human nature, sought by education, persuasion, and pressure to induce the middle class to oppose war, support free public schools, succor the handicapped, lift up the fallen, right the wrongs of women, and above all demand the freedom of the slave.

Thus the range of optimism about human nature was broad. It included some who thought that men and women had been born good, much like Adam and Eve before the symbolical fall: only later did the desire for forbidden pleasure and power bring disaster. It was hard to explain how humans born "good" could at some point somehow have built or allowed to be built inhuman institutions, however, and a larger and more impressive group maintained that people were born neither good nor bad. Plastic and neutral, they became what they were through the influence of child-rearing, interpersonal experience, and the dominating institutions which brought out either the most "bestial" or the most "human" potential. This view, thanks to its moral and religious components, its appeal to middle-class values, and its devoted activist supporters, figured, as we have seen, in the mid-century humanitarian and melioristic movements for reform.

The major revolutions in biology in the later nineteenth century and in the first decade of the twentieth only partly changed the picture. While rejecting a static universe, evolutionary theory, at least for many interpreters, confirmed the unfavorable estimate of human nature by linking man's origin to the animal kingdom and by making the related drives or instincts ineluctable. Mendelianism undermined the long-cherished view that a good environment could improve human nature by transmitting to the next generation improvements acquired in this, a view Lamarck had supported. By seeming to ascribe complex social traits to a single gene or group of genes Mendelianism opened the door to advocates of eugenics. The eugenicists sought to improve human nature by eliminating the unfit, especially the mentally disturbed and the retarded (if necessary by sterilization), and by encouraging the reproduction of the fit by selective breeding and social rewards. Later, the Freudian revolution, together with the far less influential neo-orthodox insistence on the devastating effects of man's inborn pride and lust for power, confirmed the disparaging view of an immutable human nature. The emerging ethology projected the virtually changeless instinctive basis of animal and human behavior, including aggressive protection of "homelands" (territoriality). Ethologists, with some geneticists, questioned the far-reaching importance anthropologists had given to man as a culture-creating creature. The claim was now boldly asserted that inborn instructions indicated the kind of behavior possible and thus defined the culture to be developed.

On the other hand, American contributions to knowledge and interpretations of human nature reenforced confidence in man's constructive ability. If the achievements in changing behavior through chemical and genetic engineering carried frightening possibilities, they also offered opportunities for meliorist control. In psychology, the emphasis on how learning took place was natural in a society that favored the belief that most people could learn to do anything, a capacity much needed in an industrial society. The emphasis on learning implied personal adjustment based on the measurement of "intelligence" and aptitude.

It is true that professional as well as nonprofessional critics raised objections to the emphasis on adjustment; to them it put a premium on conformity and penalized creativity, thus thwarting a well-recognized basic need. Some saw in these applications of scientific psychology support for a social status quo in which people were largely dehumanized. They also questioned the claim that measurement and adjustment prevented unnecessary frustration. Nor were critics convinced that the pyschology of personality and mental health, ignoring as they tended to do economic causes of maladjustment, could better the human condition through a clearer understanding of human nature as it was expressed in personal relations.

Undeterred by such objections, behavioral scientists claimed other achievements. Role theory, for example, showed how childhood play developed a sense of the self and "the other." Its application in business, therapy, education, and other aspects of life became common. Even more crucial was the concept of culture. Its beginnings owed much to Europeans, but in field studies and in statistical and linguistic analyses American anthropologists broadened and deepened the understanding of human nature. The culture concept stressed the ability not only to create and transmit culture but to make innovations in it. When it was discovered that man's earliest culture—symbolized by the invention of certain tools—actually influenced his anatomical structure in the evolutionary process before "human" maturity, anthropologists asserted the priority of culture to the human nature that had developed. In other words, the culture created by man contributed to the development of his human nature and opened the way for its improvement.

Yet the discovery of preliterate cultures, unique in relation to Western culture and even to each other, led some to question whether in view of the contrasts in customs and values human nature was a valid concept. Such a denial of the unity of human nature might be and was used to justify the last conquests of Indians in their coveted homelands. The same view was used both to endorse and to oppose annexation of overseas island inhabited by "wild" tribes and "inferior" people whom missionaries might bring within the orbit of the middle-class American picture of human beings.

The debate was not easily resolved. Other ethnologists, noting that even the highest primates had not developed abstract symbolical thinking and complex communication, assumed that man's culture-creating and culture-transmitting capacity was genetic. This assured the unquestionable reality of human nature. It was further noted that only human beings distinguished between mores and morals or changed the environment by cultural innovation. Others, ignoring cannibalism, observed that the earliest archaeological records show that man, unlike his closest animal kin, had reverenced and disposed of his dead in ways suggesting a belief in an afterlife and a unique solicitude for his own kind. So far as anyone knew, every culture, and no animal group, reflected this conceptualization and value.

Whether or not human nature was regarded as a real and valid concept, in the later decades of the twentieth century many intellectuals reasserted the bleak view of man. The complexities, anxieties, and problems of technological culture raised new issues. Had not men in stressing their creativity forgotten that they were creatures? If genes instructed the organism on what might be a limited range of possibilities in behavior, were not boundaries imposed on the culture that utopians had dreamed about? Had not experience shown the limitations of men and women in their efforts through social control, rehabilitation, and education to constrain the expression of unwanted endowments and customs? What were the boundaries of human ability to adapt organisms and especially personality to ever-swifter and more-traumatic technological change and even domination? The one-time "Anglo-Saxon" and frontier emphasis on a self-activating, autonomous individual could no longer be looked upon as an earmark of human nature in the American setting. In the new culture that men and women had created, could the most cherished needs, desires, and potentialities—security, appreciation, dignity, and love—be taken for granted? If not, then dissidents, even bothersome troublemakers who had lost faith in middle-class images of man and who proposed a counter-culture with spontaneous, immediate pleasures and self-fulfillment, needed to be heard. Perhaps even their ideas needed to be tested. What man might become, as well as what he was, had long defined human nature for those who claim to speak for what was most distinctive in the American experience. In any case, the degree to which such views of human nature failed to meet current needs deserved consideration.

In an unstable world of genocide, mass suicide at the behest of beguiling leaders, revolution, terrorism, staggering accretions to scientific knowlege that might mean either man's near-salvation or annihilation, the whole problem of the bearing of human nature on the future raised serious questions.

In relation to desired improvement in social life, several Americans had made proposals on the basis of their analyses of human nature. Yesterday it was Albert Brisbane, Edward Bellamy, and the old Marxists. Today it might be B. F. Skinner and Edward O. Wilson, the promulgator of sociobiology. None of the analyses and syntheses offered satisfied all of those presumably competent to make informed judgments, whether scientists, social philosophers, behavioral scientists, or ethical and religious leaders. If there was now a consensus in the intellectual community that, however important the genetic determiners of alternative behavior, some freedom still remained as to the kind of culture to be encouraged; if it was agreed that human beings do not need to fight because of innate aggressive tendencies; if few questioned that children could be brought up neither to dominate nor accept domination passively; if, in spite of growing doubt, the resources and technological possibilities at hand, at least in America, could meet everyone's basic wants and a growing measure of supplementary human needs in the esthetic and other areas; then the problem became one of how these feasible goals were to be achieved for all. The future discussion of human nature might show how obstacles to the realization of these objectives could be overcome—obstacles such as habit and indifference, sheer bigness of institutions, the problem of controlling power in an atmosphere of moral uncertainty and ambiguity, the life-enhancing and life-destroying uses of knowledge. Not inconceivably this would require new ways of thinking and feeling, a new consciousness and a new conscience. If so, such innovations would surely have to be built on the foundations of the long exploration of human nature which had engaged the thought of some of America's greatest intellectuals.

REFERENCE
MATTER

Bibliographical Note

Since the footnotes of this book indicate, in addition to specific sources, the range and nature of the materials used, little purpose would be served in repeating information about the books and articles that have been cited. In discussing the ideas of public figures who deserved recognition as members of the intellectual community, I have used the most recent editions of their writings. When these are still in progress, I have fallen back on older editions. Besides such materials, I have used sermons, theological treatises, manuals on mental philosophy and on sex, major books of psychologists, and articles in well over a hundred periodicals, addressed to the informed public and to the members of the professions whose interests involved ideas about human nature—ministers, physicians, educators, scientists, philosophers, social scientists, and men and women of letters.

Scholars who have written about ideas of human nature in other times and places provide a useful frame for the American discussion. Chu Hsi's *The Philosophy of Human Nature*, translated by J. Percy Bruce (London, 1922), should be supplemented by Donald J. Munro, *The Concept of Man in Early China* (Stanford, 1969) and *The Concept of Man in Contemporary China* (Ann Arbor, 1977). Indian, Jewish, and Islamic theories of human nature are discussed in S. Radhakrishnan and P. T. Raju, eds., *The Concept of Man: A Study in Comparative Philosophy* (Lincoln, Nebr., 1960). An early American essay "The Japanese Image of Man" appeared in *The Journal of Speculative Philosophy* in 1885 (19:133–72). Interest in the biblical views of man has been expressed by such scholars as William Lyon Phelps, *Human Nature in the Bible* (New York, 1922); Eric C. Rust, *Nature and Man in Biblical Thought* (London, 1953); and Reinhold Niebuhr, *The Nature and Destiny of Man: A Christian Interpretation*, 2 vols. (New York, London, 1941–43); rev. ed. in one vol. (New York, 1949). Eric R. Dodds, *The Greeks and the Irrational* (Berkeley, 1951), and Arthur W. H. Adkins, *From the Many to the One: A Study of Personality and Views of Human Nature in the Context of Ancient Greek Society, Values, and Beliefs* (Ithaca, N.Y., 1970), interpret Greek sources with learning and insight. The wealth of materials for the Middle Ages is impressive. These titles are only representative: Otto Friedrich von Gierke, *Political Theories of the Middle Ages*, translated and with an introduction by F. W. Maitland (Cambridge, 1958); Jorge Laporta, *La*

Destinée de la nature humaine selon Thomas d'Aquin (Paris, 1965); E. Ruth Harvey, *The Inward Wits: Psychological Theory in the Middle Ages and Renaissance* (London, 1975); and Sister Roberta Snell, *The Nature of Man in St. Thomas Aquinas Compared with the Nature of Man in American Sociology* (Washington, 1942). Paul Oskar Kristeller has discussed the issue with erudition and grace in *Renaissance Concepts of Man and Other Essays* (New York, 1972). Though referred to in the text, mention should be made again of Herschel G. Baker's *The Dignity of Man: Studies in the Persistence of an Idea* (Cambridge, 1947), revised as *The Image of Man: A Study of the Idea of Human Dignity in Classical Antiquity, the Middle Ages, and the Renaissance* (New York, 1961).

Nor is this all. E. M. W. Tillyard, *The Elizabethan World Picture: A Study of the Idea of Order in the Age of Shakespeare, Donne, and Milton* (London, 1943; Vintage Books, 1960); Gertrude V. Rich, *Interpretations of Human Nature: A Study of Certain Late Seventeeth- and Early Eighteenth-Century British Attitudes toward Man's Nature and Capacites* (New York, 1935); Arthur O. Lovejoy, *Reflections on Human Nature* (Baltimore, 1961); and Maurice H. Mandelbaum, *History, Man, and Reason: A Study in Nineteenth-Century Thought* (Baltimore, 1971) are all careful, rewarding studies. In *Models of Man: A Phenomenological Critique of Some Paradigms in the Human Sciences* (The Hague, 1972), James J. Dagenais discusses psychological, holistic, psychoanalytical, Marxist, and structuralist models. Raymond A. Bauer, *The New Man in Soviet Psychology* (Cambridge, Mass., 1952), and Ralph B. Winn, ed., *Soviet Psychology: A Symposium* (New York, 1961), describe and in part explain changing emphases on ideas about man in the USSR.

The only general view of ideas about human nature in the nineteenth and twentieth centuries in the United States is the loosely associated collection of imaginative and brilliant essays in Don M. Wolfe's *The Idea of Man in America* (Dallas, Tex., 1957; rev. ed., New York, 1970). Floyd W. Matson's *The Idea of Man* (New York, 1976) has thoughtful essays on man as killer, Darwinism, Freud, man as machine, the biological revolution, and democratic man. He has nobly defined humanism in *The Broken Image: Man, Science, and Society* (New York, 1964; Garden City, N.Y., 1966).

Besides the well-known histories of philosophy, psychology, religion, the natural and social sciences, and literature, broad syntheses in cultural history sometimes provide useful comment and interpretation. Good examples are Ralph E. Burner, *The Great Cultural Traditions: The Foundations of Civilization*, 2 vols. (New York, 1941); Pitrim A. Sorokin, *Man and Society in Calamity: The Effects of War, Revolution, Famine, Pestilence upon Human Mind, Behavior, Social Organization, and Cultural Life* (New York, 1942); and the important and little-appreciated *A Study of War*, 2 vols. (Chicago, 1942), by Quincy Wright. A second edition of Wright's book was published in 1971, "with a commentary on war since 1942."

Similar books restricted to America include the indispensable, encyclopedic study by Joseph Dorfman, *The Economic Mind in American Civilization*, 5 vols. (New York, 1946–59); Sydney E. Ahlstrom, *A Religious History of the American*

People (New Haven, 1972); Elizabeth Flower and Murray C. Murphey, *A History of Philosophy in America*, 2 vols. (New York, 1977); and James Willard Hurst, *Law and Social Process in United States History* (Ann Arbor, 1960), and *Law and Social Order in the United States* (Ithaca, 1977). Hurst discusses ideas about human nature in relation to the development of knowledge, to law, and to the legal process.

Several books on human nature, written without special reference to American conditions, put any student of the subject under obligation. Ellsworth Faris's *The Nature of Human Nature, and Other Essays in Social Psychology* (New York, 1937) exerted considerable influence. Ashley Montagu's *On Being Human* (New York, 1951, 1966), *The Biosocial Nature of Man* (New York, 1956), and *Anthropology and Human Nature* (Boston, 1957) are also pioneer work. I have thoroughly discussed in the text John Dewey's influential *Human Nature and Conduct: An Introduction to Social Psychology* (New York, 1922; Modern Library, 1957). In contrast with the social-psychological approach of Dewey, several books reflect a humanist position in either the traditional or a newer sense: Hartley Burr Alexander, *Nature and Human Nature: Essays Metaphysical and Historical* (Chicago, 1923); Lawrence K. Frank, *Nature and Human Nature: Man's New Image of Himself* (New Brunswick, 1951); Joseph Wood Krutch, *Human Nature and the Human Condition* (New York, 1959); Lewis Mumford, *The Transformations of Man* (New York, 1956); and Robert L. Heilbronner, *An Inquiry into the Human Prospect* (New York, 1974).

Several collections of essays merit attention. Distinguished authorities contributed to John R. Platt, ed., *New Views of the Nature of Man* (Chicago, 1965), as they did to "Human Nature: A Reevaluation," *Social Research* 40 (Autumn 1973): 375–483. The refreshing essays published under the title "Changing Concepts of Human Nature" in *The American Scholar* 38 (Winter 1968–69) should not be missed. Catholic positions are ably presented in *The Image of Man: A Review of Politics Reader*, edited by M. A. Fitzsimons, Thomas T. McAvoy, and Frank O'Malley (Notre Dame, Ind., 1959). The essays in *Human Nature in Politics*, Nomos 17, edited by J. Roland Pennock and John W. Chapman (New York, 1977), view politics in broad terms. John J. Mitchell's anthology *Human Nature: Theories, Conjectures, and Descriptions* (Metuchen, N.J., 1972) includes essays by Canadian, British, and French, as well as American, scholars. Milton M. Gordon's *Human Nature, Class and Ethnicity* (New York, 1978) considers, among other things, the bearing of group relations and structural processes on various sociological views of human nature. *Sociobiology and Human Nature: An Interdisciplinary Critique and a Defense*, edited by Michael S. Gregory, Anita Silvers, and Diane Sutch (San Francisco, 1978), presents essays airing the principles and assumptions of the new discipline, and exploring the humanistic implications of the convergence of the related disciplines represented at the conference on which the book is based.

In connection with research in such primary materials as the writings of Benjamin Rush, "father of American psychiatry," and his successors who contributed to the *American Journal of Insanity* (Utica, Baltimore, etc., 1844–1921), subsequently the *American Journal of Psychiatry* (1921–), and the *Journal of Mental and Nervous Diseases* (Chicago, 1874–), secondary works are useful: *One Hundred Years of American Psychiatry*, published for the American Psychiatric Association (New York, 1944); Albert Deutsch, *The Mentally Ill in America: A History of Their Care and Treatment from Colonial Times*, 2d ed. rev. and enl. (New York, 1949); the excellent work of Gerald N. Grob, *Mental Institutions in America: Social Policy to 1875* (New York, 1973); Norman Dain's splendid *Concepts of Insanity in the United States, 1789–1965* (New Brunswick, 1964); and David J. Rothman, *The Discovery of the Asylum: Social Order and Disorder in the New Republic* (Boston, 1971). Rothman regards the asylum policy as a disaster conceived to control deviance in the interest of social order, economy, and comfort for the mentally able.

The whole related field of mental health, at first called mental hygiene, has been one of the most striking and far-reaching examples of the application of views of disordered human nature. It has worked through clinics, community centers, schools, churches, social agencies, and families. The files of *Mental Hygiene* (Concord, N.H., 1917–) offer a ready source of information, as do other publications of organizations dedicated to this cause. Those associated with it have left several first-hand accounts of their experiences. These include the classic *A Mind That Found Itself: An Autobiography*, by Clifford W. Beers (Garden City, N.Y., 1908, 1953); Dr. Arthur H. Ruggles's *Mental Health, Past, Present and Future* (Baltimore, 1934); Wilbur L. Cross, ed., *Twenty-five Years After: Sidelights on the Mental Hygiene Movement and Its Founder* (Garden City, N.Y., 1934); and Nina A. Ridenour, *Mental Health in the United States: A Fifty-Year History* (Cambridge, Mass., 1961). Kingsley Davis's article "Mental Health and the Class Structure," *Psychiatry* 1 (1938): 55–65, broke new ground. It provoked controversy and called fresh attention to the interrelations between status and mental health. Valuable, too, are the essays in Arnold M. Rose, ed., *Mental Health and Mental Disorder* (New York, 1955). August de Belmont Hollingshead and Fredrick C. Redlich, in *Social Class and Mental Illness: A Community Study* (New York, 1958), and Jerome K. Myers and Lee L. Bean, in *A Decade Later: A Follow-up of Social Class and Mental Illness* (New York, 1968), developed a trend in research already under way, and in so doing gave depth and understanding to dimensions of a problem long overlooked. Louis P. Thorpe, *The Psychology of Mental Health* (New York, 1950; 2nd ed., 1960), and Francine Sobey, *The Nonprofessional Revolution in Mental Health* (New York, 1970), touch on other aspects of the movement in relation to assumptions about human nature. The stage of popularization was well under way with the appearance of Joshua L. Liebman's *Peace of Mind* (New York, 1946) and the books of Norman Vincent Peale, including *The Art of Real Happiness*, written with Smiley Blanton (New York, 1950).

The concept of the stages of life in relation to human nature has a long history. With the exception of Hall, Baldwin, Lightner, and a few others, Americans in general gave relatively little attention to this before the work of Erik Erikson. Of late years, a large number of books on childhood as an aspect of human nature have appeared to supplement the work of the pioneers. Glen Davis, *Childhood and History in America* (New York, 1976), is one representative. Philip J. Greven, *The Protestant Temperament: Patterns of Child-Rearing, Religious Experience, and the Self in Early America* (New York, 1977), contends that these patterns revealed the values and personality types of the period. Peter G. Slater, *Children in the New England Mind in Death and in Life* (Hamden, Conn., 1977); Joseph H. Hawes, *Children in Urban Society: Juvenile Delinquency in Nineteenth-Century America* (New York, 1971); and Robert M. Mennel, *Thorns and Thistles: Juvenile Delinquency in the United States, 1825–1940* (Hanover, N.H., 1973) reflect the increasing specialization in the field.

Attitudes toward birth control, considered in some of the large number of books on sex, have attracted considerable interest. In addition to titles cited in the footnotes, mention might be made of James C. Mohr, *Abortion in America: The Origins and Evolution of National Policy, 1800–1900* (New York, 1978); and James Reed, *From Private Vice to Public Virtue: The Birth Control Movement and American Society since 1830* (New York, 1978).

Much writing on the history of the family illuminates attitudes toward all stages of life. Joseph F. Kett's *Rites of Passage: Adolescence in America 1790 to the Present* (New York, 1977) is limited by its male orientation. David E. Stannard set a high standard in his *The Puritan Way of Death: A Study in Religion, Culture, and Social Change* (New York, 1977; Oxford Paperback, 1979). David Hackett Fischer's *Growing Old in America* (New York, 1977) blazed some new trails of research. Also useful are David E. Stannard, ed., *Death in America* (Philadelphia, 1975); and Charles C. Jackson, ed., *Passing: The Vision of Death in America* (Westport, Conn., 1977).

I have given relatively little attention to psychohistory, though the position I took in *Human Nature in American Historical Thought* (Columbia, Mo., 1968) seems to me to have been confirmed by the appearance since then of both ill-thought-out studies and penetrating and illuminating ones. John A. Garraty, in "The Interrelations of Psychology and Biography," *Psychological Bulletin* 51 (1952): 577–80, and Lester A. Little, in "Psychology in Recent American Historical Thought," *Journal of the History of the Behavioral Sciences* 5 (1969): 167–71, comment on psychoanalytical portraits in biography. *The History of Childhood Quarterly* (1973–76) and its continuation *The Journal of Psychohistory*, 1976–) testify to the lively interest in the field. Fawn Brodie's *No Man Knows My History: The Life of Joseph Smith* (New York, 1945; 2d ed., rev., 1971) seems more plausible, despite its limitations, than her *Thomas Jefferson, an Intimate History* (New York, 1974). It would be easy to cite a dozen or more fairly recent books of this sort. Whatever their limitations, they do not lack interest to students of human nature historically considered.

Concern with the self has of course been an enduring theme in the American interest in man; recently it has been expressed in several books that are historical in character as well as in a number that are contemporary in emphasis. An example of the latter is Paul C. Vitz, *Psychology as Religion: The Cult of Self-Worship* (Grand Rapids, Mich., 1979). Also indicative of an important trend almost certain to stimulate further investigation are Alan E. Kazdin, *History of Behavior Modifications: Experimental Foundations of Contemporary Research* (Baltimore, 1978); and Stephan L. Chorover, *From Genesis to Genetics: The Meaning of Human Nature and the Power of Behavior Control* (Cambridge, Mass., 1978).

Beyond all this, the growing bibliography in the history of a revived interest in the work ethic and in the background and development of such contemporary interests and movements as the sexual revolution, the new feminism, black liberation, the native Americans' search for identity and demand for justice, charismatic religions, and violence and terrorism impose for the historian of their bearings on human nature not only far-reaching interdisciplinary approaches but thoroughgoing cooperative ones as well.

Index

425

Reflexology, 377

Reform. *See* American Social Science Association; Antislavery; Education; Humanitarianism; War; Women

Reich, Wilhelm, 358

Reid, Thomas: on early Virginia society and human nature, 31–32; and Scottish common sense philosophy, 89, 90, 91; *Inquiry into the Human Mind: Principles of Common Sense* (1764), 130–31

Religion. *See* Christian doctrine; Revivals; individual denominations and leaders

Renaissance: influence of, on American heritage, 7, 12; pessimism and optimism about human nature, 11–12; on relation of curiosity to inductive reasoning, 13; views on Indians, 16; influence of, on Puritan theology, 45

Renouvier, Charles, 205

Reymond, Dubois, 191

Reynolds, Dr. James, 92n58

Revivals: and "declension" of religion, 176; contemporary criticisms of, 177; "preparation" and Grace, 177; role of appeal to emotions in, 177. *See also* Bushnell, Horace; Finney, Charles G.; Great Awakening; Maffitt, John M.; Nevin, Rev. John

Ribot, Theodule, 193, 197

Richet, Dr. Charles, 325

Ripley, George: case of, for equality based on mysticism, 163; on perfectionism, 155; on conscious and unconscious life, 316n7

Robinson, David Z., 308

Robinson, Edward S., 351

Robinson, James Harvey, 296

Rochefoucauld, François de la, 72, 94n61

Rogers, Carl, 358, 392, 393

Rolfe, John, 18

Roman Catholicism, 14, 20, 297–98, 352n30. *See also* Brownson, Orestes O.; Jesuits

Romantic movement: as a reaction, 148; and various kinds of "romanticisms," 148, 149; emphasis on the individual, 149; emphasis on unconscious perceptions, 149; importance of emotions and intuitions in, 149; sensitivity to beauty, mystery, and benevolence, 149; subjectivism of, 149; contradictions of, 149–50; sense of tragedy, disillusionment, and despair, 150; social explanation for rise of, 150; varying exponents of, 151–52; and sex, 158–60; views of women, 165ff. *See also* Brown, Charles Brockden; Fiction; Freneau, Philip; Fuller, Margaret; Marsh, James; Sex

Rossiter, Clinton, 260n39

Rowlandson, Mary, 8

Rush, Benjamin: on enlightenment of man, 70; on blacks and blackness, 89; on education, character, and personality, 89; opposition to slavery, 89; relation of, to deism and "enlightened" ideas of man, 89; sympathy with humanitarianism, 89; use of term *human nature*, 89; on 1780 Continental Congress, 89n49; qualified influence of Scottish philosophers, 89, 90; rationalist and empirical aspects of psychology of, 89–90; emphasis on morality and free will, 90; faculty psychology of, 90; on phrenology and cerebral localization, 90; on insanity, 90–91; on dreams, 91; on sexual overindulgence and insanity, 162

Rush, Dr. James, 189

Russian Revolution of 1917: influence of, on discussion of human nature, 292–93; John B. Watson on, 383

Sachs, Dr. Hanns, 356n47

St. Augustine, 315

Saltus, Edgar, 318–19

Samelson, Franz, 288n52

Sanborn, Franklin B., 223ff., 231

Santayana, George, 338, 384n42

Sapir, Edwin, 347, 354

Scaglione, Aldo: on question about human nature, vii

Scanlan, James P., 111

Scarr-Salapatek, Sandra, 307

Schäffe, Albert Eberhard Friedrich, 240

Schelling, Friedrich Wilhelm Joseph von, 316

Schopenhauer, Arthur, 315–16

Schöpf, Johann David: on lack of human deformity in America, vii, 28

Schubert, Gotthilf von, 321

Schwab, Joseph J., 394

DESIGNED BY IRVING PERKINS
COMPOSED BY FOX VALLEY TYPESETTING, MENASHA, WISCONSIN
MANUFACTURED BY THE NORTH CENTRAL PUBLISHING CO., ST. PAUL, MINNESOTA
TEXT IS SET IN CALEDONIA, DISPLAY LINES IN BASILEA

ⓌⒿ

Library of Congress Cataloging in Publication Data
Curti, Merle Eugene, 1897-
Human nature in American thought.
Includes bibliographical references and index.
1. United States—Intellectual life. 2. Man.
I. Title.
E169.1.C877   973   79-3965
ISBN 0-299-07970-8